THE PURSUIT OF HOLINESS
IN LATE MEDIEVAL
AND RENAISSANCE RELIGION

STUDIES
IN MEDIEVAL AND
REFORMATION THOUGHT

EDITED BY

HEIKO A. OBERMAN, Tübingen

IN COOPERATION WITH
E. JANE DEMPSEY DOUGLASS, Claremont, California
LEIF GRANE, Copenhagen
GUILLAUME H. M. POSTHUMUS MEYJES, Leiden
ANTON G. WEILER, Nijmegen

VOLUME X
THE PURSUIT OF HOLINESS
IN LATE MEDIEVAL
AND RENAISSANCE RELIGION

LEIDEN
E. J. BRILL
1974

THE PURSUIT OF HOLINESS
IN LATE MEDIEVAL
AND RENAISSANCE RELIGION

PAPERS

FROM THE UNIVERSITY OF MICHIGAN CONFERENCE

EDITED BY

CHARLES TRINKAUS

WITH

HEIKO A. OBERMAN

LEIDEN
E. J. BRILL
1974

74-174419

ISBN 90 04 03791 8

PRINTED IN BELGIUM

TABLE OF CONTENTS

Part Two

LAY PIETY AND THE CULT OF YOUTH

Part Three

HUMANISM AND THE ARTS

EPILOGUE

FOREWORD

On April 20, 21, 22, 1972 some fifty-seven medieval and Renaissance scholars met in a conference on late medieval and Renaissance religion at The University of Michigan. Drawn from the six academic disciplines of history, literature, philosophy, religion, art history and music history, there was also a representation of individuals at various levels of their careers from recent Ph.Ds. to leading scholars in these disciplines. Though these participants represented a wide range of particular scholarly interests within their disciplines, they had in common a strong concern with the importance of religious thought, feeling, behavior and expression in the late middle ages and the Renaissance (as distinguished but not separated from ecclesiology, church history and the relationships between church and state). They are listed at the end of this foreword.

The papers presented in this volume consist of an original ten prepared in advance for the conference, the ten comments prepared in response to these papers (several of which are themselves short original studies), the three shorter papers presented at the conference dinner (one of which has been expanded into a major paper), a paper expanding the remarks of one of the participants, and a paper by the conference chairman and present editor on some of the issues that led to the assembling of the conference. In addition a limited number of interventions from the floor are also included. The volume, however, is by no means the minutes of the conference but rather finds its justification and its unity in the programmed interrelatedness of subject-matter of the papers and the comments which was occasioned by the conference.

More important than the occasion which led to these papers being written was also the state of research and interpretive study of religion in this period within the several disciplines. It seemed clear to a number of scholars that the character of religion, as an integral part of late medieval and Renaissance culture, was coming to be regarded in a substantially different way than it had been, that new researches and approaches were occurring in several areas and fields, that it would be salutary to bring together some of the scholars who were involved in these new directions in order to take stock in a systematic way of these developments. That this situation was correctly estimated was evident in the positive and prompt response of the scholars invited to contribute papers or comments as well as in the eager participation of so many scholars in response to our invitations.

It is an act of utmost risk for any one historian (of any of the disciplines represented - religion, art, philosophy, music, society, culture) to venture to speak for his colleagues, and particularly so when they are among the most creative and original students of the late medieval and Renaissance periods. Nonetheless it may be helpful to the reader at least to attempt to define some of the problems, some of the assumptions and some of the hypothetical conclusions concerning late medieval and Renaissance religion that brought us together, produced these papers and discussions, and sent us away with a surprizing sense of consonance.

Speaking as an interpreter, there seemed to be in the participants a sense of the need for a new unity or a new synthesis of the religious experience of the period which individual scholars sought to express in relation to the materials and events they knew best from their own researches. At the same time there was a strong commitment to a revisionist frame of mind which wished to challenge the older interpretations, indeed to find them to be somewhat dogmatic responses to sectarian and culturally conditioned outlooks of previous generations of scholars (*pace* our own). New looks at old questions by the favored route of archival and manuscript research has seemed to present to this current generation of scholars (ranging in age from their thirties to their sixties) a strikingly different, almost unrecognizable image of the religious condition, attitudes, beliefs and practices of this period of the fourteenth, fifteenth and early sixteenth centuries. Now each scholar and participant obviously viewed and views this situation from his own experience with the materials of his researches, and each views it therefore differently. The assumption of particularity, plurality and variety is a deeply ingrained one. Yet the historian whose function it has been to search out new data or to look in a more refined way at old, and to confront old generalizations with contradicting evidence, has not been able totally to avoid the sense of some kind of structure underlying the discrete documents and events. And if older structurings have seemed to derive more from the mind of the researcher than the evidence of his sources, there seems all the more need to construct the new synthesis, or to move into the kind of researches which will tell him whether his hypotheses concerning what is going on in general might be confirmed.

The papers in this volume very much reflect this state of mind —
a strong commitment to historical "nominalism" creeping toward a
somewhat begrudging (yet hopeful) "realism". The first paper by the
eminent historian of late medieval theology, Heiko A. Oberman,
combines the remarks he made at the conference dinner and some of
the sessions into a skillful and forward-looking synthesis of late
medieval theology, Renaissance humanism and Reformation thought.
Historians have indeed experienced increasing dissatisfaction with the
unities and divisions of the older interpretations, still within the last
fifty years heavily shaped by post-Lutheran and post-Tridentine
retrospections on the period from 1200 to 1600. Oberman has striven
mightily to break the mould in which our historical visions of this
time-period have been formed. He does not see (to express it in its
crudest terms) a glorious (or over-bearing) religious unity of the
thirteenth century, the "high" middle ages, followed by a decadent
failure of nerve in the fourteenth and fifteenth centuries (where through
the medium of nominalist theology men of the age feared and doubted
the power of merely human reason to construct its image of the universe, God's and man's). Nor does he see an indiscipline and licen-
tiousness in a hypocritical blending of the sensuousness and materialism
of classical culture with religious motifs in the Renaissance. For him
the Reformation does not represent a break with its immediate past,
but a well-prepared and almost indiscernible one. The fourteenth and
fifteenth centuries are not those in which the middle ages rotted only
to be finally *aufgehoben* by modernist Protestantism, or rescued and
revived by the Counter-Reform. Rather an underlying unity characterized by a fervent piety and a merging of the sacred and the profane
which itself affirmed man's powers of action, thought and will run
through the years 1350-1550 in the North and Italy alike.

In more specific terms, and not necessarily sharing all of Oberman's
positions, William J. Courtenay has offered a finely wrought analysis
of what contemporary scholarship has asserted about "nominalism",
seeing it in variety and plurality, in its many thirteenth-century
roots, in the nuances and differences of approach in its various fields
and individuals. And yet the very "nominalism" of recent studies of
nominalism (ironically confronted with our urge to construct historical
unities by Charles T. Davis in his piece on "Ockham and the *zeitgeist*")
has not been able to part from a common characterization of these
thinkers as "nominalist", as Paul Oskar Kristeller insists in his comments — particularly in the area of logic. Nor did it escape a number

of participants that even by Courtenay's judicious account of the
revisions, there was indeed still a break from a predominant emphasis
in thirteenth-century theology on an eternal, natural universe susceptible to valid intellectual reconstruction by human logic and metaphysical projection to a subsequent emphasis on a positive scriptural
assertion of God's will and wishes, and of His promises and covenants
with man and His church, and a consequent historical, literary,
linguistic and juridical mode of comprehending God and His will.
Such also was Oberman's view of the transition, and in it he finds
the common ground between late medieval scholasticism and Renaissance humanism (as I, also, assert in my essay below).

What seems to have been at stake from the early fourteenth century
forward was the achievement of a state of holiness, whether in ultimate
unity with the divine essence (or mind, or will), or in the more proximate degrees of sanctity embodied in the assurance of acceptability
for salvation, or in the attainment of the powers embodied in sacraments,
both within and without the church. This pursuit of holiness was of
course the ancient goal of the Christian faith and as such nothing new.
But in our period it assumed its own shapes of many kinds, both old
and new. And it was not only given an urgency by intellectual doubts
concerning the earlier scholastic rationales but was also part of the
steady growth in the power and depth of religious feelings in western
Europe in clergy and laity alike. This wave of religiosity seems now
to have accompanied and indeed to have been part and parcel of the
expansion of the population and the growth of urban centers with
their burgeoning networks of economic, political and ecclesiastical
communication within and between each other. This is the primary
assumption on which the authors in this volume seem to have agreed
(though they will disagree as to timing, relative importance of different manifestations of a pursuit of holiness and as to the exact relationships of sacred and secular, clerical and laical within it). This renewed
urge toward a holy state found ways of reinforcing the traditional
ecclesiastical means of offering and aiding salvation and at the same
time continuously prompted the exploration and election of rival
ways which brought the laity or the individual closer to the divine
with or without clerical leadership and assistance. It was a time of
testings and experimentations, dogmatically proposed and hotly argued
since all the individuals' and culture's ultimate values were at stake.

From the nominalism, set forth in its newer dress by Courtenay,
the volume moves to the problem of late medieval mysticism as

possibly the most important means of transcending the partial and proximate of the *potentia ordinata*—the divinely ordained, established order of church and salvation for which, our authors are claiming, nominalism was the great strategy of reinforcement as men felt driven back upon their own intellectual and affective powers. Mysticism, on the other hand, in Steven Ozment's exposition, represents both in its Bernardine-Bonaventuran and its Dominican-Eckhardtian strains, a way to leap beyond God's covenanted order to his ultimate and absolute being and power. And related variously to the nominalist, historicistic strategy, it also gave greater impetus and license to dissent. And so Luther's dissenting theology is characterized by Ozment as "an unprecedented, unAugustinian merger of nominalism and mysticism." Taking up this theorem, Edward Cranz surveys the stages of western mysticism from antiquity and early Christianity to the late middle ages and Reformation, again to affirm a drastic break between thirteenth-century style theology and a new mode that must somehow start with subjective human means of knowing and loving. Applying this to Nicholas of Cusa, he explores the connections of Cusanus' thought with the mystical tradition, with nominalism and with Ozment's notion of the Lutheran merger.

Focussing on the primary theme of the pursuit of holiness, many aspects of general church history had to be eliminated from the program of the conference. Yet one which originated within ecclesiastical organization itself, but which is intimately concerned with the individual viator's pursuit of salvation, was the guidance offered to confessors in the administration of the sacrament of penance by means of summas for confessors. Thomas Tentler in the succeeding paper explores the nature and the spiritual dynamics of sacramental and salvational theology in this literature. His argument, that the system laid forth in these summas offered not only consolation to the penitent in his search for reconciliation and sanctity but direction and control through the sense of guilt engendered, is then sharply questioned by Father Leonard Boyle in his comment, and reasserted in a reasoned defense in Tentler's response. And this closes the first part of the volume on the "theologies of the late middle ages".

Part II, on lay piety and the cult of youth, is concerned with two related areas that have recently been attracting the interest of historians. Because studies of this type are only beginning, the papers contributed here are of a pioneering and experimental character, and are monographic in the sense of examining limited local situations. A new synthetic interpretation or a critical review of work in these areas (such as are offered in Part I) would not have been possible, as it has hardly begun. Here the pursuit of holiness is viewed from the perspective of the layman, always associated with members of the clergy of course, but expressing and revealing through the evidence gathered the power of the lay religious impulses and the variety of ways that were open to laymen in seeking sanctification—both old and new. It is the manifestation in action of the impulse to merge the sacred and profane that was enunciated in the new theologies. A. N. Galpern has emphasized the strength and perdurance of more traditional forms of lay piety in his paper on sixteenth-century Champagne, while Marvin Becker, who expanded his conference remarks into a paper, is particularly concerned with the increasing reliance on political and state organs by the Florentine laity to ensure the proper carrying out of their pious wishes, as well as with the general range of religious activities responding to lay initiative.

Perhaps the most challenging paper in the volume is Richard Trexler's study of the youth confraternities of fifteenth-century and Savonarolan Florence. In a richly documented exposition inspired by Ariès' familiar work on childhood, Trexler leads up to the hypothesis of a shift in the localization of the carriers of sanctity in Renaissance society from the traditional medieval role of the "religious", the members of the orders, to the child. Our guarantee that society may somehow be purged of our own guilty thoughts and deeds lies in the younger generation, unspoiled and untouched, yet guided and protected in its innocence. Certainly this thesis will demand further researches and comparative studies of other places, and it is sure to be challenged, though it may well in the end vindicate itself. Donald Weinstein, however, in his critique of the paper looks rather to a broadening of the issues with a special concern for the growing tendency to sanctify the state and political action.

The effort to overcome the guilt and preserve the innocence of the child is also examined in Gerald Strauss' study of the Lutheran program, also a pioneer study that is the first stage of his more extensive examination now under way. And Lewis Spitz' masterly command of the sources and literature of the Reformation enables him to make trenchant suggestions on where and how Strauss' inquiries might be pursued. Deeply involved herself in these new anthropological and psycho-historical studies, Natalie Davis contributes a welcome critique and a projection of general directions for further studies of this type.

Obviously some very important questions are raised for historians by these studies of late medieval and Renaissance lay piety and the new cult of childhood. It is not alone that leading elements of society, both economic and political, are centrally involved in these religious programs, so that, as an urban type of capitalism and a new princely type of political regime emerge, they begin to exert an influence reflecting their interests and policies in the critical area of religious experience. Rather, also, deeper, more affective attitudes seem to be asserting themselves. Basic changes seem to be occurring in the structure and value-system of European culture, perhaps originating in the economic and political transformations taking place over long periods of time, but manifesting themselves in new ways of localization of the holy. Perhaps it is not so much new studies and new interpretations of the period which are needed as new approaches to the problem of studying and interpreting the period. Perhaps, as Heiko Oberman suggests in his paper, the history of thought is itself integral with the history of behavior and is a barometer of the changing culture and value-system out of which the modern world is born. At any rate, where nominalists were trying to bridge the gap between the world of historical experience accessible to man and the divine potency by means of a trust in the existential validity of the divine promises and covenants, less theoretically oriented laymen were expressing their own trust in the presence and availability of the divine in their confident (as well as anxious) religious behavior.

Part III turns again to the area of thought and symbolization as evidence and manifestation of a new pursuit of the holy. The question of the religious role of Renaissance humanism and Platonism is weighed in my own paper and in that of Professor Kristeller. For me the problem is that of grasping humanism as but one of the expressions of crisis and change wherein more historical, rhetorical and literary treatments of human relationships correspond to a more situational demand for constantly changing decisions and actions in the far more complex, flexible and intense transactions required by the urban scene. The need for constant decisions and agreements, political, economic and social, placed a premium on persuasion and alerted jurists, notaries, writers and clerics to the relevance of ancient rhetorical culture as an instrument and a new model for their own. But in this, which was essentially a secular historical development, there could not help but be an influence and impact on the realm of religious discourse, with implications for the conception of the nature of priesthood, church, religious experience and truth. For Kristeller this relationship is also seen in similar fashion but with a proper wish not to exaggerate the religious or to forget the wide range of non-religious humanistic and philosophical studies. But again for myself there is the question of whether it was not of greater historical significance that the religious thought of the Italian humanists blended autonomously with the needs of their own society and culture than that they anticipated the later religious Reform in certain striking respects. Moreover, they were typical of their age in the very blending of the secular and religious.

But artists also were part of their culture, and the central role of art as a suggestive and symbolic environing of religious life and practice in church and cloister of the late middle ages and Renaissance is undeniable. Creighton Gilbert's study of a basic shift in emphasis from depictions of the Crucifixion to ones of the Last Supper on the walls of Renaissance refectories, and his distinction between the type of the *Last Supper* in the refectory and the *Communion of the Apostles* (stressing the Eucharist) in chapels, are striking examples of how the methodology of the art historian can be applied to the study of religious change. His paper assumes and implies a new sense of participation and sharing on the part of the live brothers dining before the dramatic frescoes of the *Last Supper* of Christ and the Apostles. It parallels the attempts of laymen and youth to enact the roles of holy persons in processions and *sacre rappresentazioni*. Yet many questions remain to be answered, as Clifton Olds points out, and Gilbert's will be only the first of such studies.

John O'Malley in his essay on the sermons preached at the papal court in the high Renaissance stresses the humanistic and Platonic influence of the theme of the dignity of man, supported by a concentration on the lessons of the Incarnation. It is Father O'Malley's view that humanist influence is present in a new style of "transformational" or rhetorical theology embodied in these sermons, where the educational and rhetorical role of the ecclesiastic seems emphasized. Paul Kristeller adds some further examples and makes some suggestions for the treatment of this direct application of humanist rhetoric to the sphere of religious practice. Also in Father McConica's careful study of the humanistic elements in Erasmus' view of the ecclesiological crisis and of the nature of the papacy and the Christian life emphasis is placed on the manifestation of a new rhetorical and situational theology. But in his use of the term "evangelical" McConica provokes some trenchant considerations by Eugene Rice and William Bouwsma of just what this term should mean and how it should be used in discussions of Renaissance religion. The question of the relationship of Renaissance to Reformation, raised earlier by Oberman, Ozment, myself and others is involved in this concept, for it implies that religious truth and authority, and the models of holiness, are to be found in the apostolic life depicted in the Evangels, but correctly understood by means of humanist scholarship and exegesis (typified by Valla and Erasmus). And the Evangels should be the incitement and inspiration for a renewed pursuit of holiness. But whether the term, "evangelical", best comprehends the humanist or Erasmian religious position, that of Luther, or contemporary types of Catholic piety, one, or all, or none, is clearly a matter of crucial historical judgement concerning the character of all three. Hence clarification of the use of such a term seems essential, and necessary for but not subordinate to the need for a new understanding of the relationships of the late medieval, Renaissance and Reformation epochs to each other. Father McConica and his commentators contribute to that clarification and exploration, yet the difficulty and subtle complexity of the issues are skillfully presented in John Arthos' ironical essay on the ambiguities of the Rome of Pope Julius.

Finally the volume presents Louise Cuyler's study of how a particular musical form was put to political and religious use by the Habsburg emperors of the Renaissance and how secular and religious elements were harmoniously combined. Lewis Lockwood moves out from the particularity of her analysis to some of the broader implications of her research. And as an epilogue to the entire volume we have Myron Gilmore's graceful exploration of the mixture of the religious and the profane in Renaissance art and letters, taking off from Erasmus' "The Godly Feast", and employing it at the last as an analogy of this modern group of secular and religious scholars examining the religious past of their own culture in this conference in a mood of serious play.

February 1973

CHARLES TRINKAUS
London

ACKNOWLEDGEMENTS

A conference and the publication of a volume of this sort are a collective enterprise and possible only through the efforts and contributions of many individuals. In the first place we have to thank the contributors for their papers and comments, and the participants (listed below) not only for the vigor with which both entered into the discussions and the interest they manifested but also for many helpful acts and suggestions. Without the kind of local support and cooperation given by the Committee on Planning and Arrangements of The University of Michigan (also listed below) such a meeting cannot happen; and gratitude is also due to the other participating Michigan faculty, and especially to those who (with their spouses) so generously entertained our guest participants. In developing the program of the conference special mention must be made of Professor Richard C. Trexler of the University of Illinois whose original idea it was to have such a get-together and who made important suggestions for the program, of Professor John W. O'Malley, of the University of Detroit and Professor Thomas N. Tentler of The University of Michigan who, along with Charles Trinkaus, had several important discussions which blocked out the program. Professors Louise Cuyler and Marvin Eisenberg made many important suggestions as to participants and papers in the fields of music and arts, as did Professors John Arthos and Frank Huntley for literature; all are of The University of Michigan. Special thanks are also due to Professor D. Noel Freedman who contributed the office and the services of the secretary of Michigan's Program of Studies in Religion.

The conference was financed by generous grants from The American Council of Learned Societies and from The Earhart Foundation of Ann Arbor, Michigan; the project is deeply indebted to both for its very existence. The publication of this volume has also been assisted by generous contributions from the Horace H. Rackham School of Graduate Studies and the Comparative Studies in History Program, both of The University of Michigan, and from the Jesuit Community at the University of Detroit for which we must be especially grateful.

February 1973   CHARLES TRINKAUS   HEIKO A. OBERMAN
London   Tübingen

THE CONFERENCE ON LATE MEDIEVAL
AND RENAISSANCE RELIGION

The Conference on Late Medieval and Renaissance Religion at The University of Michigan, April 20, 21, 22, 1972, was sponsored by The University of Michigan's Program of Comparative Studies in History and Program of Studies in Religion.

Committee on Planning and Arrangements from The University of Michigan:

John Arthos, Literature
Louise E. Cuyler, Music History
Marvin Eisenberg, History of Art
D. Noel Freedman, Near Eastern Languages, and Director of Program of Studies in Religion
Frank L. Huntley, Literature
Thomas N. Tentler, History
Charles Trinkaus, History, and Chairman of Program of Comparative Studies in History (1971-72)

Conference Participants (Institutional affiliations as of April 1972):

Marilyn Adams, Philosophy, The University of Michigan
Robert Adams, Philosophy, The University of Michigan
John Arthos, Literature, The University of Michigan
Roy Battenhouse, Literature, Indiana University
Marvin B. Becker, History, University of Rochester
Sandra Berke, History, Michigan State University
William J. Bouwsma, History, University of California (Berkeley)
Leonard E. Boyle, Pontifical Institute of Mediaeval Studies, Toronto
Paul Clogan, Literature, Case-Western Reserve University
Eric Cochrane, History, The University of Chicago
Marcia Colish, History, Oberlin College
Giles Constable, History, Harvard University
William J. Courtenay, History, University of Wisconsin
F. Edward Cranz, History, Connecticut College
David E. Crawford, Music History, The University of Michigan
Louise E. Cuyler, Music History, The University of Michigan
Charles T. Davis, History, Tulane University

Natalie Zemon Davis, History, University of California (Berkeley)
Marvin Eisenberg, History of Art, The University of Michigan
D. Noel Freedman, Religion, The University of Michigan
A. N. Galpern, History, University of Pittsburgh
Creighton Gilbert, Art, Queens College of C. U. N. Y.
Myron P. Gilmore, History, Harvard University
Hanna H. Gray, History, The University of Chicago
Harold J. Grimm, History, Ohio State University
Frank L. Huntley, Literature, The University of Michigan
Paul Oskar Kristeller, Philosophy, Columbia University
Robert Lerner, History, Northwestern University
Lewis Lockwood, Music History, Princeton University
James K. McConica, Pontifical Institute of Mediaeval Studies, Toronto
Gwynn S. McPeek, Music History, The University of Michigan
Paul Meyvaert, Literature, The Medieval Academy of America
Francis Oakley, History, Williams College
Heiko A. Oberman, Church History, Universität Tübingen
Clifton C. Olds, History of Art, The University of Michigan
John C. Olin, History, Fordham University
John W. O'Malley, History, University of Detroit
Steven Ozment, History, Yale University
Wilhelm Pauck, Church History, Vanderbilt University
Joseph Polzer, History of Art, University of Louisville
Eugene F. Rice, Jr., History, Columbia University
Robert Snow, Music History, University of Pittsburgh
Lewis W. Spitz, History, Stanford University
Nicholas H. Steneck, History, The University of Michigan
Gerald Strauss, History, Indiana University
Thomas N. Tentler, History, The University of Michigan
Sylvia L. Thrupp, History, The University of Michigan
James D. Tracy, History, University of Minnesota
Richard C. Trexler, History, University of Illinois
Charles Trinkaus, History, The University of Michigan
James A. Vann, III, History, The University of Michigan
Teresa Vilardi, History, Wooster College
Glenn E. Watkins, Music History, The University of Michigan
Carroll Westfall, History of Art, Amherst College
Donald Weinstein, History, Rutgers University
David Wilkins, History of Art, University of Pittsburgh
Charles Witke, Comparative Literature, The University of Michigan

PART ONE

THEOLOGIES OF THE LATE MIDDLE AGES

1. THE SHAPE OF LATE MEDIEVAL THOUGHT : THE BIRTHPANGS OF THE MODERN ERA*

HEIKO A. OBERMAN

Universität Tübingen

I. THREE ASSUMPTIONS

1. Our very project of investigating the shape of late medieval thought—even before it is under way—implies a number of disputable assumptions.

In the first place, what is implied is not merely an open question but rather a quest for the beginning of the modern era. Usually an inordinate amount of historical arrogance underlies such an investigation, since it assumes more or less explicitly that the merits of an epoch can be measured by its degree of proximity to our own era. It is not difficult to be sympathetic with those who are unwilling to regard such a quest as part of genuine historical research; though perhaps no longer put in that form, "each epoch is immediate to God," and should therefore be described in its own terms.

Yet we recall two significant debates. The one, dealing with the modernity of the Reformation, centered around the thesis of Troeltsch, who opposed Hegel and his disciples in arguing for the basically medieval basis and horizon of Luther and the German Reformation. Thus Troeltsch claimed to have established the non-modernity of the Reformation movement.[1] The second debate is of more recent vintage and concerned with the Italian Renaissance. Hans Baron in a paper read for the American Historical Association in 1941 opposed the thesis of C.H. McIlwain, the authority on medieval constitutional history, that the twelfth century Renaissance "seems to be on the

---

* The following contribution was first conceived as a guest-lecture. In its original form it is to be published in *Archiv für Reformationsgeschichte* 1973.

[1] Ernst Troeltsch, "Renaissance und Reformation", *Gesammelte Schriften*, IV (Tübingen, 1925), pp. 261-296. Salient portions have been translated into English by Lewis W. Spitz in *The Reformation — Material or Spiritual?* (Boston, 1962), 17-27. Cf. Gerhard Ebeling, "Luther und der Anbruch der Neuzeit", *Zeitschrift für Theologie und Kirche*, 69 (1972), 185-213; 192-200.

whole more significant in a perspective of the whole of history, than
the later development to which we usually attach the word "Renaissance." Baron argued for the "modern" face and the "precursorship"
of Renaissance Italy in the field of political ideas and came close to
the Burckhardtian thesis, which presents the Renaissance as the
first-born among the sons of modern Europe.[1]

It should be granted that these debates revealed as much about the
debators as about the periods in question. It should also be granted,
however, that this—in the eyes of skeptics—idle game is of the very
essence of the historical venture : the trek into the past, the move
ad fontes serves the reflection upon oneself and one's society in providing a critical freedom over and against the tyranny of the *Zeitgeist*.
Hence, to pose our question is at once a luxury *and* a necessity, not
unlike the true double rating of historical research as such. By "luxury"
I mean that vital dimension of our work not determined by the impatient, ever-shifting claims of relevance, that playsome freedom of
the *homo ludens* who so—and only so—chances upon new horizons of
understanding. By necessity I mean the dialectics of precision through
details and perspective through distance, that distance which allows
for the historian to function as the *homo quaerens intellectum*. Hence
we pose our question not out of a presumptuous identification of
modernity and utopia, but out of the need for perspective in order to
interpret the past to the present.

2.   In the second place, our question implies that there is good reason
to look at the later Middle Ages for the beginnings of a new era. Admittedly we no longer assume a tripartite view of history with its
periodisation of antiquity, Middle Ages and modern times. Furthermore, we distinguish today at least pre-modern, modern, and contemporary history, where the age of the Enlightenment seems to dwarf
all preceding factors of change. Yet on the penalty of introducing an
Olympic family of *dei ex machina*, we are well-advised to accept the
Joachite cradle-view of history, according to which each period gives

---

[1] Hans Baron, "Toward a More Positive Evaluation of the Fifteenth Century Renaissance", *Journal of the History of Ideas*, 4 (1943), 22-49. Cf. Karl Dannenfeldt, *The
Renaissance, Medieval or Modern?* (Boston, 1959), 35-48; 64-75. Cf. Wallace K. Ferguson, *The Renaissance in Historical Thought. Five Centuries of Interpretation* (Boston,
1948), 195-252 : The Burckhardtian Tradition in the Interpretation of the Italian Renaissance; 290-328 : Reaction against the Burckhardtian Tradition; 329-385 : The
Revolt of the Medievalists.

birth to the next in such a way that its birthpangs will precede its coming of age, *n'en déplaise* Collingwood,[1] as the best theory to date which takes fully into account the coexistence of continuity and discontinuity.

For the later Middle Ages, which we—at this point arbitrarily—set for the two centuries, ranging from about 1350-1550,[2] the cradle-theory is of particular relevance, because this period has long been regarded as an age of regression, throwing its dark shadows well into the centuries to follow. Efforts to rectify the view of the *decline* and the *waning* of the Middle Ages with that of the *harvest* may well have helped to establish a more positive understanding; at the same time, it could be taken to stress continuity at the expense of discontinuity. In keeping with the positive implications of the harvest image but as a necessary extension, we shall deal today with a few aspects of the initiation of a new season, not looking for causes but for prototypes of modern ways of life and thought.

3. A third preliminary observation leads us to a point of special concern to me. Our question assumes that it is possible to trace the shape of late medieval thought. One should be skeptical *vis-à-vis* such a claim. If we have learned one thing in the last twenty years of research, then it is to enlarge our awareness of geographical and sociological as well as religious diversification. This lesson is clearly reflected in the trend away from pan-European and national to regional and local history. Granted that the shape of late medieval thought is an abstraction for the purpose of communication, with this expression we have, nevertheless, a very concrete goal in mind : namely, to present it as the common field of all those who are involved in the pursuit

---

1 After introducing Joachim as illustration Collingwood—as it may seem, most reasonably—formulates the general rule : "Eschatology is always an intrusive element in history. The historian's business is to know the past, not to know the future..." R. G. Collingwood, *The Idea of History* (Oxford, 1949; New York, 1965³), 54. If we replace "eschatology" with futurology, Collingwood's thesis is no longer *luce clarius*! At least the historian cannot deny sharing responsibility for knowing the present— which in the newly developing field of futurology encompasses the future.

2 I cannot argue here for this form of periodisation. An excellent recent survey by Josef Engel comes to another conclusion, but notices more generally "die Tendenz zur Vorverlegung der Neuzeit" in manuals and especially in monographic literature. "Von der spätmittelalterlichen respublica Christiana zum Mächte-Europa der Neuzeit", in Theodor Schieder, ed., *Handbuch der europäischen Geschichte*, III : *Die Entstehung des neuzeitlichen Europa* (Stuttgart, 1971), 1-443; 11.

of the late medieval history of ideas, be it through late medieval
scholastic, Renaissance, or Reformation research. The separation of
these fields, often with their own chairs, their own journals and learned societies, has made for study in depth and detail, which should be
gratefully acknowledged. This separation has also had the effect that
equal mastery in all three fields has, by necessity, become rare if
not impossible. Yet the establishment of such a tripartite approach
allows for—and *de facto* encourages—*a priori* assumptions of differences which obscure and preclude a wholesome vision of the whole
period in its common features, and may lead us therefore to overlook
characteristics of each. No question taxes so much the quest for the
unity of our epoch as the question of modernity. It tends to bring out
both the centripetal forces of the time and the often confessionally
charged passion or else the cool *Vorverständnis* of the investigators.

II. The Many Faces of Crisis

We want to direct our attention to one central aspect of late
medieval thought, under which other trends can be subsumed, which
at the same time provides us with one of the clearest prototypes of
modernity. By this I mean the closing of the gap between the sacred
and the profane, looked at from the perspective of late medieval,
Renaissance and Reformation studies.

The most obvious and pervasive factor in our period is the phenomenon of crisis. There exists a consensus on the significance, although
not on the exact effects of the Black Death, which reached its high-
point in England around 1349. Preceded by an extended food crisis
on the continent, we notice in its wake both a relatively moderate
acceleration of urbanization and a strikingly rapid expansion of
existing urban centers. Whether the agrarian crisis is to be regarded
as cause or effect, is a separate question: the deflation of wheat prices
and the decline in agrarian self-sufficiency led to a dramatic trek to
the cities, which left behind ghost villages and whole ghost areas, for
Germany so carefully charted by Wilhelm Abel.[1] From around 1450
until *circa* 1520 the wheat prices reached an unprecedented drop

---

[1] Wilhelm Abel, "Landwirtschaft 1350-1550", in H. Aublin and W. Zorn, eds.,
Handbuch der deutschen Wirtschafts- und Sozialgeschichte, I (Stuttgart, 1971), 302; cf.
p. 308. Cf. W. Abel, *Geschichte der deutschen Landwirtschaft vom frühen Mittelalter bis
zum 19. Jahrhundert*, in G. Franz, ed., *Deutsche Agrargeschichte*, II (Stuttgart, 1967²),
128ff.

simultaneously in England, France, Germany and Austria. The agrarian crisis did not only affect the lower aristocracy and the payroll agrarian workers. It also hit the town communities in thrusting upon them a fast-growing urban proletariat which did not find—and was not granted !—access to the guilds or representation in the city government. The monetary crisis is clearly reflected in the increasing protest against the threat to existing reliable value systems and against the arbitrary manipulation of coinage values.

I am rather inclined to associate the effects of the new money-economy with the subsequent but equally upsetting legal crisis implied in the growing impact and usage of Roman law based on the dogma of private property with its confiscatory exploitation of the distinction between *proprietas* and *possessio*. Both developments were not only a threat to valuables and *securities*, but also to values and *security*.

The *usus pauper* of the radical Franciscans had been able to provide for a moral response as the courageous free choice for what the fate of the socio-economic forces had decreed. Yet after the condemnation of the apostolic ideal of poverty by Pope John XXII in 1323 the Church had deprived itself of a possible answer to the challenge of the times. Nevertheless, the Franciscan friars established themselves as the pastors to the plebeian city population; to the lower strata in society they related more readily than the other two mendicant orders, the scholarly Dominicans and the establishment-favored Augustinians. The reason can be found in their non-violent revolutionary eschatology, their tendency towards anti-intellectualism and the psychological rather than metaphysical basis of their theology in pulpit and confessional. Their more moderate revolutionary eschatology was based on the expectation of the seventh *status ecclesiae*, when friars would replace the prelates, all Jews would be converted, and peace would reign. The extreme interpretation led—since the condemnation of Olivi, the great theoretician of the Spirituals—an underground existence and had to find other forms of expression.

It is not surprising that the Franciscans proved to be in tune with the *Zeitgeist;* so much so that for two centuries late medieval spirituality, piety and theology outside the university halls can be said to have been dominated by them. The Thomistic revival in Cologne set off the Pfefferkorn affair, was ridiculed and then contained by the "Letters of Obscure Men," until it could find more receptive soil in what from the point of view of administration can be considered the first modern state, absolutist Spain.

The context in which the unsettling effects of all these crisis factors
could have their full impact is, however, the ecclesiastical crisis. I
regard it as a major breakthrough, that during the last international,
largely Marxist, Colloquium organized by the Czechoslovakian Academy of Arts and Sciences at Smolenice in September 1969, we were
able to agree that the economic crisis was not the cause, but rather an
aspect of the late medieval crisis issuing from the Western Schism.[1] The
Western Schism, with its concatenation of abortive solutions from
Pisa and Constance to Basel, including the seemingly reassuring
achievement of union with the Eastern Church at Florence, called
the sacred basis of existence into question to an extent hitherto
unknown. The confusion of consciences and the political strife resulting
from the claims of—at times—three obediences with their own fiscal
and administrative legislation are too well-known to be enlarged upon.

Less well-known is the role which—again—the Franciscan order
played in the debate around the thesis *ubi papa, ibi ecclesia* at the
heart of the curialist-conciliarist struggle. In a book recently published,
Brian Tierney analyzes the emergence of the dogma of infallibility.[2]
He calls for a revision of the dogmatic constitution of the First Vatican
Council—at which papal, universal, *ex cathedra*, decrees were declared
irreformable *ex sese, non autem ex consensu ecclesiae*. Tierney does so
on the basis of the discovery, that the matrix of this dogma is to be
found among the adherents of the extreme heretical wing of the
Franciscan Order at the beginning of the fourteenth century, namely
with Petrus Olivi. Hence infallibility proved to have been launched by
an accused heretic without support from the earlier tradition. The
impressive array of arguments and convincing documentation of
Tierney interests us here less than retracing one part of his argument
by taking a closer look at the texture of Olivi's intentions in his
Quaestio de infallibilitate Romani Pontificis.[3] It seems to me that
Tierney has not only rightly pointed to the significance of this text,
but also appropriately read it in the light of Olivi's later Apocalypse
commentary. Yet his conclusions as to Olivi's intentions are too
juridically conceived when Olivi's "new theory of papal infallibility"

---

[1] The leading paper at this conference, by Frantisek Graus, is now available in
English : "The Crisis of the Middle Ages and the Hussites", in Steven E. Ozment, ed.,
The Reformation in Medieval Perspective (Chicago, 1971), 76-103.

[2] Brian Tierney, *Origins of Papal Infallibility 1150-1350* (Leiden, 1972).

[3] Michele Maccarone, ed., *Rivista di Storia della Chiesa in Italia*, 3 (1949), 325-343.

is seen as "designed to limit the power of future popes,"[1]—rather, I read Olivi as contending that the emerging New Age is not to be a future of popes at all.

As a matter of fact, Olivi refers to the Apocalypse to declare that the Western Church, and particularly the First See, has been given the primacy by God himself. In passing he allows a glance at occidental feelings of superiority, providing God with a valid reason for his choice : as appears from the historical sources, "tota gens orientalis semper fuit prona ad hereses et scissuras, gens vero latina semper inventa est simplicior et stabilior in fide."[2] We find a forewarning not to simplify Olivi when we look at the text referred to (Apoc. 17, 18) in his own commentary on the Apocalypse. In this comprehensive, partly futurological, elaboration of Joachite ideas Olivi identifies Rome with Babylon. True enough, this identification applies only to the last stage of history, but Olivi knows that he lives on the edge of at once the most modern and the last times, the *novissimi*, when the succession of Christ will be transferred to the sons of St. Francis. In this light, we have to read his conclusions. The pope is inerrant and his decrees are irreformable—"nec papa nec sedes romana potest in fide pertinaciter errare." Yet when he is pope "secundum solam apparentiam," when he is not *verus papa*, then he has no jurisdictional authority at all, "quia omnis fidelis est maior eo."[3]

I do not believe that another Franciscan who wrote less than half a century later, William of Ockham, deviated theoretically from this defender of *this* infallibility of the *papa verus*; though we do not find the characteristic Olivian dimension of eschatology, which is not easily stripped away without changing the whole texture of thought, nevertheless, in his assessment of the pope, Ockham does declare the heretical pope deposed *ipso facto*, just as Olivi; and he comes to the same conclusion that "omnis fidelis est maior eo."[4] But instead of Olivi's looking toward the coming of the Third Age Ockham looks to the convening of a General Council : if a heretical pope is deposed *ipso facto*, such is the case, because all heresies have been unmasked

---

[1] Tierney, *op. cit.*, 130.

[2] Maccarone, *ed. cit.*, 337, 27-29.

[3] *Ibid.*, 342, 38f.; 343, 8f.

[4] *Compendium Errorum Joannis XXII*, obiectio cavillosa 3, ratio 1 in Guilelmus de Occam, *Opera plurima* (Lyon, 1494-96; reprint Farnborough 1952), II, fol. BB 5ra. See further Arthur S. McGrade, *The Political Thought of William of Ockham : Personal and Institutional Principles* (Cambridge, 1973), Chapters II-III.

as such by General Councils.[1] Olivi's eschatological fervor has found in Ockham a more juridically oriented expression, where the millennial dream of the *ecclesia spiritualis* has been remoulded into a reform program for the *ecclesia universalis*. These two examples suffice to show the range of variants within one and the same tradition which shaped the mood of the times. It provided particularly a ferment of crisis for a society based on "eternal" institutions, which now increasingly were surmised to be "temporal" and perhaps even dated.

In the particular case of Olivi, the epithets and powers of the pope can be so highly exalted, because the great shift is imminent. The moment is near at which the final demarcation line between Rome and Babylon will be drawn : a pope who does not live up to the high qualities of his office proves to be a pseudo-pope, a pope "quoad solam apparentiam", in appearance only. What first seems to be the highest elevation of papal office, is a test of orthodoxy which soon is to unmask the antichrist. The eyes of all true believers are on the pope : once he does err, we have entered the most modern era, the time of the last things. Though Tierney is right in pointing to Olivi for the origins of infallibility in the sense of doctrinal irreversibility,[2] we sense here a completely different climate of expectation than in 1870.

Such precarious claims and "faint praise" influenced the climate and set the stage on which the drama of the Western Schism is enacted.

---

[1] "... papa hereticus incidit in antiquam heresim per generale concilium damnatam ... quia omnis heresis est explicite per generalia concilia iam condemnata." *Dialogus de imperio et pontificia potestate*, lb. VI, c. 73 in Occam, *ed. cit.*, I, fol. 88rb.

[2] The case of papal doctrinal flexibility is argued by Pope John XXII, when he reacts to the 1279 papal defense of the *usus pauper* (in "Exiit qui seminat") on March 26, 1322 with the words : "... non debet reprehensibile iudicari, si canonum conditor canones a se, vel suis praedecessoribus editos, vel aliqua in eisdem contenta canonibus revocare, modificare, vel suspendere studeat, si ea obesse potius viderit, quam prodesse." L. Wadding, *Annales Minorum*, VI (Quaracchi, 1931[3]), 446 = *Extravag. Ioann. XXII.*, tit. 14 c. 2; E. L. Richter and E. Friedberg, eds., *Corpus iuris canonici* (Leipzig, 1879-1881[2]), II, col. 1224.

Two months later (June 4, 1322), this challenge evokes the response of the Franciscan General Chapter meeting in Perugia : "... quod pro dogmate sano Sedes Apostolica comprobavit, semper teneri debet acceptum, nec ab ea licet quomodolibet resilire..." Wadding, *ed. cit.*, VI, 448 (cf. Decr. Grat., D. 19 c. 1; Richter and Friedberg, *ed. cit.*, I, col. 58f.). For the discussion of the historical aspect of Tierney's argument it is important to point to this Perugia Chapter rather than to Olivi himself as the "origin of papal infallibility." At the same time, the very fact that papal irreversibility is formulated as protest *against* a papal ruling, supports Tierney's theological critique of the infallibility decree of Vatican I.

Its full implications are not immediately realized. At first, during the Pisan Council, such sober *grandseigneurs* as Gerson and d'Ailly thought they could avert disaster with common sense and decent diplomacy. At the opening of the Council of Constance, however, we find d'Ailly openly quoting and defending Joachim of Flora, and Jean Gerson looking for ever more radical solutions.

It may be too dramatic to call the later Middle Ages the Age of Crisis, because crisis is the turmoil caused by the passing away of one world of values and the painful birth of a new one, and this is no prerogative of any single era. Yet there have been few times when the awareness of crisis has reached and encompassed all social classes, and pervaded—though admittedly with *Phasenverschiebung*—such extensive areas of Western Europe.

III. The Search for New Security

With his categories, Paul Tillich would have described this era as in search for new symbols of security. Exactly in this way has the former Marxist, Frantisek Graus, pointed to the Hussite revolution as the crisis, not of the monetary system, not a feudal or political crisis, but as the crisis of symbols of security; he thus explained the Hussite concern with the sacraments.

In this section, I should like to pursue the late medieval effort to deal with one central aspect of the quest for new forms of security, namely, the bridging of the distance between the sacred and the profane; one could say the elimination of the ontological opposition, contrast and gap between the sacred and the profane.

In view of the present state of scholarship, we have no grounds for assuming from the beginning a common thrust pervading all late medieval movements. We are therefore well-advised to deal successively with late medieval scholasticism, the Renaissance and the Reformation. Whereas Renaissance scholarship provides us—relatively speaking—with the fewest problems, in view of the surprisingly persistent influence of Burckhardt's modernity thesis, late medieval scholasticism is still largely known, when known at all, as a chapter in the history of philosophy. Its place among the creative forces of the time is rarely mentioned. When it is dealt with, it is usually adduced to show the confusion of that epoch, the despair of reason, the divorce between faith and daily experience, and the fearful clinging to the authority of the Church. Its own self-understanding and its views on the world, on man and his society are still largely *terra incognita*. Yet late medieval scholasticism is the heyday of Franciscan thought, impregnated by ideas transmitted by the Order most deeply involved in the crises of the times.

To refer to this movement as nominalism or *via moderna*—in themselves problematical labels—is for two reasons more appropriate than to name it Scotism in the fourteenth century, after Duns Scotus, and Ockhamism in the fifteenth century, after William of Ockham. In the first place, "Scotism" and "Ockhamism" suggest too strongly a merely academic setting, whereas the ideas of the *via moderna* are on a wide scale absorbed by non-Franciscans, infiltrating even the doctrinally well-disciplined Dominican order and shaping the piety of thousands of sermons preached all over Europe—a source still largely untapped by scholarship. In the second place, nominalism proves to be the more comprehensive category, as the movement that not only survived, but even flourished long after Ockham and Ockhamism were condemned by the University of Paris in September, 1339, and again in December, 1340.[1]

I regard it as beyond the ken of the historian to determine whether the rapid spread of nominalist ideas reflects the spirit of the times in its search for new securities or whether it was a real (co-) agent in bringing forth these ideas. But the movement is not sufficiently charted if the following elements are not taken into consideration.

1. The insistence on God's *potentia ordinata* can easily leave the impression that we are confronted here with an 'establishment' theology. After all, the nominalist point of departure is that God could have decreed—*de potentia absoluta*—to create another world, to choose other means of salvation, and to establish another order. As a matter of fact, *de facto, de potentia ordinata*, however, God has committed

---

[1] Cf. Ruprecht Paqué, *Das Pariser Nominalistenstatut. Zur Entstehung des Realitäts-begriffs der neuzeitlichen Naturwissenschaft. (Occam, Buridan und Petrus Hispanus, Nikolaus von Autrecourt und Gregor von Rimini.)* (Berlin, 1970), 8ff. For the condemnation of Ockham by the Augustinian Order see Adolar Zumkeller, *Hugolin von Orvieto und seine theologische Erkenntnislehre* (Würzburg, 1841), 257f. A third reason to prefer nominalism as the more appropriate designation is that the choice of the term 'Ockhamism' is the yield of early French nationalism. The true *Inceptor* being Johannes Buridanus, the Parisian *via moderna* could well lay claim ro the title Buridanism. In the condemnations, however, the foreigner Ockham is given precedence.

himself to this world, to this Church, to this order. To remind ourselves that we are moving here in the orbit of Franciscan theology, suffices to warn us against conclusions too hastily drawn in this regard. The established reality *de potentia ordinata* is never divorced from the possibilities *de potentia absoluta*. By this, at every step, we are reminded that this, our world, is contingent, not an ontologically necessary outflow or reflection of eternal structures of being, but the result of a decree, a contract, a *pactum Dei*.

2.   Contingency is perhaps the best one-word summary of the nominalist program. This contingency is understood in two directions, embracing both the vertical relation God-world-man and the horizontal relation world-man-future. We cannot pursue now this second form of contingency, which concerns the so-called question *"De futuris contingentibus."* When applied not only to the future but also to the past, it provides for a truly scholarly basis of historical studies by its tendency to eliminate supernatural factors in the interpretation of the course of events.

Contingency should not be understood to mean unreliable, threatened by the alternatives *de potentia absoluta*. The contingency of creation and salvation means simply that they are not ontologically necessary. The point is that in the vertical dimension our reality is not the lowest emanation and level in a hierarchy of being which ascends in ever more real steps to the highest reality, God.

3.   Against the implication that our world is a mere reflection and shadow of higher levels of being, the nominalist insists on the full reality of our experienced world. Hunger for reality is so much the mark of nominalism, that it is a perhaps humorous but certainly a misleading tradition that bequeathed upon its opponents the name "realists". What is often called Ockham's razor, is the slashing away of the hierarchy of being, of ideas and concepts, which sheer speculation had invented.

4.   The protest against "wild speculation" or against "vain curiosity" is not merely a sign of anti-intellectualism. Admittedly this is not alien to the Franciscan tradition, and more generally it is a trend of the times. It is particularly noticeable in the beginning stages of the *devotio moderna*, which propagated the crusade into the interior and hence presented withdrawal as answer to the challenge of in security.

In nominalist thought we encounter the sternest opposition to the claims of intellect and reason when not verified by the tests of experience. On this basis, nominalism provided the setting for modern science, replacing the authority-based deductive method with the empirical method. The combination of *experientia* and *experimentum* allowed for a fresh investigation, by trial and error, of such basic phenomena as movement and retardation.[1] In this way the chain of causation is reduced to observable second causes, a major advance in the transition from *the* speculative law of nature to the observable *laws* of nature.

More generally it can be said that the underlying intention of nominalism is best described in terms of the late medieval revolution against the meta-categories that obfuscate reality. Just as it rejected metaphysics to establish physics, so nominalism ventured to strip theology of her distorting meta-theological shackles, with the result that the Scriptures and the prior decrees of God were emphasized at the expense of natural theology. In this attack on meta-categories I find the most revealing parallel with aspects of Italian humanism.[2]

---

[1] Anneliese Maier is generally not partial to a more positive view of progress in nominalism. Yet—in connection with questions about *intensio* and *remissio*—she observes that the empirical evidence is new : "Noch einmal : hätten sich die Früheren diese Fragen vorgelegt, so hätten sie im wesentlichen dieselben Antworten gegeben. Aber sie haben eben diese Fragen nicht explicite gestellt. Und das ist das Neue. Es ist oft hervorgehoben worden, daß der Empirismus der Neuzeit auf den Ockhamismus zurückgeht. Hier, bei der Theorie der intensio und remissio, haben wir einen der Punkte, wo diese Entwicklung mit Händen zu greifen ist." *Studien zur Naturphilosophie der Spätscholastik*, II : *Zwei Grundprobleme der scholastischen Naturphilosophie. Das Problem der intensiven Größe. Die Impetustheorie* (Roma, 1968³), 77f. Careful not to construct a causal relation she grants that it was the achievement of the impetus theory of the 14th century "an die Stelle einer rein spekulativen Betrachtung der Bewegungsphänomene eine eigentliche, an der Erfahrung orientierte Mechanik zu setzen. Mit diesem Schritt aber war die exakte Naturwissenschaft geboren." *Ibid.*, 313. Cf. A. C. Crombie, *Augustine to Galileo : The History of Science A.D. 400-1650* (Cambridge, Mass. 1953), 273. Cf. Paqué's excellent analysis of the origins of nominalism, where he—although still too much in the tradition of the German *via antiqua*—finds the modernity of nominalism in the view of language as "nachträgliches Zeichensystem für schon fertig vorliegende und verstandene Realitäten." Paqué, *op. cit.*, 266.

[2] Valla's reduction of universals to particulars is a case in point. See Charles Trinkaus who speaks once of "counter-nominalism" *(In Our Image and Likeness. Humanity and Divinity in Italian Humanist Thought* [London, 1970], I, 152), once of "thoroughgoing nominalism" *(op. cit.*, I, 381).

5. This sketch would be incomplete if in conclusion no mention were made of an emerging new image of God implied in the emphasis on God's *potentia ordinata*. God is a covenant God, his *pactum* or *foedus* is his self-commitment to become the contractual partner in creation and salvation. Here originates the Pelagianism of the *facere quod in se est*, which stands in the area of justification for the meager but sufficient human moral efforts which God has contracted, accepted or pledged to reward. In this emphasis on covenantal and not-necessary relationship between God and his world[1], as well as between God and his Church, man is no longer primarily a second cause moved by the prime mover and first cause. In the nominalist view man has become the appointed representative and partner of God responsible for his own life, society and world, on the basis and within the limits of the treaty or *pactum* stipulated by God.

Because of the frontal attack upon traditional ontology and meta-categories nominalism *could* make the impression upon contemporary ecclesiastical and secular authorities and *did* make the impression on later interpreters that it merely enhanced the climate of crisis and accelerated the late medieval disintegration of stability and time-honored structures. Nominalism did call traditional truths and answers into question in order to replace them with a new vision of the relationship between the sacred and the secular by presenting coordination as an alternative to subordination and partnership of persons instead of the hierarchy of being.

IV. Pax and the Third Age

Perhaps it is a revealing characteristic of times of crises that in them the planning for peace is particularly intensive. The two most prominent themes in treatises and reform proposals throughout the later Middle Ages are *pax* and *concordia*. From Marsilius' *Defensor pacis* through the *De pace fidei* of Cusanus, from the Joachite dreams of peace and concord in the last stage of history through the imperial reform vision of the *Reformatio Sigismundi*, reform and peace are closely associated. This state of affairs provides the necessary perspective to look upon one of the least discussed of Luther's Ninety-

---

[1] See William J. Courtenay, "Covenant and Causality in Pierre d'Ailly", *Speculum*, 46 (1971), 94-119.

Five Theses : " 'Pax, pax', et non est pax," usually bypassed by
Reformation scholars, who seize more avidly upon the seemingly
more central following thesis : " 'Crux, crux', et non est crux."[1] It
could be bypassed as merely a biblical reference, in this case from
the prophet Jeremiah (6, 14), yet as real prophecy this verse had
received a loaded meaning from St. Bernard in his widely read cycle
of sermons on the *Song of Songs* : There is peace, Bernard says, and
yet no peace : "Peace from the pagans, peace from the heretics, but
no peace from God's own children, *sed non profecto a filiis.*"[2] For all
his contemporaries the allusion to the three epochs of history was
clear. In the first period, the Church withstood the Roman persecu-
tions, and in the second, the age of the Fathers, she had been able
to deal with the heretics. Now, however, the peace of the Church
was much more seriously endangered, threatened as it was from within.

In this sense Pierre d'Ailly refers to the prophecy of Jeremiah,
which has now come true to the point of a *generalis deformatio;* in
all its scandal and horror, this had been foreseen by Joachim and
Hildegard—a thoroughgoing deformation which calls for an equally
thorough reformation.[3] Though we explicitly note that d'Ailly calls
upon the much tainted authority of Joachim—whose words, he says,
should not be held in low esteem—the conciliarist leader does not
provide an answer in keeping with the spiritual tradition from Joachim
through Olivi. Unlike them he does not assume the irreversibility of
the final apocalyptic situation. For d'Ailly the present chaos is not
the prelude to Armageddon and the last things, but a God-given
opportunity for general reform of the Church and for the re-establishment of peace.[4]

---

[1] Martin Luther, Thesis 92; *WA* I, 128, 15-17; cf. already summer 1512 : "... 'Pax,
Pax', cum non sit pax", *WA* I, 15, 10. In 1512 Pax is still in part individually understood.

[2] *Super Cantica Canticorum*, Sermo 33, 15f. : "Omnes amici, et omnes inimici ...
Ministri Christi sunt et serviunt Antichristo ... Olim praedictum est, et nunc tempus
impletionis advenit : 'Ecce in pace amaritudo mea amarissima.' ... Sed in qua pace ?
Et pax est, et non est pax. Pax a paganis, pax ab haereticis, sed non profecto a filiis."
S. Bernardi Opera (Rome, 1957 ff.), I, 244, 6-25.

[3] "Propterea extunc quidam spirituales mala haec subtilioris intelligentiae oculo
praevidentes ... et alia plura scandalosa inde sequutura praedixerunt; sicut pater in
libris Abbatis Ioachim et Hildegardis, quos non esse contemnendos quorundam magno-
rum doctorum probat auctoritas." Petrus Alliacensis, "De Reformatione Ecclesiae", in
Tractatus de materia concilii generalis (Paris, 1671), III, 69. Cf. Francis Oakley, *The
Political Thought of Pierre d'Ailly. The Voluntarist Tradition* (New Haven, 1964), 315f.

[4] "Haec autem Deus misericordissimus, qui solus ex malis bona novit elicere, ideo

The goals of conciliarism are not correctly understood when regarded as anti-papal. Such sentiments were certainly present, and the more radical aspects of Ockham's thought would later affect the decisions of the Council of Basel. In the heyday of conciliarism, however, on the long road from Pisa to Constance, the basic goal was to meet the crisis of the Church, the re-establishment of *pax* and *concordia*, or, to put it in the words of Dietrich von Niem (written in 1410), the achievement of : one pope *(capitis unius declaracio)*, one undivided Church *(membrorum una consociacio)* and moral reform by return to the mores of the early church *(morum proborum antiquorum reformacio)*.[1] Our concern in conciliar research with the *means* of implementation has lead to a deficit in attention given to the *aims* striven after. In reversing this trend we may find ourselves less mystified by the shifting development of d'Ailly and Gerson or discern more consistency in the party exchanges of Cusanus and Piccolomini.

Moving our sights from the nominalist theologian d'Ailly to a humanist professor of rhetoric, we find that Lorenzo Valla's presentation of the fraudulent basis for the so-called Donation of Constantine (1440) is by no means antipapal. In a recent study, Josef Lortz and Erwin Iserloh find here a negative, subjectivistic factor, typical of the age, which undermined the authority of the Church.[2] I am inclined to see Valla's investigation as antipapalistic, but not as antipapal. It forms his contribution to the papal efforts to come to a reunion with the Eastern Church (1439). The ultimate goal of Valla's shocking argument is formulated in his very last sentence : "Tunc papa et dicetur, et erit pater sanctus, pater omnium, pater ecclesiae, nec bella inter Christianos excitabit, sed ab aliis excitata, censura apostolica, et papali maiestate sedabit."[3] When the pope functions only as successor to Christ and not also as successor to Caesar, then

---

permittere credendus est, ut eorum occasione Ecclesia sua in melius reformetur." *Ibid.*, 69.

[1] Hermann Heimpel, ed., *De modis uniendi et reformandi ecclesiam in concilio universali* (Leipzig-Berlin, 1953), 13; cf. 42, 46.

[2] Joseph Lortz and Erwin Iserloh, *Kleine Reformationsgeschichte* (Freiburg i.B., 1969), 20.

[3] Laurentius Vaila, *De falso credito et ementita Constantini donatione declamatio*, ni *Opera Omnia* (Basel, 1540; reprint Torino, 1962 with a preface by Eugenio Garin), I, 795. These last words are introduced by the wish : "Utinam, utinam aliquando videam, nec enim mihi quicquam est longius, quam hoc videre, et praesertim meo consilio effectum, ut papa tantum vicarius Christi sit, et non etiam Caesaris ..."

he will not merely be *called* but really *be* "Holy Father", Father of all men, Father of the Church; and when war is unleashed, not by him but by others, peace will return on his apostolic command and authority.—Again, as in the case of d'Ailly, Valla sees the root of all evil, the threat to peace by greed for power, *ambitio* and *avaritia*, as lying *within* the Church. On the basis of this analysis he issued his call for reform.

This omnipresent and pervading awareness of living in a New Age, in the third epoch, witnessing a threat to the sacred realm itself, reflects and sets off reflection about the interrelationship between the sacred and the secular. Before the *dignity* of man went to seed on the European cultural scene and became mere *civility* of manners, this dignity was based on the awareness that man himself stands on the demarcation line of both worlds, forming the *trait d'union*, the link between the sacred and the secular. We find an application of this view in Valla's rejection and bridging of the gap between the secular faithful and those who have taken the monastic vows : Christians are all to be called *religiosi*. Just as in d'Ailly's call for reform, so with Valla we find not the Joachite quietistic approach, but rather the activistic partnership of the anthropology of nominalism; and what we see in Valla is more than an incidental expression of the humanist involvement in the spirit of the times. To use the words of Charles Trinkaus : "Valla represents the extreme of a humanist statement of position both on religion and human nature. But in his extremity much is revealed about humanism generally."[1]

The papal bull "Unam Sanctam" (1302) is usually regarded as an extreme papalist statement—and it is, in its designation of the Pope as the *homo spiritualis, the* spiritual man, who cannot be judged by anyone and who judges everything in both realms of Church and State. Yet this high papalogy is not novel, but a fine summary of the political consequences of that hierarchy of being where peace and justice in the world are derived from the sacred, from sanctification and legitimation through the sacraments and the jurisdiction of the Church. Without the *vera iustitia* of the Church, the Augustinian "Unam Sanctam" tradition holds that the State has to disintegrate, can only become a *latrocinium*, a robber-state—as St. Augustine put it.

Without the sanction of the sacred, the secular provide for a truly human society. If this is the case, then a relation of the sacred and

---

[1] Charles Trinkaus, *op. cit.*, II, 765.

the secular is assumed which itself must disintegrate under the on-slaught of the crisis of the later Middle Ages. When the very sources of peace and justice themselves can no longer be regarded as sacred, sanctioned and legitimated, the guarantee for peace and justice in state and society is henceforth seen in terms of a partnership between the sacred and the secular, which provides enlightened, rational man with the basis of his covenanted responsibility.

V. "Summa misericordia ... super summam miseriam directe cadit"[1]

In our final section we propose to do no more than quote three sources with some sober marginal comments. The three quotations are taken from the early writings of three later significant theologians : from the 1407 treatise on *Mystical Theology* by Jean Gerson, the 1517 *Libellus* on predestination by John von Staupitz, and Luther's *Freedom of a Christian*, written three years later in 1520. All three deal with the relation between God and man, more particularly between Christ and the sinner in terms of love and marriage symbolism. Each is mystical in tone, but not necessarily mystical in the sense of describing an unusual experience of union with God. On the contrary, what all three have in common is that this mystical experience is no longer regarded as the privilege of a few elect aristocrats of the Spirit; in accordance with the late medieval phenomenon of democratisation of mysticism, the bridal kiss and the intimate union of God and man now mark the life of every true believer.

1. We pick Gerson up at the point where he has turned to the illiterate or at least to the unschooled, for whom he emphasizes experience more than reason. After having described the preliminary stages of the penitent on the road to what he calls reformation,[2] Gerson goes

---

[1] Johann von Staupitz, *Libellus de executione aeternae praedestinationis* (Nürnberg, 1517), cap. X, n. 69.

[2] "Scito autem nisi te prius expurgaverit timoris lima per integerrimam et non fictam penitentiam, nisi mens insuper elimata peccati scoria claraque refulserit se per reformationem in novitate spiritus secundum duos primos actos ierarchicos, qui sunt purgare et illuminare, 'vanum' prorsus erit tibi 'ante lucem surgere' ad hoc culmen perfectionis : 'surgite' proinde, 'qui manducatis panem doloris', timore scilicet sine quo iustificari nemo potest ante Deum." Ioannis Carlerii de Gerson *De Mystica Theologia* [1407, 1422²], *Tractatus secundus practicus*, Cons. 12; ed. André Combes (Lugano, 1958), 215, lines 112-120.

on to say : "But when it has finally come so far that one is sufficiently pure, that is that one has a clear conscience so that one no longer ... looks at God as a judge who metes out punishment, but as the completely desirable, and lovable ..., then fly with a feeling of security into the arms of the bridegroom, embrace and kiss him with the kiss of peace which surpasses all understanding [Phil. 4, 7], so that you can say with grateful and loving devotion : "My beloved is mine and I am his. [Cant. 2, 16]."[1]

We want to make two observations. The first serves to alert us to the necessity, clearly stipulated here, for the soul to be fully purged and clean—*per reformationem*—before it can reach the *culmen perfectionis*, the embrace of the Bridegroom, where what is his, pure divinity, becomes yours and what is yours, pure humanity, becomes his. This is thoroughly traditional, and is found in the same form in St. Bernard, Ficino and Cusanus. It would not have deserved special mention, were not the other two quotations so sharply deviating. Since in the medieval exegetical tradition the individual soul and the Church are interchangeable, Gerson's view of the reformation of the Church is implied : through penance and purgation the re-establishment of the Church without spot or wrinkle. In this perspective, reformation must mean corporate purge, moral reform, withdrawal from the *negotium saeculare*.[2]

---

[1] "At vero dum eo usque pervenerit bene conscia mens et munda, ut neque gaudia neque aliud omnino vel servile vel mercennarium recogitet, neque preterea de Deo quicquam durum, asperum, negotiosum penset vel turbulentem, sicut de iudice retributore vel vindice, sed hoc unicum in mentem venerit quod sit totus desiderabilis, 'suavis et mitis' [Ps. 85,5], totus amari, 'etiam si occiderit' [Job. 13,15], dignissimus, dum ita solum placuerit amoris negotium, tunc vola securus in amplexus sponsi, stringe pectus illud divinum amicitie purissimis brachiis, fige oscula castissima pacis exsuperantis 'omnem sensum' [Phil. 4,7], ut et dicere subinde possis, gratulabunda et amorosa devotione : 'Dilectus meus michi, et ego illi' [Cant. 2,16], ...". *Ibid.*, 216, lines 122-134.

[2] The decisive point of difference between Gerson—"amor ... naturam habet congregandi seu uniendi homogenea et heterogenea, sic etiam separat et dividit" *(op. cit., Tractatus primus speculativus*, Cons. 41; ed. cit., 110f., lines 94-96)—and Luther—"vita haec non est habitatio iustitiae" *(WA Br* II, 372, 86), or "Christus enim non nisi in peccatoribus habitat" *(WA Br* I, 35, 29)—is lucidly presented by Steven E. Ozment, *Homo Spiritualis. A Comparative Study of the Anthropology of Johannes Tauler, Jean Gerson and Martin Luther (1509-16) in the Context of Their Theological Thought* (Leiden, 1969), 137; 184ff. Cf. Ozment, "Homo Viator : Luther and Late Medieval Theology", *Harvard Theological Review*, 62 (1969), 275-285 = *The Reformation in Medieval Perspective, op. cit.*, 142-154.

My second observation has a more general bearing on Luther scholarship. In Luther's own presentation of his development, he points to the *iustitia Dei* of Romans 1:17 as the key to his discovery of justification by faith. Before, as Luther indicates, he had feared and hated this *iustitia* as the punishing righteousness of God. Luther scholars have regarded this fear of the *iustitia Dei* as a unique experience of the unique man Luther which called for a unique psycho-theological explanation. Here we should be reminded, however, of Erik Erikson's brilliant analysis of Luther's preoccupation with the *cloaca*, which he interpreted in the light of Luther's unfortunate childhood experiences, his particular psychological make-up. This interpretation looks considerably less convincing when we discover the existence of a well-documented medieval *cloaca* tradition. Here we find exactly this identification of feces with the diabolic sphere of influence, which proves therefore to be a transpersonal traditional syndrome. In the same way, Gerson's description of the ascent to union with the Bridegroom de-mythologizes the uniqueness of Luther's concern with the punishing righteousness of God : Gerson describes it as a normal stage on the road to reformation through which *all* have to pass. Here again Luther can only be understood when seen as a citizen of the medieval world.

2. The second quotation stems from a precious little treatise of Staupitz which offers far more than its title indicates, "Eternal Predestination in Time and History". It is the shortest medieval *summa theologiae* known. This treatise ushers in two centuries of pre-occupation—of Calvinists, Lutherans and Tridentine Catholics alike—with the doctrine of predestination as the central core of the Christian faith.

After having described what he calls the "contract" between Christ and the Christian, the point at which the soul says "Yours is mine, and mine is Yours," he goes on to explain this union : "Already you can see how appropriate it is that the tax collectors and prostitutes precede us into the kingdom of heaven ... It follows, therefore, that those have nothing in common with their Bridegroom who do not participate with Him in sin, who claim righteousness for themselves, who spurn sinners. After all, this marital love is the highest mercy, which falls immediately upon the deepest misery, concerned as it is before everything else with the extinction of sin. For this purpose 'He gave himself up for the Church that he might sanctify her, having cleansed her by the washing with water in the Word of Life that the glorious Church might be presented before Him without spot or wrinkle or any such thing, that she might be holy and without blemish' [Eph. 5:25-27]."[1] Here purgation is not the precondition for that union in which justification takes place; instead, purgation takes place in the marriage union itself. Not purgation but sin is the precondition for fulfillment of the contract, the exchange of possessions; Christ is only interested in real sinners. Only real sinners have something to offer Him : their sin.

Earlier, Staupitz had assigned what medieval theologians called sacramental grace, *gratia gratum faciens*, to God's eternal predestination, making Christ himself the intermediary of created grace. To put this in as short a formula as possible : justification not by ascent of the sinner but by the descent of Christ; or, justification on the level of the secular sinner, not on the level of the sacred God. To put it in Staupitz's own programmatic words : "highest mercy falls immediately—without mediators—upon deepest misery." The gap between the sacred and the secular could not have been shortened more dramatically than here in justification, the central theme of late medieval theology.

3. Without further comment we turn now to Luther's proclamation of freedom by faith, perhaps his single most influential writing, widely accepted also by those who would give this freedom a more political interpretation than intended by the Wittenberg Reformer.

After having interpreted faith as trust in God and identification with his Word, Luther continues : "The third incomparable benefit of faith is that it unites the soul with Christ, as a bride is united with her bridegroom. By this mystery, as the Apostle teaches, Christ and the soul become one flesh. And if they are one flesh and there is between them a true marriage—indeed the most perfect of all marriages, since human marriages are but poor examples of this one true mar-

---

[1] "Iam vides, quam iuste in regnum coelorum praecedunt nos publicani et meretrices. Vides etiam, quare permissa sunt peccata, et quod 'omnes peccaverunt et egent gloria'. Consequens ergo est : eos nihil habere commune cum sponsa qui ei in peccatis non communicant, qui sibi iustitiam vendicant, qui peccatores spernunt. Amor enim iste sponsalis summa misericordia est et super summam miseriam directe cadit, de exstinctione peccati prae cunctis sollicitus." Johann von Staupitz, *Libellus de executione aeternae praedestinationis*, cap. X, n. 68 and n. 69. See here David C. Steinmetz, *Misericordia Dei. The Theology of Johannes von Staupitz in its Late Medieval Setting* (Leiden, 1968), 91.

riage—, it follows that everything they have they hold in common, the good as well as the evil ... Christ is full of grace, life and salvation. The soul is full of sins, death and damnation. Now let faith come between them and sins, death and damnation will be Christ's while grace, life and salvation will be the soul's; for if Christ is a bridegroom, he must take upon himself the things which are his bride's and bestow upon her the things that are his ... Who then can fully appreciate what this royal marriage means? Who can understand the riches of the glory of this grace? Here this rich and divine bridegroom Christ marries this poor, wicked harlot, redeems her from all her evil, and adorns her with all his goodness."[1]

Luther deviates in this text, with its famous *"Fröhliche Wechsel"* or *commercium admirabile*, just as sharply from Gerson as Staupitz had before him. At one point he intensifies the unprecedented marriage deal, *commercium*, with an explicit reference to the sinful bride as the harlot.[2] He differs with Staupitz's formulation on one significant point : for Luther the union with Christ is mediated through union with his word, through faith in his promises. This point should be stressed when the relation between the thought of Staupitz and Luther is analyzed. But in either case, we find a new proximity, even immediacy, between a twain that had not met before so pointedly, obliterating the gap between the sacred and the secular.

With this view of justification a concept of reformation is given which differs from the conciliar reform of Gerson. The profound misery of the Church, the allegorical counterpart to the misery of the soul, is not to be purged as a precondition in order to restore the Church without spot or wrinkle. Yet the crisis of the Church is not overlooked or taken lightly; it is seen as characteristic of the Church in time and space. Henceforth reformation will not be the structural reform of Gerson or the return to the mores of the early Church, as Dietrich von Niem had put it, or the achievement of lasting peace in the words of Valla. Luther's reformation, part and child of the crises of the

---

[1] *Luther's Works* [American edition] 31, 351f.; *WA* VII, 54, 31-55, 27.

[2] The "harlot" element is unprecedented in the medieval *commercium*-tradition and a far cry from St. Augustine's one allusion to the two *commercia*, the first of Christ's compensation to the Father and the second of his gift to the sinner, offering his death for the life of man : "Mortuus est Deus, ut compensatio fieret coelestis cuiusdam mercimonii, ne mortem videret homo. ... Qualia commercia! quid dedit et quid accipit? Mercantes homines veniunt ad commercia, ad res mutandas ... Tamen nemo dat vitam, ut accipiat mortem." *Sermo* 80, 1, 5 on Math. 17, 18-20; *PL* 38, 496D-497A.

later Middle Ages, has a dual focal point, first in the acknowledgment
of the perpetual nature of the crisis of man and his society, and secondly, the trust in the reality of the sacred embrace of the secular condition.

Looking back on the path we have travelled, we find no reason to
conclude that the Reformation movement has a unique claim upon
penetration into the modern era. We have not given "equal time" to
the Italian Renaissance, since the Burkhardtian stress upon modernity
finds ample support today and at the same time is kept under sufficient control by Kristeller's emphasis upon continuity with the
Middle Ages.[1] As a matter of fact, we find not only continuity with
the preceding medieval tradition but also striking congruity with
contemporary Scholasticism, in some respects even more profound
than the congruity of the Italian Renaissance with the learned aesthetic,
apolitical piety of Erasmian Humanism, north of the Alps. The development of Italian Renaissance humanist thought in the direction of "the
subordination of philosophy to rhetoric"[2] as the access route to wisdom
could be and was hailed by nominalists in their revolt against meta-
categories. When the debate about a "civic humanism" subsides,
we shall be left in the realm of political theory with the impressive
Renaissance achievement of a new diplomacy based on a balance-of-
power concept, emerging out of a reality-oriented, realistic grasp of
the secular condition, which is to shape the political affairs of the
future.

In view of the size of the research task confronting us, we have
dedicated more time and space to the ideas emerging from late medieval
Scholasticism. If I seem to have sided with Troeltsch in arguing for
the medieval roots and context of the Reformation movement, then
it is important to formulate *expressis verbis*, what I implicitly noted
in my enumeration of the chief characteristics of that dominant late
medieval scholastic movement which we decided to call nominalism.
If the discovery of the inductive method as the basis for reliable
scientific conclusions is the harbinger of modern research—and hence

---

[1] Cf. Paul Oskar Kristeller, *Renaissance Thought* (New York, 1961), 92-119; Id.,
Le thomisme et la pensée italienne de la Renaissance (Montréal-Paris, 1967). Adumbrations
of this view already in Kristeller's *magnum opus*, now after 35 years finally published
in its original, *Die Philosophie des Marsilio Ficino* (Frankfurt am Main, 1972).

[2] Hanna Grey, "Renaissance Humanism : The Pursuit of Eloquence", *Journal of
the History of Ideas*, 24 (1963), 497-514. Cf. Jerrold E. Seigel, *Rhetoric and Philosophy
in Renaissance Humanism. The Union of Eloquence and Wisdom. Petrarch to Valla*
(Princeton, 1968), 255; cf. 168f.

as important as the discovery of the New World; if the new understanding of the covenantal relationship between God and man as partners signifies the coming of a new season, the season of the dignity of man; in short, if the closing of the gap between the sacred and the secular carries the marks of the time to come, we dare to see in the crisis of the later Middle Ages the birthpangs of the Modern Era.

2. NOMINALISM AND LATE MEDIEVAL RELIGION

WILLIAM J. COURTENAY

University of Wisconsin

Nominalism has long been considered a major intellectual movement within late medieval society. The altered form which it supposedly gave to late scholasticism, the dominant role it played in the universities of northern Europe, the personalities that contributed to its formation and dissemination have attracted the attention of those interested in the philosophy, theology, political thought, literature, and art not only of the late Middle Ages but of the Renaissance and Reformation as well. It is natural to expect that nominalism should provide some insight into the spirit and mood of the age, and many parallels have been drawn between nominalism and other developments contemporary with it. As necessary and fruitful as this enterprise is, however, it has become difficult to realize. During the last forty years a revision has taken place in the traditional understanding of the nature and implications of nominalism. Although a new consensus has been reached on the thought of certain figures within the nominalist movement, the interpretation of the majority of figures and issues is still controversial.

It is obvious that when the interpretation of nominalism is significantly altered, the theories that relate nominalism to other late medieval developments must also be revised. It is the intent of this paper to describe briefly the changing assessment of late medieval nominalism and, for purposes of discussion, to make some tentative suggestions about how the most recent views might relate to other aspects of late medieval society, especially late medieval religion.

1. The Traditional Assessment of Nominalism

Scholars of late medieval thought writing before 1930 had the comforting assurance that they knew what nominalism was and who the nominalists were. Nominalism was the view in logic that defined universals as concepts created by the mind without real, or extra-mental, referents, and thus without meaning as a description of external reality. Building upon the atomism implicit in this epistemological and ontological premise derived from such twelfth-century thinkers as Roscelin and Peter Abelard, the late medieval nominalists, principally William of Ockham, Gregory of Rimini, Pierre d'Ailly, Marsilius of Inghen, and Gabriel Biel, attacked metaphysics, ethics, and even scientific methodology, thus undermining and destroying the major achievements of high scholasticism. The pervasive influence in the late Middle Ages of this philosophical trend with its devastating theological implications was an established fact that did not need to be questioned or re-examined. As far back as Werner,[1] Denifle,[2] and DeWulf[3] the meaning and influence of nominalism was a "given" to which other evidence and insights had to conform.

This picture of nominalism had been fashioned over several centuries and was a composite based more on the late medieval nominalists than upon their twelfth-century counterparts.[4] A particular body of ideas, all interrelated and mutually reinforced, contributed to the definition of nominalism. These recurrent ideas or themes that together compose the traditional view of nominalism are : (1) atomism, particularism, or individualism; (2) excessive stress on the omnipotence of God; (3) voluntarism; (4) skepticism; and (5) fideism. These themes reappeared in different ways and in different groupings as the various areas of nominalist thought were explained.

---

[1] Karl Werner, *Die Scholastik des späteren Mittelalters*, vols. 1-4 (Vienna, 1881-1887).

[2] Heinrich Denifle, *Luther und Luthertum* (Mainz, 1904-1909).

[3] Maurice de Wulf, *Histoire de la philosophie médiévale* (Paris, 1900).

[4] The basic elements in the traditional view of nominalism can be found in Constantine Michalski, "Les courants philosophiques à Oxford et à Paris pendant le XIVe siècle," *Bulletin international de l'Academie Polonaise des Sciences et des Lettres*, classe d'histoire et de philosophie, 1919-1920 (Cracow, 1922), 59-88; "Les sources du criticisme et du scepticism dans la philosophie du XIVe siècle," *International Congress of Historical Sciences* (La Pologne au Ve Congrès international des Sciences Historiques) (Bruxelles, 1923-24), 241-268; "Le criticisme et le scepticisme dans la philosophie du XIVe siècle," *BIAPSL*, CHP (Cracow, 1927), 41-122; "Les courants critiques et sceptiques dans la philosophie du XIVe siècle," *BIAPSL*, CHP (Cracow, 1927), 192-242; "Le problème de la volonté à Oxford et à Paris au XIVe siècle," *Studia Philosophica : Commentarii Societatis Philosophicae Polonorum*, vol. II (Lvov, 1937), 233-367; Franz Ehrle, *Der Sentenzenkommentar Peters von Candia* (Münster i.W., 1925). More recent versions of this assessment can be found in Gordon Leff, *Medieval Thought from Saint Augustine to Ockham* (St. Albans, 1958); Armand A. Maurer, *Medieval Philosophy* (New York, 1962); and David Knowles, *The Evolution of Medieval Thought* (London, 1962).

The beginning point for nominalism, the basic view that shaped the rest of the system, has traditionally been discovered in the area of logic and, closely related to that, epistemology. It has been thought that the nominalists believed that only the individual was real and that common nature was a figment of the imagination. Moreover, logic concerned the interrelation of mental concepts, not external reality, and thus logic was the study of terms and signs rather than things.

One of the results of this nominalist, or terminist, logic was epistemological skepticism, for which several explanations have been given. In some versions the stress on signs and the rejection of universals was construed to mean that there was an unbridgeable gap between the object and the knowing mind. Moreover, the primacy and autonomy of the individual, combined with the denial of the validity, or at least the demonstrability, of the principle of causality, dissolved the cause-effect relationship of object and mind. In other versions nominalism was thoroughly empirical, ascribing truth only to those propositions that were self-evident and could be known analytically or whose content was derived directly from sense experience. In both cases, in order to be true the contrary of the proposition could not be asserted without involving a contradiction. Viewed in this way, it was not external reality but metaphysical truth that could not be known by man in this life.

The traditional evaluation of the relation of nominalism to the development of science depended upon a certain understanding of the operation and implications of the nominalist epistemology. If one believed that nominalism severed the tie between the knowing mind and external reality, then scientific inquiry became impossible. Even if one accepted the view that nominalism was empirical, its scientific value could still be questioned. Was not a proper scientific method impossible where universals were rejected in favor of an atomistic view of the physical universe and the composition of matter and where the idea of relation and the principle of causality were regarded as unknowable or indemonstrable? Moreover, the nominalist view of divine activity envisaged the possibility of divine intervention and direct divine causality within the natural order, so that God might deceive man by producing an intuitive cognition of a non-existent.

Perhaps the most disturbing aspect of nominalist thought in the traditional interpretation was the effect nominalism purportedly had upon metaphysics. If truth were limited to those propositions that were self-evident or based directly on sense experience, then one could not validly speculate on form and matter nor on substance and relation. In addition, the principle of causality upon which so much metaphysical speculation was based, could not be demonstrated. Furthermore, one could not demonstrate the existence of God and other issues in natural theology that were so important for thirteenth-century metaphysics. The rejection of metaphysics as a proper scientific area of human inquiry brought about a separation of faith and reason that could only be bridged by fideism, a blind trust in the authority of the church.

Closely related to the destruction of natural theology and metaphysics was the rejection of the ethical system based on natural law and its replacement by a system of moral positivism. This developed from the nominalist stress on divine omnipotence and the primacy of the divine will, attributes of God which could not be analyzed, predicted, or judged. The order that prevails, be it the order of the physical universe or the moral order, is in no sense necessary. God could have established and still could establish a different moral order in which murder and adultery would be virtuous acts. God could even cause a man to hate him and accept such action as meritorious. The moral order which presently pertains, therefore, is dependent solely on the arbitrary will of God and can be altered.

Finally, the traditional assessment of the nominalist view of the nature of the church and society again stressed individuality and atomism. Both institutions were supposedly composed solely of autonomous individuals. Thus nominalism favored representative forms of government. The church universal and the political commonwealth were mental creations superimposed on Christendom.

It was conceded that the system thus described was accurate only as a description of late medieval nominalism. The principle of God's absolute power, of the possibility of divine intervention, was not a developed part of twelfth-century nominalism. Further, it was admitted that the system was a composite, derived from an examination of the thought of various fourteenth- and fifteenth-century thinkers, principally Ockham, d'Ailly, and Biel. The description, however, purported to be an accurate picture of the full implications of the nominalist system that was developed in the early fourteenth century and continued as a major intellectual force into the sixteenth century.

Nominalism was not, in the traditional interpretation, simply a system of thought. It was a school that had its own peculiar historical development. John Duns Scotus, Durand of St. Pourçain, and Peter Aureol were the precursors of the movement that was brought to fruition by William of Ockham around 1320. The destructive tendency of Ockham's thought, both in philosophy and theology, was recognized by his contemporaries, and he was summoned to Avignon in 1324 to stand trial. He avoided condemnation only by fleeing Avignon before the completion of the process against him. The forces unleashed by him continued to flourish unchecked in England (through the teaching of Robert Holcot, O. P., Adam Wodham, O. F. M., and Richard of Billingham) and at Paris (through the teaching of Nicholas of Autrecourt, John of Mirecourt, O. Cist., and Pierre de Guichart.).

Opposition to Ockhamism was slow to crystalize in an effective manner. Walter Chatton's critique of Ockham and Wodham produced no censures of nominalism in England during the 1330's. By the end of that decade, however, the Arts Faculty at Paris had become sufficiently concerned over Ockhamism to begin proscribing nominalist teaching. In September, 1339, the Parisian Arts Faculty censured Ockhamism and, fourteen months later, Nicholas of Autrecourt and others were summoned to Avignon to answer charges of teaching things contrary to the faith. In the next month the Arts Faculty at Paris followed that papal action by condemning a series of nominalist propositions.

The effectiveness of the prohibitions of 1339-1340 was momentary. The investigation of the teaching of Nicholas of Autrecourt dragged on, due to a change in popes and the desire of the curial commission to give Nicholas an opportunity for an adequate defense. Finally, however, action was taken by papacy and university alike. Autrecourt was condemned in 1346, and in the following year he burned his books and made a public retraction at Paris. Moreover, in that same year (1347) the Faculty of Theology condemned John of Mirecourt, and a long series of propositions, taken largely from his writings but including statements from Arnold of Villanova and Adam Wodham, were prohibited. Although no corresponding condemnation took place at Oxford (as had happened in 1277), the teaching at both universities seems to have become more cautious and conservative.

At the end of the fourteenth century nominalism (in a form less radical than Autrecourt) captured the arts and theological faculties of the newly founded German universities and dominated them in the fifteenth century as it had dominated Paris and Oxford in the fourteenth. Many of the best known theologians of this period have been placed within the nominalist school : Pierre d'Ailly, John Gerson, Marsilius of Inghen, Henry of Langenstein, and Henry Totting of Oyta. Although constantly at war with the *via antiqua* in the fifteenth century, nominalism lived on in Germany, especially through the teaching of Gabriel Biel and his disciples, to contribute, both negatively and positively, to the Protestant Reformation.

The traditional analysis of nominalism and the picture of its historical development were already undergoing modification before 1930. However, a surprisingly large portion of the traditional view has lived on to dominate even the most recent textbooks on the history of medieval thought. When parallels or contrasts are made between late scholasticism and art, literature, and religion in the late Middle Ages, it is frequently the older view of nominalism that forms the basis for comparison. For example, those familiar with Erwin Panofsky's *Gothic Architecture and Scholasticism* will immediately recognize in his description of the relation of late gothic architecture to late medieval thought the traditional description of nominalism, where the fragmentation of design and structure into meaningless and unrelated ornamentation or austere simplicity is paralleled by the critical Ockhamist movement that destroyed the synthesis of high scholasticism, with its balance, harmony, and universality.[1] The late medieval mood of pessimism, despair, and decay that Huizinga describes in his *Waning of the Middle Ages*, based largely on literary evidence, also owes something to the traditional assessment of nominalism, as his chapter on "Symbolism in its Decline" reveals.[2] The flowering of late medieval piety and mysticism is often attributed to the fideism and skepticism that followed the break-up of the thirteenth-century synthesis. Numerous theories on the origin and meaning of the Protestant Reformation, not the least of which is the view of Luther taken by Joseph Lortz, have been based on a negative assessment of late medieval nominalism, whose decadence not only required some type of theological reform but obscured the issues so that reform could not recapture the purity of pre-fourteenth century Catholic theology but rather led to a fragmentation of Christianity.[3]

---

[1] Erwin Panofsky, *Gothic Architecture and Scholasticism* (Archabbey, Pa., 1951).

[2] Johan Huizinga, *The Waning of the Middle Ages* (London, 1924).

[3] Joseph Lortz, *Die Reformation in Deutschland*, (Freiburg, 1940, 1949).

2. Revisions in the Understanding of Late Medieval Thought

The changing evaluation of nominalism and late medieval thought that has been taking place since about 1930 has not made the impact it deserves. There are several reasons for this. First of all, the statements upon which the earlier view was based can, for the most part, be found in the writings of Ockham and/or others in the fourteenth and fifteenth centuries traditionally associated with him. The question is, therefore, one of interpretation, and many of the points at issue between the old and newer views depend upon the interpretation of the nominalist use of the distinction between the absolute and ordained powers of God. Secondly, the difficulties of working in a field where there are very few printed sources has discouraged many from checking the texts on which the old and new views are based, and consequently, the number of participating scholars is relatively small. Thirdly, those who have done research in the late medieval field since 1930 have (unlike earlier scholars such as Michalski and De Wulf) generally concentrated their efforts on only one aspect of the thought of that period (for example, logic, science, theology, or political thought). Consequently, there are few recent works that treat Ockhamism or nominalism in general. Finally, vested interests (both Protestant and Catholic) committed to the earlier assessment have prolonged the life of the traditional approach in spite of the weakening evidence in support of it. Some Catholic intellectual historians of a Thomist persuasion, possibly believing that a more positive evaluation of late medieval thought would diminish the significance of Thomas and the validity of Neo-Thomist metaphysics, have ignored or rejected the revision without listening to its case and without re-examining the texts. Protestant historians have been equally committed to the view of the decline and corruption of late medieval thought. which could be viewed as one of the great justifying causes of the Reformation.

Most of those whose research has contributed to the revised understanding of nominalism and late medieval thought have utilized one of two basic approaches. There are those, first of all, who have accepted the traditional view or definition of nominalism and, upon discovering that a theologian traditionally regarded as a nominalist (for example, Ockham or Gregory of Rimini) does not maintain that system or the particular aspect of it under consideration, have removed that theologian from the ranks of the nominalists. In some cases this research was conducted by historians with no visible confessional or parochial interest, and the results of their research (perhaps quite different from what they expected) left the general understanding of late medieval thought and nominalism intact. Albert Lang's study of Henry Totting of Oyta [1] and Gerhard Ritter's work on Marsilius of Inghen [2] fall within this category. Other historians using this approach belonged to religious orders and have concentrated their research on a figure or figures within their own order. This has led some to question the motives of these scholars and to cast doubt, unjustly I think, on the disinterestedness and validity of the conclusions of their research. Philotheus Boehner and his students and followers at St. Bonaventure's fall within this category. [3] Among the non-Franciscans who have adopted this approach is the Augustinian, Damasus Trapp. [4]

On the other hand, there are those who initially take the term 'nominalism' as a neutral term that simply describes the thought of William of Ockham and his followers. Upon discovering that Ockham and other 'nominalists' did not maintain the positions once attributed to them, they proceeded to redefine the term 'nominalism' along the lines of a more accurate description of the thought of Ockham or Biel. Within this approach may be placed the contributions of Paul Vignaux (for example, his articles in the *DTC* on Ockham and nominalism as well as his later study of nominalism) [5] and Heiko Oberman (both his

---

[1] Albert Lang, *Heinrich Totting von Oyta* (Beiträge zur Geschichte der Philosophie und Theologie des Mittelalters, XXXIII, 4/5; Münster i.W., 1937).

[2] Gerhard Ritter, *Studien zur Spätscholastik*, vol. I : *Marsilius von Inghen und die okkamistische Schule in Deutschland* (Sitzungsberichte der Heidelberger Akademie der Wissenschaften, Philosophische-historische Klasse; Heidelberg, 1921).

[3] Philotheus Boehner, *Collected Articles on Ockham* (Franciscan Institute Publications, Philosophy Series, No. 12; St. Bonaventure, N.Y., 1958); Oswald Fuchs, *The Psychology of Habit According to William Ockham* (FIP, Phil. Ser., No. 8; St. Bonaventure, 1952); Matthew C. Menges, *The Concept of Univocity Regarding the Predication of God and Creature According to William Ockham* (FIP, Phil. Ser., No. 9; St. Bonaventure, 1952); Damascene Webering, *Theory of Demonstration According to William Ockham* (FIP, Phil. Ser., No. 10; St. Bonaventure, 1953); and Herman Shapiro, *Motion, Time and Place According to William Ockham* (FIP, Phil. Ser., No. 13; St. Bonaventure, 1957).

[4] Damasus Trapp, "Augustinian Theology of the 14th Century," *Augustiniana*, VI (1956), 146-274; "Peter Ceffons of Clairvaux," *Recherches de théologie ancienne et médiévale*, XXIV (1957), 101-154; "Clm 27034 : Unchristened Nominalism and Wycliffite Realism at Prague in 1381," *RTAM*, XXIV (1957), 320-360.

[5] Paul Vignaux, "Nominalisme," in *Dictionnaire de théologie catholique*, XI.1 (Paris, 1930), cols. 717-784; 'Occam," in *DTC*, XI.1 (Paris, 1930), cols. 876-889; *Nominalisme au XIVe siècle* (Paris, 1948).

early article on nominalism and his subsequent study of Gabriel Biel).[1]

The first approach concludes that a given figure was not a nominalist if his thought is more in keeping with the method and moderation of the thirteenth century. This approach has the advantage that the content of the term 'nominalism' remains intact and everyone knows what it means. The difficulty, however, may be that as more and more figures are examined and found not to conform with the traditional understanding of nominalism, we may end up with an important late medieval school of thought in which we cannot place any important late medieval thinker. The second approach takes a similarly positive attitude toward figures traditionally associated with nominalism but, believing that the term 'nominalism' is only a descriptive term for the thought of these men, also gives the term 'nominalism' a positive connotation. In this second approach the term 'nominalism' loses its specific, traditional content, and runs the risk of being redefined with every new study.

Regardless of approach, the end result of the research of these historians has been to construct a three-school, or three-movement, theory of late scholasticism.[2] There was first of all the conservative, Augustinian branch of late medieval thought (including such figures as Thomas Bradwardine, Gregory of Rimini, and Hugolino Malbranche of Orvieto), designated by the terms "right-wing nominalism"[3] or "historico-critical group".[4] Second, there was the moderate, central, or middle branch of late medieval thought (including such figures as Ockham, Pierre d'Ailly, and Gabriel Biel), to which were ascribed the terms 'moderate nominalism', 'Ockhamism', or the less radical

---

[1] Heiko A. Oberman, "Some Notes on the Theology of Nominalism with attention to its Relation to the Renaissance," *Harvard Theological Review*, LIII (1960), 47-76; *The Harvest of Medieval Theology* (Cambridge, Mass., 1963).

[2] Oberman actually designated four branches of late medieval nominalism : a conservative "right wing," a radical "left wing," an Ockhamistic, moderate, middle-of-the-road position, and a syncretistic school that combined Ockhamism and Scotism. This fourth "school," in which Oberman placed John of Ripa and Peter of Candia, was ignored in *The Harvest of Medieval Theology*, and the recent studies of Paul Vignaux make it doubtful whether Ripa and Candia should be connected with nominalism at all. Trapp seems to have a "two-school" theory, but he implies a distinction within what he calls the "logico-critical" school between moderates and extremists.

[3] "Right wing" and 'left wing" are terms used by Oberman, "Some Notes on the Theology of Nominalism ..."

[4] "Historico-critical," "logico-critical," and "modernist" are terms used by Trapp, "Augustinian Theology ..."

branch of the "logico-critical group". Finally there was the radical branch of late medieval thought (those that supposedly resembled the traditional view of nominalism, for instance, Robert Holcot, Adam Wodham, Nicholas of Autrecourt, and John of Mirecourt), described as "left-wing nominalism", "modernism", or the radical branch of the "critico-logical group". I will have more to say about the suitability of these categorizations and approaches after examining the major aspects of the revised understanding of late medieval thought as constructed in the period from 1930 to 1965.

It is inappropriate to dismiss the revision, as is sometimes done, with the suggestion that it is the product of a misguided Franciscan chauvinism. This view suggests that the Franciscans originated the revision and encouraged it in order to remove certain Franscicans, in particular William of Ockham, from the ranks of the nominalists and thus to absolve the Franciscans from contributing to the late medieval decay of philosophy and theology and, inadvertently, to the Reformation.[1] When one examines the stages in the revised understanding of late scholasticism, the absurdity of this view becomes apparent. The two earliest scholars upon whose work the revision is founded, Erich Hochstetter [2] and Paul Vignaux, were not even in religious orders. If anything, they came from backgrounds that were sympathetic to Thomas. Two other scholars whose contribution has been equally important are also "secular" in background, E. A. Moody [3]

---

[1] This charge has been made against Boehner. It more properly applies, however, to the research of Ludger Meier in his attempt to dissassociate the Erfurt Franciscans from Ockhamism. In particular, see : "De schola franciscana erfordiensi saeculi XV," *Antonianum*, V (1930), 57-94, 157-202. 333-362, 443-474; "Ein neutrales Zeugnis für den Gegensatz von Skotismus und Ockhamismus im spätmittelalterlichen Erfurt," *Franziskanische Studien*, XXVI (1939), 167-182, 258-287; "Research that Has Been Made and Is Yet to Be Made on the Ockhamism of Martin Luther at Erfurt," *Archivum Franciscanum Historicum*, XLIII (1950), 56-67; and *Die Barfüsserschule zu Erfurt* (Münster i.W., 1958).

[2] Erich Hochstetter, *Studien zur Metaphysik und Erkenntnislehre Wilhelms von Ockham* (Berlin and Leipzig, 1927); "Nominalismus?" *Franciscan Studies*, IX (1949), 370-403; "Viator mundi : Einige Bemerkungen zur Situation des Menschen bei Wilhelm von Ockham," *Franziskanische Studien*, XXXII (1950), 1-20.

[3] E. A. Moody, *The Logic of William of Ockham* (New York, 1935); "Ockham, Buridan, and Nicholas of Autrecourt," *Franciscan Studies*, VII (1947), 113-146; "Ockham and Aegidius of Rome," *Franciscan Studies*, IX (1949), 417-442; *Truth and Consequence in Medieval Logic* (Amsterdam, 1953); "Empiricism and Metaphysics in Medieval Philosophy," *Philosophical Review*, LXVII (1958), 145-163; "Buridan and a Dilemma of Nominalism," *Harry Austryn Wolfson Jubilee Volume*, vol. II (Jerusalem, 1965),

and Heiko Oberman. In fact, the only Franciscan among the major contributors to the revision is Philotheus Boehner.

A new assessment of Ockhamism or, if you like, moderate nominalism, has emerged during the last forty years through the efforts of Hochstetter, Vignaux, Boehner, Moody, and Oberman. The following description is a composite made up from their research into the thought of Ockham and Biel, and it contrasts sharply with the traditional overview presented above.

a) *Universals and the Relation of Logic to External Reality*

No one disputes the fact that Ockham gave primacy to the singular and rejected the idea that there existed a "common nature," which inhered in things that "look alike" and which produced their resemblance. For Ockham, resemblance among things of the same species exists in external reality and is experienced by man. This however, is not the result of a common nature inhering in things of the same species. One need not pursue resemblance into "an intelligible order of abstract essences and necessary relations ontologically prior to particular things."[1] Similarity among things of the same species has a genetic origin, and it is based on what each individual has in himself, not on any shared nature or essence. Socrates resembles Plato more than a donkey because Socrates has a rational soul and Plato has a rational soul; they do not, however, have a rational soul "in common."[2]

The first stage by which a natural resemblance becomes a universal concept is the natural sign. A natural sign is a concept applicable to many particulars that resemble one another before an individual mind has expressed that concept in language. When a concept is expressed in language, whether it remains a thought (mental concept) or is spoken or written, it becomes a conventional sign, or term. The concept, whether as a natural or conventional sign, is the act of understanding and is predicable of many individual things that resemble one another.

577-596; "Ockhamism," in *Encyclopedia of Philosophy*, vol. V (New York, 1968), 533-534; and "William of Ockham," in *Encyclopedia of Philosophy*, vol. VIII (New York, 1968), 306-317.

[1] Moody, "William of Ockham," 307.

[2] Ockham, *Summa Logicae*, Pt. I, ch. 17 (Boehner edition, St. Bonaventure, 1957), 53. Cf. Hochstetter, *Studien zur Metaphysik* ..., 78-117; Vignaux, "Nominalisme," 736-742; Boehner, "The Realistic Conceptualism of William Ockham," in *Collected Articles* ..., 156-174; Moody, "William of Ockham," 307-312.

Logic concerns the correct manipulation of natural and conventional signs within propositions and syllogisms. Moreover, truth or falsity is applicable only to propositions and syllogisms, not objects in external reality. For example, there is nothing true or false about the terms 'God' or 'man'. There is something true or false about the propositions 'God exists' or 'Socrates existed'. Propositional knowledge, although it is a mental creation concerned with universality rather than particularity, is directly related to and dependent upon external reality through sense experience. This is the reason why Ockham's thought is considered empirical. But before we examine Ockham's epistemology and the principle of cause and effect on which it was based, it may be helpful to examine Ockham's understanding of divine power and will which supposedly, along with the principle of singularity or particularity, destroyed the medieval philosophical system.

b) *The Dialectic of the Two Powers of God*

Because of the importance of this distinction for nominalist thought and because its meaning has been frequently misunderstood, the dialectic of the two powers deserves a fuller treatment than the other areas of nominalism. The distinction between the absolute and ordained powers of God had its origin in the late eleventh century and was the common property of the schools from the twelfth century on.[1] Simply put, the distinction meant that according to absolute power God, inasmuch as he is omnipotent, has the *ability* to do many things that he does not *will* to do, has never done, nor ever will do. By viewing God's intellect and will from the temporal standpoint and by attributing to God a distinction between the ability to act and the desire to act, theologians acknowledged an area of initial possibility for divine action, limited only by the principle of contradiction, out of which the things God did do or is going to do were chosen.

The distinction was theological, and its major function in the thirteenth century, as the discussion of the distinction in Thomas

---

[1] On the origin of the distinction see : W. J. Courtenay, "Necessity and Freedom in Anselm's Conception of God," *Wirkungsgeschichte Anselms von Canterbury* (Proceedings of the International Anselm Congress, Bad Wimpfen, Germany, 13-16 September, 1970.) to be published in 1974; R. P. Desharnais, *The History of the Distinction between God's Absolute and Ordained Power and Its Influence on Martin Luther* (Unpublished dissertation, Catholic University of America, Washington, 1966); A. Lang, *Die Wege der Glaubensbegründung bei den Scholastikern des 14. Jahrhunderts* (Beiträge zur Geschichte der Philosophie des Mittelalters, XXX.1/2; Münster i.W., 1930).

illustrates, was to affirm that God did not act of necessity; he could
have done things other than those he chose to do.[1] Thus the present
order, the order that God has established, is not identical with his

---

[1] Thomas Aquinas, *On the Power of God* (*Quaestiones disputatae de potentia Dei*),
q. 1, a. 5 (Westminster, Maryland, 1952), 29-31 : "I reply that the error of those who
say that God cannot do otherwise than he does is connected with two schools of thought.
Certain philosophers maintained that God acts from natural necessity : in which case
since nature is confined to one effect, the divine power could not extend to other things
besides what it actually does. Then there have been certain theologians who maintained
that God cannot act beside the order of divine justice and wisdom according to which
he works, and thus they came to say that God cannot do otherwise than he does. ...
Accordingly we conclude that a thing which acts from natural necessity cannot be a
principle of action, since its end is determined by another. Hence it is impossible that
God act from natural necessity, and so the foundation of the first opinion is false.

"It remains for us to examine the second opinion. Observe then that there are two
senses in which one is said to be unable to do a thing. First, absolutely : when, namely,
one of the principles necessary for an action does not extend to that action; thus if
his foot be fractured a man cannot walk. Secondly, by supposition, for if we suppose
the opposite of an action, that action cannot be done, thus so long as I sit I cannot
walk. ... For even as the divine goodness is made manifest through these things that are
and through this order of things, so could it be made manifest through other creatures
and another order : wherefore God's will without prejudice to his goodness, justice and
wisdom, can extend to other things besides those which he has made. And this is where
they erred : for they thought that the created order was commensurate and necessary
to the divine goodness. It is clear then that God absolutely can do otherwise than he
has done. Since, however, he cannot make contradictories to be true at the same time,
it can be said *ex hypothesi* that God cannot make other things besides those he has
made : for if we suppose that he does not wish to do otherwise, or that he foresaw that
he would not do otherwise, as long as the supposition stands, he cannot do otherwise,
though apart from that supposition he can." *Summa theologiae*, Pt. I, q. 25, a. 5 : "Some
laid it down that God acts from natural necessity ... But we showed above that God
does not act from natural necessity, but that His will is the cause of all things ... Others,
however, said that the divine power is restricted to this present scheme of things because of the order of the divine wisdom and justice, without which God does nothing. ...
However, the order established in creation by divine wisdom ... is not so equal to the
divine wisdom that the divine wisdom should be restricted to it. ... Therefore, the divine
wisdom is not so restricted to any particular order that no other scheme of things could
proceed from it. Hence we must say absolutely that God can do other things than those
He has done. In ourselves ... something can reside in our power which cannot reside in
a just will or in a wise intellect. But in God, power, essence, will, intellect, wisdom and
justice are one and the same. ... what is attributed to His power considered in itself
God is said to be able to do in accordance with His absolute power. ... what is attributed to the divine power, according as it carries into execution the command of a
just will, God is said to be able to do by His ordained power. In this manner, we must
say that by His absolute power God can do other things than those He has foreknown
and pre-ordained to do. But it could not happen that He should do anything which

goodness, justice, and wisdom, because they could have found expression in another system. The distinction is deceptive for the modern reader because it seems to be talking about possibilities and avenues for divine action when in fact it is making a statement about the non-necessity of the created order. Both parts of the dialectic, which must be taken together to be meaningful, face in the direction of creation, not God. Together they declare the contingent, non-necessary, covenantal character of our created world.

Potentia absoluta and *potentia ordinata* are not, therefore, two ways in which God can act or might act, normally and with the concurrence of nature in the case of the latter and extraordinarily, supernaturally, and miraculously in the case of the former.[1] *Potentia absoluta* referred to the total possibilities *initially* open to God, some of which were realized by creating the established order; the unrealized possibilities are now only hypothetically possible. Viewed another way, the *potentia absoluta* is God's power considered absolutely, that is, without taking into account the order established by God.[2] *Potentia ordinata*, on the other hand, is the total ordained will of God, the complete plan of God for his creation. The ordained power is not identical with the particular ordinances that God has willed, for those ordinances are only the most common way through which the ordained will of God is expressed.

Before considering Ockham, several aspects of the thirteenth-century understanding of this distinction should be noted. First, the distinction was not so extensively used in the thirteenth century as in the later period. It is not one that appears repeatedly in Alexander, Bonaventure, Albert, and Thomas. Second, the area of things that God cannot do because they imply contradictions is larger in the thirteenth century than in the fourteenth. Stated another way, a

---

He has not foreknown and not pre-ordained that He would do. For His doing is subject to His foreknowledge and preordination, though His power, which is His nature, is not." Cf. *Summa contra Gentiles*, L. II, ch. 23-30.

1 Ockham, *Quodlibeta*, VI, q. 1 : "Haec distinctio non est sic intelligenda quod in Deo realiter sint duae potentiae quarum una sit ordinata, alia absoluta, quia unica est potentia in Deo ad extra quae omni modo est ipse Deus. Nec sic est intelligenda quod aliqua potest Deus ordinate facere, et alia potest absolute et non ordinate, quia Deus nihil potest facere inordinate." Similar statements can be found in Rimini, d'Ailly, and Biel : see below, 40, n. 1.

2 This is the reason why the term *absoluta* is used. It does not imply that God acts or could act imperiously.

larger number of aspects of the created order are absolutely necessary for Thomas than for Ockham. Third, there is no basis in the thirteenth century for equating *potentia absoluta* with the ability of God to transcend the present order, to interrupt it by miraculous activity. Nor did the thirteenth century equate *potentia ordinata* with the particular laws by which the established order normally operated. The antinomy of miracle vs. the common course of nature was treated separately from the distinction of *potentia absoluta* and *potentia ordinata*. The latter distinction was not an antinomy, since what God ordained was chosen from the possibilities open to him and therefore they are not mutually exclusive. Furthermore, miracles were not contradictions of God's ordained will, although they contradicted particular principles that normally operated within God's ordained order.

Ockham's understanding and use of the distinction of the two powers of God did not markedly depart from previous usage, although there were some differences.[1] Ockham shared with other theologians

---

[1] Ockham, *Quodlibeta*, VI, q. 1 : "Quaedam Deus potest facere de potentia ordinata et quaedam de potentia absoluta. Haec distinctio non est sic intelligenda quod in Deo realiter sint duae potentiae quarum una sit ordinata, alia absoluta, quia unica est potentia in Deo ad extra, quae omnimodo est ipse Deus. Nec sic est intelligenda quod aliqua potest Deus ordinate facere et alia potest absolute et non ordinate, quia Deus nihil potest facere inordinate. Sed est sic intelligenda quod 'posse [facere] aliquid' aliquando accipitur secundum leges ordinatas et institutas a Deo et illa Deus dicitur posse facere de potentia ordinata. Aliter accipitur 'posse' pro posse facere omne illud quod non includit contradictionem fieri, sive Deus ordinavit se hoc facturum sive non, quia Deus multa potest facere quae non vult facere." Gregory of Rimini, *Super primum et secundum sententiarum*, L. I, dist. 42-44, q. 1, a. 2 (Venice, 1522; reprint 1955), I, fol. 162ᵛP-163ʳA : "... Deum posse hoc vel illud facere potest intelligi dupliciter : uno modo secundum potentiam ordinatam, et alio modo secundum potentiam absolutam. Non quod in Deo sint duae potentiae, una ordinata et alia absoluta, nec hoc volunt significare doctores, sed illud dicitur Deus ad intellectum recte intelligentium posse de potentia ordinata quod potest stante sua ordinatione et lege aeterna quae non est aliud quam eius voluntas qua aeternaliter voluit haec vel illa et tale vel tale esse futurum. Illud autem dicitur posse de potentia absoluta quod simpliciter et absolute potest. Econtra, illud non dicitur posse de potentia ordinata quod non potest stante lege et ordinatione sua quae nunc est; illud vero non posse de potentia absoluta quod simpliciter et absoluta potest. Patet autem quod simpliciter et absolute sine suppositione contradictionis Deus multa potest quae non potest stante eius lege et voluntate qua voluit sic se facturum. Et hoc ideo, quia illa etsi sint simpliciter possibilia, sunt tamen incompossibilia ordinationi divinae. ... Quamvis autem ista sunt incompossibilia, quia tamen illa ordinatio non est necessaria, id est, non est necessarium Deum sic ordinasse, quinimmo possibile est ipsum ordinasse et voluisse oppositum; ideo illud quod solum est impossibile ex suppositione ordinationis, utpote ei incompossibile non est absolute impossibile sed possibile,

in the late thirteenth and early fourteenth centuries an appreciation
for the usefulness of the distinction in combating Greco-Arabian
necessitarianism, and he made extensive use of the distinction to

---

et simpliciter loquendo illud Deus potest facere. Huic distinctioni satis concordat alia
antiqua, qua dictum est quod quaedam Deus non potest de iustitia quae potest de
potentia. ... Illud ergo dicitur Deus non posse de iustitia quod est incompossibile suae
ordinationi et voluntati, quae est prima iustitia. Illud autem est omne cuius oppositum
Deus vult quamquam ipsum sit secundum se possibile simpliciter." Pierre d'Ailly,
Quaestiones super libros sententiarum cum quibusdam in fine adjunctis, L. I, q. 13, a. 1
(Strasbourg, 1490; reprint 1968), D : "Unde Deum posse aliquid facere solet dupliciter
intelligi : uno modo secundum potentiam absolutam; alio modo secundum potentiam
ordinatam. Non quod in Deo sint duae potentiae, una absoluta et alia ordinata, sed
Deus dicitur illud posse de potentia absoluta quod simpliciter et absolute potest. Et
sic intelligitur Deus omnipotens, et de tali potentia semper loquar in praesenti articulo,
ut satis patet. Sed Deum aliquid posse de potentia ordinata potest dupliciter intelligi.
Uno modo stricte quod potest stante sua ordinatione qua aeternaliter voluit se sic vel
sic esse facturum, et sic solum potest illa quae ipse ordinavit se facturum, Alio modo
potest intelligi magis large, quod potest stante veritate legis seu scripturae divinae. Et
sic possibile ordinate potest dici illud quod est possibile et non obviat alicui veritati
legis ordinatae vel scripturae sacrae. Et utroque istorum modorum dicitur quod impossibile est de potentia ordinata ultimum iudicium non fore, quia licet sit simpliciter
et absolute possibile, tamen non stat cum aeterna Dei ordinatione et obviat scripturae.
Isti autem duo modi differunt, quia aliquid est impossibile de potentia ordinata primo
modo et non secundo modo, sicut si Sortes sit reprobatus, haec est impossibilis de potentia ordinata primo modo : 'Sortes salvabitur,' ut patet etc., et tamen non est impossibilis secundo modo, quia est absoluta possibilis, nec obviat sacrae scripturae, cum nec
hoc nec eius oppositum sit revelatum in scriptura. Similiter etiam aliquid est possibile
de potentia ordinata secundo modo et non primo modo, sed nunquam econverso, quia
quidquid obviat scripturae sacrae repugnat ordinationi divinae, sed non econverso. Et
ideo secundus modus est in plus quam primus, ut patet, quia quidquid est possibile
primo modo est possibile secundo modo, sed non econverso, ut dictum est. Secundus
autem modus videtur magis proprius quam primus, quia secundum primum modum
nihil est possibile de potentia ordinata nisi quod est vel erit. Similiter, isto modo cuius-
libet contradictionis de contingenti una pars est impossibilis de potentia ordinata, non
autem secundo modo, ut patet de istis : 'Sortes salvabitur', 'Sortes non salvabitur'
demonstrato aliquo viatore. Et istud faciliter patet, etc." Cf. d'Ailly, *Sent.* IV, q. 1,
a. 2 N : "Sicut dicitur quod Deus aliquid potest de potentia absoluta quod non potest
de potentia ordinata, ita dico de creatura. ... licet creatura de potentia naturali seu
naturaliter ordinata non possit creare vel annihilare, ut dictum est, tamen ista potest
de potentia simpliciter absoluta, scilicet supernaturaliter seu miraculose." Gabriel Biel,
Collectorium circa quattuor sententiarum libros, L. I, dist. 17, q. 1, a. 3 H, quotes the
passage from Ockham's *Quodlibeta*. However, in the following section, he seems to
equate *potentia ordinata* with particulars laws that can be changed from time to time
rather with the general ordained will of God (d'Ailly's first sense of *potentia ordinata*).
The same tendency noted in d'Ailly, *Sent.* IV, q. 1, a. 2, can be seen in Biel, *Sent.* IV,
dist. 1, q. 1, a. 3, dub. 2 M : "Et ideo notat hic Petrus de aliaco ... quod sicut dicitur

stress the non-necessity of divine action and thus the chosen quality of the created world. It was an important theological and philosophical tool for distinguishing relative and absolute necessity in things and events. Moreover, Ockham reduced the number of things God could not do because they implied contradictions. Specifically, he placed within the absolute power of God actions that *seemingly* contradicted God's goodness, justice, or wisdom. In this way he underscored the contingency of the present order by acknowledging other orders God *might have* established, had he so chosen. Ockham, however, did not believe these other orders were now possible.

Ockham's use of the distinction of the powers of God is a natural outgrowth of the thirteenth-century use, not a contradiction of it. Ockham was as aware as Thomas that the analogy between human and divine volition on which the distinction was based (namely, that God shares the human experience of feeling one has the physical power to do many things one does not desire to do and will never do) is basically inapplicable because of God's immutability and a-temporality, and because of the unity of God's wisdom, will, and essence. The distinction, therefore, was a statement about the created order, not the divine nature. Moreover, Ockham did not associate absolute power with miracle, nor did he identify the ordained will of God with particular willed ordinances. Confusion on this point has arisen because Ockham introduced miraculous examples into *potentia absoluta* discussions. These supernatural events were not, for Ockham, examples of divine action, *de potentia absoluta*, but were examples of historical incidents (for instance, the three children in the fiery furnace or the burning of Elijah's offering on Mount Carmel), proving that the principles involved (in this case the causal principles that fire always burns and water always quenches fire) were contingent and not abso-

---

quod Deus aliquid potest de potentia absoluta quod non potest de potentia ordinata, sic etiam creatura potest aliquid de potentia ordinata quae videlicet potest secundum ordinem a Deo nunc institutum. Potest etiam aliquid de potentia absoluta sive obedientiali secundum quam potest quicquid mediante ipsa Deus potest producere non solum secundum ordinem nunc institutum sed secundum ordinem institui possibilem. Et ita natura aliqua potest in effectus contrarios effectibus quos modo potest. Sicut de cataplasmate ficuum apposito vulneri regis Ezechiae per Esaiam prophetam quo sanatus est, ut habetur IV Reg. 20. Dicunt expositores quod ficus, secundum naturam propriam, erant contrariae sanationi ulceris, tamen ex speciali miraculo et ordinatione divina speciali induxerunt effectum contrarium." Obediential power specifically implies a contradiction of nature; cf. Bonaventure, *Sent.* I, dist. 42, a. un., q. 3 (Quaracchi edition, vol. I, 755)

lutely necessary. Miracles for Ockham, whether past or future. were always expressions of divine benevolence and compatible with the revealed nature of God. *Potentia absoluta* speculations, on the other hand, such as whether God could have become incarnate in an irrational animal, were not concerned with the appropriateness or likelihood of the postulated situation. Rather, as Vignaux points out, "the invocation of divine omnipotence—*potentia Dei absoluta*—allows the dialectical proof that separates the accidental from the essential in the object of an investigation."[1]

The distinction between the two powers of God in Ockham, therefore, is not a description of divine action, a distinction between the way God *normally* acts *(de potentia ordinata)* and the way he *occasionally* acts *(de potentia absoluta,* or miraculously). If, as Francis Oakley has argued,[2] this is the meaning of the distinction for d'Ailly (and there is some evidence that points in that direction, not only for d'Ailly but for Gregory of Rimini as well)[3], it represents a change from Ockham's usage, which is far closer to the thirteenth century. Even in the later "nominalists" the distinction excludes the idea of a capricious, arbitrary God who might change his mind and reverse the established laws that obtain in the orders of nature and salvation. God has committed himself to maintain the order that he has created, and when he occasionally acts contrary to certain principles or laws that normally operate within that order, it is for reasons that are in keeping with the broader design of his established will.

c) *Epistemology*

Working on the foundations laid by Duns Scotus and others, Ockham rejected the thirteenth-century Aristotelian epistemology of active

---

[1] Paul Vignaux, *Philosophy in the Middle Ages* (New York, 1959), 173.

[2] Francis Oakley, "Medieval Theories of Natural Law : William of Ockham and the Significance of the Voluntarist Tradition," *Natural Law Forum*, VI (1961), 65-83; "Christian Theology and the Newtonian Science : The Rise of the Concept of the Laws of Nature," *Church History*, XXX (1961), 433-457; "Pierre d'Ailly and the Absolute Power of God : Another Note on the Theology of Nominalism," *Harvard Theological Review*, LVI (1963), 59-73; *The Political Thought of Pierre d'Ailly* (New Haven, 1964), 163-197; "From Constance to 1688 Revisited," *Journal of the History of Ideas*, XXVII (1966), 429-432; "Jacobean Political Theology : The Absolute and Ordinary Powers of the King," *Journal of the History of Ideas*, XXIX (1968), 323-346.

[3] The crucial passage in d'Ailly (*Sent.* IV, q. 1, a. 2) is reproduced above, 40, n. 1. Although Rimini's usage is closer to Ockham, he occasionally opposes *naturaliter* with *absoluta*, e.g. Sent. I, dist. 42-44, q. 1, a. 2 (I, 165 F).

object informing a passive mind through the agency of sensible species, intelligible species and the agent intellect. In place of the process of extracting or abstracting the universal from the particular, Ockham asserted that the mind intuited the particular and knew it directly and immediately. Intuitive cognition for Ockham, upon which all knowledge is ultimately based, is the knowledge according to which one judges a thing to be present and existing. Nothing can deceive the mind and force it to judge that something exists or is experienced when it is not.[1]

The distinction of God's powers was examined before Ockham's epistemology because the more recent versions of the traditional affirmation of Ockham's epistemological skepticism and the non-empirical, non-scientific import of his system have centered around Ockham's assertion that God can cause, de potentia absoluta, the intuitive cognition of a non-existent.[2] Although Ockham made this assertion (it seemed to follow naturally from the theological principle, accepted by Thomas[3] and reaffirmed in the Parisian articles of 1277,[4] that God can cause directly whatever he causes through secondary means), he placed several safeguards that, regardless of their philosophic or scientific validity, seemed to him sufficient to protect the empiricism of his epistemology. First, the possibility is only de potentia absoluta, and God does not in fact act that way. Second, even if we imagine such a thing happening, one would only perceive the object to exist; one would not judge it to exist.[5]

---

[1] Ockham, Ordinatio (Sent. I), prol., q. 1; Boehner, "The Notitia Intuitiva of Non-Existents According to William Ockham," in Collected Articles, 268-300; Sebastian J. Day, Intuitive Cognition : A Key to the Significance of the Later Scholastics (FIP, Phil. Ser., No. 4; St. Bonaventure, 1947).

[2] Anton Pegis, "Concerning William of Ockham," Traditio, II (1944), 465-480.

[3] Thomas Aquinas, Summa contra Gentiles, L. III, ch. 70 : "Patet etiam quod, si res naturalis producat proprium effectum, non est superfluum quod Deus illum producat. Quia res naturalis non producit ipsum, nisi in virtute divina. Neque est superfluum, si Deus per seipsum potest omnes effectus naturales producere, quod per quasdam alias causas producantur. Non enim hoc est ex insufficientia divinae virtutis, sed ex immensitate bonitatis ..."

[4] Art. 63 (CUP I, 547).

[5] The philosophical and scientific validity of Ockham's reasoning has recently been questioned by T. K. Scott, "Ockham on Evidence, Necessity, and Intuition," Journal of the History of Philosophy, VII (1969), 27-49; "Nicholas of Autrecourt, Buridan and Ockhamism," Journal of the History of Philosophy, IX (1971), 15-41.

d) *The Relation of Nominalism to Science*

On the basis of the empiricism of Ockham's epistemology and his adherence to a highly sophisticated terminist logic, the contribution of Ockham and his followers to the development of medieval science seems firmly established. Many of those viewed as followers of Ockham are also important names in fourteenth-century science : John Buridan, Nicholas of Oresme, Albert of Saxony, Pierre d'Ailly, Henri of Langenstein, and Marsilius of Inghen. Moreover, Ockham upheld the validity of the principle of causality. Although God could do directly what he normally does through secondary causes, secondary causality does obtain in the natural order and Ockham specifically excludes *sine qua non* causality *in naturalibus*.[1]

It is interesting along this line to note that the defenders of atomism in the fourteenth century—and there were some—were not the Ockhamists but the anti-Ockhamists. Adam Wodham, a disciple of Ockham, energetically attacked the atomism of Walter Chatton, who was one of the earliest critics of the thought of Ockham.[2]

e) *Metaphysics and Natural Theology*

In this area there is some disagreement among those who have contributed to the revision. It was the belief of Boehner and those influenced by him that Ockham altered metaphysics and natural theology only in two respects. First, he concentrated on existing individuals rather than abstract essences, but he believed in and continued to use the concepts of essence and existence, form and matter, substance and accidents, causality, and relation. Ockham still affirmed that there was such a thing as metaphysics and that its purpose was to study being *qua* being. Although he never wrote a work specifically on metaphysics, it was his expressed intention to do so. Second, he reduced the number of things in theology that could be demonstrated apart from relevation, but he maintained the importance of probable

---

[1] Ockham, *Sent.* IV, q. 1, G-H; *Sent.* II, q. 4 & 5. For a discussion of Ockham's position on natural causality see : Hochstetter, *Studien zur Metaphysik* ..., 144-173; Webering, *Theory of Demonstration* ..., 143-165; Courtenay, "The Critique on Natural Causality in the Mutakallimun and Nominalism," *Harvard Theological Review*, LXVI (1973).

[2] J. E. Murdoch and E. A. Synan, "Two Questions on the Continuum : Walter Chatton (?), O. F. M. and Adam Wodeham, O. F. M.," *Franciscan Studies*, XXVI (1966), 212-288.

arguments and even felt that the existence of God could be demonstrated. The thrust of Boehner's argumentation is that Ockham did have a metaphysics and a natural theology, although they were greatly simplified and to a large extent reduced.[1]

Moody, on the other hand, believes that Ockham radically altered metaphysics. By adopting a strict definition of demonstration and by using an empiricist criterion for the evidence used in demonstration, the so-called demonstrations generally used in metaphysics and natural theology became un-scientific and only probable. Thus natural theology was eliminated in favor of a positive theology based on revelation and faith rather than reason. Moody admits that Ockham allows "that a descriptive concept of God can be formed from the concept of 'being' or 'thing'," and Moody admits that Ockham has an argument for the existence of a sustaining cause of the universe, but Ockham does not believe that the existence of one sustaining cause can be rationally demonstrated, although it may indeed be highly probable.[2]

Whether one accepts Boehner's or Moody's version of Ockham's metaphysics, the limitations on natural theology are apparent. One can no longer accept, however, the thesis that Ockham engaged in the wholesale destruction of metaphysics and disallowed natural theology in principle.

f) *Ethics*

The newer view of the ethical system of Ockham or of Biel is altered considerably by a better understanding of the distinction between *potentia absoluta* and *potentia ordinata*. The ethical system that prevails is not a necessary system, which God was forced to adopt, but a chosen system, one of several God might have chosen to institute, had he so desired. Having chosen this one, however, it is binding and God will not arbitrarily or capriciously interrupt the present order to institute a new morality. Moreover, there is a close relationship between the eternal law of God, natural law, and the positive law that obtains in the church. Man, therefore, can and should act according to the dictates of right reason within him, as supported by the customs of the church and the statements of Scripture. An ethical system does not become totally positivistic just because God was not

---

[1] Boehner, "The Metaphysics of William Ockham," in *Collected Articles* ..., 373-399.
[2] Moody, "William of Ockham," 307-308, 313-315.

forced to choose it. It is the belief of both Ockham and Biel that the ethical system reflects the wisdom and intellect of God as well as his will (these being one and the same), and the voluntary nature of the present moral order (voluntary only for God, not for man) does not prevent God from having his own reasons for choosing the present order, even if man cannot know them.[1]

g) *Soteriology*

The nominalist position on grace and salvation, although seldom a major part of the traditional exposition of nominalism (at least not in expositions of Ockham's thought), has received considerable attention lately.[2] Again, the understanding of the two powers is the crucial issue by which the nominalist position is explained. For those who saw in the absolute power of God the possibility of divine intervention and who believed this concept represented the true thought of nominalism, God became omnipotent and arbitrary in such a way that the established system of salvation was violated and God accepted and rejected man according to his own inscrutable will—a position that some have seen as an extreme Augustinianism stemming from Duns Scotus. For those who saw in the ordained power of God the obligation of divine faithfulness and who believed this concept represented the true thought of nominalism, Ockham and his followers were semi-Pelagians who believed that God was obliged to reward with grace and eventually with eternal life any man who did what was in him.

The newer appreciation of the powers of God has stressed both aspects and has seen that the dialectic of the two powers is particularly useful in soteriology because it grants freedom and omnipotence to God without undermining the operation or predictability of the present order. If the newer research sees one aspect stressed more than another, it is the semi-Pelagian aspect.[3]

---

[1] Ockham, *Sent.* II, q. 4; *Sent.* II, q. 19; *Sent.* III, q. 8; *Quodl.* III, q. 13; *Sent.* I, dist. 45, q. 1; *Sent.* I, dist. 47, q. 1; *Sent.* I, dist. 48, q. 1; Oberman, *Harvest* ..., 90-93.

[2] The nominalist view of grace and justification has long been a part of Biel scholarship. It has only recently become a major issue in the literature on Ockham. Cf. Erwin Iserloh, *Gnade und Eucharistie in der philosophischen Theologie des Wilhelm von Ockham* (Wiesbaden, 1956); Dettloff, *Die Entwicklung der Akzeptations- und Verdienstlehre von Duns Scotus bis Luther* (Beiträge zur Geschichte der Phil. und Theol. des Mittelalters; Münster i.W., 1963), 253-290; Oberman, *Harvest* ..., 146-248,.

[3] Oberman, *Harvest* ..., 146-184.

h) *Sacramental Theology*

The second major area of nominalist theology that has been a subject of revision is the Ockhamist and post-Ockhamist view of the sacraments, in particular the eucharist. In earlier views this was the area in which Ockham supposedly had crossed over into heresy and for which he was called to account at Avignon. Recent evaluations have found little that is unique or particularly heretical in Ockham's eucharistic teaching.[1] Since he was never condemned on this issue, it may be that the theological commission examining his work was equally unable to find convincing evidence of heresy. Biel, the one follower of Ockham to dwell extensively on eucharistic theology, is now considered to be within the mainstream of catholic orthodoxy on this issue.[2]

i) *View of Society and the Church*

The Ockhamist view of the nature of society and the constitution of the church has attracted the attention of several recent historians, in particular Boehner,[3] Oberman,[4] Tierney,[5] and Oakley.[6] Although there is some disagreement among these scholars on the exact nature of the political thought of Ockham, d'Ailly, and Biel, there is a consensus that Ockham's views, especially as expressed in his more considered and thoughtful studies like the *Dialogus*, are more traditional than was once thought and heavily dependent on canonist teaching. Ockham was not the originator of conciliar theory, nor did he share the attitude toward papal power and the constitution of the church expressed in *Defensor pacis*. Moreover, his view of society and the church seems less atomistic and voluntaristic than it once did. If Ockham's political thought was one of the major sources for the

---

[1] Gabriel N. Buescher, *The Eucharistic Teaching of William Ockham* (Washington, 1950).

[2] P. Anatriello, *La dottrina di Gabriele Biel sull' Eucaristia* (Milan, 1936); Courtenay, "Cranmer as a Nominalist—*Sed Contra*," *Harvard Theological Review*, LVII (1964), 367-380; *The Eucharistic Thought of Gabriel Biel* (Doc. diss., Harvard Univ., 1967).

[3] Boehner, "Ockham's Political Ideas," in *Collected Articles* ..., 442-468.

[4] Oberman, *Harvest* ..., 361-422.

[5] Brian Tierney, "A Conciliar Theory of the Thirteenth Century," *Catholic Historical Review*, XXXVI (1951), 415-440; "Ockham, the Conciliar Theory and the Canonists," *Journal of the History of Ideas*, XV (1954), 40-70.

[6] Oakley, *The Political Thought* ..., 198-211.

political thought of d'Ailly and Biel (and this seems now to be generally accepted), then these later "nominalists" can also be seen as more conservative, especially Biel, the great defender of papal prerogatives.[1]

In addition to the more favorable and positive evaluation of the contribution of moderate nominalism, described above, the history of nominalism has also been revised. For example, the relation of Scotus, Durand, Aureol, and Ockham is now seen to be more complex and is not one continuous development. While recognizing the importance for Ockham's thought of the Scotistic idea of intuitive cognition, the limitations on theology as a science, the importance of God's omnipotence as expressed in predestination and divine acceptation, and the covenantal approach to theology that Scotus inherited from the Franciscan tradition, the differences between Scotus and Ockham, especially in the areas of logic and metaphysics, seem more significant. E. A. Moody has credited Ockham with the destruction of the muddy and confused philosophy and theology of the late thirteenth and early fourteenth centuries, particularly associated with Giles of Rome, Henry of Ghent, and John Duns Scotus, and has pointed to some surprising similarities between the thought of Ockham and Thomas Aquinas.[2] Boehner and Buescher have similarly pointed up important contrasts between Ockham on the one hand and Durand and Aureol on the other.[3] Consequently, no direct line of continuity runs from 1277 and the "second Augustinian school", through Scotus, Durand, and Aureol, to Ockham.

Similarly, the lines of development that stem from Ockham have been reinterpreted, in particular the relation of Ockham to radical nominalism. Moody has shown that the Parisian decree of 1339 was not a censure of Ockhamism but only a statement that Ockham should not be taught dogmatically to the exclusion of other points of view.[4] The nominalist theses condemned in the decree of 1340 were

---

[1] See the introduction to *Defensorium Obedientiae Apostolicae et Alia Documenta*, ed. by H. A. Oberman, D. E. Zerfoss, and W. J. Courtenay (Cambridge, Mass., 1968), 3-55.

[2] Moody, "Ockham and Aegidius of Rome."

[3] Boehner, "Realistic Conceptualism ...," in *Collected Articles ...*, 156-174; and "Ockham's Tractatus de Praedestinatione et de Praescientia Dei et de Futuris Contingentibus and its Main Problems," in *Collected Articles ...*, 420-441; Buescher, *Eucharistic Teaching ...*, Kenneth Plotnik; *Hervaeus Natalis O.P. and the Controversies over the Real Presence and Transubstantiation* (München, 1970).

[4] Moody, "Ockham, Buridan ..."

inconsistent with the thought of Ockham, although they paralleled the thought of Nicholas of Autrecourt, summoned to Avignon the month before and later condemned in 1346/47. Moreover, the two major opponents of Autrecourt, John Buridan and Bernard of Arezzo, were Ockhamists, leading one to the conclusion that Ockham and Autrecourt had little in common. In addition, both Boehner and Moody have detailed important differences between Ockham and Holcot,[1] and Damasus Trapp believes he has discovered in Gregory of Rimini the major opponent of John of Mirecourt.[2] Thus, in light of recent research, radical nominalism has become a movement that had only the most tenuous ties with Ockham and lasted only two decades until it was effectively silenced by the condemnations of 1347, conceived and implemented by the Ockhamists.

Changes in the interpretation of the subsequent history of nominalism are not as dramatic. D'Ailly and Biel are still seen as close followers of Ockham, although a "revised" Ockham has been paralleled by a "revised" d'Ailly [3] and a "revised" Biel.[4] More crucial for this later period is the relationship between nominalism (in either the old or new versions) and mysticism, especially as focused in the life and writings of John Gerson.[5]

The combined effect of the research of Hochstetter, Vignaux, Boehner, Moody, and Oberman has been to establish the orthodox, non-radical character of the thought of Ockham and Biel, and, by extension, d'Ailly. This more favorable and positive evaluation of these late medieval thinkers was achieved on two fronts : by a more careful and exhaustive analysis of the thought of each figure and by severing the ties that bound these moderate nominalists to the so-

---

[1] Boehner, "The Medieval Crisis of Logic and the Author of the Centiloquium Attributed to Ockham," in *Collected Articles* ..., 351-372; Moody, "A Quodlibetal Question of Robert Holkot, O. P. on the Problem of the Objects of Knowledge and of Belief," *Speculum*, XXXIX (1964), 53-74. For a corrected edition of this quodlibet see : Courtenay, "A Revised Text of Robert Holcot's Quodlibetal Dispute on Whether God is Able to Know More Than He Knows," *Archiv für Geschichte der Philosophie*, LIII (1971), 1-21.

[2] Damasus Trapp, "Augustinian Theology ...;" "Peter Ceffons ...;" and "Gregory of Rimini Manuscripts : Editions and Additions," *Augustiniana*, VIII (1958), 425-443.

[3] Courtenay, "Covenant and Causality in Pierre d'Ailly," *Speculum*, XLVI (1971), 94-119.

[4] Oberman, *Harvest* ...

[5] Steven Ozment, *Homo Spiritualis* (Leiden, 1969).

called radical nominalism of Holcot, Wodham, Autrecourt, and Mire-court. Although it was recognized that the thought of Ockham, d'Ailly, and Biel was not identical in all respects, it was felt they had enough in common to permit them to be grouped together as if they were a school. The principal ideas that were the source and unifying elements of that movement were discovered to be more theological than philosophical. It was not the atomistic metaphysics of the individual (so long misunderstood) nor the epistemology of intuitive cognition (Scotist in origin and adopted by almost everyone in the late Middle Ages) that distinguished this movement, but rather a conception of the centrality, efficacy, and dependability of verbal, contractual agreements for all aspects of the relationship between God and man. Each individual idea in this moderate nominalist system (for example, the idea of the two powers of God, or the semi-Pelagian soteriology, or the non-necessity of the Judeo-Christian ethical system, or the idea of *sine qua non* causality in the sacraments) can probably be found in earlier thinkers or in contemporaries to whom one would never apply the terms nominalist or Ockhamist. The unique feature of Ockhamist thought was that these ideas were all present and grounded in the idea of pact, or covenant—willed verbal agreements that are no less dependable and certain because they are in origin voluntary.[1]

3. New Perspectives, 1965-1972

Certain details of the "revised" picture, particularly in regard to the historical development of nominalism, are presently being ques-tioned and altered. Inasmuch as these may lead to a different history of late medieval thought in the near future, they should be treated as a separate section.

a) *Terminology*

It is already becoming apparent that the term "nominalism," as a description of the thought of Ockham, Buridan, Rimini, d'Ailly, Biel,

---

[1] I have treated aspects of this issue in the following articles : "Necessity and Free-dom in Anselm ...;" "Sacrament, Symbol, and Causality in Bernard of Clairvaux," *Bernard of Clairvaux : Studies presented to Jean Leclercq* (Washington D.C., 1973), 111-22; "The King and the Leaden Coin : The Economic Background of *Sine Qua Non* Causa-lity," *Traditio*, XXVIII (1972), 185-209; "Covenant and Causality. ..."

and other late medieval thinkers, is no longer as appropriate as it once seemed. If Ockham did not reject generic similarity in nature or destroy metaphysics, and if the essential structure of his thought (and even more that of Biel) was theological rather than philosophical, then should not the term "nominalism" be dropped in favor of a more descriptive label? Has anything other than habit and familiarity prolonged the usage?

The case against using the term "nominalism" to designate a school or schools in the fourteenth and fifteenth centuries is strong. Even those contributors to the revision who, like Oberman, have continued to use the term, do not believe that Ockham or Biel were nominalists in the traditional sense. Even if one restricts the term "nominalism" to the area of logic and epistemology and acknowledges that Ockham did indeed reject "common nature" and stress knowledge of the particular, Ockham was not a thorough-going nominalist; nor are there valid grounds for assuming that Ockham's position on the question of universals is the key to his thought, from which all else follows.

It is not surprising, therefore, to learn that none of Ockham's contemporaries ever called him a nominalist. "Nominalist" was a twelfth-century term that described a particular position on the question of universals, and when *nominales* or *opinio nominalium* were used in the thirteenth century, they described the position of twelfth-century logicians.[1] By 1270 these labels had ceased to be used and were only reintroduced in the fifteenth century (possibly associated with the revival of Albertism and Thomism) to describe a position in logic or, more accurately, a way of teaching logic.[2] Similarly, the words *terministae* and *via moderna* are fifteenth century in origin and concern logic, not epistemology, metaphysics, or theology. When, in the fifteenth century, Ockham's name occurs in a list of *nominales*, the intent was to indicate that he shared with others a particular approach to logic, not that all those named in the list belonged to a school of which Ockham was the founder.[3] The only descriptive term

---

[1] Cf. Vignaux, "Nominalisme," 717-718; F. Pelster, "Nominales und reales in 13. Jahrhundert," *Sophia* (1946), 154-161.

[2] Ehrle, *Der Sentenzenkommentar ...*; Ritter, *Studien zur Spätscholastik*, vol. II : *Via antiqua und via moderna auf den deutschen Universitäten des XV. Jahrhunderts* (Sitzungsberichte der Heidelberger Akademie ..., 7. Abhandlung (Heidelberg, 1922; reprint 1963).

[3] C. E. Bulaeus, *Historia Universitatis Parisiensis*, vol. V (Paris, 1670), 708; Plessis d'Argentré, *Collectio judiciorum novis erroribus*, vol. I (Paris, 1728), 134, sp. 2; Stephen

in the fourteenth century was *moderni,* which simply meant any contemporary theologian or, in a pejorative sense, any opponent.

Within this mass of confusing labels Moody has shown admirable caution. He has consistently refused to apply the term "nominalist" or even "Ockhamist" to an entire group of theologians in the fourteenth and fifteenth centuries as if they constituted a school. Nominalism was and is, for Moody, a philosophical position and a method. It was essentially the application of logical analysis to philosophical and theological problems in such a way that they became problems about "the meaning and reference of terms and the truth conditions of sentences."[1] Thus nominalism was a philosophy of language, and as a method it eventually came to be known as the *via moderna.* Moody has noted that no theologian in the fourteenth century designated himself as an Ockhamist, nor was that term used to describe anyone's thought save Ockham's.[2] Moody has, therefore, chosen to confine "nominalism" to its logical, epistemological, and metaphysical meaning and to confine "Ockhamism" to Ockham. Although he sees a consistency in Ockham's thought, he does not see that consistency as the result of one or two peculiarly nominalist principles, and although he is aware of the use later theologians made of Ockham and the parallel thinking to which one can point, he does not believe that constitutes a nominalist or Ockhamist school. "Partyism" or "Schoolism" seems to be a child of the fifteenth and sixteenth centuries that should not be read back into the fourteenth century.

How is one then to describe the unity of thought among Ockham, d'Ailly, and Biel to which various scholars have pointed ? "Ockhamism" seems to be the least undesirable term. "Nominalism" should perhaps be left to the realm of logic, where it was subscribed to by many *moderni* who otherwise have little in common. The best argument for retaining "nominalism" as the proper title for the thought described above seems to be the importance that Ockham, d'Ailly, and Biel gave to the ideas of assigned value and willed verbal covenants.

Baluzius, *Miscellanea novo ordine digesta,* vol. II (Lucca, 1761), 293-294; Ehrle, *Der Sentenzenkommentar ...,* 305-321.

[1] E. A. Moody, "Buridan and a Dilemma of Nominalism," in *H. A. Wolfson Jubilee Volume* (Jerusalem, 1965), II, 577. See also "A Quodlibetal Question of Robert Holkot, O. P., on the Problem of the Objects of Knowledge and of Belief," *Speculum,* 39 (1964), 53-74; "Ockhamism," in *Encyclopedia of Philosophy* (New York, 1968), V, 533-534; "William of Ockham," in *Encyclopedia of Philosophy* (New York, 1968), VIII, 306-317.

[2] Moody, "Ockhamism," 533.

b) The "English School" of Nominalism

The radicalism attributed to the thought of Holcot and Wodham is presently being questioned. As a side product of the re-evaluation of Ockham, the radicalism of Holcot had been accentuated in the period from 1940 to 1965. Boehner had passed the onus of authoring the radical *Centiloquium* from Ockham to Holcot in 1944.[1] Moody, in an article in 1964, pointed out some logical issues on which Holcot was more radical and nominalist than Ockham.[2]

Moody's evidence still seems solid and incontrovertible, but the association of Holcot and the *Centiloquium* now appears doubtful.[3] The evidence on which Boehner based his supposition was drawn from a hasty and inaccurate reading of the Holcot texts. The impression of skepticism and fideism that one gleans from the earlier statements on Holcot's thought has been considerably dispelled by Oberman's research into Holcot's views on faith and reason, predestination and grace.[4] The texts recently published by Paolo Molteni support Oberman's findings, although Molteni's interpretation is still wedded to the older viewpoint.[5] Most attention has been given to Holcot's logic and epistemology, and in the latter area Holcot adopted the general outlines of the Ockhamist theory of cognition but reintroduced species in a manner that seems to relate back to Thomas.[6] Recently, Heinrich Schepers has argued that radical nominalism at Oxford was specifically an anti-Ockhamist movement, and Holcot, far from being a radical nominalist, was a faithful disciple of Ockham and helped lead the counter-attack against the nominalists, whose leader was the Dominican, William of Crathorn.[7] The publication of the critical edition of Holcot's *Quodlibets* and *Sentence Commentary*, now underway,

---

[1] Boehner, "The Medieval Crisis ..."

[2] Moody, "A Quodlibetal Question ..."

[3] See the forthcoming doctoral dissertation of Hester Gelber, University of Wisconsin, 1974.

[4] Oberman, "'Facientibus Quod In Se Est Deus Non Denegat Gratiam.' Robert Hoicot, O. P., and the Beginnings of Luther's Theology," *Harvard Theological Review*, LV (1962), 317-342; *Harvest* ..., 235-248.

[5] Paolo Molteni, *Roberto Holcot o.p. Dottrina della grazia e della giustificazione con due questioni quodlibetali inedite* (Pinerolo, 1968).

[6] See the forthcoming dissertations of Hester Gelber (University of Wisconsin, 1974) and Anne Brinkley (Harvard Univ., 1972).

[7] Heinrich Schepers, "Holkot contra dicta Crathorn," *Philosophisches Jahrbuch*, LXXVII (1970), 320-354, LXXIX (1972), 106-36.

should speed the process of determining the exact position of this important English theologian.[1]

Adam Wodham, the other leading English nominalist, may undergo a similar transformation. Dettloff has found nothing unusual about the soteriology of Wodham, which seems to follow Ockham closely.[2] On the issues of quantity and continuum Wodham placed himself in opposition to Walter Chatton, one of Ockham's leading opponents.[3] A recent study has pointed to the more conservative tone of Wodham's defense of Ockham's eucharistic thought.[4] However, adequate texts of Wodham's thought are even more scarce than for Holcot, and it may be some time before a new picture of Wodham can be constructed.

Even on the basis of the studies that have been done to date, the history of Ockhamism and nominalism in England appears to be quite different from what was thought five or ten years ago. As a result, radical nominalism has moved one stage further away from Ockham.

c) *The "Parisian School" of Nominalism*

Of all the nominalists that appeared in the pages of the older literature, the appropriateness of "nominalism" as a designation for Autrecourt and Mirecourt seemed most certain. In addition to internal evidence from their writings, their status as arch-nominalists was confirmed by the condemnations of 1346 and 1347. The research of Damasus Trapp, only a little more than a decade ago, assured us that Gregory of Rimini, an Ockhamist, was the central figure behind the condemnation of Mirecourt in 1347.

That assessment, however, is now open to grave doubt. In examining the views of Mirecourt on grace and justification, Dettloff found nothing out of keeping with Ockham's thought, and he therefore concluded that Mirecourt's radicalism must lie in some other area.[5] Roy Van Neste, in a recent doctoral dissertation at the University of

---

[1] The critical edition of Holcot's *Quaestiones Quodlibetales*, edited by W. J. Courtenay, H. Gelber, and Anne Brinkley, will be published in three volumes, the first to appear in 1974. The publication of the *Sentence Commentary* will follow the *Quodlibets*.

[2] Dettloff, *Die Entwicklung* ..., 329-332.

[3] Murdoch and Synan, "Two Questions ..."

[4] Thomas Mitchell, *Medieval Discussions of Quantity and the Development of Eucharistic Thought with Special Concentration on the Ockhamist Tradition* (Master's thesis, University of Wisconsin, 1971).

[5] Dettloff, *Die Entwicklung* ..., 325-328.

Wisconsin, discovered that Mirecourt's epistemology had little in common with Autrecourt and instead followed the outline of Ockham's theory of knowledge.[1] Moreover, Mirecourt rejected intuitive cognition of a non-existent, thus increasing empirical certitude at the expense of possibly incurring the anger of the Ockhamists.[2] In my own examination of Mirecourt's position on sacramental causality I found him maintaining the Thomist position against the Ockhamists.[3] Finally, one of the positions of Mirecourt most often cited as indicative of his radicalism, namely the belief in God's power to make a past thing not to have been, was not maintained by Mirecourt at all. Among those who held this opinion was Gregory of Rimini. Since this was one of the issues in the process against Mirecourt, it seems unlikely that Rimini could have been the spirit behind the condemnation of 1347.[4]

The picture of Mirecourt that emerges from these recent studies is that of a cautious, non-radical, somewhat eclectic theologian who was misjudged on certain issues. It may be some consolation to the reader's sense of disorientation in the face of the rapid change in characterization undergone by the nominalists to discover that the reputation of the "prince of the nominalists," Nicholas of Autrecourt, has remained unchanged. This may in part be due to the paucity of his extant writings upon which to base any reconstruction. However, as we know more about the figures that surrounded Autrecourt, our understanding of his thought and intention is bound to change as well.

4. On Relating the "Revision" to Other Late Medieval Developments

On the basis of the foregoing analysis it is evident that the clichés about nominalism, such as atomism, skepticism, fideism, divorce of faith and reason, can no longer be used to show parallels or dissimilarities with other aspects of late medieval society. It is not clear how

---

[1] Roy J. Van Neste, *The Epistemology of John of Mirecourt in Relation to Fourteenth Century Thought* (Doctoral dissertation, University of Wisconsin, 1972).

[2] *Ibid.*

[3] The results of this research will appear as part of a longer study, "Sacramental Causality in 14th-Century Cistercian Thought : John of Mirecourt, James of Eltville, Gottschalk of Nepomuk, and Conrad of Ebrach."

[4] Courtenay, "John of Mirecourt and Gregory of Rimini on Whether God can Undo the Past," *Recherches de Théologie ancienne et médiévale*, XXXVIII (1972).

the newer views relate, although some work has already been done in this direction. The conclusions drawn here are, of course, speculative, and are intended only to provide a basis for discussion with scholars in other disciplines represented at this conference.

If the fragmentation of the medieval synthesis can no longer be used as the hallmark of nominalism around which to build a theory of the development of late gothic art, the increased importance given to empiricism in the nominalist system should have some implications for the development of the visual and plastic arts, if not architecture. Ockhamist epistemology is not simply empirical; it is based on visual experience, and it takes the eye as the primary sense organ around which to build a theory of knowledge. The rapidity with which the mind reaches out to know the object is particularly appropriate to (and in fact is based on and illustrated by) visual experience. "Knowing" in Ockhamism is primarily "seeing." Such an epistemology certainly parallels the emphasis in late medieval and early Renaissance art on rendering the visual world with increasing accuracy.

The themes of late medieval art are supported by the theology of Ockhamism. In particular, the dignity of man, a theme both in Renaissance art and literature, lies at the heart of the Ockhamist semi-Pelagian soteriology, as has been pointed out already by Oberman.[1] The chosen quality of the present order as well as its dependability give to the world around the *viator* an intensified meaning.

The close examination of life as it is lived and the stress on the dignity of man are themes of late medieval literature as well as art. If there is a pessimistic note to certain types of late medieval literature, it cannot be ascribed to Ockhamism, which was much more positive in its outlook. Perhaps the most obvious connection between Ockhamism and late medieval literature lies in the type of theological issues one finds reflected in the poetry. In particular one recalls Chaucer's discussion of the issue of determination and free will as associated with the controversy between Bradwardine and the "Pelagians".[2] The issue of grace and justification, central to the recent research in nominalism, is also found as a recurring theme in late medieval literature.[3]

---

[1] Oberman, "Some Notes on the Theology of Nominalism ..."

[2] Geoffrey Chaucer, *The Canterbury Tales*, "The Nun's Priest's Tale."

[3] See the recent dissertation by J. F. McNamara, *Responses to Ockhamist Theology in the Poetry of the "Pearl"-Poet, Langland, and Chaucer* (Louisiana State University, 1968).

The connections between Ockhamism, art and literature are, at best, the reflection of common interests. When we turn to late medieval religion, however, the connections are much closer and stronger. Central to the revised view of nominalism is the Biblical conception of God, who remains omnipotent and free, and who communicates directly with man through covenants. The stress on omnipotence and divine power, the stress on the covenantal nature of man's relation with God, the continual use of Biblical (especially Old Testament) examples in the writings of Ockham and Biel, all mark a re-emphasis on the Judeo-Christian conception of God in contrast with the more distant and more mechanistic deity of Latin Averroism as influenced by Aristotle's Prime Mover. Gilson has already pointed out that this trend back to a Biblical conception of God was stimulated by the condemnations of 1277 and represents a reaction to Greco-Arabian necessitarianism.[1] Ockhamism was only one part of that changing conception of God, although one of the more visible and important parts. The tendency to see God as the Biblical Yahweh rather than the Aristotelian Prime Mover remained strong as long as Averroism needed to be combatted, i.e., throughout most of the fourteenth and fifteenth centuries.

One aspect of this increase in Biblical theology and the Biblical conception of God that has not been sufficiently noted is that theology became less apologetic in the process. The apologetic focus of so much of thirteenth century theology—one thinks especially of Raymund Lull, Roger Bacon's *Opus majus*, Thomas' *Summa contra gentiles*, and Raymund Martin's *Pugio fidei*—was designed to convert the Jew and the Moslem and reconvert the heretic. The emergence of a scientific theology that could be rationally demonstrated, a theology that begins with the existence and nature of God, established a common ground for dialogue between Christian and non-Christian. All this began to change in 1277. With the attack on the scientific nature of theology and the limitation of the amount of knowledge of God that could be gained through the unaided reason, theology as a tool for defending the faith and converting others was replaced by a more internal and internally consistent theological system. Perhaps the Christo-centric approach of Luther is the culmination of a long process away from a "philosophic," natural theology that could serve apologetic

---

[1] Etienne Gilson, *History of Christian Philosophy in the Middle Ages* (New York, 1955), 402-410, 498-499.

ends. May not Holcot's idea that a knowledge of God will be granted to the one who does what is in him be a residue of thirteenth-century Dominican theology in Ockhamist garb ?

If Ockhamism reduced the common ground shared by Christian and non-Christian, it encouraged a more active religious life for the Christian by guaranteeing salvation to the one who did what was in him. Although the degree of an individual's love for God and the implementation of that love in works of charity could only be judged worthy by God, the requirements were revealed in Scripture and the teaching of the church, and one could, without fear, trust God to keep his covenants. The covenantal theme of Ockhamist theology is, perhaps, the key to that system, and it was as important for late medieval religion as it was later to be for the Reformation. [1]

OCKHAM AND THE ZEITGEIST

CHARLES T. DAVIS

Tulane University

Professor Courtenay's paper is an extraordinarily useful guide to a tangled and embattled subject, the so-called nominalistic movement. Although he casts doubt on the suitability of calling it a movement, it has been so regarded for a long time, and has elicited various and violent responses. Devout Thomists, for example, have tended to regard those who adhered to this "school" as troublemakers of the most irresponsible sort. They destroyed the good world that Aquinas had made. They let the genie of individualism out of the scholastic bottle. Even so just and catholic a historian as Etienne Gilson[2] can hand down the following harsh verdict on Ockham, the great founder (or, as some would say, precursor) of the school (if, indeed, it was a school). "In philosophy itself," Gilson declares, "this apprentice sorcerer has,

---

[1] Cf. Oberman, "Wir sein pettler. Hoc est verum. Bund und Gnade in der Theologie des Mittelalters und der Reformation," *Zeitschrift für Kirchengeschichte*, LXXVIII (1967), 232-252; Martin Greschat, "Der Bundesgedanke in der Theologie des späten Mittelalters," *Zeitschrift für Kirchengeschichte*, LXXXI (1970), 44-63.

[2] *History of Christian Philosophy in the Middle Ages* (New York, 1955), 498.

not at all created, but unleashed and encouraged forces which he himself could not possibly control after setting them free."

On the other hand, devout Protestants have sometimes viewed Ockham and his followers as a cold-hearted band of logic-choppers, symptomatic of the decline of medieval religion. It was the task of Luther, they claim, to reject the perverse cleverness of the nominalist outlook and to fuse thought and feeling again under the aegis of faith.

Those who have, on the contrary, admired the nominalistic school have often hailed its members as demythologizers. They used, it is said, a new epistemology and logic to destroy the metaphysical constructions that had been reared by medieval system makers. They cut close to the bone, but the operation was salutary for the development of modern philosophy and empirical science and perhaps also for the purification of Christian theology.

Now the nominalists seem on the whole to be gaining favor among the students of medieval thought. This development is natural, for twentieth century historians have tended to be "demythologizers" themselves. They have questioned and tried to explode many previously accepted historical "universals". Who, for instance, dares now to mention scholasticism or humanism without quickly adding that these terms should be referred to methodologies rather than ideologies ? Who now is rash enough to speak of feudalism as a system ? As for those inherently ridiculous labels Middle Ages, Renaissance, and Reformation, they are tolerated only for convenience and because of their innocuous indeterminism. But they are no longer considered to have definite objects of reference. Pietism and mysticism may be the next terms to be attacked. History is becoming more and more nominalistic, and scholars (at least some of them) feel more and more that they should concentrate on particular relations between individual phenomena at the expense of the mythological universals so ingeniously fabricated and so ingenuously accepted in the past.

This nominalistic approach has not spared nominalism itself. Some historians now doubt that this term is either useful or accurate in describing the alleged philosophical outlook of a number of late medieval thinkers, who actually held divergent opinions on many problems. There is a certain irony in the fact that nominalism, the great dissolvent, is being dissolved itself.

Much valuable work has been done in the last half-century on the task of rewriting the history of late medieval theology and philosophy. In regard to Ockham, such revision has generally tended to tone down the old, highly-coloured account of his radicalism. Such scholars as Vignaux, Boehner, and Oberman, while stressing his originality, have also recognized his use of earlier concepts, and his close links with some aspects of thirteenth century thought. Following in this tradition, Courtenay notes that Ockham preserves the traditional distinction between God's *potentia absoluta* and his *potentia ordinata*. Ockham uses the concept of the *potentia absoluta* to affirm God's complete freedom and the absolute contingency of the created universe. At the same time he says that God created *this* universe. Whatever happens in it, including miracles, happens according to His *potentia ordinata*. God therefore does not treat his creation like a despot, and men need have no fear that he will fail to keep his covenants.

This interpretation seems very convincing. Various fundamental questions about Ockham's place in medieval intellectual history are, however, still unresolved. Should we consider Ockham, for example, as does Moody, basically an Aristotelian, attempting to cut away the neo-Platonic accretions that had obscured the master's true thought ? Or should we look at Ockhamism as essentially a later stage in the diffident and often hostile reaction toward Aristotle that had begun with Bernard, Grosseteste, and the Franciscans Bacon and Bonaventure ? Interesting suggestions have been made about Ockham's specific debts to the Franciscan Spiritual Peter Olivi. A. Maier [1] says that he took from Olivi his analysis of *quantitas*. J. Koch [2] says he followed Olivi in his denial that theology was a science and in his doctrines on grace, justification and the sacraments. E. Bettoni [3] says that he depended on Olivi for his solution of the problem of universals. Much more research needs to be done on these matters, but the task is made extremely difficult by the lack of critical editions, and sometimes of any editions at all, of so many important thirteenth and fourteenth century philosophical and theological treatises.

The same process of revision, facing the same obstacle of a lack of critical texts, is apparent in the study of Ockham's political and ecclesiological writings. Here, however, a learned and brilliant recent work has continued to assert the thesis that Ockham was a thoroughgoing rebel against ecclesiastical authority. This is maintained in the new version (Paris, 1956-63) of George de Lagarde's *La naissance de*

---

[1] *Archivum Franciscanum Historicum* (1953), pp. 176-181.

[2] *Recherches de Théologie Ancienne et Médiévale* (1930), 309-310.

[3] *Le doctrine filosofiche di Pier di Giovanni Olivi* (Milan, 1959), 514-515.

l'esprit laïque au déclin du moyen âge (vols. IV-V, a revision of vols. IV-VI of the old edition, Paris, 1942-46). For De Lagarde this Franciscan theologian was, paradoxically enough, the greatest and most dangerous medieval champion of the lay spirit. He was the subtle saboteur who introduced the "individualistic microbe" into the Church. "He maintains the principle of authority," De Lagarde asserts, "but destroys the substance of it so well that his acknowledgment is only an opportunity for him to marshal doubt, suspicion, and if the case warrants it, the revolt of Christendom against that authority." (V, 164) De Lagarde speaks of the "insidious subtlety and the respectful impertinence of Ockham's position in regard to the pontifical primacy." (V, 126) and says that this makes him a true precursor of Luther.

But such a view seems considerably overdramatized. De Lagarde says in shocked tones that Ockham envisages the possibility of the inerrancy of the Church being conserved by the faith of only one layman. But a similar position was advanced by the great hierocratic theorist Augustinus Triumphus and also by earlier writers. There was nothing in this theory that denied the papal primacy, for a pope who fell into heresy was believed to be *ipso facto* no longer a pope.

Already in 1944 Richard Scholz [1] came to the conclusion that Ockham "does not at all want, like Marsilius, to reverse the relationship between the spiritual and temporal powers, and place the empire above the papacy. His basic premiss concerning the relationship of the two authorities is a thorough-going traditionalism maintaining their co-existence and concordance." In an article, "Ockham, the Conciliar Theory and the Canonists"[2] Brian Tierney remarks, "It would be possible to go through a whole range of Ockham's political and ecclesiological concepts ... and point to more or less exact parallels in the works of thirteenth century canonists." As for Father Boehner, he does not hesitate to say [3] "Ockham's political ideas in their great outlines could have been developed, so far as we can see, from any of the classical metaphysics of the 13th century; for, as will be shown, they coincide with a sound Catholic political theory."

In at least one important way, however, Ockham's political and religious theories seem closely connected. Both emphasize to an extraordinary degree the freedom of man as well as of God. "Christ

---

[1] *Wilhelm von Ockham als politischer Denker und sein Breviloquium de principatu tyrannico, M.G.H., Schriften,* VIII (Stuttgart, 1944), 26.

[2] *Journal of the History of Ideas,* XV (1954), 46-47.

[3] *Collected Articles on Ockham* (St. Bonaventure, N. Y., 1958), 446.

did not ...," Ockham said in his *De imperatorum et pontificum potestate*, "forbid all principate or prelacy to the apostles ... But he forbade to them a principate of domination, which in a word taken from Greek is called despotic, which, according to the *Politics*, is the kind of principate one has over slaves; such a principate Christ did not give to the apostles, but a ministerial principate, which is the kind of principate one has over free men, and which is much nobler and greater in dignity than a dominative principate even though it is not so great in extent of power ..., even as a principate over men is nobler than a principate over beasts ..."[1]

Laymen and clerics possess the "liberty of the law of the Gospel", which means that to them belong "all such things as are found to be adverse neither to good morals nor to the teachings of the New Testament." It would be absurd if they were less free than unbelievers; therefore they have "all the rights and liberties of unbelievers, which they licitly and justly enjoyed before and after the incarnation of Christ : rights and liberties which ought not to be taken from believers against their will, since believers ought not to be worse off through being subjected to the perfect law of liberty, namely, that of the Gospel, than unbelievers were either before or after the incarnation of Christ ..."[2]

On the higher level of predestination and free will, Ockham also affirms man's freedom. In his *Commentary on the Sentences* and in his *Tractatus de praedestinatione et de praescientia Dei* he analyzes this intractable and yet central problem of the Christian faith with rigor and freshness. Starting from the premiss that God is free and can beatify whomever he chooses, Ockham says that by his disposing will God desires the salvation of all men. God's consequent will, however, depends to a large extent on human acts. If man places the obstacle of mortal, unrepented sin in God's way, he is damned. Man's merits and demerits usually decide his eternal fate, although positive exceptions may be made, as in the case of the Virgin Mary and St. Paul. Even faith in Christ may not be necessary; if a person lived according to right reason, God might ordain his salvation. Reprobation results only from sin in time. It cannot therefore be determined from all eternity, for otherwise man's fate would be necessary, and his acts would have no moral value. Ockham admits that he cannot explain

---

[1] C. 7, Ed. C.K. Brampton (Oxford, 1927), trans. E. Lewis, *Medieval Political Ideas* (London, 1954), II, 609.

[2] CC. 1, 9, *ibid.*, II, 607, 610-11.

how it is possible for God to know with certainty future contingent facts, even though one is certain by faith that He knows them. But Ockham nevertheless asserts that no future contingent comes to pass necessarily. Although God is absolutely sovereign and every created being is absolutely contingent, God in His sovereignty maintains the liberty of the created human will.

God's own will desires man's free assent even more than his salvation. God's freedom assures man's freedom. At every level Ockham combats necessitarianism and determinism, in divine creation, in human acts, and in ecclesiastical and political institutions. Although the study of Ockham and his followers is still in its infancy, it seems clearly established that his theology, and not merely his logic and epistemology, is of great interest. To establish the links between them and his political and ecclesiological thought may ultimately be more valuable than to try to establish the putative links between Ockham and his age [1].

But this is the last and most irresistible temptation even of the historian who believes himself to be skeptical and hard-boiled, indeed something of an Ockhamist. How can he resist drawing parallels between the chief object of his interest and the other important cultural aspects of the period? So Courtenay links Ockham with the new art, the new humanism, and (most convincingly) the new empirical science. But however plausible or implausible the results, the act itself of drawing such parallels presupposes the existence of a universal. This universal is the Zeitgeist. To believe in it is to postulate the psychological unity of an age. In the last analysis, all historians are realists and not nominalists, for otherwise how could they write history? How could they convince themselves that historical synthesis is possible?

It is permissible to doubt that a grand synthesis of fourteenth century thought can be constructed around the figure of the Venerable Inceptor. The age of Ockham is the age of Petrarch, of Wyclif, and of St. Catherine of Siena as well. It is also a time of popular heresy, apocalyptic expectations, and mystical devotion, all alien to Ockham's sober temper. Ockham and his followers represent only one aspect of the period (if such a term has meaning) and probably not the most distinctive aspect at that.

---

[1] Jürgen Miethke, *Ockhams Weg zur Sozial-Philosophie* (Berlin, 1969) is a remarkable effort in this direction.

All attempts to formulate theories that characterize a whole age reveal the compulsive desire of the historical realist to find universals beneath the flux of temporal phenomena. In searching for the Zeitgeist we are all Hegel's heirs. Would Ockham be amused at our faith that the Zeitgeist exists ? At our efforts to fit his nominalism into an idealistic Hegelian framework ? If we could ask him this, I wonder what his answer would be.

THE VALIDITY OF THE TERM : "NOMINALISM"

PAUL OSKAR KRISTELLER

Columbia University

If I understand Prof. Courtenay correctly, he is arguing that the study of Ockham and his school has been undergoing a fargoing revision due to the work of such scholars as Moody, Boehner and Oberman, and that consequently we should no longer speak of nominalism. I confess that I am far from convinced that this is so. I realize that research on Ockham and his school has made much progress in recent decades, and that the work of the scholars mentioned has been especially important. I also understand that the Ockhamist position on the question of universals has been subjected to a more refined interpretation that disposes of the older and cruder forms in which this position had been described. Finally, it is very obvious to me that the evaluation of the school has undergone a basic change, and that the traditional contempt for late medieval scholasticism has been replaced by a serious and widespread respect for its intellectual a-chievement. On the other hand, the chronological sequence of this change is not as clear as Prof. Courtenay suggests. For example, the traditional treatment of Ockhamism is expressed by as influential a scholar as Etienne Gilson in his *History of Christian Philosophy in the Middle Ages* as late as 1955, as Prof. Courtenay himself indicated, whereas the reevaluation of Ockhamism in the field of physical science goes back at least to Pierre Duhem's *Études sur Léonard de Vinci* (1906-13), and an objective if not friendly treatment is apparent in Franz Ehrle's *Der Sentenzenkommentar Peters von Candia* (1925). Secondly, the contribution of Ockham and his school must be seen in terms of such disciplines as logic, physics, theology and political theory which also by the standards of his own time were clearly distinct. I do not say that these fields were unrelated to each other, but their distinction makes it imperative for the historian to ask specifically how the contribution of a given thinker to one field is connected with his contribution to another field. Such a connection cannot be taken for granted from the outset. Now the position traditionally called nominalism belongs primarily to the field of logic. I see no reason at all why we should cease to characterize the logical position of Ockham and his school as nominalism (or terminism). The work of Moody and Boehner has gone a long way to provide us with a more detailed and more sympathetic interpretation of Ockhamist logic, but it never occurred to me to conclude that this logic should no longer be called nominalistic. The work of Oberman has primarily focused on the theology of the school and on its central distinction between God's *potentia absoluta* and *ordinata*. Yet I do not see that a more detailed and sympathetic interpretation of Ockhamist theology should invalidate an interpretation of Ockhamist logic, even if it turned out to be impossible to derive the theology from the logic or to associate it closely with it. To conclude, I see much progress in Ockhamist studies during the last few decades. I see a tendency to study its doctrines more completely and in greater detail. I certainly see a tendency among specialists and general historians alike to give greater recognition to Ockhamism for its acumen and for its positive contributions to late medieval and early modern thought in all the different fields listed above, and perhaps in some others. Yet I see no evidence that the traditional description of the Ockhamist position in logic as nominalism or terminism should be abandoned, or that any of the leading scholars in Ockhamist studies have advocated or accomplished such a revision.

3. MYSTICISM, NOMINALISM AND DISSENT

STEVEN OZMENT

Yale University

Mystical writings are the most promiscuous late medieval literature. They range in form from the abstrusely philosophical to the downright folksy and are the common preserve of the lettered and unlettered alike. Exaggerating very typical medieval convictions, they bridge the barriers of sex, age, social class, and "heresy." But of all its real and possible alignments none seems more odd and inconsistent with the nature of mysticism than a liaison with nominalism. How can a committed nominalist embrace mysticism? That is a problem which requires us to be both philosophers and chroniclers, taking up an enormous task of definition and taking account of a wide spectrum of concrete historical practice.

1. JEAN GERSON AND "NOMINALISTIC MYSTICISM"

Scholars have been inclined to contrast two basic types of late medieval mysticism. On the one hand, they point to a "Germanic" tradition tending to be Dominican in religious Order, Thomist in theological orientation (yet with a strong dose of Neoplatonism), concerned more with intellect (contemplation, *visio Dei*) than with will (practical piety), theocentric and "essentialist" as regards the *unio mystica*, and suspected, if not adjudged heterodox, by the church. Eckhart of course exemplifies this tradition. On the other hand, there is a "Latin" tradition tending to be Cistercian or Franciscan in religious Order, eclectic in theological orientation, prejudicial in favor of the will (love), Christocentric and volitional as regards the mystical union *(conformitas voluntatis)*, and staunchly orthodox in the eyes of the church. For this tradition of mysticism Bernard of Clairvaux and Bonaventure are the popular examples.[1]

---

[1] Cf. J. Bernhart, *Bernhardische und Eckhartische Mystik in ihren Beziehungen und Gegensätzen* (Kempton, 1912), esp. 156; E. Vogelsang, "Luther und die Mystik," *Luther-*

While such sweeping typologies have the merit of stabilizing the slippery topic of mysticism, they must necessarily ignore contradictions and nuances in one or more of the areas compared.[1] For this reason we may welcome efforts positively to relate mysticism to such an apparent mortal enemy as late medieval nominalism in the theology of the Parisian chancellor and mystical theologian, Jean Gerson. Two noteworthy attempts are those of Walter Dress, *Die Theologie Gersons : Eine Untersuchung zur Verbindung von Nominalism und Mystik im Spätmittelalter* (Gütersloh, 1931), and Heiko Oberman, *The Harvest of Medieval Theology* (Cambridge, Mass., 1963).

As the subtitle of Dress' book indicates, nominalism and mysticism are not taken to be natural bedfellows. It is argued, however, that nominalism possesses a peculiar "Ansatzpunkt" for mysticism : its theologically stringent epistemology. As Gerhard Ritter before him, Dress calls attention to Gerson's ability to pursue "metaphysics" within the framework of a nominalist epistemology.[2] But it is the

---

Jahrbuch (1937), 32ff (distinguishing Dionysian, Latin [Bernard, Bonaventure, and Hugo of St. Victor] and German [Tauler, W. Gansfort, J. Goch, and the *Theologia Deutsch*] mysticism); K. Ruh, "Zur Grundlegung einer Geschichte der franziskanischen Mystik," *Altdeutsche und altniederländische Mystik* (Darmstadt, 1964), 240-74, esp. 264-5; S. Grünewald, *Franziskanische Mystik* (Münich, 1932), esp. 121ff; and K. Bihlmeyer, "Die Selbstbiographie in der deutschen Mystik des Mittelalters," *Theologische Quartalschrift* LXIV (1933), 405-44. Two of the best historically informed definitions of mysticism are D. Knowles, *The English Mystical Tradition* (New York, 1961), 2f; and E. Underhill, *Mysticism* (New York, 1961[12]), 23 ff, 415ff.

[1] See, for example. W, Dress on the confluence of Platonism, nominalism, and Franciscan theology in Ficino's "Voluptarismus," *Die Mystik des Marsilio Ficino* (Berlin, 1929), esp. 105-07, 113-14; K. Grunewald's defense of Tauler as a "voluntaristic" mystic, *Studien zu Johannes Taulers Frömmigkeit* (Leipzig, 1930); J. Von Walter's argument that a theocentric "visio magna" is more important to Bernard than a Christocentric "conformitas voluntatis," "Die Sonderstellung Bernhards von Clairvaux in der Geschichte der Mystik" in *Christentum und Frömmigkeit : Gesammelte Vorträge und Aufsätze* (Gütersloh, 1941), 125ff, esp. 131; and H. A. Oberman's criticism of Vogelsang's typology (note 1), "Simul gemitus et raptus : Luther and Mysticism," in *The Reformation in Medieval Perspective*, ed. S. Ozment (Chicago, 1971), 219-51. As in Eckhart, one can find an essentialistic volitional union in the *Theologia Deutsch*, ed. H. Mandel (Leipzig, 1908), ch. 25, p. 53.10-17.

[2] Metaphysics, as a science, deals with "signs", not with things in themselves. Still the signs are not simply subjective constructs with no extra-mental foundation. In Ritter's words, "die Zeichnen besitzen zugleich eine reale Bezogenheit auf die 'äussere' Welt, so dass auch vom Boden der 'terministischen' Erkenntnislehre aus ein Aufbau der 'realen' Disziplinen, inbesondere der Metaphysik, möglich ist." *Studien zur Spätscholastik* II (Heidelberg, 1922/Darmstadt, 1963), 28f. Cf. Dress, *Die Theologie Gersons*, 18ff.

major theological consequence of this epistemology, the denial of demonstrative knowledge of God, which becomes the peculiar jumping-off point for mysticism. Gerson, Dress maintains, embraces the Dionysian *via negativa* both as a positive point of contact with nominalist epistemology—each denying intuitive knowledge and existential statements about God—and as a point of departure for transcending, without contradicting, this same epistemology. Dionysian negation and nominalist economy work together to prepare the way for a distinctive "affective transcendentalism."[1] The goal of the Dionysian negative way is an "agalma Dei pulcherrimum"; and in Ockham one finds room for a "notitia abstractiva deitatis."[2] As the mind engages in these demanding contemplative exercises, it is purged and humbled, made ready to follow the heart *(desiderium)*, which can finally reach into the holy of holies; through love the contemplative soul moves from abstract concept to real communion with God.[3]

Dress deals with nominalism almost exclusively from its philosophical side, in terms of its theory of knowledge. Mysticism is therefore seen as compensating for the theological poverty of nominalist epistemology. Dionysian mysticism not only knows the mental agonies of this epistemology, but it is able, through affection, to transcend its limitations.[4]

Oberman, by contrast, deals with nominalism almost exclusively from its theological side, in terms of its soteriology. Hence, where Dress leaves off—"affective transcendentalism"—Oberman begins his comparison of late medieval nominalism and mysticism. It is at the point where affection (will and love) reach out to God that the convergence of the two is seen. For Oberman, mysticism does not compensate for the philosophical weaknesses but rather agrees with the theological strengths of nominalism.

Using Gerson as his model, Oberman contrasts an "affective" or "penitential" type of mysticism, congenial to nominalism, with what

---

[1] Dress, *Die Theologie Gersons*, 51, 54, 69f. Cf. the critical response by J. B. Monnoyeur, "La doctrine de Gerson augustinienne et bonaventurienne," *Études franciscain* 46 (1934), 690-97.

[2] Dress, *Die Theologie Gersons*, 57, 59.

[3] "The simplicity after which the soul strives by purifying and 'universalizing' its concepts is not some possible content to be grasped, but freedom from all earthly things and creaturely accidents. By negation the soul is freed from the imperfect. This is really no more than a preparation for a new union with God, which can be achieved in perfect form only by affective movement, by love." *Ibid.*, 58; cf. 69-70.

[4] Cf. *infra*, 76, n. 1.

is variously described as "speculative," "essentialistic," or "transformation" mysticism. The former is said to reside in the affective power of the soul, to seek God as the "Good," and to understand union with God in terms of volitional conformity. "Essentialistic" mysticism, on the other hand, locates in the intellective power of the soul, views God as "Truth," and culminates in an intellectual intuition of transcendental reality in which the beholder loses his being in God.[1]

Oberman has made us aware of the important logical distinction late medieval theologians made between the absolute and ordained powers of God : the *potentia Dei absoluta* and the *potentia Dei ordinata*. The latter was a catch-phrase for the whole of God's *de facto* decisions from the creation to man's redemption. It represented "what is" rather than what theoretically could have been in the history of salvation; for according to his "absolute power," God could have chosen otherwise than he in fact did. In the practical terms of religious life and theological debate, however, the "potentia Dei ordinata" was simply the church with her "orthodox" doctrines and sacraments, which embodied God's "revealed will." And the "potentia Dei absoluta" was that sphere of divine freedom above and beyond this chosen system of salvation. Concretely, the former represented the"establishment;" the latter the permanent possibility of historical novelty.[2]

Oberman considers it especially important that affective mysticism, like nominalism, does not permit penetration into the intellect or being of God; rather, maintaining distance, it settles for loving conformity

---

[1] *The Harvest of Medieval Theology*, 330-39.

[2] Originally, for scholastics, the *potentia Dei absoluta* was but a hypothetical construct, God considered absolutely, in terms of his infinite possibilities, without reference to any chosen external activity. For medieval thinkers, God never acted "inordinate," never, so to speak, shot from the hip. In this sense, any and every activity of God outside himself, regardless of its rarity, must be an expression of "potentia ordinata;" to talk about God's relation to the world is by definition to talk about power in "ordered" form. In later thinkers (Pierre d'Ailly and Gregory of Rimini perhaps, certainly Gabriel Biel), the two powers of God go beyond the strictly hypothetical to embrace a distinction between God's regular and his highly irregular activities in the world. This distinction was based on actual biblical precedents, the chief of which was the direct conversion of Paul on the road to Damascus—an example of God's *potentia absoluta* breaking into the *potentia ordinata*. Cf. Oberman, *Harvest of Medieval Theology*, p. 45f, and William Courtenay's article in this volume, "Nominalism and Late Medieval Religion," *supra*, 37-43. It is in this latter, "applied" sense of the possibility of historical novelty that I find the distinction relevant to developments in the late medieval mystical traditions. Cf. especially Sebastian Franck's trial in Ulm, *infra*, 89-90.

with God's revealed will (the *potentia Dei ordinata*).[1] Despite the
analogy, at this key juncture in his typology, when the *conformitas
voluntatis* of mystical union is allied with the *potentia Dei ordinata*
of nominalist theology, it may be asked whether theological metaphors have been mixed. The *conformitas voluntatis* of mystical union,
an extremely rare experience granted a few chosen *viatores* in this
life, normally refers to a special contact with God beyond that possible
within and through the ordained means of grace (the *potentia ordinata*);
it is momentary yet real communion with the living Will of God
(potentia absoluta!) above his will system of salvation. Although
"will" is a key term in both instances, quite different things are
involved. One conformed in will with God in mystical union has not
only reaped the fullest possible benefits from the ordained media of
salvation, but he has also risen above them to God himself. Until the
latter movement is made, until the *potentia ordinata* is transcended,
it can be argued that there is, properly speaking, no mysticism.[2] And,
contrary to Oberman's apparent assumption, such transcendence can
occur, as I think it clearly does in Gerson, without thereby incurring an
"essentialist" union with God.

André Combes, a principal foil of Oberman's typology, sees the
major difference between Gerson and Ockham in the former's retention
of a qualified realist metaphysics which permits real contact between
the soul and God. Gerson, to be sure, is no advocate of an extreme
realist position, which too closely aligns man's created nature *(esse
reale)* with his archetypal being in the mind of God *(esse ideale)*. But
neither is he an advocate of what Combes considers to be the extreme
Ockhamist position which denies any real connection whatsoever.
Unlike Ockham, Gerson does not identify the divine ideas simply
with the particular *de facto* creations of the divine will. Rather,
Combes argues, he grants them an independent existence in the mind

---

[1] *Harvest of Medieval Theology*, 330.

[2] Bonaventure, for example, placed the affective "transitus et transformatio in
Deum" after the graced *viator* has beheld God as pure unity of being and a trinity of
goodness (the fifth and sixth stages of the *Itinerarium mentis in Deum*). Teresa of
Avila describes her struggle against the belief that God is present only by grace and
not in terms of his very person. *Libro de la vida*, cap. 18, 15 in *Obras completas* I (Madrid,
1951), p. 697. Cf. Dionysius the Areopagite, *On the Divine Names*, ch. 2, sect. 7 in *Dionysius the Areopagire : On the Divine Names and the Mystical Theology*, trans. C. E. Rolt
(New York., 1966[5]), 73f.

of God and, further, identifies divine intelligence and divine essence.[1]
As a consequence, there are very real lines of communication between
man and God in Gerson's theology. Man lives not only on earth as
a creation of divine will but also in heaven as an exemplar in the
mind (= being) of God. And his reunion with his origin in mystical
union is more than volitional concord. For Combes, then, Ockham
appears in Gerson's theology only to fend off the dangers of extreme
realism, just as a (moderate) realist metaphysics is present to guard
against extreme Ockhamism.[2] Gerson's mystical theology is basically
"Bonaventurian," yet sufficiently nuanced to merit the description,
"Gersonism."[3]

Although Combes is right to point up Gerson's retention of important
realist assumptions, too quickly passed over by Oberman,[4] Gerson does
carefully distinguish divine intelligence and divine essence, God's
ideas and his being, so that man's archetypal life in the mind of God
is not *ipso facto* identifiable with unity in the being of God. Such a
distinction is taken up in criticism of the "identitas realis et essentialis" of creatures with God, which Gerson found in Manichaean
doctrine and, in a different context, in speculation on the nature of
mystical union in the early writings of Jan van Ruysbroeck.[5] This is

---

[1] *Essai sur la critique de Ruysbroeck par Gerson* III[1] (Paris, 1959), 219-33; 270f.
"Selon Gerson, la créature n'est pas seulement dans l'intelligence divine en tant qu'objet
connu au terme de l'opération créatrice. Elle est dans l'essence divine, qui ne diffère
pas de l'intelligence. Nous en sommes d'autant plus assurés, que la créature tient tout
son être réel de son être idéal, et retourne vers cet être idéal même. Dans une telle
doctrine, la distinction ockhamiste entre intelligence et essence disparaît en tant que
telle. L'intelligence divine se confond avec l'essence, source et fin des créatures." *Ibid.*,
222. Cf. below, n. 5.

[2] *Essai* III[1], 217. Cf. David Schmiel, *Via propria and Via mystica in the Theology of
Jean le Charlier de Gerson* (St. Louis, 1969).

[3] Combes, *ibid.*, 223.

[4] It is questionable when Oberman insists that Gerson's criticism of the "formal-
izantes" in the two lectures *Contra curiositatem studentium* indicates that he is a "true
disciple of d'Ailly and Occam." *The Harvest of Medieval Theology*, 335. A case can be
made that Gerson's views on the perimeters of reason's competence in theological
matters are here more Thomist than Ockhamist. Cf. my article, "The University and
the Church : Patterns of Reform in Jean Gerson," *Medievalia et Humanistica* NS I
(1970), 111-126, 112f.

[5] See my *Homo Spiritualis* (Leiden, 1969), 55ff, 74f. Relevant texts in translation
are in my edition of *Jean Gerson : Selections* (Leiden, 1969), 17ff, 49ff. According to
Ockham : "Ideae non sunt in deo realiter et subiective sed tantum obiective, sicut
omnes creaturae ab aeterno fuerunt in deo, quia ab aeterno fuerunt cognitae a deo. Et

an important point of distinction between Gerson and the tradition represented by Eckhart and Tauler, with significant consequences (or parallels) in the areas of speculative anthropology and the mystical union.

Eckhart and Tauler interpreted the first chapter of John's gospel (vs. 4 : "In ipso vita erat") to mean that preexistent man was essentially one with God. For Gerson, by contrast, distance is preserved even in eternity. Preexistent man is not one with divine being, but rather participates in the Mind and Will of God; he is not essentially but "ideationally" and "volitionally" one with God. Taking up an admittedly inadequate traditional analogy, Gerson tells us that life was in God like a plan is in the mind and will of an artisan; man was one with God like an idea is one with the intention of its creator. Divine will and intellection are not to be equated willy-nilly with divine essence; preexistent man, although "in God," is not to be identified with the being of God. In this area of their speculation, it is Gerson, not Eckhart, who posits a God beyond God!

Ever problematic is the question of the nature and degree of contact with God in mystical union. The point at issue in "essential" and "volitional" unions is more subtle than the option between a loss of self in a divine abyss (the Eckhartian "gotheit" beyond the revealed God, if one wishes) and loving conformity with the revealed will of God (interpreted along the lines of the *potentia Dei ordinata* of nominalism, if one wishes). At issue, I would submit, are in fact two distinct forms of union with the being of God which, although sharply distinguished from one another by very different metaphysical presuppositions, still seem to have more in common with one another than either has with the philosophy and theology of late medieval nominalism.

Although a difficult and ever disputable affair, the metaphysical dimension of the volitional union merits observation. For Gerson, as Combes has pointedly stressed, mystical union involves a "real" relation. God and man enter union as generic likes, on the basis of a common nature, as purified spirit embraces and is embraced by pure Spirit.[1] Gerson's theological metaphysics, however, precludes essential

---

ideo nunquam invenitur quod Augustinus alicubi ponat ideas nisi in divina intelligencia, non in essentia, per hoc innuens quod non sunt in deo nisi sicut cognita et non sicut ibidem realiter existentia." I *Sent.* d. 35, q. 5 N.

[1] Cf. *Homo Spiritualis*, 77, 82. On the *similitudo* theme in Ficino see Dress, *Die Mystik des Marsilio Ficino*, 64. Cf. Oberman's comments on Biel's "eucharistic mysticism." *Harvest of Medieval Theology*, 358f.

identification of creatures with God at every level and in every form of their existence. Even in its precreated state in the divine mind the soul could be said to be God only as an idea in the mind of an artisan can be called the artisan. And at the end of time there is to be no essential return and identification of the soul with its Creator.[1]

In the present life, the unitive soul approximates its precreated "esse ideale" in the divine mind; created image corresponds to eternal archetype. For a moment, in thought and act, the soul is as God conceived and willed it, conformed as fully in mind and will to its Creator as an idea in the mind of an artisan is conformed to the intention of the artisan. Though still a creature, in mystical union, the soul is one with God's Mind and Will. And this "conformitas" is of a higher order than that which occurs in the humble embrace of God's revealed will. In the latter case, one is obedient to God; in the former,

---

[1] Oberman incorrectly makes Gerson an "essentialist" on the matter of eschatological union : "The union with the abyss, which is union with the Godhead beyond God for Eckhart—and union with the essence of God's being for Ruysbroeck—is for Gerson an eschatological event granted only to the *comprehensores*." *The Harvest of Medieval Theology*, 340. For Gerson, neither in final beatitude nor in the imperfect assimilation of beatitude enjoyed by some in this life is there essential union with God. Cf. *infra*, 75, n. 1. Gerson refuses to concede the possibility of an essential union even "de potentia Dei absoluta." *Epistola prima ad fratrem Bartholomaeum* in Andrè Combes, *Essai sur la critique de Ruysbroeck par Gerson* I (Paris, 1945), 623.4ff. We are "gods" (Ps. 81:6) "non quidem per veritatem et unitatem divinae essentiae, et locutionem propriam, sed participative et assimilative, imitative et nuncupative." *Ibid.*, 625.8ff. Despite imagery as "essentialistic" as that employed by Eckhart, note how Bernard too is careful to preserve distance even in the eschatological event : "Quomodo stilla aquae modica, multo infusa vino, deficere a se tota videtur, num et saporem vini induit et colorem; et quomodo ferrum ignitum et candens, igni simillimum fit, pristina propriaque forma exutum; et quomodo solis luce perfusus aer in eamdem transformatur luminis claritatem, adeo ut non tam illuminatus, quam ipsum lumen esse videatur : sic omnem tunc in sanctis humanam affectionem quodam ineffabili modo necesse erit a semetipsa liquescere, atque in Dei penitus transfundi voluntatem. Alioquin quomodo omnia in omnibus erit Deus, si in homine de homine quidquam supererit? *Manebit quidem substantia*, sed in alia forma, alia gloria, aliaque potentia." *De diligendo Deo*, *MPL* 182, 991 A-B. Cf. A. Forest, "Das Erlebnis des consensus voluntatis beim hl. Bernhard" in *Bernhard von Clairvaux : Mönch und Mystiker*, ed. by J. Lortz (Wiesbaden, 1955), 120-127. Although Gerson strongly criticizes such imagery *(De myst. theol. spec.* [ed. André Combes (Lugano, 1958)], *cons.* 41, 107), he would fully agree with this sentiment. It is to be noted that Ockham rejected the mixed liquids simile (or absorption imagery) of mystical union as "fantastic" in the *Tractatus contra Benedictum* XII, ed. H. S. Offler, *Guillelmi de Ockham opera politica* III (Manchester, 1956), 161-62, cited by R. E. Lerner, "The Image of Mixed Liquids in Late Medieval Mystical Thought," *Church History* 40 (1971), 397-411.

one touches God himself. For Gerson, mystical union is an imperfect "assimilatio beatitudinis", a penultimate "visio et fruitio Dei," already in this life.[1] That is the content of the *conformitas voluntatis* and concurrent *cognitio Dei experimentalis*. In "historical" terms, the unitive soul conforms to its original, archetypal life in God as did Adam before the Fall; indeed, inasmuch as the unitive soul is not able not to love God, it might be said to be even closer to God than was Adam, bridging that twilight zone between prefallen and precreated man. Gerson describes the mystical flight of the ethically and sacramentally purified soul as follows :

When the heart and mind, purified and intimately aware of God, have progressed so far that they now give no thought to carnal joy or to any servile or mercenary act, know nothing of God which is harsh, unfriendly, upsetting, or confusing, and no longer look on God as an avenger who makes retribution but know him only as the completely desirable, "sweet and gentle" [Ps. 85 (86):5], totally to be loved "even if he slay me" [Job 13:15], the most worthy—when [I say] the heart and

---

[1] When he scored van Ruysbroeck for saying that the unitive soul "convertitur seu transformatur et absorbetur in esse divinum" Gerson carefully distinguished a present and future "visio et claritas objectalis" from van Ruysbroeck's alleged defense of a "visio et claritas essentialis." "Tertia pars ejusdem libri [van Ruysbroeck's *De ornatu spiritualium nuptiarum*] prorsus repudianda rescindendaque est, tanquam vel male explicata, vel plane abhorrens et discrepans a doctrina sana doctorum sanctorum qui de nostra beatitudine locuti sunt. Nec stat cum determinatione expressa decretalis ponentis beatitudinem nostram consistere in duobus actibus, visione et fruitione scilicet cum lumine gloriae. Et si hoc ita est in beatitudine consummata, quod Deus non est visio et claritas nostra essentialis, sed tantum objectalis, quantomagis hoc erit alienum in beatitudinis quadam assimilatione imperfecta quam fas haberemus degustare hic in via. Ponit autem tertia pars libri praefati quod anima perfecte contemplans Deum, non solum videt eum per claritatem quae est divina essentia, sed est ipsamet claritas divina. Imaginatur enim, sicut scripta sonant, quod anima tunc desinit esse in illa existentia quam prius habuit in proprio genere, et convertitur seu transformatur et absorbetur in esse divinum et in illud esse ideale defluit quod habuit ab aeterno in essentia divina." *Epistola prima ad fratrem Bartholomaeum*, 618.5ff. In a much later work, the *Collectorium super Magnificat*, Gerson employed the imagery of eucharistic transformation to interpret mystical union, but, in striking contrast with Eckhartian mysticism, it is the human "accidents", not the human "substance," which are changed. "Contemplabaris, o sapientissima feminarum, quoniam in eucharistiae sacramento fit transformatio panis in essentia sua, remanentibus accidentibus. At vero dum mens in Deum transformatur, remanet quidem essentia mentis, sed accidentia nova succedunt, non fantastica, non materialia, sed deiformia, divina claritate radiante. Trnasformamur, inquit apostolus, de claritate in claritatem : de claritate communis notitiae rationalis acquisitae in claritatem fidei deiformis infusae; de claritate hac fidei in claritatem intelligentiae, et de hac demum in claritatem saporosae et sapientialis experientiae." In Combes, *Essai sur la critique de Ruysbroeck par Gerson* I, 857.22ff.

mind are so set only upon the business of love, then fly secure into the arms of the Bridegroom, clasp that divine Friend with the piurest embrace, plant upon him the most chaste kiss of peace, surpassing "all understanding" [Phil. 4:7], so that you can say with joyful, amorous devotion : "My beloved is mine, and I am his!" [Cant. 2:16].[1]

In the case of an "essential" union, on the other hand, the metaphysical presuppositions are quite different. Before its creation the soul was one essential being with God. So complete was this union that Eckhart, in a famous outburst, could boast : "Were I not, God would not be."[2] Mystical union mirrors preexistence and the eschatological event. Man's precreaturely as his eschatological existence is essential unity in God. In this life the unitive ideal is, accordingly, "oneness in God." Adamic manhood or Christ-like conformity of mind and will with God are approached only as a preparation for still more intimate contact. *Conformitas, similitudo*, is a stage on the way,

---

[1] *De myst. theol. pract.*, ed. Combes (Lugano, 1958), *cons.* 12, 216.122-135. Like Gerson's later critic. Vincent of Aggsbach (d. 1460), Bonaventure is more strictly Dionysian in excluding the intellective powers from the mystical union. The mind, like Moses, is not permitted to enter the promised land. Gerson too excludes intellection in the normal, technical sense of the term. But, vis a vis the "pure Dionysians," he consistently championed a cognitive dimension in mystical union. Vincent attacked him because he identified mystical theology with prayer or "affectus mentalis aut intellectualis supremus." Gerson, *De myst. theol. spec.*, *cons.* 43, 118.31f and *De elucidatione scolastica mysticae theologiae* (1424), ed. Combes (Lugano, 1958), *cons.* 11 and 12; Vincent, *Tractatus cuiusdam Carthusiensis de mystica theologia* in E. Vansteenberghe, *Autour de la docte ignorance : Une controverse sur la theologie mystique au XVe siècle* (Münster i.W., 1915), 197. This is an important distinction between Gerson and Bonaventure and Vincent. One should not, however, too sharply distinguish Gerson and Bonaventure at the point of the mystical union proper. Although Bonaventure maintains that, in the "perfect transitus," the "apex affectus totus transferatur et transformetur in Deum," the "transitus" still occurs "cum Christo" and is subject to the conditions of creaturely existence; one realizes Christ's promise to reside with him in paradise only "quantum possibile est secundum statum viae." *Itinerarium mentis in Deum*, ed. J. Kaup (Münich, 1961), VII, 2, 4, I fail to see in this an Eckhartian direction. Cf. however Oberman, "Simul Gemitus et raptus," 226f. Dionysius the Areopagite speaks of man's deification "as far as is permitted without sacrilege." *Dionysius the Pseudo-Areopagite : The Ecclesiastical Hierarchy*, trans. by T. L. Campbell (Washington, 1955), 25, b. 17.

[2] "In miner geburt wurden elliu dinc geborn und ich was sache min selbes und aller dinge, unde wolte ich, ich were noch niht alliu dinc, were ich niht, so enwere niht got." *Deutsche Mystiker des 14. Jahrhunderts*, II : *Meister Eckhart*, ed. F. Pfeiffer (Leipzig, 1857), 184.7-20. This passage is later exploited by Valentin Weigel, *Sämtliche Schriften* 3 (Stuttgart-Bad Cannstatt, 1966), 66f. Cf. Tauler, *Die Predigten Taulers*, ed. F. Vetter (Berlin, 1910), 331.32-332.4 (on John 1:4 : "In ipso vita erat").

not the goal. The soul for a moment in mystical union is truly God. Eckhart puts the matter so :

A great master says that his [unitive] breakthrough *(durchbrechen)* to God is more excellent than his emanation from God. When [he says] I flowed from God, all things recognized God. But there was no happiness in this, for I was but a creature among creatures. In the breakthough to God, however, I will be free in the Will of God and free from the will of God, from God's works, from God himself. For then I am above all creatures, neither God nor a creature [for such distinctions no longer exist]. Rather now and forevermore I am what I was[before my creation] ... In the breakthough to God I discover that God and I are one.[1]

With Gerson, the unitive soul, in ecstasy, swoons in the embrace of an eternal other; with Eckhart, it simply becomes the other. For both, however, mystical union is an approximation of *pre-* or *un*createdness. In both instances, the unitive soul passes momentarily beyond God's ecclesiastical establishment and revelation to enter eternity, to encounter God himself. Eckhart and Gerson are so close—yet so far apart. Yet perhaps not so distant, as mystical thinkers, that they still do not have more in common with each other than either has with nominalism. We must look to the task of definition.

2. NOMINALISM : A SCIENCE OF THE *Potentia Dei Ordinata*

The most distinctive trait of the late medieval mystical traditions, irrespective of the division on the mode of union, is the affirmation that God and man share a common nature and are really connected. This is highlighted on the anthropological level by the weight placed on the *synteresis voluntatis et rationis* and/or *Seelengrund;* in the area of soteriology it is set forth in the principle, equally widespread among mystical thinkers, that "likeness' *(similitudo)* is the *sine qua non* for saving knowledge and relationship. These common medieval doctrines, to be sure in exaggerated form, became the very pillars of mystical theology.[2]

---

[1] Pfeiffer, *op. cit.*, 284.11-22. More succinctly put : "Unser herre Jesus Kristus der bat sinen vater, daz wir mit ime unt in ime ein würden, unt niht alleine vereinet, mer : ein einic ein." *Buch der göttlichen Tröstung* in *ibid.*, 431.16-17.

[2] Gerson : "Quia Deus spiritus est et similitudo est causa unionis perspicuum est cur spiritus rationalis sic depuratus et defecatus unitur spiritui divino, quia videlicet similis efficitur cum eo." *De myst. theol. spec.*, *cons.* 41, 111.103-106. Eckhart points out that, in the highest powers of his soul, man is "gotes geslehte unde gotes sippe."

On the other hand, late medieval nominalism is distinguished, philosophically and theologically, by the insistence that man's relation to God and to his world is finally covenantal and not ontological, based on willed agreements and conventions, not on common natures and necessary connections.[1] Nominalist epistemology was "revolutionary" precisely because it challenged the traditional assumption that only like can know like.[2] Direct, intuitive knowledge of particulars replaced abstracted "intelligible species" as the immediate and sure basis of human knowledge. While far from denying a foundation for universal concepts in extra-mental reality,[3] nominalism granted such concepts existence only "in anima et verbo" : they are freely fashioned verbal "conventions," formed by the mind as a natural response to its perception of individual things.[4] Over against the moderate realism of Thomas Aquinas or Duns Scotus, for example, Ockham argued that the mind does not abstract from particulars universals in some fashion really existing in particulars in order mediately to know these same particulars. Knowing individual things intuitively, the mind "legislates" universals as tools to handle perceived species and genera. A willed verbal relation connects the mind conceptually (and surely) with extra-mental reality.

Buch der göttlichen Tröstung, 420.31-40. Regarding *similitudo* as the door to unity in God, Eckhart writes : "Also spriche ich nu von gelichnüsse unt von der minne hitze; wan nach dem, daz es dem andern gelicher ist, dar zuo unt dar nach jaget ez me unt ist sneller unt ist ime sin louf süezer un wunneclicher, unt ie me ez verrer kumet von ime selber unde von allem dem, daz jenez niht enist, dar zuo ez jaget, ungelicher sich selben unt allem dem, daz jenez niht ist, dar nach wirt ez gelicher dem, daz ez jaget, dar zuo ez ilet. Unt wan gelichnüsse fliuzet von dem einen unt ziuhet unt locket von der kraft unt in der kraft des einen, dar umbe gestillet noch benüeget niht noch dem, daz da ziuhet, noch dem, daz gezogen wirt, und daz sie in ein vereinet werdent." *Ibid.*, 431.1-11. Indeed, the soul "hates likeness," since it is penultimate, only the means to unity. *Ibid.*, 431.39f. Cf. T. Steinbüchel, *Mensch und Gott in Frömmigkeit und Ethos der deutschen Mystik* (Düsseldorf, 1952), 188 ; J. Quint, "Mystik und Sprache : Ihr Verhältnis zueinander in der spekulativen Mystik Meister Eckeharts," in *Altdeutsche und alterniedländische Mystik*, 130. The *synteresis* concept in Gerson and Eckhart is discussed *infra*.

[1] Cf. the lucid discussion by W. J. Courtenay, "Covenant and Causality in Pierre d'Ailly," *Speculum* 46 (1971), 94-119.

[2] Cf. M. H. Carré, *Realists and Nominalists* (Oxford, 1946), 110 ; P. Boehner (editor), *Ockham : Philosophical Writtings* (London, 1962³), xxvii.

[3] Cf. P. Boehner, "The Realistic Conceptualism of William Ockham," in *Collected Articles on Ockham* (St. Bonaventure, N. Y., 1958), 165ff.

[4] *Summa logicae* I, ed. P. Boehner (St. Bonaventure, N.Y., 1957), 45.54-66. Cf. criticism of Scotus' formal distinction, *Ockham : Philosophical Writings*, 37ff.

In parallel, nominalist soteriology, while far from undermining the traditional media of salvation, drew upon tradition to stress the contingent and covenantal character of man's relation to God. Grace is not in but rather "accompanies" the sacraments because God has "pledged" to be present when sacraments are performed.[1] And the *habitus gratiae*, as Scotus had already taught, is not a primary and necessary but a secondary and contingent cause of divine acceptance. In the Scotist tradition, nothing created must, by reason of its nature *(ex natura rei)*, be accepted by God.[2] And according to Ockham's "theological razor" (if such I may call his use of the following axiom), what God can do by means of secondary causes, he can also do without them.[3] It was far from inconceivable for Ockham that God, exercising his absolute power, could save a man without an inherent, transforming, supernatural *forma accidentalis*.[4] Even here, however, when Ockham's speculation *de potentia Dei absoluta* seems to align him with those mystics who emphasize God's transcendence and ineffability, he is in fact denying the most basic of mystical tenets.[5] For

---

[1] Cf. Courtenay, *Speculum* 46 (1971), 110ff. Aquinas ascribes this view to Peter Lombard and criticizes it for failing to grant the sacraments of the New Testament a material role in the conveyance of grace to the soul.

[2] Elaborated by Werner Dettloff, *Die Lehre von der acceptatio divina bei Johannes Duns Scotus mit besonderer Berücksichtigung der Rechtfertigungslehre* (Werl/Westf., 1954), and *Die Entwicklung der Akzeptations- und Verdienstlehre von Duns Scotus bis Luther* (Münster/Westf., 1963).

[3] *Ockham : Philosophical Writings*, xixff, 25f.

[4] I *Sent.* d. 17 (contra Petrus Aureoli) : "... aliquis potest esse deo acceptus et carus sine omni forma supernaturali inhaerente. Secondo, ... quacumque forma posita supernaturali in anima potest ipsa esse non accepta deo." Cited by Dettloff who comments : "Dieses Argument Wilhelms von Ockham liegt ... durchaus in der Linie der scotischen Lehre : weder der actus caritate formatus noch der natürliche gute Akt nötigen Gott ihrer Natur nach zur Akzeptation, also kann de potentia dei absoluta der eine wie der andere mit dem ewigen Leben belohnt, also im eigentlichen Sinne akzeptiert werden." *Die Entwicklung der Akzeptations- und Verdienstlehre*, 263-64, 267.

[5] Contrary to G. Leff, who concludes in reference to Eckhart and Ockham : "In both cases, the emphasis was upon God's indefinability in terms of external wisdom— ineffability for the mystic, unpredictability for the Ockhamist." "Ultimately both made for the same impasse between the world of nature and the world of faith which is the dominant fact in the religious life of the later Middle Ages." *Heresy in the Later Middle Ages* I (Manchester, 1967), 259f. Ockham's denial of real relations does not create an impasse, but rather defines the relationship between the world of nature and the world of faith in covenantal rather than ontological terms. And Eckhart in fact establishes indestructible ontological lines of communication between the world of (human) nature and the world of faith.

it is precisely in this speculation that he states most unequivocally the contingent, covenantal character of every relation between God and man.

Recent scholarship has cautioned against seeing in Ockham an active *potentia Dei absoluta*, skirting the established system of grace. Ockham's "conservatism" at the point of the *habitus gratiae* in particular and the *potentia Dei ordinata* in general has been convincingly argued.[1] Ockham supports the "establishment." Still, although regularly and in fully trustworthy fashion executed through secondary causes (sacraments and *gratia creata*), a saving relation with God is never finally dependent upon real connections between God, grace, and the soul, nor upon real relations between human activity *(facere quod in se est, fides caritate formata)* and divine reward. Man's salvation rather depends upon God's fidelity to his promises, on the trustworthiness of the word behind the "system." That is the unique thrust of nominalist soteriology, which must not be obscured by efforts to render nominalism "fully Catholic." Precisely when it speculates on the "God behind God," nominalism reveals itself as a science of the *potentia Dei ordinata*—a study of historical covenants, of God's will as expressed in Scripture and tradition, of the raison d'être of penultimate churches, priests, and sacraments, of order instituted and maintained. Nominalists perceived an unsettling "extra" dimension in the system itself; but they discovered that it was a verbal relation. In the final analysis, words are the connecting link between the mind and reality and between the soul and God. Man must come to grips with the world around him through "signs voluntarily instituted"; and he must work out his salvation on the basis of "laws voluntarily and contingently established" by God. In the final analysis, all he has is willed verbal relations.

3. MYSTICAL THEOLOGY : A SCIENCE OF THE *Potentia Dei Absoluta* [2]

If nominalism builds on willed verbal relations, mysticism looks to

---

[1] Cf. Dettloff, *Die Entwicklung der Akzeptations- und Verdienstlehre*, esp. 288ff; Oberman, *The Harvest of Medieval Theology*, esp. 30ff, 160ff; and P. Vignaux, *Luther, commentateur des Sentences* (Paris, 1935), esp. 59ff. For a strong alternative view of the matter, see E. Iserloh, *Gnade und Eucharistie in der philosophischen Theologie des Wilhelm von Ockham : Ihre Bedeutung für die Ursachen der Reformation* (Wiesbaden, 1956), esp. 279ff.

[2] On this section see my study, *Mysticism and Dissent : Religious Ideology and Social Protest in the Sixteenth Century* (New Haven, 1973).

real ontological connections between God and man. If nominalism is a scholastic science of the *potentia Dei ordinata*, mysticism can be described as a commonsense "science" of a presently active *potentia Dei absoluta*.

The mystical thinker's most basic theological postulate is the Biblical witness to God's sovereign freedom to operate beyond what He himself has established as normative. Objectively the mystical thinker looks to God's freedom to communicate immediately with men, to speak more conclusively in the depths of an individual heart than through all the official writings and ceremonies of even the most ancient of institutions. Subjectively mysticism rests on an anthropological base uniquely structured to transcend the limitations of the normal, mechanical processes of sense perception, reason, and volition. This subjective base can also be called a "potentia absoluta"—a "potentia hominis absoluta." In the technical language of the medieval theologian, it is an inalienable and irrepressible *synteresis voluntatis et rationis* or *Seelengrund*—an indestructible orientation to God, a unique receptacle for God, in the depths of the soul.[1] For nominalists, in practice, the *synteresis* is directed to the ordained *via salutis;* it is the anthropological base for ethical activity *(facere quod in se est)* which puts one in a state of grace. For mystical thinkers, the *synteresis* is directed beyond the *via salutis;* it is the locus for God's unmediated birth in the soul.

In a classical statement of the options open to the medieval theologian, Bonaventure, the *magister* of Franciscan mysticism and spirituality, set forth three possible theologies : *"symbolica,* by which we deal correctly with sensible things, *propria,* by which we correctly handle intelligible things, and *mystica,* by which we are taken up into mind-transcending ecstasies."[2] Gerson later repeats this division in his magisterial *De mystica theologia speculativa* (1402). Here he points out that "mystical theology draws its doctrine from experiences

---

[1] See Gerson's description, *De myst. theol. spec., cons.* 14, 34.24-35.31. On the history of the *synteresis* concept and its interpretation : H. Appel, *Die Lehre der Scholastiker von der Syntheresis* (Rostock, 1891) and "Die Syntheresis in der mittelalterlichen Mystik," *ZKG* 13 (1892), 535ff; H. Kunisch, *Das Wort "Grund" in der Sprache der deutschen Mystik des 14. und 15. Jahrhundert* (Osnabrück, 1929); H. Wilms, "Das Seelenfünklein in der deutschen Mystik," *Zeitschrift für Askese und Mystik* 12 (1937), 157-66; H. Hof, *Scintilla Animae* (Lund, 1952), esp. 161ff; and W. Frei, "Was ist das Seelenfünklein beim Meister Eckhart?," *Theologische Zeitschrift* 14 (1958), 89-100.

[2] *Itinerarium mentis in Deum*, I, 7.62.

within the hearts of devout souls, just as the other two theologies proceed from extrinsic effects."[1] Symbolic theology studies created things and their perfections as signs and indications of God and divine perfection. Scholastic theology scientifically investigates the sacred and traditional writings of the church. Mystical theology, by contrast, finds its authoritative "texts" in the experiences which have occurred in the history and tradition of the heart. The mystical theologian must attempt to articulate mind-transcending ecstasies which erupt from the depths of the soul. He specializes in the sphere "supra nos."

Just as there are Biblically attested exceptions to God's normal self-mediation through the priestly-sacramental system of the church, so there are psychological structures within the human soul which transcend the limitations of the soul's normal sensory, reasoning, and volitional processes. As God has retained, as a sovereign deity must, an area of freedom above and beyond his covenantal commitments to the church, so the soul knows, as an immortal being must, an area of freedom above and beyond its necessary and chosen responses to the visible world. It is this "supra" dimension, this superabundant structural freedom of God and of the soul, which makes mystical experience and theology both possible and necessary.

A particularly revealing passage appears in a sermon by Eckhart on Luke 14:16f, the story of the man who prepared a great feast and sent his servant to invite his friends. Eckhart presents the following analysis. The man who extends the invitation is of course God, and the feast is union with God. But who is the servant designated to bring the two parties together? Eckhart assigns this role to the special anthropological resource of mystical theology.

> This man sent out his servant. Now St. Gregory says that the preachers are this servant. From another point of view one could say that the angels are. But there is a third possibility. It seems to me that this servant is the spark of the soul (daz vünkelin der sele), which is created by God and inserted as a light from above. It is an image of divine nature, constantly opposed to everything that is not of God. But it is not a power of the soul, as several suggest. It is constantly inclined to what is good; even in hell it is directed to the good. The masters say that it struggles incessantly [toward God]. It is called a synteresis, and that designates both a connection [with God] and an aversion [from all that is not God]. It has two activities: bitter combat against every impurity and constant attraction to what is good.

---

[1] De myst. theol. spec., cons. 2, 8.4ff.

That attraction, in fact, is directly built into the soul and remains even in those who are in hell.[1]

Tauler puts the matter no less strongly. Only the direct presence in the soul of God himself can satisfy the "spark of the soul." "The soul has a spark, a ground in itself. The thirst of this spark is so great that God, even though he is omnipotent, can quench it with nothing save himself. He could give it the life of everything he has created in heaven and on earth, and still it would not be satisfied."[2]

Here, it can be added, we see reflected in their anthropologies the significance of the different positions taken on the mode of man's preexistence in God. For Eckhart and Tauler, the "spark" or "ground" of the soul appears to be a much more potent point of contact with God than the *synteresis voluntatis* of Bonaventure and Gerson (although the latter is no less effective a base for the soul's return to God). Bonaventure and Gerson speak of a spark "of the will," a special qualification of the normal powers of the soul. Eckhart and Tauler, by contrast, set the ground of the soul completely apart; it is a more fully independent mystical structure.

4. MYSTICISM AND DISSENT : FROM "SUPRA" TO "CONTRA"

Both in terms of its objective orientation and its subjective power mysticism departs the ordinary way to religious truth and salvation for a more immediate communion with God. It reaches further than the normal psychological functions of the soul can grasp and demands more than the normal institutional structures of the church can give. In the most literal sense of the words, the mystical enterprise is trans-rational and trans-institutional. And because it is such, it bears potential anti-intellectual and anti-institutional stances, which can be adopted for the purposes of dissent, reform, and even revolution.

The most traditional, church-supporting form of mystical theology bears a patent potential anti-intellectualism. Gerson is a good case in point. He summarizes a long tradition when he maintains that mystical theology, the way of love, is absolutely superior to scholastic theology, a way traversed only by those with a university education. Not only

---

[1] *Meister Eckhart : Die deutschen Werke*, ed. J. Quint, I (Stuttgart, 1958), 331.13ff; cf. *Das Buch der göttlichen Tröstung*, 420.31-40.

[2] *Die Predigten Taulers*, ed. F. Vetter (Berlin, 1910), 137.1-5.

is mystical theology the "most perfect knowledge possible," it is also knowledge in which even "young girls and simpletons" can excel.[1] Gerson, of course, did not intend this remark in any revolutionary anti-intellectual or anti-institutional sense. He simply uttered a Biblical truism, and he uttered it as chancellor of the University of Paris. The remark, in fact, was part and parcel of his program to reform what he considered to be an excessively cerebral theological faculty within the University. He would overcome the errant head by subjecting it to the inerrant heart—the *synteresis voluntatis*.[2] Mystical theology was a potent weapon of reform; the "supra" dimension of mysticism subserved conservative renewal without becoming the "contra" of militant dissent.[3]

Potential anti-intellectual and anti-institutional stances are more apparent features of German mysticism. When Eckhart praises the *synteresis* in the sermon cited above, he cites St. Augustine in support of the conviction that "this spark has more truth within it than everything man can learn."[4] The possible revolutionary impact of Eckhart's teaching on the "corda simplicium" was repeatedly noted in the censures of his teaching.[5] How will you keep men down in the church after they have been in the mind of God ?

A recent study has convincingly shown how, beneath the historical and sacramental relation between God and man transacted by the church, Eckhart constructed a more fundamental interplay between God and the depths of the individual soul.[6] In another context I have

---

[1] *De myst. theol. spec.*, *cons.* 30, 78.33f.

[2] See my article, "The University and the Church : Patterns of Reform in Jean Gerson," *Medievalia et Humanistica* N.S. I (1970), 111-126.

[3] In the 15th century Nicholas of Cusa is another example of mystical concepts in the service of conservative reform. J. Koch discusses Eckhart's influence on Cusa, "Nicholas von Kues und Meister Eckhart : Randbemerkungen zu zwei in der Schrift *De Coniecturis* gegebenen Problemen," *Das Cusanus-Jubiläum (August 1964)*, ed. R. Haubst (Mainz, 1964), 164-173. Further bibliography in P. Sigmund, *Nicholas of Cusa and Medieval Political Thought* (Cambridge, Mass., 1963), 62 n.

[4] *Die deutschen Werke* I, 336.1f.

[5] J. Koch, "Meister Eckharts Weiterwirken im Deutsch-Niederländischen Raum im 14. und 15. Jahrhundert," *La mystique Rhènane : Colloque de Strasbourg 16-19 Mai 1961* (Paris, 1963), 133-56, 136, 152-54. See also the bull of condemnation (March 27, 1329) in Denzinger, *Enchiridion symbolorum* (1963), 950-980, pp. 290 ff. Appeal to the King of Heaven and the Church Triumphant, over against and in distinction from the Church Militant, was an issue in the trial of Joan of Arc. *The Trial of Jeanne D'Arc*, trans. by W. P. Barrett (New York, 1932), 125f.

[6] S. Ueda, "Ueber den Sprachgebrauch Meister Eckharts : 'Gott muss ...' Ein Bei-

argued that a "natural covenant" of more basic soteriological significance than God's historical covenants can be identified in the writings
of Tauler.[1] The mystical *via salutis* exposes the operative value judgments. According to the German mystics, true self-realization entails
the suspension of normal rational and volitional activities, a shutting
down of the regular processes of the soul. The latter are immobilized
(Gelassenheit) and cut off from the external world *(Abgeschieden-
heit)*. For a moment, the soul surrenders its accustomed routine
(Entleerung) and takes refuge in its self-sufficient inner ground.
One is above popes and kings, beyond sacraments and laws, immune
to worldly praise and condemnation. Whether it be by experience
or in theory only, one uniquely discovers through the mystical *via
salutis* the ideological prerequisite for that spectrum of dissent ranging
from revolutionary activity to quietistic withdrawal : the penultimate
character of all worldly power and authority, the sovereignty of the
Self within oneself.

Despite speculations about their revolutionary importance, nominalist writings do not stand out as manuals for dissent, militant or
otherwise, in the late Middle Ages. When serious protest is made against
Christendom it is not readily traced to enthusiastic marginal comments
on Ockham's philosophical and theological writings (Nicholas of Autrecourt notwithstanding). One is reminded of Gerhard Ritter's comments
on the ultimate "philosophical harmlessness of nominalist epistemology," as well as recent defenses of the "Catholic" character of nominalist theology. As Copleston has pointed out, a theological chair of
nominalism was erected even in the University of Salamanca.[2]

---

spiel für die Gedankengänge der spekulativen Mystik" in *Glaube, Geist, Geschichte :
Festschrift für Ernst Benz*, ed. G. Müller and W. Zeller (Leiden, 1967), 266-77.

[1] *Homo Spiritualis*, 13-26, esp. 25f. Cf. also M. Greschat, "Der Bundesgedanke in
der Theologie des späten Mittelalters," *ZKG* I (1970), 44-63.

[2] G. Ritter, "Romantic and Revolutionary Elements in German Theology on the
Eve of the Reformation" in *The Reformation in Medieval Perspective*, 15-49, 22; F.
Copleston, *A History of Philosophy* III/1 (Garden City, N.Y., 1963), 164. See also B.
Hägglund, *Theologie und Philosophie bei Luther und in der Occamistischen Tradition*.
(Lund, 1955), esp. 87ff. The bravado notwithstanding, the nominalists' protest of their
orthodoxy against the edict of Louis XI (1473) bears repeating : "As for that which
is alleged against the nominalists, that their science is perverse and full of heresies,
first it is replied that in those matters which concern nominalism and realism the position
of the nominalists is always more in conformity with the faith and frequently approved
by the church, while the position of the realists is precarious and reproved in many
things by the church ... The nominalists without comparison err less than others, and

It could, in fact, be argued that the socalled "fideism" of nominalism is even more conducive to the conservation of a vibrant ecclesiastical establishment than is a more generous view of the theological reach of reason. If revelation is the absolutely exclusive access to God, then, from a practical point of view, everything hinges on the example and credibility of its custodian. In the contingency of the *potentia ordinata* lies an important mandate to reform, not to oppose and certainly not to seek alternatives to, the established church. The significant qualification, of course, is that, for an Ockhamist, the church now has its unique mediatorial role as the result of a covenant and not because of its position within a supposed metaphysical hierarchy. The church, so to speak, loses its "ontological" claim on men; it must consequently present itself to the world as an object of faith, not as the evident passageway through which all life must inevitably pass.

With mystical writings the story is otherwise. Here the foundations of medieval church and society are not only shaken, but alternative structures are given justification. Herbert Grundmann has pointed up the rootage of key mystical concepts in the idealistic piety of 12th and 13th century religious movements, many of which were censured if not condemned as heretical.[1] Gordon Leff has likewise stressed the way "Neoplatonic mysticism" subserved dissent and heterodoxy in the 14th and 15th centuries.[2] The dissent matrix of such popular late medieval mystical stories and legends as *Schwester Katrei* has also been highlighted.[3] In the 16th century the learned dissenter, who

---

always for one error found in the doctrine of the nominalists, if any are found, four or five are shown in the doctrine of the realists." L. Thorndike, *University Records and Life in the Middle Ages* (New York, 1966), 359.

[1] "Die geschichtlichen Grundlagen der deutschen Mystik," *Altdeutsche und altnieder-ländische Mystik*, 72-99, esp. 90ff; *Religiöse Bewegungen im Mittelalter* (Darmstadt, 1961²), with new material on German mysticism, 524-38. In the latter Grundmann disputes a too strong division between "genuine" and "heretical" mysticism, maintaining the common origins and ambivalent nature of accepted and rejected alike. Cf. Leclercq, et al., *La spiritualité du Moyen Age* (Paris, 1961; English : London, 1968), 243-82, 481-505.

[2] *Heresy in the Later Middle Ages* I, 31f, 307, 356-59, 386.

[3] "The whole point of such stories is that a *simple* woman triumphs over a learned theologian." F. P. Pickering, "A German Mystic Miscellany of the Late 15th Century in the John Rylands Library," *Bulletin of the John Rylands Library* 22 (1938), 455-92, 479. Cf. also G. Constable, "The Popularity of Twelfth-Century Spiritual Writers in the Late Middle Ages," *Renaissance Studies in Honor of Hans Baron*, edited by A. Molho and J. A. Tedeschi (Dekalb, Ill., 1971), 3-28. It is to be noted that even the

could choose his historical weapons, hastened to mystical rather than to nominalist writings. Especially revealing is the widespread adoption of a syncretic mystical treatise, the *Theologia Deutsch*, in the 16th century. Beginning with Luther, who edited and entitled it in 1516 and 1518, this late 14th century work by a still unidentified German author,[1] was only secondarily a guide to contemplation and sanctification.[2] Those who read and praised it were those who parted ways with the ecclesiastical establishment(s) of the 16th century. It was, for example, a widely used document for Anabaptist life and theology.[3] Thomas Müntzer and Andreas Bodenstein von Karlstadt possessed copies.[4] The eclectic radical Louis Haetzer composed an expurgated edition for use in circles adverse to the "German theology" of Luther.[5] Hans Denck wrote a series of theological propositions which were appended to the Haetzer edition as a summary and commentary.[6]

scholastics who were revived in the 15th century were those with a pronounced spirituality. See Gerson's praise of Bonaventure as a "doctor ardens," who "inflammat affectum et erudit intellectum." Letter to a Franciscan (Dec. 7, 1426), *Œuvres complètes*, ed. by P. Glorieux, II (Paris, 1960), 277. Gerson also extols Bernard in this letter.

[1] Cf. G. Baring, "Neues von der 'Theologie Deutsch' und ihrer weltweiten Bedeutung," *ARG* 48 (1957), 1-11, 7; M. Pahncke, "Zur handschriftlichen Überlieferung des 'Frankfurters' ('Theologia Deutsch')," *Zeitschrift für deutsches Altertum und deutsche Literatur* 89 (1958/59), 275-80, 279f.

[2] For conservative piety in the 15th century, best represented by the *Devotiomoderna*, mystical writings were apparently simply this. While appropriating the ascetic and ethical strains of mysticism, piety on the eve of the Reformation found the distinctive mytical speculations on the *Seelengrund* and union with God foreign. G. Gieraths, "Johannes Tauler und die Frömmigkeitshaltung des 15. Jahrhunderts" in *Johannes Tauler : Ein deutscher Mystiker. Gedenkschrift zum 600. Todestag,* ed. by E. M. Filthaut (Essen, 1961), 422-34, esp. 426f; Koch in *La mystique Rhènane*, 137; G. Ritter, *Die Heidelberger Universität* I : *Das Mittelalter (1386-1500)* (Heidelberg, 1936), 411-434 (on Johannes Wenck). R. R. Post, however, found high mytical themes (visions, ecstatic union) in the Devotionalists Henry Mande and Gerlach Peters. *The Modern Devotion : Confrontation with Reformation and Humanism* (Leiden, 1968), 334f, 342. Cf. M. A. Lücker, *Meister Eckhart und die Devotio moderna* (Leiden, 1950).

[3] G. H. Williams, "Popularized German Mysticism as a Factor in the Rise of Anabaptist Communism," *Glaube, Geist, Geschichte : Festschrift für Ernst Benz*, 290-312, esp. 294f.

[4] See Müntzer's book list, *Thomas Müntzer : Schriften und Briefe : Kritische Gesamtausgabe*, ed. G. Franz and P. Kirn (Gütersloh, 1968), 558. On Karlstadt, see H. Barge, *Andreas Bodenstein von Karlstadt* II (Leipzig, 1905), 25f, and G. Rupp, *Patterns of Reformation* (Philadelphia, 1969), 116ff.

[5] Cf. J. E. Gerhard Goeters, *Ludwig Haetzer (ca. 1500-1529) : Spiritualist und Antitrinitarier* (Gütersloh, 1957), 133f.

[6] In *Hans Denck : Schriften* II, ed. W. Fellmann (Gütersloch,1956), 111-13. Cf. Feli-

In the last years of his life, Sebastian Franck authored an extensive Latin paraphrase and, while under siege by the Calvinists, Sebastian Castellio translated it into Latin and French.[1] Together with the sermons of Eckhart and Tauler, the *Theologia Deutsch* was the model for Valentin Weigel's first writings, the foundation for his critique of Lutheran orthodoxy.[2] It has the further distinction of having received the condemnation of established Christendom. John Calvin called it the poison of the Devil[3], and Pope Paul V placed it on the Index of forbidden books, where it still remains today.[4]

In an age when the authority of tradition was crucial to historical survival, nonconformists rejoiced to find in mystical writings a tradition against tradition, a sanction for the irregular. They turned to these writings not only to confirm their high ethical ideals, but also to find an ally against the present order(s). Here they found material for the construction of alternative assessments of human nature and destiny, new "potentiae Dei ordinatae," one might say, which could compete with, even undermine, ruling ideologies and institutions. When Luther, for example, was accused of innovation, he quickly published the full text of the *Theologia Deutsch* as concrete evidence of

---

citas Dobratz, *Der Einfluss der deutschen Mystik auf Thomas Müntzer und Hans Denck* (Münster/Westf., 1960).

[1] Franck's paraphrase is reproduced in A. Hegler, *Sebastian Francks lateinische Paraphrase der Deutschen Theologie und seine holländisch erhaltenen Traktate* (Tübingen, 1901), 20-29. The Basel 1557 Latin and the 1558 Antwerp French translations of Castellio were based on the 1546 Frankfurt a.M. edition, which in turn goes back to the 1528 Worms edition.

[2] *Von der Bekehrung des Menschen, Von waarer Armut des Geistes oder gelassener Gelassenheit* and *Kurtzer Bericht und Anleitung zur Teutschen Theologey*—all in *Valentin Weigel : Sämtliche Schriften* 3, ed. W.-E. Peuckert and W. Zeller (Stuttgart-Bad Cannstatt, 1966). Cf. H. Maier, *Die mystische Spiritualismus Valentin Weigels* (Gütersloh, 1926), and W. Zeller, "Meister Eckhart bei Valentin Weigel : Eine Untersuchung zur Frage der Bedeutung Meister Eckharts für die mystische Renaissance des sechzehnten Jahrhunderts," *ZKG* 62 (1938), 309-55.

[3] H. Oncken, "Aus den letzten Jahren Sebastian Francks," *Monatshefte der Comenius Gesellschaft* 11 (1902), 86-101, 88. According to L. Keller, Luther too began to turn against the *Theologia Deutsch* in 1521-25, viewing it as a source of "Schwärmerei." *Monatshefte der Comenius Gesellschaft* 11 (1902), 145-57, 146f. Noteworthy in this connection is Schwenckfeld's complaint of Luther's turn about on Tauler : "Luther hat am ersten Taulerum commendiert, jetzt veracht er ihn." Cited by G. Maron, *Individualismus und Gemeinschaft bei Caspar von Schwenckfeld* (Stuttgart, 1961), 102.

[4] See G. Baring, *Bibliographie der Ausgaben der 'Theologia Deutsch' (1516-1961) : Ein Beitrag zur Luther Bibliographie* (Baden-Baden, 1963), 6f.

the good stock of "Wittenberg theology." Luther's most articulate
and bitter opponent, Thomas Müntzer, found in German mysticism
a Spirit = heart correlation of religious authority which could be set
against Luther's Word = ear arrangement *(sola fides ex auditu verbi)*.[1]
And when Sebastian Castellio climaxed his logical and ethical critiques
of Calvinist teaching in the *De arte dubitandi* (1563), he found an
authoritative "prophet" in a mystically influenced concept of *ratio*
(interpreted along the lines of the *synteresis rationis)* and an ideal
of human "omnipotence" in the mystical teaching of real union with
God (the central message he had discovered in the *Theologia Deutsch)*.[2]
Throughout the 16th century a safe refuge from and effective weaponry
against a repressive Christendom were found in the "supra" dimension
of mysticism.

A most revealing example of mysticism in the service of dissent,
of the transformation of the mystical "supra" into a "contra potentiam
ordinatam," is Sebastian Franck's difficulties with the Lutherans in
Ulm. Thanks to a conspiracy running from his old schoolmates at
Heidelberg, Martin Frecht and Martin Bucer, through Philip Melanchthon to Landgrave Philipp of Hesse, Franck was brought to trial in
1535 on charges of being an "obvious revolutionary and Anabaptist."
The authorities in Ulm saw in his mystical teaching an effort to create
a new church. "We are told there is now no true calling, service,
pulpit, administration, or reception of the sacraments in the Lutheran
and Zwinglian churches. Rather one awaits the appearance of the
ministerium spiritus, the true office of the Holy Spirit, which will
perhaps come from the Silesian [i.e. Schwenckfeldian] and Franckian
churches."[3] Visions of Münster come to Ulm were foreseen. The
matter was brought to a head as Franck's judges undertook to instruct
him in the distinction between the two *potentiae* of God, a distinction

---

[1] Müntzer's views are best set forth in the *Ausgetruckte Entblössung* (1524). Treatments of mysticism in Müntzer's thought are H.-J. Goertz, *Innere und äussere Ordnung
in der Theologie Thomas Müntzers* (Leiden, 1967), and M. M. Smirin, "Die Mystik Taulers
und die verschiedenen Richtungen der deutschen Reformation," ch. 3 of *Die Volks-
reformation des Thomas Müntzer und der grosse Bauernkrieg* (Berlin, 1956²), 207-71.

[2] See *De arte dubitandi*, ed. E. Feist, in *Per la Storia degli Eretici Italiani del Secolo
XVI in Europa*, ed. D. Cantimori and E. Feist (Rome, 1938), 260-64, and the *Tractatus
de justificatione* in *Dialogi IV* (Gouda, 1613). The latter treatise composes chapters
7-29 of Book II of the *De arte dubitandi* but was not included in the Feist edition.

[3] Text in A. Hegler, *Beiträge zur Geschichte des Mystik in der Reformationszeit*, ed.
W. Köhler, *ARG : Texte und Untersuchungen* I (Berlin, 1906), 136.

his mystical teaching, in their view, had erased. The following reprimand is exemplary in the extreme not only of the dissenter's tactical deployment of mystical motifs, but also of the predictable "establishment" reaction to it. The transcript reads as follows :

> Franck should not have written what he says in the 44th paradox : "The Master (God) teaches us more in one flashing moment than all external words, sermons, and Scripture until the end of time." Now it is true that, *potentia absoluta*, by his completely perfect omnipotence, God can do absolutely anything he pleases. He can, as they say, make an axe under a bench crow. But one should rather speak *de potentia Dei ordinata*, of God's orderly power, as he has employed it in his word and works. Then one sees that God gives his grace through the means of his word and sacraments placed in the hands of servants he has chosen. He also dealt with the [Old Testament] fathers by word of mouth before the Law was given. And Christ converted Paul from heaven by word of mouth.[1]

Franck learned his lessons from the sermons of Eckhart and Tauler, to whom he repeatedly appealed during the course of his trial. It was in this mystical tradition that he found resources to maximize the contingency of the *potentia ordinata*, to collapse, as it were, the *potentia Dei ordinata* into the *potentia Dei absoluta*. As his judges perceived the situation, this could only remove the mandate from vested authority, a prelude to anarchy. Their reply was no less extreme, as they moved to constrict to the barest minimum the *potentia Dei absoluta*. For Franck, historical forms are not only momentary and accidental, but finally insignificant. For his judges, the given historical forms of power and authority have final divine sanction. Even the classical instance of God's sovereign *potentia absoluta*, the direct conversion of Paul on the road to Damascus, becomes a mirror of the "ordained" Lutheran word.

Te be sure, mystical theology has also been a bulwark of the "establishment." When one looks to the Eastern church and the Catholic "Counter"-Reformation, mystical theology appears to be but the outermost boundary of the ordained *via salutis*, hardly a "revolutionary" appeal beyond it. In practice, if not in theory. the "supra" dimension of mysticism can certainly remain "intra potentiam ordinatam," either by coexisting benignly beside it or by confining itself to the task of conservative censure and reform. This does not minimize the revolutionary possibilities of mystical theology, but simply makes it clear that their exploitation is a decision extrinsic to mystical theology

---

[1] *Ibid.*, 117.

itself. Also, it must be borne in mind that, within the mystical tradition, quietistic acceptance of the *status quo* can be no less negative a judgment on the established order than militant dissent. Eastern mystics accepted the established order because they deemed it unworthy of their involvement, and Teresa of Avila and John of the Cross were suspected of being *Alumbrados*.

CONCLUSION

The elasticity of the late medieval mind is to be respected. Harvest-minded 15th century thinkers especially reveal strong syncretistic impulses. Still, we must not lose the forest among the trees. On a practical level it is understandable that certain Ockhamists enlisted mystical writings for the purposes of reform.[1] On a philosophical level, however, mysticism and nominalism appear to be diametrically opposed in their basic ideological bents. Nominalists are finally confined to the penultimate, connoisseurs of time and history. Mystics, by contrast, look to an eternal covenant behind historical covenants, to the generation before creation in time. Nominalism scrutinizes the *status quo*, knowing it to be as fully inescapable as it is contingent. Mysticism, by contrast, cultivates the possibility of flight beyond the given structures of historical reality. Nominalists elaborate the accidental nature of the *potentia ordinata;* mystics, in the final analysis, work out alternatives to it.

It is an intriguing speculation whether, beyond Gerson, Wessel Gansfort, and Biel, the young Luther might be said to represent a genuine synthesis of these diverse traditions. A devotee of medieval spirituality, he was trained in the Ockhamist tradition. Before he posted his 95 theses against indulgences, he critically annotated Tauler and Biel, edited the *Theologia Deutsch,* and fathered a disputation against scholastic theologians (Scotus, Ockham, d'Ailly, and Biel). Anarchist to Rome, he became a new pope to Orlamünde and Allstedt. Rejecting the basic axioms of both mysticism and nominalism, he still maintained parallel conclusions. His theological concepts of "sola fides" and "simul iustus et peccator" suspended the anthro-

---

[1] This seems, in the end, to be as far as Oberman wants to go. 'At the end of our investigation we may conclude that there is reason to prefer the title "mystical elements in Biel's theology" to "Biel's mystical theology." ' *Harvest of Medieval Theology,* 359.

pological *synteresis* and the unitive principle of *similitudo*, yet still supported a "copulatio animae cum Christo, sicut sponsam cum sponso."[1] His theology likewise set aside speculation on the conditions of revelation (the so-called *logica fidei* of d'Ailly and Holcot) and the Pelagian tendencies of nominalist covenant theology, yet maintained that "omnia nostra bona sunt tantum in verbis et promissis."[2] Indeed, for Luther, these two statements were interchangeable. "Real" contact with God was established through a "verbal" relation; final certitude of salvation was maintained at a distance.

As his praise of Gregory of Rimini and John Staupitz reminds us, Luther was steeped in and greatly profited from the "purer" Augustinianism of his own Order.[3] Scholars have rightly made much of this important matrix of Reformation theology. Still, it may be asked in conclusion whether the uniqueness of the latter, which finally sets Luther as far apart from the basic axioms of Augustine as from those of late medieval nominalism and mysticism, could ever have emerged here. The novelty of Luther's theology may rather lie in an unprecedented, unAugustinian merger of nominalism and mysticism. Perhaps this is the larger sense in which Luther was of Ockham's faction and the *Theologia Deutsch* taught him more about God, Christ, man, and all things than any book save the Bible and St. Augustine.[4]

---

[1] See *Homo Spiritualis*, 186, and my article, "Homo viator : Luther and Late Medieval Theology" in *The Reformation in Medieval Perspective*, 148ff. See also E. Vogelsang, "Die Unio mystica bei Luther," *ARG* 35 (1939), 63ff.

[2] *WA* 4, 272.16f (Sch. to Ps. 115:10). See theses 45-50 of the *Disputatio contra scholasticam theologiam*, *WA* I, 226. On the *promissio* motif in the theology of the young Luther, see J. S. Preus, *From Shadow to Promise : Old Testament Interpretation From Augustine to the Young Luther* (Cambridge, Mass., 1969), 245-271. In the long run Preus errs, I think, when he insists that this motif is incompatible with the *conformitas Christi* theme. They are finally two sides of the same coin, two expressions of the same new concept of faith.

[3] *WA* 2, 394f; *WA Tr* I, Nr. 173. Cf. A. Zumkeller, "Die Augustinertheologen Simon Fidati von Cascia und Hugolin von Orvieto und Martin Luthers Kritik an Aristoteles." *ARG* 54 (1963), 15-37) On nominalism and mysticism in Staupitz, see David C. Steinmetz, *Misericordia Dei : The Theology of Johannex von Staupitz* (Leiden), 1968), 152ff.

[4] Cf. *WA* 6, 195.4; 600.11; *WA* 1, 378ff.

CUSANUS, LUTHER, AND THE MYSTICAL TRADITION

F. EDWARD CRANZ

Connecticut College

Since I am an expert neither in the nominalism nor the mysticism of the later Middle Ages, it may be most useful as a stimulus to discussion of Professor Ozment's excellent paper if I engage in speculation from a larger context and thus perhaps encourage those who *are* experts to tell us more.

My starting point will be Professor Ozment's exciting suggestion, with which I find myself in fundamental agreement : 'The novelty of Luther's theology may rather lie in an unprecedented unAugustinian merger of nominalism and mysticism.

It seems to me that we are here dealing with a special case of the dominant process of medieval and Renaissance-Reformation intellectual history, the use and transformation of an ancient inheritance. We must try to understand the use in such a way as not to deny the transformation, and *vice versa;* we must also be prepared to find odd combinations of use *and* transformation.

The particular development from late medieval nominalism and mysticism to Luther represents a late stage in a long series of Christian attempts to come to terms with an ancient inheritance, mainly Platonist or Neoplatonist, on union and knowledge and symbolism. In rough fashion, we may distinguish three stages : 1. the ancient patristic synthesis in its two forms, Pseudo-Dionysius and Augustine. 2. the medieval newness, beginning in the late eleventh and early twelfth centuries. 3. the climactic final stage, with which we are here mainly concerned, which began in the late thirteenth and early fourteenth centuries and which was sparked in part by new Latin translations of crucial works of Proclus.

I shall try to trace the broadest outlines of the story under three main topics : 1. the notion of the self, or what is meant by the 'I' or the 'we'. 2. the relation of the knower to what is known. 3. the theory of allegory and of biblical interpretation. In all three cases, I think we shall find a movement away from an original substantive, impersonal solution toward one which may be called personal or historical.

On the first point, the ancients regularly gave a substantial and universal answer to the question about the self or the 'I'. In the Greek commentators on Aristotle, a man is identified with the eternal *nous* within him as this is united with the eternal intelligibles which it thinks. Themistius can even equate 'my essence' or 'my form' (τὸ ἐμοὶ εἶναι, ἡμεῖ) with the eternal and impassive active intellect.[1] In Proclus, the center of the 'I' is the 'one in us', and the goal of life is the fusion of this with the One itself.[2] Augustine in the *De vera religione* in his discussion of the love of neighbor says that each is to love what he is to himself (quod sibi ipse est, 46, 89). We are to love human nature without carnal qualification; no one can lose this, for what he loves he has in himself whole and perfect (nam quod in illis diligit, in seipso habet totum atque perfectum, 47, 90).

On the second point, the ancient tradition maintains that knowledge is a substantial relationship resulting in the union or conjunction of the knower with the known. There is the familiar text from Aristotle, 'In things without matter, what knows is the same as what is known, since theoretical knowledge and what is known theoretically are one and the same.[3] Or in John the Scot, perhaps the last great representative of this tradition, 'The knowledge of what is, is what is.'[4]

Finally, on the question of allegory, one may speak of a substantive allegory in a universe of stages. For the Greeks, the paradigm of all myth and allegory is the cosmos. In the words of the Neoplatonist Sallust, 'We call the cosmos a myth, for bodies and things appear in it, while minds and souls are hidden,[5] For the Christians, there developed a comparable substantive hierarchical structure with three levels : Israel is the image of the *ecclesia* on earth; and the ecclesia here is an image of the heavenly Jerusalem.

Such in roughest outline is the pagan inheritance and its first Christian appropriation, and I have spoken of it in such a way as to bring out the points which are common to pagan and Christian. One should, however, note that there were two main ways in which the Greek inheritance was synthesized with Christianity, the one illustrated

---

[1] Paraphrase on the *De anima* ed. R. Heinze, CIAG V, 3 (1909) 100, 16-101, 4.

[2] See W. Beierwaltes, *Proklus* (Frankfurt, 1965), 367-82, and his article 'Der Begriff des 'unum in nobis' bei Proklos' *Miscellanea Mediaevalia* II (Berlin, 1963), 255-66.

[3] *De anima* III, 4 430a2-5.

[4] *De divisione naturae* II, 8 (*P.L.* 122, 535), Cognitio eorum quae sunt, ea quae sunt, est.

[5] *De diis* III, 3.

by Pseudo-Dionysius and the other by Augustine. Pseudo-Dionysius borrows the Platonist distinction between the sensible and the intelligible, but he goes on to place God, like the One of Neoplatonism, as 'beyond' both thought and being. Augustine, by contrast follows Exodus III, 14 Ego sum qui sum; and he identifies God with being.

This ancient tradition provided for full mystic 'union' in the pseudo-Dionysiac form, and in Augustine it at least provided for immediacy in knowledge as the mind was conjoined in knowledge with the 'invisible things of God' of Romans I, 20. Why was it necessary to abandon it and set the West on a course which might lead to Ockham and Luther?

I believe that the changed context which necessitated a rethinking of mysticism and immediacy came with the 'first nominalism', or whatever one chooses to call it, of Abelard. Here the ancient unity or conjunction of knower and known was broken, and as a result the ascent to any higher stages of union was cut off. Thus Abelard, in one of his extraordinary dismissals of the whole ancient tradition of knowledge, exclaims : 'Intellection (intellectus) is an action of the soul, by which it is said to be intelligent (intelligens). The form toward which intellection is directed is some imaginary and made-up (ficta) thing which the soul manufactures for itself as it wishes and of what sort it wishes, such as are those imaginary cities which we see in sleep.[1] Abelard explains that these figments are made up, so that through them we may think about things. 'Thus words were invented so that men might have a doctrine of things, not a doctrine *of* these figments (de figmentis) but only through these figments. It was done that men might establish intellections *about things*, not about figments, but only through figments.[2]

In Professor Ozment's term, the mind 'legislates' concepts through which it can think *about* things which are absent from it. Even in Anselm, we see the loss of the immediacy which had been provided by pseudo-Dionysius and Augustine, in the lamentation which follows his great triumph in the proof of the *Proslogion*. 'But if indeed, O my soul, you have found God, why is it that you do not feel (sentis) what you have found? Why, O Lord God, has my soul no feeling of Thee, if it has found Thee?'[3]

---

[1] *Logica, Ingredientibus*, ed. B. Geyer, *Peter Aebelards Philosophische Schriften* (B.G.P.M. XX) (Münster, 1919-27), 20, 25f.

[2] *Ibid.*, 315 my italics.

[3] *Proslogion* XIV.

It is in this context that in the twelfth century we find the remarkable new developments of Christian and Victorine spirituality. In simplest terms, these developments may be said to start from an Augustinian position where the mind rises from sense to the realm of reason, intellect, and intelligence. But they accept the Abelardian conclusion that within the realm of 'reason' the mind is always thinking *about* things and never achieves immediacy or union. Hence we find the introduction of a third stage where immediacy and union can be restored. Sometimes one uses the old Augustinian terms, but beyond the first stages of sense and reason, there is now a higher third stage such as intellect or intelligence; sometimes one adopts the terminology of the affections and of will for the third and highest stage. Finally, in a very interesting, somewhat later, development, we find the introduction of a whole new set of terms such as *apex mentis, scintilla mentis*, and *synteresis*. These are 'new' in the sense that they were not to be found in the earlier Augustinian or pseudo-Dionyiac traditions. Endres von Ivánka has shown that, surprisingly enough, they derive from Stoicism, probably through Origen.[1] In their Stoic context, they referred to the *hegemonikon*, which as the 'leading part' may be taken as the Stoic answer to the question about the 'I' or the self. But the *hegemonikon*, as a portion of the *pur technikon* which penetrates the universe, was as substantive and thing-like as the other ancient answers.

In the twelfth century, however, not only these Stoic terms but also the modified Augustinian terms acquire a new resonance as they illustrate what might be called a first attempt at an account of a new Western 'I' or self. Such a self is somehow above the new realm of a reason which can only think *about* things; it is distinct from the universal human nature of Augustine as well as from the impersonal otherness of Proclus' One in us. And the new ideas provide not only for immediacy but even for a quasi-union with God, as in Bernard's well-known metaphors of the water in the wine and of the iron in the fire.[2]

The new spirituality of the twelfth century thus successfully used and transformed various ancient inheritances in order to say some-

---

[1] For this whole story, see Endre von Ivanka, *Plato Christianus* (Einsiedeln, 1964), 309-85. Part of this is found more fully in his article, 'Apex mentis, Wanderung und Wandlung eines stoischen Terminus' *Zeitschrift für katholische Theologie* 72 (1950), 129-76.

[2] *De diligendo Deo*, X, 28 (*P.L.*, 182, 991).

thing new about immediacy and union in the context of the 'first nominalism' of Abelard. But I believe that new challenges to both immediacy and union arose in fourteenth-century humanism with its suggestion of a new definition of the 'I' and in fourteenth-century nominalism with its suggestion of a new definition of God.

To take Petrarch as illustrative of the humanism, I think we find in him the position that a man is, in effect, the whole universe of his thought. Thus in the *De vita solitaria* Petrarch offers a daring revision, almost a parody, of the famous sentence from Augustine's *Confessiones* : 'Thou has made us for Thee, and our heart is unquiet until it rests in Thee'.[1] Petrarch substitutes *acquiescere* for *requiescere* and writes : A noble mind cannot rest (acquiescere) anywhere except in God, where our end lies, or in itself (praeter seipsum) and its secret concerns, or in some soul conjoined to it by great likeness'.[2] Petrarch makes this even more explicitly a 'humanist' definition where he rephrases his point ; we now find, in addition to God and the like-souled friend 'ourselves and our *honesta studia*'.[3] Petrarch insists again and again that his answer is an individual and personal one. But in any case, he has chosen his own self as a universe of the mind, and he will 'rest' in it.

I think it might be suggested that the 'new' God of nominalism has certain similarities with this new self of Petrarch. The doctrine of the *potentia absoluta* as against the *potentia ordinata* guarantees that just as Petrarch had chosen one of a number of possible answers as his 'self', so the particular order by which God is related to man is chosen or legislated and in no sense necessitated.

And along with this legislation of knowledge and of the self, I believe that in both humanism and in nominalism. we may speak of a legislated allegory, as the old substantive structure of imagery breaks down, and as we find what might be called an allegory of meaning. Thus Salutati, for example, asserts that in the sacred poetry of the Bible both the letter and the hidden senses or meanings are true. However, since it has the Holy Spirit as author, 'it is ordered to an infinite (number of) senses. One cannot think of any truth, appropriate to the letter, which that infinite wisdom did not intend from the beginning'[4]. Even for human poetry, since the resemblances oĵ

---

[1] I, 1, #1.

[2] In *Prose*, ed. Mantellotti et al. (Milan, 1955), I, 1, 296.

[3] *Ibid.*

[4] *De laboribus Herculis*, ed. B. L. Ullman (Zurich, 1951), II, 2, 17.

things (rerum similitudines) are infinite, many expositions are possible.[1] And Ockham in his *Dialogus* develops at some length the argument that in biblical passages with more than one possible sense, only through revelation could anyone know the 'first, true meaning' (intellectus).[2]

But if Abelard's reduction of intellection to 'thinking about' has created obstacles to Dionysiac or Augustinian immediacy or union, it is clear that the developments of fourteenth-century nominalism and humanism make such immediacy or union even more difficult. Nor was there any refuge in Aristotelian scholasticism. As is well known, St. Thomas cites pseudo-Dionysius constantly, but he makes little significant use of the *De mystica theologia*. Thus, he describes it in the Preface to his commentary on the *De divinis nominibus*. 'Dionysius wrote another book on this sort of removal or negation (de huiusmodi remotionibus) in which God remains unknown and hidden to us; he called it *On mystic*, that is, hidden *Theology*' (Prooemium I). And Thomas elsewhere remarks that the vision of the blessed is related to the vision of the *viator* not as seeing more perfectly is related to seeing less perfectly but rather as seeing is related to not seeing.[3] And the Stoic terms such as *apex mentis* are either ignored or reinterpreted so as to lose their old function. Thomas defines *synteresis*, for example, simply as a 'habit containing the precepts of the natural law'.[4]

Perhaps this blocking of the road to immediacy and union, whether in humanism, nominalism, or scholasticism, partly explains the great attention devoted to the late thirteenth-century translations of Proclus and also the renewed interest in pseudo-Donysius. But as the *apex mentis* theology did not result in any return to the Stoic impersonal and substantial *hegemonikon*, so the late-medieval use of Proclus and of pseudo-Dionysius did not lead finally to a revival of the union of the impersonal 'One in us' with the impersonal One in itself. Rather, it led to immediacy between the 'persons' of God and of man as outlined by nominalism and humanism. Nevertheless Proclus and pseudo-Dionysius contributed in two ways to the working out of solutions very different from their own. In the first place, they gave strong expression to the goals of immediacy and union at a time when the

---

[1] *Ibid.*

[2] *Dialogus* Pars III, Tractatus I, Liber III, Cap. XIV-XXXVI.

[3] *Quaestiones disputatae*, De veritate, XVIII, art. 1, corpus.

[4] S.T., I, II, 94, art. 1, ad 2.

West seemed unable to reach these goals; in the second place, the notion of the One as beyond being and substance helped to clear out the last Augustinian relics of a 'substantial' definition of God and of man and thus left the way open for a new 'personal' definition.

Let me try to illustrate this first in Nicholas of Cusa, a thinker in constant and close contact with both pseudo-Dionysius and Proclus.[1] He is not commonly reckoned with the 'nominalists' but he surely believed that our universals existed only in the mind[2] and more generally that man 'legislates' the whole universe of his mind; God creates a real universe, and man in his image creates a notional universe.[3]

In his notion of the 'self' Cusanus may be said to bring to philosophic clarity what had been adumbrated by Petrarch. Thus in the *De visione Dei*, we find an interesting account of 'Socratic being'. 'The being of Socrates (esse Socratis) encompasses all Socratic being (esse Socraticum), and in this simple Socratic being, there is no otherness or diversity, for the being of Socrates is the individual unity (unitas individualis) of all (the things) which are in Socrates, so that in that unique being is complicated the being of all (the things) which are in Socrates, that is, in that individual simplicity, where nothing is found to be other or diverse.'[4]

The center of the self is no longer reached, as in the ancient inheritance, by moving away from that which is temporal and particular to that which is universally intelligible or 'other'; the center now somehow embraces all these temporal particulars and complicates them within itself.

To explain the mystic vision connected with such a self, Cusanus uses the metaphor of an omnivoyant picture. The picture looks at every individual as if it looked at that individual alone. As the metaphor is generalized, Cusanus argues that each individual as he sees God actually sees the full reality of himself. God is the face of faces; each individual sees only itself in that infinite face.[5]

Cusanus' doctrine of knowledge is that of 'knowing ignorance'. Here the mind's comparing and measuring of the particulars coincides with an immediate awareness of God who as infinite and unknowable ex-

---

[1] See, for example, the opening sections of the *De non Aliud* Heidelberg edition, Vol. XIII (1944), 1, lines 1-6).

[2] See *De mente* XI, Heidelberg edition Vol. V (1937) 97f.

[3] See *De beryllo* VI, Heidelberg XI, 1, 7.

[4] Chapter XIV, ed. Paris, 1514, Vol. I, f. 106.

[5] *De visione Dei*, Chapter VI, ed. Paris, Vol. I, fol. 101; see also Chap. XV, fol. 107.

ceeds all comparison. And in his last work, Cusanus moved on to a doctrine of 'simple vision' where the mind sees simultaneously both the hidden eternal Infinite and its particular appearances.[1]

Finally, Cusanus completely abandons the old allegory of substantial, hierarchic stages. All images, says Cusanus, are disproportionate, even those of pseudo-Dionysius; they can be apprehended only through knowing ignorance where the particular and the infinite coincide.[2] And in the mystic insights of the *De visione Dei*, the image is experienced as one with the exemplar. 'Thou art therefore, O my God, shadow in such a way as to be truth; Thou art my image and the image of everyone, in such a way that Thou art our truth'.[3]

I would suggest therefore that we may regard Cusanus as a first paradoxical solution coming out of the interaction between nominalism and humanism, on the one hand, and the ancient tradition of mysticism, notably as seen in pseudo-Dionysius and Proclus, on the other. He accepts to the full the 'legislations' of the humanists and of the nominalists. He uses the Neoplatonist notions of the One in itself (and of the one in us) as beyond being and form in order to eliminate substantial definitions both of God and of man. And at the end, he is able to achieve the Neoplatonist goals of immediacy and union in very different 'personal' coincidences of the finite and the infinite. The substantial allegorical stages are gone; the union or conjunction of the mind in knowing with the intelligibles is gone; and the union of what is impersonal in us with what is impersonal in God is gone. In all three questions of self, knowledge, and of allegory immediacy and union result from a coincidence of what is most personal, particular, and historical with what is absolute.

Mutatis mutandis, I think we see a parallel development in Luther, even though the specific theologies; of Cusanus and Luther are often diametrically opposed. As is well known, Luther is familiar with and deeply moved by the whole 'mystic' tradition, from Augustine and Pseudo-Dionysius through Bernard and Tauler and the *Theologia Deutsch;* in one of his Table-talks he even discusses the Parmenides tradition and may be drawing on Proclus.[4] When he later condemns Pseudo-Dionysius, it is with the addition 'Expertus loquor'.[5] And it

---

[1] See *De apice theoriae*, ed. Paris. Vol. I, fol. 220.

[2] *Apologia doctae ignorantiae*, Heidelberg ed. II (1932), 24.

[3] Chapter XV, ed. Paris, II, fol. 107.

[4] *WA Tr* I, 108, #257; see also I, 303-3, #644.

[5] *De captivitate Babylonica, WA* V, 561.

is interesting to note that his early theological hopes even embraced the ancient identification of the knower with the known. In a Sermon of 1514, he quotes the familiar text from the *De anima* : 'The possible intellect is nothing in act of all the things which it understands; in potentiality it is all of them, and thus it is in some sense all things'.[1] And in this general context, Luther observes 'This fair philosophy, though understood by few, is useful for the highest theology'.[2] But whatever Luther's hopes, he was also a member of the 'Ockhamite faction' and therefore he must also say of the Aristotelian sentence just cited : 'but all these things if understood substantially are most false'.[3]

But as Cusanus broke with both Proclus and pseudo-Dionysius as he achieved their goals in 'simple vision', so Luther breaks with the formulae of the mystic tradition, as he achieved its goals in the personal union of faith. There is no need to cite many examples to end the story.[4]

Luther will go beyond the conformity of the will and the mind which could be found in nominalism, but he will not go back to the universality of Augustine or to the impersonality of Proclus and of pseudo-Dionysius. Thus he explains in a Sermon : 'The Lord does not say that your thoughts will be in me or that my thoughts will be in you but rather that you, you are in me, and I, I am in you (du, du bist in mir, und ich, ich bin in dir). The Lord does not speak of a mere thought (einen schlechten Gedanken) but rather that I am in him with body, life, soul, piety, and justice, with sins, foolishness, and wisdom, and that he, Christ, is in me with his holiness, justice, wisdom, and blessedness.'[5] In this coincidence of opposites, faith makes of the believer and Christ as it were one person : 'But faith makes of you and Christ as it were one person (quasi unam personam) so that you are not separated from Christ, but cleave to him, as if you were to say : 'I am Christ' and as if he in turn were to say 'I am that sinner'.'[6] And if faith is now what defines the true self or the 'I' of the saved Christian, Luther is explicit that there is nothing substantial or thing-

---

[1] III, 4 429a22 cited by Luther in a Sermon of 1515 *WA* I, 29, Clemen V, 417, 11-13.

[2] *Ibid.*, Clemen V, 417, 22-23.

[3] *Ibid.*, lines 14-15.

[4] For a good collection of passages, see Erich Vogelsang, 'Die Unio mystica bei Luther' *Archiv für Reformationsgeschichte* 35 (1938), 63-78.

[5] Sermons on John VI-VIII, *WA* 33, 225.

[6] *Commentary on Galatians*, *WA* 40, I, 285, 5-7.

like about it : 'I am accustomed to speculate in this way (sic imaginari), as if there were no *quality* in my heart which is called faith or righteousness, but in their place I put Jesus Christ'.[1]

Luther's attitude toward allegory develops in comparable fashion. He began with high devotion to the older allegorical tradition. As he tells us in his usual vigorous style. 'When I was a monk, I was an artist at allegory ... I used to allegorize sewers and everything else'.[2] But eventually Luther abandons all this, and even that paradigm of all allegory, the crossing of the Red Sea, is 'no longer allegory but simple history ... not a figure but great seriousness.'[3]

Perhaps even more important, in his later consideration of the all-important story of Sara and Agar, as allegorized by S. Paul in *Galatians* IV, 22-26, Luther affirms the same coincidence of the presently human and the divine, which we have already seen so often in Cusanus and in Luther. Luther rejects the allegorical stages which separate the present church from the anagogic Jersusalem. The heavenly Jerusalem, according to Luther is the church which is now in the world : 'It can be in Babylon, in Rome, on the sea, in a valley, or on the mountains, indeed wherever is the soul which believes and learns Christ, there is the spiritual *ecclesia*'.[4] The firm tie between the literal sense of the Bible and its spiritual reality, threatened by humanism and nominalism, is reestablished by Luther as the literal and the anagogic senses coincide in faith.

Thus at the end, I think we must agree with Professor Ozment that 'the novelty of Luther's theology may lie in an unprecedented unAugustinian merger of nominalism and mysticism'. I would suggest that for a full understanding of this merger we must learn to place it against the background of a long development in which men of the Middle Ages rethought an ancient 'mystic' inheritance in the light of new concepts of meaning and of the self. Finally, I would like at least to raise the question whether Luther's merger does not have an instructive antecedent in a previous merger affected by Nicholas of Cusa.

---

[1] Luther's addendum to a letter of Melanchthon to Brenz, May, 1531. *WA Briefe* VI, 100-101.

[2] TR, #335, Clemen 8, 44, 7f.

[3] *WA* 16, 275-6.

[4] *Commentary on Galatians* 40, I, 663, 9-664, 2.

4. THE SUMMA FOR CONFESSORS
AS AN INSTRUMENT OF SOCIAL CONTROL

THOMAS N. TENTLER

The University of Michigan

1. THE ERA OF THE SUMMA FOR CONFESSORS

Two well known events define symbolically the period of the summas for confessors. The first is the publication in 1215 of the bull *Omnis utriusque sexus*, by which Innocent III and the Fourth Lateran Council commanded all Christians who had achieved the age of discretion to confess their sins yearly to their own priests. The second is the drama enacted by Martin Luther at the gates of Wittenberg, where, on December 10, 1520, he publicly burned *Esurge Domine*, several collections of canon law decrees, John Eck's *Chrysopassus*, some unnamed works, and the *Summa Angelica*. In 1215 no summa for confessors had been written. By 1520 the last true representative of the genre had recently been completed. Between those dates there had appeared—depending on how you define them—from twelve to twenty-five summas of casuistry for confessors.[1]

---

[1] Johannes Dietterle, "Die Summae confessorum (sive de casibus conscientiae)—von ihren Anfängen an bis zu Silvester Prierias—(Unter besonderer Berucksichtigung ihrer Bestimmungen über den Ablass)," *Zeitschrift für Kirchengeschichte*, 24 (1903), 353-363; Pierre Michaud-Quantin, *Sommes de casuistique et manuels de confession au moyen âge (XII-XVI siècles)*, in *Analecta Mediaevalia Namurcensia*, 13 (Louvain, Lille, and Montreal, 1962), 34-42, 103-106. Their lists of twenty-four and twenty-five summas agree on twelve names. The authors most often entitled their works *Summa de casibus conscientiae*, but they are generally known by nicknames; those used here are in chronological order :

Raymundina (1220, 1234); (Gloss, 1240-45). Raymond of Peñafort, *Summa de poenitentia et matrimonio cum glossis Ioannis de Friburgo* [i.e., William of Rennes] (Rome, 1603).

Monaldina (before 1274). Joannes Monaldus di Capo d'Istria, *Summa in utroque iure*.

Joannina (c. 1290). Johannes von Freiburg, *Summa confessorum*.

Summa Johannis, deutsch (c. 1300). Berthold von Freiburg, *Summa Johannis*.

Astesana (c. 1317). Astesanus de Asti, *Summa de casibus conscientiae*.

Pisanella (c. 1338). Bartholomaeus de Sancto Concordio, *Summa casuum*.

Supplementum (c. 1444). Nicolaus de Ausimo, *Supplementum summae pisanellae*.

The decree of 1215 is fitting, both in tone and intention, as a prelude to the summas. Its language stresses discipline throughout. It is a papal law, universally binding. The clergy are ordered to publish it in every church so that no one can escape the obligation by pleading ignorance. It endorses the jurisdiction of the parish clergy by stipulating that everyone confess to "his own priest." It prescribes harsh penalties for those who fail in their Easter duty—they are barred from the church and denied Christian burial—and thus it gives added urgency to the requirement of confession, which would normally have preceded reception of the Eucharist (especially if communion was only once a year). The most severe sanctions are directed against priests who break the seal of confession, a salutary reminder that the discipline of the decree and of the church is applicable to all of society, which most assuredly includes the clergy. At the same time, however, it grants a pastoral office to confessors that unequivocally establishes their spiritual authority; they impose penances, which penitents must try to complete as best they can, and they act as healing experts :

> Let the priest be cautions and discreet, so that, like a skilled physician, he may pour wine and oil on the wounds of the injured man, diligently examining the circumstances of both sin and sinner, through which he may prudently learn what kind of advice he should offer, and what kind of remedy he should apply—trying various methods—to heal the sick man.[1]

For the time being we shall ignore the assumption, absolutely clear, that the penitent will be offered an effective cure, and that he should derive psychological benefits from the ministrations of his confessor. Rather we shall concentrate exclusively on the assertion of the priest's power to examine penitents and try to change their behavior.

Within five years of promulgation of *Omnis utriusque sexus*, Raymond of Peñaforte had begun the first version of his *Summa de casibus poenitentiae*. Sometime after 1234 he added a section on matrimony, to the original three. And by 1245 the *Raymundina*, as it would be called in the tradition of the summists, had a thorough gloss added

---

Rosella (and *Baptistina*) (1480-90). Baptista Trovamala de Salis, *Rosella casuum* (and *Summa Baptistina*).

Angelica (1480-90). Angelus Carletus de Clavasio, *Summa Angelica de casibus conscientiae*.

Sylvestrina (1516). Sylvester Prierias Mazzolini, *Summa summarum* or *Summa Siluestrina*.

Citations to the *Supplementum* also refer to the *Pisanella*, which is included in Nicolaus de Ausimo's summa.

[1] Oscar D. Watkins, *A History of Penance*, 2 vols. (London, 1920), II, 733-4, 748-9; Charles Joseph Hefele and H. Leclercq, *Histoire des conciles* (Paris, 1913), V², 1350-51.

to it by William of Rennes. Thus Raymond and William founded a literary tradition that would represent the authority of the hierarchical church to pastors (and teachers of pastors) whose role as minister of the Sacrament of Penance had been greatly enhanced by the decree of 1215.

If the initial event is an act of Rome, the terminal event is an act against Rome and all her works. Luther's angry defiance is a fitting symbol for the end of the era of the summists, because it represents a rejection of crucial elements of the medieval system of discipline and, of course, of the summas for confessors that had been created to explain and enforce it. The Reformation marks the end of the composition of summas for confessors, if not of their publication and circulation. Indeed, even Luther's enemy Cajetan found fault with at least the style of the summas, and he criticized them openly in his *Summula peccatorum* of 1525.[1] But it was Luther's attack that most directly opposed the tradition of the summas. For Luther rebelled against their substance, not just their form. To understand the summa for confessors, therefore, is to understand the first of the late medieval enemies of the Reformers. To understand the summa for confessors is to understand one of the principal contributions of intellectuals to control by the hierarchical, sacramental church.

2. The Literary Genre

Raymond of Peñaforte, the patron saint of canon lawyers, studied and taught canon law at Bologna, became master general of the Order of Preachers, served as papal penitentiary, and compiled the Decretals for Gregory IX. Ties with the mendicants, the university, the canon law, and the papal court make this an entirely appropriate career for the author of the first summa for confessors.

The *Raymundina* attempts to be practical and complete. Its four books cover the major kinds of sin, and present them in "cases" of conscience (it was Raymond who introduced the term into the penitential literature). Raymond's world is defined by law—positive, ecclesiastical law, and moral law, divine and natural—and he tries to apply these realms of law to concrete human situations. Book I deals with sins against God; book II, with sins against one's neigh-

---

[1] Michaud-Quantin, *Sommes de casuistique,* 104-106.

bor; book III, with problems relating to Holy Orders and Penance; and book IV, with matrimony. The *Raymundina's* organization is obviously calculated to find a place for discussion of any case. Thus Book I defines and examines problems concerning simony, Jews, Saracens, pagans, heretics, apostates, schismatics, vows, oaths, lying, sorcery, sacrilege, ecclesiastical immunities, tithes, and burial. The "De poenitentiis et remissionibus" of book III is a treatise on confession, contrition, absolution, and satisfaction that considers in the fashion of a summist the questions posed by earlier manuals of confessors. Book IV contains an elaborate investigation of betrothal, dowries, impediments, accusations, and legitimacy. Throughout, the questions are simple, the answers are clear, and the scope is impressive. That William of Rennes felt impelled to add a gloss is no argument against the clarity or thoroughness of the *Raymundina;* William merely expanded some discussions, offered additional examples for others, and proposed different solutions only on those rare occasions when his training and experience dictated.[1]

The *Raymundina* established a basic pattern, and summas for confessors retained the same purpose and orientation throughout their history. Yet in response to social and intellectual currents, there were important changes in the summas from the thirteenth century to the sixteenth century. Sometime before 1274, Monaldus di Capo d'Istria introduced the alphabetical order, making the summa of confessors an encyclopedia of casuistry and the cure of souls. Not much later, John of Freiburg incorporated the opinions of theologians into his solutions, and granted them—particularly Thomas Aquinas and other Dominicans— an authority equal to that of the *Raymundina* and the canonists. In the fourteenth and fifteenth centuries summists continued to keep abreast of opinions of theologians, collections of canon law, papal and conciliar legislation, and the experience of pastoral authorities. In view of these changes, new summas were useful and even necessary.

That the summas were thought useful, and that they influenced the discipline of the late medieval church, is supported by the evidence of the early history of printing. It is true that the *Raymundina* was probably not printed before 1603. Similarly the *Monaldina* was not printed until 1519 and never again, despite its publisher's attempt on the title page to compare Monaldus with Antoninus, Angelus, and

[1] *Ibid.*, 34-41.

Astesanus. Even the much admired *Joannina* appeared in print only four times between 1476 and 1518. Nevertheless, other summas did very well indeed. Thus the German re-working of the *Joannina*—the *Summa Joannis, deutsch* of "Bruder Berthold"—went through eleven printings in the fifteenth century and one in the sixteenth. The printing records of other summas reveal a popularity that commands our respect. A brief list of the most successful in the fifteenth and sixteenth centuries is the best means of showing this literature's apparent appeal.[1]

Pisanella : 6 incunabules (plus its inclusion, complete, in the *Supplementum*)

Astesana : 10 incunabules (Lyon 1509)

Rosella and *Baptistina :* 14 incunabules (Venice 1548), (Strassburg 1586)

Supplementum : 29 incunabules (Lyon 1519)

Angelica : 24 incunabules (La Haye 1505), (Hagenau, 1505, 1509)
(Venice 1504, 1511, 1569, 1577, 1578, 1593)
(Paris 1502, 1506, 1509, 1511, 1513)
(Lyon 1509, 1512, 1513, 1516, 1519, 1523, 1534, 1592)
(Strassbourg 1502, 1513, 1515/16, 1520, 1519)

Sylvestrina :
(Lyon n.d., 1519, 1524, 1528, 1533, 1541, 1553, 1557, 1572, 1582, 1585, 1593, 1594)
(Bologna 1515, 1524)
(Antwerp 1542, 1569, 1580, 1581, 1583, 1585)
(Venice 1569, 1578, 1581, 1584, 1587, 1598, 1601)
(Strassbourg, 1518)

One could not claim that summas for confessors were the most popular books printed before the Reformation. Nor could one claim that the summas were meant for an ignorant or uneducated audience. On the contrary, they were the creation of an intellectual elite, who were aware of the seriousness of the obligation to hear confessions and equally conscious of the complexity of the legal and moral pre-

---

[1] The figures are based on Dietterle; Michaud-Quantin; Hugo Hurter, *Nomenclator literarius theologiae catholicae*, II (reprint, New York, 1962); Jean Dagens, *Bibliographie chronologique de la littérature de spiritualité et de ses sources (1501-1610)* (Paris, 1952); and catalogues of a few libraries. The list is certainly not complete, and accurate only insofar as the bibliographical notices are accurate.

scriptions that had to be honored if the confessional were to fulfill its role as the principal place for the forgiveness of sins. The later summas continued the characteristically scholastic response of Raymond of Peñaforte, William of Rennes, and John of Freiburg. They display those qualities so deftly summarized by Erwin Panofsky as the spirit of the schools : harmony, clarity, distinctness, and, above all, totality. Their cases touch every aspect of life and their solutions draw on reason, law, theology, and pastoral experience to achieve clarity and harmony. Furthermore, without contradicting the admission that the summas were not popularized works for badly educated readers, it is still correct to insist that they were not abstract but practical. They may be erudite, but they are certainly not profound. By their very structure, by the order of their presentation and the concreteness of the cases, they make it easy for literate people of only average intelligence to use them. The summists were too scholarly to suppress all the differences among their authorities, theologians and canonists; but, for the most part, they just tried to lay down the law. Concise and definite answers are not always possible; but when they are they will be given. For we are dealing with reference books designed to give answers, not philosophical inquiries designed to evoke debate.

The enormity of their task exceeds even the length of the books. Summas for confessors were to summarize moral obligation and reconcile the demands of the external and the internal forum. They had to consider all elements of Christian society : the hierarchy, priests and religious, and, most important of all, penitent Christians of all statuses, conditions, occupations, sexes, and ages. In the face of this detail and complexity, the summists responded sensibly. The most popular summas—the *Summa Johannis, deutsch*, the *Rosella*, *Supplementum*, *Angelica*, and *Sylvestrina*—were alphabetical; and printed editions of the *Astesana* and *Joannina* are generally equipped with a full index. Thus they are all ecclesiastical and theological encyclopedias. To find the solution to a problem, one only has to find the right word. Sometimes one must search under other headings. Sometimes there are cross-references to aid in the search. For the most part, however, it takes only a short time to become familiar with the principles of organization. Once that is accomplished, the summas become handy reference works with huge stores of information readily retrieved.

hat kind of information ? What do the most expert authorities try to teach pastors? How do summas for confessors help achieve the social control envisaged in *Omnis utriusque sexus*? The answers to these questions center on such topics as the place of the priest in the operation and theory of the institution, the definition and explanation of sins, the treatment of ecclesiastical legislation, and the development of strict conceptions of obligations.

3. BOOKS AND DISCIPLINE

a) *The Confessor's Authority*

Perhaps the first task to perform if the institutions of forgiveness are to become effective in the control of behavior, is to establish the authority of the confessor. One simple way this can be achieved is through the confessor's mastery of the situation itself. If the confessor can control the encounter with the penitent, by knowing what to do in unusual as well as ordinary situations, then his position as director of the penitent's reformation is emphasized. The summas explain these details in articles such as "Confessio" and "Confessor." In difficult cases, the confessor can learn how to deal with the penitent who has been excommunicated, or who says he cannot do a penance, or stop committing a sin, or feel sorry. How such problems are solved, of course, says something about the kind of control the confessor exercises. But the simple fact that the summas try to teach confessors to answer questions about these routine, technical matters is important because this knowledge supports the authority of the priest. He is in control because he has the requisite information to conduct the confession with confidence.[1]

This expertise—and especially the essential casuistic ability to discern mortal from venial sins—the summas for confessors call "the key of knowledge."[2] There is another key, however, which is more important for the functioning of the institution and the authority of the priest : "the key of power." If a priest is ordained and has jurisdiction he may validly hear confessions and absolve from sins. He

---

[1] Cf. Michaud-Quantin, *Sommes de casuistique*, 64-65.

[2] *Supplementum*, "Confessor 2," 4; and "Clavis"; *Sylvestrina*, "Confessor 3," par. 1-4; *Angelica*, "Confessio 4"—for summaries of the expert knowledge of a good confessor. The best advice to the confessor on this subject is perhaps Gerson, *Tractatus de arte audiendi confessiones, Opera omnia* (Antwerp, 1706), II, 446B-453S.

may be ignorant. He may even be immoral. But if he holds the key of power he may forgive sins. And it is that anti-Donatist proposition, together with a variety of theories about how the Sacrament of Penance forgives sins, that constitutes one of the principal assertions of the authority of the priest.

The first task of the theory of how the sacrament forgives is to define the responsibilities of the penitent. The second is to explain how the sacramentally conferred grace is effective. In other words, the penitent has to know what he has to remember, think, say, feel, and do; and he has to know how the priest's intervention helps him. The answers to these questions are not uniform. But they all define an area of responsibility and an area of gracious support—and in doing both they make the requirements, advantages, and necessity of the Sacrament of Penance more intelligible.

There is a decided tendency in the summists to favor the view that the keys are immensely and intrinsically powerful and, therefore, that the priest's indispensable role is also extremely helpful. Since the tradition begins with Raymond of Peñaforte, it is certain that all would have been familiar with his contritionist theory in which the forgiveness of sins is granted before confession. Given this theory, Raymond answered somewhat unsatisfactorily the question, what does the priest do if sorrow forgives sins?[1] But later summas find a variety of ways to exalt the power of the keys and priestly absolution, so that theories of forgiveness are brought into harmony with a conception of sacramental efficacy *ex opere operato*.

Bartholomaeus of Pisa is an example of a summist who departs least from the *Raymundina*'s Lombardist contritionism. He follows the authority of his fellow Dominican theologians, Thomas Aquinas and Albert the Great, by supporting an indicative absolution—*ego te absolvo*. But lest anyone get the wrong idea he advises the deprecatory *Misereatur tui* to make it clear "that the priest does not absolve by his own authority but as a minister." How do the keys work? Bartholomaeus uses the Thomist explanation that the keys are an instrumental cause, disposing the penitent to justification but not directly causing it ("because this belongs solely to God"). Then he seems to emphasize sacramental efficacy *ex opere operato* as he compares Penance to Baptism and asserts that both are effective purifiers. But he reasserts his basic contritionism by reviving the example of Christ's

---

[1] *Raymundina*, III, 34, 11, p. 446.

healing of the lepers to explain that the priests do not cure, but only "show" the cure.[1] In this version of how the sacrament works, the penitent is required to become sincerely and perfectly contrite. He is still required to come to the priest—and that means that the confessional will remain a source of discipline in every way that flows from the encounter of the penitent with an authoritative priest. But in one important respect the *Pisanella* leaves social control to a process outside the confessional : it stresses the need for a sincere sorrow and difficult transformation of heart before the penitent ever gets to the priest. And that is a different way to achieve the goal of changing his behavior.

The *Supplementum* expresses an alternative view that begins to define a different process. Nicolaus de Ausimo agrees that the keys have only an instrumental causality, but, he adds, those who are not perfectly sorry can obtain grace through sacramental absolution. Moreover, he objects outright to the contritionist assertion that the priest only shows absolution : "On the contrary, it seems that they not only show someone absolved, but also absolve, albeit instrumentally, as was said above."[2] In the *Supplementum*, then, we can see some movement toward the exaltation of sacramental absolution that would characterize later summas.

In the *Angelica* we find a view of the power of the priest that fully accords with the sacramental theology of Duns Scotus. Angelus is one of those who believe that someone coming to confession with inadequate sorrow will find remission of sins there because of the power of the keys. The *Astesana* had already asserted the Scotist doctrine that the penitent who is only attrite will find forgiveness as the power of the keys raises his sorrow to adequate contrition, just so long as he does not place an obstacle against it.[3] Angelus repeats this doctrine in its entirety and then uses it to propose an argument for the necessity of confession. Angelus states that because confession is the safest and surest way to achieve forgiveness, omitting confession shows contempt for one's salvation. For only in confession can attrition be raised, not by man's merit but by God, to achieve forgiveness. Indeed, in confession one does not even have to be attrite, but only not place an obstacle in the path of grace. That benefit makes

---

[1] *Supplementum*, "Absolutio," 6; "Clavis," 6-7; "Contritio," 11.

[2] *Ibid.*

[3] *Astesana*, V, 18-19.

a penitent much more secure. For one cannot be certain he has attrition (because Angelus, like most medieval authorities on penance, does not define attrition by its motivation, as simply sorrow out of fear). He can, however, be far more certain that he is not placing an obstacle in the path of grace—that is, that he is not at the time sinning by intending to sin. One must take this path to recuperate grace, therefore, "since it is easier and more certain."[1]

The concurrence of Sylvester in this Scotist doctrine means that the two most popular summas at the time of the Reformation subscribed to the most radical version of the power of the priest. Absolution, by virtue of the keys, justifies by turning an attrite into a contrite man, unless he interposes an obstacle. But even more, Sylvester agrees that all the penitent really has to do is desire the justifying Sacrament of Penance and not interpose an obstacle by sinning at the last instant of the pronouncement of absolution. In defending this position, Sylvester even goes beyond Angelus : he argues that in some cases, by virtue of an *ornatus animae* imprinted by absolution, someone who was feigning contrition when he confessed might in fact be forgiven at some future time by some future contrition, after the fiction had disappeared.[2]

For the *Angelica* and the *Sylvestrina*, the key of power is powerful indeed. It is no wonder that Angelus saw fit to link his sacramental theory with the assertion of the practical necessity of penance for salvation. For if it is as sure as he maintains, then it is more than likely that repentent sinners searching for security will look here. If so, then a serious question is raised : do such views seriously weaken the Sacrament of Penance as a force for discipline ? Do they not hold out a forgiveness so easy that the attempt to demand even an intention to amend, not to speak of an actual amendment, is utterly defeated ?

In one sense the answer is definitely yes. The history of penance reveals a general tendency toward decreasing severity, and the popularization of Scotist sacramental theology is consistent with the pattern. But it is only common sense to associate social control with severity; hence it is easy to interpret this trend as an unmitigated failure in the attempt to enforce obedience.

---

[1] *Angelica*, "Confessio sacramentalis," 8-13, 30; "Confessio 2,"; "Confessio 7." Cf. Heiko Oberman, *The Harvest of Medieval Theology* (Cambridge, Mass., 1963), 149; and Bernhard Poschmann, *Penance and the Anointing of the Sick* (New York, 1964), 184-193.

[2] *Sylvestrina*, "Confessio 1," q. 1, q. 21, par. 24, q. 23, par. 27; "Contritio," q. 3-4, par. 5-6.

Yet severity is not necessarily the test of effectiveness. It is clear from the history of sacramental penance as a whole that changes in the institutions of forgiveness were gradual responses to the need, or demand, for a more flexible discipline. Looked at from that perspective, the response to pressure is realistic : in the long run it makes the institution viable and more likely to succeed in influencing behavior. As we noted above, the decree of 1215 promised comfort and healing and this psychological function is indispensable to the success of confession. Thus exalting the power of absolution—the "Sacrament of Absolution" as the Scotists called it—means that the institution itself is better able to offer that comfort. In the process, confession to a priest will be exalted. The rigor of a theory that demands carefully examined sorrow along with a firm purpose of amendment is lost—and that loss is not to be underestimated. But in its place is an institution that has clear-cut benefits for sinners. That gain is not to be underestimated.[1] It makes the power and authority of the confessor most convincing.

b) *Catalogues of Forbidden Behavior*

The most obvious task for summas trying to control behavior is to define the behavior that is forbidden. The summas for confessors, like the manuals, are devoted to the classification and examination of sins. Sins are identified everywhere : in articles on vices (such as "Avaritia" or "Luxuria") or on activities (such as "Usuria" or "Debitum coniugale") or on obligations (such as "Abbas" or "Votum" or "Restitutio"). The line between a mortal and venial sin is drawn. Sins are weighed according to their presumed gravity. There is, in short, an enormous amount of information about sin in the summas. It is not presented in so handy a form as in the manuals, which list varieties according to

---

[1] This trend toward a sacramentalist and attritionist theory refers only to the summas; it would be totally misleading to portray a general attritionist or Scotist theology in manuals or devotional literature; see Joseph Mausbach, "Historisches und Apologetisches zur scholastischen Reuelehre," *Der Katholik*, 15 (1897), 48-65, 97-115; *idem*, "Katholische Katechismen von 1400-1700 über die zum Bussacramente erforderliche Reue," *Der Katholik*, 16 (1897), 37-49, 109-122; Nikolaus Paulus, "Die Reue in den deutschen Beichtschriften des ausgehenden Mittelalters," *Zeitschrift für katholische Theologie*, 28 (1904), 1-36; *idem*, "Die Reue in den deutschen Erbauungsschriften des ausgehenden Mittelalters," *ibid.*, 449-485; "Die Reue in den deutschen Sterbebüchlein des ausgehenden Mittelalters," *ibid.*, 682-696; *idem*, review of E. Fischer, *Zur Geschichte der evangelische Beichte*, in *Historisches Jahrbuch*, 24 (1913), 786-792.

any number of systems of categorization (such as the seven deadly sins, the sins against the Ten Commandments, sins against the Holy Spirit, sins against the corporal and spiritual works of mercy, and so on). Nevertheless the information is detailed, and designed to give an impressively large number of ways to sin.

Recent studies of medieval sexual and economic morality have demonstrated the detail and complexity of moral theologians' treatment of sin, and many of them have correctly used the summas for confessors as evidence.[1] The treatment of sins of aggression or violence would yield an ethic of similar detail, although it might not be so coherent. In a study of the role of the summas for confessors in controlling behavior, however, it is equally important to establish how this information on sin was supposed to be used. How was the confessor to learn what the penitent had done? How was he to explain to him what was wrong and how he should change?

It is a cliché of the literature that the penitent is obliged to make a complete confession. That imperative is so widely understood and exceptions to it are so esoteric,[2] that we can take it as the principal requirement of a good confession. To aid the penitent in the fulfillment of that requirement, a variety of simple aids in the examination of conscience were written.[3] The summas, on the other hand, are vast enterprises written for confessors. And although it is not inconceivable that laymen read them, we must assume that this was rarely the case. Yet if they were never intended to be read by penitents, they were to reach penitents all the same. As we have already seen, the foundation of the institution is a priest with authority : he runs the actual confession, and he absolves, sometimes with added benefits. Thus it is consistent with this conception of the sacrament to find the catalogues of forbidden behavior directly communicated to the priest, who in turn uses his knowledge to interrogate the penitent.

The basic rules on interrogation had been proposed by Raymond of Peñaforte, and his advice continued to influence all authorities on confession :

---

[1] John T. Noonan, *Contraception* (Cambridge, Mass., 1965); *idem, The Scholastic Analysis of Usury* (Cambridge, Mass., 1957); Josef G. Ziegler, *Die Ehelehre der Pönitentialsummen* (Regensburg, 1956); cf. Siegfried Wenzel, *The Sin of Sloth* (Chapel Hill, 1960).

[2] Henry C. Lea, *A History of Auricular Confession and Indulgences* (Philadelphia, 1896), I, 348-353.

[3] Michaud-Quantin, *Sommes de casuistique*, 69-72, 82-83.

After [the priest] has heard the confession, let him begin to inquire distinctly and methodically ... Nevertheless, I advise that in his questions he not descend to special circumstances and special sins; for many fall severely after such an interrogation who otherwise would never have dreamt of it.[1]

It is difficult to believe that Raymond had anything in mind except sexual sins when he advised against descending into detail. But whatever he meant by caution, later summists did not take it as a directive to neglect the first part of his advice—that the confessor inquire distinctly and methodically.

The *Astesana* urges confessors to "scrutinize the conscience of the sinner in confession as a physician scrutinizes wounds and a judge a case," because interrogation can disclose things that penitents hide out of confusion or simplicity. Thus the interrogations should follow three guidelines. First, they should investigate common sins—transgressions of the Ten Commandments, instances of the seven deadly sins, and abuses of the five senses, their likely aggravating circumstances, and the special vices usual in particular statuses or professions. Second, only well-known sins should be investigated. Enormities, such as sins against nature, should be approached generally, with circumspection and circumlocution. Third, confessors should not descend too far into details, especially in sins of the flesh.[2]

If we take the rule for questioning as a whole we find that Astesanus has only expanded the *Raymundina's* directions, with greater emphasis placed on both the command to investigate and the command to be cautious. For our purposes, his emphasis on diligent interrogation, which continues in later summas, is more important. The *Pisanella* advises questions on the seven deadly sins. The *Supplementum* agrees with the urgency of interrogation, but adds that the confessor ought to investigate according to articles of faith, the sacraments, the Ten Commandments, the works of mercy, and others.[3]

The *Sylvestrina's* offering on this subject is in part identical with the *Astesana*. But Sylvester also provides some more careful reflections on the proper approach to interrogation. The confessor should ask questions when he thinks the penitent's memory may need help, when he does not understand the penitent, or when the penitent has not been clear. Still he should not ask all the questions he possibly

---

[1] *Raymundina*, III, 34, 30, p. 465; cf. *ibid.*, 26, p. 462.

[2] *Astesana*, V, 16.

[3] *Supplementum*, "Confessor 2," 5.

can; and he must take care lest he annoy the penitent. If Sylvester advises caution, however, he also encourages a thorough investigation. He tells confessors first to inquire whether the penitent is under any kind of excommunication. Then he lists some standard ways to identify sins—the Ten Commandments, the seven deadly sins (which he identifies with the mnemonic SALIGIA), the seven sacraments, the works of mercy, the senses, and the articles of faith. In advising what to do with these catalogues of sin—which he only mentions by category and does not enumerate—Sylvester says he follows the judgment of the *Angelica* : a confessor is required to ask questions only when he thinks circumstances demand it; he need only guard against the charge that his negligence harms the penitent.[1]

Of all the summas, however, the *Angelica* comes out most decisively for careful scrutiny. The list of questions in this highly esteemed summa is monumental. In one folio edition almost twenty-four pages are devoted to "Interrogations," along with cross-references to articles that treat each moral problem in detail. It is a casuist's index, whose completeness far surpasses all rivals. It can lead one to the discussion of such sins as invocation of demons, severity towards parents, dissimulation of holiness, abortion, and going to the baths with Jews. The very thoroughness of this exhaustive list must have been an encouragement to be thorough in the conduct of confession. It is true that the *Angelica* dutifully repeats the usual cautions against descending into details and special circumstances; and those cautions must be taken seriously. But in introducing the section on interrogation, Angelus combines admonitions for restraint with reminders of a sterner responsibility. He warns that questions should be asked wisely and astutely to uncover sins hidden through ignorance or shame. The confessor is obliged under pain of mortal sin to ask relevant questions, if he seriously suspects the penitent is not telling all because of ignorance, or forgetfulness, or negligence. Strangely enough, if the confessor suspects the penitent of willfully hiding sins, he is not obliged to ask questions; on the other hand, if the motive leading the penitent to hide things seems to be shame, the confessor is again obliged to persist. In general, the *Angelica* teaches, if the confessor omits questions out of inadvertency or forgetfulness it is probably not a serious sin. But if the confessor omits them out of negligence it probably is. On the whole, then, the weight of the *Angelica*'s authority is on the side

---

[1] *Sylvestrina.* "Confessor 3," qq. 14-15, par. 17-18.

of a thorough examination by the confessor in any doubtful cases : not only its specific directions and threats, but the sheer bulk of the section on interrogations lead to that conclusion.[1]

c) *Confessors and Ecclesiastical Law*

The summas' most ambitious disciplinary task was to summarize ecclesiastical regulations of every sort so that confessors could understand, obey, and enforce them. Raymond of Peñaforte, faithful to his profession, introduced this obsession with positive law into the genre. Huge sections of the *Raymundina* are devoted to such questions as excommunication, clerical irregularity, restitution, religious vows, impediments to matrimony, wills, and tithes. Raymond's successors continued this tradition, and the exposition of legal cases is perhaps the most prominent feature of the summas. Their task was to represent law in the forum of penance and make conformity to the regulations of the hierarchy a strict matter of conscience.

In one sense, one might classify most of the summas' moral cases related to issues in law; for canon law covers most areas of life. Still, topics like excommunication and marital impediments are peculiarly the province of lawyers. And it is important to recognize that authorities on pastoral care were determined to make hierarchical legislation on these matters known and respected. We can see just how faithful the summas for confessors were to these sources of authority by considering one example of regulation : episcopal reservations.

It was customary in medieval and Reformation Europe to "reserve" the absolution of some sins to higher authorities. The practice probably began in the ninth century, when penitents went to Rome for absolution. The twelfth and thirteenth centuries saw the general confirmation of this practice for the papacy.[2] In the same period, episcopal reservations were firmly established. But the history that summas for confessors are most aware of is the decree of Benedict XI, who defined nine cases reserved to bishops.

The *Pisanella* identifies these cases for confessors. Four, Bartholomaeus tells us, are reserved *de iure* : sins of priests leading to irregu-

---

[1] *Angelica*, "Interrogationes."

[2] A. Bride, "Réserve. Cas réservés," *Dictionnaire de théologie catholique*, 13², 2441-2461; Edward V. Dargin, *Reserved Cases according to the Code of Canon Law*, Dissertation in Canon Law, Catholic University of America (Washington, D.C., 1924), 7-9; H. C. Lea, *History of Auricular Confession*, I, 314-346.

larity; arson; sins incurring solemn penances; and major excommunications. Five are reserved *de consuetudine* : homicide; forgery; violation of ecclesiastical liberties; violation of ecclesiastical immunities; and witchcraft and divination. The *Supplementum* adds mutilation to the customary case of homicide. But Nicolaus also notes that all of the cases cannot be known, and confessors receiving a license to hear confessions should know what sins are reserved to the Bishop in that diocese.[1]

This is the common conclusion. As Sylvester tells us, the *Rosella*, the *Pisanella* and the *Supplementum* agree. The differences he criticizes in the *Angelica* are not substantive. But Sylvester's extensive discussion is especially informative, because it reveals the difficulties inherent in too close adherence to the letter of the law and the power of the episcopacy.

"How many customary episcopal cases are there?" he begins. If one is talking about "the special custom of various dioceses," the answer is "innumerable." And although he upbraids the *Angelica* for saying that there is no custom, because the bishop can reserve few or many cases, Sylvester quickly comes to almost the same conclusion. He asserts the validity of Benedict's list; "there are five that always, or almost always, are reserved to bishops." But he still has to admit that "sometimes they add more and sometimes fewer." The dilemma is a real one for Sylvester, however, because the episcopal authority he is representing conflicts here with the privileges of his order. The problem is also real for the institution as a whole; and Sylvester's response to it is characteristic of the summas' attitude toward authority and reform.

The *Sylvestrina* attacks the notion that bishops can reserve cases at will. In the case of the mendicants, it argues, such action would violate the privileges of the Franciscans, Dominicans, and some others, which come from the pope himself. The most telling argument against the bishops is that reservations *ad libitum* nullify the spirit of the papal legislation : "that from freely confessing to the said friars people might have their consolations in the Lord." In the case of curates and other religious, the bishop who exercises his prerogative to reserve cases without a good reason commits a sin. He may legitimately deny authority over certain cases to particular priests. He may legitimately reserve cases for the common good. But, Sylvester warns : "it is not

---

[1] *Supplementum*, "Confessor 1," 1.

expedient for the common good to reserve so many cases; rather it puts a snare in the path of salvation."[1]

In the face of a maze of legislation limiting the powers of simple curates, Sylvester raised a voice of protest. He was in good company. Jean Gerson in particular saw the dangers of reservations—and ecclesiastical censures in general. And while Sylvester might not have welcomed the support, Luther also protested against reservations on the same basic principles.[2] Sylvester was thus a reformer. He even threatened bishops, the very authorities the summists were generally so busy upholding. Yet after all, he adhered to the primary purpose of the summas. He maintained the binding force of episcopal regulations. Curates must obey. They must not absolve from sins the bishop reserves. And interest in pastoral reform could never lead him to ignore, much less overthrow, ecclesiastical law.

d) *Strict and Binding Obligations : Restitution*

In defending the legal network of reservations, the summas for confessors undermined the discipline that stems from the authority of simple confessors, but asserted all the more forcefully the right of the hierarchy to claim a dominant role in controlling the faithful. In their treatment of restitution, however, they introduced a concept that, on the one hand, limited the free working of sacramental absolution (because it imposed a condition on it) but, on the other, gave to confessors another network of cases that priests could use to discipline penitents. We cannot concern ourselves here with the legal sentences of satisfaction imposed in the external forum by canon law courts, although it is in that aspect of social and legal history that we are most likely to determine how important restitution was in the lives of late medieval Christians. That it was important to the authorities who wrote on the forgiveness of sins, however, is utterly beyond dispute. They looked on the obligation to restore damages—for loss of reputation and other intangibles as well as property—as an absolutely binding condition for the remission of sins. And their rigid and sweeping prescriptions made it certain that many people—perhaps

---

[1] *Sylvestrina.* "Casus,"; "Confessor 2," 5-6; "Confessor 3," q. 1, par. 5.

[2] Gerson, *Opera omnia*, II, 413-414; II, 415A-C; II, 460-462; II, 310-311, 321-322; I, 441A, 445D-446A; Martin Luther, *To the Christian Nobility of the German Nation*, III, 6; cf. Antonius of Florence, *Confessionale—Defecerunt scrutantes*, 3.

especially the wealthy and powerful—would find their consciences deeply disturbed by these strict demands for justice.

The summas for confessors are naturally the most luxuriant source of cases requiring restitution, for their authors are well-versed in the technicalities of moral theology and canon law and they like to give complicated problems the full treatment. Thus the *Raymundina* discusses this obligation and begins with the following definition:

> Likewise there are some sins for which no one may do penance unless he restores or renounces—if indeed he can—what he has sinfully received [quod male accepit]: namely, simony, pillage or plunder, arson, robbery, sacrilege, usury, and dishonorable and fraudulent commerce.

For a full explanation of these cases, Raymond refers his reader to "special titles," presumably to Book II where there are sections "On Usurers," "On Stolen Goods," "On Secular Business," and the like.[1] With the advent of the alphabetical summa, restitution is treated in a separate article, which is highly complicated and generally long. The *Supplementum*, for example, has an eight-part discussion that in one edition runs for over eighteen folio pages. But we possibly gain the best insight into the minutiae overwhelming the casuistry of restitution from the *Angelica*.

To make restitution, Angelus tells us, means to return to its pristine state; and because divine and canon law also speak of "correcting," "restoring," and "satisfying," he decides that the best way to define it is to call it "any satisfaction that must be done to someone else." His treatment, in four parts, is voluminous. "Restitution 1"—"Who is obliged to satisfy?"—has in one edition about twenty columns and ten folio pages. Its 216 entries range from simple cross-references to other articles in the summa, to lengthier treatments of such topics as "Buyer," "*Turpe lucrum*," and "Usurer," the last in twenty-five items and running to over five columns. The next three parts are not so long as "Restitution 1," but in dealing with the questions "To whom and in what order is it to be done," "When one is obligated to do it," and "How its obligation is to be removed," he takes up almost five pages. Thus the *Angelica* devotes slightly under fifteen double-columned folio pages in this edition to approximately 250 separate considerations of how, when, whether, and from whom satisfaction is required for certain sins. The penchant for totality, which we saw in Angelus's

---

[1] *Raymundina*, III, 34, 47, p. 478; *ibid.*, II, 5-8, pp. 166-256.

"Interrogations," is quite as dramatically displayed in "Restitution."
The range of cases would satisfy the most curious and scrupulous
mind. Adulteresses who conceive sons from their illicit unions—and
sons so conceived—are discussed elsewhere, under "Adultery." There
are similar cross-references for lawyers, alchemists, ambassadors,
clerics, pluralists, physicians, prostitutes, and deflowerers of virgins.
The confessor who absolves without proper powers will find how he
is to make restitution for that sin under "Confession 5." Other cases,
however, are solved in the article "Restitution" itself, and one interesting example is the determination of satisfaction for homicide. Angelus
relies on Scotus, who teaches that the murderer is to labor for the
rest of his life against heretics or infidels, or else to spend it in prayer,
almsgiving and the like. The requirements that Scotus describes sound
like a simple penance, however, and Angelus seems to think of them
as such when he adds immediately that, if the murderer cannot or
does not wish to comply with this lifelong obligation, he must perform
some satisfaction chosen by a good man and, beyond that, to appease
the offended as much as he can. If the victim supported dependents
then there are explicit directions that satisfaction be made according
to the best estimate of how long he would have lived and how much
he would have provided for those dependents :

> And if the victim supported some people, [the murderer] is held to as much satis-
> faction to them as the victim would have given them value or money. And he will
> estimate according to the time he would likely have survived and been productive
> —just as the *lex hereditatum* estimates the calculation.

Because restitution is based on this calculation, one must consider
the victim's occupation, quality, age, wealth, and the like, so that a
proper restitution can be made. No restitution is strictly demanded
if the murder was done in self defense—even, it seems, if the act was
excessive, "because it is difficult to moderate a just annoyance [quia
difficillimum est iustum temperare dolorem]." If you execute someone
by order of justice you need not make restitution. But mutilation and
amputation require full restitution : satisfaction of the wounded man,
payment for medical attention and reparation for losses in earnings
incurred.[1]

---

[1] *Angelica*, "Restitutio." The *Sylvestrina's* article "Restitutio" is divided into eight
sections and 65 sub-sections; it takes up 22 1/2 double-columned pages. These articles
alone are longer than many, if not most, manuals.

It takes very little imagination to relate the *Angelica*'s exposition of cases of restitution to social control. Some danger is posed to the authority of the priest whose keys—already restricted by reserved cases—only work on condition of satisfaction for some sins. But that very condition again represents an affirmation of discipline. It is coercive, not in law courts but in the court of conscience. The obligation to restore is indeed strict and binding, designed to serve justice and deter from sin.

4. CONCLUSION

The most difficult problem in estimating the influence of the summas for confessors is to determine who read them. We know they were published in many editions and presumably bought and read. Certainly they must have been used to teach cases of conscience, both to future curates and to mendicants. Yet whether they were widely circulated among the secular clergy is only a matter of speculation.

Nevertheless, they are reliable guides to the theory and practice promoted by the clerical elites. There is enough consistency among the summists to show that they agreed on at least the basic beliefs about sin and forgiveness. In their organization and detail we can discern the outlines of a whole system of discipline. One might argue that it was especially the papacy, which in 1215 had made the obligation to confess its own, that benefited from this literature. And the fortunate circumstance that all of the summists were Franciscans and Dominicans, who owed their privileges, especially of confession, to the papacy, could only accentuate their papal loyalties. Yet all forms of ecclesiastical authority benefit from their efforts, right down to the curate. In the end, the great winner in this literature is the system of social control.

We have seen specific elements of that system developed in the summas : catalogues of sins; expositions of ecclesiastical law; broad application of moral and legal principles; and assertion of the authority of the confessor in theory and practice. These "cases" and discussions are parts of a more general set of assumptions on which the control of the Sacrament of Penance and, ultimately, the whole Roman Catholic Church depended. The summas for confessors taught this set of assumptions, in spirit and letter. They taught, in their massive, encyclopedic way, that morality was definable; that human authorities could define it; that all men were responsible for knowing and practicing it; that those who did not were guilty and should feel guilt and remorse; and that sinners were accountable not only to God, but also to men. who bound and loosed for Him. The core ideas are familiar : law, guilt, and absolution. Together they formed a total system and represented a choice : ecclesiastical institutions of forgiveness would control primarily through sanctions in the forum of conscience. Public sanctions and penalties are minimized. Excommunication, citation before ecclesiastical courts, public acts of expiation, and, in general, public shame continue as forces for social control. But in the Sacrament of Penance they become subsidiary to, and at the same time are incorporated into, a culture of guilt.

Originating in the canon law, the external forum, the summas for confessors nevertheless pursued the obvious and logical choice of addressing themselves to cases of conscience. Angelus de Clavasio puts that choice as clearly as possible :

> Nothing has been said here that I have not thought to be in agreement with justice and truth, especially in the forum of conscience, which I have judged more in need of satisfaction than the forum of contentions; and for that reason I have not followed at times the common opinion of the doctors, especially the canonists and lawyers, because it did not seem to me to conform to the truth of theology and conscience.[1]

The implication of Angelus's casuistic principles is that he will be attentive to the need to heal—to offer psychological benefits—which, as we noted above, is the other part of the charge of *Omnis utriusque sexus*. All of the summists, but especially Angelus and Sylvester, try to fulfill this pastoral office. It was in the cure of consciences, which we have only touched on, that the summists differed most from pure canon lawyers. And we have seen in Sylvester's criticism of reservations a concrete example of conformity to "the truth of theology and conscience" instead of the letter of the law.

Heinrich Boehmer suggested that Luther burned the *Angelica* in public because it treated the cure of souls "entirely as a branch of ecclesiastical jurisprudence," in which "man's whole religious behavior was viewed as the fulfillment of a number of external legal duties having no inward relation." He argued further that "Luther singled out the *Summa Angelica* from among the three or four famous Summae of this sort (handbooks for confessors) because it probably represented the extreme of this legalistic treatment of ethical and religious ques-

---

[1] *Angelica*, "Prologus."

tions."[1] But Boehmer was, at best, half right. It is true that Luther's anger at the "Summa Worse Than Diabolical" was directed at the invasion of religion by laws that Luther did not find evangelical or religious. But it is not true that it was the worst of the summas in these terms—it was probably one of the two best, as Angelus had expressly intended. Still less is it true that the *Angelica*—any more or less than the *Sylvestrina*, the *Pisanella*, the *Astesana*, the *Joannina*, the *Supplementum*, the *Rosella*, or the *Raymundina*—succeeded, or even tried, to make religion external. Quite the contrary, they tried to make all obligations binding internally.

Luther was, however, correct in his assessment of the *Angelica*, and the rest. This most laxist of the summas, which Sylvester had excoriated as "bold and dangerous in its habit of deciding," contained the most "consoling" doctrine of penance. If one searched for certitude in the Roman Catholic Sacrament of Penance, it could be found here. It remained, for millions, a completely satisfying theology. But the *Angelica* embedded that theory of forgiveness in a total system of control, in which the human conscience was free and responsible, in which guilt was "imputed" to individuals, and sins were recalled one by one and in detail before a priest who held keys and could absolve penitents who were properly disposed. The summas knew about doubt, and despair, and troubled consciences, and they tried to take care of them. But they could not cure perplexity and scrupulosity for Luther, because they were completely wedded to the system of control that had made Luther despair as a monk. They treated symptoms, but, for Luther, they caused the disease.

It would be a grievous exaggeration to take Luther's experience as a model for the psychology of the whole Reformation. Nevertheless, it does provide us with a useful insight. When we reconstruct the moral, sacramental, and ecclesiastical theology of the smumas, we discover immediately that they are intended to bring guilt down on people who deviate. That is not to deny that they try to strengthen the pusillanimous, or offer reconciliation to the sinner, or console the anxious. But their system of social control is predicated on an ecclesiastical authority's theology of law, guilt, and absolution.[2]

---

[1] Heinrich Boehner, *Martin Luther : Road to Reformation* (New York, 1967), 376-377.

[2] Among several denunciations of the *Angelica* (in, for example, the *Lectures on Genesis, On Marriage Matters, The Babylonian Captivity*), Luther's remarks in *Lectures on Galatians (Luther's Works*, 26 [St. Louis, 1963], 405-6) show most clearly his condem-

That system was nothing new at the end of the Middle Ages. But with the aid of powerful currents of reform, that system may have been reaching not fewer but more souls. Anti-clericalism and anti-papalism may have roots in clerical incompetence and Roman corruption. It may, on the contrary, have roots in clerical and Roman efficiency. In the years between the invention of printing and the scene at the Wittenberg gates on December 10, 1520, a vernacular summa for confessors is printed twelve times; a pastor in Frankfurt-am-Main composes a vernacular manual of confession that includes a section for children; a Carmelite priest writes a vernacular manual in response to requests by pious Nuremberg laymen; and short works in Latin on confession by Antoninus of Florence and Andreas de Escobar appear in scores of editions each.[1] The evidence suggests that the Sacrament of Penance, bolstered by preachers of repentance and a literature that preaches the theme "poeniteas cito," is gaining as a system of social control. And helping it along is that learned and popular genre, the summa for confessors.

Was 1520 the real end for the summas? Certainly not. A quick look at the success of the *Sylvestrina* and the *Angelica* in the 16th century printing statistics should disabuse of that illusion. If no more were

---

nation of that summa as a cause of psychological suffering : "Therefore it is impossible for men who want to provide for their salvation through the Law, as all men are inclined to do by nature, ever to be set at peace. In fact, they only pile laws upon laws, by which they torture themselves and others and make their consciences so miserable that many of them die before their time because of excessive anguish of heart. For one law always produces ten more, until they grow into infinity. This is shown by the innumerable *Summae* that collect and expound such laws, and especially by that diabolical one entitled 'the Angelic.' " I think this passage has a better explanation of why Luther burned the *Angelica* than Boehmer's or Luther's own (*Why the Books of the Pope and His Disciples were Burned*, in *Luther's Works*, 31, 381-395).

[1] For Bruder Berthold's *Summa Johannis, deutsch*, see Rudolf Stanka, *Die Summa des Berthold von Freiburg. Eine rechtsgeschichtliche Untersuchung.* Theologische Studien der Osterreichischen Leo-Gesellschaft, 36 (Vienna, 1937). Johann Wolff, *Beichtbuchlein des Magisters Johannes Wolff (Lupi), ersten Pfarrers an der St. Peterskirche zu Frankfurt a.M., 1453-1468,* ed. by F. W. Battenberg (Giessen, 1907). For the anonymous *Peycht Spigel der sünder* (Nuremberg, 1510), see N. Paulus, "Reue in Beichtschriften," *ZfkTh,* 28 (1904), 15-17; cf. N. Paulus, "Johann Romming und dessen Beichtbüchlein für die Nürnberger Schuljugend," *Der Katholik,* 21 (1900), 570-575. The *Gesamtkatalog der Wiegendrucke* contains extensive information on Antoninus's *Confessionale* and on Andreas de Escobar's *Modus confitendi;* for his *Lumen confessorum* see Michaud-Quantin, *Sommes de casuistique,* 71-72.

composed, it may have been because the existing ones were enough
to discourage competitors, and perhaps because far-sighted critics like
Cajetan saw a limited future for the genre in the church of the Counter-
Reformation. But we should not let that make us believe that the
system of social control that emerges in the Counter-Reformation is
substantially different from that represented in the summas. The
Fathers of Trent may have reformed it and found new ways to teach
it; but their system of social control would remain the same as it
had been when Luther, in the monastery, learned it and felt guilty.

THE SUMMA FOR CONFESSORS AS A GENRE, AND ITS RELIGIOUS INTENT

LEONARD E. BOYLE

Pontifical Institute of Mediaeval Studies, Toronto

Among other things I find that Dr. Tentler's presentation of the
origins of *Summae confessorum* is not wholly accurate. It is true, as
Tentler says, that the genre is connected with the well-known constitution *Omnis utriusque sexus* of the Fourth Lateran Council in 1215.
But far from being caused by that decree, as Dr. Tentler implies, the
genre was already in existence before the Council, as will be clear to
anyone who has had to study the manuals of Robert Flamborough
(c. 1210) and Thomas Chobham (c. 1215), both of which have had
recent editions.

Dr Tentler may well object that the works of Flamborough and
Chobham, not to speak of several other works of this kind that antedate
Omnis utriusque sexus, are *manuals* for confessors, not *Summae confessorum*, but then, if we are to be precise, neither is the *Summa de
casibus* of Raymond of Peñafort which, according to Dr Tentler, is
'the first summa for confessors'. Raymund, of course, did write a
Summa, but he did not call it a *Summa confessorum*. The first *Summa*
for confessors explicitly to be called a *Summa confessorum* is, in fact,
that of John of Freiburg in 1298, some sixty years after the revised
edition of Raymund's work. So, if Dr Tentler is willing to call Raymund's *Summa de casibus* a *Summa confessorum*, then the manuals
of Flamborough, Chobham and others before or at the time of the
Fourth Lateran Council may likewise be given that title, although
just as anachronistically.

If Dr Tentler's opening statement, 'In 1215 no summa for confessors had been written', is as unacceptable as it is anachronistic, his later statements about the fate of the genre are also not quite accurate : 'By 1520 the last true representative of the genre had recently been completed' (103); 'The Reformation marks the end of the composition of Summae for confessors, if not of their publication and circulation' (105). One has only to glance at e.g. the historical introduction to Prümmer's *Manuale theologiae moralis* (a modern and widely-used manual of practical theology for confessors) to see how, if anything, the tradition of the *Summae confessorum* thickened rather than changed direction after 1520 and really had a field-day in the 17th and 18th centuries with works such as the *Instructorium conscientiae* of Lopez (1585), the *Medulla theologiae moralis* of Busembaum (1645), and the *Tribunal confessariorum* of Wigandt (1703).

As I see it, the modern movement to aid priests engaged in the hearing of confessions began about 1210 with Robert of Flamborough, an English penitentiary of St Victor in Paris, and it grew in strength after the pastoral reforms of the Fourth Lateran Council in 1215. Its greatest exponents in the 13th and 14th centuries were the Dominicans Raymund of Peñafort (*Summa de casibus* c. 1225, revised in 1234) and John of Freiburg (*Summa confessorum*, 1298). Since Raymund is regarded by Dr. Tentler as the author of the first *Summa confessorum*, it may be useful to note just why Raymund composed his *Summa de casibus* and just where he stands in the summist tradition.

Far from conceiving his *Summa* as 'an instrument of social control', Raymund was simply helping out the brethren of the fledgling Dominican Order, which had unexpectedly found itself committed to the hearing of confessions. In 1221, some six years after the Order had been founded, Honorius III had added confessions to the Order's express function of preaching and had urged the bishops of Christendom to give the Order every encouragement in this respect. As a result, manuals of practical theology were hurriedly put together at various centres of the expanding Order so as to allow the Dominicans to fulfill this papal commission. At Bologna, the chief centre of the Order, a *Summa* for confessors was put together before May 1221 by Conrad Höxter; in 1222 the Dominicans of St Jacques combined to produce a handy vademecum for the Dominicans of the Paris area; another handbook appeared at Cologne in 1224; while in 1225 a first version of a *Summa de casibus* was composed at Barcelona for the

Dominicans of Spain by Raymund of Peñafort, a former professor of law at Bologna.

It was in this way that a tradition of manuals for confessors began within the Dominican Order which Raymund dominated in the 13th century and John of Freiburg in the 14th and 15th. In turn, these Dominican manuals (and their Franciscan counterparts from 1300 onwards) inspired a number of manuals of the general pastoral care and of sacramental practice, such as the *Oculus sacerdotis* of William of Pagula about 1320 and the *Manipulus curatorum* of Guido de Monte Rocherii about 1333.

What really was the purpose of these manuals and *summae*? Simply that of helping out priests in the *cura animarum* who did not have access to the great commentaries and specialized writings of the major scholastics. In the spirit of the constitution *Cum sit ars artium regimen animarum* of the Fourth Lateran Council (a constitution which they, unlike Dr. Tentler, also invoke on occasion along with *Omnis utriusque sexus*), the authors of these manuals and *summae* aimed at nothing less than the formation of an educated clergy. Through these manuals and *summae* the decrees of popes and councils, and the teachings of theologians and canonists on any and every aspect of domestic, social and economic life, were conveniently placed at the disposal of priests who were often far removed from any contact with scholastic circles. Written, as their prefaces often explicitly state, "ad informationem simplicium sacerdotum", these manuals and *summae* contributed in no small way to the spread of the latest theological positions on the sacraments and pastoral practice in general, as well as to a spread of a knowledge of the universal law of the church.

Dr Tentler, on the other hand, sees the *Summae confessorum* as 'an instrument of social control'. They helped, he says, 'achieve the social control envisaged in *Omnis utriusque sexus* (109); they 'controlled behavior' (see 114); 'Their task was to represent law in the forum of penance and make conformity to the regulations of the hierarchy a strict matter of conscience' (117).

Apart from the fact that *Omnis utriusque sexus* is a straightforward pastoral constitution which was, in effect, summing up a pastoral situation that had existed in many dioceses for years before Fourth Lateran, the assertion is a little too strong that the *Summae confessorum* made 'conformity to the regulations of the hierarchy a strict matter of conscience'. If by 'hierarchy' Dr Tentler means a 'local hierarchy', then I can only say that the *Summae confessorum* as such, not to speak of local English, French, German, Italian or Spanish manuals, have little or nothing to say about 'regulations' of the local 'hierarchy'. And if by 'hierarchy' he means the church as a whole, then he encourages a very limited view of the scope of these *summae*.

The 'task' of the *summae* was first and foremost to present confessors (and their penitents through them) with a detailed and informed exposition of the law of God and of the basic requirements of Christian belief and practice : the commandments, the sacraments, virtues and vices, etc. Since the laws of the church (Dr Tentler's 'regulations of the hierarchy' ?) were for the most part devised to ensure a proper observance of these fundamental beliefs and practices, any informed treatise on these matters had perforce to give prominence to these laws or 'regulations'. In so far as the *summae* treated of these laws, their purpose was not so much to impose law (in Dr. Tentler's sense) as to allow confessors to see the precise relationship of the law of the church to these beliefs and practices—and this in order that confessors might better educate the consciences of their penitents.

The education of confessors and penitents on these essential matters and their ramifications may indeed be termed 'social control', but not if, as Dr Tentler states, 'social control' means making 'conformity to the regulations of the hierarchy a strict matter of conscience'. Like any Christian teacher, the authors of *Summae confessorum* had 'conformity' to the law of God as their primary and overall goal. 'Regulations of the hierarchy' are rightly seen by them as secondary to that law and as 'instruments' of its fulfillment.

Dr Tentler, however, does not make much of this aspect of the *summae*. He sees their 'social control' not in the fundamental terms of education and the law of God but in terms of guilt-complexes : 'When we reconstruct,' he writes, 'the moral, sacramental, and ecclesiastical theology of the summas, we discover immediately that they are intended to bring guilt down on people who deviate'. And although he allows that 'This is not to deny that they try to strengthen the pusillanimous, or offer reconciliation to the sinner, or console the anxious', his firm conclusion, nevertheless, is that 'their system of control is predicated on an ecclesiastical authority's theology of law, guilt and absolution'.

This is all too negative and sweeping. It presents a picture which may find some foundation in one or two of the *Summae confessorum* of Luther's early years but which is not true of the genre as such.

General conclusions about the genre are, in fact, wholly impossible

9

if one omits (as Dr Tentler does) a detailed examination of that *summa* which dominated the period 1300-1500 and gave the name to the genre : the *Summa confessorum* of John of Freiburg. For John of Freiburg's *Summa* radically changed the character of manuals for confessors and dealt a severe blow to the popularity which Raymund of Peñafort and his approach had enjoyed for more than two generations.

Where Raymund, because of his legal background, is narrowly legalistic in treating of the problems of conscience with which a confessor might be faced, John of Freiburg, a theologian by profession, makes sure that Raymund's legal sources (which he faithfully repeats) are balanced by quotations from theological writings. Raymund, for example, has nothing at all on the sacrament of Order as such, but plunges at once into the impediments to the reception of the sacrament.[1] John of Freiburg, on the other hand, proceeds at this point to devote some 54 questions to the theology of the sacrament, giving long quotations from Albert, Aquinas and Peter of Tarentaise. Again, where Raymund is severely legal in the title *De poenitentiis et remissionibus* (3.34), John of Freiburg has some 86 long questions on the theological and moral virtues and the corresponding vices (faith, hope, charity, blasphemy, etc.), taken in the main from the *Secunda secundae* of Aquinas. His departure from the content of Raymund's *Summa* is significantly introduced by the words, 'Post haec (Raymund and legal sources) *descendo ad spiritualia*'.[2]

Since it was John of Freiburg's balance of law and theology that provided the headline for most of the manuals and *summae* for confessors after 1300, I feel that Dr Tentler does not do justice to the *Summae confessorum* when he concentrates so much on Raymund and 'regulations of the hierarchy' and guilt-complexes.

---

[1] *Summa de casibus*, 3.22.

[2] *Summa confessorum*, 3.34, qq. 202-288.

INTERVENTION RE FATHER BOYLE'S
COMMENT ON TENTLER,
"SUMMA FOR CONFESSORS"

WILLIAM J. BOUWSMA

University of California (Berkeley)

Father Boyle takes particular issue with Professor Tentler's conception of the Summas for Confessors as an instrument of social control. His point was that the authors of these works were not motivated by any concern to control Christians and thus to serve the interests of the hierarchy. They only wanted to help confessors to perform a delicate and difficult spiritual task.

This might well be true, but it does not respond directly to Tentler's point. As I understand his paper, Tentler was concerned not with the motives of any group of men, but with the function of the summas within a social system. His underlying point would be that ideas, institutions, and even books may well perform certain functions or roles independently of the intentions of their creators.

RESPONSE AND RETRACTATIO

THOMAS N. TENTLER

Father Boyle objects to my definitions of two terms : "summa for confessors" and "social control." We do not disagree because I have been "inaccurate," "anachronistic," limited, or too negative and sweeping. Rather, we differ in the meanings we attach to those two terms. I understand his objections and can even sympathize with them. Nevertheless, I would rather retain both terms and their meanings as I have used them in this essay.

It is not novel to identify Raymond of Peñaforte as the originator of a literary genre distinct from manuals for confessors. Pierre Michaud-Quantin has stated that proposition as clearly as could be : "le dominicain catalan a fondé le genre littéraire des *Summae confessorum* proprement dites ..."[1] If Michaud-Quantin's reasons for this distinction [2] are not universally persuasive, they are good enough to exculpate anyone who accepts them from the charge of anachronism and inaccuracy. It is true that other historians define and use these terms differently, and Father Boyle's criticisms would find much scholarly support.[3] Nevertheless, my own experience with this literature validated Michaud-Quantin's distinction between manuals and summas, and justified my restricting this essay to the "summas" listed in footnote one (which specifically notes that most of the genre are called "summa de casibus" and not "summa confessorum").

There is an inner coherency to these works obvious to anyone who uses them. Whether you call them "summas for confessors" or "summas of casuistry," Raymond of Peñaforte and William of Rennes belong, whereas Alain de Lille, Robert of Flamborough, and Thomas of Chobham do not. That the line goes directly from Raymond and William to Monaldus and John of Freiburg (and not from any of the other so-called predecessors) is evident to anyone who opens the *Monaldina* or "the" *Summa confessorum*. The *Astesana* and *Pisanella* are equally obvious continuators of this line. Popular works such as William of Pagula's *Oculus sacerdotis* and Guido de Monte Rocherii's *Manipulus curatorum* may be conscious of this genre and borrow substantially from it, but they do not belong to it : these books do not look like summas and they do not contribute to the development of the summas. It is true, and irrelevant, that John of Freiburg is spiritually akin to all pastoral and moral authorities who emphasize theology more than canon law, and that his summa marks a change in direction for this literature. But in terms of the history of a genre, the summas I have identified originate with the *Raymundina* and terminate with the *Sylvestrina*. Others might be included, but it is best to confine our attention to the ones I have listed, whose characteristic traits are unmistakable. They are generally known by nick-

---

[1] Michaud-Quantin, *Sommes de casuistique*, 40.

[2] *Ibid.*, 9-12, 15-19, 21-24, 43-48, 98-106.

[3] Thomas of Chobham, *Summa confessorum*, ed. by F. Broomfield, Analecta mediaevalia Namurcensia, vol. 25 (Louvain and Paris, 1968), XVII-XVIII; S. Kuttner, "Pierre de Roissy and Robert of Flamborough," *Traditio*, 2 (1944), 493-495; J. J. F. Firth (ed.), *Liber Poenitentialis of Robert of Flamborough*, Pontifical Institute Studies and Texts, 18 (Toronto, 1972), 10-12. Cf. Pierre Michaud-Quantin, "A propos des premières Summae confessorum. Théologie et droit canonique," *Recherches de théologie ancienne et médiévale*, 26 (1959), 268, 274, 300.

names (especially the *Astesana, Pisanella, Rosella, Baptistina, Supplementum, Angelica, Tabiena,* and *Sylvestrina*). From an organization into four or more books in Raymond of Peñaforte, John of Freiburg, and Astesanus of Asti, they changed definitively into alphabetical encyclopedias in the 14th century. Their interdependence is obvious from the titles of their articles, which generally run from "Abbas" to "Uxor" or "Zelus," with long articles under "Confessio," "Confessor," "Contritio," "Debitum coniugale," "Excommunicatio," "Restitutio," "Satisfactio," and so on. When non-alphabetical summas were printed in the 15th and 16th centuries they were often supplied with an alphabetical index containing these very same article titles. Can anyone seriously contend that works so similarly organized as these, with such similar contents, do not form a genre? Can anyone seriously contend, moreover, that the ancestors of Nicolaus de Ausimo, Angelus de Clavasio, and Sylvester Prierias Mazzolini were Alain de Lille or Thomas of Chobham rather than Raymond of Peñaforte, William of Rennes, and John of Freiburg?[1]

Summas for confessors also differ from later works of casuistry including those by Hermann Busenbaum, Louis Lopez, and Martin Wigandt, whom Father Boyle partiularly mentions. All of these authors abandon the encyclopedic form and the attempt to achieve encyclopedic breadth. Busenbaum's work is closer to a long manual; Lopez and Wigandt offer more academic and intricate excursions into cases of conscience. All reveal changes necessitated by new moral and new institutional conditions. They are much more concerned with general principles of casuistry than summists, and thus they have more detailed, as well as up-to-date, consideration of the concepts of conscience and culpability. They and the summas have common theological roots in the 13th century, it is true, and they even occasionally refer to later summas. But casuists from the Reformation on do not organize their works around the opinions of Raymond of Peñaforte, John of Freiburg, or even Angelus de Clavasio. Rather they take up the more challenging ideas of modern doctors—Victoria, De Soto, Azpilcueta, Lessius, Escobar, Sanchez, Diana, Molina, and others like them. Later casuists write for confessors, and concern themselves with such topics as restitutions, absolution, and the conjugal debt; but

---

[1] Neither Broomfield (pp. LXIX-LXXV) nor Firth (11-20) contend that Thomas of Chobham or Robert of Flamborough influenced in any significant way the works I have called "summas for confessors."

they do not compose "summas for confessors" and they do not depend primarily on summas for confessors.

Summas for confessors are unique because they try to be academic, complete, concise, simple, and, above all, usable. I have tried to suggest that this rare combination of intellectual and pragmatic qualities is explicable in part by the summa's appearance at a particular time in the history of the church, when the yearly obligation to confess became papal and universal; when canon law was expanded, refined, and more effectively applied; when universities collaborated with the hierarchy by organizing and disseminating the sciences necessary to run the church; and when Dominicans and Franciscans—ordinary confessors and leaders of the intellectual establishment—began to make their momentous contribution to the theory and practice of sacramental, auricular confession. That is why *Omnis utriusque sexus* seemed a fitting *symbol* for the beginning of this literary genre. It is well known that books for confessors were written before 1215, just as it is well known that the obligation to confess antedated 1215. It should be equally evident that the statute itself grew out of a long religious movement that led to the decision to emphasize confession and at the same time produced books on confession. It should be just as obvious, however, that it was no ordinary statute—and it would be pointless to cite the numerous authorities who have argued for its far-reaching effects. As a symbol, moreover, *Omnis utriusque sexus* is indeed appropriate, not only for the reasons historians have given, not only because medieval churchmen at every level can be shown to have heard of it and to have attempted to enforce it, but also because even a cursory reading reveals its disciplinary content, its involvement in social control. It deals with jurisdiction, investigation, obligations, sanctions, and behavioral change. That is roughly what religious historians and ecclesiastical authorities call discipline and sociologists call social control. I prefer the latter term because it encourages students to look at aspects of an institution that ecclesiastical authorities (and authors) do not explicitly identify as part of their resources for performing an actual, social task.

Thus we must now turn to "social control," the second term at the heart of the differences between Father Boyle and me. Neither the term nor the reality should be any more objectionable then "casuistry," (which is an inevitable product of any attempt to make moral principles relevant to human conduct, and which is one of the essential features of the summas that most clearly betokens their participation

in social control). What does the term mean ? Perhaps the best explanation for our purposes is supplied by William Gamson's *Power and
Discontent*.[1] Although dealing with an entirely different problem—
contemporary political authorities' control over "potential partisans"
who try to enter and influence the political process—Professor Gamson
has two discussions that show why, in spite of the apparently enormous
differences in empirical data, the sociological concept is illuminating
when applied to summas for confessors.

Gamson's first discussion—"persuasion" as a means of social control
—warns that differences in labels do not necessarily constitute differences in things :

> There is an interesting variety of words used to describe this social control technique
> [persuasion]—some of them highly pejorative and others complimentary. The
> approving words include education, persuasion, therapy, rehabilitation, and, per-
> haps more neutrally, socialization. The disapproving words include indoctrination,
> manipulation, propaganda, and "brainwashing." The choice of words is merely a
> reflection of the speaker's attitude toward the social system and its agents. If one
> believes the authorities are faithful agents of a social system which is accorded
> legitimacy, then they are "socializing" potential partisans when they exercise social
> control. If one sides with the potential partisans and identifies with their grievances
> against the authorities, then this latter group is using "manipulation" as a form of
> control. The behavioral referent, of course, may be identical in both cases; the
> choice of word reflects two different perspectives on the same relation.[2]

The terms Father Boyle and I use may not differ so dramatically as
some of Professor Gamson's examples, but the problem is still one of
attitude toward ecclesiastical authorities. Father Boyle objects to such
language as "guilt," "controlled behavior," "conformity to the relations of the hierarchy," "impose law," and, above all, "social control."
He prefers "the formation of an educated clergy," "the spread of the
latest theological opinions," "a spread of knowledge of the universal
law of the church," "conformity to the law of God," "education and
the law of God," "exposition of the law of God and the basic requirements of Christian belief and practice," "educate consciences," and so
on. But these are merely different words for the same thing; and it is
at best naive to suppose that by calling techniques of persuasion
"education" and norms "the law of God" one refutes the almost

---

[1] William A. Gamson, *Power and Discontent* (Homewood, Ill., 1968), 115-134. Although Gamson says that he treats this problem from the point of view of "authorities,"
he admits that "control has a pejorative ring," and he notes the possibility of calling
authorities "leaders" as well as "controllers."

[2] *Ibid.*, 125-126.

truistic observation that hierarchical and priestly authorities are in command, and that summas are designed to present a coherent system in which they can order, threaten, persuade, and control.

Indeed, even those "spiritualia" of John of Freiburg to which Father Boyle refers are a Thomistic contribution to social control. For they describe obligations and identify or define sins. They tell confessors what Christians must believe, and how Christians are to conduct themselves with unbelievers. They talk about the sins of blasphemy, despair, presumption, and hatred. They even get down to dancing, plays, and feminine dress. To call them "spiritualia" does not remove them from the realm of social control any more than to note that they originate with a theologian rather than a canonist. Angelus de Clavasio must be understood in the same way. He was, as I noted above, one of the least legalistic of the summists : often laxist in moral theology; thoroughly Scotist in sacramental theory; always concerned for the pastoral effect of his opinions, and therefore explicitly favorable to theologians as opposed to canon lawyers. But he set himself the same task as John of Freiburg and all other writers on confession, and that task included social control.

Professor Gamson's second discussion, which examines actual forms of persuasion, applies directly to my analysis of the summas for confessors as instruments of social control. He describes techniques for achieving acceptance of superiors such as "surrounding authorities with trappings of omniscience" and "making them distant awe-inspiring figures possessed of tremendous intelligence and prescience plus access to privileged information that is essential for forming judgments"; "personal contact and the humanization" of authorities" that results in identification with and trust in them; and simply getting people to "do their duty" by obeying legitimate commands, even at the risk of their own and others' comfort and safety. If these explanations of persuasion are perfect summaries of some of the summas' most prominent techniques, Gamson's conclusion is an uncanny description of their basic strategy :

> Perhaps the most powerful and common means of social control is simply the conveying of expectations with clarity and explicitness coupled with clear and direct accountability for the performance of such expectations. As long as legitimacy is accorded in such situations, individuals will regard their noncompliance as a failure and any interaction which makes such a personal failure salient is embarrassing, unpleasant and something to be avoided.[1]

---

[1] *Ibid.*, 126-134.

This formulation of the most effective means of social control—clear and explicit expectations, clear and direct accountability—describes the essence of institutional penance's social control. The characteristics of summas for confessors described above are totally consonant with the achievement of control in that form. They are, if any books ever were, devoted to the clarification, definition, and publication of expectations, as well as to the assertion of the legitimacy of the authority of priests over penitents and the hierarchy over the church. Legal structures—in the form of reservations, excommunications, and restitution—are central. But I have tried to emphasize further—in opposition to anti-Catholic historians who have seen medieval religion as external and ritualistic—the crucial role given to conscience and, therefore, to guilt. The summists tried to help ecclesiastical authorities get catalogues of forbidden behavior thoroughly internalized. That too is social control.

It is useful for historians to be aware of constant elements in social systems—to be aware, for example, of the similar functions of medieval ecclesiastical institutions and modern political institutions. But it is essential to go beyond that recognition, to analyze medieval techniques of control and explain their relationship to a system of authority. If intellectuals played a significant role in that system, then it is only natural to ask specifically how law and theology, lawyers and theologians, and a legal and theological literature worked for the integration and control of society. My essay tried to contribute some answers to those questions. It also tried to suggest that in Martin Luther the church encountered a "deviant" who recognized that a system of people and ideas controlled him and that, for his own cure, he had to delegitimize that system—the ideology and the persons in authority. For that task no summa for confessors, not even the *Angelica*, would do. To meet Luther's challenge, moreover, the summas were again inadequate. Another literature, a new educational system, a different style of persuasion was necessary. But that is another history.

PART TWO

LAY PIETY AND THE CULT OF YOUTH

1. THE LEGACY OF LATE MEDIEVAL RELIGION IN SIXTEENTH CENTURY CHAMPAGNE

A. N. GALPERN

University of Pittsburgh

The Middle Ages continued to wane well beyond the fifteenth century, which Johan Huizinga studied so brilliantly. A Frenchman of the 1380s could have recognized his own times in the religious practices of one hundred and fifty years later. France offers an especially good opportunity to study the impact of the past on the religion of the sixteenth-century laity because the country lacked sustained, effective direction from a clerical elite. Her Calvinist ministers and their adherents were just strong enough to antagonize tepid Catholics into supporting Papal stalwarts in a bloody and successful defence of tradition. And her bishops were too jealous of their relative autonomy to accept direction from Rome, too varied in their interests, until the seventeenth century, to undertake a strictly Gallican reform. The evidence from France enables us to follow religious currents downstream from the late medieval, fourteenth and fifteenth, centuries, and watch them dilute as they are joined by the newer sixteenth-century waters. The mix varies from one Christian to another. In other places Protestant Reformers in power tried to dam up the older currents, and derided any leakage as papist survivals. Still elsewhere, their Catholic counterparts built and manned sluices in hopes of blending careful doses of novelty into tradition. Either way the surviving evidence obscures a range of religious needs and aspirations which no theologian could encompass and no administrator constrict. The sixteenth century, John Calvin and Archbishop Cisneros of Toledo notwithstanding, was hardly noted for clarity or even tidiness. For the springtime of the Reformation and the autumn of the Middle Ages fall within the same general period, which was perhaps as distant from the world of Descartes as from that of St. Thomas Aquinas.

The present paper will seek to evoke, within the first half of the century, the traditional strain in the diffuse and ambiguous French religious mood, and to interpret that strain as a continuing and lingering response to the generalized crisis of the later Middle Ages. An attempt, however tentative, to make the parallel lines of economic and social inquiry, on the one hand, and religious inquiry on the other, converge, seems timely, given the significant but somewhat cloistered work in these two fields for the pre-Reformation period.[1]

This subject cannot of course be studied from archival sources on the national level. But what portion of a country whose population was approaching sixteen million souls does one choose for its exploration? Given the diversity that was (and is) France, no city and its hinterland, no diocese or province could be considered either representative of the kingdom as a whole, or a mean between extremes. Still, some places were more distinctive, more alive with their own individuality, than others. The wheatlands of the Ile-de-France, which were abundant enough to insure the greatness of Paris, stand out even in a country known for its rural wealth.[2] The mercantile centers of Rouen and Lyons, one for the Atlantic, the other for overland, trade, were rich and vibrant cities, parts of the wider, European world.[3] The cloistered interior of Brittany lived on its meager agricultural resources and its rich, particularistic traditions. The list could be extended, but not indefinitely. It is unlikely ever to include Champagne.

For the great moments and special qualities of this province, by and large, lay buried in the past. True, Reims was still in some ways the clerical capital of France. The kings came to its cathedral for coronation, to be anointed by the archbishops with the sacred chrism, and acclaimed by peers and people as their God-given sovereign. But by the twelfth century the city had lost its earlier intellectual eminence and political influence to Paris. During that same period in the southern

---

[1] For cogent syntheses and comprehensive bibliographie see the two relevant volumes in the *Nouvelle Clio* series : Jacques Heers, *L'Occident aux XIVe et XVe siècles, aspects économiques et sociaux* (Paris, 1966), and Francis Rapp, *L'église et la vie religieuse en Occident à la fin du moyen âge* (Paris, 1971).

[2] Marc Bloch, "L'Ile de France," *Mélanges historiques* (Paris, 1963), II, 707; Heers, 52; Guy Fourquin, *Les campagnes de la région parisienne à la fin du moyen âge* (Paris, 1964).

[3] Michel Mollat, *Le commerce de la Haute Normandie au XVe siècle et au début du XVIe* (Paris, 1952); Lucien Romier, "Lyon et le cosmopolitanisme au début de la Renaissance française," *Bibliothèque d'humanisme et renaissance; travaux et documents*, XI (1949), 28-42.

part of the province the counts of Champagne, vassals stronger than the Capetian kings, brought both power and civilization to Troyes, while they fostered fairs that became the hub of international commerce. But by the fourteenth century the province had become part of the royal domain, and the fairs had shrunk to the size of the local markets.

Champagne in the sixteenth century was at once too far from Paris and not far enough—too far to be galvanized by the capital and share in its animation, too close to enjoy life on its own. She had no university until the cardinal of Lorraine founded one at Reims in 1547 to help defend the faith, no provincial estates, and no parlement. Both as a high court of appeals and as the administrative agent of the royal will, the parlement was a crucial institution, which gave strength and character to a province. Generally speaking, then, for matters judicial, political and intellectual, Champagne depended on guidance from outside.

The province that I have studied was one of the more prosaic parts of France, worth studying for the very reason that it was unlikely to have bred a religious climate all its own. Long removed, by our period, from the main currents of trade, it was not at all isolated from new fashions and new ideas. For it is easier to build a good road than to grow a bumper crop on the chalk plains that stretch in a broad north-south belt from Reims to Troyes. Champagne's vocation, ever since men have settled the area, has been to link more important places to one another. And although hardly wealthy, the province was not yet truly poor. The meadows along the river valleys that flow north and east toward Paris, the rye fields above the meadows, and the sheep walks between valleys, the vines along the face of the north-south ridges that ring the Parisian Basin, and the timber on their back slopes, sustained the *bonnes villes* of Troyes, Reims and Châlons, and dozens of *bourgs* as well. The province does have an ill-reputation, which it owes to the trials of the seventeenth century, and to the criticisms of eighteenth-century improvers, crystallized and enshrined in the *Encyclopedia*.[1]

---

[1] Jean-Marie Pesez et Emmanuel Le Roy Ladurie, "Le cas français vue d'ensemble," *Villages désertés et histoire économique XIe-XVIIIe siècles* (Paris, 1965), 214-227; Roger Dion, "Le 'bon' et 'beau' pays nommé Champagne pouilleuse," *L'information géographique*, XXV (1961), 211.

The area of Champagne is sizable, stretching from the gateways to
Paris to the sixteenth-century eastern frontier, and from the Ardennes
forest to the limits of Burgundy. And despite its geographic coherence,
Champagne was neither an economic unit nor—in institutional terms—
a religious one. The ecclesiastical province of Reims extended from
the diocese of Châlons into the Low Countries. The archbishop-duke of
Reims and the bishop-count of Châlons were powerful territorial lords,
whom the counts in Troyes had never been able to subject. The province of Sens, for its part, included the diocese of Paris as well as Troyes.
But our business is not really the institutional structure of religion.
In fact, to consider a single bishopric runs the danger of looking at
the laity through the eyes of the clergy, instead of the other way
round. Most important, since the sources are scattered, a comprehensive picture can emerge only by combining materials from several
archival depots. And finally, the inclusion of a wider area enables us
to glean a good deal of information on urban-rural religious relationships, though not enough, unfortunately, to study the countryside for
its own sake.

Our evidence consists, first, of parish ledgers, which are most
plentiful for the city of Troyes. They give the numbers and sometimes
the names of participants in confraternities, the donations of parishioners to their church and the occasions on which they contributed,
the relative éclat with which the various holidays were celebrated,
and the effort and expense in building and embellishing the churches.
A hundred and fifty wills from the city and region of Reims for the
second quarter of the century not only stipulate or request a specific
place of burial and provide for funeral arrangements, but make bequests to the poor and provisions for pilgrimages by relatives or
palmers. Granted that a testator's motives, as he drew up his will in
contemplation of death and more often than not in the face of it,
were more narrowly religious than in the normal course of his life. I
would argue, nevertheless, and hope to demonstrate, that he was
drawing upon and emphasizing underlying feelings that were in him
all the time. Granted, too, that the wills are not numerous enough to
show the frequency of attitudes and gestures. They do in their diversity
demarcate the range of acceptable religious behavior. Taken together,
the information they supply —and which cannot be found elsewhere—
enables us to turn hints into hypotheses. The texts of mystery plays
are a further body of evidence, to be read in conjunction with the
iconography of the stained-glass windows and statues that still grace

scores of parish churches as well as the cathedrals of Champagne.[1] The few memoirs by contemporaries are crucial in interpreting as well as observing the religious scene.[2] Almanacs, books of hours and other works of devotion addressed to the faithful by local and Parisian printers complete this list.[3] The body of the paper should establish that, in the matter of religious practice and belief, the various parts of Champagne were complementary.

First, however, we need to survey the condition of the province at the turn of the sixteenth century. Champagne was then still slowly recovering from the late-medieval depression. Recently historians have emphasized that much of southern Germany and Italy, of Iberia, the Low Countries and England weathered this period relatively well, and in some cases even became more prosperous.[4] Champagne, like France in general, however, suffered terribly. The Great Death of 1348 and its sequels was not the only problem. The second half of the Hundred Years War, and the war of supposedly disbanded but unpaid companies against the civilian populations between campaigns, tortured the province, plundering merchants and driving peasants away from their farms. The crown, fighting for its life against the English, and under-

---

[1] BM (Bibliotheque municipale), Troyes, MS. 2282 is a copy of three of the four days of a play performed at the end of the fifteenth and beginning of the sixteenth centuries, which is based on the *Mystère du vieux testament*, a cycle of plays then current in France, and on the Parisian cleric Arnoul de Greban's Passion. See Louis Petit de Julleville, *Les mystères* (Paris, 1880), II, 411-413. Canon Guillaume Flameng, *La vie et passion de Monseigneur Saint Didier, martyr et evesque de Langres* (Paris, 1855), is a second Champenois text, commissioned for a performance in 1482.

The basic studies of the art of the period are Raymond Koechlin et J.-J. Marquet de Vasselot, *La sculpture à Troyes et dans la Champagne méridionale au seizième siècle* (Paris, 1900), and Paul Biver, *L'école troyenne de peinture sur verre* (Paris, 1935).

[2] Nicolas Pithou, *Histoire ecclésiastique de l'Église de la ville de Troyes ... de la restauration du service de Dieu et de l'ancien ministère en ladicte église ... jusques en l'année 1594*, BN (Bibliothèque nationale), Collection Dupuy, MS. 698, of which the first part was probably prepared for, and is summarized in, the contemporary, Genevan, official *Histoire ecclésiastique des églises réformées au royaume de France*, ed. G. Baum et E. Cunitz, 3 vols. (Paris, 1883-1889), offers trenchant if caustic descriptions of the behavior of his Catholic contemporaries. The diary of the observant and intelligent cleric of Provins, Claude Haton, *Mémoires*, 2 vols. (Paris, 1857), is so revealing that it will be used below, even though it begins only at mid-century.

[3] Examples are *Le Grant Calendrier et Compost des Bergers* (Troyes, 1528 and 1541), and *Les presentes heures à lusage de Chalons ... faictes à Paris pour Symon Vostre Libraire* (Paris, 1512),

[4] Heers, passim.

mined by the great lords, princes of the blood who hoped to comandeer the hulk of France for their own purposes, could provide no protection to the lands in its own domain.

The second half of the fifteenth century was a time of rebuilding for France, of peasants who left the mountain regions, which were becoming choked with people, for the fertile plains on which the wars had been fought. They did not flock to Champagne. A demographic study of the southeastern part of the province proves that the rural population did not begin to recover its losses, from its own resources, until after 1470.[1] Reims, too, found it hard to make good the past. It had become a sluggish town of small handicrafts and food trades, which served the clerical population of consumers.[2] A municipal census in 1482, a year of grain shortage, showed 10,678 residents, including the peasants of any means who had come in, temporarily, from the countryside, but not the more than 2,000 of the city's own "miserable and poor people who beg their life." The city did not dwarf Châlons, with its 9,228 inhabitants in 1517. Troyes was more populous and dynamic, with 15,309 residents and half again as many indigents in 1482, and 23,659 people in 1500. The city was embarked on a brief but bright moment in its history, which would last through the half century.[3]

If progress in most parts of Champagne was slow, then at least the general direction was clear—more people, increasing activity and greater security, too. For the French crown was strong once more, and its officers, while their kings played at war in Italy, exercised royal authority in a way that had not been seen for two hundred years. Until the religious wars of the later sixteenth century threatened France with disorganization once more, and a heady, expansive economy began to suffer from both monetary and demographic inflation, the people of Champagne would see better times than their forefathers had. But did their religion reflect the improvement of the present, or even expectations of the future, rather than the misfortunes that lay behind?

---

[1] R. Fossier, "Rémarques sur les mouvements de population en Champagne méridionale au XVe siècle," *Bibliothèque de l'École des chartes*, CXXII (1964), 196.

[2] P. Desportes, "La population de Reims au XVe siècle, d'après un dénombrement de 1442," *Moyen âge*, LXXII (1960), 482.

[3] Desportes, 467, n. 23, for the 1482 figures for Reims and Troyes; BN, Dupuy, 228, fol. 115 for the 1500 count at Troyes; and Maurice Poinsignon, *Histoire générale de la Champagne et de la Brie* (Châlons, 1896), I, 580.

A central theme of traditional religion, which can be read in the wills and on the stained-glass windows, was the demand by Christians for the prayers of their fellows. 'Guillemette, widow of the late Colas Vinot, has given this present window in the year 1522; pray God for those who live and for all the dead,' reads an inscription at the bottom of a set of panels portraying St. Nicholas in the church of Saint-Parres-aux-Tertres near Troyes.[1] Gibrian Pirche, receiver in the *élection* (tax court) of Reims, and his wife, established an annual pension of 25 livres in 1538 for a daughter who was about to enter a nunnery "so that the said Jehanne be more inclined to pray and serve God our creator for the salvation of her soul and of her late relatives and friends, and for all others."[2] This phrase, granted, is a formula which does not disclose the Pirches' inner thoughts. It tells us, rather, what they were expected to think. Only after Jehanne's religious obligations to her family have been stated does the contract note that the pension would also help provide for the material necessities. Prudent families often sent a girl to a convent to avoid the expense of dowering her. Pious families, it would seem, regarded the daughter who became a nun as a spiritual asset.

The quest for prayer extended far beyond the immediate family. In 1532 Claude Berthier, bourgeois of Troyes, Nicole Dorigny, his curate at St. John's parish, and Odard Hennequin, their bishop, together gave the parish 800 livres in order that the priest celebrating High Mass on Sundays and holidays turn to face the congregation, and ask them to say a Pater Noster and an Ave Maria for the three, Berthier's wife, their relatives, and all the parish dead.[3] Since the donors were of similar social origin, all members of prominent bourgeois families, their partnership in the endowment is not surprising. What merits our attention is a bishop felt the need for laymen's prayers. The captain (royal military officer) of the *bourg* of Chaource, south of Troyes, and his wife gave a window of the Passion to a rural church in 1512, with an inscription that began by citing their names and ended with 'pray God for them and for us all when we are gone.'[4] Emile Mâle, the superlative historian of art, was struck—and more than a little offended—by the concern of donors of stained glass, at the

---

[1] Biver, 31-32, fig. 16.

[2] AD (Archives départementales), Marne, 4 E 16694 (3 June 1538).

[3] A. Assier, *Comptes de la fabrique de l'église Saint-Jean* (Troyes, 1855), 44-45.

[4] Biver, 99, fig. 77.

end of the Middle Ages, to perpetuate their own memory. The only French inscription that he could consider "truly Christian" was in the village church of Montangon, northeast of Troyes : 'In 1533 men good but unknown had this window mounted; it concerns them not to name here their names, but God knows them.'[1] Surely most people in Champagne would have considered such anonymity flippant rather than modest, arrogant rather than pious, because it meant that the donors felt no need for religious aid from their fellow Christians, and implied that they might not give any in return.

The town crier of Troyes who walked the streets from midnight to two in the morning, announcing "Wake up, wake up, you who sleep, and pray God for the souls of the dead, whom he wants to forgive," typified an era.[2] His words conveyed the intense concern of Christians for the souls agonizing in purgatory, as well as the great opportunity they sensed, and responsibility they felt, to abridge this suffering. No wonder people bought indulgences so freely, both in the parish church and from monks traveling with a relic belonging to their abbey.[3] Hucksters could make extravagant claims for the efficacy of their relics, in sixteenth-century Europe, only because laymen wanted very much to hear about and believe in the ease of release from purgatory. Advertising always depends upon a tacit understanding between buyer and seller. The line between orthodox opinion and abuse was very fine, moreover, until the Council of Trent. A sixteenth-century window in honor of the Eucharist at St. Alpin's parish church of Châlons shows a priest celebrating mass, while the small, nude figure of a soul ascends from the furnace of purgatory to be wrapped by an angel in a white robe.[4]

---

[1] *L'art religieux à la fin du moyen âge*, 5th ed. (Paris, 1949), 190.

[2] Théophile Boutiot, *Histoire de la ville de Troyes et de la Champagne méridionale* (Paris, 1870-1880), III, 237, based on the municipal accountbooks from 1505 to 1579, and verified by me for 1563-64 : AC (Archives communales), Troyes, C 182.

[3] At Chaource, for example, at the beginning of the century the parish church offered a pardon in St. John the Baptist's name several times a year : AD Aube, 108 G 5, cahier 1 (1512-13), fol. 1. The ledger-book of the fabric of the Cathedral of Troyes for 1501-02 lists payments by 14 monasteries and other institutions for the right to offer indulgences in the diocese : AD Aube, G 1573, fol. 11v. The provincial Council of Reims decided (without success) in 1564 to banish outside vendors of indulgences, indicating that the practice was still widespread : Dom G. Marlot, *Histoire de la ville, cité et université de Reims*, 1st ed. from the original seventeenth-century French MS. (Reims, 1843), III, 370-372, citing documents since lost or destroyed.

[4] Abbé Etienne Hurault, *Les vitraux anciens de l'église Saint-Alpin à Châlons-sur-Marne* (Paris, n.d.), 8.

The importance that most men and women attached to their own funerals helps to show that Catholicism at the end of the Middle Ages was in large part a cult of the living in the service of the dead. A testator envisioned his "obsequies, services and funerals" as he dictated his will; the prolixity of the formula suggests the elaborateness of these proceedings, which mobilized the spiritual resources of the community in the defence of the individual soul.[1]

Damoiselle Guillemette Coquillart, wife of an attorney of Reims, projected in 1542 what may have been the most elaborate funeral for a lay, private person in sixteenth-century Champagne. Her testament, by defining the limits which fervent piety and a full purse could reach, will serve as a foil for the rest. The notary found the lady, as his formula states, "dressed in her clothes, speaking with ease, going and coming"—in other words, well, and not in the immediate shadow of death. Like all testators, nevertheless, "Thinking of sovereign matters, considering that nothing is more certain than death nor more uncertain than its hour, and not wanting to be deceased from this world intestate, wanting rather to provide for the salvation of her soul, she has made this testament and ordonnance of last will and by it disposed of the goods that God has lent her, in the manner that follows."[2]

She ordered, for the day of her death, if possible, vigils at St. Peter's, her parish, and then a high mass, the *grande recommandise* or full set of prayers for the commendation of her soul, and thirty low requiem masses. Her husband and brother, meanwhile, whom she named as executors, were to distribute two *poissons* of wine and eight *setiers* of rye to the poor at their discretion, but as soon after her death as they could.

On the day of her burial, the clergy of St. Peter's, not only the six canons but "all the other priests who constantly frequent the said church," as another, more precise, testatrix stated,[3] together with those of St. James' parish, would conduct the body from her home to church, and aid in chanting the appropriate psalms along the way. The four mendicant orders at Reims—Franciscans, Dominicans, Augustinians and Carmelites—were to join the convoy. Two two-pound

---

[1] The phrase appears in AD Marne, 4 E 272 (15 January 1537), and 4 E 16704 (19 November 1549).

[2] AD Marne, 4 E 16670, 1541-42, fol. 49-53 (10 May 1542). She was the wife of Hon. Homme et saige Maistre P. Petit licen en loix advocat dem. a Reims.

[3] Nicole Coquebert, widow of Nicolas Forest, merchant of Reims, whose will in other respects is similar to the one we are considering. AD Marne, 4 E 278* (5 February 1550).

torches, carried by young novice friars, would flank each of the processional crosses of the six churches. Adult friars, one from each order, would march at the sides of the bier, holding an edge of the cloth that covered it in one hand, and a candle in the other.

Damoiselle Coquillart "wanted and ordered" burial in the chapel of St. Peter's Confraternity in the parish church. The chapel served as a family burial place, since her mother's remains already lay there, and her sister-in-law had also selected it.[1] For the day after her burial our testatrix requested three masses of the Trinity, five low masses in honor of the wounds of Christ, and a high mass of Notre Dame. She asked that her "principal service" be held on the next Sunday, if possible, with all six of St. Peter's canons participating in the vigils, the usual three high masses—of the Holy Spirit, Notre Dame and Requiem —the *grande recommandise*, and thirty low masses. The laymen would receive 4 sols, the women 3, and the canons 2 sols, 6 deniers. Thirteen poor people—a number symbolizing God and the twelve apostles, as another testator pointed out [2]—were also to be present. They would each offer a candle and be given 2 sols.

From the day following her death, a daily low mass would be said at St. Peter's for a year's duration, for the remedy of her soul, and those of her late relatives and friends. After each mass the priest would recite Psalm 129, the *de profundis*, while standing on her grave. She ordered one high and thirty low requiem masses for the "anniversary and end of the year," which was to be observed on the day after her principal service, or as soon thereafter as feasible. An identical service would be performed at St. James's, and other, varying, services held at the four mendicant orders, the Hôtel-Dieu (a hospital and home for the poor), and the Church of Hernonville, north of Reims, where her daughter was a nun. She instructed, finally, the officers of the eleven confraternities outside her own parish to which she belonged "to do their duty towards her soul"—in other words to hold a service.

No doubt some of the Rémois who knew the Damoiselle Coquillart considered her a bigot, to use a term then in vogue for those who practiced their religion incessantly, but other testaments differ from

---

[1] Jehanne, widow of the Hon. Jehan Coquillart, was the sister-in-law. AD Marne, 4 E 16692 (21 June 1536).

[2] Pierre Pirche, merchant of Reims. AD Marne, 4 E 16696 (5 February 1550).

hers in degree rather then in kind.[1] Our 157 wills from Reims for the years 1525 to 1552 include men and women from the families of artisans, merchants, legal practitioners, bourgeois landlords, *anoblis* or men in the process of becoming noble, canons of the cathedral and collegial churches, as well as laboureurs or prosperous peasants, vinegrowers, and their wives from villages in the region. About half of the resident testators invited all four mendicant orders. Three people besides Damoiselle Coquillart asked that novice friars, who obviously represented innocence, carry the lights.[2] Pierre Natier, one of these testators, not only wanted four novices around his bier, but also thirteen little children in the procession, each holding a small pot of incense and a candle.

During the sixteenth century, the friars were the butt of satire—a weapon which is only directed against men and institutions that enjoy at least some, and usually much, popular credit. Their invitation to funerals is our first indication that they continued to serve the religious needs of a good number of the Catholics of Champagne.

Testators did not slight the secular clergy for the friars. They invited, if they could, a phalanx of priests in order to multiply the number of prayers. In rural churches this was a common practice for testators of mark or means. Dame Jacquelyne de Laignes, widow of the captain of Chaource, ordered "thirteen psalms by thirteen priests" around her body on the day of death, and left 3 sols "to each priest, up to the number of fifty, who will say a mass in her intention."[3] It would seem that a similar offer at Reims might convoke a synod of the ragamuffin clergy, but five residents of the city extended the invitation.[4] In 1574, to introduce a piece of later evidence that illuminates this subject, Damoiselle Claude Godet, widow of an *échevin* (municipal magistrate) of Châlons, wanted "to be paid on the day of

---

[1] A "bigotte," depicted with her hands joined in prayer, is among the figures in a dance of drath that appears in *Les presentes heures a lusage de Châlons* (Paris, 1512), sig. il.

[2] Jehanne, wife of Didier Clermont, carter : AD Marne, 4 E 16692 (26 March 1533); Nicolas Goujon, escuyer, seneschal of Reims and seigneur of Tours-sur-Marne : 4 E 16707 (5 January 1552); Pierre Natier : *ibid*. (7 October 1552).

[3] AD Aube, 108 G 29 (30 September 1527).

[4] Damoiselle Margueritte Cuissotte, wife of Thierry de lospital, escuyer, seigneur of Casel ?, AD Marne, 4 E 16695 (16 April 1539); Barbe Fort, wife of Hon. Nicolas Chiertemps, 4 E 16700 (11 August 1545); Nicolas Ribaille, *ibid*. (17 August 1545), Nicole Coquebert, n. 22, and Nicolas Goujon, n. 26, above.

her said burial all the masses that will present themselves," a rather contemptuous if revealing phrase which stresses the task at hand and slights the men who would perform it.[1] Well-off artisans and peasants, who had to be more prudent, stipulated a specific number of masses. Baudinet Bonhomme, *pothier d'estain* (pewterer) of Reims, wanted ten for his first and third services, and twenty for the principal one.[2]

To serve these needs the secular clergy had to be numerous. It was not limited to the holders of benefices, who were supported by endowed property. Rather it included "the stipended habitués who continually serve *in divinis* or who are necessarily required [in a particular church] to perform the divine service ..."[3] Mary Magdalene's parish of Troyes had twenty of them in 1549.[4] But even the habitués were insufficient in number to meet the laypeople's periodic but insistent religious needs. This task fell to the clerical supernumeraries "... who are not stipended but who frequent it [the church] and go to the divine service performed there when it suits them, without constraint."[5] In practice the laity, and priests of means acting as individuals, provided much if not most of the work for these day laborers, in the form of funeral processions, anniversary masses, and as we shall later see, confraternity festivals.

The demand for numbers precluded highly selective standards for the recruitment of the clergy. Many testators insisted that every priest who participated in their funeral be dressed "in a decent garb," for fear that shabby-looking clerics would mar the solemnity of the occasion, and cast a shadow on the social importance of the deceased. Only two, however, made specific reference to the qualities they wanted in a priest. Monseigneur Charles de Roye, who was a great lord of France as well as the count of Roucy, a village northeast of Reims, directed in 1543 that his masses be said "by churchmen of good and honest life, whom his heirs and successors will elect." Perhaps only a man of exalted estate could hope that such a demand might be met. Canon Nicole Moyen of Reims was more realistic. He asked in 1546

---

[1] She was the widow of Noble Homme Jacques Godier, AD Marne 4 E 6366 (15 May 1574).

[2] AD Marne, 4 E 16707 (23 June 1552).

[3] AD Aube, 10 G layette, carton 2 (20 October 1507). Bishop Jacques Raguier of Troyes, as plaintiff against St. Urban's Collegial Church, in a case of disputed authority over a member of the *familia* of one of St. Urban's churchwardens.

[4] AD Aube, G 1345, fol. 110, cited by J. Roserot de Melin, *Antonio Caracciolo, évêque de Troyes (1515-1570)* (Paris, 1923), 177.

[5] AD Aube, 10 G layette, *loc. cit.*

that the two hundred masses he commissioned be said "by churchmen not suspect of bad life, if possible."[1] The personal failings of the clergy were not, however, of crucial importance to a people who expected ritual action rather than moral example or intellectual leadership from their priests. Humanists like Thomas More, who envisioned a utopia staffed "by priests of exceeding holiness, and therefore very few," had an entirely different conception of clerical function in mind.[2]

Not all testators were scrupulously concerned about their funerals. Maistre Garlache Sonyn, *enquesteur* or investigator for the king at his court in Reims, wanted "burial in whatever church seemed good to [his wife] Damoiselle Marie Sollet, and that to it be convoked and called whatever priests and other persons, and also be carried so many and such torches for the reverence of the crosses that will be there, and that for the remedy and salvation of his soul so many and such services, prayers and orisons that will seem good to his wife, praying and calling upon her to do her duty in this as she would wish the said testator do for her in a similar one."[3] A noticeable but not substantial minority of Rémois testators used variations on this formula.[4] They chose a means of expression which gently masked their disinterest while it saved the appearances, explicitly recognizing and paying proper lip service to the norms of the community. One exceptional case by a man calling himself Catholic classes the others as conventional. In 1556 the *anobli* Denis Grossame asked his brother to do his duty in having services performed, but stated that he intended no "solemnity" during his burial, and only a small lantern and a candle for light.[5]

Unlike Garlache Sonyn, who slurred over the saints in his will, traditional Catholics were careful to pay them due homage. In general they approached these exemplars of humanity in the same way that

---

[1] Roye was related, through the marriage of one of his daughters, to Anne de Montmorency, constable of France. AD Marne, 4 E 16698 (22 August 1543). Canon Moyen : 4 E 16701 (4 August 1546).

[2] *Utopia*, ed. Edward Surtz, S. J. and J. H. Hexter, in *The Complete Works of St. Thomas More* (New Haven, 1965), IV, 226-227.

[3] Hon. Homme et saige Mᵉ Garlache Sonyn licencie en loix enquesteur pour le roy au siège de Reims. AD Marne, 4 E 16704 (24 December 1549).

[4] 20 of the 157 wills leave at least a major portion of the rites to the discretion of executors. But precise quantitative statements from sixteenth-century notarial archives are apt to be misleading because one never knows to what degree the clientele of a notary whose records have survived is representative of the whole.

[5] Noble et scientifique personne Maistre Denis Grossame licencie en loix seigneur dyrnal et vendeul. AD Marne, 4 E 16671 (29 January 1556).

poor people approached their betters : by offering prayer in exchange for patronage and favor. The saints' superabundance of merit enabled them to intercede with God for the living and the dead, and filled the treasury from which the pope drew indulgences—a classic case of the strong carrying the weak.

A person's Christian name governed his initial allegiance. The choice depended most often, not on the parents' preferences, but on the names of the sponsors at baptism, one of whom passed down his saint to the infant. For the first-born, ideally, the godparents were a set of grandparents. Jehan Pussot, carpenter of Reims, recorded in 1570 that his eldest daughter "was named Perette, by my father[-in-law] Pierre Pinchart and his wife." Twenty-one years later Pussot and his wife sponsored Perette's eldest, Jehan.[1] This practice emphasized continuity within the family. It also permitted a Catholic to consider the saint as a more distant but more powerful godparent—and even to address him as such. Claude Enfer, merchant of Chaource, invoked "Monsieur St. Claude, my godfather," in his will.[2]

The surviving evidence does not make clear what responsibilities human godparents undertook. Testators often left small sums of money to godchildren; clerics complained, as was their wont, that godparents neglected their religious duties. Canon Gentien Hervet, in his catechism for the diocese of Reims, berated them for considering their obligations fulfilled once they had charged the parents with teaching the child his beliefs—a criticism which suggests that godparents were not totally unconcerned.[3]

What men and women expected of their saintly godparents, on the other hand, is very clear indeed. At Ervy a stained-glass baptism of Christ, dated 1510, includes the window's donor, drawn to half the scale of the Biblical figures, in the lower left-hand corner. An elderly person, he kneels like all donors before a prayer bench, his hands piously joined. Three even smaller figures, his adult sons, kneel behind him. Next to them stands a massive and majestic St. James, the donor's name-saint, who visually dominates and visibly protects the group. The saint has his hand on the old man's shoulder, and his eye

---

[1] Jehan Pussot, "Journalier ou mémoires," *Travaux de l'Académie de Reims*, XXIII, No. 1 (1855-1856), 154; XXV, No. 1 (1856-1857), 15.

[2] AD Aube, 108 G 29 (29 May 1557).

[3] *Catechisme et ample instruction de tout ce qui appartient au devoir d'un chrestien ...* (Paris, 1568), 9.

on someone in front and above him whom the window does not show. In the corresponding panel on the right, St. Anne presents the donor's wife to the unseen figure, while the woman's five daughters look on.[1]

This pattern recurs throughout Champagne, and continues until the religious wars put a stop to window-making.[2] In other provinces Emile Mâle found more complete illustrations, which identify the unseen figure as the Madonna with the Christ Child in her arms. She is a middle link in the chain of prayer that leads from man to God.[3] The essential function of the name-saint, then, was to protect his dependents beyond the grave, and to intercede for them with the powers above. For this reason, donors who died after commissioning a window, but before it was completed, were nevertheless shown with their saint.[4]

I have found no contemporary evidence, however, to justify Mâle's calling the name-saint a patron.[5] This term was reserved to the responsibilities of saints to groups, as opposed to individuals. The merchant Claude Enfer distinguished between "Monsieur St. Jacques my patron," to whom the parish church of Chaource was dedicated, and "Monsieur St. Claude my godfather."[6] The Church of Nogent-sur-Seine was named for St. Laurence, whom the priest Claude Haton identified as the "patron and godfather" of one Laurent Gravier.[7] Men and women, in their wills, were much more likely to commend their soul to the parish patron than to their name-saint. Half the testators of Reims did so, enough to indicate a common practice that stopped short of being a formula. By contrast only two Rémois, a chaplain in the cathedral and the pious nobleman Nicolas Goujon, invoked name-saints.[8] The difference between the will and the window was that the testator was appealing to the community for support immediately after his death, while the donor was thinking of the long run, when his neighbors and priests would themselves be gone, and the parish

---

[1] Biver, 156, fig. 156.

[2] For representative Champenois examples see Mâle, *L'art religieux*, 162, n. 1.

[3] *Ibid.*, 162-163.

[4] Three of the Cathedral of Troyes's nave windows, erected at the turn of the sixteenth century, furnish examples. Biver, 67-69, fig. 40; 71-72, fig. 42; and 73-75, fig. 44.

[5] *L'art religieux*, 167, and Ch. 5, passim.

[6] See *supra*, 154, n. 2.

[7] Claude Haton, *Mémoires* (Paris, 1857), I, 341.

[8] Discrette personne Messire Jehan Goirton prestre cure de Vendy? coustre clerc et chaplain de l'ancienne congregation de Notre-Dame de Reims. AD Marne, 4 E 16671* (7 July 1552); Goujon, n. 26.

patron's attention focused on other, living persons. Only the name-saint could offer permanent support. The window, as Mâle pointed out, would serve as a perpetual reminder to him.[1]

The intensity and joy with which parishioners celebrated the festival of their patron provides a further indication of his importance. The church-wardens of St. James in Troyes ordered the portal and treasure of the church covered with tapestries. They had the floor strewn with festive branches and leaves, and gave flowered hats to the girls who solicited donations for the vestry. A friar came to deliver a sermon, for this was one of the four holidays on which the vestry was obliged to pay a preacher.[2] After—and often during—Mass in church, it was time for play outside, which took the form of street dances, as indicated by the admonishment of the Cathedral Chapter of Troyes in 1599 to St. Aventin's parishioners to stop dancing while services were being held.[3] This secular aspect of the festival was as important as the religious side, for it gave men and women the opportunity to show conviviality toward one another while they honored the saint whose patronage they all shared.

In evil times Catholics appealed beyond their parish to the patrons of towns and regions. To quell a fire in 1530 the clergy of Troyes carried in procession the relics of three protectors of the diocese—those of St. Loup, located in the abbey of that name, who was credited with preserving Troyes from Attila, of the Cathedral's St. Helena, whose bones a thirteenth-century bishop had brought back from the sack of Constantinople, and of St. Hoylde, a Champenois virgin, of St. Stephen's Collegial Church.[4] The peasants of the surrounding countryside, during a severe drought twenty-six years later, marched village by village to the Cathedral of Troyes, in hopes that St. Mathie, another local virgin, whose relics were housed there, and St. Helena, would intercede with God for rain.[5]

Relics of the saints also served to cure personal ills. One layer of sixteenth-century Champagne's religious topography was a fine mesh of pilgrimage sites. Residents of Reims had a healing saint within a

---

[1] *L'art religieux*, 162.

[2] AD Aube, 14 G 16-14 G 54.

[3] AD Aube, G 1292, fol. 218 (27 January 1599).

[4] Marie-Joseph Des Guerrois, *La sainctete chrestienne ... au diocese et ville de Troyes ...* (Troyes, 1637), 419.

[5] Nicolas Pithou, *Histoire ecclésiastique* (see 145, n. 2), fol. 88[r]; Haton, I, 31.

few miles, at St. Brice's village church on the plain. Or they could climb to the point where the vineyard-clad "Mountain of Reims" approaches the city most closely and faces it most directly, to reach St. Lie's relics, in his chapel near the market village of Ville-Dommange. The bones of St. Fery, at the Church of Verneuil-sur-Aisne, were twenty-six miles away, almost a full day's journey west. St. Bertaud's Abbey was north and a bit east of Reims, thirty-seven miles across the plain. He at least was known to history. Fifteenth-century popes, for the purpose of rebuilding the hospital attached to the abbey, had granted indulgences to his pilgrims. Paul II, issuing one of them in 1466, noted that innumerable poor, sick and especially mad people *(phreneticos)* were the saint's clients.[1] To the south lay the relics of St. Peter's Abbey in Avenay, where the Mountain faces the Marne, and those of St. Radegonde, at the Church of Mareuil-sur-Ay in the valley below, and of St. Gond, at his abbey in the marshes at the foot of the Mountain of Vertus. Beyond the province, Rémois went to St. Claude in Franche-Comté, known for his help to the crippled and the maimed, and to St. Fiacre, near Meaux in Brie, who aided those afflicted with hemorrhoids and other rectal complaints.[2]

These shrines and others are identified for us by the instructions of fifteen female testators and three males, that either palmers or relatives make the pilgrimages which they themselves had vowed but could not hope to accomplish.[3] By sending another they would be "discharged towards God and the Blessed Saint," as Damoiselle Coquillart phrased it, after citing her promise to St. Claude. Our list, of course, only suggests the density of the network. Village priests, in response to a bishop's questionnaire of 1727, reported many more shrines, while noting that a good portion of them no longer attracted anyone.[4]

---

[1] *Acta sanctorum* (Antwerp, 1643 f). Reprint (Brussels, 1865-1970), 16-19 June, 100-102.

[2] The curative functions of the saints, as well as the regions in which they were venerated, are catalogued in Louis Réau's masterful and comprehensive *Iconographie des saints*, Pt. III of his *Iconographie de l'art chrétien* (Paris, 1955-1959). See also Paul Pedrizet, *Le calendrier parisien à la fin du moyen âge* (Paris, 1933).

[3] For documentation see my unpubl. diss. (Berkeley, 1971), *Change without Reformation : Religious Practice and Belief in Sixteenth-Century Champagne*, 70-71, n. 28.

[4] A. Poulin, "Les pèlerinages du diocèse de Reims à la fin de l'ancien régime," *Nouvelle revue de Champagne et Brie*, X (1932), 152-185, and his *Les pèlerinages du diocèse de Reims* (Charleville, 1927).

Sixteenth-century ecclesiastical visitations, which could have had much more to report, are mute on the subject.[1]

The eighteenth-century priests, as professionals, were quite specific on what ills a given saint could cure. It would be difficult to establish, however, the degree to which sixteenth-century laypeople had a clear understanding of the division of labor among the locally known healing saints. Their reputation, especially when it was not buttressed by indulgences, depended on the word-of-mouth advertising that followed successful cures. Then, too, time, money, and the desire—or disinclination—to travel were important criteria in choosing among shrines.

Peasants threatened by agricultural crises, as we noted a moment ago, sought aid from the saints in town. City dwellers, we now know, went to the countryside for relief from individual problems. The principle of reciprocity once again appears as a crucial element in sixteenth-century religion.

In the person of the Virgin, all the attributes of the saints were united. Every testator invoked her by formula, as "the glorious Virgin Mary," but some were more precise and more intimate. To the squire Nicolas Goujon, who used the chivalric idiom, she was "his well-beloved mother Mary dame and mistress."[2] More simply, Adam Maure, merchant of Bar-sur-Aube, addressed her as "the glorious Virgin Mary his mother."[3] Another merchant, Robert Gillet of Reims, explained in 1569 the theological basis for this parentage by recommending his soul "to the suffrages and saintly prayer of the glorious Virgin Mary Mother of God and of all the saints of paradise."[4] But even if a Christian could not be certain of an immediate welcome to the community of saints on high, he could have faith that Mary's gentle hand would guide him through purgatory and toward that ultimate goal.

The Virgin was also the patron of churches, not merely of cathedrals like Notre-Dame de Reims and collegial churches like Notre-Dame en Vaux of Châlons, but of simple villages like Pont-Sainte-Marie outside of Troyes, which celebrated its annual festival with gusto on Assumption Day.[5] Marian shrines did not require relics to draw the faithful.

---

[1] Neither AD Marne, G 254 (Reims depot), Visitations of the Doyenné de la montagne, nor G 286, of the Doyenné of Epernay, mention pilgrimages.

[2] AD Marne, 4 E 16707 (5 January 1552).

[3] AD Aube, 330 G 6 (24 July 1530).

[4] AD Marne, 4 E 16749 (19 May 1569).

[5] Pithou, *Histoire ecclésiastique*, fol. 318r.

The churches of Notre-Dame de l'Épine, outside of Châlons, and of Notre-Dame de Liesse, a day's ride from Reims to the Laonnais in Picardy, enjoyed a national reputation.[1] While the peasants around Troyes were marching to the city's cathedral in 1556, those further down the Seine Valley went to the Belle-Dame of Nogent-sur-Seine, a miracle-working statue around which a chapel had been built.[2] The village church of Notre-Dame de Voulton, near Provins in the same region, attracted worshippers from the Brie champenoise.[3] A company of men who had gone on pilgrimage to the Holy Land in 1532 made their last stop of the return trip at Voulton, fulfilling a vow.[4] Last but hardly least, everywhere small statues of the Madonna, in building niches and on street corners, were venerated by neighbors. A Notre-Dame de pitié stood at the end of an alley of Troyes. According to Nicolas Pithou, who may have exaggerated in order to explain its desecration by iconoclasts in 1561, the statue was ordinarily dressed in silk clothes. Especially on Sundays, a lamp burned before it. "Great and enormous idolatries were committed there daily."[5] Truly every Catholic was a ward of the Virgin.

Catholics had the opportunity to demonstrate their loyalty to the Virgin and the saints by belonging to confraternities. These were voluntary associations of men and women, under the patronage of a specific devotion, which met at a particular church. The surviving records suggest that every village church, no matter how small, had at least one such group. In some rural and all urban parishes, there were several, offering a wide choice of devotions to honor. Each met at a specific altar, often in its own chapel. Though clerics might join, the pious confraternity was essentially a laypeople's association, whose members elected their officers from among themselves. It was distinct from the guild confraternities of artisans or professional men, in which membership was compulsory. Here the religious unity reinforced a solidarity that already existed at the same time that it placed the members under the protection of the patron saint of their craft.

---

[1] R. Mandrou, *Introduction à la France moderne (1500-1640)* (Paris, 1961), 285.

[2] Haton, *Mémoires*, I, 31.

[3] *Ibid.*, II, 820-821; André Richard, *La Belle Dame de Nogent-sur-Seine* (Nogent, 1843).

[4] Denis Possot, *Tresample et Abondante description du Voyiage en la terre sainte dernierement commence lan de grace mil cinq cens trente deux ... depuis la ville de Nogeant sur Seine jusques a la saincte cite de Hierusalem ...* (Paris, 1536), sig. Pi.

[5] *Histoire ecclésiastique*, fol. 168.

Occasionally an urban pious confraternity was important enough to attract people from the town as a whole. St. Remy's was but a modest parish of Troyes, yet its Confraternity of the Cross had 337 members in 1555.[1] By way of rough comparison, only 68 people participated in the parish's most important local confraternity in 1517, that of the patron, St. Remy himself (for this and subsequent references to the confraternities of Troyes, see Table 1). At nearby St. James's,

Table 1

Confraternity Membership at Three Parishes of Troyes

	St. Remy's Parish 1517 AD Aube, 20 G 6		St. James' Parish 1503 AD Aube, 14 G 16		Mary Magdalene's Parish, 1521 AD Aube, 16 G 50	
Jan.	St. Maur	24	St. Maur	19	St. Maur	57
	St. Sebastian	13	St. Sebastian	10	St. Sebastian	64
Feb.					St. Blaise	114
March			Annunciation	25		
April					Translation of Magdalene's relics :	72
May	St. Avoie	36				
June			St. Claude	14	St. Claude	43
					St. Syre	22
			Holy Sacrament	22	Holy Sacrament	89
July			St. James	40		
					St. Anne	26
August					Assumption	95
			St. Roche	22	St. Roche	52
					St. Fiacre	50
Sept.					St. Michael	17
					St. Ursula	5
Oct.	St. Remy	68				
					St. Loup	18
Nov.			St. Andrew	6		
Dec.	St. Barbara	13			St. Barbara	43
			Immaculate Conception :	34	Immaculate Conception :	125

during the first three decades of the century, the patron's was the best attended confraternity. Mary Magdalene's parish was larger and more affluent, and the number of confraternities greater. Here the

---

[1] AD Aube, 20 G 135.

patron occupies a quite respectable, but by no means a commanding, position.

An entire group of confraternities was dedicated to the mysteries of the Virgin's life. For more than two hundred years the mendicant orders had been propagating her cult. Pope Urban VI established, and the Council of Basel in 1441 confirmed, the Visitation as a festival day. The Franciscan Sixtus IV (1471-84) promoted the doctrine of her Immaculate Conception. The Annunciation, during the same period, emerged from semi-oblivion to an important place in the festival cycle.[1] Each of these devotions, as well as that of the Virgin's mother, St. Anne, was honored by numerous confraternities in Champagne.

Despite this emphasis on the Virgin and the patron saints, the confraternity as an institution did not necessarily deflect Christians from the direct contemplation and worship of Christ. Those honoring his mysteries were among the most popular in Champagne. The drawing power of the Confraternity of the Cross is a case in point. Nicolas Pithou mentions a confraternity of the Name of Jesus at the Hospital St. Bernard. It brought in so much revenue, according to him, that the guardian of the Franciscans founded a similar one in order to fill his own coffers, too.[2] Confraternities of the Holy Sacrament for Corpus Christi Day, moreover, commonly existed in rural as well as urban parishes.

Together these three types—patron, Virgin, Savior and Holy Sacrament, comprised about one-half of the confraternities at urban parishes. Almost all the rest were devoted to the healing saints, like Maur, who was invoked by those with gout and rheumatic disease; Edmund, by pregnant women; and Sebastian and Roche, by those who feared the plague.

A few confraternities were dedicated to saints who were neither parish patrons nor directly linked to the cure of physical ills. The most important was St. Barbara, to whom one prayed to avoid a sudden death, which would prevent him from receiving extreme unction. The Augustinians of Reims maintained a confraternity in honor of St. Nicholas of Tolentino, the protector of souls in purgatory.[3]

---

[1] E. Delaruelle, E.-R. Labande et Paul Ourliac, *L'église au temps du grand schisme et de la crise conciliare (1378-1449)* (Paris, 1964), II, 777-779; Pedrizet, *Le calendrier parisien*, 113-114.

[2] *Histoire ecclésiastique*, fol. 39.

[3] Marlot, *Histoire de ... Reims*, IV, 29, and pièce justicative No. XI, 616.

In general, the friars of Champagne were particularly active and successful in promoting confraternities at their monasteries. Our discussion will not give them due credit, since the surviving sixteenth-century confraternity records come almost exclusively from the parish and collegial churches of Troyes and southern Champagne. But the wills from Reims remind us of the importance of the mendicant orders. To cite a striking, if belated, example from 1581, the merchant Nicolas Frizon patronized confraternities at all four orders : St. Barbara's at the Franciscans, St. Nicholas of Tolentino's at the Augustinians, the Trinity at the Dominicans, and the Assumption and the Holy Sacrament at the Carmelites.[1]

Regardless of what devotion it honored or where it met, festivals and funerals were the business of the pious confraternity. It celebrated its saint's day or other holiday to a greater degree than the ordinary ceremonies of the church provided. For the festival, members purchased a candle from the officers, at their desk in the church. They designated one of their number, either in turn or by auction, for the honor of guarding the baton, or ceremonial staff, during the year to come. He or she was expected to make a special offering to the confraternity. All the members, carrying their candles and accompanied by the torches of the confraternity, conducted the new *bâtonnier*, in procession, to his house to deposit the staff. They returned to the church for the celebration of a high mass. On the following day Requiem Mass was sung for the benefit of the souls of deceased members.

This was the simplest pattern, but one that was frequently embellished. Several confraternities commissioned sermons at their churches for the Sunday before the festival.[2] The Confraternity of the Cross preferred to hear its preachers in the open air, in front of an imposing calvary on the main square of Troyes known as the Beautiful Cross.

The processions, too, could become elaborate affairs. The lower panels of a stained-glass window given by the Holy Sacrament Confraternity of St. Alpin's parish of Châlons to the church depict twelve members acting out the Last Supper. They receive communion from a priest, as the apostles received it from Christ. In the next panel their costumes are visible. Dressed as the apostles they march behind a dais sheltering the Holy Sacrament. The window dates from the beginning of the

---

[1] AD Marne, 4 E 16749 (10 February 1581).

[2] For example, St. Gibrian's Confraternity at St. Remy's Abbey, Reims. AD Marne (Reims depot), H 1308, fol. 12 (1546).

sixteenth century; the twelve were in the vanguard of the confraternity's actual procession on Corpus Christi Day. As the inscription on the window said :

DOUZE CONFRERES GENS DE BIEN	EN CESTE EGLISE ET EN CE LIEU
EN DOUZE APOSTRES REVESTUS	DOUZE HOMMES EN LA PROCESSION
SONT ACCOUSTRES PAR BON MOIEN	LE JOUR DIST DE LA FETE DIEU
POUR DECORER LE DOULX JHESUS	DENOTENT L'IMITACION [1]

The requiem mass, performed the next day, could take on major proportions. The Holy Sacrament Confraternity of Chaource paid forty-three priests to say Mass in 1521, and thirty the next year.[2] Thirty-four, including several canons who were members, officiated at the confraternity of the same name at St. Urban's Collegial Church of Troyes.[3]

In rural churches, a confraternity may have participated rather extensively in the ordinary responsibilities of the parish, and have been more an adjunct of the vestry than a wholly separate entity. At the village of Courtauld each testator who mentioned the confraternities in his will left a sum to be divided among all of them at the parish, without mentioning any by name.[4] It may well have been common practice here for the pious parishioner of means to belong as a matter of course to every confraternity—or at least to have them all participate in his funeral. A ledger from Pel lists some twenty-seven confraternities; by "confraternity," these villagers must have understood the celebration of a holiday in the accustomed way.[5]

Confraternities also played an important part in the permanent decoration of the church. Occupational confraternities often, perhaps commonly, commissioned an image of their patron. The vine-growers

---

[1] The inscription, lost during the restoration of the window, is quoted by E. Hurault, *Les vitraux anciens*, 7. See also Mâle, *L'art religieux*, 177-178.

[2] AD Aube, 108 G 45.

[3] AD Aube, 10 G 757[4], Cahier No. 4, fol. 11.

[4] AD Aube, 139 G 5.

[5] AD Aube, 307 G 2.

honored St. Vincent, whose name was similar to their own. Those of
the village of Creney offered a window in his honor; at Bouilly they
placed a statue of the saint in the confraternity's own chapel.[1] The
goldsmiths of Troyes, who met at Mary Magdalene's parish, told the
legend of St. Eloy in their window—the saint had been a goldsmith
himself. The inscription below expressed their desire "to obtain remission of their sins and full grace ... and that the peace of God be
given for this good deed, in paradise."[2] Their claims on plenary grace
may seem presumptuous; one suspects that, in decorating its chapel,
the typical urban professional confraternity was acting out of mixed
motives. For the guild was demonstrating its piety—and civic spirit
and wealth, too—not merely to its patron and to God, but to the other
guilds and the town as a whole. This was one of the ways in which
it could hope to maintain or increase the prestige of its members as
individuals, and the part they might play, as a group, vis-à-vis the
other guilds, in municipal affairs.

Pious confraternities were even more important as donors than the
guilds. Mâle was prepared to conjecture that any otherwise unattri-
buted stained-glass window had been donated by one of them.[3] They
were, clearly, one of the most important patrons of late medieval art.
I have already referred to the lower panels of the Holy Sacrament
window at St. Alpin's Church in Châlons, which portrayed twelve of
the confraternity members as apostles. The window as a whole is in
honor of the Eucharist. Its upper panels depict, first, the Hebrews
receiving manna in the desert. "By manna," an inscription informs
the faithful, "is signified St. Jesus our Savior; by means of his purified
blood, all salvation rests in him alone." The second panel is a representation of the Last Supper.[4] At the Cathedral of Troyes, St. Sebastian's Confraternity took on the major task of subsidizing one of the
nave windows, which was being erected at the turn of the sixteenth
century. In twenty-four panels, the window recounts the saint's legend.
Below, in the triforium, a second set of panels shows a crowd of men
and women, identified as the members by an inscription reading,

---

[1] Creney : Male, 171. Bouilly : Société française d'archéologie, *Congrès archéologique.* 113e session, Troyes, 1955 (Orléans, 1957), 386.

[2] Mâle, 171.

[3] *Ibid.,* 176.

[4] See *supra,* 163, n. 1.

"The Confraternity of St. Sebastian gave this window in the year of 1501. May God keep them."[1]

It is important to ask what sort of people were likely to belong to a pious confraternity. Was participation widespread, or was it limited —either to a small elite of the devout, or, perhaps, to specific social groups? The membership lists from St. James's parish of Troyes show that half the participants in 1526 belonged to but one of the nine confraternities of the church. At the other extreme, a handful of people joined several. They were ultra-devout, a small minority of the whole. This information cuts two ways. Not many persons in the parish took the trouble to show their special respect to several devotions (though enough to indicate that it was not considered bad form to do so). But if the number of frequent participants, of "goers," was limited, then confraternity membership was that much more widespread. It encompassed a greater part of the community than would have been true otherwise, had the confraternities been composed merely of a small knot of people accustomed to seeing one another from festival to festival.

Table 2

Frequency of Participation in the Confraternities of St. James' Parish, Troyes, in 1526 (AD Aube, 14 G 18)

Total number of parishioners who joined confraternities	Number of confraternities they joined								
	1	2	3	4	5	6	7	8	9
93	46	14	17	4	3	3	-	3	3

Of course, some of those who belonged to but one or two confraternities at their own parish—or even none at all—participated at other churches. We have met the merchant Frizon, who favored the friars' confraternities of Reims. There was also our model testatrix, Damoiselle Coquillart. She was a member of the patron's confraternity at St. Peter's, her own parish, and would be buried in its chapel, beside her relatives. But she also instructed her executors to fulfill her financial obligations to eleven other confraternities at two other parish, and four mendicant, churches.

---

[1] Biver, 65-67, fig. 39.

The confraternity rolls of St. James's list artisans, too. Jehan Huon, saddler, was a member of the Confraternity of the Conception from 1525 to 1552.[1] Blaise Chantefoin, a glovemaker, took the baton of the Annunciation in 1554, and one Felizon, potter, joined St. Gond's in 1583.[2] This list could be lengthened, without telling us, however, what proportion of the total such men made up, for the occupations of only a few members are given.

One point can be made. Men and women met in a pious confraternity who did not meet elsewhere in the highly class-conscious sixteenth century. And they met, if I may use the term, as soul-brothers and sisters (confrères and consoeurs). There was an opportunity for human contact, for elbow rubbing, between the artisans on the one hand, and the rich merchants and *anoblis* on the other. Pierre Pion took a candle at St. Roche's rather regularly from 1525 to 1532.[3] An aspirant to the nobility, he had just built a chateau at the nearby village of Rumilly-les-Vaudes, which our group of pilgrims on their way to the Holy Land, a few years later, thought worthy of mention as a tourist attraction.[4] But we should not exaggerate the possibility of fraternization. At other churches, other confraternities, there was much less room for social diversity. The Confraternity of St. Gibrian at St. Remy's Monastery of Reims imposed a 35-sol entry fee.[5] At Chaource the Holy Sacrament Confraternity was entitled to the best robe of the deceased, which was then sold at auction, usually to the next of kin. An estate which did not contain a suitable robe paid in coin : a minimum of 1 livre in 1521.[6]

Emile Mâle's interest in the confraternities as patrons of art led him to comment on their more general significance. "Never had man been less isolated," he wrote with reference to the fourteenth and fifteenth centuries. "Divided into small groups, the faithful formed innumerable confraternities. It was always a saint who brought them together, for

---

[1] AD Aube, 14 G 18-14 G 20. His craft is identified in 14 G 21, fol. 26.

[2] Chantefoin : AD Aube, 14 G 26, fol. 20. Nicolas Pithou identifies his occupation, for Chantefoin, by 1556, "had some entry and knowledge into the true religion," *Histoire ecclésiastique*, fol. 95ʳ. Felizon : 14 G 37, fol. 6.

[3] AD Aube, 14 G 18-14 G 21. In the years for which we have records, 1525-1527, 1530 and 1532, he is absent only in 1527.

[4] *Congrès archéologique*, 300. Possot, *loc. cit.*

[5] AD Marne (Reims depot), H 1308 (1535-1536), fol. 2.

[6] AD Aube, 108 G 45.

the saints were then the bonds that united men."[1] But the principle of association extended far beyond the confraternity. Georges de Lagarde points to the cellular construction of society during this period. Both church and state were weak and disorganized, compelled to acquiesce in the partition of their authority if they were to govern at all. This was the age of the estates, not merely (and not mainly, in France), the representative assemblies, but "the social and political groups which shared the effective domination of a country."[2] The estates were mutually hostile, for as soon as one of them gained an advantage, it was challenged by another, which claimed a share in the newly won privileges and prerogatives.[3] Cities enjoyed a greater or lesser measure of autonomy; within them guilds jostled one another for position, but joined together to question the direction of municipal life by the upper crust of urban society. The villages in Western Europe strengthened their community organization. During the early stages of the long-term depression, they were forced to defend themselves against the expedients of their seigneurs, who were struggling for economic survival. If a seigneur became a rentier, after conceding defeat, then his peasants had to take a more active part in regulating their own affairs.[4] And what was true of secular society holds for the church. Pope and anti-pope hurled anathemas at one another, while they attempted to keep the conciliar movement at bay. Bishops defended themselves against their cathedral chapters, which resisted the pretensions of other collegial churches. Franciscans and Dominicans could not amicably divide the spoils they had won from the secular clergy.

To cap the argument, it is typical of times of depression, when men are preoccupied with security, for them to gather together in protective associations, rather than to act boldly as individuals, taking the greater risks that promise greater gains. Mercantilism, the conviction that there is only a limited amount of wealth (and power, and prestige), which

---

[1] *L'art religieux*, 167.

[2] "La structure politique et sociale de l'Europe au XIVe siècle," in *L'organisation corporative du moyen âge à la fin de l'ancien régime. Études presentés à la commission internationale pour l'histoire des assemblées d'états*, III (Louvain, 1939), 104.

[3] Lagarde, *La naissance de l'esprit laïque*, Vol. 1 (Saint-Paul-Trois-Châteaux, Vienna, 1934), Ch 7.

[4] L. Genicot, "Crisis : From the Middle Ages to Modern Times," *The Cambridge Economic History of Europe*, 2nd, ed., Vol. 1 (Cambridge, 1966), 733-734.

cannot be increased, but only wrested from the grasp of others, dominated the later Middle Ages.

In religious behavior, too, people leaned on one another, and joined
together. Robin Horton observes that "the relationships between
human beings and religious objects can be ... defined [in part] as
governed by certain ideas of patterning and obligation such as characterize relationships among human beings. In short, Religion can be
looked upon as an extension of the field of people's social relationships
beyond the confines of purely human society."[1] This meant that in
the later Middle Ages, access to the benefits that religion could offer,
whether in this world or the next, was only open to people if they
acted within and through small groups—the family, the confraternity,
the guild, the parish, the village or urban community. It also meant
that the fragmentation of political authority, and the interposition of
corporations as mediators between sovereign and subjects, clouded
men's understanding of divine power. For the never-ending tug of war
within both church and state made it difficult to know just how much
authority the ruler had relinquished. Under these circumstances, men
could not clearly perceive the relationships within the celestial hierarchy.[2] The great and unresolved religious question of the later Middle
Ages was the degree of responsibility and independent initiative that
God had devolved on the Virgin—and on the saints, those independent
power brokers in an age of bastard feudalism.

But were people satisfied with the religious efficacy of their petty
groups, particularly since they were well aware of the tremendous
hostility between the corporations into which they were organized?
Fifteenth- and sixteenth-century preachers were continually harping
on the characteristic vices of each estate. In theory they were encouraging their listeners to reform. In practice they were reflecting
the tensions that charged social relations.[3] Claude Haton observed,
with reference to the Franciscans and Dominicans, that "commonly
in people of an estate there is a certain envy which throws them one

---

[1] "A Definition of Religion, and Its Uses," *Journal of the Royal Anthropological
Institute*, XC (1960), 211.

[2] The concordance between the polity of a society and its conception of the supernatural is the brilliant starting point for what proves to be a disappointing book. Guy
Swanson, *Religion aud Regime* (Ann Arbor, 1967).

[3] See for example Claude Haton's recollections of the sermons delivered by a Dominican during the Lenten season of 1555 at Provins. *Mémoires*, I, 13.

against the other."[1] Surely people knew that the boons they asked for would be granted them only as Christians united in true fellowship.

The annual festival of Corpus Christi provided an opportunity to neutralize the animosities that made harmony so difficult to achieve. Human solidarity was the key note of Corpus Christi, the day on which people reaffirmed the unity of the groups to which they belonged. In cathedral towns the representatives of the clerical and lay corporations gathered to march in a general procession that wound through the city streets and culminated in a high mass at the cathedral. Then marchers from each parish began processions of their own. The church-wardens of Montreuil-sur-Barse, east of Troyes, noted in 1549 that the inhabitants followed "the good custom" of accompanying the Holy Sacrament to the end of the village.[2] They demarcated its limits, and so defined its territory, in the process.[3] "In every parish of Provins," wrote Claude Haton in his entry for 1570, for the Octave of Corpus Christi, "the residents organize a confraternity of the Holy Sacrament, to which, until this day, "they have shown a great devotion, faith and honor." After the processions, mass, and the family dinner, "the neighbors of each street and canton assemble, through their mutual friendship, up to twelve, fifteen or twenty, more or less, depending on the number of residents ... to play and take recreation together, men on one side, women on the other, each one with another. Some men play at bowls ... others obtain the meat for supper, which is prepared at the house of one of them, in which men and women join to sup, each paying his own way as at a tavern." Any newly married man or new arrival was required to pay the company for his welcome, according to his means—i.e., in order to be accepted by the neighborhood. Weather permitting, the tables were set up in the street, "in view of all the passers-by who want to watch, and by this means they maintain peace, concord and amity with one another, a matter to be truly praised, since at the said assemblies, the poor as well as the rich are received, if it pleases them to come." After supper the festivities took on an increasingly joyous tone, much to Haton's regret.[4]

---

[1] *Ibid.*, 12 ("... communément en gens d'un estat y a quelque envie qui court les ungs sur les aultres").

[2] AD Aube, 279 G 1, obiter dictum in the inventory, item 23.

[3] In his *conclusion générale*, A. Friedmann, *Paris, ses rues, ses paroisses, du moyen âge à la révolution* (Paris, 1959), makes the point that, in general, processions that followed parish boundaries inculated parishioners with a feeling of solidarity.

[4] *Mémoires*, II, 611.

Haton's description, recorded in 1570, may perhaps reflect an attempt to revive a spirit of community which sixteenth-century social changes were progressively undermining.[1] If so, then the people of Provins were drawing on a meaning which the holiday had long held. In 1520, when Henry VIII and Francis I decided to exhibit friendship, they took advantage of the season of the English king's arrival on the continent to meet on Corpus Christi Day. Henry set out from within the enclave of Calais, then an English possession, with a fully armed escort while Francis and his retinue crossed the frontier. Hall's *Chronicle* offers a faithful image of how the events of the day were interpreted in retrospect, which is more useful than precisely what happened. It indicates that men in both parties had doubts about the motives of their late hereditary enemies. The English were unsettled because they were outnumbered, and the French because, one may assume, strength in numbers had not helped them in the past.[2] But after pausing on opposing hillocks, the kings "spurred their horses fiercely," according to a contemporary French pamphlet; they galloped to the valley bottom, embraced in the saddle, dismounted, took each other's hand, and entered the gilded tent that gave its name to the Field of the Cloth of Gold. The great lords of both kingdoms then joined them, and participated in a toast, repeated several times, to "Good friends, French and English."[3] During the days that followed, affairs of state mixed with revelry. The two Renaissance monarchs, like the people of Provins, professed at Corpus Christi time to forget old grievances, showed their neighborliness, and tied the knots of sociability in more or less honest pleasure.

Occasionally, granted, this holiday was violent rather than pacific. "It was on the Monday before Corpus Christi Day, in the year 1381," wrote the chronicler Froissart, a colorful but intelligent collector of reminiscences, that the villagers of southeastern England, wrought up by the itinerant preacher John Ball, "left their homes to go to London to see the king and be freed from serfdom." After pillaging the churches

---

[1] On the relationship between the loosening of communal bonds and the rise of witchcraft accusations in later sixteenth-century England see Alan Macfarlane, *Witchcraft in Tudor and Stuart England* (New York, 1970), 197, and Keith Thomas, *Religion and the Decline of Magic* (New York, 1971), 562-563.

[2] Edward Hall, *Hall's Chronicle* (London, 1809), 608-610.

[3] The French pamphlet, otherwise unidentified, is given in Great Britain. Public Record Office. *Letters and Papers, Foreign and Domestic, of the Reign of Henry VIII* (London, 1862-1932), Vol. III, Pt. 2, No. 869.

of Canterbury, whose archbishop was Lord Chancellor, "they left the next morning for Rochester, with all the common people of Canterbury with them. They drew in all the people from the villages they went near, and they passed by like a tornado leveling and gutting the houses of lawyers and judges of the king's and archbishop's courts, and showing them no mercy." Outside London they met with men arriving from other counties on Corpus Christi Day as they had intended.[1]

At a moment when the members of village communities, town parishes and guilds were about to express their solidarity, they were easily roused against enemies who were outsiders—landlords, clerics doubling as officers of state, and the king's evil counselors. In form, the English peasant revolt was a wave of Corpus Christi processions.

La fête-Dieu, the festival of God, was the formal French name for Corpus Christi. Colloquially, the procession in particular, and by extension the holiday in general, was called *le sacre*,[2] which is best rendered as the anointment or consecration of the Holy Sacrament. The people used a day officially devoted to celebrating the means by which they communed with their Maker to manifest a sense of community among themselves. Ideally, this end was served by the very act of taking communion, throughout the year. The evangelical humanist Marguerite of Angoulême, sister of Francis, has her party of travelers in the *Heptameron*, published in 1558-59, "hear the Mass and receive the Holy Sacrament of union, at which all Christians are made one ..."[3] In the sixteenth century most men and women took communion a few times a year at best.[4] But people craved a sense of unity, and derived great satisfaction from proving to themselves that they had achieved it. And so they put great effort into making Corpus Christi festive. Tapestries were hung from windows along the procession routes. Parishes in Troyes provided flowered hats for some of the

---

[1] *Œuvres de Froissart*, ed. Kervyn de Lettenhove (Brussels, 1867-1877), IX, 392-398. I have quoted from C. Brereton's abridged translation. *Froissart : Chronicles* (Baltimore, 1968), 213-214.

[2] Emil Littré, *Dictionnaire de la langue française* (Paris, 1956), VI, 1807. For further examples of this usage see the *Histoire ecclésiastique des églises réformées au royaume de France*, ed. G. Baum et E. Cunitz (Paris, 1883-1889), "le grand sacre [Corpus Christi procession] d'Angers," I, 345; and "le jour qu'ils [Catholics] appellent leur Sacre," II, 634.

[3] (Paris, 1866), ix.

[4] H. O. Evennett, *The Spirit of the Counter-Reformation* (Cambridge, Eng., 1968), 38.

women who marched.[1] Taken together, such details help to show that the holiday was celebrated with as much gusto as the day of a parish's own patron—and for much the same reasons.

The clergy, as leaders of Corpus Christi processions, as celebrants of the private masses which linked the living and the dead, and in many other ways as well, performed the rituals that alone could sustain harmony and promote unity. It is well known that the Catholic clergy occupied the pivotal position of mediators between man and God; it was perhaps even more the case that the function of the priesthood at the end of the Middle Ages—as understood by the laity—was to act as intermediaries between men and between groups.

This is not to imply that traditional Catholics were necessarily satisfied with their priesthood. A major grievance may have been the awareness that the rituals they valued so highly did not always realize their purpose. Corpus Christi, Rabelais commented, was a day for women to show off their finery [2]—by definition, in competition with one another. Haton lamented that a series of processions to implore rain in 1573 was "more performed through pride, curiosity, and worldly honor than by saintly devotion, especially on the part of some clerics more than that of the simple people, and it seemed the said processions were held at Provins by envy of one church for another."[3] Ideals were tarnished in practice; the clergy did not always do its duty, nor act with the appropriate humility, since it was divided by the very kinds of rifts that these rituals were intended to heal. Such feelings do not invalidate our case, though they do help to redefine what the "simple people" took the term "clerical abuses" to mean. When men and women realized that their attempts to cultivate harmony were unsuccesful, whom did they blame but the clerics, those servants of God who could not unite laymen while they were themselves at each other's throats?

If the inability of the clergy to restore harmony among men disturbed many orthodox Catholics, then the insecurity of their relationship with God must have troubled them even more. No one during our period stood alone before the divine. But even with all the human aid they could muster, men and women toward the end of the Middle

---

[1] On the flowered hats see, for example, AD Aube 15 G 13, fol. 7^r, and 14 G 16A, fol. 26.

[2] Pantagruel, *Œuvres complètes* (Paris, 1955), 264.

[3] *Mémoires*, II, 722.

Ages, like Adam and Eve after the Fall, "hid themselves from the presence of the Lord God." In a period of recurrent plague, economic crisis and political commotion, it would have required strong faith and some imagination to have real confidence in his beneficence; people sought, in view of his ominous attitude, to protect and insulate themselves from his gaze. They preferred, rather, to identify as closely as possible with the sacrifice of the Son, who had died to save them from the Father's wrath. Jesus became the symbol of suffering. Christians who empathized with the Passion, and helped him to carry the Cross, could expect in return to transfer their burden of sin and guilt onto his shoulders, leaving them with an immense sense of relief, though not perhaps the feeling that their soul was truly cleansed. The Virgin, mother of them all, but localized and particularized in the shrines and statues that made her accessible to the individual believer, became the symbol of compassion. Tolerant, forgiving and understanding, she would use her influence to plead the case of souls which would otherwise sink straight to hell of their own dead weight of sin.

Sixteenth-century media conveyed these themes. The fourteen performances of Passion plays staged in the towns of Champagne from the 1480s to the 1530s, and attended by audiences that sometimes numbered in the thousands, imprinted the full measure of Christ's suffering and the Virgin's sorrows on the minds of spectators, and invited them to share in both.[1] She conceived and he lived and died on the stage just as they had done fifteen hundred years ago. The audience experienced the Biblical drama as if they themselves had been in the Holy Land.

The books called "Hours," compilations of prayers published in Paris for the use of the laity, provided literate men and women with a similar opportunity from day to day. Simon Vostre's *Hours According to the Custom of the Diocese of Châlons*, dated 1512, includes a service in honor of Notre-Dame de pitié. The reader, at matins, is instructed to ask the Virgin "that it may please you to have me, miserable sinner, participate in the merit of the sword of sorrow by which your soul was pierced ... so that I may entirely accomplish the commandments

---

[1] Partial lists of the performances are given in Petit de Julleville, *Les mystères*, II, 174-185, and Octave Beuve, *Le théâtre à Troyes aux quinzième e seizième siècles* (Paris, 1913). For additional performances listed in archival records see Galpern, *Change without Reformation*, 105-106, n. 2. On the size that the audience might reach see AC Châlons, BB 7, fol. 238 (1531).

of God, and that in hope of the general resurrection I may avoid damnation and welcomely bear the acts and burdens of our Lord, which
he has given me, in order that I may achieve enduring joy. Amen."[1]
The Hours enjoyed wide circulation. In 1520 two merchant-booksellers
of Châlons ordered eight hundred from a Parisian printer who had
supplied them, and Rémois merchants, too, in the past.[2] Guides to
piety, moreover, reinforced the Hours. A young matron earns the
admiration of a master of theology, in a Troyen tract entitled *Here
Begins a Little Instruction and Manner of Living for a Laywoman*....
She has informed him that, among other practices, "every day I bathe
myself in the vermilion wounds of Jesus Christ, with full confidence
that he will purify my faults with his Passion."[3] The anonymous
author must have been a Franciscan, since he praises "our good
saintly father, Brother Olivier Maillard," a fifteenth-century preacher
of that order. A supplementary tract, bound with the *Little Instruction*, offers counsel on the manner of "hearing the Mass devoutly."
"You must not read your Hours, nor the Pater Noster or Ave Maria,
but only think of our Lord ... on Sunday, at the Mass, how he was
at the Garden of Olives, sweating blood and water ... on Saturday,
how he was taken down [from the cross] and placed on the lap of
his gentle mother."[4]

Every person in Champagne, literate or not, could learn from and
react to the works of sculpture which individuals and confraternities,
during the opening decades of the sixteenth century, commissioned
from local artists. In 1515 Dame Jacquelyne de Laignes had an Entombment of Christ placed in her family chapel within the church of
Chaource. Two soldiers guard the chapel entrance. Standing six feet
tall, they must have appeared larger than life to contemporaries.
Their commanding presence at the entry helps to differentiate the
chapel space beyond from the rest of the church, while their grave

---

[1] *Les presentes heures* (Paris, 1512).

[2] AD Marne, 4 E 6188, fol. 210 (8 October 1520), printed in Amédé Lhôte, *Histoire
de l'imprimerie à Châlons-sur-Marne, 1488-1894* (Chalons and Paris, 1948), pièce justicative No. 3, 169).

[3] *Cy commence une petite instruction et maniere de vivre pour une femme seculiere
comme elle se doit conduire en pensees parolles et œuvres tout au long du iour tous les iours
de la Vie pour plaire a nostre seigneur et amasser richesses celestes au proffit et salut de
son ame* (Troyes, n.d.).

[4] *Sensuit cy apres une petite maniere comment une femme seculiere se peult conduire
devotement et vertuesement pour le proffit et salut de son ame* (attached to the above).

and reserved mien establishes an air of utmost seriousness, and suggests that they are themselves aware of the significance of the event. A third soldier sits resting on a stone, nearby. Opposite the three, and facing the worshipper, Joseph of Arimathæa and Nicodemus lower Christ's body into the sepulcher, while the Virgin, St. John, Mary Magdalene and the two other Marys look on. Their contained, silent sorrow is more expressive than lamentation, more realistic than the caricature of grief; it sustains the atmosphere of dignity and momentousness, and invites the visitor to participate in a living scene, instead of keeping him at arms length from a mere copy in stone. Off to a side, finally, kneel the figures of the donor and her late husband, reduced to a scale that is smaller than life.[1]

This art envoked the pity of the spectator, so that he might vicariously experience the suffering of those whom he worshipped. Other subjects for sculpture sought to replicate contemporary life and experience. Mary as the Madonna became progressively less divine in the course of the later Middle Ages.[2] "At St. Urban's of Troyes, for example [at the beginning of the sixteenth century], the Virgin is a young Champenois with a high forehead, her eyes slit into a tight smile, candid and yet malicious; as for the Child, chubby-cheeked, curly-haired, smiling, busy with a large grape, he is the Word incarnate in a little Champenois boy." "Nowhere," Emile Mâle continues, "were the artists further from respect than in Champagne."[3] St. Anne had become a bourgeoise matron, dressed to show off her estate; the male saints were depicted as craftsmen, practicing the trades that they patronized.[4] Whether poignant or realistic, the statues served to bring Jesus, the Virgin and the saints as close to the Christian people as possible, and helped to compensate for the distance that they felt separated them from God the Father.

Among the possible objections to this general argument is the fact that important indicators of what I have called late medieval religion reached their apogee at the turn of the sixteenth century, when the worst had passed. Confraternities were then popular and well attended. The Passion play had only recently taken its definitive form, and was

---

[1] William Forsyth, *The Entombment of Christ. French Sculptures of the Fifteenth and Sixteenth Centuries* (Cambridge, Mass., 1970), figs. 65-71.

[2] Mâle, *L'art religieux*, 149.

[3] *Ibid.*, 149-150.

[4] *Ibid.*, 157-161.

now performed before thousands of spectators in the towns of Champagne. Stained-glass windows depicting traditional themes were being commissioned in the hundreds, statues in the thousands. It should cause no surprise, however, that men were still subjectively responding to a crisis period that had ended. Cultural patterns, once launched, may embark on a life of their own, and take their time in responding to social changes which one might think ought to finish them off without delay. Or to put it another way, the very end of the crisis—domestic peace and order, greater assurance of life and increasing wealth—made it possible for people in Champagne to stage the plays, pay for an art and patronize confraternities which were more relevant to the difficult and unpleasant past than to the present. The greater the lack of fit, the more severe the ultimate correction (or overcorrection, depending on one's point of view) had to be. This said, let it be acknowledged that a more sophisticated and precise analysis and dating of the eve of the Reformation is needed, and awaits the marshalling of complementary evidence from many different regions of Europe.

2. ASPECTS OF LAY PIETY
IN EARLY RENAISSANCE FLORENCE

MARVIN B. BECKER

The University of Michigan

"In the long run, utility is simply a figment of our imagination and may well be the fatal stupidity by which we shall one day perish."

Nietzsche

Anyone examining the *provvisioni* of the Florentine signory will be struck by the numerous enactments of successive governments dealing with religious confraternities, pious foundations, and public charities. After a reading of these provisions, a very unsurprising hypothesis emerges : during the course of the fourteenth and fifteenth centuries, management and control of activities of these bodies came increasingly under the purview of the signory. The documents indicate particular reasons for this development; numerous requests were made by religious organizations for governmental funding in time of crisis. When the communal councils voted subventions, a measure of government supervision was almost certain to follow. The first amply documented crisis was the Black Death, and the year 1348 marked a historical moment at which governmental regulation was initiated on a large scale. Medical and health problems were so colossal that traditional philanthropic institutions were in need of subsidies. In the wake of the Black Death private benefactions and testamentary gifts increased astronomically, and for the following two decades the government acted to guard the swollen patrimony of the confraternities and pious foundations, while at the same time exercising stronger control over public charity. The problem of accountability and proper dispensation of resources was a matter of mounting civic concern. This trend toward regulation, so noticeable during the second half of the fourteenth century, was not confined to confraternities and pious foundations, but extended to a variety of other quasi-public and ecclesiastical organizations as the authority of the state grew.[1] A consequence of augmented state power

---

[1] The present study is part of a more general inquiry into the validation of laic roles in the early Italian Renaissance. For a description of the boundaries of this problem,

was the signory's repeated efforts to stamp out seditious behavior and politicking by the religious confraternities. The signory was especially anxious to curtail religious demonstrations because they might provoke unrest among the populace. Fear of secret brotherhoods of workers was also intense, and the Ciompi revolution of 1378 did little to allay these anxieties. Also, there was apprehension over the activities of *fratellanze* in the *contado;* these associations were viewed as undermining Florentine hegemony over Tuscany. These brotherhoods might well become centers for instruction in heresy. Less political but more influential was heightened public interest in problems of sanitation and hygiene. Those confraternities most directly involved in the administration of health care and the distribution of foodstuffs came to work in closer collaboration with communal officials. The signory legislated on these vital matters and also appointed captains, treasurers, and notaries to oversee their activities. Governmental intervention was frequently aimed at preventing the frivolous, even fraudulent, waste of charitable endowments. There is reason to believe that public supervision found favor in the eyes of would-be benefactors who often preferred to have lay rather than ecclesiastical control exercised over their bequests.[1]

---

see my article "An Essay on the Quest for Identity in the Early Italian Renaissance," in *Florilegium Historiale*, ed. J. Rowe and W. Stockdale (Toronto, 1971), 295-312. It is essential to recall that the clericalized church of the late Middle Ages did not possess a highly articulated theology pertaining to the role and place of laity in the church. Cf. L. Landini, *The Causes of the Clericalization of the Order of Friars Minor, 1209-1260, in the Light of Early Franciscan Sources* (Chicago, 1968). On the subject of charity, it should be understood that no presumption exists that lay philanthropies reduced the incidence of poverty in Renaissance Florence, Venice, or any other Italian urban center. On the trend toward Florentine regulation of pious foundations, confraternities, guilds, the Parte Guelfa, and other quasi-public bodies, see *Camera del Comune, Entrata*, beginning with vol. 32 for the years immediately preceding the Black Death and *Provvisioni* starting with vol. 36. (All documents mentioned in this article are to be found in the Archivio di Stato at Florence.)

[1] See the advice of Ser Lapo Mazzei to Francesco Datini : "Oft have I had it in mind to say to you, if you add not some words to the Will you have made, the Bishop of Pistoia is like to get your whole fortune—and will squander it to free himself from debt, and in horses and banquets ..." Mazzei concluded by advising Datini to add a codicil to his will stating that the Commune of Prato or its consuls or men appointed by Prato or Florence should nominate the poor people to whom his fortune was bequeathed. Cf. Iris Origo's sensitive study *The Merchant of Prato* (New York, 1957), 366-367. For a discussion of control over workers by the Florentine government, see N. Rodolico, *Il Popolo Minuto* (Bologna, 1899), and his *I Ciompi* (Florence, 1945);

During the fourteenth century responsibility for care of the indigent, infirm, aged, orphaned, starving, dying, and dead devolved upon the Republic. Hospitals, foundling homes, centers for poor relief—in fact all charities—grew more and more dependent upon government. Many times a petition would be presented to the signory by a citizen or corporate group raising questions as to the integrity or efficiency of particular executors of charitable foundations. After an inquiry the need for establishing principles of accountability would become apparent. Also, disputes between patrons and heirs on the one side and communal officials on the other were endemic. The terms under which the original benefaction was inaugurated were ambiguous, and the signory became a court of last resort. The tendency over the second half of the fourteenth century was to displace the original patron or religious order in favor of administration by a public body. Moreover, the intention of the patron was reassessed in terms of civic needs. These developments were accelerated when confraternities and pious foundations petitioned for tax exemptions, subsidies, and even protection from ecclesiastical exactions. By early Quattrocento the state came to serve as regulator and benefactor of philanthropic institutions.[1]

When the signory assumed the role of supervisor of charity, it availed itself of the services of the Republic's numerous guilds and fraternal organizations. These associations of laymen were regularly charged with administering pious works and philanthropies. The communal councils confirmed these functions so that they might manage endowments and benefactions more efficiently. Frequently, this involved displacing clerical executors in the name of eradicating abuses, real or imagined. The impulse was clearly to make more income available for maintenance of hospitals, infirmaries, orphanages, houses for the aged, and centers for alms-giving. Artisan and merchant corporations as well as the religious confraternities were entrusted with the sacred obligation of ministering effectively to Christ's poor. It is well to remember that the poor man in his misery was a replication of Our Lord Christ. Unlike earlier philanthropies directly sponsored by corporate bodies exclusively for their own membership, these new

---

G. Brucker, "The Ciompi Revolution," *Florentine Studies*, ed. N. Rubinstein (London, 1968), 314-356.

[1] For a sampling of this type of governmental enactment, see *Provvisioni*, 67, f. 241r; *ibid.*, 78, f. 221r; *ibid.*, 109, f. 76v; *ibid.*, 160, f. 212r.

trusts involved a concern for the well-being of the community as a whole.[1]

When the signory assumed these prerogatives it contended that it was only serving the original philanthropic intentions of the benefactor. Such claims were made most frequently during times of crisis when, as we have seen, the needs of the sick and poor were great and the pious foundations themselves required large infusions of communal money. Since certain of these foundations became public institutions for medical assistance and poor relief, they were of course the first to be regulated in the interests of public sanitation. Leading communal magistracies such as the Eight, intervened in the management of philanthropies in order to improve hygienic conditions in the city.

In late medieval Florence decisive political roles were played by a host of corporate bodies. In spiritual matters they were ideologically committed either to the pope or the emperor and, therefore, intensely partisan. In the case of leading confraternities, they played a military role in combating heresy during the middle years of the thirteenth century. At the same time, the guilds were being organized into a militia for defense of the Republic against its internal enemies. Indeed, if one were to catalogue the political world of the thirteenth century, one of its most prominent features would be the numerous *societates* and *fraternitates* performing limited and sometimes contradictory functions. It might be well to recall that these associations, while quasi-public, were often pitted against one another (the Guelf party versus Ghibelline). Not surprisingly, these associations practiced a philanthropy designed to insure its restricted membership against the many risks of quotidian life. This corporate sense of charity also can be viewed in the activities of the extended family, where the individual was protected by his kinsmen. Not only was the *consorteria* physically supportive, but guild and confraternity supplied spiritual reassurance and charitable benevolence. By mid-fourteenth century, however, this corporate world was losing much of its vitality. While the confraternities and guilds remained at the center of philanthropic life, the part

---

[1] B. Pullan, in his recent book *Rich and Poor in Renaissance Venice* (Cambridge, Mass., 1971), 133ff., finds a comparable impulse at work in that city. He also suggests that this broader sense of community had its origins in Tuscany. The present inquiry indicates that this is the case, with the Tuscan beginnings antedating Venetian developments by perhaps half a century. It should not be assumed, however, either in the instance of Venice or Florence, that the new philanthropy actually reduced the percentage of indigent. In a subsequent study I hope to discuss this question.

they played was largely administrative. Further, the signory acted to curb the activities of those quasi-public bodies which had been so divisive in past Florentine politics.[1] The state became the guarantor (ideally) for maintenance of civic order, and the once politically partisan corporate units took on a benign and charitable face when engaging in the construction of an extended Christian community.

The great benefactions of late Trecento and early Quattrocento were made by men who preferred having state officials as executors rather than ecclesiastics. In this transition a variety of precedents were established : the right to alienate property under governmental supervision; the right to sell shares of communal stock when part of the original benefaction; and finally, to liquidate unprofitable investments. The Republic acted to protect the captains and syndics of pious foundations and confraternities from civil litigation by disgruntled heirs. In the Quattrocento these officers were empowered to loan money to the government at rates of interest varying from five to fifteen percent. This they did in the "name of charity" and for "love of country." Very large bequests were now being made with sizable blocks of public bonds. Confidence in the state as a trustworthy executor of pious benefactions was a benchmark of lay spirituality by early Quattrocento.[2]

I

While the politics of those centuries of communal revolution have been carefully investigated, the religious dimensions of these movements have been neglected. Central to these struggles throughout north and central Italy over the late Middle Ages was the quest of a laity for spiritual authentication. Italian townsmen in the twelfth and thirteenth centuries were as anxious to gain an ample share of the spiritualities of the late medieval world as they were of winning political office. Civil contests were linked to intense struggles by an

---

[1] G. Brucker, *The Society of Renaissance Florence* (New York, 1971), 83-84; U. Morini, *Documenti inediti o poco noti per la storia della Misericordia di Firenze (1240-1525)*, (Florence, 1950), doc. II, X, XII; L. Passerini, *Storia dei stabilimenti di beneficienza e d'istruzione gratuita della città di Firenze* (Florence, 1853), 419-424.

[2] *Provvisioni*, 190, fols. 43v-44r; *ibid.*, 191, f. 121v. L. Passerini, *op. cit.*, 355-356 quotes the comments of the Florentine chronicler Giovanni Cambi who described the office of Cistercian overseer of the accounts of Santa Maria Nuova "chome d'un bancho di merchante," lending to the commune, motivated by "la carita e amore."

urban laity to achieve spiritual influence and representation in the church. The consequences were an increase in the membership of middling families in the cathedral chapters, the councils of the bishop, and organizations supervising church construction. The right to build private chapels, bury one's dead close to the altar of the cathedral, and place their children in one of the prestigious monasteries of the city was quintessential to an urban laity. At the heart of these impulses was the aspiration to have greater clerical empathy and religious support for the trying earthly pilgrimage of townsmen seeking to satisfy spiritual and secular demands. Being businessman, husband, soldier, father, patriot, politician—and above all, Christian—induced tensions to mount as roles multiplied.[1] In earlier centuries the laity had secured a place in Christian society simply by imitating monks and clerics; now the goal involved an attempt by secular men to find models of piety in order to validate these assorted, and often conflicting, roles. The thrust was away from a culture whose principal remedies had been asceticism and withdrawal toward a religious program dramatizing that problematic world where lay virtues would find both their justification and limit.

Of course the force of lay piety was general throughout Europe, but citizens of Italian communes had a greater opportunity to reach their spiritual objectives : first, they possessed the necessary political power; secondly, because of the *retardataire* character of Italian culture, the claims of an urban laity were honored more readily.[2] The culture lacked many of the formal ingredients of an aristocratic, scholastic, and curial civilization. The absence of courts, dynasties, and monastic centers of classical studies allowed lay culture to surface more easily since competing forces were weaker. The failure to establish those literary genres connected with the medieval civilizations of the North permitted Italian letters to be more vulnerable to the aspirations of an urban laity contending for spiritual and psychological acknowledgment of its problems. It was not that the Italian townsman was so different from his French counterpart, but rather that political and cultural conditions lent him the opportunity to dramatize his religious hopes.

---

[1] M. Becker, "Individualism in the Early Renaissance : Burden and Blessing." *Studies in the Renaissance*, XIX (1972), 273-97.

[2] M. Becker, "Towards a Renaissance Historiography," *Renaissance Studies in Honor of Hans Baron*, ed. A. Molho and J. Tedeschi (Dekalb, Ill., 1971), 151-153.

Florence was a great center for the expression of laic piety, and before attempting to analyze leading aspects of this movement we might note certain features of its society and economy. Most striking was the phenomenal growth of the city : its population increased by 300 percent within a century. As of 1278 it stood at 73,000 inhabitants. It is not, however, with the fact of number that we should be concerned, but rather with the curious character of the attendant social change. This was a startlingly nouveau society, and the greater share of its leading families were, as the chroniclers put it, "men of recent origins." Equally relevant to our inquiry is the gradual undermining of the feudal nobility. At approximately that time almost half of the urban nobles were scions of wealthy businessmen. Meanwhile, the seventy-four *consorterie* of the *contado* were substantially reduced in prestige and power. Our concern is not with the pursuit of social data but rather to attempt to assess the cultural consequences of this burgeoning and oddly mixed society. First, we must consider briefly the implications of this democratization for spiritual life. If there is any single generalization concerning upper-class bourgeois behavior in the thirteenth century, it would treat the alacrity with which the *popolani grassi* sought to participate in religious life. Over a third of the churches in the city were in the hands of laity; the populace had already joined the clergy in ousting the simoniacs. Now Florence became the first Italian town where the companions of St. Francis were to preach. In 1218 they were given a fixed establishment under the protection of Cardinal Ugolino (the hospital of San Gallo); three years later the convent of the Clares was founded at Monticelli. Florence was the first center for lay monasticism with the establishment of the Third Order of the Franciscans. It should also be noted that the greatest number by far of manuscripts of the *Fioretti* survives to this day in Florence.[1] In 1221 the chapter of the Cathedral gave the Dominicans the church of Santa Maria Novella; only seven years later the Franciscans were to receive Santa Croce. In the decade of the forties the *Laudesi* of Santa Maria Novella were formed to sing hymns in Latin and the vernacular composed by clerics and laymen. This *compagnia* had no parallel in Western Europe, and every night it assembled to sing these *laudi*. Also of interest is the fact that most of the surviving manuscripts in the *volgare* are in the Tuscan tongue.

---

[1] G. Petrocchi, "Inchiesta sulla tradizione manoscritti dei 'Fioretti di San Francesco,'" *Filologia Romanza*, III (1957), 311-325.

For the next century and a half democratization of spiritual life proceeded with an intensity difficult to match in any part of Europe. No single explanation will cover this multi-faceted phenomenon, but surely the fact that the city had no proper nobility to monopolize the spiritualities was a prime factor. A visit to Santa Croce reveals the high rate of religious investment that Florentine burghers made when given an unrivaled opportunity to enter the sacred portals and bury their dead. This of course was new : before the thirteenth century lay burials inside churches were rare, with the privilege usually reserved for royalty. Now the new aristocracy of the Bardi, Castellani, Peruzzi, Rucellai, Strozzi, and others entered the holy precincts *en force*. The commune entrusted construction and maintenance of those buildings most closely identified with the soul of the city (the Baptistry, Duomo, San Miniato) to the *arti* of those self-same merchants and bankers. The artistic revolution initiated by Cimabue and Giotto opened the sacred world of Christ and his apostles to a burgher audience no longer distanced from the holy personages. In fact, the highest moments of the Christian drama were to occur in a historical milieu not so different from the ordinary world of a burgher patriciate.

The burgher conscience was informed by the popularizings of Dominicans and Franciscans, and nurtured by a socioeconomic milieu in which they could continue to participate in the benefits of a religious community. The absence of a *true* nobility allowed for the quickening of lay spirituality. In Trecento art and religion we can observe the elevation of the values of domesticity and the round of family life to the status of a cultural ideal. Lay piety provided support for this program with the citizenry participating in numerous religious confraternities. By the late thirteenth century these organizations had proliferated in Florence so that the Arno city stood first among all the towns of Tuscany. In fact, surviving documentation suggests that she outstripped virtually all urban centers in the founding of these pious bodies.[1] Moreover, changes in the structure of the confraternities paralleled those already noted in the field of communal administration. Over the fourteenth century the tendency was toward

---

[1] At the end of the fourteenth century, Florence had at least forty-two confraternities, while in all of central Italy they numbered seventy, and in north Italy about forty. Cf. G. Monti, *Le confraternite medievali dell'alta e media Italia* (Venice, 1927), I, 147-193; II, 23; I. Hijmans-Tromp, *Vita e opere di Agnolo Torini* (Leiden, 1957), 20.

greater secular control of both confraternities and the disposition of charity. Within the sodalities the shift was in the direction of giving the laity a stronger voice and this was replicated by governmental intervention and control. The fourteenth century was the locus for further democratization of the spiritualities as laity came to play roles once the exclusive preserve of monks and clerics. Burghers were anxious to imitate Christ and his apostles—especially those acts of charity and mercy which were at the heart of the ministry of the Redeemer and his disciples. An industrial city such as Florence, where a third of the population depended upon the prosperity of wool manufacturing, provided ample opportunity for such benevolence. Further, economic changes were weakening traditional corporate structures that had previously been so supportive. Indeed, as the individual's isolation increased and he lost guild and *consorteria* support, he might be aided by the many charitable institutions founded between the mid-fourteenth and mid-fifteenth centuries.

II

Preachers, humanists, even sculptors, affirmed that the paths of the Florentine patriot and Christian pilgrim did in fact converge in the City of Man; no necessary contradiction existed between one's duty to God and obligation to his fellows.[1] Though the burgher odyssey might be wearing, still, the quest for salvation had a persistent social and political dimension. The art of early Quattrocento Florence proclaimed a new ideal : A Christian community located in a more ample social space generated by broader human concerns could be realized in historical time. Love of God could be reconciled with love of country; and citizen interest could transcend the constricted and narrow allegiances of the world of the *consorteria* and medieval corporation. The message of leading humanists such as Coluccio Salutati underscored this notion of extended sociability.[2] The idea of *caritas* was

---

[1] M. Becker, *Florence in Transition* (Baltimore, 1968), II, 55-68. G. Brucker in his *Renaissance Florence* detects a marked shift in Florentine behavior as citizen resources were being increasingly devoted to civic and social problems; cf. pages 209-210. See also Ser Lapo Mazzei, *Lettere di un notaro a un mercante*, ed. C. Guasti (Florence, 1880), II, 313-316, 319, 324.

[2] This facet of Salutati's thought has not been sufficiently featured by scholars. Separation of civic life from the ethos of *caritas* was not prominent in writings of most humanists of the early Quattrocento. Moreover, affirmation of citizen obligations and

transvalued into a generalized conception of philanthropy. An enduring monument to this new concern were the frescoes of the Brancacci Chapel, where the young Masaccio depicted a radically new sense of Christian community. The Apostles were ordinary men performing simple acts of charity in city streets and in a countryside identical to a Tuscan ambience. Further, these pious gestures served to create a network of interpersonal relationships that was at the center of this sacral community. The anguish of Adam and Eve was more deeply felt because their alienation was juxtaposed against that world of good works constituting the ideal Christian community.[1]

The writings of chroniclers also serve to highlight the transition from a conception of sanctity as being the special preserve of orders and individuals, to one in which holiness is viewed as a function of the collected good works of a community. Recent scholarship has stressed the fact that the Florentine Quattrocento was a time of increased civic benefactions. Indeed, the traditional historical interpretation accenting the onset of secularization as a hallmark of the Florentine Renaissance is not helpful in this regard. Economic indicators suggest that in representative zones of the Florentine *contado* there was a sizable augmentation of gifts to ecclesiastical foundations. The ownership of land by hospitals and other charitable institutions almost doubled between 1427 and 1498. This amazing growth was matched by the endowments of foundations in San Gimignano. In 1315 the ecclesiastical corporations of the city and district owned 12 percent of all taxable wealth. In 1475 this figure rose to 28.8 percent, with the patrimony of hospitals far outstripping those of monasteries and convents. Similar patterns have been noted for the town of Pistoia, where the number of hospitals increased almost threefold during those

---

the social nature of the *true* citizen prompted Salutati and others to define *caritas* as that virtue which alone can "foster the family, enlarge the city, and guard the kingdom." Against this position his opponents argued that as far as sociability was concerned, bees and ants must be rated more highly than men : "Who does not know of the great prudence that exists in the forms of society of bees and ants and similas insects ? Both justice and compassion are much more developed among certain animals than among certain men." Cf. E. Garin, *Italian Humanism*, trans. Peter Munz (Oxford, 1965). Of course Salutati promised to write *De vita associabili*, unfortunately never written or lost; and throughout his life he remained eminently concerned with the theme of social responsibility.

[1] F. Hartt, *History of Italian Renaissance Art : Painting, Sculpture and Architecture* (Englewood Cliffs, New Jersey, 1969), 158-164.

years. Of course the most celebrated of these benefactions was the Ceppo of Francesco Datini, whose original bequest was the enormous sum of 70,000 florins.[1]

Recently, scholars have described this upsurge of civic charity as a "new direction in Christian piety," and nowhere was this impulse more prominent than in Tuscany. Leadership was assumed by Siena and Florence, and in both centers pious foundations were consolidated with tighter administration of trust income. The Observant Franciscans brought a new awareness to problems of philanthropy as they sponsored the assimilation of small charities into larger, more efficient, organizations. The formation of great foundling hospitals like the Innocenti in Florence became a model for all of Europe, even winning praise from Martin Luther. San Bernardino, who as a young man cared for the sick, served on the board of yet another model hospital, Santa Maria della Scala in Siena, popularizing the conception of extended responsibility of citizens for the poor, the infirm, and the aged. The keystone of his faith was *caritas* and he proclaimed that all men were the body of Christ. Ultimately, all goods should be held in common and no one should have a surplus when others stood in need : "While in his true fatherland in heaven, man may be destined to lead a contemplative life, it is his calling in this world to act and to love. Even the keys of wisdom are in the hands of love." He and Sant'Antonino, prior of the Dominican friary of San Marco and later Archbishop of Florence, were spokesmen for a philanthropy responding to the breakdown of corporate exclusiveness. Both were economic thinkers whose ideas pertaining to labor and the responsibility of the rich toward the proletariat marked them as the leading theorists of their century. In addition to subtle analyses of wage theory and the needs of workers, Sant'Antonino formed the first religious confraternity dedicated to the assistance of those "worthy poor" who were too "shamefaced" to seek welfare.[2]

---

[1] E. Fiumi, *Storia economica e sociale di San Gimignano* (Florence, 1961), 216-223; E. Conti, *La formazione della struttura agraria moderna nel contado fiorentino* (Rome, 1965), III, part 2, passim; D. Herlihy, *Medieval and Renaissance Pistoia* (New Haven, 1967), 245-49. B. Pullan, *op. cit.*, 133ff discusses the debate over this question in recent scholarship as it pertains to Italian other than Tuscany. Cf. also G. Brucker, *op. cit.*, 209-211.

[2] Works on the social theories of these two saints are legion; especially valuable is R. de Roover's *San Bernardino of Siena and Sant'Antonino of Florence : The Two Great Economic Thinkers of the Middle Ages* (Boston, 1967).

The Catasto of 1427 permits us to indicate particular areas of change in philanthropy. Most notable is the size of the patrimony of religious confraternities in relation to the guilds. The former held three times more real property than the latter. While the guilds remained as administrators, it was the confraternities that moved to the fore in the field of philanthropic activities. It is probable that by the early Quattrocento virtually all Florentines above the poverty level were enrolled in one or more of the city's numerous confraternities. These laic associations were among the principal beneficiaries of more than 100,000 florins in alms and legacies for the year 1427. One example of spectacular gains was the hospital endowed by Bonifazio Lupi : in 1362 he donated 300 florins to purchase land and construct a building for the care of the "infirm poor." The hospital received sizable testamentary grants, and by the 1430's the value of its buildings was 24,000 florins and the income from its properties stood at 700 florins. Santa Maria Nuova was founded about 1288 by Folco Portinari, the father of Dante's Beatrice, to care for the sick; originally it had but twelve beds, and if we place four in a bed, as was the medieval practice, it accommodated forty-eight. Over the next century care was provided for 300 patients annually, and the income of the hospital from communal subsidies and legacies rose astronomically. The foundling hospital of the Innocenti was of course a favorite of the Florentines, and by mid-fifteenth century it was furnishing care for orphans at the rate of approximately fifty new children each year. In most instances poor relief and health care were the responsibility of the membership of the confraternities. In fact, without their energy and funds these pious institutions could not have survived. The Misericordia, the Bigallo, and scores of others were the sinews of these holy enterprises.[1]

---

[1] Figures presented from the Florentine Catasto of 1427 are taken from C. Canestrini's *La scienza e l'arte di stato* (Florence, 1962), 150-152; they have been corrected in D. Herlihy's printout, which he has kindly made available to me. The totals presented in my paper, however, remain approximations, since it will be necessary to investigate the patrimony of charitable foundations as well as bequests of donors. The problem of exaggeration of pious bequests remains; also, the amounts actually distributed to the poor are still unknown. Herlihy corrects Canestrini's population figures as well as the total given for Florentine households. For the patrimony of the Bigallo and Misericordia, see H. Saalman, *The Bigallo* (New York, 1969), doc. XIX. According to the Catasto, the Bigallo-Misericordia Compagnia listed assets of over 18,000 florins, and ten hospices were under its jurisdiction. For Santa Maria Nuova, see L. Passerini, *op. cit.*, 301-345. For the hospital of Bonifazio Lupi, see G. Brucker, *op. cit.*, 210-293; L. Passerini, *op. cit.*, 216-227.

In 1427 the total for alms and legacies by Florentine citizens was approximately 108,000 florins; this figure represented about one-sixth of the sum of all income enjoyed by citizens. If we add to this the yearly revenues of churches and pious foundations. then another 130,000 florins must be entered. The aggregate income for spiritual purposes reached 238,000 florins, and this figure was around thirty-five percent of the income of the citizenry. Such a sum was probably more than that realized by all landed investments. It should also be noted that ecclesiastical holdings in Florentine territories were well in excess of 1,500,000 florins.

The Quattrocento state became increasingly concerned with the administration of public assistance. In a city where at least sixteen percent of the population were at the poverty level, and another thirty percent barely subsisted, welfare was to be a pressing matter.[1] The years between the 1340's and '80's had been a time of worker unrest, with the Ciompi revolution of 1378 and the *minori* government (1378-1382) serving to frighten the oligarchs. In the decades immediately thereafter we note the founding of great hospitals, hospices, and orphanages in greater numbers than ever before. At this time too the signory grew intensely interested in increasing the income of pious trusts and preventing mismanagement of ecclesiastical foundations. The government repeatedly intruded into the philanthropic activities of the confraternities to maximize efficiency. The high incidence of worker and artisan unrest had been prompted in part by the dismantling of *minori* and *minuti* organization; under the stress of competition and economic individualism, many traditional corporate supports eroded. The conception of philanthropy became more generalized as the state assumed responsibilities once the preserve of a multitude of quasi-public associations. Expressive of this new ethos was the selection of the officials over the funded public debt to serve as guard-

---

[1] It is of interest to note that poverty statistics for Florence do not differ appreciably from those of other European cities in the fourteenth and fifteenth centuries. Despite the acceleration of civic philanthropy in such wealthy centers as Venice and Florence, we do not know what percentage of the poor were actually ministered to by the confraternities. In the case of Venice, the figures presented in Brian Pullan's recent study indicate that only eight percent of the city's poor were beneficiaries of the charity of the Scuole Grandi. (I wish to thank Professor Reinhold Mueller of Hobart College for this information.) For a discussion of poverty levels in other European centers, see M. Mollat, "La notion de la pauvreté au Moyen Age," *Revue d'Histoire de l'Église de France*, LII (1966), 14-19.

ians of the patrimony of widows and orphans. Also illustrative of this trend were a series of enactments establishing a state insurance system for provision of dowries for girls.[1]

III

This movement toward an extended sense of civic responsibility was encouraged both by political exigencies and the desire of a large segment of the laity to participate directly in that round of acts of charity which would make them worthy in the sight of God. Quattrocento ritual and ceremony firmly placed the laity in sacral space as they literally acted out the *imitatio Cristi;* the confraternities were centers in which this burgher drama was to unfold. A close connection obtained between laic spirituality and Florentine humanism; confraternities were the locale for delivery of sermons and orations by leading humanists. Laic interest in questions of salvation and immortality were pre-eminent in the writings of these literati throughout the Quattrocento. Ficino and others were the focus for groups of pious laymen seeking spiritual illumination in philosophical and theological discussion. That the men of the confraternities could assemble to consider problems of doctrine was itself a dramatic manifestation of intellectual democratization. Further, the humanists themselves had democratized the role of priest and stood in relationship to their disciples as cleric to parishioner. Since the time of Petrarch literati assumed the part of lay confessor; now this role was generalized in the confraternities.[2]

The political ideas of eminent humanists like Coluccio Salutati have been well explicated, but occasionally they have been separated from their religious matrix. The Florentine chancellor's appreciation of the

---

[1] For a discussion of the *Monte delle doti*, see M. Becker, *op. cit.*, 71-72, 152, 236-237. Nunneries regularly petitioned the signory for the right to collect dowries of those girls who had entered convents. (I wish to thank Professor Anthony Molho for this information.)

[2] On this theme, see C. Trinkaus, *In Our Image and Likeness* (University of Chicago Press, 1970), I, especially chapters 1 and 2 on Petrarch and Salutati, 1-102; P. O. Kristeller, "Lay Religious Traditions and Florentine Platonism," *Studies in Renaissance Thought and Letters* (Rome, 1956), 99-122. For the names of leading humanists delivering sermons before the prestigious confraternity of the Magi, see R. Hatfield, "The Compagnia de' Magi," *Journal of the Warburg and Courtauld Institutes*, XXXIII (1970), 125-134; among those noted were Girolamo Benivieni, Donato Acciaiuoli, Cristoforo Landino, Pier Filippo Pandolfini, and Alamanno Rinuccini. For Marsilio Ficino's connections with the confraternity movement, see P. O. Kristeller, *op. cit.*

associative life was rooted in his ample definition of charity. Always empathetic to the spiritual strivings of a laity, he proclaimed the primacy of faith existentially understood as well as the overarching need for *caritas* if the human community was to flourish. Without the history of the charitable and civic-minded actions of our forebears, even Holy Scripture would lose its appeal and fail to inspire men with compassion and love. What is evident in the writings of Salutati is his conception of a Christian community capable of realization through the civic and philanthropic actions of ordinary men not so different from those who followed Our Lord during his ministry on earth.[1]

Humanists of the next generation challenged the ideal of voluntary poverty. In its stead they opted for justification of wealth in terms of its social and political benefits. Again, Bruni, Poggio, and others were responding to the dissolution of traditional forms of communal life. A reading of their histories of Florence discloses that they had almost no comprehension of older corporate structures. The crisis they confronted during the first part of the Quattrocento induced an understanding for the role of wealth in sustaining civic life. The broader community could no longer be supported by the restricted allegiances of the past; institutions of the commune such as the guilds and *Parte Guelfa* were too parochial. Feeling for one's city and fellows required contempt for those hypocritical friars preaching the doctrine of voluntary poverty. Underlying humanist polemics against monasticism was the implicit rejection of any claims that the clergy held a monopoly over God's sacred manna. Neither Poggio nor Lorenzo Valla denied the value of monastic institutions, but they did attack any denigration of the spiritual prerogatives of laity. Firm endorsement of the dignity of the secular odyssey sometimes encouraged an invidious, ironic comparison between monk and layman. The former, it would seem, took the easier path toward salvation living under vows, while the latter selected the hard road when remaining in the world of temptation. Monks appeared to care more for salvation of their own souls than for the spiritual well-being of others. In securing the spiritual

---

[1] Quintessential to this conception of community was Salutati's elevation of the *mercatores et artifices* to an equal status with the *milites* of the city. Democratization at the upper levels of society was a growing theme in vernacular and humanistic literature during Salutati's lifetime. Cf. E. Garin, "I cancellieri umanisti della repubblica fiorentina da Coluccio Salutati a Bartolomeo Scala," *Rivista Storica Italiana*, LXXI (1959), 185-208. For an assessment of the status of the merchant at an earlier time, see A. Sapori, *Le marchand italien au Moyen Age* (Paris, 1952), pp. xxiv-xxvi.

dignity of the laic role, Bruni, Poggio, and Valla also contended that contempt for honest work and praise of mendicity destroyed the very fabric of civilization. Indeed, those lofty eras in world history had frequently been times of great civic wealth. The intention of many humanist polemics against monastic targets was to enhance the possibility of realizing a "true" Christian community where affluent citizens would be fully cognizant of their social responsibilities. In the interests of such a community humanists authenticated laic emotions and drives.[1]

The centrality of the confraternity occurred at a historical moment when older forms of sociability were in decline. The claims of spirituality advanced by the nobility and higher clergy were not to be displaced. Throughout the Quattrocento Tuscan artists and literati were able to portray life styles rooted in the world of traditional hierarchy. For example, we find the painter Piero della Francesca depicting the heraldic aspirations of Sigismondo Malatesta, while at the same time demonstrating an acute sensitivity toward the burgherlich world of the confraternity, with its simple values of a humanity dependent upon divine mercy and protection. Sir Kenneth Clark describes one Piero brilliant at making the illusion of heraldic fantasy convincing, and another equally capable of confirming "the illusion of reality and depth" for his bourgeois patrons.[2] The members of the company of the Madonna della Misericordia who gave him his first commission, were depicted as kneeling within the "cave of the Virgin's cloak." The space they occupy and the air they breathe has all the properties of an everyday world—"only a little finer and more luminous." The burgher world of spirituality had achieved parity with that of curia and court. Artists and literati could dramatize just as effectively the merchant viator as the knight.

The confraternities relinquished their political role, assuming in its stead extensive cultural and social responsibility. Their popularity was assured, and by the Quattrocento they included in their ranks virtually all the citizens of Florence. Youth confraternities multiplied

---

[1] C. Trinkaus, op. cit., pp. 103-170; E. Garin, Italian Humanism, 43-56; F. di Zenzo, Saggi su l'umanesimo (Naples, 1968), 99-120.

[2] K. Clark, Piero della Francesca (London, 1968), 22-32. Of interest is the fact that Piero was first mentioned in a Florentine document in which Domenico Veneziano (7 September 1439) received payment for frescoes in the choir of S. Egidio, the chapel of S. Maria Nuova.

as did charitable foundations for dowring girls.[1] Hospices for the aged, orphanages, and hospitals were among the principal charges of these lay companies. There is a paradox in this : at a time when Florentine society was more atomized than ever, the idea of a Christian community took hold. So persuasive was this ideal that humanists were to argue that the bonds of spiritual community could not even be severed by sin. Again, the Brancacci Chapel is illustrative of this ideal. Masaccio's frescoes show Adam and Eve being expelled from Eden. The scriptural message is clear : as punishment man falls into the world of suffering and death, process and mutability. But for Masaccio, loss of the Edenic state is only a preliminary to the re-creation of another more durable community marked by man's exquisite concern for his fellows.[2]

The backdrop for this new vision was an urban society of heightened competition, decline of the corporate ethic, and erosion of the supports of family business and *consorteria*. The confraternities were agencies for social and spiritual insurance at a moment when contemporary sensibilities dwelled upon economic risks. Evidence from the Florentine *catasti* of the fifteenth century discloses that the upper classes were beginning to feel the adverse effects of downward mobility; they appear to have been reproducing themselves at a rate greater than the capacity of the economy to absorb them. Of great interest is the fact that Sant'Antonino and others were proclaiming that religious confraternities must now assume responsibility for the fallen rich ("the shamefaced") in addition to their usual sacred charges.[3]

The idea of charity was presented as a collective enterprise. In humanist writings, as well as in religious ritual and civic pageant, the City of God was understood to be the Christian community of those having charity in their hearts rather than self-love. Demarcations between the lives of the clergy and laity would diminish as Florence found favor in the sight of God. The apotheosis of a secular

---

[1] R. Trexler, "Ritual in Florence : Adolescence and Salvation in the Renaissance," below 200 f.

[2] A. W. Skarstrom, " 'Fortunate Senex' : The Old Man, A Study of the Figure, His Function and His Setting," Chapter IV. (Dissertation, Yale University, 1971.) U. Procacci, *All the Paintings of Masaccio*, trans. P. Colacicchi (New York, 1968).

[3] Vespasiano, *Renaissance Princes, Popes and Prelates*, trans. W. George and E. Waters, with Introduction by M. Gilmore (New York, 1963), 157-163, W. Gaughan, *Social Theories of Saint Antoninus from his Summa Theologica* (Washington, 1950), 45-47. Cf. above, 188, n. 1.

city was regularly dramatized by writers of distinction such as Gregorio Dati, Matteo Palmieri, Gianozzo Manetti and others. Again, the role of the confraternity was vital. Within these companies laymen could re-enact the sacred drama of Christ, take common meals, join in hymn singing and prayer, confess, and listen to sermons composed by their own members—all this under secular auspices. Pledged "to observe the laws of God" and rules of civic comportment, the brothers were charged in their statutes to "see if there is anyone among you who trusts himself to be Christ and will govern you according to the precepts of Christ."[1] The official envisioned was in fact the *governor* who was a type of lay abbot. On Holy Thursday it was decreed that "the governor will wash the feet of the brethren and will offer a simple meal to commemorate this day on which Christ washed the feet of his disciples and then shared a meal with them." The confreres were then reminded that their chief mission was charity and they were ordered to distribute bread and wine to the poor of the city and countryside whom the orderlies were to identify. "And each [brother] who takes these alms [to distribute] must indicate the name of the pauper to whom he is giving them before he leaves ... so that each one knows who has been visited and who has not, to avoid a double distribution to one, and nothing to another."

Philanthropy was being converted into a way of life rather than a series of isolated gestures. Charity lost much of its dramatic and episodic character as it was transvalued into a systematized sequence of interrelated acts. The shift was from the corporate to the communital, with confidence placed in the *virtù attiva* of ordinary citizens now judged capable of fulfilling their civic obligations and performing the daily round of "sante operazioni." How different was the assessment of Dati from such Trecento chroniclers as Stefani, who repeatedly reminded his readers that it had been "the good people" who had called for the crucifixion of Christ. In the eyes of leading commentators of the first part of the Quattrocento, it was the concord of the city nurtured by citizen dedication to charity and civic good works that gained for Florence the mercy and love of God. So sweet was the melody orchestrated by this harmony that it ascended to heaven, moving the saints to defend the city from its enemies and advance it above all others in Italy.[2]

---

[1] R. Hatfield, "The Compagnia de' Magi," *op. cit.*, 124-125; G. Brucker, *op. cit.*, 206-208.

[2] G. Dati, *L'Istoria di Firenze dal 1380 al 1405*, ed. L. Pratesi (Norcia, 1904), 140,

The culture resonating from the confraternities was part of a network of ideals serving as a bridge to a larger society, with religion and
civic veneration interlaced. The thrust toward democratization of the
spiritualities had culminated with secure placement of the laity within
the frame of a sacred community. The confraternities took responsibility for numerous public festivals in which the political allegory of
the Holy City was explicated in gaudy detail. The Magi, most famous
of these companies, enrolling some seven hundred members, performed a "sacred representation" on Epiphany in which Florence was
transformed into the "image of Jerusalem." The beginnings of the
sacre rappresentazioni were in the *laude* composed to be sung by the
religious guilds. Among writers of *laudi* in the fifteenth century were
leading humanists as well as the mother of Lorenzo de' Medici, while
authors of sacred representations included Lorenzo himself and his
kinsman Lorenzo Pierfrancesco. The origins of secular drama were
also in the companies : Politian's *Orfeo*, which marked its beginnings,
was patterned after the *sacre rappresentazioni*. The correspondence
between the Platonic Academy and the companies has already been
noted; as has the fact that members of the Academy also composed
sermons to be delivered to the confraternities. The observation that
these lay congregations, not the universities, were to serve as sponsors
of the "new culture" of the sixteenth century is of course apposite.[1]

At first glance much of the art and literature of Quattrocento
Florence seems without roots in the social world. Unlike the culture
of the Dugento and Trecento which was nourished by the world of
hierarchy, corporatism. and commune, this new civilization appears to
be abstract and lacking in social dimension. Main currents in Florentine
thought after the 1430's have been described as formalistic and evasive—a flight from the political and economic issues of the day. A
vast literature had emerged focusing on themes of *caritas, amore,
humanitas,* and purification of the *anima.*[2] Solicitude of men of letters

---

171; Marchionne di Coppo Stefani, *Cronica fiorentina,* ed. N. Rodolico in *Rerum Itali-
carum Scriptores,* new ed. vol. XXX (Città di Castello, 1903-1955), rub. 564.

[1] P. O. Kristeller, "Lay Religious Traditions and Florentine Platonism," *op. cit.,*
100-112; P. Toschi, *Sacre rappresentazioni Toscane dei secoli XV e XVI* (Florence,
1960); E. Garin, *Science and Civic Life in the Italian Renaissance,* trans. P. Munz (New
York, 1969), 90-91.

[2] For bibliography and a discussion of the literature on these topics, see M. Schiavone's
introduction to his edition of Ficino's *Teologia Platonica* (Bologna, 1965), I, 3-71. Cf.
also Schiavone's *Problemi filosofici in Marsilio Ficino* (Milan, 1957).

toward the spiritual problems of the laity had deepened. The priestly role of humanists was accented as poets and philosophers sought to describe the possibilities of spiritual communion among men. God was a necessary partner in the reconstitution of a Christian community. The quest for unity and religious peace was to be realized when men, secure in the value of their own humanity, formed societies animated by a mutuality of spiritual concerns. Much underlying these new ideals was a continuation of older literary themes; from its inception Florentine humanism had addressed itself to the problem of the loss of a sense of community. Civic humanism sought to present alternatives to a citizenry confronted by an erosion of corporate ties. Efforts were made to authenticate new social values and formulate codes of behavior more relevant for individuals living in greater isolation. To modern scholars the stress on charity and love might indeed look evasive until one realizes that they surfaced with compelling social force. These virtues alone could foster the family, guard the city, and even enlarge a Florentine empire. Men were regarded as God's creatures charged with the solemn obligation to care for one another; man's dignity did not reside in solitary experience or in strategic personal relationships. Neither pride of caste nor cultivation of autonomous feelings of self-hood were sufficient to endorse this *dignitas;* instead, man's consciousness of his solidarity with all men was quintessential.[1]

Such a view represented the deepening of the sentiments of lay piety as the claims of an extended sociability found a treasure-trove of religious metaphors. This response to the falling away of traditional social and political supports represented an attempt to discover effective principles for constituting a society. The model for community was lodged in the world of the confraternities and academies. These associations were crucial to the thought of a Ficino or a Pico, for there men demonstrated the talent for mutuality and love. Ficino's *Commentary on the Symposium* could be enacted as a *love feast,* with its ready analogue in the *prandium caritatis* of the sodalities.[2] The seven works of temporal mercy were no longer seasonal gestures or occasions for

---

[1] E. Garin, "Problemi di religione e filosofia," *Bibliothèque d'Humaisme,* XIV (1952), 70-82; C. Trinkaus, *op. cit.,* II, 459-592.

[2] R. Sears Jayne, *M. Ficino's Commentary on Plato's Symposium,* in *The University of Missouri Studies,* XIX (1944); *Commentaire sur le Banquet de Platon,* text and translation by R. Marcel (Paris, 1955); L. Tonelli, *L'amore nella poesia e nel pensiero del Rinascimento* (Florence, 1933).

special ceremonies. Love was the key to Ficino's theology as well as to his epistemology; but also on a more mundane level it was the lifeblood of a Christian community and nurture of the brotherhoods. Finally, Neoplatonic philosophers and poets depicted the movement of the human soul from love of God to love of *humanitas* as evidenced through acts of civic piety. For Manetti and others the life of Socrates became a model for laic sanctity : an ordinary citizen gained immortality by conquering his self-love when sacrificing his life for an ideal spiritual community.[1]

IV

Emblematic of this new conception of *caritas* was the greatest single philanthropic monument to be constructed in Florence in the first half of the fifteenth century—the Ospedale degli Innocenti.[2] Begun in 1419 by Filippo Brunelleschi, it was located at the end of a recently opened street (via dei Servi), which runs from Santissima Annunziata to the Duomo. The Foundling Hospital and its piazza provided Florentines with a radically different stage for noble action. On each side of the square a great loggia was planned with a short flight of steps leading up to it. Never before had so large and rational a space been constructed to express man's humaneness. In the first of the great buildings completed in 1424 in the new style (the Foundling Hospital), we note its "airy plan" and many courtyards expressing exactly this "rational humaneness." The poetry of the open-arcaded loggia on the ground floor fronting on the Piazza dell'Annunziata was an invitation to all men to initiate a new era of peace and trust. Here amidst the beauties of proportion and ornament, exactly measured to sacred scale, Florentines could carry on "sacred conversations." Deeds of mercy and acts of charity were placed in a civic setting of harmony and concord.

That this new world was visionary is indisputable. But the "imaginative increments" of this idealized polis arose from close connections with social and political change. First, democratization of the spiritual-

---

[1] E. Garin, *La cultura filosofica del Rinascimento italiano, Ricerche e Documenti* (Florence, 1961), 102-182. On Manetti, see Garin's *Italian Humanism*, 56-60; for Matteo Palmieri and the "Transition to Platonism," see *ibid.*, 66-69. Cf. also C. Trinkaus, *op. cit.*, 683-721.

[2] F. Hartt, *op. cit.*, 115-119; P. Hendy, *Piero della Francesca and the Early Renaissance* New York, 1968), 17-25; E. Luporini, *Brunelleschi : Forma e Ragione* (Milan, 1964), 79ff.

ities converted the physical city into a model of the New Jerusalem;
in fact, the facade of Santissima Annunziata did resemble Quattrocento imaginings of the Holy Sepulchre. In Florence burghers could
readily translate private piety into a public tableau. Just as pictorial
space was opened to the merchant pilgrim who joined the holy personages, so too civic space came to include the ordinary citizen. Not
checked by a true aristocracy, a court, or a curia, spirituality took on
public dimension as it was refracted through the prism of merchant
life and action. The energies released elevated the polis to a community
of lay monks, and the confraternity became a paradigm for this new
society. Ideas of *caritas* and *amore* became programmatic, and in the
century after the 1340's, when communal politics lost so much of
its cohesion, the signory sought to institutionalize the public expression
of these qualities. Government by corporate interest groups and juridically defined cadres was in crisis. A more impersonal and individual-
ized politics was emerging, and this in turn was predicated upon the
increased atomization of society. These changes left the individual
more isolated, while at the same time permitting philanthropic impulses to break the customary bounds of limited familial allegiances
and restricted corporate obligations. The drive to extend these concerns was an amplification of lay piety guided by a century of governmental control.

At the heart of the Quattrocento dilemma induced by economic
change, was the failure of a battery of collective ideals. These values
had their locus in kinship groups, juridically defined social cadres,
consortiums of nobles and commoners, and a plethora of self-regulating
corporate bodies. All of these contributed to a belief in an organic,
non-competitive society in which men subordinated egoistic impulses
to *il bene comune*. Of course the efficacy of such doctrines was in
serious dispute, but their verity was rarely challenged. That men could
not always satisfy the claims of "distributive justice" did not invalidate this commanding concept. In the hundred years after 1340, corporate
and associative energies, once so vital, atrophied and were ritualized.
The best thinkers in Florence, from Bruni to Machiavelli and Guicciardini, recognized this failure and sought to discover new principles
that might animate civic life. What few men could face was the clear
emergence of self-interest and competition as predominating over
traditional Christian and communal values. Lay piety, always strong
in Florence, projected a comprehensive vision of a new ideal of community—that of Christian brotherhood—acted out by humble citizens

in the ordinary round of civic life. This vision was elevated to an
enduring art form by the generation of Brunelleschi and Masaccio
when the frontiers between philanthropy and sanctity were opening
to merchant pilgrims.[1]

---

[1] Since writing this paper I have learned from Professor Richard Goldthwaite that
pious foundations sold annuities to finance their building programs. And, of course,
Santa Maria Nuova served as a bank. Cf. above, 181, n. 2.

3. RITUAL IN FLORENCE :
ADOLESCENCE AND SALVATION IN THE RENAISSANCE*

RICHARD C. TREXLER

University of Illinois

The recent interest in the development of the modern family and the modern concept of childhood and youth has been largely sparked by the seminal work of Philippe Ariès[1]. In his view, the modern child produced the modern family. The new child was himself the result of pedagogical innovations and aristocratic sensibilities which, over a long period of time, drifted down to the middle and lower classes from the leisure class, and to society at large from the schools. Late medieval and early modern teachers had perceived that children and youth learned different disciplines best at certain ages, and this specification of curriculum had led in the seventeenth century to the discovery of child psychology. The child was no longer an "idiot" whose parents waited for him to grow up, but a particular human being with behavioral modes valuable in themselves, which could be rightly enjoyed by the parents. Around this new creature grew the family, a unit for the child's protection and self-expression.

This paper contributes to the growing literature which is attempting to elaborate upon Ariès' views of this evolution from medieval to modern family and generational institutions.[2] It is specifically about urban Florence; emphasis is not placed upon private aristocratic or patrician sensibilities, but on the creation of social instrumentalities—

* I am especially grateful to my research assistant, Miss Jane Goldberg, and to Professor Rab Hatfield, for their help.

[1] P. Ariès, *Centuries of Childhood* (New York, 1965).

[2] See especially D. Hunt, *Parents and Children in History. The Psychology of Family Life in Early Modern France* (New York, 1970); N. Davis, "The Reasons of Misrule : Youth Groups and Charivaris in Sixteenth-Century France," *Past and Present*, n. 50 (1971), 55f, 61f; J. Thirsh, "The Family," *Past and Present*, n. 27 (1964), 116-122; R. Goldthwaite, *Private Wealth in Renaissance Florence : A Study of Four Families* (Princeton, 1968), 234-275.

confraternities for boys—aimed at acculturating the adolescents of Florence.[1]

The canon Delaruelle asked in 1963 if the boys' confraternities of the quattrocento were the first such groups specifically intended for youth.[2] The answer seems to be affirmative. Why did such sponsored pious groups appear in Italy at the beginning of the Renaissance ? What were their goals ? How did they evolve ? What was their relation to the religious and educational currents of the period ?

We will see that adolescents emerged in the quattrocento as the male "saviors" of society, a role which traditionally had been reserved to the monasteries and governments. The youth were incorporated as the monasteries declined. How did organized religious and other integrative activities bridge the gap from a traditional society in which incorporated holy men had functioned as the ritual saviors of society to the new society in which an age group would fill the same role ?

In northern Europe, the fifteenth century witnessed an ever-heightened attempt to bring students into colleges and subject them to greater discipline. One of the spurs to this enclosure of young students was the influential sermons of Gerson on the rearing of the young. Like other moralists and educators of the fifteenth century, he saw the problem of unruly students as part of the indocility of the young

---

[1] Goldthwaite, *Private Wealth;* on 293-303 the author has provided a bibliography of recent works on Italian familial history. See also the study by R. Starn, "Francesco Guicciardini and his Brothers," in *Renaissance Studies in Honor of Hans Baron,* eds. A. Molho and J. A. Tedeschi (Dekalb, 1971), 409-444. C. Bec, *Les marchands écrivains. Affaires et humanisme à Florence 1375-1434* (Paris, 1967) provides the best analysis of family sensibilities at Florence during this period.

[2] E. Delaruelle, "La vie religieuse dans les pays de langue française à la fin du XVe siècle," in *Colloque d'histoire religieuse* (Grenoble, 1963), 14. In all the following, I adhere to the most common quattrocento usages of the following terms : infant : until the child speaks; childhood (*puerizia* or *fanciulezza*) : until ca. twelve or thirteen, the age of puberty; adolescence (an *adolescente* or *giovanetto* and sometimes *fanciullo*) : from ca. thirteen to twenty-five; youth (*iuvenis* or *giovane*) : from twenty-five ot forty, after which point I speak of the adult or *uomo fatto.* "Young people" is meant to convey a generality for those less than thirty. This admittedly anachronistic procedure has the advantage of mirroring contemporaries' formal conception of ages, and prevents textual misunderstandings. On the question of these formal age differentiations, see Ariès, *Centuries,* 18-25 ; I. Del Lungo, *Dino Compagni e la sua cronica* I (Florence, 1879), 1100f; D. Herlihy, "Vieillir à Florence au Quattrocento," *Annales E. S. C.* XXIV (1969), 1339. A variant series of ages was offered by the Florentine humanist Matteo Palmieri in E. Garin (ed.), *L'educazione umanistica in Italia* (Bari, 1949), 114.

as a whole.[1] In Italy as well, new pedagogical directions were contemporary with attempts to harness young people as a whole.

The traditional youth groups of medieval Europe did not lend themselves to social planning. Their main purpose was diversion, achieved through such means as parody, masquerades, dances, and other forms of festive nonsense. In the small communities of Europe, such *badie* or *charivaris* could function as a type of social control element enforcing accepted village norms.[2] But in the cities they often proved more conducive to disorder than to burgher piety. The Florentine evidence suggests that the modern youth club, distinguished in the early period by its pious and deliberate pedagogic thrust, was an urban creation at odds with the old communal or rural gang.

Youth had long played a major role in Florentine festive brigades, organized to provide both amusement and visual pleasure. Villani's descriptions of the brigades of the outgoing duecento and early trecento can be summarized in the following fashion.[3] The groups were occasional, organized mainly for the festivities of May Day. They were competitive, brigades from different sections of the city vying with each other to please the citizenry. They were financed by rich families. While young people may have predominated (Villani speaks of brigades of *gentili giovani* in the 1290s),[4] participation does not seem to have been limited to them. Villani would have us believe that in the good old days, the brigades were composed of noble youth, while in his own latter days, grown *artefici* and *popolo minuto* walked the streets as play emperors, dukes and the like.[5] This too obvious dichotomy between past purity and present decline is dubious. I should imagine that the traditional brigade of this and later times was com-

---

[1] E. Delaruelle *et al*, *L'Église au temps du Grand Schisme et de la crise conciliaire (1378-1449)*, *(Fliche et Martin*, XIV, part 2), (Paris, 1964), 845ff.

[2] N. Davis, "Charivaris," 55 *et passim*. The Italian counterparts to the French charivaris were concentrated in rural northwestern Italy; G. C. Pola Falletti Villafalletto, *Associazioni giovanili e feste antiche* I (Milan, 1939), and the same author's *La juventus attraverso i secoli* (Monza, 1953).

[3] I draw my summary from *Croniche di Giovanni, Matteo e Filippo Villani* I (Trieste, 1857), (book) VII, (chapter) 89 (1283); VII, 132 (1289); VIII, 70 (1304); X, 219 (1333); XII, 8 (1343).

[4] *Ibid.*, VII, 132.

[5] Cf. Villani's characterization of the 1283 brigade as "la più nobile e nominata che mai fosse nella città di Firenze e Toscana," with that of 1343 during the dictatorship of Walter of Brienne : "Fu movitura e consentimento del duca per recarsi l'amore del popolo minuto, per quella isforzata vanità; *ibid.*, VII, 89; XII, 8.

posed of a few rich youth (and some not so young) financed by their fathers, who in turn mobilized groups of lower class young people and adults.[1] In any case, Villani and other trecento chroniclers made no clear and lasting distinction between *uomini* and *giovani* in describing the leisure-time institutions of Florence. This lack of differentiation continued until the latter part of the trecento.[2]

Children and adolescents at school do not seem to have been corporatively organized. At all educational levels—schools for reading and writing (ca. seven through twelve years old), through those for arithmetic (ca. twelve through fourteen), to those of latin grammar (ca. fourteen to eighteen years old), town students visited their lecturers and returned home each evening.[3] We are unable to speculate as to the degree of solidarity school associations may have engendered. Debenedetti has shown that the school masters had organized,[4] but nothing suggests that the school was the institutional base for any youthful social activity in Florence.

---

[1] The historian Cambi, for example, described a Carnival in 1499 where were "raghunati assai duomini tutti plebei, el forte, benchè e' Messeri alchuni fussino fanciulli da bene per segnio"; I. a San Luigi (ed.), *Delizie degli eruditi toscani* XX (1785), 136. An example of old leadership is provided by Doffo Spini, who led the group of Compagnacci against Savonarola. He was fifty years old. His approximately nine associates from the nobility were called *I Vecchi;* these had a group of some 300 *giovani* at their beck, "i più scoretti della città"; J. Schnitzer (ed.), *Quellen und Forschungen zur Geschichte Savonarolas III : Bartolommeo Cerretani* (Munich, 1904), 54f; P. Villari and E. Casanova (eds.), *Scelta di prediche e scritti di fra Girolamo Savonarola* (Florence, 1898), 481.

[2] From then on, the *brigate* were by definition *de' giovani;* see for example the Alberti and Castellani brigades of 1386 in which *giovani* were wonderfully dressed; *Biblioteca Nazionale, Firenze* (hereafter *BNF*), *Fondo Panciatichi* 158, f. 150r; almost all of the numerous brigades described by Bartolommeo Del Corazza in his *ricordi* were of *giovani;* G. O. Corazzini (ed.), "Diario Fiorentino di Bartolommeo Del Corazza, anni 1405-1438," *Archivio Storico Italiano* (hereafter *ASI*) ser. 5, vol. XIV (1894), 243f, 254, 255, 276. In religious processions, however, the lack of distinction continued for some time. In his famous first description of a *festa* of S. Giovanni Battista (ca. 1405), for example, Goro Dati speaks of "compagnie d'uomini secolari" wearing angels' dress; C. Guasti, *Le feste di San Giovanni Battista in Firenze* (Florence, 1884), 5. The first mention of young people participating as a distinct unit in a religious procession would seem to be Del Corazza's description of the entry of Martin V into Florence in 1419, when "gioveni, de' maggiori della terra e più politi," accompanied the Corpus Christi; see Del Corazza, "Diario," 257, 271-274, 285, 292f.

[3] See the summary in R. Davidsohn, *Storia di Firenze*, 8 vols. (Florence, 1956-68), VII, 211-223.

[4] S. Debenedetti, "Sui più antichi doctores puerorum a Firenze," *Studi Medievali* II (1906-7), 338-342.

In these early centuries, therefore, there was no extra-familial group instrumentality for the stated purpose of indoctrinating young people in religious and other social values. The typical trecento school of the master certainly imparted these values de facto; many of the instructors were clerks and priests, and the textbooks for reading and writing had a strong ethical content. Yet instruction in social piety was not formalized.[1]

The parent who sought such training for his sons outside the home had little choice. Florence's monasteries and friaries do not seem to have allowed externs to attend their schools, for here in Florence, as elsewhere in Europe, the move was to limit these conventual schools to those who had vocational intentions.

The only possibility in Florence of an education which would insure training for secular youth in piety as well as in grammar came through the existing adult confraternity system. At the end of the duecento two of these sodalities maintained schools at the churches where they met. Details are sketchy, but it seems that instruction was provided by religious persons, and that the best students, upon terminating their courses, had preferential but nonobligatory access to the religious life.[2] Apart from these distant forerunners of the boys' confraternities of the quattrocento, no pious group specifically for young people has left its trace in the Florentine records. Fleeting as their appearance is, these confraternal scuole provided the only instrument outside the

---

[1] Davidsohn and Debenedetti seem to have assumed that lay schools had uniformly lay teachers, which was certainly not the case. What was missing was formal religious instruction within the school's framework. Informally, in the Christian age any teacher, lay or ecclesiastical, imparted religious norms : "Nam pueri religiosi nascuntur, atque educantur, et in religione firmissimi permanent, quousque in adolescentia ratio excitetur ..."; M. Ficino, Opera Omnia I (Turin, 1962), 4. In 1514, the Council of the Lateran V ordered school masters to teach the catechism to children, and forbade them from teaching anything else on feast days other than "religion and good manners"; P. Tacchi Venturi, Storia della compagnia di GesV in Italia I (Rome, 1950), 339f.

[2] The Necrology of the Dominican friary of Santa Maria Novella relates that Fra Uguccio di fu Lapo Morelli († 1301) before he entered the order, was "a teneris annis cum multa devotione cum allis pueris nostre Societatis Beate Virginis"; R. Davidsohn, Forschungen zur Geschichte von Florenz IV (Berlin, 1908), 430. For both this society and the one at the collegiate church of S. Lorenzo, see also Davidsohn, Storia, VII, 225f. Fathers may have used these societies as a means of insuring the future of their sons in an overpopulated society. For confraternities created to guarantee members' daughters' entrance into a nunnery, see Archivo di Stato, Firenze (hereafter ASF), R. Diritto, 4892, ff. 293r-297r (1516).

family for an education which would not neglect religious acculturation.[1]

In the trecento there were no lay sodalities statutorily limited to
giovani or *fanciulli*.[2] Confraternities were for *uomini* or *donne* or both.
They were organized into *laudesi*, indoor groups for singing church
music, and the *disciplinati* or flagellants, characterized by stern internal discipline and by their participation in outdoor processions.[3]
These confraternities increased during the quattrocento, and became
more diversified in type. Companies bearing "standards" or baldach-
ins appeared at the end of the trecento, and in early quattrocento the
so-called "night companies" made their debut. With the traditional
laudesi and *disciplinati*, the new companies of the standards and the
night companies formed a rich web of secular sodalities into which
poured a large number of Florentine citizens and *artefici*. The articulation of fraternities into age groups was a part of this wider confraternal organization. While several scholars have recognized the
growing importance of the confraternities in Florentine cultural life
during the quattrocento, the creation of special confraternities for
young people has not caught their attention.[4] A description of their

---

[1] Parental concerns on this score had spurred the development of the college within
the Northern European university, and the expansion of the oblate system within the
Mendicant orders; see J. R. H. Moorman, *The Grey Friars in Cambridge, 1225-1538*
(Cambridge, 1952), 104-111.

[2] Richa's assumption that a company of *fanciulli* had existed in the friary of San
Marco since the outgoing thirteenth century is incorrect; G. Richa, *Notizie istoriche
delle chiese fiorentine*, 10 vols. (Florence, 1754-62), V, 329-331. See also G. M. Monti,
Le Confraternite Medievali dell'Alta e Media Italia I (Florence, 1927), 149-190. Writing about 1405, the Dominican reformer Giovanni Dominici made no mention of pious
organizations for children or youth in his pedagogic recommendations to parents;
G. Dominici, *On the Education of Children*, ed. A. Coté, (Washington, 1927).

[3] In 1419, "Flagellants and *laudesi*" were still used to describe the range of lay
confraternities; *Archivio di Stato, Firenze* (hereafter *ASF*), *Provvisioni*, 109, ff. 160v-
162r (19 Oct. 1419). In the Diary of Del Corazza, the "compagnie cogli stendardi" which
took part in processions were the same as the "compagnie de' battuti" or "di discipline";
Del Corazza, "Diario," 242, 249, 279f.

[4] Monti has attempted to quantify the secular trend, and in terms of numbers of
confraternities founded, the quattrocento is indeed remarkable. But a full-length study
of the Florentine confraternities will be necessary before we know how many people
were involved, the average life span of the foundations, and what classes of the population were involved in them; important articles on the cultural significance of the con-

origins and development will focus attention upon this particular institution.

Our first evidence of a confraternity specified by age is contained in a petition of 1396 directed to the Signoria of Florence by the captains of the "venerable and devout" society of San Matteo, meeting in the Augustinian church of Santo Spirito. Made up of "honest and devout youth," the society was growing rapidly. It asked for and received annual alms of the type normally given to ecclesiastical entities by the *Mercanzia* and guild consuls.[1] It was the first non-ecclesiastical group to receive such funds. Once the first of these groups of *iuvenes* was established, others quickly followed.[2]

The process of age delineation continued, and soon the first companies for adolescents appeared on the scene. The oldest may be that of the Nativity (also called "of the Archangel Raphael"), established in 1410 by a goldsmith. It met for some years in the hospital of the Scala.[3] A second company, that of San Niccolò del Ceppo, purport-

---

fraternities are : P. O. Kristeller, "Lay Religious Traditions and Florentine Platonism," in his *Studies in Renaissance Thought and Letters* (Rome, 1956), 99-122; E. Garin, "Desideri di riforma nell'oratoria del quattrocento," now in his *La cultura filosofica del Rinascimento Italiano* (Florence, 1961), 166-182; R. Hatfield, "The Compagnia De' Magi," *Journal of the Warburg and Courtauld Institutes* XXXIII (1970), 107-161. For the constitutions and matriculation of one company of flagellants, see the recent publication by O. Marinelli (ed.), "La Compagnia di Disciplinati di S. Domenico in Firenze," *Bolletino della deputazione di storia patria per l'Umbria*, ser. 1, vol. LXVI (1969), 211-240.

[1] "Per devotos iuvenes et honestos dicat societas creata fuit," *ASF, Prov.*, 85, ff. 247r-248r (8 Dec. 1396).

[2] Among the subsequent companies of *iuvenes* was that of S. Michele Archangelo, meeting in the Servite church, and "recently made" when its *capitoli* were approved by the bishop on 23 Nov. 1420; *ASF, Notarile antecosiminiano* S 672 (1417-21), at the date. In 1419 the commune approved a payment for candles to "certain societies of youth" participating in the celebration of S. Giovanni Battista; *ASF, Prov.* 109, ff. 49v-50r (12 June). It is unclear whether these latter groups were pious or festive.

[3] Del Migliore in recording this information in his *Zibaldone* said that it aimed at teaching Christian doctrine to *giovanetti*. I have been unable to find any verification for the traditional assertion that this and the other boys' confraternities were called "confraternities of (Christian) Doctrine." It will become clear in what follows that no reference is made to catechetical training in any of the quattrocento records of these companies. For the early wanderings of the company, whose statutes of 1468 are extant, see Monti, *Confraternite*, I, 183. When the famous *cartolaio* Vespasiano da Bisticci was "di non molta età," (born 1421), he was encouraged to join the company of *fanciulli* of ser Antonio di Mariano. Ser Antonio was the custodian of this company (see below, 213, n. 4); *Vita di uomini illustri del secolo XV* (Florence, 1938), 145 (*Vita* of the Cardinal Albergati, † 1443).

edly transferred to the Ceppo from Oltrarno in 1417. Morçay tells us that it had earlier been a *scuola di lezione*.[1] A third company, that of the Purification, is said to have issued from the overcrowded company of the Nativity in 1427.[2] The documentation for the institution of these first three companies remains inconclusive. With the establishment of the company or *scuola* of *giovanetti* of San Giovanni Vangelista in the same year, we finally enter upon firm ground. Both its *capitoli* and the episcopal approval are extant.[3]

By 1435, a Florentine prelate could refer to "several" societies of boys or children in the city.[4] Their rapid growth generated quick demands for their limitation. An important papal bull of June 24, 1442 [5] shows the custodians of four such Florentine companies for boys complaining to the pope about this needless multiplication. One reason for this proliferation, they said, was that the boys themselves were creating new clubs, and removing their custodians at will. Eugenius in his letter recognized the existence of four groups for *pueri* : S. Giovanni Vangelista, S. Niccolò, the Nativity, and the confraternity of the Purification. Acceding to the recommendation of the four custodians, the pope set up a commission composed of the custodians of these confraternities, the abbot of the newly reformed *Badìa Fioren-*

---

[1] The same author cites no evidence for his assertion that its statutes were approved by the archbishop in 1450; R. Morçay, *Saint Antonin. Archevêque de Florence (1389-1459)* (Paris, 1914), 91. In the document cited at 208, n. 2, it is called a *societas adolescentium*. The confraternity's history is thoroughly confused because there was at least one and perhaps two other confraternities *del Ceppo*; see L. Passerini, *Storia degli Stabilimenti di Beneficienze di Firenze* (Florence, 1853), 188; L. Santoni, *Raccolta di notizie storiche riguardanti le chiese dell'arci-diogesi di Firenze* (Florence, 1847), 96; E. and W. Paatz, *Die Kirchen von Florenz*, 6 vols. (Frankfurt, 1940-54), II, 97-100; IV, 292-295.

[2] The group's *capitoli* were approved by the archbishop April 3, 1448; Monti, *Confraternite*, I, 184, citing Del Migliore's *Zibaldone* cited above. On June 29, 1444, the company or *scuola* of *fanciulli* was given possession of its new quarters around S. Marco; Morçay, *Antonin*, 473f. It retained them till 1506; Hatfield, "Magi," 127.

[3] Membership was limited to those between thirteen and twenty-four years of age. Copies of the *capitoli* and archiepiscopal approval of 2 July 1427 may be found in the *BNF*, Cl. 31, cod. 11, ff. 8v-9r, and in the *ASF, Not. antecos.* J 7 (1417-27), at the date July 2, 1427. Morçay erroneously identifies this company with one founded in 1388; *Antonin*, 91. Despite its statutory age limits, in the document cited at n. 29 below it is called variously a *societas puerorum et iuvenum* and a *societas ... puerorum et adolescentium*.

[4] See below, 209.

[5] Printed in C. C. Calzolai, *Frate Antonino Pierozzi* (Rome, 1960), 83f.

tina, and the prior of the Observant Dominican house of San Marco.[1] Without the advice and consent of a majority of these six men, no new groups could be created; the removal of custodians by the boys could not be legal, and elections to vacant custodianships could not be formalized. The archbishop was charged with his traditional right to approve such creations and elections. Unlike many other legislated bodies, the commission established by Eugenius did function. In 1453, we find it consenting to the boys' election of the custodian of a fifth confraternity, that of the *iuvenes et adolescentes* of Sant' Antonio da Padova, meeting in the monastery and church of San Giorgio.[2] According to D'Ancona, this company was founded in 1441.[3] There may have been more than five such groups in the city at this time. This document shows only that the four mentioned in Eugenius' bull were controlling elections in at least one other club.

One of the important provisions of Eugenius' bull of 1442 was that it forbade any group of boys besides the original four and those approved by the commission to call itself a "society" and to take part in public processions dressed in white. Various boys' groups were obviously competing for processional posts. Despite Eugenius' guidelines, this pressure continued and the San Giovanni celebration of 1453 was marred by confusion.[4] Therefore, in 1454 the commune asked the archbishop for a list of clerical entities and lay confraternities authorized to participate in the Patron's procession. Antonino's response listed seven confraternities of *fanciulli*. Of the five we have mentioned previously, four are directly listed in this document, while the fifth is probably included under a variant name. The company of Santa Brigida listed by Antonino is scarcely known. According to Del Migliore, the last of the seven, that of San Bernardino, was founded in 1451, the year after the Saint's canonization.[5]

---

[1] The abbot of the *Badia* was the Portuguese reformer Gomez da Silva; see G. Batteli, *L'abate don Gomez Ferreira da Silva e i Portoghesi a Firenze nella prima metà del quattrocento* (Rome, 1940). The prior of San Marco at the time was the saintly Antonino Pierozzi.

[2] S. Orlandi, *S. Antonino* II (Florence, 1960), 313-316. In this document its membership is said to include *iuvenes et adolescentulos*. The "nominatio et deputatio" by the forty-four members took place on March 31, 1453; the assent by the commission and the archiepiscopal approval followed on June 1, 1453.

[3] A. D'Ancona, *Origini del teatro italiano* I (1891), 406. The group's *ordinamenti* of 1466 are extant; Monti, *Confraternite*, I, 186.

[4] For one aspect of this confusion, see *ASF, Prov.* 145, ff. 86v-87r (19 June 1454).

[5] "Regole di frati come vanno a processione secondo la nota del vescovo Antonino

After this point, it is difficult to follow the institutional development of the boys' clubs. Their particular relation to the great movement of *fanciulli* under Savonarola, for example, remains to be clarified.
In Benedetto Varchi's time, about 1530, there were nine boys' confraternities in the city.[1] Thus from mid-quattrocento to mid-cinque-
cento a net gain of only two groups had been made.

In the year 1435, the Camaldolan general and scholar Ambrogio
Traversari addressed Pope Eugenius on the subject of boys' confraternities. To learn something of the organization and social position of
these groups, we can do no better than to start by citing his remarks :

> Hear now something equally pious, most Holy Father : Our city has several societies
> of noble, middle-class, and poor boys *[puerorum]*. At the head of each is a faithful,
> grave, religious, and God-fearing man who rears these [boys] and who, in secular
> dress, drills the recruits for the militia of the Eternal King. Following their rule, they
> observe continence in everything. They flee from inane spectacles and all games, and
> they abstain also from the idle talk [of the games and spectacles]. They confess
> more frequently, and take communion often. And while during the remaining
> days of the week they exercise their individual trade under the supervision of
> their relatives, on Sundays and feast days they all meet at a designated place
> where they give themselves over to the praise of God *[divinis laudibus]* and use
> their time for worthwhile colloquies. When however they have left their childhood
> years behind, they transfer to another group where older people meet, and continue
> in similar works. Many of them, once they have tasted the goodness of innocence,
> enter the religious life.[2]

In another letter on the same subject, Traversari gives us more
information on their position and social utility. Speaking of one such
scuola, he says :

> The leaders of the city are repeatedly pleased to send their sons to be nourished
> in this school and to be educated in this school of Christian virtue. In it nothing
> impious is learned, nothing other than good habits is imbibed ... [Through this
> training] they often remain innocent amidst the obscene railery of criminals ...
> On Sundays and feast days, when greater license for lasciviousness is usurped,

---

come mi dette Baccio Falsamonstra"; *ASF, Signoria e Balia, Carte di Corredi* 45, f.
18v. The document bears no date. But according to an unsubstantiated remark of Gori,
Antonino drew this up in 1454; P. Gori, *Le feste fiorentine attraverso i secoli. Le feste
per San Giovanni* (Florenec, 1926), 20f. For the company of S. Brigida, see Paatz, *Kirchen*,
I, 406f. The company of S. Bernardino met in the Franciscan church of Santa Croce.
Its *capitoli* were written in 1471; Monti, *Confraternite*, I, 186, citing the Del Migliore
Zibaldone.

  [1] B. Varchi, *Storia Fiorentina* (Florence, 1963), I, 591 (IX, 36).
  [2] A. Traversari, *Latinae Epistolae* ... ,ed. L. Mehus, II (Florence, 1759), c. 40.

they gather together, and after salubrious admonitions, they either recite the psalms or sing hymns together. And if perhaps someone has occasionally or lightly violated the rules, penance is meted out and the crime is confessed. Formed and indoctrinated in this way, they return to their parents' homes and, the parents being presented with such a specimen of religion, the boys [contribute] through example and incitement to the good morality of the family ... [If the boys] decide to remain laymen, they retain the taste of supernal grace which they received in their tender years. To whatever magistracies of the city they are elected, they cultivate justice before all else.[1]

The main purpose of these confraternities or schools was obviously to remove the boys from the chaos and spontaneity of the street, and to provide a leisure-time activity under competent direction which would aid the formation of a pious character.[2] Separation of age groups was one of the means used to achieve this character. In itself the division according to ages reflected only the corporate mentality of the time : children were of a different sect than youth, youth than grown men.[3] Such a division did not assume that youthful piety was to be reached through different activities than those of the men's confraternities. In fact, one of the striking aspects of these clubs is the markedly adult character of their internal group practices. The decision to create corporations of young people was new; the legal instruments for doing so were old. The *capitoli* of the new groups followed the classical associative formulas for grown men. The boys of the Vangelista were to be between thirteen and twenty-four years of age. These adolescents proclaimed in their constitutions, however, that it is they who have decided to organize. It is these boys who "make the constitutions", choosing the goals and methods of their group.[4]

---

[1] *Ibid.*, c. 134; printed in E. Garin (ed.), *Il pensiero pedagogico dello umanesimo* (Florence, 1958), 304. Both of these letters were written in 1435.

[2] Vespasiano da Bisticci tells us, for example, that as children Piero and Donato Acciaiuoli entered a company of *giovani* with their tutor "to flee youth to whom good manners were foreign ... All this was done to form well the habit of virtue"; *Vite*, 355 (*Vita* of Donato Acciaiuoli). The Vangelista, like an adult sodality, outlawed gambling, whoring, and blasphemy; *BNF, Cl.* 31, cod. 11, ff. 3v-4r (cap. III).

[3] "When he became older," for example, Donato Acciaiuoli moved from the company of youth to the night company of S. Girolamo; *Vite, loc. cit.* In earlier times an occasional adult confraternity seems to have had *pueri* or *adolescentes* attached to it in some capacity; see above, 204, n. 2, and the 1278 *capitoli* of the adult company of S. Egidio, where *fanciulli* above fourteen or fifteen might be admitted; Monti, *Confraternite*, II, 153.

[4] Vogliendo dunque alcune divote persone deta danni tredici in quattuordici et non piu cominciare et dare principio al bene operare ..."; *BNF, Cl.* 31, cod. 11, ff. 2r-3r.

The similarity to adult modes was more than merely legal. The youngsters effectively controlled by vote all the offices of the con-fraternity. From their midst the *fanciulli* of the Vangelista elected their governor (second in command in the confraternity) and his two counsellors. Together with the guardian of the confraternity, these three boy-officers then elected the boy-*infermieri* who would act as masters of the novices.[1]

The *confratelli* also had a determinant voice in the election of the adult men who were attached to the groups. The confessors, for example, were directly elected by the boys from a list of four candi-dates submitted to them by their adult custodians or guardians, as they were sometimes called. As for this latter official, there are traces in the *capitoli* of a desire to prevent the boys from removing him at will : If on his death-bed the guardian revealed to the group's confessor his choice of a successor, that choice was to be honored. Still, the boys themselves retained the greatest authority : Each year the confessors, together with the three boys serving as governor and counsellors, were to reaffirm the guardian.[2] We have seen that before 1442, the boys exercised these rights to the fullest, dismissing their guardians at will and instituting new groups when they encountered opposition. Eu-genius' decision to appoint a commission of grown men to advise and consent was a small step toward controlling organizations which, des-pite their youthful membership, retained the democratic associative principles common to the corporations of their fathers.[3]

The internal activities of the clubs, as they are revealed in the *capitoli* of the Vangelista, were as adult as their election procedures, not significantly different from the traditional activities of the non-flagellant men's confraternities. They met on the first and third Sundays of each month and on all Sundays of Advent and Lent. On Holy Thursday the guardian washed the feet of the boys, a traditional confraternal practice. The boys were to confess once a month to the group's confessor, take communion together on the feast of the Evan-gelist, and attend mass every morning "or at least try to see the body

---

[1] *Ibid.*, ff. 5rv.

[2] *Ibid.*, ff. 4r-5r.

[3] For an overview of the long process by which university students were stripped of their medieval corporate privileges, see E. Durkheim, *L'évolution pédagogique en France* I (Paris, 1938), 146-156. Compare the long battle of the Dominican students at Padua to retain their traditional rights in L. Gargin (ed.), *Lo studio teologico e la biblio-teca dei Domenicani a Padova nel tre e quattrocento* (Padua, 1971), 16f, 19-36.

of Christ."[1] As in the confraternities of the *uomini fatti* the brothers suffered correction by the guardian when they violated the *capitoli*. Finally, novices were accepted in typical adult fashion : voted on during the second meeting of their novitiate, they were formally installed during the third gathering, dressed in white and singing the *Veni Creator* and *Te Deum*.[2]

At their inception, then, the boys' confraternities were democratic in their operation and adult in their practices. These "schools of virtues"[3] were not, however, without controls imposed by elders. Internal control was fostered in the Company of the Purification by allowing only the older boys to vote on certain affairs,[4] a custom found also in a Pistoian confraternity of *fanciulli* in 1516.[5] A more important control element was the dependence of the boys' groups on confraternities of *uomini fatti*. Thus the Purification was under the protection of the men's confraternity of S. Girolamo.[6] The Vangelista had a similar relation to the adult confraternity of S. Paolo.[7] And the boys' group of S. Bastiano was fathered by the men's company of S. Jacopo, which decided to alleviate its overgrowth by "making two companies in one body, one company of the men of the night of S. Jacopo and S. Giovanni Gualberto, the other of *fanciulli* under the title of the glorious martyr S. Bastiano."[8] The Pistoian boys of the

---

[1] *BNF*, Cl. 31, cod. 11, ff. 3rv.

[2] *Ibid.*, ff. 5r-6v.

[3] See above, 209. The Pistoian boys' confraternity of the Purità, founded in 1516, also referred to itself as such; P. Vigo (ed.), *Una confraternità di giovanetti pistoiesi a principio del secolo XVI* (Bologna, 1887), 45.

[4] Decision made by "guardianus societatis puerorum purificationis beate Marie seu Sancti Marci, una cum gubernatiore et consiliariis et pueris natu maioribus"; Florence, *Biblioteca Laurenziana*, Fondo *Biblioteca di San Marco*, cod. 370 : *Chronica conventus Sancti Marci de Florentia*, f. 17r (1496).

[5] Vigo, *Confraternità ... pistoiesi*, 60.

[6] The 1543 acts cited above (208, n. 2) refers to "Pierus Mariani, custos societatis ... [sic] que congregatur apud hospitale Sancti Mathei seu dictum *l'ospedale di Lelmo* de Florentia." This is without doubt the Purificazione, as a comparison of the papal bull of 1442 and the 1453 document makes clear. Del Migliore had read an old document in the archive of San Marco on the night company of San Girolamo, "ad quem protectio et cura dicte societatis [dei fanciulli della purificazione alias di S. Marco] spectat"; F. Del Migliore, *Firenze Città' Nobilissima Illustrata* (Florence, 1684), 256.

[7] See *ASF*, *Comp. Relig. Soppr.* 1579, containing information on relations between the companies. I owe this information to the kindness of Rab Hatfield.

[8] This information comes from a memorial of the parent company's cinquecento historian, who says that it took place in 1460; cited in Richa, *Notizie*, X, 352ff. In the

Company of Purity gathered in the same meeting place as the *uomini* of S. Matteo, and the prior of that company approved the boys' election of a guardian.[1]

A further element of control by elders and parents may be mentioned, but without the documentation one would like. The guardians of these boys' confraternities may have come from the companies of *uomini fatti* and formed an elite of pious laymen. The guardian of the confraternity of the Vangelista, for example, was at the same time one of the twelve Buonomini, a prestigious confraternity created in 1442 to aid the shamed poor of good family.[2] The original home of this same boys' group was donated to it by another member of the Buonomini.[3] Further, in one short period, three members of one family headed confraternities : Piero succeeded his father Mariano as guardian of the Purification, while ser Antonio di Mariano governed the company of the Nativity.[4] Further research may show that a relatively small group of citizens was the motivating force behind much of the drive to organize the boys.[5]

The firmest control exercised by adults was, however, not institutional at all, but through monetary support. As we shall see, the

---

process of founding the Pistoian boys' confraternity of the Purità, the men's sodality of S. Matteo assigned two of its *giovani* to the Purità to provide guidance; Vigo, *Confraternità ... pistoiesi*, 6.

[1] *Ibid.*, 6, 50.

[2] This was Jacopo di Biagio dell'Ancisa, *cimatore* or tailor's cutter, custodian in 1453; on the Buonomini, see my forthcoming "Medieval Charity and the Defense of Urban Elites," in F. Jaher (ed.), *The Rich, the Well-Born and the Powerful. Elites and Upper Classes in History* (Urbana, 1973), 64-109.

[3] Luigi d'Urbano di messer Francesco Bruni bought the property of S. Trinità Vecchia from the Gesuati in 1438 and then donated it to the Vangelista in 1441 ; Monti. *Confraternite*, I, 188. On Bruni, see Trexler, "Charity," 89.

[4] A document cited by Morçay records that in favoring the Purification, Cosimo de' Medici "tutte le partite di per se pagò et tolse per la compagnia di Mariano"; Morçay, *Antonin*, 474. Thus in 1444 one Mariano must have been guardian. It may be assumed that Piero di Mariano, the guardian in 1453, was his son, and that ser Antonio di Mariano was another son. It will be recalled that the Nativity fathered the Purification; see above, 207.

[5] Ser Alessio di Matteo Pelli, notary who acted as Cosimo's procurator in handing over the Purificazione's new quarters in 1444, was also a member of the Buonomini; see Morçay, *Antonin*, 474. On Pelli, see Trexler, "Charity," 89. According to a tradition going back to Del Migliore, but which I have not been able to document, the original Buonomini came from the membership of the night company of S. Girolamo; Del Migliore, *Firenze ... Illustrata*, 256.

boys' activities were costly, and financial support came from lay
benefactors. We know next to nothing about Florentines' attitudes
toward having their children in these companies. On the one hand
they wanted their boys to receive pious instruction, while on the other
the majority probably did not want their children so exposed to clerical
ways as to develop a vocation for the religious life. Duecento adult
confraternities may have supported schools so as to channel surplus
sons into the religious life, but with population at a much lower level,
the average middle and upper class Florentine of the quattrocento
wanted a pious son, but not a religious one. A father might be forced
to place a surplus daughter in a nunnery; a son could be emancipated.[1]
The religious vocations desirable to a Camaldolan monk like Traversari
were not so attractive to the average father,[2] and the Savonarolan
period was marked by parental recriminations against the reformer
who had won their sons to the religious life. The same values hindered
increased membership in the Pistoian confraternity of the Purità.
When three boys chose a life of religion in 1517, parents reacted by
withdrawing their sons—and their financial support—from the group.[3]

Lay leadership of these confraternities was an evident attempt to
prevent boys from being seduced into the religious life. Who then were
these guardians and, just as important, who were the boys who matriculated in the companies of the *fanciulli*? As limited as our information presently is, and as misleading as matriculation lists can be
in assessing the tone of social groups, some limited overview of their
social composition may be offered.

The guardians were small shopkeepers rather than civic leaders.
In 1453 one carried the title "ser"; he may have been a notary. One
guardian was a dyer, another a shoemaker, while a third was a small
wool master. This shopkeeper leadership seems to have been preserved
in subsequent years.[4] True, in 1483 the guardian of the Purification

---

[1] On this problem, see below, 217.

[2] See Traversari's enthusiasm for the confraternities as generators of vocations
above, 209.

[3] "Imperochè molti per timore haveano che non andassino alla sancta religione, da
propri padri e madri hebbeno comandamento che non andassero all decta compagnia,
nè al convento di San Domenico si appellassino ..."; Vigo, *Confraternità ... pistoiesi*,
p. 59; see also 64f.

[4] The founder of the Nativity, it will be remembered, was a goldworker; see above,
206. In 1453, the custodians or guardians of five companies were Antonio di Paolo,
tintore (del Ceppo); Onofrio di Filippo di Bartolommeo, *calzaiuolo* (S. Antonio da Padova);

was a *dominus* Domenico di Stefano, and in 1495 one ser Chiaro di Giovanni.[1] Yet in the 1490s the guardian of the company of the Vangelista was a brass worker named Cristofano di Miniato. The fact that in 1491 this confraternity performed a *sacra rappresentazione* written by Lorenzo de' Medici and that Lorenzo's twelve-year old son Giuliano was the *messere* of the boys during this time, did not necessitate a change in the social quality of the group's leadership.[2] None of the known guardians of these groups during the quattrocento played any discernible role in government, and none was of significant financial standing in Florence.[3]

What of the boys serving under such honest but relatively humble citizens? A perusal of the matriculation of the company of S. Antonio da Padova in 1453 reveals that its forty-four members were predominantly of artisan background.[4] Of those whose occupations are listed, six were shoemakers, as was the guardian of the group. There were four flax dressers, three mercers, and two each of barbers, goldsmiths, silk merchants, and thread sellers, plus an assortment of five other artisans. The only crafts listed which pertained to the major guilds were the mercers and *setaiuoli;* the others were minor guildsmen.

Those without occupational designations included one patrician, a Gianfigliazzi, three members of the Salvetti and Da Filicaia families, and two sons of notaries or priests. The last eight matriculants also have no given occupation. They were probably too young for such a designation.

Since the company of Sant' Antonio was for "adolescents and youth," the average age of the matriculated was probably higher than the clubs strictly for adolescents. Its social tone was probably quite similar to the others : sons of honest burghers, plus a sprinkling of patricians exercising much influence among their *confratelli*.

We have sketched the creation and growth of the new boys' confraternities, said something of their internal organization and activities, and tried to relate them to a wider picture of confraternal diversifi-

---

Jacopo di Biagio, *cimatore* (Vangelista); Ser Antonio di Mariano (Nativity) and his brother Piero di Mariano; Orlandi, *S. Antonino*, II, 314f.

[1] Richa, *Notizie*, V, 330f.

[2] See below, 228, n. 4.

[3] I could trace none of them in the Catasto lists of 1427 published by L. Martines, *The Social World of the Florentine Humanists* (Florence, 1963), appendices.

[4] *ASF, Not. antecos.* B 386 (1453-54), f. 10v. Rab Hatfield was kind enough to transcribe this matriculation for me.

cation within the city of Florence. Before proceeding any further, however, it is necessary to mention the creation of another type of confraternal organization during the quattrocento. I refer to the foundation of two important *scuole* under mixed secular-ecclesiastical direction located in the cathedral church and in the Medici parish church of San Lorenzo. Differences there were between these *schole clericorum* and those of the secular *fanciulli*. Yet these were less important than the commonality of certain of their aims and practices.

The *schola puerorum ordinandorum* was instituted in the cathedral of Florence in 1436 through the joint efforts of Pope Eugenius IV and the commune.[1] Acting for the commune, the Florentine wool guild matched an investment by the pope in the communal funded debt, and the perpetual interest from this sum was to finance the salaries of a master of plain-chant and grammar and thirty-three student-clerks. The master was to be a priest erudite in both fields; the boys were to be natives of the dioceses of Florence or Fiesole, and at the time of their entrance to be between ten and fifteen years old.

This *scuola* was for externs; like the boys of the confraternities, these clerks lived at home or in rented quarters. Two occasions brought them to the seat of the *scuola*. The first was for instruction in song and grammar, the second and more important was to participate in cathedral ritual. The stated purpose of the *scuola* was to meet the increased needs of the enlarged cathedral for singers and altar boys through grammatical and voice instruction.[2] The ritual expected of the boys was extensive : it involved a procession from their school to the cathedral and their presence in church "at all times of all days

---

[1] This sketch is based on two bulls of Eugenius IV printed in J. Lami, *Sanctae Ecclesiae Florentinae Monumenta* II (Florence, 1758), 1147ff (23 March 1436), and 1465f(Oct. 4, 1441). The first of these has been reprinted in A. Seay, "The 15th-Century Cappella at Santa Maria del Fiore in Florence," *Journal of the American Musicological Society* XI (1958), 45-55. The bull of 1441 may also be found in F. A. D'Accone, "A Documentary History of Music at the Florentine Cathedral and Baptistry during the Fifteenth Century," (Harvard, diss., 1960), II, 6f. A list of the known masters of the *Scuola* is found in Richa, *Notizie*, VI, pp. 105f. On the background to the Eugenian investment, see J. Kirshner, "Papa Eugenio IV e il Monte Comune," *ASI* CXXVII (1969), especially 354.

[2] Dictam ecclesiam in clericorum in cantu et grammatica peritorum numero adaugere"; Lami, *Monumenta*, II, 1147. The institution of this school preceded by only two days the consecration of the rebuilt cathedral. For Eugenius' encouragement of such *scuole* in other cathedrals, see D'Accone, "History," I, 96.

on which it happens that masses and canonical hours and other divine offices are celebrated in the said church."

Eugenius seems to have intended not only to augment the solemnity of divine services, but to create a seminary-type institution which would produce diocesan priests of assured competence and experience. Each boy received a stipend of nine florins a year for the ten years of his membership in the *scuola*. It was assumed that when the boy reached canonical age he would take Holy Orders (from about twenty-two for subdiaconal orders to twenty-five for sacerdotal orders). If at any time the boy gave up his intention, or if at the age of twenty-five had not taken the Holy Orders, he was required to return all the salary he had received during his years in the *scuola*.[1]

The arrangement was an attractive one. A father could enter his boy, receive the income from the *scuola*, and at worst pay back the sum (without interest) if he withdrew the boy at twenty-two or twenty-three. For this the boy received free instruction—we will see later what some of that was. Very importantly, the *scuola* bound him to a regular attendance at divine services and consumed his time during Sundays and feast-days, when divine services were almost continual. The scheme was so successful that just six years after its foundation, Eugenius had to restrict the number of boys being sent to the school, while at the same time correcting an already apparent abuse : it is evident that fathers and tutors were using the school to procure the stipend, instruction, and discipline, and then withdrawing the young people to avoid sacred orders.[2]

---

[1] "Et quod quilibet puerorum praedictorum cum pervenerit ad aetatem, per quam secundum canones possit ad sacros ordines promoveri, ex tunc teneatur et debeat ad ipsos ordines se facere promoveri. Si quis autem antequam ad sacros ordines promotus fuerit, vel ad annum vigesimum quintum, ut praemittitur, pervenerit, a proposito clericatus duxerit divertendum, volumus, ac praesentium tenore statuimus, ut talis, ut praemittitur, divertens, quicquid perceperit ex huiusmodi scholastriae emolumentis, ipsis consulibus refundere teneatur"; Lami, *Monumenta*, II, 1148.

[2] Magistro ... inhibemus, ne ultra numerum triginta trium praedictorum clericorum, ac aliorum viginti, qui tamen omnes ecclesiae cum superpellicetis deserviant, non possit alios aliter recipere aut retinere ... Si quis autem cuiuscumque status ... existat, qui aliquem de clericis dicti collegii sine licentia praefati episcopi, et dilectorum filiorum consulum artis lane Florentinae, qui pro tempore fuerint, abstraxerit, seu removerit, quidquid salarii nomine clericus ipse recepterit, restituere memorato collegio teneatur..., ad quod etiam clericus ipse obligatus existat; et nihilominus, qui huiusmodi clericos abstraxerint, et qui eos retinuerint, poenam ipso facto excommunicationis incurrant, a qua non possint, nisi huiusmodi salario restituto, absolvi"; *ibid.*, 1465.

Certainly the founders' intentions were not the same as those who promoted the confraternities of boys. The former aimed at insuring a supply of priests and a decorous divine service. The twelve clerks in the *scuola* founded by Cosimo de' Medici at San Lorenzo in 1458 were being referred to as "novices" at the beginning of the cinquecento. Further, it would seem that scientific instruction was given in these clerical *scuole;* by 1441, the pope had to arrange the hierarchical position of other masters who had attached themselves to the cathedral school.[1] Yet the similarities to the confraternities are many. In both types boys from puberty to twenty-four or -five were being organized under masters or guardians. Both involved the boys in pious activities, especially on Sundays and feast-days. The church *scuole* as well as the confraternities fostered social piety. At San Lorenzo, the boys were to be instructed not only in plain-chant and grammar, but piety and ecclesiastical discipline, were to receive not only lessons, but good habits.[2] As we shall also see, the church schools developed thespian activities similar to those of the confraternities. The organization and development of boys' groups in Florence during the quattrocento remains the prime social fact. The *scuole* of the young clerks were definitely part of that phenomenon.

Adolescent groups were not originally conceived as different from those of the confraternities of the *uomini fatti*. What of their historical

---

[1] The Lorenzan designation is contained in a protocol of 1520 against a master who "negligentemente faceva quello se li apparteneva circa il dar letioni, et costumi alli nostri novitii et cherici, per cui la nostra scuola al tutto era guasta et corrotta"; D. Moreni, *Memorie storiche ... S. Lorenzo. Continuazione* I (Florence, 1816), 64f. See also 63, where the boys are referred to simply as "novices" (1510). The Eugenian reform : "Quod si scholasticum memoratum virum in grammatica et cantu peritum eligi contigerit, utrumque officium grammaticam et cantum docendi exercere possit, prout in praefatis literis nostris continetur. Si autem in altera dumtaxat peritus esset, possit alius eligi, qui alteri facultati satisfaciat. Regimen autem collegit memorati penes grammaticae praeceptorum volumus permanere; Lami, *Monumenta*, II, 1465. Despite these seeming references to a scholastic curriculum, I have been unable to find any quattrocento evidence in A. Gherardi's documents on the *Studio Fiorentino* that the cathedral school was related to the Florentine University, or at all subject to the communal officials of the *Studio*. According to Davidsohn, however, the theological college of that *Studio* was called after 1495 the *Collegio Eugeniano;* Davidsohn, *Storia*, VII, 279.

[2] Non solum docere bonos mores, et grammaticam pueros sive clericos, sed etiam eos imbuat arte canendi, intelligendo de cantu, qui vulgo dicitur fermo"; Moreni, *Memorie*, I, 67 (1528). For Cosimo's intentions, see *ibid.*, 54.

development ? Did they evolve in a fashion distinct from those of their fathers ? Were activities developed which were thought more suitable to their tender years ?

To provide an answer, we divide this activity into four segments :

1. internal activities of the traditional type, called "practices of the old law" by one confraternal writer of the early cinquecento ;[1]
2. their oratorical activities;
3. their processional activities;
4. their *sacre rappresentazioni* and other dramatic presentations.

We possess no information on the more traditional activities of the Florentine boys' groups during the quattrocento, and that includes those of the Savonarolan period. Yet if we examine the *ricordi* of the Pistoian confraternity of the Purità (1516-17), we see that little had changed in their indoor activities : correction, self-accusation, confession, individual prayer, and the "external cult" of the group *laudi*.[2] The only peculiarity of the boys' domestic activity were their "corporal exercises." It will be remembered that the boys had been organized to avoid the lasciviousness of Carnival and other feasts, and it seems that in order to accomplish this, the boys remained together for most of those days. The guardians and confessors of the companies realized that spiritual exercises could not hold the boys' attention throughout the day. They were just as aware that some of the boys would yearn for the customary street diversions on feast days. Consequently, the boys elected or were assigned a *messere* from among their midst—as was the custom of the typical street or carnival gang—who was responsible for supervising his colleagues in dignified physical diversions such as games of ball. This *messere* further provided the boys with meals, an expense and responsibility usually assumed by the governors of adult confraternities. In such a fashion honest sport or diversion was encouraged, and the boys could "come through Carnival without horrendous sin."[3] The inability of young people to con-

---

[1] Vigo, *Confraternità ... pistoiesi*, 23f.

[2] Conspicuously missing from this most extensive description of a Tuscan boys' group is any mention of catechetical or doctrinal training. Tacchi Venturi conjectured that a "libretto della dottrina christiana, la quale è utile et molto necessario che li puti pizoli et zovenzelle limpara per sapene ...", included among Antonino's works and printed at Venice in 1473, was written for the boys of the Purification; Tacchi Venturi, *Storia della compagnia di Gesù*, I, 337f.

[3] Vigo, *Confraternità ... pistoiesi*, 49-69.

centrate over a sustained period of time was the rationale for these amusements. And to this extent the particular proclivities of the young were recognized. Yet such innocuous games were viewed here—as to some extent they were by humanistic pedagogues—as concessions to the weaknesses of the young, rather than as creative activities. The games were there to permit a quick return to the adult practices they were cultivating.[1]

The orations delivered in these confraternities were typical of confraternal life as a whole. Those still accessible to modern scholars were delivered before at least eight different confraternities. Five of these were of *uomini fatti*, while the other three were read in the boys' confraternities of S. Niccolò (del Ceppo), S. Antonio da Padova, and the Nativity.[2] Our limited evidence suggests that the orations to the boys were given by boys, and not by grown men.[3]

Many of the boys in these groups could not understand the humanistic latin of their speakers. But this would not detract from the edification offered the boys by such fine examples of maturity. In these centuries, Latin awed rather than bored. Besides, dignified bearing and gestures as much as the words marked the successful speaker. Here is the reaction to a sermon delivered to the Pistoian confraternity of the Purità by a boy of childish years, standing before a scaled down rostrum and addressing his brothers :

> [He] explained the meaning of the words "company", "fraternity," and "purity," and to what end [the company] had been instituted and many other things, exhorting purity of conscience and right, honest, and virtuous living in these early years [of life.] He pronounced the said sermon not with artificial gestures, but with ones taught by God, [and] with such grace that he reduced many of the bystanders to tears and to great devotion.[4]

---

[1] It is significant that not only the ball games, but the *rappresentazioni* or sacred plays which the Pistoian group performed were considered "external" activities, while sacramental reception and individual prayer were internal; *ibid.*, 23f, 58, 68f. See also below, 221.

[2] This information is culled from a list in A. Bandini, *Specimen Literaturae Florentinae Saeculi XV* II (Florence, 1751), 160ff. See also on the orations Kristeller, *Studies*, 105f; Garin, *Cultura filosofica*, 167, 178f; Hatfield, "Magi," 128-135.

[3] The budding humanist Giovanni Nesi (born 1456), for example, delivered one oration to the rectors of S. Niccolò at the age of sixteen. At eighteen, he addressed the boys of S. Antonio da Padova, and then between the ages of nineteen and twenty-two this "adolescent" spoke three times to the Nativity; Bandini, *Specimen, loc. cit.*

[4] Vigo, *Confraternità ... pistoiesi*, 40f.

The processional and dramatic activities of the boys' groups were as innovative as the "practices of the old law" and the orations were traditional.[1] In discussing these creative activities, I shall first consider their processional activities devoid of any dramatic or narrative content, and reserve my comments on their dramatic and semi-dramatic activities, whether in procession or at rest, for a later point.

Secular confraternities played an increasingly important role in Florentine processions during the quattrocento, and it is against this background of a growing secular imprint on public religious expression that the boys' new role must be understood. In the celebrations attending the conquest of Pisa (1406), for example, twenty companies marched in the procession. In the following year, there were twenty-two.[2] In 1454, Archbishop Antonino authorized seven companies of *fanciulli*, thirty-seven flagellant companies from the city, and thirty-six from the *contado*.[3] In early cinquecento, a memorialist recommended to the political authority that all the companies of *fanciulli* be permitted to march in the general procession on the eve of S. Giovanni, but only twelve to sixteen of the men's companies, "so as not to tire" the spectators.[4] A few years later, Varchi tells us that there were thirty-eight flagellant companies which marched in processions.[5]

The growing importance of the companies in these processions was at the expense of two competing images : the political representation of the city by the procession of its geo-political subdivisions or *gonfaloni*, and the representation of the clergy. These remained, of course, but with the growing elaborateness of the *feste*, it was the secular companies which benefitted most.

Certainly the propitiative processions of the commune in crisis remained more traditional, with the clergy in a prominent position in front, and "the people" in back. The indiscriminate mixing of different social classes in these crisis processions was in the strongest contrast with the representation of political order in the celebratory procession.[6]

---

[1] As early as 1305, a Sienese confraternity required its lay director to deliver a sermon to his successor; Kristeller, *Studies*, 104.

[2] These companies were called "compagnie cogli stendardi" or simply "stendardi"; Del Corazza, "Diario," 242, 245.

[3] See 208 above.

[4] C. Guasti (ed.), *Le feste di San Giovanni Battista in Firenze* (Florence, 1884), 27.

[5] Varchi, *Storia*, IX, 36.

[6] On "clamare," as this propitiative organization was called, see C. Torrente, *Las Procesiones Sagradas* (Washington, 1932), 6f; G. Meersseman, "Disciplinati e penitenti

But increasingly the order emphasized in the latter type was more the cumulation of private groups than the public or political structure.

Accompanying this increase in secular participation and the privatization of representation was the juvenescence of all the groups represented. We see it in the desire to have *giovani* representing Florence in its embassies to foreign lands.[1] At home, *giovani* rather than *uomini fatti* came to represent each of their families in the *gonfaloni* which assembled for the offering to S. Giovanni and the accompaniment of the Corpus Christi.[2] By 1419 richly dressed *giovani*, "the most polished" in the land, were those who surrounded the sacred host.[3] The confraternities of *uomini fatti* at the beginning of the quattrocento started to incorporate numbers of *fanciulli* into their processional ranks. Goro Dati tells us (1405) that the "companies of secular men" in the S. Giovanni procession had angels dressed in white amongst them, and from this point on angels formed a standard part of celebratory processions.[4] In 1428 another chronicler was dazzled by youthful pages bedecked with rich clothing, through which shone "their angelic faces."[5] Soon it would be companies of boys, and not single children, who would present the image of innocence to the Florentine populace.

---

nel duecento," in *Il Movimento dei Disciplinati nel settimo centenario dal suo inizio* (Perugia, 1962), 68. Chroniclers in Florence liked to refer to an undifferentiated mass of people following the clergy in these propitiative processions, but a closer look suggests that they were ordered according to sex and age group, if not by political organization : "Ricordo che giovedi a di 16 dottobre 1455 comminciano a farsi le processioni solenni per impetrare la vitorio divino contro al turco, e 4 giorni cioe ogni di a uno quartiere sempre multiplico il popolo. E da prima e fanciulli e fanciulle, poi in ultimo le donne assai vestite di bianco, cioe con camice sopra e panni, e uno + rossa nel petto"; *ASF, Carte Strozziane* II, XVI bis, f. 21r (*Libro di Francesco di Tommaso di Francesco Giovanni*). On processional orders, see below, 262; also Trexler, "Ritual Behavior in Renaissance Florence : The Setting," *Medievalia et Humanistica*, III (1972), 125-144.

[1] A law of 30 April 1498 ordered that in order "to learn about statecraft," a *giovane cittadino* fiorentino danni 24 in 40" was to play a full part in every embassy sent abroad"; *ASF, Prov.* 189, ff. 17v-18v. See also F. Guicciardini, *The History of Florence* (New York, 1970), 150.

[2] See *ASF, Prov.* 129, ff. 214rv (Dec. 22, 1438); *ibid.* 132, ff. 151v-153r (Aug. 9, 1441).

[3] "Giovani, de' maggiori della terra e più politi"; Del Corazza, "Diario," 257; see also 271-274.

[4] Dati is cited in Guasti, *Feste*, 2. I suspect that the habit of placing young people in the front of an adult group was by no means new; for an example of the duecento, see Davidsohn, *Forschungen*, IV, 432 (a procession in a cloister). But the importance of and attention given young angels clearly increases in the quattrocento.

[5] Hatfield, "Magi," 146.

From Pope Eugenius' letter of 1442 regulating the four original companies, we may assume that the groups were already taking part in public processions. Our first documented evidence, however, comes from 1454. Of the seven companies which Archbishop Antonino approved, the humanist Matteo Palmieri in his description of the year's S. Giovanni procession mentions three as having taken part.[1] He seems in fact to be describing four : About thirty members of the confraternities of Jacopo di Biagio (the Vangelista) and of Nofri di Filippo (S. Antonio da Padova) paraded together just after the cathedral clerks (the *Scuola Eugeniana?*) and immediately before the float representing S. Michele Archangelo. Following this float came an equal number of boys from "the company of Antonio and Piero di Mariano" (probably the Nativity governed by ser Antonio di Mariano, and the Purification headed by his brother Piero).[2] They were followed in the procession by a long line of floats or *edifizi*, each probably sponsored by different companies. The incorporated boys were by now the public image of youth in the life of the city, asexual innocents reflecting the institutionalization of secular innocence : "The *fanciulli*," reads a report from 1455, "were all dressed in white with the red cross on their shoulders, [and] went singing and psalmonizing with great melody." Here were the seeds of the great Savonarolan processions of the 1490s.[3] Yet the Florentines do not seem to have recognized the new role of the young in their processions. Not until the advent of the great Dominican are we again informed of the boys groups' participation in procession.

We turn now to the most complex and fascinating aspect of boys' confraternal life in the quattrocento : their dramatic and representational endeavors. These are well known, for they have attracted the attention of historians of drama. Our interest is more social in nature. A new relationship between Christian ritual and social order can be traced in these adolescent dramatic presentations. In them is mirrored a new pedagogy of social acculturation. As the statues started to move

---

[1] Cited in Guasti, *Feste*, 21.

[2] It is interesting that these boys' companies, which Palmieri generically called "compagnie de' fanciulli di disciplina," were the only ones in the procession whose names he gave; see *ibid.*, 22.

[3] *BNF, Conv. Rel. Soppr.* C-4-895 (Priorista of Paolo di Matteo Pietrobuoni), f. 170v. For another description of the same procession, see above, 221, n. 6; for the Savonarolan processions, see below, 251 f.

in late trecento and early quattrocento, as the representations of Jesus and his Mother and the Saints came to be played by real people, the faces were those of children and young people. When the bourgeois of Florence saw their everyday concerns and ideals represented in theatre, it was an adolescent voice and face which reflected these values.[1] Before analyzing this important socio-cultural fact more closely, however, let us summarize the scanty information on the confraternities' dramatic activities.

Children and young people first emerge in representational roles under the aegis of confraternities of *uomini fatti*. In the period between the 1370s and the 1420s, these groups had gradually substituted live representatives of the sacred statues and paintings which had been and long remained an important part of representations of sacred history. The chronicler Pietrobuoni emphasized that in the representation of the Assumption in the church of the Carmine in 1422 "a living man instead of *misser domenedio* [went] to heaven."[2] A few years later the same chronicler tells us that the Compagnia de' Magi in its processional public presentation of the story of the Magi included an infant Christ played by a three year o.d *fanciullo*, Francesco d'Andruccio de' Ricasoli. In one hand the child held a goldfinch; "with the other he did things so spontaneously natural that a man of forty could not have them done better."[3] Already in this report of 1428 we trace the amazement so common to the Florentines of the quattrocento on finding that young people, in this case a child scarcely removed from the breast, could be taught to artfully simulate "natural behavior" by careful indoctrination. Perhaps hard adult experience was not necessary before men learned to formalize their behavior.

Sometime before mid-century the boys' clubs first became responsible for their own presentations. Palmieri's description of S. Giovanni's celebration in 1454 seems to contain the first evidence that a boys' sodality was solely responsible for a representation. The *edifizio* of St. Michael which separated the four clubs in that parade may have

---

[1] See the remarks on adolescents as actors in the often suggestive book of C. Molinari, *Spettacoli fiorentini del quattrocento* (Venice, 1961), 63, 69.

[2] "Eando uno huomo vivo invecie di misser domenedio in cielo"; *BNF, Comp. Rel. Soppr.* C-4-895, f. 107r (May 21, 1422).

[3] "Uno fanciullo di circha a tre anni fasciato e lle mani isvolte; in sull'una [fu] uno calderugio vivo, et coll'atra faceva cose pronte naturali che huomo di quaranta anni meglio non avarebbe fatto. Iddio pareva in quel corpo del fanciullo Francesco d'Andruccio da'Richasoli"; cited in Hatfield, "Magi," 146.

been produced by the Vangelista, for this angel was one of the patron saints of the confraternity.[1] Another scholar has suggested that the float of the Nativity in the same procession was probably presented by the boys' group of the same name.[2] These identifications are based on the principle that each confraternity honored its patron saint or titulary name.[3] In subsequent processions, the boys' groups continued to play their role along with the companies of adults in providing the public with instruction, devotion, and amusement.

There is some evidence that in most of these early processional productions, children played children's parts and adults—or at least grown youth—played the adult roles. Cosimo de' Medici is only the best known of many adults who represented sacred figures in the quattrocento *spettacoli*.[4] Even in the indoor *rappresentazioni* viewed by prelates attending the Council of Florence (1439), the visitor's eye was not caught by children performing adult roles, but by a verisimilitude which "made the *giovani* look just as [the sacred personages] do in the pictures."[5]

All of the representational roles mentioned up to this point were of figures in sacred history. Florentines had learned that the young could be taught to play the young of sacred myth, to ape their pictorial representations through clothes and their godly innocence through perfected gestures. All of this was amazing to contemporaries; they could not help but be pleased at these manifestations of youthful piety and gravity. Yet there was more to come. Florentine processions, wonderful mirrors that they are of the dreams, fancies, and ideals of the society, yielded in 1468 a description of *social imitation* stunning in its forthrightness, one showing that the boys were learning not to be gods and saints, but the very alter egos of their fathers : grave yet innocent, just but unspoiled, heroic but sexless.

The description is of a Magi processional festival :

Thus, as the appointed time arrived, all involved convened in the square of the city. They had represented as well all the optimates and leaders of the city, as if

---

[1] The Confraternity honored him "perche il di di santo Michele del mese di Maggio si ragiono di dare principio alla nostra squola ..."; *BNF, Cl.* 31, cod. 11, ff. 7v-8r.

[2] Hatfield, "Magi," 114.

[3] Cf. for example Dati (1405) speaking of the lay companies "facendo bellissime rappresentazioni di que' Santi e di quelle reliquie a cui onore la fanno"; cited in Guasti, *Feste,* 5.

[4] Cosimo paraded in more than one *festa* of the Magi; Hatfield, "Magi," 136f.

[5] See the two descriptions printed in D'Ancona, *Origini*, I, 246-253.

Herod had sent these in the capacity of legates in order that they might escort [the embassy of the Magi] to the king; the conformity of which representation of the citizens to real citizens was so great that it hardly would seem believable. For they had so carved their faces and countenances in masks that they might scarcely be distinguishable from the real. And their very sons had put on their clothes, which they then used, and they had learned all of their gestures, copying each and every one of their actions and habits in an admirable way. It was truly lovely for the real citizens who had convened at the public buildings to look upon their very selves feigned, with as much beauty and processional pomp as the regal magnificence and the most ample senate of the city, which they would proudly conduct before them.[1]

Social ideals emerge from a play within a play. The sons involved were surely physically mature—the Magi was not a confraternity of *fanciulli*.[2] Still, the important element in this illusion was its reflection of a societal search for the reproduction of the father or older generation, to be realized by instruction in acting while the sons were still young. The method was a perfected ritualization of the gestures of their fathers. The father represented in this festival was not the private figure, with all his weaknesses and dark sides, but rather a normative elder, decked out in his own mask of senatorial splendor, the perfect father of official Medicean culture : grave and opulent, theatrical, and individual in his personal idiosyncracies.[3] Is it not striking to find in this complex urban culture a ceremony of rite of passage so similar to that found in more primitive cultures ? This festive practice and the solemn rite of exclusion at age twenty-four from the company of the Vangelista—both carried out at an age of social rather than bio-logical maturity—point to a new *social* function of secular Christian ritual, the recreation in that society of a group both infinitely better

---

[1] This written by the Dominican Giovanni di Carlo, and is translated in Hatfirld, "Magi," 116. NB this passage by the humanist pedagogue Vergerio : "Quanto a ciò bellissima è la costumanza praticata fin dall'antico in Roma, dove la gioventù condu-ceva i senatori, chiamati i padri, nella curia ... e alla fine in folla li reconduceva alle loro case"; Garin, *L'educazione*, 64, referring to Valerius Maximus.

[2] Fra Giovanni di Carlo was apparently referring to its members when he spoke of "socia quedam iuventus" performing the Magi ca. 1466-69. On the internal organi-zation of this important company, see Hatfield, "Magi," 119-28.

[3] This essentially private image preserved the luster of public dignity, since the "actors" were members of the city councils. Note also that the Signoria of Florence joined the march of the Magi, and thus became a part of the representation, "not indeed as Florentine citizens," said Fra Giovanni di Carlo, "but wholly as their images and shadows"; Hatfield, "Magi," p. 117.

than, yet the same as, the dominant social class. The monastic life had once monopolized that role for this male society. Now it was to be the boys. The Thespian muse in the hands of the young was more than mere make-believe. It regenerated social norms and gave hopes of a New Age—fathered by the Old.

We will return to this problem. For now we must conclude our review of the activities of the boys' companies by examining their fixed dramatic productions. During the quattrocento, boys' groups performed both sacred plays and classical comedies. In all probability the so-called *sacre rappresentazioni* came first. The first known performance was in 1449[1], Based on biblical or hagiographical stories, and performed in and around churches and cloisters, they included all the basic elements of theatre : a script, a musical score for the *laudi* included in them, scenery, and the bare bones of dramatic action. Rossi has pointed out how markedly Old Testamental and Evangelical the surviving Florentine plays are : a heavy emphasis on social and familial order characterizes one after the other.[2] Isaac, boy that he is, submitted himself to his father Abraham and to God with all the mature deliberation of a grown man :

> Quanto è ignorante, cieco, stolto e pazo
> Chi va cercando fuor di Dio, letizia !
> Qual cosa è più bestial ch' esser ragazo
> Del mondo, e del dimon pien di tristizia ![3]

A prostrate Ismael and Agar plead God's forgiveness :

> Signor, dal quale noi siam stati creati,
> Che, senza te, nessun saria,
> E se noi meritammo esser cacciati
> E d'aver d' un po' d' acqua carestia,

---

[1] In that year the "Abramo ed Isac" of Feo Belcari was performed in the Cistercian church of S. Maria Maddalena; D'Ancona, *Origini*, I, 260. According to V. Rossi, the earliest datable text of *sacra rappresentazione* is the "Rappresentazione del dì del giudizio" by Feo Belcari, with additions of Antonio di Meglio († 1448). "Beato Bernardino" is one of the actors, and this dates its composition after the friar's death († 1444), but its performance probably after his canonization (1450). Rossi opts for the period 1444-1448; *Il Quattrocento* (Milan, 1964), 282.

[2] *Ibid.*, 283. Molinari has made the point that at least three Florentine *sacre rappresentazioni* on the theme of the Prodigal Son were written during the quattrocento; Molinari, *Spettacoli*, 77.

[3] "Abramo ed Isac" by Feo Belcari; A. D'Ancona (ed.), *Sacre Rappresentazioni dei secoli XIV, XV e XVI* (hereafter *SR*), 3 vols. (Florence, 1872), I, 55.

Per la tua grazia siamo or liberati,
Onde a te laude e gloria sempre sia,
Qui ci starem, Signor, fin che a te piace;
Chè guerra è senza te, teco ogni pace.[1]

Upon which another boy throws himself at the feet of his earthly father and says :

O caro padre mio,
    Io sono uno Ismael :
E come a Dio quel,
    A voi chiego perdono;
E se tal stato sono
    Ch'io merti esser cacciato,
Datemi, se v'è grato,
    Come a lui acque e pane.[2]

Historians of Italian drama have long assumed that the *sacre rappresentazioni* of the quattrocento were performed by adolescent confraternities. The evidence for young actors is convincing : several of the plays start with apologies for infelicities because "we are only *fanciulli.*"[3] The protestations in themselves might persuade one that the confraternities of boys were those who, from the start, undertook their performance. Still, our available evidence is slim : although we know of two such plays written in the 1440s, one of which was performed, it is not until 1491 that we have proof that a company of boys—the Vangelista—performed a *sacra rappresentazione.*[4] In the same year, we are informed that *a group of young monks* performed "The Judgment of Solomon" in a Florentine monastery.[5] At this time, the young

---

[1] "Abramo e Agar," anonymous; *ibid.*, 36f. In the title of a 1556 Florentine edition of this play, one reads : "E prima per annunziazione è un padre con duoi figliuoli, un buono e un cattivo, per esempio universale de'padri e de'figiliuoli"; *ibid.*, 2.

[2] *Ibid.*, 37.

[3] For a selection of such apologies, see D'Ancona, *Origini*, I, 401-405.

[4] "Ricordo fo come, a' dì xxi di dicembre mcccclxxxx Piero mio fratello ed io Bartolomeo faciemo l'entrata, questo dì sopradetto, nella conpagnia de'fanciugli di santo Giovanni evangelista ... El carnasciale sequente fu messere di detta conpagnia Giuliano di Lorenzo di Piero di Cosimo de' Medici ... ; e feciesi detta festa el secondo di quareima, di detto anno ... E la sopradetta festa fu la rappresentazione di santo Giovanni e Pagolo"; from the *ricordanze* of Bartolommeo Masi, cited in H. A. Mathes, "On the Date of Lorenzo's *Sacra Rappresentazione di San Giovanni e Paolo*. February 17, 1491," *Aevum* XXV (1851), 324-329; Masi's exit from the company in 1507 is printed in Monti, *Confraternite*, I, 190.

[5] The author was a priest. One of the young monks played the courtesan with too

novices at San Marco were also performing *sacre rappresentazioni*.[1] Perhaps the young novice nuns and girls boarded in the nunneries were already performing the *rappresentazioni* before audiences of older nuns and an interested public.[2]

Thus it is not certain that secular *confratelli* were the first performers of these sacred plays. It may turn out that the impulse for these *rappresentazioni* came from ecclesiastical institutions seeking to educate their novices *and boarders*, (those not fully committed to the religious life), through dramatic representations.[3]

It has been almost a century since Isidoro Del Lungo discovered the strongest evidence for this hypothesis : it happens that the first identifiable group which we know to have performed a play in quattrocento Florence was not composed of laymen at all, but of clergy—the clerks of the *Scuola Eugeniana!* [4] Del Lungo was so surprised that clerks were studying Terence and, as he thought, performing the pagan's works in churches, that he missed the larger social significance of his find : clerks of the church *scuole* were at one with lay adolescent groups in filling a social need for youthful piety through acting.

The correspondence in which Del Lungo made his discovery con-

---

much conviction, which was remembered in later years by Pope Leo X ; G. B. Picotti, *La jeunesse de Léon X* (Paris, 1931), 29.

[1] Speaking of Savonarola's relations to the young friars, the biographer refers to "li spettacoli delle rappresentationi, le quali in tanto odio erano venute che tutti li suoi figliuoli, per persuasione del servo di Dio, giurorno di mai più fare o aiutare" ; P. Ginori Conti (ed. attrib.), *La vita del beato Ieronimo Savonarola* (Florence, 1937), 46 ; see *ibid.*, 90, where they swear never to "dire o dectare" the same. For evidence that the Carmelite and Servite friars made and accompanied *edifizi* in the S. Giovanni procession of 1514, see Giovanni Cambi, *Istoria* in *Delizie*, XXII, 45.

[2] D'Ancona, *Origini*, I, 404 ; II, 157-172.

[3] As has been long realized, the salutations of "padri e fratelli" in the prologues of many *sacre rappresentazioni* could refer to abbots and fellow monks or friars. Or consider this prologue to the anonymous "Re Superbo" :

A laude e gloria sia del buon Iesù
e di San Bernardino predicatore,
che presti a' servi suoi tanta virtù
che mostriamo un esemplo d'un signore
il qual superbo più ch'ogni altro fu ...

L. Banfi (ed.), *Sacre Rappresentazioni del Quattrocento* (Turin, 1963), 471. This sounds to me as if it were recited by Franciscan novices or fellow friars. For a variant interpretation, see D'Ancona, *Origini*, I, 405.

[4] Both of the relevant articles of Del Lungo were reprinted in his *Florentia. Uomini e cose del quattrocento* (Florence, 1897), 357-387.

tains some invaluable information on the attitude of a boys' teacher toward youthful dramatic representations. From a letter to Lorenzo de' Medici from Piero Domizi, the master of the cathedral school, we know that in August, 1476, the clerks were prepared to perform a play called "Licinia," perhaps written by the master himself. The church of Ogni Santi was one of the projected sites. The letter makes clear that the clerks were competing with other dramatic groups for the attention of Medici.[1] A second letter shows that Lorenzo had attended a performance by the clerks in Ogni Santi during the Florentine year 1477 (25 March 1477-24 March 1478). It is implied that the play was the master's own. Medici's visit had so inspired the master that he was now determined to prepare more comedies for presentation. Still, the priest was concerned about his students' welfare, and felt it necessary to ask for Lorenzo's mature advice :

> Terence is certainly a divine poet, and Donatus has rendered him more divine. If only all these things were not read to the clerks ! How very difficult it is to censor the reading so that they [boys] do not imbibe passionate habits, since especially the wit of boys is so perceptive. By the choice of God it is necessary that I supervise their discipline on Sundays. To do this I have written a serious little work in which I admonish [them] to develop those foundations of the life of adolescents from which exactly the cult of God is formed; [that] there is not much constancy in the man who considers divine precepts only in retrospect; [that] he is happy who leads a good life, and many other such things.[2]

The master-priest sent his little play to Medici with the implicit recommendation that Lorenzo, in the interest of the boys' spiritual health, favor the performance of this Christian text rather than a pagan one. There is some reason to believe that Domizi was genuinely concerned. He was probably the author of a Latin comedy on the conversion of St. Augustine, known to have been performed in Ferrara in 1494.[3] Furthermore, there was bitter opposition to the budding revivals of pagan theatre in Florence, and we may imagine that training clerks in Terence provoked the especial ire of the "little hooded [friars] with feet of wood."[4]

---

[1] "Il perchè oggi eravamo in ordine, se voi degniate d' udire e vostri cherici insieme col maestro : essi ve ne priegono, acciò che noi non siàno più schacciati degli altri. Volendo verremo costì chè siamo pochi : se none, degnate d'essere contento che la nostra Licinia si reciti in vostro nome ..."; *ibid.*, 382 (letter of Aug. 19, 1476).

[2] *Ibid.*, 383.

[3] Tiraboschi recorded "una commedia latina in versi iambici sulla conversione di Sant'Agostino, scritta da Piertro Domizio sacerdote"; *ibid.*, 385.

[4] This was Poliziano's description of the opponents; *ibid.*, 361.

Domizi, however, was competing with another group of boy-clerks for the favor of the city's lord; Del Lungo was probably right in supposing that this competition came from the church of San Lorenzo, whose *scuola* of clerks was in all probability responsible for the production in 1488 of Plautus' "Menaechmi."[1]

The long development which we have traced had seemingly reached its culmination. Boy-clerks and lay adolescents alike entertained the lord of the city and an admiring clientele with impressive regularity. The boys had something to teach, and they in turn shone in the brilliance of Lorenzo's sun. One young angel recorded his participation as a member of the Vangelista in the performance of Lorenzo de' Medici's "San Giovanni e Paolo" :

> Lorenzo de' Medici was there to see the said *festa* ... along with many other upstanding men and such a crowd that it was a marvelous thing. And all the boys of the company stood on the stage, especially those who were wearing linen clothes. Piero and I, Bartolommeo, were among those to stand there.[2]

And another play began with one of these angels stepping forward and saying :

> Cari, diletti padri, e frate' nostri
> Noi vi preghiam per l'amor del Signore
> Poichè siate adunati in questi chiostri,
> State divoti e non fate romore :
> Le fatiche son nostre, e' piacer vostri
> E ogni cosa ci fa far l'amore :
> No'v'abbiam ragunati in questi poggi
> Per fuggir le pazie che si fanno oggi.[3]

We have now concluded a summation of the activities of boys' confraternities during the quattrocento. Starting with typical adult practices, they developed thespian activity peculiar to them and to the semi-ecclesiastical *scuole* of at least two Florentine churches. In the cinquecento at least two of the sodalities evolved into philodramatic institutions.[4] But in this same century, professional adult actors appeared, and the relationship between adolescence and acting lost

---

[1] *Ibid.*, p. 379. Reumont discovered from a letter that a performance took place on May 12, 1488, and published this information in *ASI*, ser. 3, XX (1874), 190-191.

[2] Cited in Mathes, "On the Date of ... *San Giovanni e Paolo*," 325f.

[3] In the anonymous "Giuseppe Figliuolo di Giacobbe"; D'Ancona, *SR*, I, 62f.

[4] These were the Nativity and the confraternity of S. Niccolò del Ceppo; D'Ancona, *Origini*, I, 405. On the evolution of the Vangelista, see *ibid.*, 412.

much of its earlier sociocultural significance. The golden age of these youthful dramatic productions had been contemporary to a spate of new pedagogical thinking. I shall argue that there was a strict tie between the two. With the decline of the one went that of the other.

In the preceding hundred years, however, some exciting social innovations had been tried. Fathers had come to recognize the potential of adolescence, whether their sons were in the confraternities, *scuole* of the secular churches, or in the houses of the Mendicants. By corporate segregation from public life, biologically mature adolescents could be indoctrinated and taught to act out the ideal and even the seamy daily needs, thoughts, and gestures of their elders, male or female, without losing their innocence. The social institutionalization of adolescence could not only end street crime and moral perversion by the sons of citizens, it could create a society with all the norms of the present, all the gestures of the elders, but a New Age of justice and gravity. The century had been astonished by the educability of the new generation, and had been quick to parade its institutions of innocent gravity. The success of Savonarola sealed the conviction that the young were the salvation of the world, that without an institutionally indoctrinated adolescence, only a revolution of the corrupt could await a sinful society.

I turn now to an analysis of the nexus education-ritual-acting, as it has emerged in this review of juvenile activities.

The ritual protection of the city of Florence had traditionally been entrusted to four social groups. The priests were agents who performed divine services. The monastic element, apart from the world, protected the city through communal ritual and saintly life. The government in procession periodically renewed the contract of the *popolo* with God, his Mother, and the Saints. An additional but less important element in this ritual schema was the confraternal system of lay men and women, who prayed together for the good of the city. Consequently, to placate God, the city relied not only on purity (the monastic element), but upon the ritual mechanics of sinners (priests, governmental members, *confratelli*). It was not wholly reliant on the Donatistic efficacy of its monks and nuns; the *saeculum* as well was capable through the mechanics of its ritual of influencing the divine will.[1]

---

[1] For an elaboration of the above sketch, see my "Ritual Behavior in Renaissance Florence : The Setting," 125-144.

This ritual schema may be conveniently divided between outdoor and indoor activities. The procession was the typical outdoor ritual. Its ideal had always been order : a lineally designed spectacle of intermeshing parts, all together moving at a steady rate. In it no particular person was distinguishable, for it had no biographical or narrative element. Its purpose was rather to display the assembled political or social order. Inside the church, monastery, or confraternal oratory, however, commemorative ritual had an important place : the washing of the feet, the mass, flagellation, etc., all recalling the life of the various people of Christian tradition.

Adolescents, children, and youth had played no specific part in this traditional ritual pattern. In the fifteenth century, they enriched Florentine ritual experience by their new, organized, presence. What had been the precedents for child and adolescent ritual ? What was the immediate background to their emergence as a ritual element ? And what prospects did the new importance of adolescent ritual offer the city of Florence ?

Traditionally, young people filled no social role until they had left behind their childishness and adolescence. Society was for *iuvenes* and adults, and until one reached the mid-twenties one was a private being, whose training in social piety was entrusted to the mother and to the master grammarian. It is in the handbooks for these teachers that we find the guidelines for traditional acculturative practices. The Dominican Giovanni Dominici painted a charming picture of how the young person should be schooled in respect for religion, the anchor of all values :

> The first regulation is to have pictures of saintly children or young virgins in the home, in which your child, still in swaddling clothes, may take delight and thereby may be gladdened by acts and signs pleasing to childhood ... Make of such pictures a sort of temple in the house ...[1]
>
> But make a little altar or two in the house, dedicated to the Saviour whose feast is every Sunday. You may have three or four different colored little vestments, and he and the other children may be sacristans, showing them how on all feasts they should variously adorn this chapel ... They may ... have in place the little bell and run to ring it at all hours as is done in the church. They may be dressed in surplices as acolytes, sing as well as they know how, play at saying Mass, and be brought to the church sometimes and shown how real priests do it, that they may imitate them. Teach them to preach after they have heard preaching

---

[1] G. Dominici, *Education of Children*, 34f.

> several times in the church ..., you and the family remaining seated while they
> speak from above, not laughing but commending and rewarding them when they
> have imitated the spiritual office. Pardon them punishment due when they take
> refuge at the altar and, kneeling down, ask as a favor from Jesus that you will not
> strike them, so that they may early accustom themselves to have recourse to the
> True God in their troubles and demand grace from Him who alone can give it.[1]

The school master's pious responsibilities are brought out well in
the statutes of a rural school in Piedmont :

> Item. He has promised to preserve these students in the fear and love of Christ
> and with good habits, so that they will be reverent, obedient, humble, dignified,
> and not say turpitudes or other bad words, nor be mendacious, especially to their
> parents. Item. He has promised to lecture on some devout and spiritual authorities
> on feast days after mass and vespers, and to lead them two by two to church and
> order them so as to insure that the students remain still, dignified and devout,
> penitent and alert.[2]

Florentines liked to be told that in the good old days, children had
been brought up in this fashion.[3] Even if they had been, however, the
fact was that once the child reached twelve or fourteen, the age of
puberty and of some discretion, no social institutions had ever existed
to take over the familial training in acculturation.[4] At the very age
when motherly authority waned, and fatherly attention emerged, the
boy found that he could exercise his will alone.[5] True, the young
novice in the religious order spent his first year in a regimen of acculturation, and the brigades in Florence offered another type of
training in sublimation, but neither of these choices was attractive.
The religious life—whether deservedly or not—was in disrepute, and
the brigades were scarcely the place to learn respect for elders. Bands
of boys were to the domestic quiet of the city what foreign mercenaries
were to diplomatic tranquility.

The immediate cause of the intense interest in boys as social beings

---

[1] *Ibid.*, 42f.

[2] Garin, *Pensiero*, XXV.

[3] See the sermon of Savonarola on this subject, abstracted by L. Scremin, "Savonarola
educatore e la psicologia sessuale," *Genesis. Rassegna di studi sessuali ed eugenica* XII
(1932), 91f.

[4] As mentioned above, some confraternities of adults accepted boys from about this
age on; training of the young was, however, no part of their intended work; see above,
210,, n. 3.

[5] On this turning point, see Dominici, *Education of Children*, 44, and Matteo Palmieri, cited in Garin, *L'educazione*, 114.

was a crisis in the structure of the Florentine family. Men were marrying extremely late, while an alarmingly high percentage of young girls was entering the nunneries.[1] The results of these trends were demographic : an increase in the passive population and a consequent increase in family extinctions;[2] and moral : an assumed increase in extramarital hetero- and homosexual activity [3] and an assumed decline in youthful reverence for elders. What was responsible for the late male marriages and for the monasticization of the females? The following is not a sufficient answer, but only presents elements which throw light on the problem of the family.

Dowries rose rapidly throughout the quattrocento. This in itself causes an increase in the number of nuns, and it was not uncommon that the father had to consign several, if not all but one, of his daughters to the religious life. There was a second reason for the increase of female religious. Because of the late marriage age of males, mothers often found themselves widowed with several childern.[4] The girls could be placed in a religious habit more easily than in a marriage bed. Mothers readily chose this course, and they were encouraged in this by the testamental dispositions of their dead spouses, which commonly

---

[1] In an important article on the subject, David Herlihy reports an average age of 39.75 years for the fathers of 1005 infants born in Florence in twelve months of 1426-7, and a average age of 34 for males reported marrying in 1427-28; for the necessary refinements of this characterization, see his "Vieillir à Florence," pp. 1340f, 1344, 1346. During the quattrocento, the percentage of the female population of the city in the convents rose from approximately 2.5 to approximately 13%; see my "Le célibat à la fin du Moyen Age : Les Religieuses de Florence," *Annales E.S.C.*, XXVI (1972), 1337.

[2] Our evidence on family extinction is indirect. Certainly there was great concern about the problem, and communal steps to meet it. See A. Molho, *Florentine Public Finances in the Early Renaissance* (Cambridge, Mass., 1971), 138, 176. Alberti wrote his books on families partly because so many were dying out; *I Libri della Famiglia* (Turin, 1969), *Prologio*, and 128-132.

[3] This was the opinion of contemporary chroniclers, but it had also been that of countless commentators from the beginning of the commune. All of the demographic indices do suggest that conditions were ripe for a percentual increase. Herlihy has shown that of the males between eighteen and thirty-two years of age, in his sample of 4,456 males, only a quarter were or had been certainly married; Herlihy, "Vieillir à Florence,". 1348. The consequent importance of the orphans' institution in Florence during the quattrocento was not surprising. S. Bernardino explained the ubiquity of homosexuality from men's desire to avoid generating children; Scremin, "Savonarola educatore," 93.

[4] Herlihy, "Vieillir à Florence," 1342.

made a religious life possible for their daughters, but the married life inaccessible.[1]

Males were encouraged by humanistic and other moralists to marry late, and this climate of opinion made it all the easier to accommodate the demographic and financial impracticality of early marriages.[2] First, the pool of eligible females from one's own social level was declining. Secondly, the father's early death meant that his business was sold or died with him, for the orphaned boys were often too young to assume these responsibilities. Thirdly, the estate of the deceased father was often dissipated in the absence of a party capable of defending its interest. Poor boys and girls! Their plight became such a defined societal image in the quattrocento that The Orphaned Boys and The Girls Forced to Enter the Nunnery were among the social corporations which appeared before the crowds during Carnival.[3]

The moral component of this dilemma was no less severe. David Herlihy has demonstrated how reliant Florentine society became upon mothers for the acculturation and education not just of children, but of adolescents and youth as well. Yet how limited were her legal and moral resources for the task! And for a masculine society, what a disgrace. With his daughters in the nunnery and his sons—if sons there were—unmarried, many a Florentine father died convinced that his name died with him. Worse, many lived too long, to see that name besmudged by the activities of unmarried sons, who wasted their limited substance in the lascivious company of a *brigada*. What was to become of a society whose regeneration rested so heavily upon the weak, sensual, shoulders of the female sex?

It is not surprising that prevailing opinion held the family to be a poor place to rear the male members of the next generation.[4] The

---

[1] The normal procedure for the straitened father was to leave enough to dower his daughters in a nunnery, but not for marriage.

[2] The pedagogue Vegio recommended men marry at thirty-six, while others suggested thirty; Herlihy, "Vieillir à Florence," 1346. Archbishop Antonino believed that in his day "nimis cito contrahunt matrimonium ...," but saw the moral quandry : "sed si differunt perpetrant innumera mala"; cited in Scremin, "Savonarola educatore," 89. Savonarola recommended marriage for men at thirty-five or -six; J. Schnitzer, *Savonarola* (Milan, 1931), II, 324.

[3] Herlihy, "Vieillir à Florence," 1342, 1348.

[4] Vergerio praised the practice of some peoples of sending their sons abroad or at least away from the immediate family. This removed the sons from the indulgence of parents, and the boys pursued their studies with greater alacrity when away from home; Garin, *L'educazione*, 66. Vergerio wrote : "And even if in regard to educating sons

continual warnings of the humanistic pedagogues to preserve the children from the baleful influences of women has as its Florentine background a factual situation in which, to an alarming extent, the mother was the only available one to rear them.

The threat to masculinity was not something one talked about in polite company. When San Bernardino da Siena insisted upon the subject of homosexuality in a sermon at Siena, shamed parents started to leave, and the preacher railed at their shame and over-sensitive ears.[1] Despite the reticence of contemporaries, however, the problem of boyish femininity left its traces. A traditionalist like Dominici and even a progressive pedagogue like Maffeo Vegio da Lodi warned against females who gave boys names "which smack of femininity."[2] Bernardino chastized his female listeners most forcefully :

> O woman who has a son already a little man, make him look pretty, dress him up so that he is pleasing ... Do you know what he is ? There's no danger, you know, you don't have to put anything on him. He is a male. If he were feminine you wouldn't do such things, because she would get pregnant. Because the boy doesn't get pregnant, your're content to do what you do ...[3]

Children were scarcely five when, dandified by their mothers, they were first titillated by their own flesh, left exposed to suit the sensual tastes of mother and father.[4] Fathers were commonly considered poor examples for their progeny. From childhood sons frequented the obscene banquets of their fathers, lived in houses with lewd pictures, heard the name of the Lord blasphemed.[5] Under the care of a sensual mother and an indulgent father, little could be expected. Boys in well-to-do families who grew up in virtue were a miracle to the pedagogue Pier Paolo Vergerio[6], and Vincent Ferrer was convinced that all boys had

---

much is left to education in the home, still some things are usually ordained by law. I am of the opinion they all ought to be, for a well behaved youth is of the highest importance to the commonweal"; Garin, *L'educazione*, 61. For Gregorio Correr's view, see Garin, *Pensiero*, 707f. Although several writers thought parental indulgence an almost insuperable obstacle, no one argued that the family *could* not be a fit place for youngsters' maturation, but that it *was* not.

[1] Cited in Scremin, "Savonarola educatore," 95.

[2] Garin, *Pensiero*, 177.

[3] Cited in Scermin, "Savonarola educatore," 96. For the opinions of other Italian preachers on the extent of homosexuality, see *ibid.*, 89.

[4] *Ibid.*, 92, citing Savonarola.

[5] See, e.g., Gregorio Correr as cited in Garin, *Pensiero*, pp. 707; for Savonarola's description, see Scremin, "Savonarola educatore," 92.

[6] Garin, *L'educazione*, 66.

lost their virginity by the time they reached age fifteen.[1] Was it not better to remove children from their families, even send them abroad, to escape such bad influence ? Vergerio was not the only humanist to think so.[2] The crisis of the family was rooted in demographic and financial fact and in a climate of opinion. Its result was double : the ideological vaunting of the Roman family and the creation of new institutions to supplant and supplement the existing social institutions for the acculturation of children and adolescents. For the rich and patronized, this meant humanistic schooling; for other elements of the middle class and for the resident scions of the rich on Sundays and holy days, the confraternity. The two were united in their cause and in much of their method. Let us glance briefly at the humanist boarding school to discover those points at which it reflected the familial and social preoccupations just sketched, and those at which it bore an affinity to the Florentine boys' confraternity.

Rarely in the history of Western education have teachers been so idealized by their students as they were by the "graduate" of the schools of humanistic master-teachers. A substantial literature sprang up vaunting the persons and methods of a master like Vittorino da Feltre, written by students who were glad to call themselves the creatures of such an outstanding pedagogue.[3] These writers were not so much creating an intellectual paternity as describing the teacher and his technique of approach to young people. In listing the master's students, as he often did, the panegyrist was not so much doing it to recall the friends he had made at school—there is practically no indication of strong ties of friendship between students—as he was guilding the crown of the pedagogue by mentioning the princes and scholars who had sat at the feet of the master. These students found both a father and a mother in their master, and their parents had found an invaluable servant. While in fact pedagogues like Guarino were shamelessly obsequious toward their patrons, in the mythology of humanism the teachers were the equals of men of power, calling

---

[1] Scremin, "Savonarola educatore," 989.

[2] See above, 236, n. 4.

[3] See the still fundamental work by W. H. Woodward, *Vittorino da Feltre and other Humanist Educators* (Cambridge, 1897), 1-95. For the more recent literature, see Garin, *Pensiero*, 736. An example of a creature of Vittorino can be found *ibid.*, 623. For examples of Guarino's and Vittorino's flattery, see *ibid.*, 335-37, 613f.

princes their brothers, raised equal to the papal chair by respectful pontiffs.[1]

The figure of Vittorino da Feltre sums up the qualities of the humanist educator. He combined the best features of the mother—individual attention to the specific personality of each student, warmness and understanding—with those of the ideal father—sternness, encouragement to perform, wisdom, dispassion, a lack of sexuality and other forms of luxury. He cried repeatedly, yet produced students who did not.[2] He flagellated daily, but his students did not.[3] He was of course a virgin who watched over the health of his charges "just as much as parents do with their children."[4] The humanistic school was a type of family, with an indispensable moral legislator at its head, a lay abbot, or, if one likes, an ideal Prince of a small absolutist territory.

To the extent that humanistic education had a political goal at all, its aim was to produce good princes from the sons of princes, and good servants of the prince from the other students. These latter made good functionaries, but not equal participants in an acerbic civil life. In fact, Alberti believed that the failure of the teacher to repress voluptuousness was a cause of treason, while others warned of rebellion and insubordination among the incorrectly educated.[5] Vergerio felt the

---

[1] For one account of Vittorino before the pope, see Garin, *Pensiero*, 623.

[2] *Ibid.*, 613, 641.

[3] *Ibid.*, 519, 629.

[4] *Ibid.*, 541, 693, 695, 702. For Francesco da Castiglione's comparison of Vittorino to the ascetic S. Antonino, see *ibid.*, 549. On the humanist school as family, see Sassuolo da Prato's enthusiasm, *ibid.*, 517.

[5] "La voluptá. Questa in sé conduce i tradimenti inverso la patria, produce eversioni della repubblicha, di qui sono i colloqui coll'inimici"; cited in Garin, *L'educazione*, 150. "Quos si contra nimia cum licentia educaverint, ne mirentur postea si delicatiori licentiorique vitae assuefacti dent se ignaviae et socordiae, coinquinent se omni labe turpidinis, fiant eis rebelles, si tanquam equi indomiti—quod sacra docent verba [*Eccl.* 30, 8]—evadant duri et praecipires ..."; Vegio cited in Garin, *Pensiero*, 178. A close study should be made of the meaning of "buon vivere civile" in the pedagogic texts. Was the ideal a professional and bureaucratic, or a political *vivere?* It is certainly true that finished students were meant to "ornament" public places and in that sense there was a definite choice of the "active life" in most pedagogic writings; for examples of training to speak well in councils, see *ibid.*, 526. Still, I could find little evidence of a desire *to increase political participation through correct education* (an exception *ibid.*, 188), but repeated suggestions that a good education for the *fanciulli* insured a stable *res publica*. The professional or bureaucratic tone extended from the courtly pedagogues of the North into Florentine circles. Alberti believed "man was born in order to be useful to other men"; his recommendation to his *giovani* nephews remained representa-

new education must dissipate the native egalitarianism of the young. They had to learn that they were not the same as the *cattivi* and lay aside their readiness to believe others were suffering unjustly.[1] Because they had never worked for a living, the young were too ready to be generous, and had to learn measure : "The man who has accumulated with his own sweat is not so ready to squander his property."[2]

Vivacious students, those quick to play and associate with their fellows, were sought out by the educator.[3] They had to come free and remain free, not servile in their attitude to the Prince, but straightforward and honest : Quick-witted, alert, sparkling, learned, spirited; courtly, honestly obsequious, "good citizens," humanistic technocrats, realistic, worthy emissaries of a hopefully—but not necessarily—enlightened bearer of power.

The success of the school rested on its segregation from the outside world. This in turn depended on adequate financing. Through both parental support and, if necessary, the charity of the teacher, the student must have no worries about subsistence. Any controls over food and board must be imposed for pedagogic, not financial, reasons. Financial integrity once insured, the master had to guard his charges from circumstances which might open the door to sensuality, so destructive of order and learning. The student was to be allowed neither isolation nor solitude nor unoccupied time. For it was in such unattended moments that the boys lost their chastity, and, "before all, the boys must be kept chaste."[4]

---

tive of post-Cosiman pedagogy : "E datevi a conoscere quelle che sono necessarie a chi desideri essere, quanto merita la virtù vostra, pregiato e amato da' nostri cittadini, e adoperato in le admministrazione della republica"; "De Iciarchia," in *Opere Volgari*, ed. C. Grayson, II (Bari, 1966), 214. For a different view, see Garin, *Pensiero*, pp. XI-XII, XIV; *L'educazione*, 1-4; *Italian Humanism* (New York, 1965), 37-77.

[1] "Aggiungi che i giovani sono anche di animo compassionevole, senza malignità, e di umore benigno, perchè, nati da poco, credono che gli altri siano come loro, che hanno commesso piccoli peccati, e ritengono quindi di vederli soffrire ingiustamente ... Bisogna impiegare un conveniente sistema d'educazione, facendo in modo che mano a mano acquistino buoni costumi e che siano attenuati o, meglio ancora, sradicati del tutto i cattivi"; Garin, *L'educazione*, 61.

[2] "Sono, infatti, i giovani naturalmente splendidi e liberali, perché non hanno ancora provato il bisogno, e non si sono guadagnate con le loro fatiche le ricchezze in cui nuotano. Non è solito infatti scialacquare il proprio, chi lo mise insieme col suo sudore"; *ibid.*, 58f.

[3] Platina, cited in Garin, *Pensiero*, 676, 683; see further *ibid.*, 611-613, 677-679.

[4] Vergerio, cited in Garin, *L'educazione*, 62. For examples of the model of the abnegatory master financially aiding his students and even their parents, see Garin, *Pensiero*, 517, 603, 693, 701, 703.

The medieval monastery had also faced this eternal problem of the youth group : set up to remove boys from the sensuality of the streets, its monosexual composition provided an ideal setting for homosexuality. If women could be avoided in such a setting, and the pedagogical illusion be created that learning was asexual and unerotic, the problem of association was not automatically solved. Solitude allowed boys to be procured—masturbation was only slightly hinted at.[1] Association with older boys was discouraged by one writer, for they knew about sex while the young did not.[2] Grave, older men, who had left sexual passions behind, were more fitting companions.[3] Leisure time created a vacuum into which only sensuality could rush. The teacher had to know what a boy was doing every minute, and the boy's time had to be compartmentalized to the fullest extent.[4] This included time away from studies, which was to be carefully organized to teach princely students battle skills and inure all students to physical hardship. At all times, said Vergerio, the students should be submitted to some norm.[5] Sexual activities, the alternative to a carefully planned program

---

[1] A boy off by himself is chained by one thought, said Vergerio. "E come non è bene lasciar soli quelli che sono tentati dalla disperazione, così neanche quelli che hanno l'animo assillato dal piacere"; Garin, *L'educazione*, 62. For solitude, "maximum ad vitia lenocinium," see Prendilacqua cited in Garin, *Pensiero*, 598; also Vegio *ibid.*, 180. Cato's warning that boys left alone were in danger of being approached by bad men was seconded by Alberti, in Garin, *L'educazione*, 129. Idleness, solitude, lasciviousness or sensuality were the vices regularly described as the worst "illness" of adolescents.

[2] Palmieri, cited in Garin, *L'educazione*, 115f. The delicacy of the educated was supplemented by the directness of the preachers; both were talking about the same thing; on the preachers, see above, 237 and below, 255.

[3] See Vergerio, in Garin, *L'educazione*, 65. The patriarchal proclivities of Alberti need no mentioning. The main difficulty with exposing young people to the average master was the latter's reputation for corruption. Bernardino told his listeners about the pedagogues' reputation for homosexuality : "A Genova è uno statuto che niuno toscano può essere maestro di scuola solo per tal caso"; cited in Herlihy, "Vieillir à Florence," p. 1349. This helps to explain Vittorino's fame for producing good and pious teachers, as well as the Albertian myth of the concerned, yet patriarchal pedagogue-father.

[4] "Itaque neque noctu, neque interdiu ab his discedere. Si qua necessitas dabatur, spectatae virtutis ac fidei custodes adhibebat; saepe enim dicere solitus est, neminem, nisi sapientem, tuto sibi posse committi"; Prendilacqua on Vittorino, in Garin, *Pensiero*, 598; "Fuit in Victorino summa dividendi temporis diligentia, ut singulis exercitationibus singula ferme momenta designarentur, neve inertiae quicquam permitteretur"; *ibid.*, 628. Francesco da Castiglione wrote in the same vein; *ibid.*, 544. See also Vergerio in Garin, *L'educazione*, 62.

[5] "Ma poichè non possiamo sempre attendere a qualche lavoro, e qualche volta

of recreations, fatigued and wasted the sexless virility thought necessary to learning.[1] Vittorino, ascetic and virginal though he was reputed to be, would reluctantly encourage marriage for those students who were sensually inclined. As for those who became involved in homosexual activities, they were immediately excluded from the school.[2]

The subject matter in these schools was not narrowly technical, as that of the traditional schools was, but liberal. Consequently, acculturative instruction in religion and in the social graces was an important part of the whole. Indocility made intellectual progress impossible. It was essential that God be spoken of with the greatest reverence, and that cult ceremonies not be held up to ridicule. "What in fact would ever remain venerable and venerated among men if the divine majesty were to lose its value?" On the other hand, the silly emotions of women in things of religion had to be avoided.[3] To achieve this balance, the dedicated Vittorino led his boys to church and taught them the proper behavior in the presence of the divine majesty.[4]

In addition to this training in religious behavior, the humanistic schools imparted instruction in the normative social and intellectual

---

bisogna concedersi un certo respiro, anche per questo voglio darti qualche norma"; Garin, *L'educazione*, 100; on the same subject, see *ibid.*, 90-100, 112, 116f; *Pensiero*, 585, 683.

[1] "Infatti l'amore gustato anzi tempo contamina anima e corpo"; Vergerio in Garin, *L'educazione*, 62; "Adolescentes ab usu venereo, quoad fieri poterat, coercebat, continua opera, sobrietate; quod hinc firmari corpus et ingenium, illinc enervari et mentem tolli diceret"; Platina describing Vittorino in Garin, *Pensiero*, 676. These views are similar to those of Savonarola : "E nella parte sensitiva non è alcuna potenza che più tolga la operazione delle altre potenze dell'anima e massime delle potenze della ratione, che la potenza del tatto nell'atto della lussuria ... La libidine è cosa veementissima che è data agli animali per conservare la specie ..."; cited in Scremin, "Savonarola educatore," 87.

[2] "In mares quos ferri vidisset, eos omnino ex gymnasio summovit, quod hoc crimine nil tetrius aut flagitiosius putaret"; Garin, *Pensiero*, 676. "Nunquam uxorem habuit; nunquam in aliquo concupiscentie genere lascivisse memoratur. Abhorrebat precipue vitium soddomiticum. Si quem adolescentum qui apud se erant illo infectum esse offendisset, nulla poterat vel magna in eum animadversione satiari. Narravit mihi quidam summe sinceritatis vir, qui a Victorini confessore hoc audierat, illum scilicet usque ad mortem perpetuam celibem perdurasse : que profecto quanto rarior est inter mortales, tanto gloriosior est laus"; Francesco da Castiglione describing Vittorino, in Garin, *Pensiero*, 540. On Vittorino's lifelong attachment to his mother, see Herlihy, "Vieillir à Florence", 1344. For his abhorrence of powders and perfumes, see Garin, *Pensiero*, 677.

[3] Vergerio. cited in Garin, *L'educazione*, 64; see also Vegio and Aeneas Piccolomini in Garin, *Pensiero*, 177, 229-231.

[4] *Ibid.*, 545, 609, 611, 679.

graces of contemporary society. The theatre for their performances was usually composed of their fellow students and master : success was acting the perfect adult in front of one's adolescent colleagues.[1]

To accomplish this, the boys learned that spontaneity of expression was undesirable : "Quickly said is poorly said."[2] The same was true for writing. "There is never a need to begin to write without first having warmed and stimulated the mind by reading that which one proposes to imitate." Vittorino insisted upon this with great warmth.[3] This approach to speaking and writing was naturally carried over from content to physical action :

> [Vittorino] was scrupulous in carefully correcting in the youth not only defects of pronunciation, accustoming them to an agreeable, fluid, clear [and] sweet pronunciation if their diction was too closed or open, harsh or shrunken, hard or weak, but he rendered harmonious the step, the act of the body, the movement of the head, of the feet, of the hands, into a graciousness full of decorousness.[4]

The results of this incessant training in manners and gesture were gratifying to the teacher and a joy to the parents. What consolation it was that the petulance of a young noble like Carlo Gonzaga could be tamed. Panegyrists recorded how the boy had repented his misdeeds before Vittorino and his fellows—with the greatest poise, of course.[5] Vittorino's training of Alessandro Gonzaga had been so successful that the boy could not bring himself to join in infantile games in Vittorino's absence, "because I have him always before my eyes, observer and

---

[1] *Ibid.*, 189, 527. A passage in Alberti is highly instructive :

O giovani studiosi, Dio buono, beati voi quando qui e quivi e dirimpetto sederanno mille e mille e più volte mille omini *in teatro* o in qualche altro *publico spettaculo*, o giovani, beato a qualunque di voi potrà dire seco : "Qui, fra tanto numero di nati simili a me, niuno è omo tale a cui merito io volessi *potius* esser simile che a me, e a quelli che sanno più di me ..." O gaudio maraviglioso ! O incredibile contentamento ! ... "De Iciarchia," 214 f (my italics).

[2] Garin, *Pensiero*, 234, 641; *L'educazione*, 60.

[3] Garin, *Pensiero*, 691; see also *ibid.*, 187.

[4] Platina, *ibid.*, 691. Cf. Alberti's advice : "Queste sono el cavalcare, el danzare, l'andar per via, e simili. Ma vi bisogna soprattutto moderar e gesti e la fronte, e' moti e la figura di tutta la persona con accuratissimo riguardo e con arte molto castigata al tutto, che nulla ivi paia fatto con escogitato artificio, ma creda chi le vede che questa laude in te sia dono innato dalla natura"; "De Iciarchia," 229f. Alberti's own displeasure at gauche public presentation follows the above passage, adopted from a "prudente antiquo."

[5] Garin, *Pensiero*, 609.

judge of all my thoughts."[1] But the greatest star in Vittorino's firmament was Federigo, future ruler of Urbino. "Judged by many as dowered beyond the human condition," even in his childhood Federigo's "precocious indolence" caused people to flock to the court to see him :

> Tempering with singular courtesy his regally shining spirit, calling each by his name, greeting each with extreme gentility, often going to meet others, he was used to attracting the attention and spirit of all to such an extent that nothing was considered more decorous and marked with such affability.[2]

Vittorino cried in the face of such natural spirit and indolence. And in addressing the now mature Federigo, the master's panegyrist saw his rhetorical skills put to the test in assessing Vittorino's contribution to the formation of this student :

> To Vittorino belongs only a part of your glory. But as much of the beautiful as is owed to him—and it is much—just as much he owes to the reflection of your splendor. With his care he has educated you, bettered you, made you more handsome, you who by natural disposition were oriented toward the highest dignity. And you, through the grandness of your innumerable virtues, have rendered him immortal among those who come after.[3]

Such results could not help but be a consolation to civil society at large. The schools enabled men to rely on justice from their educated princes, and selfless service from the princes' courtiers, "creatures" first of the pedagogue, then of the prince.[4]

Humanist education and the new urban confraternities had much the same social causes and methods, a similar tone and acculturative content. Fundamental and obvious differences there were : part as against full-time segregation, an essentially moral as against a primarily scholastic curriculum, and so forth. For all that, both were seen as contributing to a re-masculinization of the family line in the face of styles and customs which obscured the differences between male and female. Both produced young people who could contribute to the moral regeneration of the family and society at large. Both were based on the assumption that through the repression of sensual and aggressive appetites in biologically mature adolescents, careful training in segre-

---

[1] *Ibid.*, p. 608.

[2] *Ibid.*, p. 613.

[3] *Ibid.*, p. 616. The writer was Prendilacqua.

[4] Federigo d'Urbino was considered the prime example of a prince whose education had contributed to an enlightened rule; see *ibid.*, 614.

gated atmospheres could produce father images in youth of tender years. Their methods were also similar : the avoidance of solitude, of contacts with older boys, the systematic utilization of all leisure time, training in gesture and expression, in acting and oration.

In all this there is a definite echo of monastic institutions. Society still required the corporate separation of some group to the end of preserving the extant order of things. But among the humanistic students and the *confratelli*, the suppression of sex and aggression was to be ingrained in adolescence, whereas in traditional monasticism heroic and individual asceticism had been a day to day, lifelong struggle with the enemy of the human race. This task was from now on a generational, rather than a corporative, function. In this relocation of institutional rites of passage from a monastic corporation to an adolescent generation to come, only the teacher remained the traditional monk : virginal, emotional, ascetic for life, a continual flagellant.

During the quattrocento, the "little angels" or *giovangelo* slowly became a societal ritual object, one whose correct manipulation could result in the preservation, even salvation, of the natural and civil order. Parents had always been consoled by the prettification of their children at home, just as they derived a sense of solidarity by dressing up the statues and paintings of their patron saints which they kept in their homes. Now, in the quattrocento, the energies of the adolescents were being institutionally harnessed in much the same way that the society authenticated its more traditional ritual objects : through silken clothes, angels' robes, and other accoutrements designed to preserve the "shining brilliance" of powerful ritual objects, while neutralizing the anarchy in the breast of undisciplined adolescents.[1]

---

[1] For elaboration, see my article, "Ritual Behavior." In the following remarks on acting and ritual, I have benefitted from the classical work by Huizinga, *Homo Ludens* (Boston, 1950), and the fine work by R. Caillois, *Les jeux et les hommes* (Paris, 1958). In certain areas, however, I have supplemented their works with modern sociological and anthropological literature. The latter distinguishes between young and old people at play ; attributes important sociocultural functions to the play of the younger generation ; recognizes the sacramental function of certain masques, mimes, and plays ; considers the role of the play's law-giver (without imputing to him a non-metaphysical, purely technocratic attitude toward the players) ; for bibliography and the freshest approach to formalized behavior, see Julian Huxley's symposium, "A Discussion on Ritualization of Behaviour in Animals and Man," *Philosophical Transactions of the Royal Society of London*, ser. B, CCLI (1966), 247-526. On the persistent association between technique and ritual in preindustrial society, see the remarks by K. Thomas,

Their position in the ritual panoply of the commune was unique. In one sense they were pure object : manipulated by pedagogues, compared to horses, plants, and clay, the boys of the ideal confraternal group responded to directions in much the same way as the machines used to feign natural motion in the festivals and representations. And Florentines reacted to these actors' ability to reproduce an adulthood which showed none of the signs of the indoctrination behind such art, with much the same amazement rendered these machines, all of whose parts and motors were hidden from the naked eye.[1] Still, they were their parents' children, and in their humanity supplemented and replaced the ritual position of the monks and the government in the placation of the Godhead.

Adolescence became a new fetish of a deeply religious society. The teacher was the individualist, the manipulator of this sacred stuff. The essentially new aspect in this realignment of sacrality was that the new cult object was a purer and more direct reflection of societal values and personnages, a direct affirmation of the present, while at the same time a generational guarantee of the future. In their dramatic performances the confraternal adolescents presented Everyman : the saint, the obedient son and mother, the patriarchal father, the whore and lost son, the devil, the greedy man, even the Virgin who fears Joseph will find her with the handsome Annunciation angel. These youngsters imitated in the *sacra rappresentazione* all the bad as well as all the good.[2] The inevitable victory of obedience and chastity was

---

"Work and Leisure in Pre-Industrial Society," *Past and Present*, n. 29 (1964), 50-62. For the dual function of youth as repository and purist manifestation of established values, see S. N. Eisenstadt, "Archetypal Patterns of Youth," in E. Erikson (ed.), *The Challenge of Youth* (New York, 1963), 32f.

[1] D'Ancona refers to the union in the *sacre rappresentazioni* of "l'industria de'-meccanismi e la venustà della dizione"; *Origini*, I, p. 217. For an epilogue to the contemporary wonder at these machines which made them seem not feigned, but "verissimo," see Vasari's *Vita* of Cecca.

[2] For the anxious Maria, see D'Ancona, *Origini*, I, 249. The author of the "Dì del Guidizio" thought it necessary to present the bad in order to choose the good :

    E farem quelle rappresentazioni
    che si dice che fian nel detto giorno,
    con certe contenzion tra' rei e' buoni
    che faran più divoto e più adorno
    quest'atto, e per le predette quistioni
    potrá comprender chi sarà da torno
    el gaudio che procede da far bene,
    e quanto è vizii sien cagion di pene.
    L. Banfi, *Sacre rappresentazioni*, 113.

the victory of the social organization of innocent youth: as in the best drama, the play controlled the actors.

By the 1490s, the Italian peninsula was full of prophets and humanists speaking of a new age and of the destruction of the old.[1] The image of youth and adolescence as being the salvation of the world was *au courant*. The Nineties were to impose upon the Florentines a choice between two kinds of salvation by adolescence. Savonarola was to bring a new type of boys' movement with him, one building on the past, but looking to an innocent, utopian future. Before considering the innovations of these prophetic years, let us summarize the world image which the boys' clubs had offered their viewers.

That image was apolitical. The "little old men" of the confraternal stage showed a society where political masks were unnecessary because the bonds of authority were clearly recognized and eulogized. How much elders could learn from such innocent obedience![2] The preservation of the social order and of the family name was best achieved through submission to a prince whose fatherly characteristics were carefully worked out by Lorenzo himself in his "S. Giovanni e Paolo."[3] The old society had been marred by the sexual and political eroticism of an undisciplined youth and adolescence. The old David had confused the perverse judges of the older generation. The confraternal David, it was proclaimed, would *save* these elders.[4]

---

[1] For Florence, see C. Vasoli, "L'attesa della nuova èra in ambienti e gruppi fiorentini del quattrocento," in *L'attesa dell'età nuova nella spiritualità della fine del medioevo (Convegno del centro di studi sulla spiritualità medievale* III), (Todi, 1962), 370-432; D. Weinstein, *Savonarola and Florence* (Princeton, 1970), 57-66.

[2] The feeling was expressed in a letter of Castiglione after seeing a performance at Urbino: "Io non dico ... nè come una delle commedie fosse composta da un fanciullo, recitata da fanciulli, che forse fecero vergona alli provetti, e certissimo recitarono miracolosamente, e fu pur troppo nuova cosa vedere vecchiettini lunghi un palmo servire quella gravità, quelli gesti così severi, parasiti, e ciò che fece mai Menandro"; cited in D'Ancona, *Origini*, I, p. 402. There is a slight difference between this praise of the perfectly acting boy and the more traditional theme of the man who had never been a boy; for examples of the latter, see R. Ridolfi, *The Life of Francesco Guicciardini* (New York, 1968), 7; Vespasiano, *Vite*, 355 (Donato Acciaiuoli); I. Gråberg da Hemsö (ed.), "La vita di Giovanni da Empoli ... scritta da Girolamo da Empoli suo zio," *ASI* III, *Appendice* (1846), 22.

[3] P. Toschi, "La teoria del principe nella rappresentazione sacra di Lorenzo de' Medici," *Rivista Italiana del Dramma* IV (1940), 3-20.

[4] "Come altra volta fu suscitato el spirito di Daniello giovinetto da Dio in confusione delli antiqui iudici perversi, così pare che suscitassi Dio el spunto di questi

It was a private image, one of idiosyncratic imitations upon a private, not a public, stage. In the old order, sinful men had manipulated God through their ritual processions. God had been pleased by this processional reflection of the political base of Florentine civic organization. The Innocents—and innocence is a private virtue—the "children of [the] new age" were, men had now learned, the only ones who could "sooth an angered God."

> Deh, Jesu, apri el pecto tuo et piovi
>   quel tanto tuo pretioso liquore
>   di gratia tal che horamai si rinnovi
>   la tua Pistoia nel tuo puro amore :
>   el nostro dono, a lei come a noi giovi;
>   qual ti sia accepto, che ti diamo, el quore,
>   et voi ci date venia de defecti.
>   qual mertiamo essendo giovanetti.[1]

> Se si mostra adirato
>   ad ragione el Signore
>   deh fa che sia placato
>   dal pueril decore,
>   di purità amatore ...[2]

The new ideology of youth and adolescence was vigorously proselytized, not only by Lorenzo, Poliziano and other new Jesus' teaching in the temple, but by the confraternities. The Pistoian brotherhood of the Purità carried banners reading : *Ex ore infantium, Ecce ancilla Domini, Exultavit infans in utero meo*, and of course, *Sinite parvulos venire ad me, talium est enim regnum celorum*.[3] They preached to the city fathers the idea of salvation by the young :

> Godi dunque città di Cathilina
>   di questo puro et pueril consortio
>   a le cui prece la bontà divina
>   fa che tu fai da quel demon divortio. [4]

> Onde la adulta età dal età verde
>   resta, come vedete, subiugata;
>   beato è dunque quello el qual mai perde
>   questa excellente dote a Dio sì grata ...[5]

---

pochi giovinetti ... non in confusione ma in salute delli loro seniori et del popolo pistolese"; Vigo, *Confraternità ... pistoiesi*, 4.

   [1] *Ibid.*, 13.
   [2] *Ibid.*, 15.
   [3] *Ibid.*, 10f.
   [4] *Ibid.*, 21.
   [5] *Ibid.*, 20.

How strikingly different was the view expressed in this verse from the traditional belief that the salvation of the family and of the commonweal depended on the good example set by parents for their children. A role reversal of sorts had taken place, and the organized and educated young people now saved what of the old society could still be salvaged. Never before had the "reverence for age" been so scrupulously and publicly manifested as in the dramatic action of quattrocento Florence.[1] Yet increasingly, Florentines looked to the condition of the young to determine the future of the planet. There were signs :

> And on the said sixteenth day [of July, 1497], there were about thirty cases of plague, and quite a few died of fever as well. Note that all those who died were heads of households from about twenty to fifty years [of age], and not *fanciulli*. This appeared to verify the dictum of the Frate abbout the renovation of the church and of the world.[2]

Videt ne contemnatis unum ex his pusillis.[3]

In his description of a public function of the Pistoian Purità, a contemporary remarked :

> It was considered a spiritual success. They gave the *popolo* quite an example and edification by marching in procession so composed and devoutly. Certainly example is more moving than speaking.[4]

Savonarola presented Florentines with just this alternative : ordered processional motion rather than fixed representational acting. As the city fathers had once processionally placated the ire of God, so now would the Florentine young people. The difference was innocence and purity.

> I tell you, the Lord wants these boys. From among the elders he will take one here and there, [but] the others will be discarded, for they have become old in evil.

> I tell you boys that you have to be the good citizens who will enjoy the good which God has promised this city. A time will come when you will see many officials come to ask your advice on governing [they city]. And they will choose to govern as you govern yourselves.[5]

---

[1] See Giovanni di Carlo's pleasure at this fact in Hatfield, "Magi," 150.

[2] Landucci, *Diario*, 155; see also *ibid.*, 158.

[3] Vigo, *Confraternità ... pistoiesi*, 11.

[4] *Ibid.*

[5] Savonarola, cited respectively in Scremin, "Savonarola educatore," 98, and P. Luotto, *Il vero Savonarola* (Florence, 1900), 222.

With Piero de' Medici's departure in November, 1494, the Dominican Girolamo Savonarola, spiritual leader of Florence, assumed political and social importance in the life of the city which no religious personage before him had ever attained. From the first, the friar insisted on a general moral reformation in Florentine society. Without it, no re-organization of the res pubblica, important as that was, could have any hope of success.

A central theme of this moral reform was the redirection of children and adolescents toward Christian virtue. Two successive phases can be distinguished during which the prophet approached the realization of this goal from different angles. The first period lasted until early 1496. During this time, Savonarola emphasized the parents' role in reforming the young. In the subsequent period, he relied more and more on the virtue of children who had come of age in the new dispensation and been subjected to the stern but sweet piety of a reformed city. The politization of the young fell within this latter period, and was partly the result of Savonarola's realization that a majority of the men who had grown up in the old corruption were incapable of reform.[1] It is this later period of the prophet's activity which will be the focus of our attention. Who were the Savonarolan boys? What were their activities? Who opposed them? What function did the prophet's boys fill in this supercharged period of political activity? How did these boys fulfill a century of hope in the young, and in what way did events transform the character of that hope?

The average age of Savonarola's *fanciulli* was lower than that of the earlier boys' confraternities. Three independent contemporary sources estimated the ages of the boys in the procession of Carnival, 1496 (16 February). The Milanese ambassador said the oldest was not more than fourteen while a Florentine observer believed that they ranged in age from six to sixteen or seventeen. Another stated that all the *fanciulli* were aged from five or six up to sixteen.[2] From Savonarola's sermon of four days later, we know that in church, boys over

---

[1] This was shown most clearly in the preacher's continual diminution of these included within the Ark and the New Jerusalem.

[2] Respectively : P. Villari, *La Storia di Girolamo Savonarola e de' suoi tempi*, 2 vols., (Florence, 1926), I, cxiii-iv (Paolo Somenzi); U. Scoti-Bertinelli, "Il carnevale del 1495 a Firenze," in *A V. Cian. I suoi scolari dell'università di Pisa* (Pisa, 1909), 89f (Bruno di Nicholaio di Matteo Lagi); (the author erred in dating the document 1495; it refers to 1496); Landucci, *Diario*, 135.

twenty were excluded from the stands.[1] The final indication of the upper age limit comes from Jacopo Nardi, who probably had himself been a Savonarolan *fanciullo*. This historian estimated that in one day some 1300 boys eighteen and under had received communion from Savonarola in the cathedral.[2]

The extensive participation of the very young was considered the greatest miracle of all. The Milanese ambassador, for example, after giving his exaggerated estimate of 10,000 boys, noted that 4000 were between the ages of six and nine.[3] And the Florentine diarist Landucci's statement that "all were between the ages of four or six and sixteen" suggests this same wonder.[4]

The chronicler Piero Parenti intimated that the age group from eighteen to thirty warily eyed, but did not participate significantly in the movement. After describing the burning of the vanities by the *fanciulli* in 1497, the historian noted that opinions on this and other Savonarolan policies had split families down the middle. "And not only [were] the *cittadini del regimento* [divided], but the *garzoni* from eighteen to thirty [years old] had divergent opinions."[5] Their support or disdain for the friar's activities was expressed in the time honored

---

[1] "Però farete che quelli che sono da dieci anni in giù, voi gli teniate a casa, e quelli che sono da dieci in su lassateli venire alla predica; ma non si vuole che là nel tribunale de' fanciulli vi vadino quelli che sieno maggiori di venti anni, e gli guardiani delle compagnie stieno là e proibischino che non si facessi scandolo"; *Prediche sopra Amos e Zaccaria*, ed. Paolo Ghiglieri, (Rome, 1971), I, 115 *(Predica IV*, Feb. 20). When the reform of the boys was drawn up, the *ordinatori* had the authority "di scacciare e' maggiori che non erono del loro collegio"; Ginori Conti, *Vita ... Savonarola*, 122.

[2] J. Nardi, *Istorie della città di Firenze* (Florence, 1888), I, 91 (II, 21).

[3] "Et li maggiori non passavano li 14 anni de etade; de anni 6 fin in 9 gene era circa 4^m"; Villari, *Storia, loc. cit.*

[4] "E note che furono stimati seimila fanciugli o più, tutti da 5 o 6 anni insino in 16"; Landucci, *Diario*, 125. The estimates of the number of boys in this procession varied from the 10,000 of Somenzi to the 1700 of Lagi. On the following Palm Sunday, the estimates were much closer. The contemporary Fra Placido Cinozzi explained why : "El numero de'quali ascese a più che a cinquemila, e quali di industria furon numerati, perchè in fatto questa fu giudicata cosa molto mirabile e stupenda"; cited in P. Villari and E. Casanova, *Scelta di prediche e scritti di Fra Girolamo Savonarola* (Florence, 1898), 10. Still, a subsequent biographer makes the same crowd-counters total up 8000 boys; Ginori Conti, *Vita ... Savonarola*, 128. For the best description of the Palm Sunday procession, with emphasis on the "si tenera età" of the boys, see Hieronymo Benivieni, *Commento di ... sopra a piu sue canzone e sonetti dello amore et della belleza divian* (Florence, 1500), cc. cxiv-cxiir.

[5] Cited in Schnitzer, *Quellen*, IV, 160.

Florentine fashion : two groups of *garzoni* elected *messeri* and prepared to "combat each other in soccer and defeat each other."

The assumption that Savonarola's boys were eighteen and below is confirmed by three independent sources who depict the *fanciulli* as Savonarolan and the *giovani* as those generally opposed to the asceticism of the friar. All these sources, consequently, permit a cautious statement about Savonarola's policy : He aimed at exposing children to his political pedagogy from the time they reached the age of reason and started school. Secondly, he seems to have recruited a substantial if not the preponderant part of his *fanciulli* from those not yet past puberty. The prophet's emphasis was on unsullied purity. Even in choosing the leaders, of the boys, Savonarola's trusted colleague Fra Domenico considered "not so much age as purity of life and natural judgement."[1] The institutionalization of boys aged six to eighteen as against these thirteen to twenty-four may have been dictated by the disinterest of the older boys or perhaps preferred by the Friar because this age limit more clearly marked off the innocents from those who had sexual experience.

The boys' strong sense of group cohesion rose from their common participation in processions. In certain other activities, however, participation was limited by age. Savonarola did not want any of them taking communion before they were eleven, and this excluded many from one of the *fanciulli* rituals most consoling to the parents.[2] Secondly, he excluded boys below ten from his sermons.[3] The famed responsory *laudi* and the equally famous disciplined attendance at sermons was, consequently, a theatre limited mostly to young adolescents. Luotto has further suggested that the inquisitorial activities of the *fanciulli*, who searched out vanities and broke up games, was the province of the older boys. Certainly they played the leading role among their *confratelli*.[4] It may well be that they were responsible for more directly political activities.

---

[1] Benivieni, *Commento*, c. cxvʳ. The three sources mentioned were the *Piagnoni* Landucci, Cambi, and Nardi, who says flatly that the *giovani* were opposed to Savonarola; *Istorie*, I, 99 (II, 25). Parenti adheres to this division between *fanciulli* and *giovani* except at one point; see Schnitzer, *Quellen*, IV, 227.

[2] Luotto, *Il vero Savonarola*, p. 191. Luotto made this point of selective participation in *fanciulli* activities to counter Pastor's and Perrens' criticism of Savonarola for allegedly indiscriminately exposing the very young to the seamy side of life.

[3] See above, 25, n. 1.

[4] Benivieni tells how Fra Domenica da Pescia, charged by Savonarola with the

Contemporaries were just as unable to agree on the social composition of Savonarola's *fanciulli* as on the makeup of the prophet's following as a whole. The characterizations range from *plebe* to *tutti nobili giovani*.[1] A reasonable assumption would be that their makeup was similar to the confraternities of the earlier quattrocento, a mélange of aristocrats, burgher patricians, and smaller artisans, with the leaders being the older boys of superior social standing.[2] The report that no one dared trouble the boys seeking out vanities because they were the sons of nobles might lead one to suspect that just such high-standing youngsters were placed in these delicate, more political tasks.[3]

In considering the organization of these boys, our first question would naturally be : What was their organizational relationship to the older groups ? A biography of Giovanni d'Empoli written in 1530 by his uncle provides our only source. This contemporary observer wrote :

> On feast days, he always went to the Company of the Vangelista. And note that at that time all the *fanciulli*, and especially those of the Companies, met together through the exhortation of Father Frate Ieronimo da Ferrara, who at that time preached against the low vices and sins committed in the said city, especially games [of chance] and blasphemy. They had constituted from among themselves officials, that is *messeri*, counsellors, and other officials who went around extinguishing games [of chance] and other vices. A son of Messer Luigi della Stufa, called Prinzivalle, was made *messere* for their company, and Giovanni was made one of the counsellors. He was the right hand man of the said *messere* and his performance was praised.[4]

This passage makes sense if one bears in mind the fact that the inquisitorial activities of the Savonarolan *fanciulli* were underway

---

organization of the boys, "raccholti subito epiu experti e epiu ad questo effecto non tanto per anni quanto per purita di vita e naturale iudicio accommodati giovanetti, incomincio come dilligentissimo pastore ad investigare el desiderio, la inclinatione e el consiglio di ciaschuno circha ad questa loro nuova reforma : Et considerato per la uniformita di tutti e per el maturo loro consiglio ..."; Benivieni, *Commento*, c. cxvʳ.

[1] On the natural *Piagnone* claim that the boys were noble, see Schnitzer, *Quellen*, III, 38. Parenti describes 4000 boys processing on Carnival, 1496, "tra nobili et ignobili, di cui la maggiore parte erano"; *ibid.*, IV, 94.

[2] See above, 215.

[3] "Eron questi figliuoli di persone da bene et nobili et per questo davon grandissimo spavento." Ginori Conti, *Vita ... Savonarola*, 124.

[4] Gråberg da Hemsö, "Vita," 22. The author goes on to say : "E spesso i fanciulli si ragunavano in San Marco a consigliarsi"; *ibid.* At the end of Lent, 1496, Savonarola told the *fanciulli* : "Voglio che abbiate un luogo fuora di San Marco dove vi raduniate e che stiate da voi"; Luotto, *Il vero Savonarola*. 226. Whether the subsequent organizations ever had their own quarters is unknown.

before the prophet's first attempt to gain governmental recognition for his new organization of the boys. Originally, it would seem, the boys' activities centered in the traditional confraternal groups. In addition to the Vangelista, we know that the Purification (in San Marco) was functioning in 1495.[1] Then, in Mardi Gras, 1496, the boys ordered themselves according to quarter for their procession.[2] Shortly thereafter Savonarola made the decision to incorporate them according to the political subdivisions of the city. We do not know whether the traditional groups were submerged by the new organization, but the new political organization dominated men's minds.

"Woe to the city administered by *fanciulli*," cried the Augustinian preacher Gregorio da Perugia from the pulpit of Santo Spirito, when the city council considered the request of the *fanciulli* that their new organization be approved by the commune.[3] The petition had been brought to the Palace by a solemn embassy of *fanciulli*, which ascended the steps of the city hall, saying they were sent by Christ and Mary, and demanded that their petition be heard.[4] In itself this curious act must have concerned many older Florentines, for the individual *fanciulli* had no legal status. More unsettling still was the purpose and content of the proposed reform. Savonarola explained that the proposed political structure would "begin to order the *giovani* [sic] in a good life style, and from the tender years on (such a model) would show them how they will have to govern in the future. For it is of the utmost importance which habits they form."[5]

Across the river Fra Gregorio thundered that such a constitution meant establishing "a small government of the Republic," that is, a puppet government.

> I am amazed that the Florentines, who are considered so expert, [and] men of the most acute spirit, have come into such decline and lowness, that the very *fanciulli* emerge with the upper hand and want to govern.[6]

---

[1] Without evidence, D'Ancona says that the Vangelista was reformed by Savonarola; *Origini*, I, 411. For the aggregation of the Purification to the spiritual benefits of the Observant Dominicans in 1495, see Richa, *Notizie*, V, 330f. According to Passerini, the confraternity del Ceppo was "one of the fraternities" which took part in the burning of the vanities; Passerini, *Storia ... beneficienza*, 192.

[2] Landucci, *Diario*, 124f.

[3] Cited by Parenti in Schnitzer, *Quellen*, IV, 112. This took place in March, 1496. See J. Schnitzer, *Savonarola* I, 314, 320, n. 51.

[4] Ginori Conti, *Vita ... Savonarola*, 125f. Parenti in Schnitzer, *Quellen*, IV, 105.

[5] *Ibid.*, 106.

[6] *Ibid.*, 105.

To this author's knowledge Florence had never had a company or confraternal structure based on the political geography of the city. It is almost certain that no such division or groups had ever been approved by the government. Consequently, this *novità* appeared to the Florentines as something much more than the traditional communal approval accorded new religious sodalities. It must have seemed an attempt to enforce the *fanciulli* morality upon the citizenry with governmental authority, using the internal political structure of the city as a base for this reform. Each quarter's company was to be fitted out with a custodian, counsellors, confessors, etc. as well as with two purely social magistrates : the correctors, whose tasks were to hunt out vanities and luxuries, and the *elemosinieri* or alms collectors, whose aggressive tactics did not endear them to some Florentines.[1] One other official, the *paciere* of each quarter, was to keep peace among the boys of the quarter. Though this office's authority may have been meant to extend only to members of the quarter's *compagnia*, the catholic claims of the Savonarolan boys to represent *the fanciulli* of Florence meant that it would function as a control element for all the neighborhood's *fanciulli*.[2]

The very dedication of the boys, depressing to some in its earnestness, frightened many Florentines. All the youngsters had cut their hair above the ears. All had taken to simple, clearly masculine clothing; there was to be no question as to their gender, their innocence, their group appurtenance.[3] All had vowed to give up the excursions to Fiesole and Monte San Gaggio to see and participate in the *rappresentazioni*[4] : in normal times these plays were considered devout, said Savonarola, but to his sons they appeared completely carnal.[5] No schools of dancing and fencing for them.[6] And they were such implacable foes of homosexuality that during the boys' heyday people feared to even mention the unmentionable sin.[7] Overnight, it seemed, the boys changed from undisciplined individuals to pious and grave examples to all the *saeculum*.

---

[1] The most extensive description of the new quarter organizations is in Ginori Conti, *Vita ... Savonarola*, 122f.

[2] "Haveano a tenere et comporre pace infra loro et fuora di loro, fra gli altri fanciulli del lor quartiere ..."; *ibid.*, 122.

[3] *Ibid.*, 119f.

[4] *Ibid.*, 122.

[5] *Ibid.*, 46.

[6] *Ibid.*, 122.

[7] Landucci, *Diario*, 124.

To give a political base to an organization with these liabilities was asking too much of enough members of the Grand Council to insure the petition's defeat.[1] As Savonarola and his boys learned, fathers reared in Medici tyranny did not easily surrender their private pleasures. The prophet also understood very well the determination of the older generation to exclude the young from high political office and from important magistracies. If the young, how much more so the children! The city patriarchs were anguished by reports that foreign people were amusing themselves over the boy government of Florence.[2]

Savonarola had no intention of instituting a government of young people. Yet as the year 1496 wore on, he increasingly identified the New Jerusalem with the *fanciulli*, and used them as political activists. They lobbied at home and in the Palace for the implementation of their program.[3] During this year, they became the active element in Florentine public life in a socio-ritual sense. In place of the privacy of the old theatrical confraternities, Savonarola stressed the public activity of his boys. In procession they assumed the emphasis on order which had once been the dominant tone of public ritual. They represented again the public order of the commune rather than the scenographic elements of the private world of the confraternities. Christ, King of Florence, and Mary, its Queen, looked down upon the republic and saw, as in an earlier time, the political order of the city offered to them—by innocent activists. And they were pleased. The crucifix of redemption was "in the hands of holy purity."[4] Placation and salvation had again become a public thing.

---

[1] See Cerretani, cited in Schnitzer, *Quellen*, III, 38.

[2] Parenti, cited in Schnitzer, *Quellen*, IV, 105ff; see also Luotto, *Il vero Savonarola*, 186f. For the discomfort over the stories that the city was governed by friars, see *ibid.*, 137.

[3] Savonarola often cautioned the boys to exercise restraint and intended that their liberty of action be strictly supervised by their magistrate. To those who objected to the *fanciulli*'s sociopolitical activity, Savonarola responded : "Tell me, are the boys magistrates? Are they of the Eight?" See Luotto, *Il vero Savonarola*, 186, 194-206.

[4] Landucci, *Diario*, 124. The procession of the Savonarolan quarters was not a perfect reproduction of the traditional procession of the administrative sections of the city. The latter was based on the *gonfaloni*, four to a quarter, whereas the former was probably organized only according to quarters. The only tradition of quarter organization for processional purposes was a quattrocento festival division which is only imperfectly documented; see Hatfield, "Magi," 115-120. See also Vasari, cited in D'Ancona, *Origini*, I, 234. On the political evangelism of the *fanciulli*, see G. Gnerghi, "Gerolamo Savonarola e i fanciulli," *Rassegna Nazionale* CXVII (1901), 345-70, esp. 362.

At this juncture, the one male age group with no political weight in the commune was the *giovani*. Their younger brothers and their fathers were involved in civic affairs. But of the *giovani*, only those aged twenty-nine and above had access to the Grand Council. Since only members of that Council had the right to fill the important officialities of the commune, *giovani* below twenty-nine were effectively excluded from honorable positions in the communal bureaucracy. With little concrete evidence to support me, I suspect that the Savonarolan period saw a reaction away from the preciosity of golden youth which had marked the Lorenzan period.

Savonarola could sympathize with the political plight of the *giovani* while remaining dubious about their moral redemption. Perhaps at his urging, an exception had been included in the law instituting the Grand Council which permitted the annual selection of twenty-four *giovani* aged twenty-four and above as candidates to the Grand Council for election to that body.[1] The stated purpose for this yearly rejuvenation of the Council was "to encourage the *giovani* and incite the *uomini* to virtue."[2]

Giovani were in these as in other times and places the bellweathers of the political winds. Virile, passionate, and often otherwise unoccupied, they could influence how long, and how strongly, the wind would continue to blow from San Marco. This explains Parenti's interest in their own type of festive politics, and the *Piagnone* Pagolantonio Soderini's decision to place one of his sons among the Compagnacci, a group of *giovani* dedicated to the humiliation of the Dominican friar.[3] Savonarola and his followers realized the importance of this group, and many of them supported moves designed to ease their admission to the Grand Council and therewith the right to hold office.[4]

A first modest step in that direction was taken in November, 1495,

---

[1] On Dec. 13, 1496, Savonarola told his listeners that when the Council was instituted, he had favored "everyone" entering, "because liberty was then in its beginnings, and it was necessary to experiment"; Villari, *Storia*, I, 502. The following information on the Grand Council is based on N. Rubinstein, "I primi anni del Consiglio Maggiore di Firenze," *ASI* CXII (1954), 154-229, 321-347; for the exception to the basic law, see *ibid.*, 166f.

[2] Villari, *Storia*, 287f.

[3] For Parenti, see Schnitzer, *Quellen*, IV, 160; for Soderini, see Guicciardini, *History*, 137.

[4] It is unclear whether Savonarola himself was in favor of this move; see below, 259, n. 2.

with the reordering of the bags from which members of the Grand Council were drawn to fill most important offices in the communal bureaucracy. Whereas before no age distinction had been made among those in the Council, now the Council was divided into three age groups. Each member over 45 had three chits deposited in the bags for the offices. Those between 35 and 45 had two such chits and, most important, those from 25 to 35 had one.[1] From a practical point of view, this was the first time that *giovani* of this age had any access to these offices. In the very same days, however, the same Council rejected the recommendation of one of its committees to open the doors to *giovani* twenty-four years old and above. Despite the pressing need for this action, the Council maintained the standard minimum of twenty-nine years.[2]

What made such a step seem important to the commission was the fact that the Grand Council, the supreme instrument of the New republic, was plagued by non-attendance, but more seriously, by the all too limited number of those eligible to take part in Council deliberations and voting. Together, these problems meant that quorums were difficult to meet. Two legal conditions for participation could be modified to increase the eligible. One was to soften the requirement that members be paid up in taxes. The other was to drop the legal age minimum. Not surprisingly the Council, after a great deal of deliberation, opted for their sons over the lesser propertied.[3]

The election of the arch-*Piagnone* Francesco Valori as *gonfaloniere della giustizia* was the signal for Savonarola's followers to carry through this and other pending reforms. Three crucial acts of his two month office should be mentioned. The first was the purging from the Grand Council of certain "bad," pro-Medicean members who had obtained seats illegally.[4] The second was the passage of the constitutions of the boys, left in abeyance for almost a year because of the strong majority opposition to their implementation.[5] The third was lowering the legal

---

[1] Rubinstein, "I primi anni," 331.

[2] *Ibid.*, 186. This had been maintained despite the cooption of some *giovani* each year aged twenty-four and above. The minimum age for entitled appurtenance had remained at twenty-nine.

[3] The law was passed Jan. 18, 1497; *ibid.*, 197.

[4] Dated Feb. 1; *ibid.*, 190. Savonarola had called for these ousters in a sermon on Dec. 13, 1496; see the passages in Villari, *Storia*, I, 502f.

[5] This was forced through in January after repeated readings; Parenti, cited in Schnitzer, *Quellen*, IV, 155; see *ibid.*, III, 38.

age minimum for the Grand Council from twenty-nine to twenty-four for any successive three month period in which a statutorily fixed minimum of eligibles could not be reached.[1]

Certainly the long-awaited communal approval of the boys' constitutions was gratifying to Savonarola. But lowering the age for participation was probably not as warmly endorsed by the prophet as it was by many of his followers in the Council. According to the *Piagnone* historian Jacopo Nardi, a *fanciullo* himself in these years, Valori "and other men of good mind" believed that the younger *giovani* were less open to the threats of vengeance used by dissatisfied factions in the Council. Adding them to it would preserve the commune.[2] In other words, the *Piagnoni* felt that the young *giovani* would side with them, partly in thanks for now having greater access to the Council and to the magistracies.

> But a result followed which was quite different from that which the said Francesco [Valori] and the other men of good mind had believed. For the degenerate *giovani*, [once] multiplied in the Council, allied themselves in the elections of magistrates on the side of the *Arrabbiati* [opponents of the *Piagnoni*], and consequently they ruined or at least had little love for the Council.[3]

This pattern of *giovani* opposition to the prophetic impulse of Savonarola clearly affirmed itself in the remaining year and a half of Savonarola's life. It was a company of *giovani*, the so-called *Compagnacci*, which became the principal extragovernmental opponent of the *frate*.[4] They smeared the pulpits where the Dominicans preached, created rackets during sermons, circulated defamatory writings, defied his moral asceticism by staging lavish and ostentatiously obscene banquets, and attacked the boys in processions. In the sources for the period, as has been mentioned, impieties were almost uniformly as-

---

[1] Rubinstein, "I primi anni," 187 (Jab. 18, 1497). The *giovani* had to be paid up in taxes, and this reduced the otherwise admissible *giovani* from ca. 500 to ca. 200.

[2] "Credendo pure d' acconciarlo meglio col farlo di maggior numero, e perciò manco esposto alle offese di chi per via di sètte lo volesse alterare,'; Nardi, *Istorie*, I, 38 (II,25). It has been assumed that Savonarola was opposed to admitting the *giovani;* see for example R. Ridolfi, *Vita di Girolamo Savonarola* (Rome, 1952), I, 276; Villari, *Storia*, I, 505. Yet the language of Savonarola in his political sermon of Dec. 13, 1496, upon which this assertion is based, is ambiguous. In his work on the Grand Council cited above, Rubinstein does not express an opinion.

[3] Nardi, *loc. cit.*

[4] Villari says that it was the Compagnacci which benefited from the age lowering; Villari, *loc. cit.*

cribed to the *giovani*, who were put into clear relief to contrast them with the saintliness of the *fanciulli*. Certainly there was much stereotyping in such opinions, but as much truth. It is a striking fact that in no account of any Savonarolan procession is there any indication that *giovani* participated.

True to his prophetic calling, Savonarola from the first had sought out the holy purity of the very young. He had turned the *fanciulli* to evangelistic social activism before puberty, educating them in Christian militancy at a time when children were traditionally still under the influence of their mothers. His influence over the young adolescents had not been meager : we have seen that he was able to marshal 1300 young people between the ages of eleven and eighteen to a solemn communion one Christmas morning. His failure to attract a militant segment of the *giovani* to his banner was the failure of a peaceful man who indoctrinated his followers with an abhorrence of aggression. The confraternities of the quattrocento had not produced a docile *gioventù*. Neither did the Dominican, nor did he really try. His hopes rested with the children and young adolescents, and those hopes failed. It was just a little time, said the diarist Landucci, but "God be praised that I live in this little bit of holy time."[1]

Ritual is creative for a community to the extent that it reflects both structure and the formless energy upon which vital order rests. The moment that ritual is emptied of those elements in which spectators see some formless element of themselves reflected, it becomes "mere ritual," "very beautiful, but devoid of spirit," as the *Piagnoni* were wont to say.[2] Creative ritual's motion is never arrested. On the other hand, the ritual in which direction is not arrested, but diverted, threatens always to lose its formal nature, and become "destructive." The ritual contract broken, the results of such ritual destruction can in themselves be creative—a new social order may result.[3] Within the

---

[1] Landucci, *Diario*, 124.

[2] Lucotto, *Il vero Savonarola*, 145; Cambi, *Istorie*, in *Delizie*, XXII, 45. Erikson calls "true ritualization" "an unexpected renewal of a recognizable order in potential chaos. Ritualization thus depends on that blending of surprise and recognition which is the soul of creativity, reborn out of the abyss of instinctual disorder, confusion of identity and social anomie"; E. H. Erikson, "Ontogeny of ritualization in man," in Huxley, "A Discussion of Ritualization," 349.

[3] See the interesting articles by F. E. Williams, "The Vailala Madness and the Destruction of Native Ceremonies in the Gulf Division," *Territory of Papua. Anthropology*, report n. 4 (1923), and "The Vailala Madness in Retrospect," in *Essays Presented to C. G. Seligman*, ed. E. Evans-Pritchard *et al* (London, 1934), 369-379.

social order, however, creative ritual must contain elements of both play and action, a dialectic of form and anti-form, if it is to survive, and if it is to engage both participants and observers.[1]

For a short period in 1496 and 1497, the processions in Florence accomplished this end. Contemporaries were incredulous upon seeing how successfully the processions achieved their task of "eliminating all confusion," as the historian-politician Parenti put it.[2] The conditions for this success were optimal : the city was threatened from abroad, the city's spiritual guide seemed above in these years, and the Florentines generally agreed on the necessity of recreating the republic. Consequently, the processions of these years could reflect the citizen's unity of purpose while eliminating the confusion over means.

The Florentines did not simply parade their *fanciulli*, their hopes for the future, in these processions. When we recall the socio-political activities of these same *fanciulli*, we see that the boys portrayed the present, and not only the future; engaged in political action, and not merely the immortalization of the idiosyncrasies of politically powerless fathers.

The organization of these devotional activities betrayed a prophetic and thoroughly public processional community. Private confraternities of men found no entrance to them.[3] Women were not permitted to lean out the windows to watch processions, and were sometimes excluded from sermons altogether.[4] At other times, Savonarola insisted on a rigid separation of the sexes.[5]

It is sometimes assumed that the processions of the Savonarolan period were for the boys alone. This is not at all the case. In fact, only the Carnival processions of 1496 and 1497 seem to have been

---

[1] A typical game example of this interplay is the break-through in the American football game, where the skilled runner evades the structures set up to restrain him. This brings the crowd to its feet. In the world of religious cult, this principle is seen in the continued renewal of cult by the addition of new miracle-producing relics or images.

[2] Schnitzer, *Quellen*, IV, 62f.

[3] The traditional adult companies are mentioned only once during the Savonarolan period : according to Nardi, they took part in a procession of Oct. 27, 1496, when the miraculous image of Impruneta was brought into the city; *Istorie*, I, 87 (II, 19).

[4] Landucci, *Diario*, 90-94.

[5] *Ibid.*, 107; Nardi, *Istorie*, I, 47 (I, 19). The separation of the sexes at church was traditional, but seems to have eased during the quattrocento; for an earlier example of the separation of the sexes in procession, see above, 221, n. 6. For the Savonarolan period, see below, 262.

limited to *fanciulli*.[1] These processions were intended as invectives
toward the devil, who usually reigned on this date, and were considered
the boys' own ersatz *feste*.[2] But all the other public processions of the
period, including the Carnival procession of 1498, included men and
women, girls and boys.[3] The boys came first, organized according to
quarter, each company carrying the quarter's banner. From the Palm
Sunday procession of 1496 on, they were dressed as angels, a costume
assumed as well by the little girls on that memorable day.[4] In subsequent processions, the order was fixed : first the companies of boys
in twos; then the men, then the young girls, and finally the women.
Each of these groups was ordered according to height.[5]

Contemporary chroniclers placed so much emphasis upon the boys
in these processions because of their incredible discipline and docility.
Some called the processions "processions of *fanciulli*," when they were
much more than that, while another observer called one of them "the
most solemn procession of the quarters," when it seems that only the
boys were arranged in quarters, while the rest of the men, women,
and girls were arranged according to sex and size.[6] Clearly, the boy
activists had become the desired representation of the city's segments
before God. Their processional behavior was the parents' assurance
that they were in or were nearing the New Jerusalem.

The Savonarolan processions were both propitiative and celebratory.
Propitiative certainly in their order : the boys led the procession as
the priests usually did, and "the people" came behind. Yet organizing
these activist innocents into quarters made the processions celebrations

---

[1] No mention of other than boys was made by either Landucci, *Diario*, 124f, or
Lagi; Scoti-Bertinelli, "Il Carnevale ..." (full citation above, 250, n. 2). The same is true
for 1497; Nardi, *Istorie*, I, 92f. (II, 21); Ginori Conti, *Vita ... Savonarola*, 129-135;
Parenti, cited in Schnitzer, *Quellen*, IV, 159-161.

[2] Benivieni, *Commento*, c. cxiv^v; Ginori Conti, *Vita ... Savonarola*, 130, 134.

[3] For the 1498 Mardi Gras, see Villari, *Storia*, II, lii; Parenti, cited in Schnitzer,
Quellen, IV, p. 232; Ginori Conti, *Vita ... Savonarola*, 132f.

[4] Landucci, *Diario*, p. 128. In the earliest processional appearance of the *fanciulli*,
they had processed "sanza veste"; Scoti-Bertinelli, "Il carnevale," 89f.

[5] The most extensive descriptions : Parenti, cited in Schnitzer, *Quellen*, IV, 159-
161; Ginori Conti, *Vita ... Savonarola*, 127ff., 129-135; Benivieni, *Commento*, c.
cxiv^v; Somenzi, cited in Villari, *Storia*, II, lii.

[6] A good example of the equation of the processions with the boys is Landucci,
who calls the Palm Sunday, 1496 procession "for boys," and then describes its incorporation of all elements; *Diario*, 128. Simone Filioepi refers to the "procession of the
Quarters"; Villari and Casanova, *Scelta*, 486.

of the new polis. The parents who followed bore witness that only public committment could open the gates of the New, innocent, Jerusalem.

During the quattrocento Florentines learned that the segregated indoctrination of adolescents outside the family and away from the streets could reproduce ideal adult types. This discovery did not, however, modify society's opinion of the natural proclivities of the adolescent. When Alberti described hunting as a "childish toy," he was disparaging such pastimes in a thoroughly traditional fashion.[1] The Renaissance in Italy discovered no new values in uninhibited childishness and adolescence. No Florentine father revelled in the juvenile behavior of his children as does the modern father. If mothers did, they always had, and such maternal coddling was understood as another example of the basic sensuality and light-headedness of the weaker sex. The artistic putto, and not the vivacious infant Christ, imaged the ideal young person : *vecchiettini* with the wings of angels.[2]

How could society make its adolescents into utopian fetishes, while conceding no inherent value to their spontaneous behavior ? From one point of view, the answer is evident : Parents' joy in their children's individual growth is a private joy; the young person's self-expression can be socially valued only in a culture where the rights of the private realm are taken to be natural.

Throughout Europe the emergence of this private realm and this new joy in children, so well described by Ariès, was accompanied by growing political absolutism.

In Florence, the quattrocento saw the debilitation of the decision-making powers of the old political class, and its slow conversion to bureaucracy and professional service to the Medici. Such an evolution could not be accomplished without the greatest strains being placed upon traditional life patterns. In earlier times, family prestige had been solidly based on political influence, and the ritual procession of family and civic glory before God and men had reflected the communal organization of real power. With the increasing subversion of political

---

[1] Né ti chiamerò bene operoso se tu consumerai tutto il dì allo sparviere a'cani, alle reti e simili. Simile occupazioni sono trastulli fanciulleschi, concessi ora agli omini gravi per recreare d'animo ..."; Alberti, "De Iciarchia," 239.

[2] For a different view, see Garin, *Pensiero*, p. XIV; Goldthwaite, *Private Wealth*, 264. Ariès examines the different types of representations; *Centuries*, 34-37, 43-48.

forms by the Medici, this old union of ritualistic and political action came to an end. Lorenzo's opponent Alamanno Rinuccini complained about the honored families being driven into their homes by the new "Caesar" : "Both by example and words he did away with all the things which in the old days had graced and given reputation to the citizens, like marriage feasts, dances, *feste*, and ornate dress."[1]

At a stage when public manifestation still seemed a natural part of political activity, the confraternities of adolescents stepped into this breach between the traditional publicity of the republic and the familial privacy of the new world of political authoritarianism. These grave boys represented on the one side a world of private virtues, but on the other a hope of public salvation for families whose survival had been customarily tied to processional prestige. To do this successfully, youthful asceticism, not boyish miscreance, was the order of the early Florentine Renaissance. The socialized and indoctrinated adolescent on the stage and in procession was ritually efficacious before he became privately consoling. He was a social ideal before becoming a private, familial diversion.

ADDENDA

After finishing the final draft of this paper, I found a reference to a company of *fanciulli* called the Purità, founded ca. 1474 in the Dominican church of Santa Maria Novella and composed, according to the source, of sons of *gentili uomini e di stato*. The following is a letter of May 12, 1476 to a Rinuccini, ambassador in Rome for the Florentine government : "A Santa Maria Novella è nuovamente una congregazione di fanciulli, chiamasi Purità, per quello nuovo miracolo di che se'informato. Sono tutt figliuoli di gentili uomini e di stato, hanno qualche dubitazione che per utilità di quello altare nuovamente fatto nel luogo del miracolo, i frati del convento non faccino regnare costì qualche supplicazione contro all loro libertà. Quando t'accaderà dira'ne qualche parola alla S. ta del papa, in modo che quando ne fussi supplicato, la S. ta Sua sia informata, ed a questa compania sia conservata la loro libertà; *Ricordi storici di Filippo di Cino Rinuccini dal 1282 al 1460 colla continuazione di Alamanno e Neri suoi figli fino al 1506*, ed. G. Aiazzi, (Florence, 1840), 246. On the Florentine group *della Pura*, see S. Orlandi, *"Necrologio" di S. Maria Novella* II (Florence, 1955), 332, 338.

---

[1] *Ricordi ... Rinuccini*, CXLVIII.

CRITICAL ISSUES IN THE STUDY OF CIVIC RELIGION IN RENAISSANCE FLORENCE

DONALD WEINSTEIN
Rutgers University

Let me begin with a word of admiration which is no mere conventional opening gambit : Trexler's paper is one of the most significant and exciting in this area of studies that I have heard or read. By asking big questions, by boldly applying concepts from anthropology, comparative religion and the sociology of religion, and by exercising a powerful imagination he has drawn together—often from the most innocent-seeming evidence—an original picture of religion, youth, the family and the state in their dynamic interrelations.

This functioning interrelation is, I believe, the main point of Trexler's approach, suggesting that the social structure must be seen in its wholeness, that its various components, including religion, attain meaning for us, as they did for fifteenth century Florentines, only in relation to each other. Thus the religious behavior of Florentine men and women can only be understood in terms of the familial, societal and political context of values and relations that gave rise to that behavior. Conversely, an understanding of Florentine religious behavior and ideas is necessary to understand the social institutions which it was designed to serve and helped to shape.

If this approach is valid, then one the of main questions raised or implied by the work of Trexler, Charles Trinkaus, Marvin Becker and myself, just, modestly, to name a few of the people present at these meetings, answers itself; that is, that there was a specifically, characteristically *civic* set of religious modalities arising out of the special experience of Italian communal life, as a special case of the medieval urban experience in general.

Some of the main aspects of this religious phenomenon—and this is *my* list, which Trexler or some of you may wish to modify or reject —are the following :

First—*laicization*. By this I mean the dominant trend toward the replacement of clerics by laymen as educators, transmitters of religious values and culture leaders generally. To some extent laymen were, if not supplanting, then coming to take their places alongside priests as spiritual counselors and, in their ritual activities, reinforcing or supplanting the ordered as well as secular clergy as advocates and inter-

mediaries for the secular community. I use the term lay *men* here
advisedly. There is a problem with respect to women and I am not
entirely convinced by Trexler's formulation of it. The work of Ariès,
Duby, Herlihy and others suggests that the conjugal family came into
its own in the period here discussed, that in the family women played
a larger part than ever in the education not only of infants but of
youth, even as women were losing their civil rights. Trexler acknowledges this but declares that confraternities for boys and humanist
schools were designed to remove middle and upper class youth from
the protracted influence of their families. If so, it seems doubtful that
they were very successful. Humanist schools were for the very few.
Even such a wealthy man as Giovanni Rucellai records in 1473 that
he had a resident tutor for his two sons. Confraternities engaged their
members on weekends and holidays. Fifteenth and sixteenth century
Italian artists celebrated the family and the maternal virtues in a
variety of iconographical representations, and it is difficult to escape
the conclusion that there was a general sanctification of lay life, to
use Ariès' phrase. In deploring the excessive influence of the mother
and the family milieu, celibate preachers and educators were vainly
bucking a strong tide. Ariès quotes the Italian in England in the late
fifteenth century who was struck by the emotional coldness of the
English, who could put their children out at the age of seven or nine,
instead of keeping them in the bosom of their own families as, presumably, his countryfolk did. Florentine diarists like Giovanni Rucellai
and Luca Landucci, the first one of the richest men of Florence, the
second a simple apothecary, present an affecting picture of deep
devotion for their wives and children and a strong family unit.

The second of the features of civic religion is *the emergence of the
young*, whether as ritual saviors, to use Trexler's phrase, or as the
special objects of intense religious and educational concern. David
Herlihy in his *Annales* article, on "Growing Old in Fifteenth Century
Florence," identifies some of the special conditions of bourgeois life
that encouraged such developments and made Florentine culture a
youth culture to such a remarkable extent. Trexler has worked into
this the religious dimension which was largely lacking in Herlihy's
paper; but I would repeat here the same question I have just raised
and for the same reasons : should the emphasis be placed upon the
opposition to feminine influence or should such opposition be taken
as a symptom that feminine influence was much stronger than in the
more traditional family set-up ? Perhaps this is the place to raise

another question relating to the family. Trexler's contention that the immediate cause of the intense interest in boys as social beings was a crisis in the structure of the Florentine family is based on Herlihy's figures on marriage age. These are drawn from the Florentine catasto of 1427. But Herlihy begins with 1427 because that is when statistical data first became available; there is no evidence that the situation the data describes is *new*. On the contrary my own reading of Herlihy's article suggests to me that late male marriage and its consequences was characteristic of bourgeois communal life. Therefore, it may be misleading to isolate the Quattrocento as a crisis period when the proper context is the late medieval commune. In this connection I am also doubtful about Trexler's attempt to link the growing emphasis upon childhood and conjugal family life with the decline of republicanism and civic participation in the fifteenth century. If this were so it would be difficult to relate childhood to the Savonarola movement as Trexler does so effectively, for one thing because the Savonarola movement stood for an enlargement, not a restriction, of citizenship as active participation in the affairs of the republic. After Savonarola others took up the effort to organize the boys for religious purposes. Pietro Bernardino, leader of the sect known as the *Unti*, or Anointed, was also called Pietro dei Fanciulli, and this association with the republicanism of the Savonarola years may have been one reason for Pietro's persecution by an anti-*piagnone* government. How much of the discussion of humanist educators and their apolitical stances is relevant to the Florentine situation? Vergerio's book was dedicated to a prince of Padua and Vittorino da Feltre had little to do with Florence.

A third feature of the civic religious phenomenon is *secularization*. Trexler uses this term where I used laicization, but I doubt he would disagree that it can be applied to mean at least two other things— one, the transfer of the scene of religious ritual from reserved monastic or ecclesiastical space to public, civic space, of which it seems to me the climactic development described in his paper is the Savonarolan effort to transform Florentine geopolitical divisions, the wards of the city, into ritual regenerative ones through the organization of the fanciulli. We could add many examples of the penetration of religious locales with civic symbols and vice versa. The second meaning of secularization here is the religious legitimation of formerly worldly and temporal activities and institutions. The idea of the holiness of family life is an excellent example. One thing secularization most assuredly does *not* mean in this context is a decline of Christian faith,

a loss of spirituality, or a tendency to assign purely rational or im-
manentist meanings to human worldly activities and institutions.
Quite the contrary, it was the effort to find spiritual meaning in those
aspects of human life that had formerly been excluded from the perimeters of the holy, the effort to sanctify the secular. This is not to
deny that there were areas of thought where secularization in the sense
of asserting purely worldly, non-spiritual values was taking place. One
thinks of Petrarch's preoccupation with fame and Machiavelli's with
politics *per se*, but we are talking here about everyday life and about
behavior that was mainly non-reflective.

A fourth aspect of civic religion results from the progress of secularization in the sense I have just used it, and that is, *the attribution of
holiness* both potential and actual, *to the city itself*. In conceiving of
Florence as the New Jerusalem Savonarola was, so I have tried to
show, at least, adjusting his own formerly universalist ideas to the
needs of the Florentine civic religion. Werner Stark says that fully
developed religious ethnocentrism has at least three strands; holiness
may be ascribed to the soil, or it may be ascribed to the population,
to their minds or bodies or even their chromosomes, or it may be
ascribed to the constitution under which the privileged people live.
Florentines expressed their religious election in all these ways. Florentine mythology taught her people that she had been born as the
daughter of Rome at the very geographical center of Italy, itself the
heart of the world, that she partook of Rome's mission to rule, that
she had been destroyed by barbarians but rebuilt by Charlemagne,
the second founder of the Christian Roman Empire, who had recon-
secrated her churches on Easter Sunday, that her people were divinely
gifted with spirit and intelligence and her city the noblest and fairest
in all the world, while her government was divinely endowed. Other
cities had comparable mythologies. Religious ethnocentrism was not
unique to the Italian commune; it was as old as the idea of the sacred
ruler and the chosen people, but nowhere did it develop so fully, at
least before the advent of modern nationalism, as in the Italian communes with their intense rivalries and their competing claims to the
Roman inheritance.

In general then, Trexler's paper presents us with the picture of civic
religion as a *collective, public* thing. Socialization through religion was
a function of group ritual activity, even though some of its objectives
may have been familial and private. The manipulation of angelic
children for purposes of regeneration was likewise public and political.

So thoroughly were spiritual and temporal localities and occasions interchangeable as to make it virtually impossible to distinguish the sacred and the profane as separate realms. I might add, with only mild exaggeration, that in the milieu of the Savonarola movement the implications of the civic religion were at last fully drawn—salvation itself took on a *collective* and an *immediate* aspect.

All this is a necessary counterweight to the still dominant impulse of scholars to concentrate upon the individual, private and reflective aspects of religion. If we study piety exclusively through the formal statements of theologians, moralists, clerics and humanists we are inevitably going to end up with a picture of medieval and Renaissance religion that is true for a very small segment of society—its intellectual elite—and maybe not even very true for that segment; indeed, we may find we have created a picture in our *own* image and likeness. If we are looking for evidence—I refrain from using the word progress—of spiritual development in the sense of greater individualism, say, or a more refined attitude toward image worship, or a disenchantment with, and of, relics and the rest of the material paraphernalia of magical religion, we will find it—if we find it anywhere—among the intellectual elite. Whether and to what extent such spiritual developments were characteristic of larger segments of society and what forms it took is a question that neither the more traditional scholarship which approaches the history of religion as a branch of intellectual history, nor Trexler's type of scholarship which approaches the history of religion as a branch of social history, has yet undertaken to answer, so far as I can see. In a paper on "Images and Human Dignity" which he presented at the AHA meetings in 1970 Trexler argued that image worship, characterized by the phenomenon of participation and power-exchange was "a reasonable religion for an urban society," much more reasonable and economical than the rationalist, impersonal and abstract conceptions of philosophers and humanists, so scornful of magic and cult activity. Reasonable it may have been; but I argued then and I would repeat now that lay piety was much more complex, and that to focus on its magical elements is to ignore such other aspects of late medieval spirituality as the rise of lay preaching, the cultivation of interior or mental prayer and the general tendency to develop more complicated and differentiated symbol systems which expressed increasing cosmological and metaphysical sophistication. For example, it may be pertinent to note that in his paper on the Company of the Magi in Florence Rab Hatfield shows how that important confrater-

nity, originally organized to present the Epiphany pageantry of the
Kings and to take part in the procession for the Feast of the Baptist,
evolved, in the course of the fifteenth century, into a very different
kind of religious organization, a society of personal and semi-private
devotions, emphasizing meditation upon the Eucharist and the Crucifixion and the virtues of penitence, and of hope for eternal life. To
be sure, some of the members of the Magi were the leading thinkers
and literary figures of Florence—that intellectual elite again—but not
all of them, and such groups as the Magi were just where intellectuals
and laymen met and interacted; that is a prime part of their historical
importance. Again, consider Pietro Bernardino, the leader of the
Anointed and the fanciulli I mentioned earlier. Pietro was an unlettered artisan, or perhaps even a laborer, the sources disagree; but
they do agree that his knowledge of Scriptures was considerable, while
the sermons we have by him reveal him as a passionate advocate of
orazione mentale or interior prayer. In short, the history of lay piety
in the late medieval and Renaissance period has many dimensions not
yet explored. How those we have explored correlate to social factors
such as class, sex, age groups, education and occupation, as well as
to the differences between town, communal, provincial and rural
settings is just barely beginning to be perceived; Trexler's work on
ritual and civic society not only contributes enormously to that perception but points out where we should look further and even some
of the things to look for. And *that*, I consider, is what creative historical
thinking is all about.

INTERVENTIONS ON "RITUAL IN FLORENCE"

WILLIAM J. BOUWSMA

University of California (Berkeley)

Professor Trexler attaches a good deal of importance to the problem
of homosexuality (and hence of the masculine identity of young
Florentines), which—on the basis largely of the conclusions of Herlihy
about the age of marriage and its implications for family relationships
—he sees as coming to a head in the late fourteenth and fifteenth
centuries and thus helping to push the establishment of youth con-

fraternities. But "Florentine homosexuality" is an old stereotype that finds expression in Dante (and I suspect earlier) and is repeated into the seventeenth century. It would be difficult to demonstrate that it had any special basis in Florentine experience, so that Florence was different in this respect from other communities, or that it posed a special danger to Florentine society in any particular period.

(Trexler replied—fairly enough—that the point has to do less with the objective situation than with the Florentine perception of a special threat from this direction. Perhaps his paper could make this more clear, but in any case he would need then to show that Florentines were more concerned about the matter at this time than in other periods of their history if the point is to be useful in explaining the formation of the youth confraternities. Actually, I am not sure that he needs it, since he also develops the explanation along other lines.)

DAVID WILKINS

University of Pittsburgh

The art historian reads the historian's work not only for what it will tell him about the context within which works of art were produced, but also in the hope that a piece of historical information will provide a clue to the solution of some art historical problem. One such problem has been the motivation behind a large number of paintings representing *Tobias and the Archangel Raphael* produced in Florence during the later Quattrocento. Some interesting and valid suggestions were forwarded by Gertrude Coor-Achenbach in *Marsyas* (3, 1943-1945, 71-86), but to these must now be added Prof. Trexler's brilliant analysis of the particular role played by organized youth during this period. I suspect that an investigation of these paintings (and of the popular dramas on the same subject) and of the oldest and most important company for *pueri*, the Nativity (also called "of the Archangel Raphael"), would lead to some convincing relationships between these phenomena.

4. REFORMATION AND PEDAGOGY : EDUCATIONAL THOUGHT AND PRACTICE IN THE LUTHERAN REFORMATION

GERALD STRAUSS
Indiana University

Reformers were ambivalent on many matters, on none more so than the future. Judgment day was near—to some it was imminent [1]—and all earthly things were transitory and fleeting. At the same time meticulous planning, organizing, and providing for many generations to come suggests a strong sense of permanence. The laws and institutions of the Reformation were made to last. Why establish so well if time was running out ?

In children the future is tangible for us and, to an extent, controllable. Children in our midst give us a hold on the generation to come. By molding the young we shape the future—or so we hope and trust. Protestant reformers were no less eager to mold and shape than men in other times and societies. Endeavoring to make their achievement permanent by directing the minds and forming the characters of the new generation, they devised educational procedures which they hoped would ensure right thinking and right conduct in the young.

The history of schools and schooling in the German Reformation is well-known. [2] It was an impressive achievement to have founded and funded so many elementary and secondary schools, gymnasia, and universities and to have provided them with able masters and sound curricula. In the history of formal education the Reformation era

---

[1] See, for example, Johann Carion's statement in his *Chronica* ... (Wittenberg, 1532), 169 recto; also Johann Mathesius, in his sermons on Luther, 1566. Mathesius writes that Luther rescued mankind *zur letzten zeit vorm jungsten tage* and *vorm ende diser welt.* Johannes Mathesius, *Ausgewählte Werke* III (Prague, 1898), 4; 14.

[2] Karl Hartfelder, "Erziehung und Unterricht im Zeitalter des Humanismus;" Ernst Gundert, "Die Reformation," both in K. A. Schmid et al., *Geschichte der Erziehung* ... vol. II, 2. Abteilung (Stuttgart, 1892); Friedrich Paulsen, *Geschichte des gelehrten Unterrichts auf den deutschen Schulen und Universitäten vom Ausgang des Mittelalters bis zur Gegenwart* (Leipzig, 1885); Karl Schmidt, *Geschichte der Pädagogik* ... (ed. Richard Lange, Köthen, 1883); Georg Mertz, *Das Schulwesen der deutschen Reformation* (Heidelberg, 1902).

holds an important place. But scholars in the history of education tend to look mainly at the mechanics of this formidable educational enterprise : schools established, instructors appointed, *Schulordnungen* and curricula, textbooks, class organization, fees and salaries, attendance requirements, and so on. On what pedagogical principles did all this teaching and learning rest? What attitudes toward the child prevailed among the reformers and how much did they know about him? What were the purposes of education and were these purposes reflected in instructional procedures? Was class room activity guided by informed principles? Such questions as these have not usually been answered; indeed, they are not often asked.[1]

The aims of public education were self-evident to the German reformers in the first generation of the Reformation. Basic instruction in the articles of the Christian faith was to prepare the ears and hearts of all for receiving the word of God when it was preached. Second, education in citizenship must make the unformed child into a useful member of society by showing him how to find and hold his place in the social and political order, taking care that he accepts the virtue of hard work and develops habits and behavior suitable to his station. Third, minds capable of higher education must be identified and prepared for the gymnasium and the university. To accomplish this last objective—one which was held, at least in the first decades of the Reformation, to be of an importance equal to the other two—the rudiments of knowledge taught in primary schools had to be sound enough to support the higher learning offered at advanced levels.

It doesn't matter whether we speak of these objectives as education or training or (in the terminology of modern child study) socialization.[2] In the early sixteenth century they were simply common-sense conclusions drawn from perceived needs for the immediate and distant future. The mass of surviving documents reveals general agreement among reformers and pedagogues on the purposes of education. "The hope of our commonweal rests on our youth" say Bucer, Capito and Hedio to the City Council of Strassburg, urging its members to undertake the reform of the entire school system so that the city might bring up its youngsters as "Christians toward God and useful citizens in the

---

[1] Philippe Ariès' noted *Centuries of Childhood : A Social History of Family Life* (tr. Robert Baldick, N.Y., 1962) refers only occasionally to events outside France.

[2] On socialization see David A. Goslin (ed), *Handbook of Socialization Theory and Research* (Chicago, 1969) and William Kessen, *The Child* (New York and London, 1965).

world"[1] Luther suggested the formula "Fear of God, good discipline, and an honest life"[2] for defining the objectives of basic education. A proper school, Luther says, is one where "children are trained in skills, discipline, and divine service, learning to know God and his word and grow into men and women capable of governing churches, land and people, households, children and servants."[3] Not every child can become a priest, a cleric or a lawyer, but all should read and write Latin, for how else can those with the gifts for higher study prove their merit?[4] The crying need for more and better pastors was, of course, uppermost in the reformers' intentions, as well as the wish to instill in minds innocent of the ways of the world safeguards against false teachings, distractions, and temptations. But they appealed no less vigorously to the authorities' sense of civic responsibility, arguing that schools and schooling were no less vital to a society's welfare than markets, roads and bridges.[5] "No worldly activity or estate can be kept in working order except by skilled men and women," Luther said, and went on to argue that the requisite skills, far from being merely manual, could be properly acquired only in properly established schools.[6]

Traditional educational institutions were clearly inadequate to this purpose. Seen from the point of view of the reformers, medieval schools were irrational and chaotic. A bewildering number of types of schools —cathedral, parish, monastic, municipal, private, and many others— were operated without proper supervision and according to no recognized standards. Abuses of all kinds were commonplace as scholars

---

[1] From a memorandum prepared mainly by Bucer but signed also by Capito, Hedio, Zell, Altbiesser, and Schwartz and handed to the Council in August, 1524. See E.-W. Kohls, *Die Schule bei Martin Bucer in ihrem Verhältnis zu Kirche und Obrigkeit* (Heidelberg, 1963). In a similar phrase, the *Ordnung der Visitatoren* for Torgau in Saxony in 1529 speaks of the advance of *"gemeiner nutz und regiment"* bound to result from good schools. Cf. Emil Sehling, (ed), *Die evangelischen Kirchenordnungen des 16. Jahrhunderts* I (Leipzig, 1902), 677-8.

[2] WA Tr., 5, No. 6103.

[3] From "Eine Predigt, dass man Kinder zur Schule halten solle" (1530), WA 39, 520.

[4] *Ibid.*, 545-6. In the *Unterricht der Visitatoren* of 1528 Luther recommends that in each Latin class the most talented boys are to be selected (*die geschicktisten auswelen*) to go to the higher form. Cf. Sehling I, 173. The most explicit statement is in Bugenhagen's *Braunschweigische Schulordnung*, 1528 in Reinhold Vormbaum (ed), *Die evangelischen Schulordnungen des sechszehnten Jahrhunderts* (*Evangelische Schulordnungen* vol. I, Gütersloh, 1860), 16.

[5] Luther writing to Elector Johann, November 1526, WA Br., 4, No. 1052.

[6] Luther, "An die Ratsherren aller Städte deutschen Lands, dass sie christliche Schulen aufrichten und halten sollen" (1524), WA, 15, 44.

led a precarious existence and money was a paramount consideration for teachers and students alike.[1] Religious instruction, where it existed at all, was unsystematic and superficial, and in all subjects teaching principles and performance varied widely from place to place and time to time. The itinerancy of a sizable part of the student population was a scandal in the eyes of the reformers who concurred emphatically with the proverb, "Once a wandering scholar, always a wastrel." Thomas Platter's memoirs offer a distressing catalogue of difficulties placed in the way of a youngster in search of an education according to the old manner.[2] This familiar source can be augmented with numberless references in the Reformation literature to the unwholesome conditions prevailing in a confused and unprincipled educational situation badly in need of reform.

What seemed wanting most in the old process was unity of purpose conscientiously pursued and rigorously enforced. In matters of education—and not only in these, of course—reformers believed strongly in uniformity and direction. Since truth was one and not subject to human manipulation, they saw no reason for encouraging multiple approaches to what was right and good. There never was any doubt among Reformation pedagogues that educational practices should be authoritatively established and conducted. The dangers of leaving such vital matters to the several judgments of many men were so great and, in the context of the 1520's, so immediate, that reformers never seem to have speculated on the possibility of less authoritarian ways of accomplishing their purposes. As they saw it, direction and supervision were the only alternatives to chaos.

Uniformity was one of the rules unquestioningly accepted as a guiding principle. Constantly recurring words in territorial and municipal school ordinances are *Gleichförmigkeit* (uniformity) and "*gleichlich*" (equal or same). Not only the catechism, but also grammar, were to be taught to all from the same books, in the same manner, and at the same hours of the day and week.[3] In Breslau the City Council

---

[1] These are evident in descriptions such as Thomas Platter's and in the injunctions and proscriptions enacted during the Reformation. See for example the statement in the Württemberg *Schulordnung* (Vormbaum, 68-9). Also Kohls, *op. cit.*, 218, note 22. Needless to say, there were some notable exceptions including the school of Schlettstadt and the schools operated by the Brothers of the Common Life.

[2] Thomas Platter, *Lebensbeschreibung* ed. A. Hartmann (Basel, 1944).

[3] See the detailed rules for instruction in grammar in the Württemberg *Schulordnung* of 1559, one of the most influential of all German school ordinances. Printed in Vormbaum, 80-1. On uniform catechism instruction, see *ibid.*, 160.

instructed masters throughout the city to adhere "for the sake of uniformity" to the curriculum established at the school of St. Elizabeth.[1] In Strassburg, government and preachers saw to it that instruction was carried on "identically" in all municipal schools.[2] Administrative economy and the wish to drive remaining medieval schools out of business were not the main reasons for this insistence. The chief reason was concern for singleness of belief and purpose. Diversity and multiplicity cause confusion. Simple minds need steady guidance from hands directed by unswerving standards : "Teach [the catechism] plainly, without changing, adding or removing a word, so that ... all things everywhere will be done the same and children and simple-minded people become accustomed to hearing the selfsame words ..., a practice which prevents the young from being thrown into confusion."[3] It is well known that sixteenth-century authorities developed a passion for legislating in minute details. Many school ordinances held teachers and pupils in a net of painstakingly prescribed hourly tasks so close-meshed that reading about it today makes one wonder how the love of learning could have survived the choking of spontaneity.[4] But individual judgment and natural impulses were precisely the temperamental traits most deeply distrusted, while innovation and experiment were thought to arise from the unfortunate human tendencies to covetousness, greed and the refusal to be satisfied. Stability could come only from order, hence the nuances of constancy and established propriety which ring in the universally used term *Ordnung* and its adjective *ordentlich* : in accordance with, in compliance with *Ordnung*, the way things ought to be.[5]

The disturbing experiences of the 1520's in Germany could only serve to strengthen the resolve of pedagogues to make the principles

---

[1] Breslau *Schulordnung* in Vormbaum, 184.

[2] Kohls, 75-6.

[3] From catechism instructions for County Mansfeld printed in Johann Michael Reu, *Quellen zur Geschichte des kirchlichen Unterrichts in der evangelischen Kirche Deutschlands zwischen 1530 und 1600*. Part I : *Quellen zur Geschichte des Katechismus-Unterrichts*, volume 2, "Mitteldeutsche Katechismen," section (1) : "Historisch-bibliographische Einleitung" (Gütersloh, 1911), 263.

[4] See for example the instructions for the German schools in the Stralsund *Schulordnung* of 1560 in Vormbaum, 479-80.

[5] Needless to say, the term *Ordnung* is older than the Reformation. But the extensive ecclesiastical and social re-ordering undertaken by the reformers caused the term to proliferate. See the entry *Ordnung* in Jacob and Wilhelm Grimm, *Deutsches Wörterbuch* vol. 7 (Leipzig, 1889).

of authority and conformity pervasive in their educational foundations. Where so many mental aberrations led to such widespread tumults, only the firmest direction could restore and preserve order.[1] To speak of Protestant schools as "instruments of magisterial education" as does Wilhelm Maurer in his book on Melanchthon's early years,[2] is therefore only to draw the political sum of the many charters and regulations creating schools in the 1520's, 30's and 40's. Secular governing bodies were not always as impatient as churchmen to get on with the organization of countrywide or city-wide educational systems, but diligent prodding persuaded most that well thought-out and carefully organized curricula would yield political as well as social benefits.[3]

Schools instituted under these circumstances were bound to represent the magisterial outlook. The state being in most instances the agent in the founding of new schools, political ends were inevitably fused with religious values in the resulting establishments. Religious leaders, for their part, were comfortable in the thought that the state's power to compel could be called upon where pulpit persuasion failed to convince the faithful that schooling was necessary and good.[4] The establishment of school systems came to be accepted as a political responsibility. By 1537, when the Schmalkaldic League required it of all its members,[5] over thirty school ordinances had been promulgated in cities and territories.[6] Municipal and territorial authorities were appointed consisting of secular and ecclesiastical officials working jointly to determine curricula and faculty appointments, lay down rules for

---

[1] Melanchthon, in the final section of his *Widder die artickel der bawrschafft* (*Melanchthons Werke in Auswahl*, ed. Robert Stupperich, vol. I Gütersloh, 1951, p. 214) written immediately after the peasant defeat, says that schools are now needed *da durch die leut zu frieden und erbarkeyt erzogen werden.*

[2] Wilhelm Maurer, *Der junge Melanchthon* (Göttingen, 1967-69), 463. Maurer emphsizes the impact upon Melanchthon of the Wittenberg disturbances and the knights' and peasant rebellions. Melanchthon's image of himself as "praeceptor" is closely tied to these experiences. Cf. *ibid.*, 415f.

[3] Cf. Luther's "An die Ratsherren aller Städte ..." (1524) WA 15, 9-53; "Eine Predigt, dass man Kinder zur Schule halten solle," (1530) WA 30, 2, 508-88; "Unterricht der Visitatoren ..." (1528) WA 26, 236-40 on schools.

[4] E.g. Luther, "An die Ratsherren aller Städte ..." (1524) WA 15, 33; "Ein Predigt, dass man Kinder zur Schule halten solle" (1530) WA 30, 2, 586-70.

[5] Mertz, 13. Reference to schools is also made in the Schmalkald Articles of 1537 under No. 12 : "*Von der Kirche.*"

[6] See the list of sixteenth-century *Schulordnungen* given in Mertz, 162-5.

student conduct, select books, work out lesson plans and establish inspection and examination procedures. Wherever possible, control was centralized. Teachers were chosen locally, but their formal appointment was usually the prerogative of high officials such as the Württemberg *Kirchenräte* who named only candidates whom they had thoroughly examined for professional qualifications, reputation, and religious orthodoxy.

Frequent visitations and periodic official examinations enabled the authorities to keep in close touch with classroom instruction. Religious teaching, once thought to be the province of the home and the pulpit, was incorporated in the curriculum by means of catechism and Bible study. Sunday was free, of course, a day to be spent in family worship. But the authorities took no chances, suspecting that many parents were negligent about taking children to church, and arranged for group attendance at weekday sermons.[1] In this and other matters the authorities declined to trust the good sense of parents. Preachers were told to appeal to parishioners to send children to school (instructions advise "serious admonitions accompanied by descriptions of the great benefit to be derived from good schooling"[2]). Catechisms included among the violators of the fifth commandment those "who fail to bring up their children to be God-fearing and well behaved."[3]

If such requests fell on deaf ears, the authorities were prepared to intervene. Education was now understood as a social duty; parental indifference could no longer be countenanced. Explicit statements to this effect were not lacking. "God has endowed each person with particular gifts so that he may be useful to his community. Parents shall note each child's special skills and have him educated accordingly so that God's gifts will not be wasted." And what if parents neglect this duty ? "In that case children cease to be in the charge of their parents but belong instead to God and the whole community. God gives life to talented boys so that their gifts shall benefit an entire community."[4] These benefits—the practical products of schooling—were often catalogued. Education meant not only a steady supply

---

[1] E.g. Strassburg, memo by Johann Sturm to Council cited in Kohls, 217 note 21.

[2] Württemberg *Schulordnung* of 1559, Vormbaum, 98. Another example : instruction to superintendents and pastors in Albertine Saxony, 1557 in Sehling I, 316.

[3] From Caspar Aquila, *Des kleinen Catechismi Erklerung* ... (1538) printed in Reu I, 2 Section (2) : "Texte," 173ff.

[4] From Ambrosius Moibanus of Breslau, *Catechismus* (Wittenberg, 1535) printed in Reu 1,2 (2), 737.

of "good schoolmasters, good preachers, good advocates, good physicians," but also an increase in the number of "God-fearing, hardworking, honest, upright, obedient, friendly, peaceable, happy and satisfied citizens."[1] To quote still another school ordinance : "There can be neither Christian life nor civil order except where young people are brought up in the fear of God and the practice of obedience."[2] The quiescent, orderly, fruitful life of everyone's fondest hopes where men live at peace with God and themselves could never come to be unless the conditions for it were first implanted as right thoughts and attitudes in the minds and hearts of the young.

About the qualities of mind desired in the young there was general though largely implicit agreement. Their characteristics will become clearer if we first contrast them with modern pedagogical aims as stated in the literature of educational psychology. A recent book defines these aims as follows : The young person is to be enabled

1. To make intelligent and autonomous choices of life goals which will serve the satisfaction of individual desires without violating the interests of the community ;
2. to take on responsibility for his own actions ;
3. to develop a critical faculty for acquiring knowledge and for judging the contributions made by others ;
4. to learn skills and knowledge relevant to problems arising in human existence ;
5. to develop flexible and intelligent attitudes to new situations and problems ;
6. to learn to employ the multiplicity of individual experiences in solving these problems ;
7. to work cooperatively with others in solving problems, not primarily to win approval but in accordance with his own socially acceptable motives and goals ;
8. to see himself in the many facets of his personality ; to accept himself and his feelings ;
9. to develop respect for what is profound in life including processes which escape the rational understanding of men.[3]

The sixteenth-century counterparts to these educational objectives are almost diametrically their opposite. Far from setting out to prepare the child for the exercise of independent critical judgment, encouraging flexible attitudes, cultivating the mind to absorb and assimilate the greatest possible number of experiences and impressions

---

[1] Braunschweig *Schuleordnung* of 1528 in Vormbaum, 10-11.

[2] Albertine Saxon *Schulordnung* of 1543 issued by Duke Moritz. Printed in Sehling I, 287.

[3] Reinhard and Anne-Marie Tausch, *Erziehungspsychologie* (2nd ed. Göttingen, 1965), 4.

while convincing him that his personality is complex and ambiguous, the pedagogues of the Reformation attempted, by means of rigorous mental and physical discipline to subdue those traits which promoted in the adult person contumacy, self-absorption, assertiveness, curiosity, and the restless search for new satisfactions. In accordance with their theological commonplaces the reformers saw the greatest danger to man's soul and society in his tendency to relate all human experience to himself and to take his own senses as the measure of all things. Their model of man was of an essentially passive being prepared to acquiesce rather than struggle, distrustful of his own inclinations and reluctant to act on them, ready to yield where his strivings conflicted with received norms. There were satisfactions to be found in life and no reason not to enjoy them. But at no moment must man forget the insignificance and transitoriness of earthly existence as measured by the life eternal, the promise of which is man's highest good.

Reformers were under no illusion about the distance separating this model from real men as they observed them. Nor where they, in view of men's inherent resistance to reform, optimistic about succeeding with the process of mind-shaping and personality-shaping through which they hoped to close the gap. Adults could be reached only from the pulpit and through the more heavy-handed means of imposing Christian standards available in marriage and morals courts. For the indoctrination of children, however, there existed a much more hopeful prospect. When taken at an early age, before attitudes are permanently rooted, children, unlike their elders, are open to influence, and as the twig is bent, the tree's inclined. School-entering age, generally six or seven, was the auspicious moment for starting the conditioning process. Most men who expressed themselves on the subject of child development seemed to think that at age seven the child undergoes some fundamental changes. "In the seventh year," wrote Luther after observing his son Hans,[1] "men begin to change. Children under seven have no unclean thoughts. They do not think of murder and adultery, though they may start feeling the temptation to steal sweets." Infantile innocence is a wonderful thing to see, Luther said.[2] He never tired of watching his own and other children amuse themselves in their guileless way. Their artless games put him in mind of the pristine

---

[1] WA Tr, 3, No. 3611a.

[2] *Ibid.*, 2 No. 1532.

state of man.[1] Infants have the right faith, he wrote,[2] "they live in innocence, are ignorant of sin, envy, anger and greed, and are happy in their good conscience. They fear no dangers in war and pestilence, nor do they dread death. And when they are told of Christ and the life to come they believe it in all simplicity and chatter merrily about it."[3]

Alas, this happy condition is soon contaminated by the appearance of what Luther calls *"rechte Gedanken,"* by which he means rational thoughts.[4] This development occurs at age seven or eight. Without reason children would not be capable of learning; on the other hand rational faculties also bring the onset of cunning and calculated self-serving. From then until puberty at about twelve for girls and fourteen for boys,[5] children "begin to experience the world"[6] and acquire those animal drives so deplored by the reformers. This, then, is the age at which to seize them, while they are malleable and before the typical human traits of willfulness and obstinacy are firmly settled in their natures. To quote on this point a catechism widely used in Saxony and Thuringia : "If we wish to increase the kingdom of Christ and populate our community with honorable, God-fearing Christians we must make our beginning with children. They are the seed which we must cultivate. As for their elders, they are too far gone in sin. There is no longer any guiding or teaching them, as daily experience with them tells us, for the world is too corrupt."[7]

The general suspicion in which human nature was held—man a slave to passion and resolutely resistant to advise and entreaties[8]— came to be codified in many ecclesiastical ordinances establishing church and school systems in Germany. The *Kirchenordnung* of Hessen, for example, asserted that "our corrupted nature and the instigations of the

---

[1] *Ibid.*, 5, No. 6099; 4, No. 4027.

[2] *Ibid.*, 1, No. 7230.

[3] *Ibid.*, 1, No. 660. Many similar statements *passim* in Tr.

[4] *Ibid.*, 2 No. 1532. I think the adjective *rechte* should not be taken as meaning "right" in the sense of correct thoughts, but "thoughts proper," i.e. rational thoughts.

[5] "The age at which nature begins to assert itself." Cf. the statement by the Augsburg physician Bartolomäus Metlinger quored in John Ruhräh, *Pediatrics of the Past* (New York, 1925), 97. See also Luther in WA Tr 3 No. 2980a and b.

[6] *Ibid.*, 3 No. 3711a.

[7] Nikolaus Hecko, *Catechismus* (1554) in Reu I,2 (2), 243-4.

[8] Melanchthon, *Loci praecipui theologici* (1559) (*Melanchthons Werke in Auswahl* II, 1, 261-3).

evil one have made us obstinate and surly toward matters affecting
our own redemption and salvation.''[1] This axiomatic proposition is
one explanation for the extra-ordinarily explicit way in which the tasks
of officials and public servants—school personnel among them—were
spelled out. If no man may be trusted, nothing could be left to the
individual discretion, certainly not the intellectual and moral teaching
of children.[2] The same assumption defines adult attitudes toward the
young. Distrust of human nature was bound to determine pedagogical
ideas. By nature "inclined to frivolity and all sorts of wickedness,"[3]
defenseless against temptations, the young must at all ages be protected from themselves. Expectations of good sense were evidently low.
Documents refer to "young and simple" boys and "poor, senseless
young folk easily led astray, scatterbrained and quick to forget."[4]
Einfältig—simpleminded, gullible—is the adjective most often associated with children. When exposed to unprepared minds, even rudiment-
ary learning was fraught with dangers. School ordinances warn teachers
of the tendency of young people to misinterpret their reading or draw
wrong conclusions from it. Terence was a perilous author to have in
the curriculum for this reason, and the Württemberg school ordinance
gravely instructs teachers to explain to their young charges that when
a wicked character gets away with a nasty deed (for example Micio
in the *Adelphi)* his escape is only temporary, for God will surely
punish him in the end.[5]

Of course, careful distinctions are usually made between the great
mass of ordinary children and those few who are gifted to learn and
retain. The latter were to be singled out and advanced, and a fine
system of gymnasia and preparatory schools existed for their special
training. A vaguely formulated notion held that intellect developed

---

[1] From the 1574 redaction of the *Kirchenordnung* of Hessen, 1566, printed in Reu
I,2 (1), 430-1.

[2] Individual schoolmasters sometimes saw a more elevated role for themselves. Cf.
Ortholph Fuchssperger, *Leesskonst* (Passau, 1542) printed in Johannes Müller, *Quellen-
schriften und Geschichte des deutschsprachlichen Unterrichtes bis zur Mitte des 16. Jahrhunderts* (Gotha, 1882). Fuchssperger claims that good teaching "cannot be defined in
fixed regulations but must be left to the schoolmaster, who should try to determine
each child's sense and iunderstanding." Reference on p. 169.

[3] *Visitationsabschied für die Stadt Dönelb* (Saxony, 1555), in Sehling I, 548.

[4] Saxon *Kirchenordnung* issued by the Elector August, 1590, quoted in Reu I, 2 (1),
140.

[5] Württemberg *Schulordnung*, 1559 in Vormbaum, 83.

gradually at age fifteen or so, at least in boys of superior *ingenium* or disposition.[1] Conscience, too, makes its appearance about then, although references to this sense are few. Luther held that since the young do not possess conscience, they require discipline.[2] Once conscience has developed a person may place some reliance on his motives, conscience exercising a restraining function which was picturesquely described in one of Paul Eber's Catechism sermons given in Wittenberg in 1562 :

> When we fall into sin, [Eber writes] we soon feel it in our hearts, which accuses and indicts us by bearing, pounding, and knocking like a judge and executioner. For conscience is nothing else than the living voice of a hangman who is saying to us "you have done wrong. There is a judge and he will punish you, you may be sure."[3]

It is not clear from what was being said whether conscience was thought to grow naturally with age or must be awakened in each individual. In either case, techniques existed—as we shall see—for amplifying the hangman's voice. As for intellect, it was thought to be a natural faculty possessed by each person to some measure. Since it was a power for evil as well as for good, the intellect was the object of much anxiety among pedagogues. The thinking faculty may well have been considered a neutral agent depending for its effects upon the material with which it works, material accumulated by experience in the form of impressions. On the contribution of experience all Reformation pedagogues agreed. The world is wicked, and little good can come of living in it. Innocent natures are soon contaminated.[4] *Ingenia* had to be guarded from unaccustomed and confusing choices, for a child is quickly bewildered and perturbed.[5] Compounded of natural endowment [6] and impressions gained in experience, a person's character is victim to all the unpredictable influences of its surround-

---

[1] The Heidelberg *Schulordnung* of 1587 (Vormbaum, 355) refers to *alle diejenigen, so zu irem verstand kommen, als die primani, secundani, auch wol tertiani.*

[2] WA Tr 4 No. 4082 : *Conscientia nondum est in pueris; illi sunt disciplina educandi.* He continues : *postea veniente conscientia Moses est lapidandus.*

[3] Published 1578. Printed in Reu I,2 (2(), 88.

[4] Cf. Luther, WA Tr 4 No. 4506.

[5] Pomeranian *Schulordnung* of 1563 in Vormbaum, 168, where uniform curriculum, books, etc. in the territory are justified by asserting that children forced to transfer would suffer a shock to their *ingenia*.

[6] E.g. Ortholph Fuchssperger, *Leesskonst* (see 282, n. 2 above), 169 : *die angeborn natur ...*

ings : "Aristotle says : 'the soul of a child is an unwritten tablet upon which nothing is written. One may, however, write on it what one will.' " Thus Bartholomäus Metlinger, a physician and writer on pediatrics in Augsburg.[1] Although the *tabula rasa* concept was certainly not universally accepted [2] Reformation pedagogues generally agreed that behavior was influenced by means of habituation. Wenceslaus Linck, the Wittenberg theologian and preacher in Nuremberg, asserted that "man from birth is like a blank slate [*ein blosse Tafel*]." We write on it, he adds, by means of upbringing and teaching.[3] Before "the world" hardens it, a child's nature is pliant; seized in time, it can be moulded to conform at least in external matters to the accepted norms of the Christian life.

This moulding process was seen as a problem in conditioning. "External discipline," defined as "the ability to direct one's outer organs—eyes, ears, tongue, hands, feet, and so on—in accordance with God's law,"[4] was a matter of habituation. School ordinances constantly reiterate this point. Pupils must do such-and-such "so that they may be accustomed to it."[5] Reading these lengthy documents one soon realizes that the reason for their painstakingly meticulous regulations for conduct in and out of school is not so much a faith in their intrinsic merit. It is rather an implicit belief in their power to inculate good habits, and these were conceived as a permanent, deep-rooted, almost automatic discipline for life to counteract natural instincts and make the young impervious to the corrupting influence of "the world."

Zucht, discipline, was uppermost in the minds of Reformation pedagogues. Reading the documents one has the feeling that no other term appears as often in the educational literature of sixteenth-century Germany. The proverb said "Teaching without discipline is a soup without salt," and Reformation educators agreed. Children must be

---

[1] Bartolomäus Metlinger, *Regiment der jungen Kinder, wie man sie halten und erziehen soll* ... (Augsburg, 1497), quoted in Ruhräh, 97.

[2] Metlinger himself goes on to cite an alternative interpretation offered by Avicenna, that wicked actions are a sign of "a bad streak in the nature."

[3] Wenceslaus Linck, "Der christliche Adel" in *Wenzel Lincks Werke* (ed. W. Reindell, Marburg, 1894), 279.

[4] Sebastian Fröschel, *Catechismus, wie der in der Kirche zu Wittenberg nu vil jar ... ist gepredigt worden* (Wittenberg, 1559) printed in Reu I, 2 (2), 63.

[5] "Damit si gewönt werden." E.g. Württemberg *Schulordnung*, 1559 in Vormbaum, 160.

brought up to obey, of course. (Luther bases this duty on 1 Timothy 1.9 "the law is not laid down for the just but for the lawless and disobedient") and the first lessons in dutiful submissiveness must—or should—necessarily come in the home. Sermons and catechisms made much of this domestic responsibility, urging parents to be firm with their offspring "especially in these times when we all see young people growing up to a wild, dissolute, godless life, and more often than not as a result of parental neglect, for once bad habits are formed no preaching, admonishing, or punishments can correct them."[1] The Württemberg school ordinance, declaring that where discipline is lacking no fear of God can exist, told preachers to persuade parents and guardians to be severe with their children *("unter der rutten halten und inen nit zu leis and mild sein")* and ordered schoolmasters to report to the magistrates all cases where a pupil's conduct gave grounds for suspicion of parental permissiveness.[2] In this matter as in most others the authorities were always ready to intervene. Normally, however, patient persuasion was thought to suffice; hence the many references in the catechisms for parentally guided domestic discipline :

> *Question :* When do parents act contrary to their calling ?
> *Answer :* When they give free rein to their children, allowing them to grow up like wild beasts in wickedness, obstinacy, profaning, lying, cheating and dissembling; when they leave them their will in all things without discipline and punishment. In the end such parents will have their reward, namely disappointment and sadness. Those parents on the other hand who keep their children in strict discipline and under the rod will see honor reflected on themselves and will redeem their souls from hell.[3]

The literature of the time offers many dispirited catalogues of contemporary social evils seen as the consequence of parental permissiveness.[4] These should probably be taken with a grain of salt. But it was an agreed-upon assumption that the social order depended on the disciplined conduct of each of its members. It was further taken for granted that the individual's acquisition of this behavioral discipline would never come out of his rational understanding of its social pur-

---

[1] Sebastian Fröschel, *Catechismus* in Reu I, 2 (2), 61.

[2] Württemberg *Schulordnung*, 1559, in Vormbaum, 92-3.

[3] Johann Spangenberg, *Des kleinen Catechismi und der Haustafel kurtzer Begriff* (Wittenberg, 1541) in Reu I, 2 (2), 297.

[4] As for example in Jörg Wickram's *Die siben Hauptlaster* (1556) printed in *Bibliothek des litterarischen Vereins, Stuttgart*, vol. 229, 181.

pose, and his consequent voluntary acceptance of it as a kind of
categorical imperative. Conscience—as we saw above—tended to be
understood as an after-thought to reprehensible action. It was *bad*
conscience aroused by an offensive act. Good action never followed
from an initiating command of conscience. Discipline therefore depended not on appeals to the inner man, but on habituation of the
external senses. First in the home, later in the school, habituation was
accomplished by means of constraints and incentives, especially by
constraints, for the natural drives were thought to furnish more than
enough of the necessary stimuli to action.

Since so many disciplinary prescriptions emphasize the rod as an
indispensable aid to habituation, it ought to be said that few authorities recommended indiscriminate use of penalties. Most advised parents
and masters to be reasonable. While the proverbs asserted that to
spare the rod was to spoil the child,[1] school regulations advised humane moderation. As is well known, Luther was himself insistent on
avoiding excess in inflicting punishment.[2] He counselled the liberal use
of enticements along with penalties : "Let children and pupils be
punished in such a way that the apple is always seen with the rod."[3]
It may well be, of course, that official calls to moderation in administering punishment should be seen as reflections of brutal practices
actually in use. The Nordhausen school ordinance of 1583, for example,
orders teachers to refrain from "acting tyranically, striking boys until
they are bloody, kicking them, lifting them from the floor by their
hair or ears, beating them about the face with a cane or a book."[4]
It stands to reason that some at least among the masters must have
inflicted sadistic punishment on boys. But there is no evidence to
support the claim of Philippe Ariès that severe corporal punishment
in schools shows "the insistence on humiliating childhood, to mark it
out and improve it."[5] On the contrary, most ordinances advised not
only restraint, but also patience : first use kind words, they said, then

---

[1] For an interesting collection of contemporary proverbs relating to the upbringing
of children, see Karl Friedrich Wilhelm Wander, *Deutsches Sprichwörter-Lexikon*(Leipzig,
1867-80), vol. II under *"Kinder."*

[2] E.g. WA Tr 3 No. 3566; 5 No. 5571; 5 No. 5819, and many others.

[3] *Ibid.*, 2 No. 3566.

[4] Nordhäuser *Schulordnung*, 1583 in Vormbaum, 380. For another example see
Württemberg *Schulordnung*. 1559, in Vormbaum, 945,

[5] Philippe Ariès, *op. cit.*, 262. Ariès speaks always primarily of France, although he
implies the general application of his observations. See also p. 254.

sterner warning. Only if this too is fruitless resort to the rod, but use it sparingly, never touching the head and avoiding words and actions tending to degrade the child. If nothing helps, urge the parents to remove the child from school. "But don't be precipitate in offering this advise, for it may be that the last will be the first. Consider in all things the age and disposition of the child."[1] Minor misdeeds might be overlooked for the time being; but do not fail to inform the pupil at an opportune time that he will not be so lucky again, for he must never be allowed to think that even the slightest transgression escapes the master's notice.[2]

Letting him feel constant surveillance was one means of inculcating disciplined behavior in the young person. Surrounding him with a maze of do's and don't's was another. Each moment of the pupil's school day was precisely regulated. His private life, too, was hedged with constraints. Every school ordinance gave under the heading *Zucht* a formidable list of prescriptions and proscriptions obviously designed to minimize choice, limit freedom of self-expression, and weaken personal judgment, while at the same time cultivating habits of conformity, deference, and assent. Obedience and reverence were the appropriate attitude to received values and to the authorities representing them, to God first, of course, for "where a child feels fear of God, discipline will soon follow,"[3] and to the lesser powers in appropriate measure. "First and foremost pupils must be brought up to know God and show obedience and reverence to government, parents, and all their elders."[4] Obedience "is the state for which God has created all rational creatures." Out of a sense of dutiful obedience we perform good works.[5] For young people these works arise specifically from the fourth commandment :

> The good works of children, pupils and subjects *[Unterthanen]* are that in their hearts they must love, honor, and esteem their father, mother, schoolmaster, and government, obeying all external demands honestly made of them and thanking God for the benevolent reign under which they live.[6]

It would be obvious even if the phrase just quoted from a widely

---

1 Württemberg *Schulordnung*, 1559, in Vormbaum, 95.
2 Electoral Saxon *Kirchenordnung*, 1590, in Vormbaum, 275-6.
3 Württemberg *Schulordnung*, 1559, Vormbaum, 92.
4 *Markgräflich Badisch-Durlach'sche Schulordnung*, 1536, in Vormbaum, 30.
5 Sebastian Fröschel, *Catechismus* in Reu I, 2 (2), 76.
6 *Ibid.*, 77.

used Wittenberg catechism did not make it explicit, that early school-ing was seen by pedagogues as preparation for good citizenship. Today's schoolboys were tomorrow's subjects,[1] and the correct habits of deference and compliance must be developed at an early age when they would be likely to take root. "Honor thy father and thy mother" was the beginning of all dutiful submissiveness. Broadened to extend to all who in wielding authority could claim to stand *in loco parentis*, the fourth commandment put it into young minds that as adults their proper views of authority should be defined by the divine command to honor and the Christian duty to love :

> *Question :* Who are father and mother ? *Answer :* Our parents and our lords. *Question :* What do you mean by the word parents ? *Answer :* Our natural parents ... *Question :* Who are our lords ? *Answer :* Our spiritual and secular rulers, schoolmasters and teachers ... *Question :* What shall be our attitude toward these ? *Answer :* We shall honor them. *Question :* What do you mean by honor ? *Answer :* To serve them, obey them, love and cherish them, for they are appointed over us to stand in God's place. *Question :* What are God's promises to pious children ? *Answer :* God promises them that they will fare well and live long on earth.[2]

In similar language nearly all catechisms made it clear that "the fourth commandment applies not only to natural children and parents ... As children must honor their parents, so must parishioners honor their preachers, subjects their rulers, domestic servants their masters, and pupils their teachers."[3] Even the complex theological issue of the Mosaic law and its relevance to Christians was sometimes cast into pedagogical terms. Melanchthon described the law as a "disciplinarian [*Zuchtmeister*] toward Christ."[4] Melanchthon's separation of functions between ministers who preach Gospel and religion and schoolmasters who instruct in the law [5] was lost in the later teaching practice of most established school systems, where religious instruction became part of the curriculum and schoolmasters explained the creed as they

---

[1] The word *Unterthan* used in the excerpt from Fröschel's Wittenberg catechism came into prominence in the early sixteenth century. Cf. Grimm, *Wörterbuch*, vol. 11, 3.

[2] Hieronymus Opitz, *Examen laicum*, 1583, printed in Reu I, 2 (2), 526.

[3] Chilian Friederich, *Fragestücken : Von den Stücken des Catechismi* (Magdeburg, 1572) printed in Reu I, 2 (2), 467.

[4] Melanchthon to Johann Oeder of Memmingen, July 1524, in Otto Clemen (ed) *Melanchthons Briefwechsel* (Leipzig, 1926) I, 350. Also *Loci praecipui theologici*, 1559, in *Melanchthons Werke in Auswahl* I, 1, 239. The reference is to Paul, Gal. 3.24.

[5] Wilhelm Maurer, *op. cit.*, II, 450-1.

expounded Aesop.[1] Teachers examined pupils on the points of sermons immediately after they had heard them,[2] and daily exercises in the catechism were obligatory almost everywhere.[3] All children had to learn the catechism by heart. Normally the regulations stressed the virtue of rote memorization,[4] though an occasional writer deplores the practice, at least for older pupils.[5] Periodic official examinations in catechism articles were also common.[6]

In one way or another most catechisms affirmed the existing social order and taught the child to accept his place in it. For every "calling" the appropriate and inappropriate kinds of conduct were described and buttressed with citations from Scripture.[7] The order of society was represented as fixed, each individual enjoying a designated place in it :

> *Question* : Which are the estates and orders ordained by God ? *Answer* : In the spiritual realm of God they are bishops, pastors and preachers. ... In the secular realm, which is God's also, they are lords and subjects such as heads of families and landlords, family members and tenants, parents, children, servants, journeymen, laborers, old people and young people, widows and orphans, rich and poor. All these are estates appointed and ordered by God so that pious Christian and God-fearing men and women may live here on earth according to his word, will and command, knowing that God takes gracious pleasure in each person's calling so long as he conducts himself in the spirit of Christian faith.[8]

The teacher's responsibility for inculcating these ideas must have been clearly understood by most schoolmasters, as the nature of their office was made clear to them upon appointment to it. The Württemberg school ordinance, for instance, specifies that candidates for teaching positions were to be familiarized with the provisions of the ordinance, particularly with the definition of his calling as "a high, holy and God-advised office and, through implanting in the minds of children the

---

[1] E.g. *Unterricht des Visitatoren* ... in Sehling I, 172-3. See also for Strassburg Kohls, 75-6.

[2] E.g. Württemberg *Schulordnung*, 1559, Vormbaum, 92.

[3] *Ibid.*, 91. See also Bugenhagen's statement in *ibid.*, 36-7.

[4] For memorization rules : Württemberg *Schulordnung*, 1559, in Vormbaum, 164-5; Sebastian Fröschel, *Catechismus* in Reu I, 2 (2), 81-2; Bugenhagen quoted in Vormbaum, 36-7.

[5] E.g. Matthias Flacius, *Ein einfeltige christliche Unterweisung der gewachsenen Jugend* (1577) in Reu I, 2 (2), 114-5.

[6] Albertine Saxon *Kirchenordnung*, 1580, Sehling I, 423.

[7] E.g. Johann Spangenberg, *Des kleinen Catechismi* ... in Reu I, 2 (2), 296-7.

[8] Justus Menius, *Catechismus* written for Eisenach, 1532, printed in Reu I, 2 (2), 172.

creed and the fear of God, an instrument for the preservation of the pastorate and the secular authority.[1]

For the school boy, the assimilation of approved values and behavior depended upon more than habituation by reiteration, drill, and rigorous surveillance. Curricular and extra-curricular regulations may have shaped his mind and defined his conduct. If observed, regulations could accustom him to a useful, orderly life. But there was within him also the urge to resist the rules. This inclination—the deplorable human inclination to obstinacy and rebelliousness—had to be subdued if disciplined behavior was to become reliable and constant. The young person's natural tendency to relate all things to his own senses had therefore to be broken and his search for standards turned from the instinctive impulses within to the regulatory authorities without.

Effective means for accomplishing this purpose were available in the doctrines about sin and guilt contained in every catechism. These formidable attacks on egocentrism must have filled the young person if not with self-hatred, at least with self-doubt. They were certainly designed to undermine confidence in his own judgment. Out of his own moral resources, he was told, he could never observe the law. Nor could he when acting on his natural drives serve his own best interests :

> *Father* : Can we love God out of our own nature? *Son* : No we cannot. *Father* : Why is this so? *Son* : Because our entire nature is so thoroughly poisoned with self-love that we cannot bring ourselves to love God as we love ourselves. ... For this reason, also, we are not able to do as much good unto our neighbor as we want to lavish on ourselves.[2]

All natural instincts, desires, motives, arise from self-love and must be repressed. Even informed and disciplined purposes cause us to go wrong :

> *Question* : Tell me, dear child, and speak the truth, did you keep the holy ten commandments. *Answer* : Alas, no, for I own and confess that I have not kept them. Indeed I have violated them flagrantly and often, outwardly through wicked actions, inwardly with evil desires. *Question* : And having failed to keep the commandments, are you by God's anger condemned to eternal death and damnation?

---

[1] Württemberg *Schulordnung*, 1559, Vormbaum, 95. Catechisms also tried to instill attachment to denominational orthodoxy. See, for example, the outburst against sectarians in Caspar Aquila, *Des kleinen Catechismi Erklerung* (Wittenberg, 1538) in Reu I, 2 (2), 180.

[2] Ambrosius Moibanus, *Catechismus* (Wittenberg, 1535) in Reu I, 2 (2), 729.

Answer : Yes, I confess myself guilty, knowing that I am deserving only of God's wrath, which is eternal death and damnation.[1]

The larger catechisms abounded in cautionary (some readers may think sadistic) descriptions of punishments inescapably following upon inevitable transgressions :

Question : Show me out of Scripture what will happen to those guilty of ingratitude. *Answer* : Jeremiah says in the eleventh chapter, 'cursed be the man that obeyeth not the words of this covenant;' 'Even his prayer is an abomination to God' (Proverbs 28). God will scorn such a man in his deepest anguish, (Proverb 3) and not hear him, but he will punish him severely with many diseases (Leviticus 26), to wit : fever, swellings, pestilence, inflation, war, fire and hailstorms, sores and boils, and altogether so much terror, misery, suffering, curses, confusions, and frustrations (Deut. 28) that he must fall into despair.[2]

The author of this catalogue of horrors, Caspar Aquila, who was superintendent in Saalfeld in Saxony, evidently felt that the results of his teaching were beneficial in proportion to the number of threats and self-vilifications contained in it :

Question : What have you learned from the ten commandments ? *Answer* : I have learned the knowledge of our damnable sinful life. ... For the ten commandments are a book of vices to us in which we read clearly what we are before God without the Grace, namely idol worshippers, miscreants, blasphemers and despisers of God's divine name, cursed robbers of his holy temple, and renegades to his eternal word. Item, we are disobedient abusers of our fathers, we are child murderers and envious dogs, killers, whoremongers, adulterers, thieves and rogues, deceivers, dissemblers, liars, perjuring tale bearers, false witnesses, insolent misers. In sum, we are wild insatiable beasts against whose evil nature God erects the commandments as if they were high walls and locked gates.[3]

Stronger language than this even can be found in Osiander's Nuremberg *Catechism or Sermons for Children* of 1533, where the author lingers long and vividly on the terrifying miseries consequent upon the transgressions which must follow from our depraved nature.[4] Common sense will tell us, of course, that many of these phrases, unthinkingly memorized by rote as the rules demanded and (we hope) sparingly expounded by humane educators, passed in and out of children's ears

---

[1] *Ordnung der Kinderlehr für Buttelstadt*, 1588, in Reu I, 2 (2), 212.

[2] Caspar Aquila, *Des kleinen Catechismi Erklerung*, 1538, in Reu I, 2 (2), 178-9.

[3] *Ibid.*, 182.

[4] Andreas Osiander, *Catechismus oder Kinder-Predig* ... in Reu I, vol. 1 "Süddeutsche Katechismen," section 2 : "Texte," 462-4. See especially passages on 545-6, 500.

without leaving so heavy a burden of shame as they were intended to
do. It should also be emphasized that the long lists of threats were
followed in each catechism by firm and often very moving assurances
of God's bountiful love for his wretched and forlorn human cratures.
Descriptions of barely imaginable punishments were intended to open
hearts to ardent desire for God's grace.

Still, it is astonishing to realize how closely the procedures just
described correspond to practices found by psychologists in cultures
where socialization depends on, or is aided by, the stirring up of guilt
feelings in children. In the very young obedience is ensured by arousing
fear of punishment (in Freudian terms "objective anxiety"). Older
children, who have begun to reason and reflect, require a more subtle
kind of control. Fear of punishment continues to play a part, but
deviation from approved behavior now tends to be linked to feelings
of shame and remorse. Having been taught to blame himself whenever
he has strayed from the code, the child experiences guilt feelings
("moral anxiety" in Freudian terms) or anticipations of guilt feelings,
whenever the thought of such deviation crosses his mind.[1] Where
punishment and blame are tied to the child's need for love, the threat
of withholding love acts as a powerful dissuader from divergent
behavior.[2]

Sixteenth-century catechisms presented their teachings about God
and man as an analogy of the parent-child relationship and its complicated reciprocal bonds and ambiguous emotions : authority and
love, obedience, respect and defiance; anger and hatred, pity, forgiveness, remorse.[3] "Love-oriented techniques of punishment," as they
have been called because "they threaten the child's attainment of the
goal of ... love, yet keep him oriented toward that goal"[4] are surely
inherent, along with crude scare tactics and severe external discipline,
in the reformers' attempts to convince the young that self-serving,
"un-Christian" acts could lead only to grief. Distress over God's withdrawn love and the deep wish to regain it may well have operated as
an inner command to promote the adoption of evaluative behavior

---

[1] John W. M. Whiting and Irvin L. Child, *Child Training and Personality : A Cross-
Cultural Study* (New Haven, 1953), 226. See the entire chapter on "Origins of Guilt"
for highly suggestive comments.

[2] *Ibid.*, 240-1.

[3] For a clear statement of this see the excerpt from Georg Rhau's *Kinder Glaube*
(Wittenberg, 1539) in Reu I, 2 (2), 206, beginning "*Das Gott unser lieber Vater ist ...*"

[4] Whiting and Child, *op. cit.*, 261.

identified with the deity whose approval and affection were being longed for. The element of love is prominent in all the teaching catechisms to which reference has been made here. They do not dwell on it with the deliberation and linguistic abandon devoted to the various forms of punishment. Nor do they elaborate on its affective issue. But it is always invoked at emotionally powerful junctures in the religious message when the bereft, forlorn human victim of his own wrong instincts sees the restoration of divine love as the only remaining hope of comfort, peace and solace.[1]

We can only guess, of course, at how much of this message was actually taken in by those who heard it. Very little, most likely, at least of its theological substance. We also do not know whether Reformation educators had much success in making their pupils adopt the value and behavior pattern whose inculcation they saw as their chief pedagogical responsibility. If they did, it may well be that the extent to which the principles of conduct were internalized as moral imperatives depended not on any comprehension of their religious meaning, but instead on their function in helping to fulfill the young person's desire to win, possess, and enjoy approval and love. Reformation pedagogues must have been aware of this fact. They did not think it presented any conflict with their theological presuppositions. The human need to love was obviously basic. The use of this basic need in their pedagogy reveals a more differentiated understanding of the human psyche than we would imagine from the schoolmasterly routines and petty repressive authoritarianism they exhibited in their class-rooms.

---

[1] I realize that these statements are an oversimplification. Interesting conclusions can be drawn, I think, from the different kinds of emotional responses anticipated from references in sermons and catechisms to God and to Christ. More cogently presented arguments about this and related aspects of the sixteenth-century religious literature for children must await closer analysis.

FURTHER LINES OF INQUIRY FOR THE STUDY OF "REFORMATION AND PEDAGOGY"

LEWIS W. SPITZ

Stanford University

Essentially there are three kinds of papers delivered at scholarly conferences such as this. The first kind represents the summation of years of research, offering a near definitive statement based upon very extensive and even exhaustive research. The guesswork has been eliminated, the solutions appear in firm outline, and the statement has a certain perfection and air of finality. Most mortals can deliver such a paper only three or four times in a single career. The second kind offers on a more limited topic the scholar's observations based upon a reasonable but still limited amount of research, offering plausible suggestions and reasonably well founded conclusions. This is the often dull variety of paper most common at conventions, the excitement of discovery subdued and the freshness of untested hypotheses dimmed. The third kind is the type presented at the outset of a major research enterprise. The adventure of exploring *terra incognita* is there, the sense of anticipation, the willingness to be led by new sources, the readiness for surprises, the freedom to exploit new methodologies and the ancillary sciences. This paper is of the third variety, unique, daring, and intensely interesting. My own response will endeavor to be helpful in this bold venture by raising a few questions which should perhaps be dealt with in the course of the author's further study.

The prospect is very good for the emergence here of an important book, one which will do for the German cultural area in the Reformation era what Phillipe Ariès did in his *Centuries of Childhood. A Social History of Family Life* (New York, 1962) based largely on the French experience. The prospectus offered for going beyond the formal histories of education to the nature of the impact on the young, the general aims of education, the qualities of mind desired in the young, the political responsibility for education, the differences made between gifted and ordinary pupils, between rulers and subjects, all this is very promising indeed. I should like to address my remarks to four questions : 1. How does the Lutheran program compare with the pre-Reformation pedagogical aims, with contemporary Catholic, and contemporary Calvinist intentions in Germany and in other lands ? 2. What development is evident within the Lutheran tradition from the pre-Luther catechisms, to Luther, to Melanchthon, and the emergence of the territorial *Schulordnungen?* 3. How do the aims of education as assessed on the basis of the catechisms and *Schulordnungen* relate to the three major contributions of Protestant education, universal literacy, a humanistic curriculum, and the divine vocation of the teacher? 4. What can be said by way of clarification on a variety of miscellaneous observations made in the paper but for the sake of economy of space not fully developed?

1. A comparison of Lutheran catechetical materials with pre-Reformation, with Catholic and with Calvinist catechetical materials.

A. Pre-Reformation materials. Reformation catechetical materials were derived genetically from the pre-Reformation confessional materials such as the *Summa* of confessors discussed by Professor Tentler and the manuals for confessors. The word catechism itself is a derivative of κατηχέω and appeared as *catechisare* in Irenaeus, Tertullian and Augustine for the teaching of Christianity to neophytes or for preparing Christians for participation in the Sacraments. Augustine wrote *De catechizandis rudibus*. In his *De fide et operibus* Augustine used the word in the sense in which Luther employed it for his small catechism of 1529 and Luther may indeed have encountered it there. Luther used the word catechism and many of his opponents and rivals subsequently adopted the word. The medieval antecedent, the books of preparation for confession, were in part by the elite for the elite, "how to" books for professionals as Professor Tentler described them. The manuals range from fairly technical to very popular kinds of handbooks. Johann Nider, *Die vier und zwanzig güldnen Harfen* is nothing else than the *Collationes* of John Cassian. *Dat licht der sele* was a translation of the *lumen animi* and *die Hymelstrasse* was a translation of the *Scala coeli*. In Book VI, chapter 15 of his *Epitome theologicae veritatis* Albertus Magnus wrote of the "Cathecismus et exorcismus tamquam preparatorii praemittuntur in baptismo." Most of the confessional books of the 14th century, as Professor Oberlin of Strassburg has shown, operated not with the Ten Commandments but with the Seven Deadly Sins. But at the very end of the 14th and all through the 15th century the Ten Commandments became so prominent as to virtually exclude all other parts of the confessional catechism (in contrast, Luther's catechism found a balance of the six chief parts). An example would be Heinrich Herp, *Speculum aureum decem praeceptorum* (Basel, 1496). But the seven deadly sins were included and the distinctions between the *venalia* and *mortalia* drawn. It is interesting to recall that Luther early on preached a sermon on the Ten Commandments followed by one on the Seven Deadly Sins, but in the introduction he wrote : "People make great distinctions between the sins and I do not know whether it is useful for the confession or not, for the confessing children tax their memory thereby and it is a burden for the confessor." He then spoke of various distinctions and says : "But one still does not establish thereby whether one loses time with this and bothers the father confessor. One is more concerned about maintaining a distinction than with achieving true repentance for the sins." Neither in his prayerbook nor his catechism did Luther allow any space for the Seven Deadly Sins.

The older catechisms had many parts—Seven Deadly Sins, Seven Cardinal Virtues, Ave Maria (which Luther kept in his Prayerbook and which was still included in the Wand Catechism of Zurich in 1525), Nine Alien Sins, Five Crying Sins, the Silent or Secret Sins, Six Works of Mercy, Seven Gifts of the Holy Spirit, Twelve Fruits of the Holy Spirit, the Sins against the Holy Ghost, Eight Blessings, Five External and Five Internal Sins were included in the suggested confessional questions. Some examples of this kind of manual would be that of Ludolf von Göttingen, or Johann Herolt, a much read author, whose *De eruditione Christi fidelium* had nine parts : 1. The Ten Commandments, 2. Alien Sins, 3. Major Sins, 4. Works of Mercy, 5. Lord's Prayer, 6. Ave Maria, 7. Creed, 8. Sacraments (seven, of course), 9. Gifts of the Holy Spirit.

In the 15th century the confessor stood before a tribunal over all estates and classes and over all ages. He was not a teaching, admonishing Christian brother, but a judge who pronounced God's judgment in His stead and applied temporal *poena* or penances, though his competence was limited and the instances differed. He often instilled a fear-motivated piety during this period. The confessional began with children of seven. Bartholomeus di Chaym of Milan wrote : *Quod puer et puella passunt peccare mortaliter a septennio et supra, cum tunc sunt doli capaces ... Sic ergo interrogari potest de infra scriptis : si confessus est integre singulis annis, sicut tenetur quilibet a septennio.* Johannes von Freyburg says that as soon as a person has reached the age of reason, and knows what good and bad are, he should confess once a year. Guido de Monte Rocherii in his *Manipulus Curatorum* says that all must confess *"qui possunt discernere inter bonum et malum."* Respect for authority must be inculcated and these books gave examples of how to get children to confess only real sins, how to shock the sleepy or slothful. Chaplain Johann Wolff of Frankfurt's *Beichtbüchlein* of 1478 suggested as examples true and improbable sins to be confessed by the children coming to their first confession : "I threw rocks at the people's chickens, ducks, and geese;" "I killed the emperor with an axe;" "I found a Heller and did not return it;" "I stole ten dozen gulden from the council in Frankfurt." In all the confessional books of the 15th century the confessors were to ask the Ten Commandments as well as the Creed and Lord's Prayer. In the 15th century, then, the children were taught in the confessional what in the 16th century they were taught in the catechisms.

There were many writings on the Ten Commandments for the *periti*, the wise and learned confessors. Nicholas de Lyra, remembered for his *Postillae* and by the rhyme *"Si Lyra non lirasset, Lutherus non saltasset,"* wrote a very influential *Praeceptorium seu expositio in decalogum.* Others who wrote such works include Jean Gerson (*De parvulis ad Christum trahendis* and *Donatus moralisatus*), a jurist Antonius de Butrio of Bologna, Johann Nider, Gottschalk Hollen (an Augustinian), Heinrich Herp (a Belgian cleric), Michael of Milan (a Dominican), Nicolaus Dünckelspühel of Vienna. But there was a massive literature beneath these authors designed for unlearned father confessors and intended for immediate practical village and town application. Archbishop Antoninus of Florence's book of confession was very influential throughout the 15th century. It was used as a source by such works as *Der Spiegel des Sünders* in the North, which often translated whole pages of it. It appeared up to 1500 in more than 72 editions, according to Hain-Copinger. Panzer's *Annales* lists a whole array of editions after 1500 in Latin and German with variant titles such as *Tractatus de instructione seu directione simplicium confessorum;* or *Summula confessionis de audientia confessionum;* or *Confessionale, Interrogatorio, Specchio di conscienza,* and *Medicina del anima.* Engelhard Kunhofer wrote a *Confessionale continens tractatum decem praeceptorum et septem viciorum capitalium* (Nuremberg, 1502). The *Speculum christianorum* deals with the second table of the law and appeared in many editions, according to Hain-Copinger. Jodocus of Windsheim wrote the *Summa Rudium.* Many such works seem to have been written in the vernacular, and one is reminded of Wycliffe's *The Lantern of Light.*

In addition to the regular *Beichtbücher* there were other ascetic and catechetical readers. A Franciscan, Marcus of Lindau, wrote *Das*

Buch der zehn Gebote, which was published in Venice in 1483, and in Strassburg in 1516 and 1520. Johann Bämler published in Augsburg in 1472 a book of morals drawing together the ethical teachings of Cato and Solomon, presenting an interpretation of the Ten Commandments and ending with :

> Nun helf uns der barmherzig Got,
> Dasz wir also halten seine Gebot,
> Dasz uns dardurch werd geben,
> Hie in Zeit Gnad und dort ewigs Leben.
>   Amen.

Another major popular work was the *Sele Trost* which was an *Example-Book* on the Ten Commandments. This beloved people's book tells the "dear child" that some people read Tristan and Isolde and some read about Theodoric the Ostrogoth, but he should read the Scriptures. There were also many illustrated books, many showing the devil fondling breasts and doing other forbidden deeds. Hans Baldung Grün did woodcuts of the Ten Commandments in 1516 and in the same year Lucas Cranach the Elder did his painting of the Ten Commandments for the *Rathaus* in Wittenberg. He also provided woodcuts for Luther's 1520 sermon on the Ten Commandments. Hymns for children and laymen were often didactic, and Luther himself wrote such hymns as "Disz sind die heilgen zehn gebot" and "Wilt du leben seliglich," both in 1524. Mathesius tells us that Luther designed his catechism for children and it gave him great joy to hear them on the street corners reciting the questions and answers to each other. It should be noted that catechisms were also used in instructing adults and were recommended for reflection in preparation for confession and participation in the Lord's Supper.

It is quite obvious that the Lutheran catechetical materials must be carefully compared with these pre-Reformation materials before a judgment can be ventured regarding the inculcation of sin and guilt, fear-motivated piety, moralism, subservience to authority, and other related questions. They, too, took a dim view of unbelievers, heretics, and doubters.

B. Contemporary Catholic materials. The Catholic catechisms and instructional materials in Luther's day in part imitated Luther's catechism, but in part drew upon pre-Luther confessional literature. The *Catechismus Romanus,* for instance, had the same chief parts as Luther's catechism although they were arranged in a different order, which may be of some significance (Creed, seven sacraments, ten commandments, and the Lord's Prayer). Again, Georg Witzel who turned evangelical and returned to Catholicism (Luther thought that for the right amount of florins he could turn him Lutheran again), wrote catechisms obviously influenced both by Luther and earlier Catholic sources. His *Catechismus. Bekehrung der Kinder der Kirche, ebenso gesund als kurz;* his *Neuer und kurtzer Catechismus;* and his *Grosser Catechismus* (Mainz, 1545), drew on Luther, but in the preface to the large catechism he explains that he found useful questions provided by various catechisms published in Venice sixty years before, evidently a reference to the Franciscan Marcus of Lindau's book on the Ten Commandments (1483) or to Eckart Ratdolt's confessional of the same year. D. Johann Dietenberger published a catechism in Mainz (1537) which he divided into four parts, the creed, God's commandments, prayer, and sacraments, the *Catechismus Evangelischer bericht und Christliche unterweisung der fürnehmlichsten stück des waren heyligen Christlichen glaubens, allen Christglaubigen, besonder den eynfeltigen Layen sehr gut nütz und zu wissen von nöten, auffs aller kürtzest in schrifft verfaszt durch D. Johann Dietenberger. Zu Meyntz bei Ivo Schäffer anno MDXXVII.* Bishop Johansen of Meissen's catechism was made up of questions and answers on the creed and the ten commandments, *Christliche Lere zu gründtlichen Unterricht des rechten Glaubens und Gotseligen wandels, Durch den Hochwirdigen in Got Fürsten und Herrn, Herrn Johansen, Bischofen zu Meyssen.* The celebrated Johan Gropper provided a handbook of the chief articles for schoolchildren in this order : 1. Creed, 2. Ten Commandments, 3. Seven Sacraments, 4. Three Divine Virtues, 5. the Seven Gifts of the Holy Spirit, 6. Beatitudes, 7. the Seven Deadly Sins in conflict with the Seven Cardinal Virtues, citing Irenius and the fathers, and concluding with the sum of the Old and New Testaments, *Hauptartikell Christlicher underrichtung zur Gottseligkeit. Johan Gropper, keiserlicher Rechten Doctor.* Johann Fabri, Contarini, Jodochus Lorichius, Georg Matthaeius, and, of course, Peter Canisius *(Kleiner Catechismus)* did highly influential Catholic catechisms.

Since the question of social and even political control perhaps by the device of inducing feelings of guilt and fear of punishment in the young subjects has been raised, it might serve a useful comparative purpose to sample a catechism by one of Luther's Catholic contemporaries on this very point, that of Brother Dederich of Münster, an Observantine, *Bruder Dederich von Münster von dem Observanten Orden.*

Ein fruchtbar Spiegel oder Handbüchlein der Christenmenschen gemacht oder zusammengetragen von Bruder Dederich von Münster, made up of the Creed and the Ten Commandments. The following somber passage is in an early section on the curses of God against those who do not keep his commandments :

God says in the fifth book of the Bible that if you will not listen to the voice of God your Lord and do not keep his commandments, all these curses shall befall you. You shall be accursed in the city, in the field, in your barns, cursed is the fruit of your body, your field, and all your possessions, cursed will be all your going in and your coming out; the Lord will send you pestilence, hunger, and affliction in all your works, until he has utterly destroyed and damned you. Likewise you shall build a house and then die and another will dwell therein; you shall take a wife and another will sleep with her; you shall plant a vineyard and shall not drink of its wine. Likewise many other more powerful plagues are written of these, which I shall not mention for the sake of brevity. Now note, all men, that all these plagues are temporal plagues, which the Jews feared most of all, but they did not know with such preciseness as we do about hell. O we Christians, how much more must we fear eternal punishment, as Jesus says : You are my friends, therefore keep my commandments. Therefore all those are God's enemies who do not keep his commandments. O how severely God will speak in his anger to them in the hour of death. Depart from me you accursed ones into eternal fire. Depart from me, for I am the life, but you shall die eternally. Depart from me, I am the divinity, and you shall be with the evil foes in great misery. Depart from me, you accursed one, you shall be filled with all which is evil and painful, you shall be robbed of all good. Depart from me, you accursed ones, into eternal fire, where darkness is, which one can experience, in which there is eternal sobbing, weeping, crying out, burning, blaspheming, cursing, gnashing of teeth, hunger, thirst, dying instead of death, eternal melancholy instead of comfort. O the miserable separation of the soul from God, who cannot enter into heaven, can never see Jesus, can never speak to Mary, the mother of Christ, and must burn eternally in everlasting fire with the evil foes. Oh woe unto us; if we do not keep God's commandments, for it would have been better for us if we had never been born than to have to remain lost forever. O almighty God, grant that we with all men be converted and may in this time do penance and improve for all of our failings, until we die and depart hence, and now and hereafter and for all times may we keep your holy commandments. Amen.

The impression that the pre-Lutheran and much contemporary Catholic confessional and catechetical instructional materials make is that of a Christianity which as J. Toussaert puts it, was 80 percent morals, 15 percent dogma, and 5 percent sacraments [J. Toussaert, *Le Sentiment religieux*, III, p. 67, cited in Jean Delumeau, *Naissance et affirmation de la Réforme* (Paris, 1968), p. 356].

C. Contemporary non-Lutheran Protestant materials. Since this study clearly calls for a comparative approach, an examination of the Calvinist literature is also indicated, in the Germanies as well as outside. In addition to Calvin's own catechism and the Heidelberg catechism of 1563, other materials were prepared especially in the Palatinate and under the direction of the French Huguenot Toussain, influential throughout the Reformed states in the Empire. Since the church/state relation struggle was particularly acute at the time of Frederick III the Pious, and since Erastian views also affected England, the use of education for preparing obedient subjects should be examined with care. The catechism of Alexander Nowell (1570), a Marian exile in Strassburg, and later dean of St. Paul, for example, asks the question :

> M. What shall we then say of them that be disobedient to parents or magistrates, or do misuse them, yea, or kill them ?
>
> S. Commonly all such do either continue a most vile and miserable life, or lose it most shamefully, being taken out of it with untimely and cruel death, or infamous execution. And not only in this life, but also in the world to come, they shall for ever suffer the everlasting punishment of their ungodliness. For if we be forbidden by the commandment of God, as here next followeth, to hurt any men, be they never so much estranged from us, yea, even our adversaries and deadly enemies, much more to kill them, surely it is easy to perceive how much we ought to forbear and beware of all doing of any injury to our parents, of whom we receive our life, inheritance, liberty and country ...
>
> M. But it is much more heinous for a man to offend or kill the parent of his country than his own parent.
>
> S. Yea surely. For if it be for every private man a heinous offence to offend his private parents, and parricide to kill them; what shall we say of them that have conspired and borne wicked armour against the commonweal, against their country, the most ancient, sacred, and common mother of us all, which might be dearer unto us than ourselves, and for whom no honest man will stick to die to do it good, and against the prince, the father of the country itself, a parent of the Commonweal; yea, and to imagine the overthrow, death, and destruction of them whom it is high treason once to forsake or shrink from? So outrageous a thing can in no wise be expressed with fit name.

A handy volume containing the English and Scottish catechisms of William George, Ezekiel Rogers, Samuel Rutherford and others is Alexander F. Mitchell, *Catechisms of the Second Reformation* (London, 1886), a copy of which is in the Newberry Library.

A comparative study of Lutheran, Catholic and Calvinist, and smaller sectarian education could profitably range well beyond a catalog of similarities and differences to raise such theological questions as to what extent the kingdom of God is conceived in terms of the Old

Testament paradigm and such cultural questions as to whether they
collectively represented a Hebraic conception of man as opposed to a
classical conception which experienced a momentary revivification
during the Renaissance.

2. Developments within Lutheranism. Luther has often been adulated
as the Pestalozzi, not to say the Comenius or Montesori, of the 16th
century. Mathesius boasted that his catechism was in as widespread
use as Donatus. But there was a considerable number of evangelical
catechisms in use before Luther's appeared in 1529, and many other
Lutheran catechisms were written and used afterwards which were
quite independent from his. Gustav Kawerau edited the two oldest catechisms of the Lutheran reformation by P. Schultz and Chr. Hegendorf.
Ferdinand Cohrs has edited in five volumes *Die evangelischen Katechismusversuche vor Luthers Enchiridion*. Some of the free imperial
cities evolved their own educational materials and a comparison with
that produced under the aegis of the consistories of the territorial
princely states is essential. One might suggest the examination of the
evangelical catechisms of Ravensburg (1546/1773) and Reichenweier
(1547, 1559). edited recently by Ernst-Wilhelm Kohls, or of *The Catechism of the Free City of Gengenbach of 1545* in Baden, especially since
no copy of this source was included in J. M Reu's *Quellen zur Geschichte
des Katechismus des Katechismusunterrichts*. The authors, Kyber,
Lindner, and Montanus, say that they would like to have simply used
Luther's, but since Luther had said that the people will be less confused
if localities stay with catechisms of long usage, they would stay with
their local evangelical version. Their catechism shows, incidentally,
traces of such pre-Lutheran evangelical catechisms as Gerhart of
Kitzingen's *Schöne Frag und Antwort*, 1525, Johann Bader's *Gespräch-
büchlein*, Andreas Althamer's *Katechismus*, 1528, Johannes Brenz's
Fragstück, 1529, Wolfgang Capito's and Konrad Sams' *Christliche
Unterweisung*, 1529. A few questions immediately suggest themselves.
Did Luther put the Ten Commandments first and then the Creed to
emphasize the dialectical relationship of law and gospel ? Did he thereby follow earlier evangelical catechisms ? Did later ones imitate him ?
What was Melanchthon's specific influence in concrete cases ? Were the
Schulordnungen somber and repressive by design and were they markedly different from earlier or from free city catechisms ? Some of the
catechisms seem to be much more gospel oriented and wholesome than
the *Schulordnungen* cited in the paper seem to be. Hegendorff, for

example, far from calling divine curses on mankind describes as evils warfare, sickness, storms, pestilence, the death of the body and asks the Lord to deliver his children from such scourges. Progression, or devolution, must be explored even while comparisons are made.

3. Aims of education. It has been repeatedly asserted that the three outstanding features of Protestant education were 1. the drive to universal literacy, 2. the promotion of the *humaniora* on various levels of education and 3. the emphasis upon teaching as a divine vocation. How and to what extent were these overall aims realized on the elementary level? Was universal literacy, achieved for the first time in history in Scotland and in two German states, compatible with the aims of princely rule? What of the recent assertions of Klaus Dockhorn at Aachen that rhetoric was a controlling influence in Luther's theology, and, if true, was this reflected in the fact that a rhetorical in preference to a dialectical or logical approach to learning metamorphized elementary instruction? Ariès refers to the place of rhetoric in elementary schools. Was the teacher merely a *Zuchtmeister* or was he also a minister or servant? Incidentally, Melanchthon had the phrase "the law is a schoolmaster to lead us to Christ" on authority higher than his own. The term *Zucht*, or discipline, seems to be far less frequent in the Lutheran catechetical literature than such terms as *Bericht, Kinderbericht, Unterweisung*, and *Unterricht*, which mean teaching or instruction rather than discipline. Does a historian who reads the Lutheran catechisms have a different mental cast in responding to their teachings if he was first taught Luther's *Small Catechism* by cheerful American schoolteachers than by post-Prussian schoolmasters? Although the 16th century Lutheran schools were clearly not predecessors of modern progressive education, they were clearly also not by design instruments of political repressive manipulation. Is to suggest that they were insufficiently disciplined subjectivity or creative insight?

One check as to whether the stress upon divine law and the sin/grace dialectical emphasis ever subconsciously, by design, or inadvertently employed for the conditioning of obedient subjects would be an examination of the religious instruction given to the young princes. A single instance must suffice here, the case of Württemberg. There the preceptor Sebastian Coccius (1508-1562) was influenced by humanist educators such as Erasmus, Melanchthon, Vives, and Johannes Sturm. His methodology developed in the context of evangelical educational pedagogy and played a part in the Brenzian reform. He was instrumental in developing the Schwäbisch-Hall *Schulordnung* of 1543 and influenced the *Grosse Schulordnung* of 1559. The territory, then, developed a Lutheran educational system. What is fascinating to note is that Prince Christoph of Württemberg received the same catechetical instruction as the children who were one day to become his loving subjects, which may suggest that the basic intent of religious instruction was to develop a sound relationship to God above all. A comparison with the education of Eberhard im Bart in the century preceding would be of value.

There is a great danger in assuming that the educational system was designed to retain permanently the three estate system and freeze the young in their father's professions in a Diocletian fashion. Luther's teachings on vacation are so widely misunderstood that an emphatic word on that point may be called for. A vocation according to Luther is a vocation to a life of service, not to a specified occupation. Reason and above all consideration for the needs of society and one's fellow men must determine one's specific occupational vocation and a change should not be made lightly. Not only did the universities continue to serve as instruments of social mobility, but the practice of encouraging the able elite to continue on from the lower levels served that purpose. The reformer himself encouraged the youth to seek out vocations of service suitable to their abilities, as the many letters to students in his *Briefwechsel* demonstrate.

Like the sense of vocation the question of conscience requires careful handling, for there was a subtle shift in reformed theology from the scholastic conception of conscience. From the paper before us one could gain the impression that the pedagogical aim of the elementary instruction was simply the development of a negative conscience, which would be a critical departure from the intention of the magisterial reformers.

4. Random comments. Even for a study centering upon German Lutheranism an analysis of Scandinavian Lutheran educational aims would provide a valuable control group. The question of subtle shifts in mental cast from the reformer to the epigoni requires sensitive treatment. Luther, for example, rebuked a Puritanical Silesian schoolmaster for not using the comedies of Terence on moral grounds. One should look, too, to see whether Luther's edition of Aesop's fables was used in the schools and how it was applied. There are many directions

in which this study could go. The reformers lived in a period of heavy eschatological mood, not unlike our own. We, like they, must carry on. You will recall that when Luther was asked what he would do if he knew with absolute certainty that the world would come to an end the next day, he replied, "I would plant an apple tree today." With the schoolchildren in his train he planted in a kind of Arbor Day ceremony an oak tree at the end of the main street in Wittenberg which still stands today.

In *The Civilization of the Renaissance in Italy,* Jacob Burckhardt wrote even of his own great *Versuch :*

> In the wide ocean upon which we venture, the possible ways and directions are many; and the same studies which have served for this work might easily, in other hands, not only receive a wholly different treatment and application, but lead also to essentially different conclusions.

The special advantage of standing on the threshold of a major research project such as "Reformation and Pedagogy" is that the subject is still susceptible to many different kinds of treatment in the author's own hands.

BIBLIOGRAPHY

Ariès, Philippe, *Centuries of Childhood. A Social History of Family Life* (New York, 1962).

Austin, Robert, *The parliaments, rules and directions concerning sacramental knowledge : Contained in an ordinance of the Lords and Commons of the 20th of October 1645. Drawn into questions and answers ... with an addition of Scriptureproofs : and some brief directions for self-examination ...* (London, 1647).

Bellinger, Gerhard, *Der Catechismus Romanus und die Reformation; die katechetische Antwort des Trienter Konzils auf die Haupt-Katechismen der Reformatoren* (Paderborn, 1970).

Bohemian Brethren, *Die deutschen Katechismen der Böhmischen Brüder. Kritische Textsausgabe mit kirchen- und dogmengeschichtlichen Unterweisungen und einer Abhandlung über das Schulwesen der Böhmischen Brüder, nebst 5 Beilagen und einem namen- und Sachregister von Joseph Müller* (Berlin, 1887).

Caemerer, Richard R., *The Education of Representative German Princes in the Sixteenth Century,* unpublished diss., Washinggton University, St. Louis, Mos., 1944.

Canisius, Peter, *S. Petri Canisii doctoris ecclesiae Catechismi Latini et Germanici. Editionem criticam curavit Fridericus Streicher, S. J.,* 2 vols. (Rome, 1933, 1936).

Catechismus Romanus, The Catechism for the curats, compos'd by the decree of the Council of Trent, and publish'd by Command of Pope Pius the Fifth (London, 1687).

Cohrs, Ferdinand, ed., *Die evangelischen Katechismusversuche vor Luthers Enchiridion,* 5 vols. (Berlin, 1900-1907), in the *Monumenta Germaniae paedagogica.*

Dockhorn, Klaus, "Rhetorik und germanistische Literaturwissenschaft in Deutschland," *Jahrbuch für Internationale Germanistik,* III, no. 1, 168-185.

Dod, John, *A plaine and familiar exposition of the Ten Commandments. With a methodicall short catechisme, containing brieflie all the principall grounds of Christian religion* (London, 1615).

Eames, Wilberforce, *Early New England catechisms; a bibliographical account of some catechisms published before the year 1800 for use in New England* (Worcester, Mass., 1898; reissued in Detroit, 1969).

Geffcken, Johannes, *Der Bildercatechismus des fünfzehnten Jahrhunderts und die catechetischen Hauptstücke in dieser Zeit bis auf Luther* (Leipzig, 1855).

Gouge, William, *A short catechisme, wherein are briefly handled the fundamental principles of Christian religion needfull to be knowne by all Christians before they be admitted to the Lord's table* ... 7th edition (London, 1635).

Kawerau, G., *Zwei älteste Katechismen der lutherischen Reformation (von P. Schultz und Chr. Hegendorf)* (Halle a. S., 1890).

Kuepper, Joseph, *Das Schul- und Unterichtswesen im Elsass von den Anfängen bis gegen das Jahr 1530* (Strassburg, 1905).

Kohls, Ernst Wilhelm, *Evangelische Katechismen der Reformationszeit von und neben Luthers Kleinem Katechismus* (Gütersloh, 1971).

—— *Die evangelische Katechismen vor Ravensburg 1546/1733 und Reichenweier 1547-1559; ein Beitrag zur oberdeutschen Katechismusgeschichte des 16. Jahrhunderts* (Stuttgart, 1963).

Mitchell, Alexander Ferrier, *Catechisms of the Second Reformation ... historical introduction and bibliographical notices* (London, 1886).

Moufang, Franz Christoph Ignaz, ed., *Katholische Katechismen des 16. Jahrhunderts in deutscher Sprache* (Mainz, 1881).

New England Primer : Containing the Assembly's Catechism; the account of the burning of John Rogers; a dialogue between Christ, a youth, and the devil; and various other ... matter ... with a historical introduction, by Rev. H. Humphrey ... (Worcester; New York, 1900, reprint).

Norwell, A., *A Catechism, written in Latin; together with the same catechism tr. into English by T. Norton; appended is a sermon preached by Dean Norwell, Jan 11, 1563*; edited for the Parker Society by G. E. Corrie (Cambridge, 1853).

Ochino, Bernardino, *Il catechismo, o vero Institutione christiana ... in forma di dialogo ...* (Basel, 1561).

Painter, F. V. N., *Luther on Education* (St. Louis, Mo., 1965, PB).

Schultz, Robert C., "The Theological Significance of the Order of the Chief Parts in Luther's Catechism," *Teaching and Faith*, Carl Volz, ed., Twenty-Fourth Yearbook of the Lutheran Education Association (River Forest, Ill., 1967), pp. 45-56.

Sohm, Walter, *Die Schule Johann Sturms und die Kirche Strassburgs in ihren gegenseitigen Verhältnis 1530-1581* (Münich and Berlin, 1912).

Thorseby, John, *The lay folks' catechism, or the English and Latin versions of Archbishop Thoresby's instruction for the people; together with a Wycliffite adaption of the same and the corresponding canons of the Council of Lambeth* (London, 1901).

Ursinus, Zacharias (1534-1583), *The summe of Christian religion : delivered by Zacharias Ursinus in his lectures upon the catechism authorised by the noble Prince Frederick, throughout his dominions ...* tr. by Henrie Parrie, out of the Latin editions (Oxford, 1587).

Vormbaum, Reinhold, ed., *Die evangelischen Schulordnungen des sechzehnten Jahrhunderts. Evangelische Schulordnungen*, I (Gütersloh, 1860).

Watts, Isaac, *The young childs' first and second catechism of the principles of religion; to which is added a preservative from the sins and follies of childhood and youth. Also examples of prayers and graces, etc.* (Edinburgh, 1804).

5. SOME TASKS AND THEMES IN THE STUDY
OF POPULAR RELIGION

NATALIE ZEMON DAVIS

University of California (Berkeley)

I.

Historians of popular religion in Europe have often proceeded as if their most important task were to separate the grain from the chaff. Not to winnow souls, but beliefs and rites : they distinguish between beliefs and practises that are "truly" religious and those which are "superstitious" and/or "magical." In the late sixteenth century, for instance, Brother Noel Taillepied, having published a description of the holy places, processions and confraternities of Rouen, went on to write a *Treatise on Ghosts*. There he distinguished between false appari-tions, caused by melancholy or trickery, and true ghosts of the dead, who, despite the wicked lies of the Calvinists, did appear to living persons, as could be verified by Scripture, the Fathers and historical example.[1]

We are still sorting our data about popular religion into Brother Taillepied's categories. Let us consider as an example the important and fruitful inquiry on "French religious practise," opened some forty years ago by the French sociologist Gabriel Le Bras. By religious practise, M. Le Bras did not mean all the actions of peasants and city folk in cajoling, coercing or otherwise dealing with the sacred; he meant specifically Catholic religious practise, as defined over time by canon law and the elite of the Church. Thus, one might note the spread of crosses throughout the medieval countryside, and then comment that they were symbols of orthodoxy, of the victory of Christ over the land, but also objects of "superstition," "of a primitive cult... in which the religion of the Spirit has little part." [2]

Establishing the boundary between superstition and the religion of sacrament and spirit has continued to be the important concern

---

[1] Noel Taillepied, *Psichologie ou traité de l'apparition des Esprits* (Paris, 1588).

[2] Gabriel Le Bras, *Études de sociologie religieuse* (2 vols.; Bibliothèque de sociologie contemporaine; Paris, 1955-56), I, xi-xii, 1-24, 96-99, 197-98.

of the French school of religious history. For instance, Jacques Toussaert's study of *Le sentiment religieux en Flandre à la fin du moyen âge* concludes that late medieval Flanders was a Christian country in an official and formal sense only. Its laity were largely indifferent to communion and confession; naive, excited and sensationalistic in matters of faith; and timing sporadic religious activity to occasions defined by family, natural catastrophe and folk tradition rather than by parish solidarity and spiritual needs. Jean Delumeau finds the situation in late seventeenth-century France somewhat changed, but little improved by the work of the Counter-Reformation. The rural clergy was now educated enough to teach the catechism; the people did their Easter duty; the parish mass was the center of religious life. Yet the conformity to Christian practise and communion was outward only. The peasants were in fact polytheistic and deeply magical, making use of pagan rites and deflecting Christian sacraments to this-wordly ends. And who can blame them, asks M. Delumeau, when they lived in a technologically backward society, which left them at the mercy of famine and disease; when they were still for the most part illiterate; and when the clergy which was to enlighten them stooped too often to techniques of terror and dazzling ceremony ? [1]

These and similar studies have enriched enormously our understanding of the late medieval and early modern periods, but they have paid a price for evaluating lay piety primarily in terms of its deviation from one historical norm or religious ideal.[2] Can we learn as

---

[1] Jacques Toussaert, *Le sentiment religieux en Flandre à la fin du moyen âge* (Paris, 1963). Jean Delumeau, *Le catholicisme entre Luther et Voltaire* (Nouvelle Clio, L'histoire et ses problèmes, 30 bis; Paris, 1971); "Ignorance religieuse et mentalité magique sous l'ancien régime," paper presented to the annual meeting of the Society for French Historical Studies, Ottawa, March, 1972; "L'ancien régime : foi ou magie ?", *Le Monde*, July 7, 1972, 14.

[2] Among these studies are the fine articles of Le Bras himself, listed and in some cases reprinted in the *Études*; É. Delaruelle, É.-R. Labande, and Paul Ourliac, *L'Église au temps du grand schisme et de la crise conciliaire (1378-1449)* (Histoire de l'Église depuis les origines jusqu'à nos jours, Vol. 14; Paris, 1964), part 5; Francis Rapp, *L'Église et la vie religieuse en occident à la fin du moyen âge* (Nouvelle Clio, L'histoire et ses problèmes, 25; Paris, 1971); Thérèse-Jean Schmitt, *L'organisation ecclésiastique et la pratique religieuse dans l'archidiaconé d'Autun de 1650 à 1750* (Autun, 1957); Jeanne Ferté, *La vie religieuse dans les campagnes parisiennes (1622-1695)* (Bibliothèque de la société d'histoire ecclésiastique; Paris. 1962); Louis Pérouas, *Le diocèse de La Rochelle de 1648 à 1724, Sociologie et pastorale* (Bibliothèque générale de l'école pratique des hautes études, VIe section; Paris, 1964).

much as we would like about the *meaning, modes* and *uses* of popular religion to peasants and city dwellers, if we judge it by the standards of Chancellor Jean Gerson, Cardinal Carlo Borromeo, or even the generous Erasmus? Can we understand the complex relations of believers to their saints or the significance of two centuries of rites of flagellation, if we think of them only as "aberrations", as expressions of mass ignorance, weakness and neurosis? If we stamp as superstition peasant ceremonial dancing or the fires and leaping on the feast of Saint John the Baptist, will we be able to see how they were intended to protect the biological and agricultural life of the village? how they perpetuated in sacred celebration moods of festivity and joyful ecstasy sorely lacking in the religious life of official post-Tridentine Catholicism?

A second limitation of this approach is the particular cast it gives to the relations between clergy and laity. It tends to assume that authentic religious doctrine and pure religious sensibility are first and foremost in the hands of a spiritual elite among the clergy. From them it passes outward to other clerics and downward to the laity. Though individual reformers may arise from among the people, the laity, especially the peasants, are perceived as passive receptacles. Under favorable circumstances they are able to absorb a religious message; but emotional and close to the primitive, they are prone to distort it in "magical" and mechanical directions.

However appropriate this view may be in explaining popular misinterpretations of, say, Catholic doctrine on the efficacy of the mass or Calvinist doctrine on providence, it obscures certain features of religious life. After all, laymen and lay women were sometimes active, indeed innovative, in sacred matters, whether it was in establishing new shrines, elaborating religious drama, striking out in religious violence, ordering and illustrating religious material in new ways in printed books, setting up new arrangements for charitable giving, or thinking up "heretical" ideas.

Furthermore, certain suppositions about the possibilities for attracting supernatural aid for concrete, this-worldly ends were shared by learned priest, Protestant divine and peasant alike. They all thought witches could tap such power for physical or sexual harm. Puritan clergymen agreed with village wise women about the practical uses of divination by Bible or Psalter (when to take a journey? how to find a thief?). On into the eighteenth century, French bishops were authorizing the use of rites of exorcism and excommunication to get rid of caterpillars and harmful animals.[1] Does not then the relation between learned clergy and semi-literate laity seem not only a struggle of religion against "magic" but also a struggle between central and village authorities for power over the countryside ? As Keith Thomas has said in regard to the Catholic Church :

> Although theologians drew a firm line between religion and superstition, their concept of "superstition" always had a certain elasticity about it... In general, the ceremonies of which it disapproved were "superstitious"; those which it accepted were not. As the Council of Malines ruled in 1607 : "It is superstitious to expect any effect from anything, when such an effect can not be produced by natural causes, by divine institutions, or by the ordination or approval of the Church"... If the people were going to resort to magic anyway, it was far better that it should be a magic over which the Church maintained some control.[2]

Keith Thomas' *Religion and the Decline of Magic* makes the changing boundaries between "magic" and "religion" in Tudor and Stuart England its central subject. In one massive study he integrates material on three areas of human relations with the sacred : Catholic and Protestant doctrine as preached by the learned and understood and practised by the unlearned; a wide range of popular religio-magical beliefs and practises, which existed alongside of that doctrine, in more or less comfortable relations with it; and the practise and per-secution of witchcraft. In regard to the *truth* or *authenticity* of these practises, Mr. Thomas makes no distinctions; his pages abound with village healers, astrological advisers and Puritan preachers who com-pete for credence and authority in relative equality. In regard to the *functions* of the beliefs and practises, however, Mr. Thomas does make distinctions, derived from the initial campaign of the Protestants against popish "magic" and from the concepts of anthroplogists, especially Bronislaw Malinowski. Magic comprises those methods and practises intended to tap supernatural power for solving concrete problems and misfortunes. Religion, in contrast, has wide functions of explanation and consolation; supplies a moral code; and has import-ant connections with the social order, reinforcing it, expressing it, and sometimes criticizing it.[3]

---

[1] Schmitt, *Organisation*, xcii n. 27. Also see Le Bras, *Études*, 235 n. 1.

[2] Keith Thomas, *Religion and the Decline of Magic, Studies in popular beliefs in sixteenth and seventeenth century England* (London, 1971), 48-49.

[3] *Ibid.*, 26-28, 46-47, 73-77, 151-54.

The functional approach can be helpful to historians, allowing them to see uses of popular religion even when they may disapprove of its rites and beliefs. Thus in the eighteenth century David Hume could argue that "polytheism or idolatrous worship" had among its fruits a spirit of tolerance and courage not so readily prompted by the jealous high deity of theistic religions. And Jules Michelet could claim that the pacts, sabbaths and charms of witches provided medieval serfs and peasant women a needed sense of community and a hope for revenge against Catholic church and seigneur. Or finally, to give a contemporary example, the distinguished Marxist historian Christopher Hill points out that Puritan Sabbatarianism was more than a matter of "fanaticism and Bibliolatry"; it served to develop the regular rhythm of work and rest necessary to the "ethos" of an increasingly urban and industrial society.[1]

Mr. Hill's distinction between mere Bibliolatry and the "rational" uses of Sabbatarianism and Mr. Thomas' distinction between mere magic and the broader uses of religion return us to our initial question about the historian's propensity to sort religious behavior into approved and disapproved categories. Mr. Thomas characterizes magic as "ineffective" techniques and rituals which will be needed so long as no more attractive alternative is available to deal with human helplessness. Its social locus is primarily the lower strata of society, among the peasants and urban poor, for whom the Puritan doctrine of self-help could hardly appear convincing. Peasants have a "ritual method of living"; the suggestion is that it is shallow in regard to meaning and morality. Political radicals use religious or ancient prophecies to validate their movements; the suggestion is that with a more realistic understanding of history, they would outgrow the need for such sentiments.[2]

My intention here is not to dispute the value of Mr. Thomas' book. It is surely one of the most important contributions to the history of European religion in recent decades, and its conceptual framework is much more complex than can be suggested here. My point is just that a premature evaluation of the functions of religion and magic, an insistence on sorting their function into those which are "rational"

---

[1] David Hume, *The Natural History of Religion*, ed. H. E. Root (Library of Modern Religious Thought; London, 1956), ch. 9. Jules Michelet, *La sorcière* (2d ed.; Brussells, 1863). Christopher Hill, *Society and Puritanism in Pre-Revolutionary England* (London, 1964), ch. 5.

[2] Thomas, *Religion*, 667-68, 277, 112, 76-77, 422-29.

and those which are not, may limit our historical insight unduly. A "ritual method of living" may be rich in meaning, even if poor in doctrine, and may make a statement about the character of the cosmos, social relationships and obligations. Clifford Geertz' deciphering of the levels of meaning in the Balinese cockfight shows us how far we can go in explaining the character of game or rite.[1]

How then may we improve our strategy for the study of popular religion in Europe? We continue to examine distinctions between religion and magic, Christian and pagan, rational and primitive as they are made in varying ways during the late medieval and early modern periods — as evidence about the periods, not as categories which exhaust the possibilities for our analysis. For ourselves, we examine the range of people's relation with the sacred and the supernatural, so as not to fragment those rites, practises, symbols, beliefs and institutions which to villagers or citydwellers constitute a whole. We consider how all of these may provide groups and individuals some sense of the ordering of their world, some explanation for baffling events or injustice, and some notion of who and where they are. We ask what feelings, moods and motives they encourage or try to repress. We look to see what means are offered to move people through the stages of their lives, to prepare for their future, and to cope with suffering or catastrophe. And further, we try to establish the ways in which religious life gives support to the social order — what Thomas O'Dea has called "the priestly function" of religion, the way in which it "sacralizes norms" — and in which it can also criticize, challenge or overturn that order.[2]

---

[1] See also E. P. Thompson's review article, "Anthropology and the Discipline of Historical Context," *Midland History*, I, no. 3 (Spring, 1972), 41-55; and Hildred Geertz, "*Religion and the Decline of Magic* : An Anthropologist's View," a paper presented at the annual meeting of the American Historical Association, December, 1972, New Orleans, and forthcoming in the *Journal of Interdisciplinary History*. On the general problem of rationality and irrationality in analyzing religion, see the articles by Steven Lukes, Martin Hollis and John Torrance on the topic "Sympathy for alien concepts" in *Archives européennes de sociologie*, VIII (1967), 247-81, and Bryan Wilson (ed.), *Rationality* (Key Concepts in the Social Sciences; New York, 1970). Clifford Geertz, "Deep Play : Notes on the Balinese Cockfight," in *Myth, Symbol and Culture, Daedalus* (Winter, 1972), 1-37.

[2] Clifford Geertz, "Religion as a Cultural System," in Michael Banton (ed.), *Anthropological Approaches to the Study of Religion* (A.S.A. Monographs, 3; London, 1966), 1-42; M. E. Spiro, "Religion : Problems of Definition and Explanation," in *ibid.*, 85-122; Thomas F. O'Dea, *The Sociology of Religion* (Prentice-Hall Foundations of Modern Sociology Series, Englewood Cliffs, N.J., 1966), ch. 1.

Along the way we are attentive to the relations between laity and clergy in all their variety, but do not assume that the communication between them on religious matter goes in only one direction — from the clergy downward. Bernd Moeller's study of lay piety on the eve of the German Reformation, a more vital piety than that of the clergy, can be a helpful model here.[1] We are careful not to adjudge a human problem "concrete," "everyday," or "empirical" when it occurs in a peasant's breast and "spiritual" and "ethical" when it occurs in the breast of a saint or religious leader. A peasant uneasy about his sexual impotency and Saint Teresa fighting desire, a chambermaid worrying about whether or whom she should marry and Théodore de Bèze wondering whether he should break his vows and marry the chambermaid Claudine Denosse are not struggling with problems of a different spiritual order, however their solutions may vary in significance for others.

Finally, as historians we are ever concerned about the context for popular religious life and for religious change. Two recent books which do this effectively are François Lebrun's *Les hommes et la mort en Anjou aux 17e et 18e siècles* and Brian Pullan's *Rich and Poor in Renaissance Venice*.[2] The former places the quest for miraculous cures, confraternities for the dying, funeral customs, prayers for the dead and the like in relation to the circumstances of death — demographic, economic, medical and legal. M. Lebrun finds remarkable continuity over more than two centuries in the facts of demography and the character of religious response. In Mr. Pullan's *Venice*, it is the changing forms of charity and welfare which are linked both with urban developments and with the changing religious sensibility of the Counter-Reformation. For instance, Mr. Pullan shows that increased concern for social distance transformed confraternities of flagellants into organizations in which the poor brothers whipped themselves and the rich brothers gave them charity.

Finding the sources of change in popular symbols, practises and rites is a major and difficult task for historians. When we are trying

---

[1] Bernd Moeller, "Frömmigkeit in Deutschland um 1500," *Archiv für Reformationsgeschichte*, 56 (1965), 3-31.

[2] François Lebrun, *Les hommes et la mort en Anjou aux XVIIe et XVIIIe siècles, Essai de démographie et de psychologie historiques* (École pratique des hautes études, VIe section, Civilisations et sociétés, 25; Paris, 1971). Brian Pullan, *Rich and Poor in Renaissance Venice, The Social Institutions of a Catholic State, to 1620* (Cambridge, Mass., 1971).

to explain change in doctrine or innovation by an individual religious leader, we may limit the difficulty by narrowing our context — say, by falling back on the nature of theological debate or of the innovator's life. But if we are looking at change in large groups or in widely accepted symbols and practises, then it is impossible to regard these as closed systems. Here we historians are likely to turn for assistance, explicitly or implicitly, to one of the current theories about "the birth of the gods." [1] Some may look for historical circumstances which inspire new fear and trembling; some, following Durkheim, will look for features of social organization or disorganization which call forth new gods, demons or witches; some, with Marx and Engels, will turn to class attitudes and aspirations; and some, with Freud and Erik Erikson, will turn to relations within the family. My purpose here is not to identify all the assumptions or theories that help historians search for explanations of religious change, and even less to make a critical assessment of them. I would stress only three points. First, we must be aware of what these assumptions are and not allow them to be simplistic just because we are dealing with "masses" rather than "elites." Second, since religious life is so rich in meaning and uses, we should expect that we will have to draw upon more than one area of human experience to provide the context for change. Third, we should think of popular religion not only as a projection or product of social life, but should see it in creative encounter with other social activities. As Clifford Geertz has said, religion not only describes the social order, it also shapes it.[2]

II.

The fine essays in this collection by Richard Trexler on fifteenth-century Florence and A. N. Galpern on sixteenth-century Champagne show how much can be learned about lay piety from an intensive local study followed by imaginative analysis. Several of the tasks discussed above they carry out with singular success. Both papers disclose to us central features of Catholic piety in the fifteenth an sixteenth centures — the confraternity and the processional — and

---

[1] Frank E. Manuel, *The Eighteenth Century Confronts the Gods* (Cambridge, Mass., 1959), ch. 4 : "The Birth of the Gods." Guy W. Swanson, *The Birth of the Gods* (Ann Arbor, 1960), ch. 1.

[2] Geertz, "Religion," 35-36.

both consider the important role of religion in marking stages of life and connecting age groups — the youth with their elders, the living with the dead. The papers do not make the boundary between religion and magic their main concern, but rather Mr. Trexler and Mr. Galpern distinguish between traditional or late medieval and more modern features of popular religion. Neither author insists that one of these religious forms is "better" or more rational than the other, though both of them assess religious organization in terms of its suitability to the needs of a given period. I want to comment on the significance of some of these points and to raise queries both about the explanations offered in these papers for religious change and about the contrast between traditional and more modern religious forms.

For Mr. Galpern the confraternity with its patron saint was a creation of the specific economic and political circumstances of the fourteenth and fifteenth centuries. Political and economic insecurity and the scarcity of commodities and resources led to *associations* in religion as well as in other areas of life. Political decentralization was projected into religious symbolism by means of the Virgin and a host of saints, who shared authority with the Lord.[1] That this style of religious life persisted and even developed well into the sixteenth century is the result of cultural lag, so Mr. Galpern claims. Though economic revival and improved political order might have made it more "relevant" for people to discard their confraternities and saints in favor of bold individual action and risk-taking, this did not happen because "cultural patterns, once launched, may embark on a life of their own and take their time in responding to social changes."

Mr. Galpern does us a service by suggesting that we look for connections between the scarcity of wordly goods and human generosity on the one hand, and the scarcity of divine grace on the other. Still there are some unsatisfactory aspects to his argument. Scarcity, insecurity and political disorder were not peculiar to the fourteenth and fifteenth century, but were broadly characteristic of pre-industrial Europe. The ups and downs in these regards were not all expressed in religious life. It seems implausible to explain the confraternity, which predates the fourteenth century and lasts almost to the French Revolution, by the special events of the fourteenth and fifteenth centuries. It also seems unwarranted to judge religious association as

---

1 See Guy W. Swanson, *Religion and Regime* (Ann Arbor, 1967) as well as his *Birth of the Gods* for an analogous approach to the relation of political life to religious symbols.

merely defensive and religious individualism as creative. In fact, the
religious confraternity showed itself capable of a variety of uses.
Where it failed, it did so not because it was an association, but because
it was the wrong kind of association.

Let me elaborate a little upon these claims. Already in the twelfth
century we can find confraternities established in parts of Italy and
the Languedoc, and they multiply especially in the thirteenth, fourteenth and fifteenth centuries. What is impressive about the confraternity as a form is its flexibility and its ability to lend itself to
such different memberships over six hundred years. Medieval village
"kingdoms", committed to supplying wax to the rural parish, gave
way in seventeenth-century France to Confraternities of the Rosary
or the Holy Sacrament, whose devotions were more private or more
controlled by the local clergy. In cities, a confraternity might have
hundreds of members or only a few dozen and might draw (as these
papers suggest) from every quarter of town or from a single parish,
from diverse occupations or from one. During the mid-sixteenth
century in France, when the king and city councils were eyeing confraternity treasuries with some greed and when Calvinists were organizing conventicles and consistories, the membership of the confraternities dwindled. But then in the late sixteenth century they
revived and new ones were formed, the laity sometimes taking on the
charitable and educational functions which Brian Pullan has described
for sixteenth-century Venice and other Italian cities. If by 1700 the
heyday of the confraternity was over and the parish was the major
organizing unit for urban religious life, nevertheless many of the
older confraternities still continued. In the diocese of Angers, nine
confraternities for people on their deathbed (Confréries des Agonisants
— anyone over six was eligible for membership) were founded in the
last half of the seventeenth century.[1]

---

[1] For evidence on confraternities, see Le Bras, *Études*, II, 423-62, I, 63; Delaruelle,
et al., *L'Église*, 666-94, G. M. Monti, *Le confraternite medievali dell'alta e media Italia*
(2 vols. Florence, 1927); André Gouron, *La réglementation des métiers en Languedoc au
moyen âge* (Études d'histoire économique, politique et sociale, XXII; Geneva, 1958),
337-65; É. Levasseur, *Histoire des classes ouvrières et de l'industrie en France avant 1789*
(2 vols.; 2nd ed.; Paris, 1900), I, 574-99, II, 131-37; J.-C. Schmitt, "Apostolat mendiant
et société. Une confrérie dominicaine à la veille de la Réforme," *Annales. Économies.
Sociétés. Civilisations*, 26 (1971), 83-104; Toussaert, *Sentiment*, 478-93; A. N. Galpern,
"Change without Reformation. Religious Practice and Belief in Sixteenth-Century
Champagne" (Unpublished Ph.D. dissertation, Dept. of History, University of California at Berkeley, 1971), 75-105; Noel Taillepied, *Recueil des Antiquitez et Singularitez*

And yet, there were limits to what confraternities could do. Over any extended period of time, they could not sustain an effective role of integration across boundaries of wealth and poverty, sex or geographical origin. If the confraternity was connected with a craft, then the role of widows and workers was minimal. Journeymen, as in the shoemakers' trade in Troyes, preferred to form their own religious grouping if they could. If the confraternity had a few hundred members of diverse economic background, then, like the Scuole Grandi at Venice, it finally broke down into "orders of rich and poor." In Troyes, Mr. Galpern's evidence does not show either a wide social distribution among the membership of confraternities or a significant participation of females. In Rouen in the first part of the sixteenth century, out of thirty-seven confraternities, only six mentioned female members and these in small proportion.[1] As for foreign residents in a city, though one might find them mixed perforce in craft confraternities, they are rarely found in other confraternities *together* with local inhabitants. Rather, as in sixteenth-century Lyon, there were separate confraternities of Germans, of Florentines, of Lucchese. Finally, there were segments of urban society which provided virtually no members to confraternities. Though urban winegrowers were likely to have a religious brotherhood where they existed in any numbers, most unskilled workers, day-laborers, and serving-girls were never involved in such societies.[2]

In short, confraternities were the creative foci of lay religious activity for centuries, their influence extending beyond their membership to those who watched their processions or benefited from their occasional charity. But local and particularistic in character, devotion and imagery, they could not engage and unite all city people. The brotherhood and sisterhood of the Calvinist movement in the mid-

---

de la Ville de Rouen (Rouen, 1587), 58 ff.; Pullan, *Rich and Poor*, 216-38; T.-J. Schmitt, *L'organisation*, 196-209; Ferté, *Vie*, 75-76; Pérouas, *Diocèse*, 501; Lebrun, *Les hommes*, 457.

[1] Levasseur, *Histoire*, I, 599, no. 7; Pullan, *Rich and Poor*, 63-83; Galpern, "Change," 94-101; Louis Martin, *Répertoire des anciennes confréries et charités du diocèse de Rouen approuvées de 1434 à 1610* (Fécamp, 1936), 143-60; Henri Hauser, *Ouvriers du temps passé*, *XVe-XVIe siècles* (5th ed.; Paris, 1927), 156; J. C. Schmitt, "Apostolat," 100-02.

[2] In Lyon, the Germans and Florentines each had a confraternity at the Dominican monastery, the Lucchese at the recently established convent of the Observant Franciscans, just outside the city walls. Most of the members were merchants or bankers. The wine-growers, who had plots in the northern part of the city, had a confraternity at the cathedral of Saint Nizier.

sixteenth century owed its strength partly to the fact that it was organized around symbols less exclusive than one or two saints and among those craftsmen, foreigners and women, who had been little integrated into the confraternities. The later success of the Counter-Reformation in cities was due partly to the fact that it accorded some scope to voluntaristic confraternities among laymen, while strengthening the unity of the more inclusive parish.[1]

Thus, the history of confraternities might better be related, not to economic contraction and short-range political disorder, but to the more slowly changing features of life that influence people's sense of community, of boundaries between the self and others, and of the character of social relationships. Such features of life would include changes in rates of literacy and geographical mobility and in sex and class differentiation; the growth of political institutions that cannot be easily reconciled with city walls, and village or regional limits; and the expectations bred from ritual about what human relationships should be like.

III.

Among the innovations in the history of confraternities is that unearthed by Mr. Trexler — the organization of young males. Religious imagery and practise in the Middle Ages had not, of course, ignored the young. The sacrament of confirmation, though by no means universal and received at varying ages, was respected, and was believed to assist the child or young adult in warding off the devil and even ill health. The innocence and wisdom of children were well known *topoi*; the offering of children to monasteries as oblations was a feature of early medieval piety, while lay children were sometimes assigned a special role in the late medieval processional. Adolescents were occasion-

---

[1] On the composition of the Protestant movement in France in the mid-sixteenth century, see E. Le Roy Ladurie, *Les paysans de Languedoc* (Bibliothèque générale de l'école pratique des hautes études, VIe section; 2 vols.; Paris, 1966), I, 342-43; N. Z. Davis, "Strikes and Salvation in Lyons," *Archiv für Reformationsgeschichte*, 56 (1965), 54, and "City Women and Religious Change in Sixteenth-Century France," in Dorothy McGuigan (ed.), *A Sampler of Women's Studies* (Ann Arbor, 1973). John Bossy's important article "The Counter-Reformation and the People of Catholic Europe", *Past and Present*, 47 (May, 1970), rightly stresses the growth of "parochial conformity", but much oversimplifies the picture in regard to the relation of the Counter-Reformation to confraternities and the demise of the confraternities (59-60). See the sources in n. 1, p. 316, above.

ally marshalled for religious movements like the Children's Crusade. [1] But the establishment of distinct religious organizations, directed by adults, through which lay males might pass during their early or later adolescence evidently began only in the fifteenth century. We can find examples of them later in places other than Florence. By 1587 in Rouen, there was a confraternity in honor of Saint Bonaventure, supported by the Enfants de la Ville; and at Paris during the reign of Louis XIII, there existed a Confrérie des Enfants des Petites Écoles. [2]

Historians will want to follow Mr. Trexler's lead and look for such confraternities elsewhere. From what we now know, they appear to be part of a cluster of developments, occurring primarily in cities from the fifteenth through the seventeenth centuries, intended to provide a more controlled and ordered socialization for adolescents outside the family. Disciplined college systems replaced freer living arrangements for students in France; the tutor's surveillance over his pupils at Oxford and Cambridge was strengthened; humanist and Jesuit educational schemes were geared in part toward the improved internalization of norms; special manuals were written for confessing the young, such as Jean Gerson's *Breve maniere de confession pour les jeunes*; and special hospitals and programs were set up for the training and education of poor orphans. [3] As with the boy's confraternities in Florence, the precise age groups affected by these institutions might vary from case to case, some even dipping down to include boys before the age of puberty. This comes not from confusion among adults about the onset of puberty. The medical literature of the period reported that the sexual maturation of boys, their "age of adolescence",

---

[1] Toussaert, *Sentiment*, 102-04; T.-J. Schmitt, *L'organisation*, 166-68; Ferté, *Vie*, 307-08; Thomas, *Religion*, 37-38. I am grateful to John Coughlan for his discussion of the offering of children to monasteries.

[2] Taillepied, *Recueil*, 58; *Le calendrier des confréries de Paris*, ed. J.-B. Le Masson (Collection des documents rares ou inédits rélatifs à l'histoire de Paris, 9; Paris, 1875), 59.

[3] Philippe Ariès, *Centuries of Childhood, A Social History of Family Life* (N.Y., 1962), part 2. Professor Lawrence Stone, in a series of lectures given at the University of California, Berkeley in April, 1973 on Oxford University (Una's Lectures) described the growth in surveillance of students by tutors in the late sixteenth and seventeenth centuries. Irene Q. Brown, "Philippe Ariès on Education and Society in Seventeenth and Eighteenth-Century France," *History of Education Quarterly* (Fall, 1967), 357-68. N. Z. Davis, "Poor Relief, Humanism and Heresy : the Case of Lyon," *Studies in Medieval and Renaissance History*, V (1968), 226, n. 27, 246-49; Pullan, *Rich and Poor*, 231, 259-63; Yves Poutet, "L'enseignement des pauvres dans la France du XVIIe siècle," *XVIIe siècle*, 90-91 (1971), 87-110.

ordinarily began at fourteen. The long debate, still unresolved at the
Council of Trent, over when children should start to confess and receive
the sacrament of penance always assumed that *sexual* sins could start
occurring only around age fourteen. The question was how much
discretion children had in regard to other matters before that time
and how well they could understand the significance of absolution.
Some authorities said at twelve or fourteen; some said at seven;
Savonarola thought ten to eleven about the right age.[1] Since opinion
was so divided about the character of late childhood, it is not surprising that institutions designed to bring up adolescents in a more
disciplined way could sometimes include younger boys.

What of the context for the formation of and subsequent support
for these institutions ? Mr. Trexler makes several suggestions for the
youth confraternities of Florence. A demographic situation in which
marriage for men was very late and in which mothers were playing an
overwhelming role in child-rearing was producing licentious soft
young males, fond of fornication and/or homosexuality. There were
not traditional organized groups outside the family to counter this
immorality, Mr. Trexler goes on, since the male festive brigades had
recreational purposes only and just made matters worse. As the new
humanist schools would change this picture for the patrician lads,
so boys' confraternities, sponsored by adult laymen, would change it
for the sons of the lesser merchants and artisans, who evidently made
up the bulk of the membership. Once under way, the theatrical and
processional life of these pious and innocent adolescents had such
impact that by the 1450's they became "the public image of youth
in the city." Finally, for unspecified reasons, they became central
in the religious and political symbolism of Florence. Innocent and
segregated lay adolescents (if I understand Mr. Trexler's argument
aright) now replaced meritorious monks in trying to win God's favor
for the whole community. The boys' confraternities prepared the way
for Savonarola's young activists, who literally and figuratively were
expected to usher in a new order of things.

Let us consider this picture more closely, for what it may help us
learn about Florence and about similar developments elsewhere. Late
marriage for males is surely significant for the formation of groups

---

[1] Hierosme de Monteux, *Commentaire de la conservation de santé* (Lyon, 1559), 202-03.
Henry Charles Lea, *A History of Auricular Confession and Indulgences in the Latin
Church* (Philadelphia, 1896), I, 400-04; Toussaert, *Sentiment,* 107; T.-J. Schmitt, *L'or-
ganisation,* 168-69.

in which adolescents can enjoy brotherly relations, either with their peers or with males of somewhat mixed ages, until the time they found families of their own. On the other hand, the *particular* features of family life which Mr. Trexler has singled out as creating the need for the boys' confraternities — very late marriage for males, the predominant role of the mother in child-rearing and the consequent effeminancy of the sons — were especially characteristic of the patricians and less so of the more modest merchant and artisanal families,[1] whose sons were in the confraternities. This suggests that other factors in Florentine life were also stimulating the formation of the new youth groups. What might they be? Brian Pullan has shown that one of the functions of the Scuole Grandi in Venice, with their splendid processions and important charitable gifts, was to grant some honor and authority to prosperous non-patricians, otherwise cut off from real political power.[2] So in Florence, it may be that non-patrician families were initially the most anxious that their sons have a disciplined adolescence, both to give them a different style from the "golden youth" and because they could not count on their sons taking their rightful place in the world if they passed their teens in the traditional or freer fashions of other social classes.

Furthermore, the new confraternities should be seen not merely in terms of the moral and social aspirations of certain families, but also in terms of aspirations for Catholic reform, which anticipate the piety and organization of Counter-Reformation. Though sponsored and supervised by laymen, the confraternity youth were taking communion and confession regularly. As religious reformers surely approved the new Florentine cathedral schools for the proper training of future priests, so they must have joined with Ambrogio Traversari in applauding the boys' confraternities. Already in the early years of the fifteenth century, Jean Gerson, then responsible for schools and choirboys in Paris, had said, "If you want to reform the Church, you've got to start with the children." [3]

But did these movements go far enough in Florence to warrant Mr. Trexler's suggestion that "pious and innocent adolescents"

---

[1] David Herlihy, "Some Psychological and Social Roots of Violence in the Tuscan Cities," in Lauro Martines (ed.), *Volence and Civil Disorder in Italian Cities, 1200-1500* (UCLA Center for Medieval and Renaissance Studies Contributions, V; Berkeley, 1972), 145, and n. 48.

[2] Pullan, *Rich and Poor*, 8, 75.

[3] Delaruelle, *et al.*, *L'Église*, 845-47, 846, n. 2.

became *the* image of youth in Florence and finally replaced monks as saviors ? This seems to exaggerate the evidence. It is true that a vanguard critic like Lorenzo Valla was already arguing in the 1440's that the lay vocation was equal in merit to the religious vocation, as Charles Trinkaus' work has shown us. [1] It is true that both the boys' confraternities and monasticism had in common certain pious styles and a Christian inversion of wordly values. Nevertheless, there were limits to this laicization of religious life. The Dominican friar Giovanni de Carlo, who (as we have seen in Mr. Trexler's quotation) appreciated the sons dressed as their citizen fathers in the Magi procession of the 1460's, was not so sure the sons symbolized regeneration for Florence. Considering the civil wars and evil times that followed afterward, he thought the procession an *evil* portent : "Thus many acted not indeed as Florentine citizens, but wholly as their images and shadows." [2] The later success of Fra Girolamo and other preachers and the scramble for a few of the prophet's ashes after his death suggest what force the professed religious still had. The apothecary Luca Landucci, whose sons were among Savonarola's "blessed and pure minded troops", certainly thought the friar more of a savior than the boys. [3]

Indeed, Landucci's diary included no *single* image of the collective behavior of boys and young males. In addition to Savonarola's supporters, he spoke of "certain young men (*giovani*) called Compagnacci", members of a festive Company or brigade, who attacked Savonarola in words and deeds and could marshal boys (*fanciugli*) to their side. He mentioned the various games traditionally played by boys (*fanciugli*) at carnival times, such as putting up barriers across the streets and making passersby pay a fine. And finally, he talked of groups of boys (*fanciugli*) who initiated violent action against political or religious targets — against the corpse of a Pazzi conspirator, dug up and dragged through Florence in mockery; against Jews in the wake of the sermons of Bernardino da Feltre; and against an iconoclast who had desecrated images of Our Lady, stoned to death and dragged through the streets. [4]

---

[1] Charles Trinkaus, *In Our Image and Likeness, Humanity and Divinity in Italian Humanist Thought* (2 vols. paginated consecutively; London, 1970), 674-80.

[2] Rab Hatfield, "The Compagnia de' Magi," *Journal of the Warburg and Courtauld Institutes*, XXXIII (1970), 117.

[3] Luca Landucci, *Diario fiorentino dal 1450 al 1516*, ed. I. del Badia (Florence, 1883), 178, 125. Translated phrase from Luca Landucci, *A Florentine Diary from 1405 to 1516*, trans. Alice de Rosen Jervis (London, 1927), 102.

[4] Landucci, *Diario*, 163, 169-70, 124, 21-22, 53-54, 66. Also, on the assaults by boys,

Now festive companies and boys' street gangs predate the adolescent confraternities in Florence, and they last, along with the religious groupings, all through the sixteenth century.[1] They are also found elsewhere in Europe. Mr. Trexler may well be right in characterizing the boys' confraternities as the more "modern" form among the three. But his picture of the traditional forms in Florence seems inadequate, making it hard for us to understand the full difference between carnival and confraternity and the reasons why the traditional forms continue to have some vitality. Where Mr. Trexler sees mere "diversion" and "amusement", "festive nonsense" and "the chaos and spontaneity of the street," one may find deeper meaning, social uses, and design.

As I have shown in another place,[2] festive companies or brigades (or "abbeys" or "kingdoms of misrule," as they were called in some places) derive from rural youth groups, whose rites and games prepared young unmarried males for adult roles and also served the village in distinctive ways. These last included noisy masked charivaris, or *scampanate*, as they were called in Tuscany, in which the youth had a festive license to mock people who had violated sexual or domestic norms. It should be noted how such play addresses itself to one of the central and perennial issues of adolescence in the West : the conflict between the upsurge of passions, sexual and other, and the increasing demands of conscience. One way to ease this tension is to let the youth become the uproarious voice of the community's conscience.

In large cities, these festive societies changed somewhat in character. Some became confined to the elegant sons of patrician families. Others lost their age specificity and were organized within a craft (such as the law clerks of the Bazoche in France) or neighborhood. The dramatic activity of these societies became more complex and ornamental and they took on certain new functions that need not concern us here. But certain of the old ones remained. In Florence, competitive races

---

see Gene Brucker (ed.), *The Society of Renaissance Florence, A Documentary Study* (N.Y., 1971), 72-73, 248-50. Fra Bernardino was preaching against the Jews and for the establishment of a Monte di Pieta.

[1] Samuel Berner, "Florentine Society in the Late Sixteenth and Early Seventeenth Centuries," *Studies in the Renaissance*, XVIII (1971), 226-27.

[2] N. Z. Davis, "The Reasons of Misrule : Youth Groups and Charivaris in Sixteenth-Century France," *Past and Present*, 50 (Feb., 1971), 41-75, with full bibliographical notes on the subject. On the Tuscan term *scampanate*, see Giuseppe C. Pola Falletti-Villafalletto, *Associazioni giovanili e feste antiche, loro origini* (4 vols.; Milan, 1939), III, 449 ff.

and sports, festive rivalry between different quarters of town, even the seemingly "inane" adolescent carnival games of stone-throwing, hut-building, and barring and fining female pedestrians — all these can be connected to rites and procedures which dramatize the relations and obligations within the city of categories of age, of sex, and to some extent of class. Especially the spirit of *scampanate*, of criticism and punishment, persisted. We hear it in March, 1498, when mocking young men burlesqued Savonarola's prophetic imagery by going about with lighted lanterns looking for lost keys. We see it three months later at the feast of San Giovanni, where one of the floats jeeringly celebrated the prophet's fall, dragging around a gigantic effigy of his corpse, which the authorities had not permitted on the real day of his death.[1] The boys' street gangs, which among other activities dragged corpses and lapidated enemies of the community, may be a special urban adaptation of the rural festive society, which usually kept youthful cruelty bounded by the conventions of the charivari.

What then is the comparison between the traditional organizations of male youth and the adolescent confraternities? Both emerge from a society in which males did not marry in their teens, as we have seen, and also in which the generations did not have fundamentally divergent views about the conduct of adult life. The sponsors of the confraternities, however, were somewhat mistrustful of young people left to their own devices. The traditional groupings acted rather independently of the expressed wishes of parents, were ordered less by statutes than by unwritten prescriptions for adolescent behavior, and timed their activities both to seasonal festivals and to local events. The confraternities were more controlled in all these regards, as Mr. Trexler has shown us. Both traditional groupings and confraternities had an important public life. For the former however, the moods were comic, spirited, turning the world upside-down in mockery, or cruel; while for the latter, we have learned from Mr. Trexler, the range of moods was more limited — serious, pious, chiding the world through their grave and angelic demeanor. The confraternity boys might be allocated the role of propitiating God through their innocence. The traditional groupings were granted the license to serve as the community's conscience, sometimes in actions which grown-ups might be hesitant to initiate themselves. It seems apparent that

---

[1] Landucci, *Diario*, 165-66, 179-80.

Savonarola's boys, who sang like sweet angels *and also* tore off women's ornaments, broke up gambling games and invaded taverns,[1] were the heirs of both the boys' confraternities and the traditional groupings.

Finally, the different types of organization had different relations to religious institutions and practises. The activities of the traditional groups were undertaken by laymen, except in the special case of the Feast of Fools at Christmastime, that upside-down revelry of young clerks and chaplains which in the fifteenth century was beginning to be banished from Europe's cathedrals and was surely frowned upon at the new cathedral schools in Florence. Yet the traditional groupings had some meaningful connections with Catholic religious life. In northern Italy and northern Europe, festive leaders were sometimes called Abbots, a joking inversion which implied that one accept real abbots. In some places festive societies actually supported a confraternity and carried on masking and foolery on their saints' day. Everywhere some of their festivities took place on important Catholic feast-days, and everywhere iconoclasts, Jews and heretics were among the objects of punishment for the street gangs.[2] The connections of the newly founded boys' confraternities with religious institutions, events and personnel were, of course, much closer than this, with likely gains in adolescent self-control and losses in adolescent autonomy.

Perhaps the most interesting contrast, however, is that between the organization of adolescence, whether of the traditional or the tamed variety, in Catholic areas and that allowed in Protestant areas of Europe. Protestantism initially attacked paternal authority, papal, abbatial and priestly, and rallied to its support many young men and adolescents (male adolescents were notorious statue-smashers). It ended up reaffirming the authority of the father within the Christian family and giving little scope to youth groups. Children might associate in catechism classes, and Anglican confirmation or Puritan conversion experiences might provide individual rites of passage for teen-agers in early or late adolescence. But all confraternities and special religious organizations were to disappear within the Christian community, and traditional festivities and organizations were attacked by Puritans

---

[1] *Ibid.*, 123, 126-27.

[2] Pola Falletti-Villafalletto, *Associazioni*, I, 2, 24; Jean Savaron, *Traitté des confrairies* (Paris, 1604), ff. 10ᵛ - 12ʳ; Taillepied, *Recueil*, 61. On the important role of boys, male adolescents and youth groups in religious violence in sixteenth-century France, see N. Z. Davis, "The Rites of Violence : Religious Riot in Sixteenth-Century France," *Past and Present*, 59 (May, 1973).

and Calvinists with much greater zeal than even the Counter-Reformation was able to mount. When youth groups and carnival play persisted in Protestant areas, it was in spite of the Church. [1] Though the problem needs fuller investigation, one might say tentatively that Protestantism cut down on the religious resources available for creating a distinctive collective identity or organization for male or female adolescents. It may thereby have left the field more open to secular institutions ultimately to play this role.

IV.

A similar transformation occurred in regard to the treatment of death and the relations between the living and the dead. This whole subject is a complex one, involving, as it does, attitudes toward death and dying; funeral rites, burial customs and other means of marking death and mourning; and expectations for the after-life. Recent decades have seen some valuable studies on these topics, in addition to the important work of François Lebrun mentioned above : on the changing literary treatment of the *Ars moriendi* in England and the Continent; on changing attitudes toward Hell; on the dance of death and other artistic treatments of dying, Purgatory and the Last Judgment; on tomb sculpture and tombstones; and on perpetual chantries and chantry priests. [2] I want here to raise only two points,

---

[1] *Ibid.*, on youthful Protestant iconoclasts. Hill, *Society and Puritanism*, chs. 13, 5; Thomas, *Religion*, 57; Davis, "Reasons of Misrule," 72 and n. 99.

[2] Among many studies one may cite, Alberto Tenenti, *La vie et la mort à travers l'art du XVe siècle* (Paris, 1952) and *Il senso della morte et l'amore della vita nel Rinascimento* (Turin, 1957). Philippe Ariès, "Contribution à l'étude du culte des morts à l'époque contemporaine," *Revue des travaux de l'Académie des sciences morales et politiques*, 119, 4th ser. (1966, 1), 25-40 and "La mort inversée. Le changement des attitudes devant la mort dans les sociétés occidentales," *Archives européennes de sociologie*, VIII (1967), 169-95. Nancy Lee Beaty, *The Craft of Dying, The Literary Tradition of the Ars Moriendi in England* (Yale Studies in English, 175; New Haven, 1970). D. P. Walker, *The Decline of Hell, Seventeenth-Century Discussions of Eternal Torment* (London, 1964). James M. Clark, *The Dance of Death in the Middle Ages and the Renaissance* (Glasgow, 1950). G. and M. Vovelle, *Vision de la mort et de l'au-delà en Provence d'après les autels des âmes du purgatoire, XVe-XXe siècles* (Cahiers des Annales, 29; Paris, 1970). T. S. R. Boase, *Death in the Middle Ages, Mortality, Judgment and Remembrance* (Library of Medieval Civilization; N.Y., 1972). Erwin Panofsky, *Tomb Sculpture. Its Changing Aspects from Ancient Egypt to Bernini* (N.Y., n.d.). Allan I. Ludwig, *Graven Images. New England Stonecarving and its Symbols, 1650-1815* (Middletown, Conn., 1966). K. O. Wood-Legh, *Perpetual Chantries in Britain* (Cambridge, 1965).

suggested by Mr. Galpern's essay and by the previous discussion of confraternities and youth.

Mr. Galpern comments that "Catholicism at the end of the Middle Ages was in large part a cult of the living in the service of the dead." His evidence for Champagne — and the picture is the same elsewhere in Europe — is the intense concern about masses for the dead souls in Purgatory. Indeed, this was still an important feature of popular Catholic piety at the end of the Ancien Régime. Purgatory was still a favorite theme for altar-pieces in Provence. Though the Counter-Reformation ultimately cut down on the hosts of penurious chaplains and chantry priests, anniversary masses and other masses for the dead continued to be founded for both wealthy and poor. The crier continued to ring his bell in the middle of the night and summon Christians to pray God for the dead. The repose of their souls was still mentioned at Sunday mass; the church bells in town and village still sounded through the night of November 1-2 in anticipation of the service for the dead and the procession to the cemetery on All Souls' Day. The ghosts of persons in Purgatory still returned to haunt, advise or seek assistance from the living.[1]

Together with prayers to the saints for intercession and help, this set of practises and beliefs enables us to accept as a valid metaphor André Varagnac's characterization of the dead in traditional Catholic Europe as an "age group." [2] They came to the living not only in memory or history, but in genuine converse and exchange. What were the major characteristics of this association? First, it was a corporate connection, establishing relations that went way beyond the individual family. Though heirs were expected to establish masses for dead relatives if the testator had not done so, the prayers were said by priests and others; collection boxes were set up for masses for those who had died poor; and confraternity and parish were generally involved in services for their dead. Ghosts that visited the living might be the

---

[1] Vovelle, *Vision*, 37-42. Delumeau, *Catholicisme*, 58. Lebrun, *Les hommes*, 487-90; Ferté, *Vie*, 333-34. Both Mr. Galpern's evidence from Champagne and my research in the notarial archives in Lyon show that the social spread of those founding anniversary masses is wide in the sixteenth century. Toussaert's claim that only the well-off could afford them seems incorrect (*Sentiment*, 220). I have found servants, journeymen, and semi-skilled workers saving several days' wages to found anniversary masses (Davis, "City Women," n. 25).

[2] André Varagnac, *Civilisation traditionnelle et genres de vie* (Sciences d'aujourd'hui; Paris, 1948), ch. 7 and 244.

souls of relatives, but also of friends, even of strangers. The living
were rarely kin to their saints, but were related to them only through
confraternities or other conventions. Secondly, the connection was
not just one of the living serving the dead, but was reciprocal. The
living did for the souls in Purgatory; the saints in Paradise did for the
living.

Thirdly, the services which the living performed for the dead were
limited and defined. Ritual did not require the living to be attentive
to all wishes of the dead, but rather to help soften for them the penalty
for sins which they, the dead, had committed. Ghosts returned ordinarily not just for any quarrel with the living, but under certain well-
known circumstances : to arrange for proper rites for a person who
had died unshriven or unburied; to obtain more masses and pilgrimages for the repose of a soul; to seek revenge for a murder; to have
the living make restitution for ill-gotten gains or other debts of the
dead; to compel the living to follow the last wishes of the dying,
especially in regard to burial or charitable gifts; to give notice of
impending or actual death; to give counsel, especially in regard to
amendment of life; to request that the living moderate their mourning.
Moreover, the ghosts were not merely the souls of the older generation,
of parents or ancestors, but rather, as suited the pattern of dying in
pre-industrial Europe, they were brothers, sisters, spouses, children,
friends and associations.[1]

The Catholic connection between the living and the dead, then,
provided the former with rites and beliefs by which they could express
their love and anger toward their own dead — their sense of loss and
their guilt — without undue self-consciousness. It was a conservative
influence, but only in certain directions. Indeed, on some issues saints
encouraged the living to movements of resistance or innovation.

The Reformation, of course, swept away Purgatory and prayers
for the dead and to the saints. Ghosts died hardest, and on into the
eighteenth century in England there were still those who believed,
in the face of Protestant teaching, that an apparition was really the
soul of brother James and not devilish trickery. Yet this is not enough
for us still to consider the dead as an "age group" in Protestant society.

---

[1] Taillepied, *Psichologie*, ch. 15 and *passim*; Johan Huizinga, *The Waning of the
Middle Ages*, trans. F. Hopman (1st published 1924; N.Y., 1954), 150. K. M. Briggs,
*The Anatomy of Puck, An Examination of Fairy Beliefs among Shakespeare's Con-
temporaries and Successors* (London, 1959), ch. 9. Thomas, *Religion*, 596-97.

What are the implications of this important change ? In some interesting pages on this subject, Keith Thomas suggests that it assisted the
process whereby "men's actions [became] less explicitly governed
by concern for the wishes of their ancestors or their spiritual welfare."
"Men grew prepared to accept innovation, unmoved by the prospect
of their ancestors turning in their graves." [1] There is some truth in
this assessment, but it distorts the picture. Clearly the subject needs
to be fully studied, but let us here consider some suggestions.

The cutting of the Catholic connection with the dead freed energies
and resources for uses for the living and the unborn. *How* these energies and resources were used depended on the historical context. Not
all ties with ancestors were severed, and it could well be argued that
the ending of ritual services to the dead strengthened other kinds
of connections with the past with which religion had been in tension.
We have seen, for instance, that the Catholic forms did not assign
importance exclusively to one's parents and grand-parents and that
they called attention less to the acquisition of property than to its
charitable uses. But the early modern period is marked by the slow
economic and legal evolution of private property, the control, manipulation and fruits of which belonged to the patriarchal family — not
to individuals, villages, larger cognatic groups or clientage systems.
Similarly, the patriarchal family was increasingly attentive to planning
the marriages and careers of children, not merely for the sake of the
progeny, but for the sake of the continuous advancement of the
family. Family histories, composed in circles that extended far beyond
the aristocracy, celebrated the rise in family fortunes and passed on
the formulas for marital felicity and worldly success that sons and
daughters were enjoined to follow. Is it not possible that the cessation
of prayers for the repose of souls gave added vividness to the historical
continuity of the family (in seventeenth-century England, even the
illicit ghosts began to groan to their relatives about money and investments); whereas in France, these strong sentiments for family and
property developed, but were moderated by Catholic religious sensibility until the rupture of the Revolution? A comparison of autobiographies by French and English women in the seventeenth century
would, I think, provide some evidence for this contrast. [2]

---

[1] *Ibid.*, 606, 602.

[2] On the writing of family histories, see Charles de Ribbe, *Les familles et la société
en France avant la Révolution d'après des documents originaux* (2 vols.; 3rd ed.; Paris,
1874), I; Paul Delany, *British Autobiography in the 17th Century* (London, 1969), 8-10,

Further, we may note that the elimination of prayers for the dead did not eliminate the need for mourning. The Protestant funeral sermon, when it could be paid for, and the tombstone, which in Puritan New England was erected even by simple farm families in the seventeenth and eighteenth centuries, were immediate responses to bereavement. But what of the months that followed? The ending of the Catholic ritual connections may have had the paradoxical consequence of binding the living even closer to their dead relatives, in self-conscious concern and guilt. Where Petrarch made Saint Augustine the judge of his spiritual conflicts, Nathaniel Hawthorne made his Puritan "great-grandsires" the judges for his worldly career and shouldered some of their sins besides.[1]

In short, as Protestantism reduced the religious resources available to mark off youth as a stage of life, so it cut out the dead as a kind of "age group." In both cases, however, the field was left open to other psychological and social codes to define the relations between the generations in their own way.

Furthermore, in parallel to the contrast between the traditional youth groups and the boys' confraternities, there is a contrast between certain late medieval or traditional attitudes toward the event of death and the more "modern" attitudes, encouraged alike by both the Counter-Reformation and Protestantism. In some ways the dance of death and allied images and practises resemble an Abbey of Misrule. By allied images and practises I mean *those which mixed the macabre and the comic*; on the one hand, trembling and terror before the corpse and its decay, on the other hand, revelry, mockery and easy familiarity with death. In many urban and rural communities, the interval between a death and the funeral feast included both aspects. Prescribed measures were taken to contain the "contagion" of the death to the corpse and to help the soul of the deceased find its way out of the

---

ch. 10. There are *livres de raison* and autobiographies by Catholic women in seventeenth-century France which express consciousness of the family and its history, such as that by Jeanne du Laurens (completed in 1631). But it is significant that the most outstanding ones, such as that by the Quietist Madame Guyon, do not place a high evaluation on the fortunes of their family. In the autobiographical work of Anne Lady Fanshawe and Lucy Hutchinson, however, religious sensibility converges with consciousness of the family's development. See also Bossy, "Counter-Reformation," 68-70 for a contrast between Protestant and Catholic treatment of the family unit.

[1] Thomas, *Religion*, p. 604; Ludwig, *Graven Images, passim*; Trinkaus, *In Our Image*, pp. 4-17; Frederick C. Crews, *The Sins of the Fathers, Hawthorne's Psychological Themes* (N.Y., 1966), 31 and ch. 2.

house as quickly as possible (covering all reflecting objects, emptying pails of water, etc.). At the same time, the wake and the feast following the funeral were occasions of joking and merriment. The wake moved back and forth from lamentations and prayers to horseplay, dancing and singing; the funeral meal involved abundant food and unrestrained drinking, and in many regions dancing as well.

Cemeteries were likewise places where the macabre and the comic were at home. As Noel Taillepied said, ghosts were often seen there. In the Cemetery of the Innocents in Paris, bones were displayed in charnel houses. And yet up to the eighteenth century all kinds of business went on in this dangerous place : peddling, chatting, soliciting by prostitutes, the pasturing of animals in rural parishes — and dancing. References to dancing among the tombs can be found from the eleventh to the mid-seventeenth centures. Similarly, on All Souls' eve, there was heavy drinking by the bell-ringers for the dead and dancing by the villagers.[1]

Of course, the dance of death itself is the example par excellence of the mixture of the comic and the macabre. Whether danced in masks or costumes (as it was in the fourteenth and fifteenth centuries), painted, preached, or printed in the editions that appeared in Paris, Lyon, Troyes and elsewhere, the *danse macabre* presented skeletons or desiccated corpses doing a terrifying and funny dance with a string of surprised partners. A funny dance ? Yes, because the dead dance with such intentional and burlesque awkwardness and their partners are so unwilling. Because the viewer identifies not only with the unprepared living, but with the grinning and powerful dead, who deflate all worldly pretensions and plans and overturn all worldly hierarchies and bear off king, pope and peasant.[2]

---

[1] Toussaert, *Sentiment*, 212-13, 219; Ferté, *Vie*, 332-34; Lebrun, *Les hommes*, 259, 477-78; Delaruelle, *et al.*, *L'Église*, 774; Taillepied, *Psichologie*, ch. 15. Arnold Van Gennep, *Manuel de folklore français contemporain* (3 vols. in 9 parts; Paris, 1937-48), I, pt. 2, 649-814. Bertram S. Puckle, *Funeral Customs, Their Origin and Development* (London, 1926), chs. 4, 6.

[2] Among many sources on the *danse macabre*, Delaruelle, *et al.*, *L'Église*, pp. 765-69; Clark, *Dance of Death*, and Curt Sachs, *World History of the Dance*, trans. B. Schonberg (N.Y., 1937), 261. For my analysis of the mixture of the macabre and the comic and its functions, I am indebted to Vivian Mercier, *The Irish Comic Tradition* (Oxford, 1962), ch. 3. On the dance of death as inversion, I have found helpful a paper by the folklorists Roger Abrahams and Barbara Babcock-Abrahams, "On Death, Dancing and Nonsense," given at a conference in Folklore and Early European Culture, sponsored by the Center for Medieval and Renaissance Studies, Ohio State University, Feb., 23-24, 1973. I have also benefited from a discussion with Frederick C. Crews.

Now the moral and spiritual quality of these images and practises has been evaluated very critically by twentieth-century observers. They certainly do not think they are funny. In the celebrated and beautiful pages of Johan Huizinga's *Waning of the Middle Ages*, they are said to spring from an impious disgust with death. The author of *Homo Ludens* saw no ludic element in the dance of death, but only a perverse relishing of hideous decay, appropriate to a sensualistic culture. Death can be interpreted in several ways, Huizinga said — in a spirit of tenderness, consolation or elegy. In the late medieval images and practises, he caught only a crude non-Christian meaning, fear of one's own death, or a worldly social message, the levelling brought about by death. Other writers have echoed or shared Huizinga's sentiments. They characterize the practises described above as "atrocious obsession," "cynical irreverence," "denaturing of mourning", and "an appetite for repulsion." [1]

As in the case of the traditional festive societies and adolescent street-gangs, I would like to suggest that these images and practises had a wider range of meaning and uses than that, and, for those who accepted them, did not seem in great tension with Christian piety. First of all, they expressed not only a horror of death, but also a triumph over that horror. The reality of the decayed flesh and bones could be accepted in the mixture of shivers and laughter. Playing at death allowed one to become familiar with its mocking power to destroy and criticize worldly life, as carnival inversion allowed mock abbots and kings familiarity with power and the license to criticize social or domestic behavior. It was a way of learning what death was about, especially important for young people and children, who were not excluded from wakes or any funeral activity and for whom death might come at any time. In some places the young were expected to dance after the funeral of one of their age group. So too playing at ghosts, which according to Taillepied was done not only as a joke but also to frighten children into diligence and obedience, was both a technique of control and a way of getting a feel for the Other World. [2]

Moreover, there were certain values affirmed by combining revelry with the macabre. Most important was the affirmation of life, rejoicing to be still among the living and affirming that life must go on, despite

---

[1] Huizinga, *The Waning*, ch. 11. Rapp, *L'Église*, 153; Toussaert, *Sentiment* 219; Ferté, *Vie*, 332, Boase, *Death*, 102.

[2] Taillepied, *Psichologie*, ch. 6.

the breach of death. Nor was this only a private sentiment; all the customs we have looked at were group affairs and the art forms were intended for public display. The traditional Irish wake included sexual ribaldry, and Vivian Mercier has convincingly connected it with rituals of fertility and rebirth. Curt Sachs has also shown how frequently funeral dance has erotic elements, intended to express renewal of life. The evidence for sexual play at Continental wakes and funeral feasts is less precise than in Ireland, but the free eating, drinking and dancing evoke a similar mood. Rabelais' picture of Gargantua mourning his wife Badebec, who had died in childbirth, exemplifies this festive connection between death and renewal. Gargantua thinks alternately of his lost wife and his new-born son, cries and laughs, shouts and drinks, misses his sexual partner and plans for a new one, fears his own death, and writes a comic epitaph for Badebec while merrily rocking Pantagruel.[1]

And, as in Rabelais' scene, the deceased were not ignored in the midst of these affairs, though the feelings expressed were mixed. He or she was lamented and talked about, sometimes with joviality. His soul, possibly still in the vicinity of house or cemetery, was feared, roused, pitied and wished on its way. It is possible that there was a perceived connection between macabre laughter and Christian belief. Christianity was a tragic religion only for the damned, who in practise Catholics seem to have assumed were a minority, compared to the great middle class of souls in Purgatory. For them and the blessed, there was finally a happy ending. "Il vault mieulx pleurer moins et boire dadvantaige !" said Gargantua of Badebec, "Ma femme... est en paradis pour le moins, si mieulx ne est; elle prie Dieu pour nous, elle est bien heureuse." [2] Why not dance at a wake?

In any case, these images and practises did have connections with Catholic religious life, just as did the traditional festive societies and

---

[1] Mercier, *Irish Comic*, 49-63; Sachs, *World History*, 104-08, 163, 248-49, 366; Van Gennep, *Manuel*, I, part 2, 779; François Rabelais, *Œuvres complètes*, ed. Jacques Boulenger and L. Scheler (Bibliothèque de la Pléiade; Paris, 1955), 181-82 (Book II, ch. 3); Mikhail Bakhtin, *Rabelais and His World*, trans. H. Iswolsky (Cambridge, Mass., 1968), 70 and 70, n. 18, 283.

[2] Rabelais, *Œuvres complètes*, 182. A forthcoming book by Kathleen Rogers Cohen on the transi tomb, or a tomb showing the corpse of the deceased, in the fifteenth and sixteenth century, argues that its significance changed over time, but in the Renaissance it symbolized Christ's Resurrection and the promise of human resurrection (*The Changing Meaning of the Transi Tomb in 15th- and 16th-century Europe*, University of California Press, 1973).

boys' street gangs. Most obvious is the sponsorship of the dance of death by fifteenth-century preachers and clerics as a means to induce repentance and amendment of life. On the other hand, the horseplay and license of the wake and dancing among the tombs were criticized by clerics as "pagan" well before the Counter-Reformation. Practitioners went right on, however, and might have defended themselves (as did practitioners of "superstition", when rebuked by the doctor of theology Jean-Baptiste Thiers in the late seventeenth century) by asserting that all their conduct was in conjunction with holy things, with Catholic prayers, Catholic ritual and feast days like All Souls'.[1]

With the Reformation and Counter-Reformation, clerical attitudes hardened toward "pagan" practises, and the mixture of the comic and the macabre in the dance of death was less and less to learned taste. Holbein's marvelous *Pictures of Death* represented both the culmination of the older tradition and the turning toward a new approach. Mocking, grinning death is present, but he is not involved in a literal dance. Instead he intrudes in a *picture of life*, that is, on the everyday surroundings of the living, accosting them or creeping up on them in a sly and mischievous way. The Christian message is ever insisted upon, with a Biblical quotation above every print. And instead of the older "Debate between the body and the soul" or "Exhortation to live well and die well" that had accompanied the printed editions of the *Danse macabre*, we have essays of a quite different tenor. In the first edition (Lyon, 1538), they were written by a Christian humanist, much influenced by Erasmus' thought, who ignored the physical horrors of decay and the discomforts of Hell or Purgatory, and stressed the importance of a life of truly charitable works as preparation for death. The next seven editions, published in Lyon from 1542 to 1562 in Latin, French and Italian, had essays by Protestant writers, who proclaimed that the only medicine for the soul was absolute faith in Christ's redemption. After Holbein, variations on the dance of death continued to be engraved and printed (including Thomas Rowlandson's satirical *English Dance of Death*, as late as 1815), but the motif was no longer central in the vision of the learned.[2]

---

[1] Toussaert, *Sentiment*, 212-13; Jean-Baptiste Thiers, *Traicté des superstitions* (1679), republished in *Superstitions anciennes et modernes* (Amsterdam, 1733), 109-10.

[2] N. Z. Davis, "Holbein's "Pictures of Death' and the Reformation at Lyons," *Studies in the Renaissance*, III (1956), 97-130. Arnold Pfister, "Über Tod und Totentänze." *Basler Bücherfreund*, III (Nov. 1927), 111-66.

Instead, there was a rich development of other attitudes toward death, based on certain medieval precedents or on humanist or Protestant modes of thought and feeling. As the boys' confraternities were intended to tame festive misrule and independent adolescent zeal, so the new sensibility tamed death a little, making it no more familiar, but less horrible and less comic. It was a matter of the utmost gravity and seriousness. Savonarola's advice to the Florentines that they keep a little ivory skeleton at hand and look at it often embodies the private and quiet spirit found in seventeenth-century paintings of meditation on death. For the seventeenth-century Anglican priest Jeremy Taylor,

> Christ... hath taken away the unhappiness of Sickness, and the sting of Death, and the dishonours of the Grave, of dissolution and weakness, of decay and change, and hath turned them into acts of favour, into instances of comfort, into opportunities of virtue : Christ hath now knit them into Rosaries and Coronets, he hath put them into promises and rewards, he hath made them part of the portion of his elect : they are instruments, and earnests, and securities, and passages to the greatest perfection of human nature, and the divine promises.[1]

This quiet death reproved wordly priorities with gentle irony instead of noisily overthrowing hierarchies as in the dance. To the growing number of Protestants who thought of death primarily in terms of God's punishment of their personal enemies, it said, "Ah, but you will be next." As for traditional funeral customs, one can imagine what Calvinist and Puritan divines thought of them, for they even condemned dancing at weddings as "a preamble to lewdness" and an invitation to the Devil. In Catholic lands, the new attitude can best be exemplified by the successful Counter-Reformation campagn to stop the irreverent goings-on in cemeteries. By the last half of the eighteenth century, as François Lebrun has pointed out, the cemeteries were properly walled and policed, silent and — empty. Somehow by banning "misrule" from the cemeteries, the authorities had also robbed the graveyard of its power to attract the living.[2]

---

[1] Rapp, *L'Église*, 152. Jeremy Taylor, *The Rule and Exercises of Holy Dying* (London, 1847), 77-78 (ch. 3, section 1). This work and the whole question of changing attitudes toward death are fully discussed in Beaty, *Craft of Dying*.

[2] *Ibid.*, 247; Thomas, *Religion*, 106, H. P. Clive, "The Calvinists and the Question of Dancing in the 16th Century," *Bibliothèque d'humanisme et renaissance*, XXIII (1961), 296-99. Lebrun, *Les hommes*, 480-86.

At the beginning of this essay, we considered some of the difficulties that can arise in understanding popular religion if we insist on sorting behavior first and foremost into categories of "religious" and "magical", or "rational" and "irrational". It turns out that the categories "traditional" and "modern" may put similar obstacles in the way of understanding. Not that we should discard them, when they help us link together certain documented cultural characteristics of a whole society or of certain classes within it. Still, either because historians are more familiar with "modern" forms or because they have some continuing commitment to evolutionary schemes, behavior dubbed "traditional" is often hard for them to explicate. This paper has stressed the meaning and uses of traditional forms by way of compensation. Among the general characteristics of "traditional" popular religion that emerge are its willingness, first, to give organizational expression to "the internal articulations" of society [1] and even to encourage such articulation (as was the case with the dead) and, second, to give ritual expression to a wide range of feelings and moods, from the cruel to the comic. In however many respects this religious life was prescribed, it could achieve psychological flexibility from the abundance of its ritual. Also we have noted the possibilities of serious social criticism in rite or play which vigorously turns worldly values or hierarchies upside down. Should we properly use the word "traditional" for this? Not if we mean by that adjective that such forms of behavior are wholly unsuited to contemporary culture.

---

[1] Bossy, "Counter-Reformation," 68.

PART THREE

HUMANISM AND THE ARTS

1. THE RELIGIOUS THOUGHT OF THE ITALIAN HUMANISTS, AND THE REFORMERS: ANTICIPATION OR AUTONOMY?

CHARLES TRINKAUS

The University of Michigan

For the intellectual historian who has ventured into the study of the history of religious ideas there is the awareness that he has but traced the course of a single thread or two within the seamless garment of history. And yet he cannot entirely refrain from looking at the results of his researches in their general historical bearing. So it is with the history of the religious thought of the Renaissance and the Reformation that there is an obligation bearing on the historian of Italian humanist religious writing to consider its relationship both to the wider context of its own epoch and to that of the subsequent, possibly more dramatic, Reform. Each of these two critical phases in the formation of the modern world has been given distinctive, highly differentiated characters by some at least of its historians, and these periods have sometimes been seen as representing even opposite values to our contemporaries. Yet each of them, however interpreted, has been regarded well-nigh universally as revolutionary in its breaking of continuity with past tradition and in its introduction of viable new approaches to man's material and spiritual life. This essay will, then, venture anew with full awareness of complexity and necessary tentativeness into the historical problems of the relationships of Italian humanist religious thought with late medieval scholastic theology and with (necessarily but a few) ideas of the Reformers, weighing but not finally answering the delicate question of dependence, independence and interdependence.

Moreover, it plunges into the context of an almost chaotic variety of historical interpretations of the broadest range of evidence and human activities with its thin line of *Ideengeschichte*. For the more these epochs are studied the more different aspects of each are singled out as granting to it what historians insist must be its "revolutionary" essence. Changes in the economic structure, in political ideas and behavior, in legal institutions, in family life, in moral attitudes, in education and higher culture, in philosophy and science, in the relationships of church and state, in methods of warfare, in constitutions, in attitudes toward past historical periods and tradition, in religiosity, in theology, in ecclesiology, in the functioning of ecclesiastics, in church finance, in the conception and usage of the sacraments, in church governance, in the attitude toward Scriptures and Tradition, in the final authority in religious matters, in epistemology or metaphysics, in the need for grace for insight or justification, in the role of works, in the status of man as conceived in relation to God—all of these changes and many others are singled out as the one critical element that either produced the revolutionary character of the period or was its chief consequence. While all these separate aspects of these periods may be supposed to constitute the strands from which a seamless garment is woven, to the working historian they too often rather seem but the scattered fragments of colored glass from a broken mosaic that it is his task to cement together once again and so reconstruct the splendid whole of history.

In our particular instance we have set out to show (what I cannot think should have been anything but obvious) that the humanists of the Italian Renaissance, as men living in a strongly (if not deeply) religious era, were themselves heavily concerned in their writings with religious questions, and made from their own standpoint and through their own humanistic intellectual disciplines some important contributions to the history of Christian thought.[1] But such has been the historiography of the Renaissance since the time of Voltaire (and indeed since the time of Erasmus, Luther and Bellarmine) that this period came to be looked upon as the tragic interval when Christian Europeans lost their bearings and flirted with sensualism and the alluring doctrines of a pagan Epicureanism. Or, on the other hand, the Renaissance has been interpreted as chiefly responsible for the ensuing blasphemies of the Reformation, or as the inevitable consequence of a medieval Catholicism that departed from its evangelical origins and blended far too promiscuously with the secular world. Or, from a non-religious perspective, the Renaissance has been hailed, and is still hailed, as the harbinger of the Enlightenment, of the repudiation of

---

[1] This was, certainly, one major goal of, *In Our Image and Likeness : Humanity and Divinity in Italian Humanist Thought*, 2 vols. (London and Chicago, 1970), though I should not wish it to be judged as innovative as this sounds nor limited to this purpose. The ensuing paper is based heavily on this book but seeks to explore an issue only peripherally touched upon in it. Future citations will be to *IOIAL*.

the ecclesiastical domination of secular life characteristic of medieval society, as the first feeble expression of, if not an atheistic or agnostic view of the cosmos, a blithely irreligious outlook, as the first phase of modern secular culture and of a bourgeois civic community where ethics and politics had become fully secularized and human energies turned toward the practical solution of purely earthly problems. Thus a combination of secular and religious historiography manages to dispense with both the Renaissance and the Reformation (Catholic or Protestant) as mutually alternative aberrations or interruptions in the smooth and continuing flow of the course of European history (with the alternative period functioning as the glorious seed time for the revolutionizing of the modern world).[1]

But assuming the continuing historical existence and relevance of the Catholic and Protestant Reformations, is it possible to read the Renaissance out of European history as either mere decadent continuation of the medieval past or as abortive and unnecessary revolutionary caesura ? Is it possible to look at the art of the Italian Renaissance without observing the overwhelmingly religious and Christian character of its subjects ? For even where classical subjects come to be depicted, it has been made amply clear how Christian was their allegorical meaning. It is true that the Church was the great patron of the arts as their principal consumer and thus dictated this subject-matter, yet often enough the patrons of ecclesiastical art were also laymen. It is also true, whether with clerical or lay patronage, that Christian theme is often unfolded against a richly sensuous background of colors and forms sometimes revealing artists' and patrons' delight in the lush or the lovely of this world (and the next), sometimes manifesting almost photographically the lavishness of the contemporary scene and its material life. A celestial vision of both worlds may indeed have displaced the agony and the asceticism, but the Christian conceptualization cannot be denied.[2]

---

[1] It would require a history of modern historiography to document this assertion properly, and Ferguson's well-known *The Renaissance in Historical Thought* (Cambridge, Mass., 1948), would merely begin it. The point is, however, to stress the mythological aspects of our *Renaissance-Begriffe*, which may well play an analogous role in our historical perceptions to that of Antiquity in the Renaissance, itself. Lewis W. Spitz is preparing the welcome companion-piece : *The Reformation in Historical Thought*.

[2] The oft-mentioned vista of Renaissance Florence as a frontispiece for manuscripts of *De civitate Dei*, perhaps overlooks the irony that this view is simultaneously city of man and city of God. Cf. A. Chastel, *Art et humanisme à Florence au temps de Laurent le Magnifique* (Paris, 1959), 182 and n. 4.

Patrons of the arts and of letters, ecclesiastical or secular, were unquestionably men who regarded themselves as religious and Christian, however much the secular ruler or patrician may have engaged in the worldly arts of commerce, politics and war. How then could they be regarded as a social or institutional source for the development of a non-religious outlook? Indeed it would seem that one of the vast and crucial phenomena of this period was the blending of the religious and the secular such as is increasingly coming to interest at least some historians of the arts, culture and society. But for evidence of the conscious recognition or pursuit of a new conception of religion more satisfyingly blending the human and the divine, should one not look at the men of letters and the philosophers (as well as to the direct manifestations in behavior)? For new ideas or new structuring of old ideas would seem to find expression from men of ideas however much their social environments may be thought to engender the conditions that provoke new thinking. And one should look, perhaps, at new types of thinkers, uncommitted by institutional and professional connections to established ways of thought and expression. Such at least are some of the assumptions we must make in seeking for the general historical significance of Italian humanist religious thought and for its relations with other contemporary intellectual and pratical movements and with preceding and succeeding phases of culture. And we must, as we have been striving to do, stress continuity and change simultaneously.[1]

Humanism, as an efflorescence of the rhetorical tradition, was medieval as well as Renaissance, as we well know from Alcuin's influence at the court of Charlemagne, or from the potency (however disputed) of John of Salisbury and his school in twelfth-century Chartres. Yet mid-fourteenth-century Petrarchan humanism was new for its time, building out of the isolated fragments of a rhetorical and classical revival of the late thirteenth century, especially from Dante's circle presided over by Brunetto Latini, from the Paduan cenacolo of

---

[1] As Professor Oberman argues above, thought also is history. However, I would certainly stress the importance of documenting and analyzing what Professor Trexler calls "religious behavior", whether popular, elitist, lay or clerical, illiterate or erudite, and I would certainly expect there to be important divergences. But in the final analysis, thinkers and writers remain members of their culture however much their critical and articulate self-consciousness seems to place them above or aside it. The "outsider" is always also "insider."

Albertino Mussato and others, from Arezzo, and even from Bologna of the great university where Dante's Giovanni del Vergilio taught.

In the dark shadows and nauseating fumes of the depths of the *Inferno*, Dante presents his picture of the disastrous sins and crimes that were characteristic of his day. And it was, indeed, these new modes of social behavior, sins according to Dante's perspective, perhaps secularism according to a later conception, that lay the basis for the great moral, religious and philosophical crisis of the early and middle Trecento. For these souls of the *Inferno* were Dante's fellow Italians and Florentines. And Dante had to look nostalgically backward a good century to find many who were suitable for Paradise. The world of the early fourteenth century did not fit easily into the older Christian vision, though the earlier medieval past also had its share of spectacular sinners.

One must be aware of movements and counter-movements, currents and cross-currents, deeply shadowed relief and delicate nuance in history. And the fourteenth century manifested all of these : from the serene joy of a Giotto fresco or the *Fioretti* of San Francesco to the gloomy *Speculum humanae vitae* and the death frescoes of the Campo Santo. Nonetheless by mid-century, domestic disasters such as harvest failures, bankruptcies and revolutions, national tragedies such as the slaughter of the flower of French chivalry in the opening battles of the Hundred Years War, the ominous symbolism of the kidnapping at Anagni and the quartering of the Roman papacy at Avignon, were crowned by the Black Death with its bitter harvest of corpses and deserted towns and villages.

Much has been written of the melancholy and despair which followed in the wake of the Black Death, of its impact on literature and the arts, of its stimulation of widespread penitential movements, including the spectacular processions of flagellants. In very fact the most profound transformation and uprooting of medieval institutions and modes of behavior and perception, of affectivity and thought, were already occurring. It is too complicated to weigh here whether these drastic external events, and prime among them the epidemics of bubonic plague which crossed Europe only to return again and again for the next half-century and more, were the sole causes of the profound changes that were to come, or whether they only hastened them on. Yet even earlier there had begun a religious crisis of even more profound and lasting dimensions than these political and demographic crises, one that did not find its resolution for more than two hundred years. When it did (and such as it did in the Reformations), it left Europe divided into warring sects not hesitating to smite, stab, burn, slay in behalf of creed and dogma. Thus it is our perception that the complex question of the inter-relations of late Middle Ages, Renaissance and Reformations finds a unity in the common condition of response to a great and enduring crisis.[1]

This spiritual crisis which in the fourteenth century succeeded to the momentary and fragile thirteenth-century sense of triumph witnessed on the popular level a host of religious movements seeking a revival of piety, a return to the ideal of the Apostolic Life, a preparation for the coming of the Third Age of monkly brotherhood, or, if it so turned out, Armageddon. The serenity of Giotto and the optimism of the early decades proved to be not its major but its minor key, and the depths of anxiety and despair were everywhere to be seen. The degradation and corruption of ecclesiastical institutions were only too evident.

The religious and spiritual crisis also had its intellectual side, and Renaissance humanism together with Ockhamism, the *via moderna*, were manifestations of it.[2] While my chief concern is with humanism, it is necessary to comment first on the historical role of the Ockhamist movement in order to clarify and understand that of the humanists. The process by which the medieval world-view (if it can be argued that there was a single one) broke down was long and complex. Four-teenth-century Ockhamism and Petrarchan humanism were two paral-lel modes of asserting a repudiation of preceding thirteenth-century scholastic efforts to forge a unity between revelation and reason, to build an ever more refined Aristotelian metaphysical structure out into the non-perceptual space of faith and theology. In this repudiation Ockhamism made its major impact in the two principal problem areas where inherited Christian theology was being challenged by historical events, namely the theoretical and the moral.

---

[1] "Crisis" is admittedly a problematical term that can also exploit a dramatic pseudo-pathos. Yet if there has to be a turning-point in history it is perhaps better that it should be grasped in the perduring, chronic sense of two centuries or so rather than bursting out every three or four gears. I am enough of a structuralist to believe that "secular" change is the historian's proper concern.

[2] *Pace* the important statements earlier in this volume by Oberman, Courtenay and Kristeller on the use of nominalism, *via moderna*, Ockhamism. Since there is no agreement (nor perhaps should be), I use these terms interchangeably but not totally indiscrimi-natingly. *Via moderna* is the most generic, Ockhamism the most specific, nominalism possibly the most satisfactory.

When in the twelfth and thirteenth centuries a conception of a rationally comprehensible, naturally determined universe, drawn from secular (i.e. Greco-Arabic) science, was projected against the prevailing anthropomorphic, mythopoeic Biblical vision of the creation, somehow these two views of the universe had to be reconciled, or one of them vindicated against the other. The growth of secular natural philosophy at the arts faculties of the universities, first the northern and then more and more importantly the Italian, meant indeed that from the beginnings of scholastic thought there were those who saw no possibility of a theoretical reconciliation but at best separate and parallel realms entertained by reason and faith. The growth of Ockhamism and the *via moderna* in this context meant, on the other hand, that an even more critical and direct assault on the stronghold of thirteenth-century scholastic theology (already challenged by natural philosophy) was taking place.[1]

The older theology was undermined by the Ockhamists' twin denials that perception and comprehension of earthly things could validly be extrapolated into a theology, and that the all-powerful God of the Christian faith could be constricted by the requirements of a logically rational metaphysical system. In place of rational theology, the Ockhamist sought a direct, intuitive approach to God in a renewed theology of revelation and faith, if not a down-right fideism. The contemporary spread of fourteenth-century mysticism indicates that simultaneously a more direct approach to the Deity was being sought in many quarters. Such are the intellectual and theoretical dimensions of the great Renaissance-Reformation religious crisis, and this was not resolved, if it was then resolved, until the age of Galileo and Newton.[2]

However, it was the religious and moral aspects of this crisis that were of significance for understanding the humanists' role. The same awakening and expansion of European societies which brought Greek science, logic and metaphysics to the Latin West in translations of

---

[1] These comments are my distillation of the literature discussed above by Courtenay and cited there. The last sentence here indicates that Professor Courtenay's salutary stress on the modifying tendencies of recent scholarship and on the links of fourteenth-century scholasticism with thirteenth still leaves the impression of a significant discontinuity, which now needs to be more carefully stated.

[2] Despite Professor Oberman's emphasis on somewhat different elements I am gratified by the substantial agreement that seems to exist on the general "shape" of the history of this period—an agreement at which we arrived by quite independent routes.

Arabic and Byzantine manuscript texts had generated the proto-
modern worlds of the medieval commune and the Renaissance city-
state, of the industrial towns and the international commercial and
financial community, of rural crisis and agricultural expansion, of the
national monarchies and the territorial princely states. New, demanding, activist, ambitious modes of experience and behavior drew many
sectors of the European populace into its networks. It was not simply
an early phase of a bourgeois revolution; it was much more complexly
an enormous quickening of the tempo of life, an outpouring of human
energy from an expanding population that bore its fruits not only in
the new centers of material wealth and new types of economic, political
and ecclesiastical activity in the greatest variety. but also in new kinds
of misery, suffering, inner tensions, competitiveness, warfare and domestic violence. The responses of the men of the eleventh, twelfth and
thirteenth centuries to their rapidly changing conditions of life were
magnificent in their efforts to create effective new modes of order—the
consolidation of the Church through the centralizing Hildebrandine
reforms and the creation of the papal and episcopal bureaucracies and
an ecclesiastical judicial system, the new urban and feudal types of
political organization, the revival and institution of a secular juridical
system based on Roman law, the evolution of the university as the
training ground for these new professions. Yet both the elements of
disorder and anarchic conflict on the one hand, and those of order,
organization, professionalization, on the other, transformed and challenged the traditional religious experience and conceptions of an
acceptable moral life.

In breaking down the thirteenth century's theological and philosophical syntheses, the Ockhamists were equally concerned with the
seeming untenability of a moral theology that rationalized the good
civic life, set forth in Aristotle's *Ethics*, as the secular equivalent of
Christian charity. Almost more critical than the problem of epistemology (the knowledge of God, the relationship of faith and intellect)
in the Ockhamist school was the problem of the relationship of free will
and grace, analyzed by theologians in incredible complexity, and leading
frequently to a dual system where the good citizen freely and deliberately acted in this world with restraint and responsibility according to
natural moral canons but found himself entirely dependent on supernatural grace for his salvation as a justified Christian.

At the same time it was averred that by God's ordered power His
covenant with believers meant that He would not withold his grace

from those who had done their voluntary best to live virtuously, according to the principle *facere quod in se est*. This combination of a theology of grace and a voluntarist ethics would appear simultaneously among the humanists.

Although there were many other motives for the revival of the rhetorical tradition and classicism in the Italian humanist movement, certainly the Petrarchan pattern also needs to be understood in the context of the same religious and moral crisis that in the north had given birth in those very years to Ockhamism. Humanism, the classical-Christian rhetorical tradition, did not require, nor did it develop a systematic philosophy or a theology. A number of individual humanists, however, did develop philosophical and religious positions of their own and made greater contributions to the history of late medieval religion than has sometimes been thought. Thus, though any systematic comparison of two philosophical or theological systems, nominalist and humanist, is out of the question (because of the unsystematic character of most humanist religious writings, at least), still there are some striking parallels between the theoretical postulates of the rhetorical tradition (where, as in the case of Salutati or Valla, they are formulated) and those of nominalism. The anti-metaphysical stance, the tendency toward epistemological probabilism as far as universals are concerned, the preoccupation with the relation between word and thing, with signs, language and reality are common to both, as well as a direct factual concern with human motivation and action. Where the two traditions differed was essentially in the more practical, action-oriented character of humanist writing, which contrasted with the theoretical interests of the scholastics of the *via moderna*, in the usual humanist avoidance of any systematic analysis of epistemological issues, though not of the structure of speech and language. The humanists who talked about the Ockhamists were, by and large, from Petrarch on, contemptuous of the endless intricacy and the *ventosa sophistica* of these *Brittani* and "prattling dialecticians". But both movements shared, perhaps unknown to themselves, a common repudiation of those thirteenth-century scholastic systems that sought an accommodation with Aristotle. As Petrarch's invective *De sui ipsius et multorum ignorantia* shows so clearly, he was even more opposed to the Artistotelian natural philosophy of his own day, which seemed to abandon concern with faith and any effort toward a Christian life. The early humanists tended to confuse the intellectualistic arguments of the Ockhamists with those of the natural philosophers and the physicians in a broad condemnation of the irrelevance of all scholastic philosophy. Petrarch did not take into account the quasi-fideism and the anti-intellectualist voluntarism of the nominalists, so similar to his own.[1]

He had a greater sympathy and bond with those clerical intellectuals of the fourteenth century who attempted to revive the theology of St. Augustine. Critical in Petrarch's image of the saint was the latter's conflict between his experience of a quest for happiness and his intellectual position of Christianized Neoplatonism.

While it is necessary to reject the thesis that Petrarch and Salutati were influenced by the order of Augustinian Hermits in any formal way, it is also true that they found a close spiritual kinship with the ideas of such Augustinians as Dionigi of Borgo San Sepolcro and Luigi Marsili. Moreover, the ideas of such a major figure in the order as Gregory of Rimini have a striking parallel to those of some of the early

---

[1] There has, of course, been a stress on the humanists' attacks on scholasticism as directed against their contemporary nominalists and natural philosophers, particularly by Professor Kristeller in his classic "Humanism and Scholasticism in the Italian Renaissance" of 1944, reprinted most conveniently in his *Renaissance Thought* I (New York, 1961). His *Le Thomisme et la pensée italienne de la Renaissance* (Montréal and Paris, 1967), might also seem to indicate a continuity with thirteenth century scholasticism. Moreover, such recent studies of Lorenzo Valla as Mario Fois, *Il pensiero cristiana di Lorenzo Valla nel quadro storico-culturale del suo ambiente* (Rome, 1969), 64-8; Giovanni di Napoli, *Lorenzo Valla, Filosofia e Religione nell' Umanesimo Italiano* (Rome, 1971), 25-77, 110-124 as well as Cesare Vasoli, *La dialettica e la retorica dell' Umanesimo : 'Invenzione' e 'Metodo' nella cultura del XV e XVI secolo* (Milan, 1968), tend so stress humanist criticisms of nominalism. However, as Kristeller knows, admiration for Aquinas was limited in numbers, and Valla's praise of him, as Di Napoli also is aware, was for his piety, not his theology. What seems to be true is that the humanists, especially Valla, were very critical of nominalist dialectic, and of Aristotelian metaphysical categories. They seem not to have been aware, or possibly to comprehend, that nominalist "Covenant" theology and the *potentia ordinata* demanded precisely the kind of textual-historical approach the humanists were dhemselves advocating. Salutati most definitely took the categories of his theological discussion from contemporary scholasticism and, while not agreeing with all of it, certainly coincided in viewpoint on a number of points. In Valla's case where scholastics made a strict separation of theology and philosophy, he could only approve, but where theology was 'contaminated' by dialectic and metaphysics, he would heartly disapprove. The most recent study of Valla seems to place its emphasis rightly on the revolutionary character of Valla's theological conceptions and methods, which were central to the development of the culture as a whole and not limited to humanists. In fact, Vallas greatest support came from figures such as Cusanus and Bessarion. Cf. Salvatore I. Camporeale, *Lorenzo Valla, Umanesimo e Teologia* (Florence, 1972).

humanists. Gregory, who is usually counted as belonging in some respects to the nominalist school, turned to man's internal subjective experiences as a reality-basis on which a Christian theology could be constructed, and in this deliberately imitated the alleged founder of his order. As is well known, Petrarch constructed his *Secretum* around just such a self-analysis of his inner experiences in his search for an existentially authentic religious vision that might overpower the distracting and fragmenting allure of secular motives. He replaced the Ockhamists' logical analysis with psychological analysis.[1]

When we look more closely at Petrarch's surprizingly developed religious philosophy, we discover, what our knowledge of him could predict, that he is exclusively concerned with the subjectivity of belief and the sense of salvation, with how the individual regards himself in this life in relation to the divine promises. Men everywhere are overcome with despair. Even in the Carthusian monastery where his brother Gerardo was a monk, he feels that the brothers' most dangerous enemy is their despair of justification. But was it not also within the fold of the Augustinian Hermits that Brother Martin Luther first experienced his sense of despair and of divine hatred that led him to his subjective theology of *sola fide*? Let us look at a few passages from Petrarch's treatise addressed to the Carthusian Brothers, his *De otio religioso*.[2] I do not know if one can ever answer the question posed in our title—anticipation or autonomy?—but the amazing closeness of Petrarch's religiosity to Luther's will permit us to face it in all its sharpness.

As in Luther's case, despair stems from man's consciousness of his weakness and his sins. Mankind's enemy would not dare to assert that anything is beyond God's power, as he would then lose all credence. Instead he insinuates that while God can do all and wishes to give all goods to mankind, it is man himself who is unfit and unworthy to receive such gifts, and many begin to meditate as follows:

> God indeed is the best; but I am the worst; what proportion is there in such great contrariety? I know ... how far envy is removed from That Best One, and on the contrary I know how tightly iniquity is bound to me ... I. confess the mercy of

---

[1] U. Mariani, *Il Petrarca e gli Agostiniani* (Rome, 1946); IOIAL, chap. I; cf. H. A. Oberman, *The Harvest of Medieval Theology* (Cambridge, Mass., 1963), 57-98 and passim. G. Leff, *Gregory of Rimini* (Manchester, 1961).

[2] Ed. G. Rotondi [Studi e Testi, 195] (Vatican City, 1958), cit. as Rotondi. References will be to Rotondi and IOIAL where the Latin is given in the notes.

God is infinite, but I profess that I am not fit for it, and as much as it is greater, so much narrower is my mind, filled with vices. Nothing is impossible to God; in me there is a total impossibility of rising, buried as I am in such a great heap of sins. He is potent to save : I am unable to be saved. For however great the clemency of God, certainly it does not exclude justice, and mercy as immense as you wish must be reduced to the measure of my miseries...[1]

It is this sense of the nothingness of man's efforts at sanctity that seems to have pervaded the later Middle Ages, and it underlay one of the central doctrines of the Ockhamist school, the emphasis on God's absolute power. His *potentia absoluta* could not be related in any rational way to human insights and experiences; only faith in His promises could reassure. So, too, Petrarch finds the doctrine of the infinitude of God's power so overshadows man that it renders hope that man can win salvation through his own powers and merits utterly ridiculous. At the same time, it produces the great assurance that despite enormous distance between the divine and the human, God will save man. Thus he counsels that divine omnipotence should be measured psychologically, not rationally :

These thoughts and others of the same sort which enter souls, when they bring them a salutary fear and dispel torpor, are to be considered as a sort of silent counsel of angels loving us; yet when they take away all hope and trust, they are to be avoided as hostile errors and dangerous roads to ruin. For where do they lead the soul which follows them except to desperation, the worst of all evils ? But nothing should terrify us, since the divine power is not limited by any conditions of nature, nor does it employ the force of its own action only toward those things which are properly disposed, but brings order to those which are indisposed. The mercy of God by far transcends human misery and justice... ... Anyone who considers that He will not show mercy to someone who wishes forgiveness, or that He is only able to show mercy in proportion to man's sin, thinks badly about God and has a poor opinion concerning His power and mercy, since the sin of a man, however great it is, is certainly finite, the goodness of God infinite, His power infinite. ... We seem worthy of punishment, unworthy of mercy, and in both we are not mistaken : for it is our part to be afflicted, His to be merciful. And it is a worthy thing for His dignity to swallow up our lack of dignity, which certainly could not happen if the sin of man could impede the mercy of God.[2]

Finally, passing over a long discussion of the dynamics of faith, we come upon a statement which is appositely close to Luther's doctrine. After quoting St. Paul, Romans vii : 22-23, "For I delight in the law

---

[1] Rotondi, 24-5; IOIAL 29, 334 n. 58.
[2] Rotondi, 25; IOIAL, 30, 335 n. 63.

of God after the inward man : but I see another law in my members warring against the law in my mind, and bringing me into captivity to the law of sin which is in my members." Petrarch asks :

Who indeed does not fear what he sees the Apostle fearing ? Or who in such great danger would hope for any other gift except that according to the apostolic counsel "by walking in the spirit he should not fulfil the lust of his flesh ?" And since this, as I have said, without God granting, cannot be done, he should say with the same Apostle, mourning and fearing, "O, wretched man that I am, who shall deliver me from the body of this death ?"; and resuming hope solely through the mercy of God he should reply to himself, "I thank God through Jesus Christ our Lord"; to that One who alone is able to succor in this internal and domestic battle it must be cried out; He must be humbly beseeched that He should liberate us from the body of this death, *whence the merit of man does not liberate but the grace of God alone* [unde meritum hominis non liberat, sed gratia Dei solius], to Whom nothing, I do not say is impossible, but not even difficult.[1]

Petrarch, of course, was putting forth the doctrine of *sola gratia*, not *sola fide*. But the anticipation of the latter is clear enough, and there is much in Petrarch's psychological emphasis on the necessity of faith in the soul of the Christian that can link his position with Luther's. With respect to those scholars and commentators on Luther who stress the uniqueness of his theological position, and its insight, one may point to the great closeness of inner religious dynamics of the two positions. Yet at the same time one may raise the question whether it was, after all, theology which brought about the Reformation. After all this statement of Petrarch's and so many similar ones that do indeed anticipate Luther, did not by themselves bring about the ecclesiastical separation of Christendom into new schisms and churches. Perhaps the basic differences between the two men lay in their historical circumstances and roles. It is clear in this instance that the Reformation, however much European history may have been leading up to it in the preceding two centuries, was not a matter of the history of ideas alone but involved the whole concatenation of events culminating in the successful break from Rome, "successful "in that Luther's break became a historical break, and Luther's heresy became a new orthodoxy, whatever one may think of more recent oecumenical views that the heresy was not a heresy, the break not an intended break, and that canonically the schism is capable of repair.[2] The rejection of the exter-

---

[1] Rotondi 66-7; IOIAL, 40-1, 340-1 n. 86.

[2] Cf. Hubert Jedin, "Mutamenti della interpretazione cattolica della figura di Lutero e loro limiti," *Rivista di Storia della Chiesa in Italia*, 23 (1969), 361-77.

nals of religion, both sacramental and ecclesiological, remained only an implied one for Petrarch who never questioned either the sanctity of the sacraments, the validity of monasticism, or the authority of popes and bishops, however, severely he criticized the abuses and corruption of the Avignonese curia. The crucial difference lay in the degree of finality about these questions, and Petrarch, however much he seems to anticipate Luther theologically, must be seen as playing a role that was autonomous to the development of the religious thought of the humanists in Italy (and his other readers) where his ideas had their chief consequences.

Fittingly, we are also able to make a comparison between Petrarch and Calvin. Much as Petrarch the humanist admired Cicero, Seneca and Horace for their literary gifts and for their powers of persuasion, which men of his time should emulate in calling men back to virtue, he also severely criticized their conceptions of the relationship of human virtue to divine power. There is an implied Pelagianism in the rhetorical notion that man can call man to virtue, as there was equally in the Thomist notion of the approximation of Aristotelian civic virtue to the golden rule, and as there was in the Ockhamist notion of man's freedom to be virtuous in humanly conceived terms, though dependent on grace for justification (which was presumed not to be witheld from the man who had done his very best to fulfil the divine commandments: *facere quod in se est*). Petrarch follows the same path as the nominalists, for he sharply criticizes the claim of the honored pagans that virtue is a sufficient goal for man.

> Thus when the illustrious pagan philosophers refer everything to virtue, the philosopher of Christ (*Cristi philosophus*) refers virtue itself to the author of virtue, God, and by using virtue enjoys God, nor ever stops with his mind before he has reached Him. For thus he will hear a certain great philosopher of Christ saying, "Thou hast established us for thy sake, and thus our heart is restless until it rests in Thee."[1]

Not only is virtue not the goal for the "philosopher of Christ" (Erasmus was not the first by any means to use this phrase), but virtue itself depends on divine grace. Petrarch then quotes Horace : "It is enough to pray God who gives and takes away that He should give life and wealth : I will myself bring peace to my soul," and Cicero : "Then death is waited in most serenity when a man is able to console

---

[1] Rotondi, 92; IOIAL, 45, 342-3 n. 97; Aug. Conf., I, i.

himself with his own praises [for his virtues] while life is declining."
Jean Calvin in the final edition of the *Institutes* similarly discusses the
ancients' claim to virtue as within the power of man :

> Moreover some of them have advanced to such a degree of presumption as to boast
> that we are indebted to the gods for our life, but for a virtuous and religious one to
> ourselves; whence also that assertion of Cicero, in the person of Cotta, that, since
> every man acquires virtue for himself, none of the wise men have ever thanked
> God for it. "For," he says, "we are praised for virtue, and in virtue we glory;
> which would not be the case, it it were a gift of God, and did not originate from
> ourselves." And a little after : "This is the judgement of all men, that fortune must
> be asked of God, but that wisdom must be derived from ourselves."[1]

Petrarch replied to this classical argument that man's virtue, which
the pagan attributes to himself, is not his at all but is directly a gift
of God.

> What thence besides sin remains which, since it is voluntary nor derived from any-
> where else than from the soul itself, certainly is established as the sole property
> of man ? Therefore there is no matter of consolation or glory for him from what is
> in the power of others; in what is in his own power, moreover, there is much matter
> of shame and fear; no one is such a slave of sin that he does not know this.[2]

One may recall at this point that Calvin, though carefully reserving
to the eternal decree of divine predestination man's spiritual powers :
to be virtuous, to become justified, to inherit eternal life, nevertheless grants a very full range of secular capacities to man, himself,
and especially praises the ancients who had first developed them—the
lawyers, natural philosophers, rhetoricians and logicians, physicians
and mathematicians.

> We shall not be able even to read the writings of the ancients on these subjects
> without great admiration; we shall admire them, because we shall be constrained
> to acknowledge them to be truly excellent.[3]

---

[1] Ioannis Calvini, *Institutio Religionis Christianae*, ed. Wilhelm Baum, Eduard
Cunitz, Eduard Reuss, Vol. II (1559 ed.) (Brunswick, 1869), I, i, 3, col. 187, Quin etiam
eo licentiae quidam eorum proruperunt, ut iactarint deorum quidem esse munus, quod
vivimus; nostrum vero quod bene sancteque vivimus. Unde et illud Ciceronis in persona
Cottae, quia sibi quisque virtutem acquirit, neminem ex sapientibus unquam de ea
gratias Deo egisse. Propter virtutem enim laudamur, inquit, ut in virtute gloriamur.
Quod non fieret si donum esset Dei, non a nobis. Ac paulo post: iudicium hoc omnium
mortalium est, fortunam a Deo petendam, ab se ipso sumendam esse sapientiam. The
English translations are John Allen's.

[2] Rotondi, 100; IOIAL, 45, 343 n. 99.

[3] *Institutiones*, ed. cit., II, ii, 15, col. 198, Imo ne sine ingenti quidem admiratione

Yet, Calvin argues, the Fathers of the Church, particularly the Greeks, extolled human powers too greatly for fear both that they would

incur the derision of the philosophers ...; and, in the next place might administer to the flesh, of itself naturally too torpid to all that is good, a fresh occasion for slothfulness.[1]

Petrarch, it is well known, was much concerned with *accidia*, his own and others'. *Accidia* was his version of the old sin of sloth or indolence. Moreover, as we have seen, the state of despair, which led to distrust in God's mercy, was the true form of this very sloth.[2]

In his most popular Latin prose work, *De remediis utriusque fortunae*, Petrarch inaugurated the discussions in the Renaissance of that most central of humanist concerns[3] : the nature, powers and condition of man. And Calvin, in the very chapter of the *Institutes* from which we have been quoting, sets forth his interpretation of this very same theme. "Man, in His Present State, Despoiled of Freedom of Will, and Subjected to a Miserable Slavery" is his translated title. Calvin wishes to make clear within the terms of his theology what may properly be said on the dual themes of the dignity of man and the misery of the human condition, and he takes it as an occasion to criticize his predecessors, both Christian theologians and pagan philosophers. And he wishes to set forth his doctrine in such terms that it will avoid the twin dangers of man's falling into slothfulness through excessive discouragement concerning his powers, or of his arrogating to himself, through excessive pride in his capacities, the honor which rightfully belongs to God. His purpose is not only expository but rhetorical as well,

for man, being taught that he has nothing good left in his possession, and being surrounded on every side with the most miserable necessity, should, nevertheless, be instructed to aspire to the good of which he is destitute, and to the liberty of

---

veterum scripta legere de his rebus poterimus; admirabimur autem, quia praeclara, ut sunt, cogemur agnoscere.

[1] Ibid., II, ii, 4, col. 188, Ex quibus veteres mihi videntur hoc consilio vires humanas sic extulisse, ne si impotentiam diserte essent confessi, primum philosophorum ipsorum cachinnos, quibuscum tunc certamen habebant, excuterent; deinde carni suapte sponte nimis ad bonum torpenti novam desidiae occasionem praeberent.

[2] Cf. Siefgried Wenzel, "Petrarch's Accidia," *Studies in the Renaissance* VIII (1961), 36-48.

[3] Cf. Klaus Heitmann, *Fortuna und Virtus, Eine Studie zu Petrarcas Lebensweisheit*, *Studi italiani*, I (Cologne-Graz), 1958. Citations will be to Bibl. Vatic., Cod. Urb. lat. 334.

which he is deprived; and he should be roused from indolence with more earnestness than if he were supposed to be possessed of the greatest strength.[1]

Interestingly, the entire point of Petrarch's treatise was to supply an encyclopedia of remedies, not for the accidents of fortune, but for their psychological impact on men. Indeed, Book I is intended to reduce the false state of elation induced by favorable events by stressing in situation after situation the false picture of man's truly miserable condition that the fortunate man entertains in order to induce him to regain his sobriety. Book II supplied the remedies for bad fortune, in similar fashion consoling against the state of melancholy that unfavorable events, both major and trivial, bring about. It is in chapter 93 that he addresses the general state of despair produced by thought of the misery of the human condition—*accidia* again. And here Petrarch sets forth what was to be the first of the Renaissance treatises on the dignity and excellence of man. Commencing with man's creation in the image and likeness of God, passing through the capacities of mind and soul, human inventions, the bounties of nature, man's superiority to animals through his creativity, Petrarch comes climactically to man's salvation and deification through the Incarnation :

> Add the immortality of the soul and the road to heaven and for a small price an inestimable reward, and what I knowingly delayed until the end is so great that I would not understand them through my own powers unless I had learned through the teaching of faith : the hope of resurrection, and that this very body after death will be reassumed, indeed agile, and shining and inviolable with much glory in resurrection, And what surpasses all dignity, not only human but angelic, humanity itself is so conjoined to divinity that He who was God is become man, and likewise one in number He begins to be God and man, perfectly containing two natures in himself, so that He makes man God, having been made man out of ineffable God, and His humility is the highest happiness and glory of man ... Does the human condition not seem to you much ennobled in this one person ? And does his misery

---

[1] *Institutiones*, ed. cit., II, ii, 1, Hominem arbitrii libertate nunc esse spoliatum et miseriae servituti addictum—title of Cap. II ; Nam ubi omni rectitudine abdicatur homo, statim ex eo desidiae occasionem arripit; et quia nihil ad iustitiae studium valere per se dicitur, illud totum, quasi iam nihil ad se pertineat, susque deque habet. Rursum vel minutulum illi quidpiam arrogari non potest, quin et Deo praeripiatur suus honor, et ipse temeraria confidentia labefactetur. Ad hos ergo scopulos ne impingamus, tenendus hic cursus erit, ut homo nihil boni penes se reliquum sibi esse edoctus, et miserrima undique necessitate circumseptus, doceatur tamen ad bonum quo vacuus est, ad libertatem quo privatus est, aspirare, et acrius ab ignavia excidetur quam si summa virtute fingeretur instructus.

not seem much purified ? But what, I pray, can man, I do not say hope, but choose, but think that is higher than that he should become God ? Behold, now he is God.[1]

And Petrarch completes his exposition with a refutation of the main defects of man as alleged by Innocent III in his famous *De miseria humanae conditionis*.

It is significant that Calvin also sees the importance of right doctrine for its consolatory and encouraging effects (though also regarding it as unassailably true, of course). He, too, deals at length with the question of man's creation in the image and likeness of God in *Institutes* II, xv. Let me quote but one passage, holding traditionally that the term "image" applies to man's soul :

> For although the glory of God is displayed in [man's] external form, yet there is no doubt that the proper seat of his image is in the soul. I admit that external form, as it distinguishes us from the brutes, also exalts us more nearly to God : nor will I too vehemently contend with anyone who would understand by the image of God that
> "... while the mute creation downward bend
> Their sight, and to their earthly mother tend,
> Man looks aloft, and with erected eyes
> Beholds his own hereditary skies",

a passage from Ovid's *Metamorphoses* frequently quoted in works on the dignity of man. Calvin resumes :

> Though the soul, therefore, is not the whole man, yet there is no absurdity in calling man the image of God with relation to the soul; although I retain the principle just laid down, that the image of God includes all the excellence in which the nature of man surpasses all the other species of animals. This term, therefore, denotes the integrity which Adam possessed, when he was endued with a right understanding, when he had affections regulated by reason, and all his senses governed in proper order, and when, in the excellency of his nature, he truly resembled the excellence of his Creator. And though the principal seat of the Divine image was in the mind and heart or in the soul and its faculties, yet there was no part of man, not even the body, which was not adorned with some rays of its glory.[2]

---

[1] Urb. lat. 334, f. 230r; IOIAL, 190-1, 398 n. 9.

[2] *Institutiones*, ed. cit., I, xv. 3, Quamvis enim in homine externo erfulgeat Dei gloria, propriam tamen imaginis sedem in anima esse dubium non est. Non infitior quidem, externam speciem, quatenus nos distinguit a brutis animalibus, ac separat, simul Deo propius adiungere. Ne vehementius contendam, si quis censeri velit sub imagine Sui, quod quum prona spectent animalia caetera terram, os homini sublime datum est, coelumque videre iussus, et erectos ad sidera tollere vultus [col. 136]. Quamvis ergo anima non sit homo, absurdum tamen non est, eum animae respectu vocari Dei imaginem; etsi principium quod nuper posui retineo, patere Dei effigiem ad totam praestantiam, qua eminet hominis natura inter omnes animantium species. Proinde

Calvin, of course, regarded the Fall of man and the Incarnation as integral parts of this theology and hastens to add :

> There is no doubt that Adam, when he fell from his dignity, was by this defection alienated from God. Wherefore, although we allow that the Divine image was not utterly annihilated and effaced in him, yet it was so corrupted that whatever remains is but horrible deformity. And therefore the beginning of our recovery and salvation is the restoration which we obtain through Christ who on this account is called the second Adam because he restores us to true and perfect integrity.[1]

Calvin's theology of God and man is intricate, and I do not intend to discuss it further here, except to point to one other interesting parallel to Petrarch. In the very next chapter, having set forth the original dignity and excellence of man, Calvin wishes to deal with "God's Preservation and Support of the World by His Power and His Government of Every Part of It by His Providence."[2] Here he seeks to do two things : vindicate God's *potentia absoluta* by showing that God can and does operate outside the laws of nature, thus giving a sense of the personal providence of God toward individuals. And, as a corollary of this, he wishes to refute the notion of fortune as something separate from divine providence. His purpose is to overcome the sense of helplessness and despair that either an over-deterministic naturalism or a too accidental, fortune-ridden view of the external world will induce in man. The similarity of the purposes to those of Petrarch, both in Petrarch's opposition to the Aristotelian natural philosophers and in his efforts to refute and undermine the conception of fortune, is striking.

And so we must raise again the question of the relationship of Petrarchan humanism to the Reformation. And again my historian's

---

hac voce notatur integritas qua praeditus fuit Adam quum recta intelligentia polleret, affectus haberet compositos ad rationem, sensus omnes recto ordine temperatos, vereque eximiis dotibus opificis sui excellentiam referret. Ac quamvis primaria sedes divinae imaginis fuerit in mente et corde, vel in anima eiusque potentiis, nulla tamen pars fuit etiam usque ad corpus, in qua non ecintillae aliquae micarent [cols. 137-8].

[1] *Ibid.*, I, xv, 4, col. 138, Quin Adam, ubi excidit e gradu suo, hac defectione a Deo alienatus sit minime dubium est. Quare etsi demus, non prorsus exinanitam ac deletam in eo fuisse Dei imaginem, sic tamen corrupta fuit, ut quidquid superest, horrenda sit deformitas. Ideoque recuperandae salutis nobis initium est in ea instauratione quam consequimur per Christum, qui etiam hac de causa vocatur secundus Adam, quia nos in veram et solidam integritatem restituit.

[2] *Ibid.*, X, xvi col. 144, Deum sua virtute mundum a se conditum fovere ac tueri, et singulas eius partes sua providentia regere.

judgement intervenes. Petrarch was the poet and rhetorician writing two centuries earlier, and however much he needed to enter into theological questions in his concern with the psychological state of his contemporaries and their need for renewed self-confidence and faith, he did not evolve an elaborate theology, nor did he contemplate reform of sacraments or church. Calvin, though his *Institutes* (as Quirinus Breen has cogently argued) [1] were written in a rhetorical and humanistic style and intention, did certainly have the goal of root and branch reformation. All that Petrarch wished and hoped for was renewal, quickening, renovation and revival within the existing structure. There is an implied criticism of the clergy in that he, a semi-layman, should endeavor to undertake this renewal, but it was never more than an implication, and Petrarch remained on the best of terms with numerous clerical friends. What his religious writings helped to bring about was a consciousness of the need for an extra-institutional, personal renewal of religion. It was also his purpose to bring about a revival of classical letters and of Roman civic virtue. His *Viri illustres* are grave, noble models of lay moral responsibility. Making it quite clear that he understood their limitations because they were pre-Christians, he had no more trouble reconciling their moralism with his theology of grace than did Dante.

Petrarch's own most illustrious follower, Coluccio Salutati, made three major contributions to humanist religious and moral thought in his treatises : *De seculo et religione, De laboribus Herculis* and *De fato et fortuna*.[2] Particularly this last work is relevant to our discussion, for he sought to make the connections between divine providence, grace and free will, between natural order, chance, and fortune systematically clear where Petrarch had established their relations more by implication and juxtaposition and taken many positions in such a loose way as to be charged with inconsistency. Salutati was a graver, more responsible, but less gifted and spontaneous man. If any of the humanists may be said to have resembled the classical model of a Ciceronian statesman, surely it was he. Doctrinally he perhaps came closer to achieving in this treatise the position which Calvin sought to uphold. Man should trust and rely absolutely on the divine providence and foresight which utilized the natural order discovered by the philo-

---

[1] In his *Christianity and Humanism : Studies in the History of Ideas* (Grand Rapids, Rapids, 1968), chap. 4, "John Calvin and the Rhetorical Tradition," 107-129.

[2] Cf. IOIAL, chap. II.

sophers only as means to God's ends. Simultaneously man should accept on faith that he has free will and strive to fulfil the divine commands. God in his power could upset natural orders at any instant and produce the seeming accident of change; He could turn man's will to nought by his intervention through fortune. Like Calvin, Salutati was deeply influenced by the Stoic conceptions of a rationally provident deity and universe and of an innate sense of political and moral order in mankind. But also like Calvin, he viewed man's powers and nature's orders as circumscribed and limited by the *potentia absoluta* of the omnipotent God. He was concerned, moreover, in detail with the central problems of fourteenth-century nominalist theology, those concerning grace, free will and contingency, and addressed himself to them in an effort to revindicate the providence of God toward particulars and the viability of a theology that sought to establish credible connections between the insights of faith and the experience of men. As Calvin did after him, he referred to the theories of the Ockhamist school as windy sophistry *(ventosa sophistica)*, yet he derived many of his philosophical positions from the nominalists. Following the precedent of both Scotus and Ockham he asserted the primacy of the will and urged upon his contemporaries that they had the inner strength of will to conform to right reason if they submitted to the divine commands and patiently waited the dispensations of His providence, whether for seeming good or ill. Men were justified through divine grace and providence, but sinned and were damned of their own will with merely divine prescience. In either case men were fully responsible for their actions and the consequences in a state of coefficiency with providence.[1]

Yet Salutati, despite the similarity of some (but decidedly not all) of his theological positions to Calvin's, despite also some difficult moments in his career when he was compelled to criticize and oppose the papacy for its worldliness, for the schism, for its anti-Florentine political actions, was in no sense a reformer. His very piety and gravity led him constantly to orthodoxy and conservation. He retained the central medieval conception of the higher sanctity and greater merits of those who bound themselves by vows. He believed merits and sins begot greater rewards or punishments, though not salvation or damnation. Yet he anticipated many aspects of the Reform in both his theology and his emphasis on a lay piety (which did not contradict his

---

[1] *Ibid.*, 76-102.

doctrinally conservative view of the monastic life). He was a man purely of his age. therefore, responding thoughtfully and appropriately to its immediate religious problems, which indeed did also anticipate many of the problems of the Reformation era. Judging by his attitude toward the gerat schism, however, it would seem as unthinkable for him as it was for Erasmus to countenance any destruction of the unity of Christendom.

One must, moreover, speak briefly of Salutati's humanism in relation to the organized religious culture of his day. Severely criticized by the Dominican, Beato Giovanni Dominici, for both his interpretations of classical poetry in a Christian sense through allegory and for his more Franciscan stress on the primacy of the will, we have in Salutati's reply a humanist manifesto of the value of the *studia humanitatis* both for the necessary training of the clergy and for the advancement of Christian learning and faith in the *studia divinitatis*. He himself had carried out the programmatic items of his manifesto in many important ways so that it is possible to conclude that he not only contributed a *theologia poetica*, finding Christian religious insights concealed by allegory in the pagan myths of Hercules and other figures, but that he also was an outstanding practitioner of what Petrarch and the humanist movement in general sought to achieve in its religious concerns, namely something that might well be called *theologia rhetorica*. Though I have not found a contemporary use of the term, it does seem appropriate for the humanists' conception of putting all the language arts and sciences—the secular study of the word—at the service of the propagation of the Divine Word, which is often enough repeated by them and manifested in their religious writings. Moreover the German Cardinal, Nicholas of Cusa, who was closely associated with many Italian humanists, did indeed give this concept of the nature and task of theology his blessing, calling it in his *Idiota : theologia sermocinalis*. And Salutati as a matter of fact spoke of his own discipline as *scientia sermocinalis* or *philosophia sermocinalis*.[1]

Although one cannot in a brief essay give more than a fragmentary notion of the extent and character of Italian humanist religious thought, it seems impossible to skip over Lorenzo Valla and Giannozzo Manetti. Of all the humanists who in any way are thought to have anticipated

---

[1] For Salutati, *Ibid.*, 555-62. Cusanus—cf. *Texte seiner philosophischen Schriften*, ed. Petzelt (Stuttgart, 1949), 314-5, Unde haec est sermocinalis theologia, qui nitor te ad Deum per vim vocabuli ducere modo quo possum faciliori et veriori.

Reformation thought Valla is certainly the best known, especially for his *De ... donatione Constantini declamatio*, his *Adnotationes in Novum Testamentum* (now attracting scholars with the recognition of a manuscript of the version Erasmus edited, and the edition of an earlier version by Perosa), and his *De libero arbitrio dialogus*. I shall not specifically discuss these works nor his *De professione religiosorum dialogus*, seemingly unknown to the Reformers though anticipating in some ways their desanctification of the monastic life, nor his *De mysterio Eucharistiae sermo*,[1] notable for its nominalist interpretation of the sacrament. Possibly the most original mind of the Italian Renaissance, Valla simultaneously assumed the most thorough-going rhetorical stance in rejection of both ancient and medieval metaphysical philosophy and developed the most intellectually consistent vision of God and man. Basing himself on his analysis of language as the empirical reflection of human experience, he combined his own version of a nominalism with a linguistic positivism when it came to the Scriptures and the knowledge of the divine. But more than that, he asserted by a philological critique of ancient and humanist ethics a naturalistic view of human nature built around the will as an elementary reaching out of the organism toward gratification in pleasure, love, or divine fruition. It is not only that his so-called Christian-Epicureanism anticipates that of Erasmus, but that he was able to develop a unifying insight into the thought of St. Augustine that reduced it to a harmony with classical Platonic eros-philosophy, hedonism, eudemonism and a Pan-Epicureanism. His thought presents the paradox of a rejection of classical philosophy and ethics and an affirmation of Christianity through a Biblical literalism which at the same time by the character of his vision of human psychology and of man's concept of the divine managed to reunite the entire range of Christian and classical ethics and theology. Thus charity and fortitude become one, and self-sacrificing and self-gratifying love, both springing from the same basic drive, develop into the one or the other according to both the depth of vision and the magnanimity or strength of soul of the individual. Radical in the fullest meaning of the term, Valla's anthropology was beyond the capacity of his time to comprehend. He has been too superficially accepted as a forerunner of the Reformation by Protestant scholars and, in the past, too superficially rejected as an enemy of the Church by Catholics, some of whom are today rushing to claim him. To him,

---

[1] Cf. IOIAL, chap. III and 674-81, 633-8.

of all the humanists, the term "autonomy" belongs. For though he had an enormous influence that can only partly be documented on subsequent humanist thought, Italian and northern, as well as in a fragmentary way on Protestant, Catholic and Radical Reform ideas, he best represents the humanly-centered conception of the role of the scholar and thinker as the analyst of the word, both human and divine, that was the hallmark of Italian humanist religious thought.[1]

Giannozzo Manetti, in many respects also a pioneer in the development of Biblical scholarship, remained apparently unknown to the Reform period and certainly unappreciated. I shall not discuss this aspect of his work, except to point out that he was the first humanist to master Hebrew and to make a new Latin translation of the Hebrew Psalter, that he also made his own translation of the Greek New Testament and discussed in a cautious way the problem of scriptural and philosophical translation, rejecting the freer more rhetorical canons of earlier humanist translations for a stricter more literal method in the name of scholarly precision and theological truth. Moreover, he embarked on a new mode of interpreting Old Testament and New Testament history, seeing the Old Testament not simply as the prefiguration of the New but as the historical record of the religious history of the Hebrews and of the Jews, distinguishing between them as separate and different stages of religious development of God's people.[2]

The work of Manetti which was best known was, of course, his treatise on the *Dignity and Excellence of Man*, for which we are still awaiting a modern edition, not to mention an English translation. Going far beyond his predecessors, in many ways akin to if not influenced by Valla, Manetti more than any other of the humanists built his vision of man around the critical Genesis passage 1:26, "And God said, 'Let us make man in our image, after our likeness.' " Due to his excellent library of Latin, Greek and Hebrew philosophical and religious works, which today forms the nucleus of the Vatican Fondo Ebraico and a large part of its Fondo Palatino Graeco and Latino, Manetti was able to draw on a wide range of both patristic and classical sources for his combination of the patristic vision of man as the divine image and the probably Posidonian synthesis of Stoicism and Platonism,

---

[1] Cf. IOIAL, 160-70. For Catholic studies of Valla cf. Fois and Di Napoli sup. cit. Camporeale, sup. cit., though a Dominican, manages to avoid sectarian apologetics.
[2] IOIAL, 571-601, 726-734.

which as Cicero reports it in Book II of *De natura deorum* is the most laudatory classical discussion of man surviving. Certainly Manetti's views of man, though stated cautiously and with intended orthodoxy, and in large part through excerpts, were in content bold and far-reaching. Certainly he was far more extravagant in his picture of man's reaching toward divinity through his earthly actions than either Luther or Calvin could tolerate. God honored man in making him the most beautiful, the most creative, the most wise, the most opulent and the most potent of all His creatures. Moreover he is less concerned to stress the Incarnation as the correction and restoration of man after the Fall than to suggest that it was meant to complement man's great gifts received through his creation in the divine image, for God would have sent his Son incarnate in a human person even if man had not sinned in order to shower further glory upon him. Certainly in this aspect of his theological vision Manetti represented an autonomous Renaissance position even though the theme of the dignity of man remained important in the ideas of Catholic and Protestant thinkers of the Reformation period.[1]

Ideas such as Manetti's exercised an influence through their transformation into the more systematic philosophical ones of Ficino, Pico and other Platonists of the late Quattrocento and the Cinquecento. Their philosophies are generally well known and their connections with northern Reformation thought have been discussed by others such as Eugene Rice,[2] Sears Jayne [3] and Lewis Spitz.[4] More systematically than their humanist predecessors, and more explicitly, they linked together the qualities of divinity with the achievements and aspirations of humanity, which were regarded as tokens or signs of man's immortal destiny. They have been hailed by Frances Yates as the initiators of a new vision of man as a *magus*, controlling, manipulating, creating with the materials of nature, like God the Creator. But they were shown the way to these aspirations by Manetti and other humanists. Their theological positions were complex but not always as unorthodox as they have been charged. Their classical-Christian synthesis and their

---

[1] *Ibid.*, 230-58.

[2] Eugene F. Rice, Jr., *The Renaissance Idea of Wisdom* (Cambridge, Mass., 1958); "The Humanist Idea of Christian Antiquity : LeFèvre d'Étaples and His Circle," *Studies w.s. in the Renaissance*, IX (1962), 126-60.

[3] Sears Jayne, *John Colet and Marsilio Ficino* (London, 1963).

[4] Lewis W. Spitz, *The Religious Renaissance of the German Humanists*, (Cambridge, Mass., 1963).

stress on the immortality of the soul had an influence at the Fifth
Lateran Council through Luther's fellow Augustinian Hermit, the
Cardinal Egidio da Viterbo.[1] But since the direction sought was a
broadening and diffusing of the sources of doctrine, rather than a
narrowing down and tightening, it was doomed to be rejected by
Protestant and Catholic Reformer alike, though enjoying a vogue with
some figures in both camps. In these days of reviving Oecumenism,
it is perhaps arousing new interest.

We cannot conclude this discussion of the autonomous and the anti-
cipatory aspects of Italian humanist religious thought without turning
to a third option and a third religious movement, namely the enormously influential employment of humanism for religious ends by Erasmus and his followers. The influence of Valla and other Italians on Erasmus is well known-of, if not in detail and depth very well known. Nor is
there agreement on the nature of Erasmus' religious thought, itself,
which would be important for a valid comparison. I am not an Erasmus
scholar, and must follow in the footsteps of my betters. With the recent
work of Spitz [2] and Kohls [3] and others,[4] we know how complex and
changing his theological ideas were. Even more recently Béné [5] has
emphasized the deep influence of Augustine, especially his *De doctrina
Christiana* on Erasmus, and this approach is congenial to the point
of view I am about to put forth—but from the sidelines or from another
battle-front as it were.

It seems to me that if the religious works of the Italian humanists
may be characterized as efforts to develop a *theologia rhetorica*, even
more should this conception apply to Erasmus. It must be remembered
that humanists writing on religious subjects were trying to reach and
influence a wide range of readers, lay and clerical. They conceived of
their writings as literature (*bonae litterae*), not science (*scientia*, though
there are exceptions), however much their writing sprang from doctrinal
preconceptions. One can speak of their religiosity and their religious

---

[1] Cf. John W. O'Malley, *Giles of Viterbo on Church and Reform, A Study in Renaissance
Thought* (Leiden., 1968)

[2] Spitz, *op. cit.*, chap. IX, "Erasmus, Philosopher of Christ," 197-236.

[3] E.-W. Kohls, *Die Theologie des Erasmus*, 2 Vols. (Basel, 1966).

[4] e.g. E. V. Telle, *Érasme de Rotterdam et Le Septième Sacrement* (Geneva, 1954);
W. P. Eckert, *Erasmus von Rotterdam Werk und Wirkung*, Vol. I, *Der humanistische
Theologie* (Cologne, 1967).

[5] Charles Béné, *Érasme et Saint Augustin, ou influence de Saint Augustin sur l'humanisme de Érasme* (Geneva, 1969).

thought much more readily than of their theology, because it was rarely that systematic. They produced lay sermons, both formally and in the disguise of dialogues or treatises. Salutati's *De fato* and Valla's *Disputationes dialecticae* are exceptions in that they do attempt to deal with basic theological and philosophical questions systematically, but they are humanistic and not scholastic in form. The great influential works of Erasmus also turn out to be extended or collected lay sermons, significantly in print. Such were the *Colloquies*, and such was the *Enchiridion*, one of the main texts from which scholars have sought to extract his theological ideas. Erasmus is constantly attempting to influence the attitude and behavior of his reader. True enough this does represent a religious position, and it seems to me one that might also aptly be called a *theologia rhetorica*. We should remember, too, his great work of editing, translating and commenting on the Scriptures and the Fathers, in which he follows the precedents of Traversari, Manetti, Valla and other Italians. We perhaps have here a *theologia philologica*. Together the two terms may be said to comprise what Cusanus called *theologia sermocinalis*, although the broadened conception that humanists such as Valla had of rhetoric might justify *theologia rhetorica* as sufficiently inclusive. In respect to this conception of the role of religious thought and writing, which is to be sure not devoid of a specific theological content, it seems to me that Erasmus most perfectly fulfils the promises and programs of the religious thought and studies of the Italian humanists. It is a true case of anticipation here, and fruition as well. More than anyone he made actual what was their ideal.

In token, rather than proof of this. I would point to one of his last great works to be completed : the *Ecclesiastes sive Concionator Evangelicus*, otherwise known as the *De ratione concionandi*.[1] It bears the notion of a "churchman" rather than a "cleric," or better still a Christian orator, for the words *Ecclesiastes* in Greek and *Concionator* in Latin mean identically, from *ecclesia* and *conventio*—popular assembly —the haranguer or orator, the man who addresses the congregation. (The Latin verb *contio* is a contraction of *conventio*.) Erasmus' book is indeed a handbook for a Christian orator, inspired by, if not directly modelled on, such works as Cicero's *De oratore* or the *Institutio oratoria* of Quintilian, so critical in Valla's thinking. To quote Erasmus' preface : "We divide the argument into four books. In the first we demonstrate the dignity of the office and in what virtues it is necessary

---

[1] In *Opera omnia* (Leiden, 1704), Tom. V, cols. 767-1100.

for the *Ecclesiast* to be endowed. In the second and third we adapt
the teachings of rhetoricians, dialecticians and theologians to the use
of discourse *(concionandi)*. The fourth, as a kind of catalogue, groups
together and shows to the *Ecclesiast* what principles or ideas he ought
to look for and in what part of Scripture they may be found."[1]

Thus he has divided his work according to the traditional subjects of
rhetoric, the character of the orator, the art and parts of the oration,
and finally dialectic, used here in the new humanist and old Ciceronian
sense of invention, the finding of the appropriate topics or *loci* for the
most persuasive discourse. Any study of the book will show that, while
it is full of doctrine that can be pulled forth from the interstices as it
were and put together in some kind of scheme, it is in literal fact a
study of sacred linguistics and rhetoric, and in a fully technical sense.

Can we now conclude, in what is a most fragmentary account of a
vast and complex subject, that the religious thought of the Italian
humanists, itself complex and various, was a series of limited responses
to the profound crisis of Christianity that began in the early fourteenth
century and ran at least to the late sixteenth century, only to find a
regrettable and provisional solution by fission? As such it was bound
to anticipate and even influence in some respects the religious ideas
of the Reform, both Protestant, Catholic and Radical. Historically,
however, it did not seek reform in the drastic ways that it came about
but in a milder spiritual transformation and quickening. Can we consider that it had in its inherited rhetorical notions of discourse and
verbal communication as central to human experience the ideal of
developing and practicing a *theologia rhetorica*? This is a notion that
we find best exemplified in the work of Erasmus, though there are
also important elements of such an approach to religion in Luther,
especially in Melanchthon, definitely in the ex-humanist Calvin, and
most assuredly in Ignatius Loyola. Thus, as a normal part of the
historical process, the humanists did anticipate the Reformers, but
much more significant is their rather unsystematic elaboration of a
characteristic and autonomous position of their own.

---

[1] *Ibid.*, cols. 767-8, Summam argumenti in quattuor libros digessimus. In primo
demonstravimus muneris dignitatem, et quibus virtutibus oporteat esse praeditum
Ecclesiasten. In secundo ac tertio quae sunt in praeceptionibus Rhetorum, Dialecticorum,
ac Theologorum, ad usum concionandi accommodamus. Quartus velut elenchus com-
monstrat Ecclesiastae quas sententias ex quibus Scripturae locis petere debeat, quem
tamen hactenus absolvimus, ut studioso lectori viam modo commonstraverimus, alioqui
res erat nec unius nec exigui voluminis.

THE ROLE OF RELIGION
IN RENAISSANCE HUMANISM AND PLATONISM

PAUL OSKAR KRISTELLER

Columbia University

I should like to make a few comments on the theme of our conference. These remarks will be largely retrospective, indicating how the approach to our subject has changed during the last thirty years or so, and also stating very briefly my own view on the links that connected Renaissance humanism and Renaissance Platonism with the religion and theology of their time.

The word religion has been used rather loosely in recent years, and when the unlearned humanism of the twentieth century is often considered as a kind of religion, one is easily tempted to consider the learned humanism of the fifteenth century as a religious movement, a temptation that I have stubbornly tried to resist. Things have been further complicated by the recent tendency to consider all intellectual concerns as belonging to either science or religion, and when confronted with this bleak alternative, all other concerns including the arts and the humanities when banished from the stern and exclusive temple of science might be driven to seek shelter, in order to avoid extinction, under the more hospitable roof of religion. I am inclined to posit a broader system of culture where the arts, philosophy, humanistic scholarship and other concerns find a legitimate place besides religion and science. And when speaking of the Renaissance, we should enquire more specifically about Christianity and its role, and about the attitudes of the leading currents of the Renaissance towards Christianity and the Church. This is a broad and complex subject that includes many diverse and overlapping facets some of which have been treated in the papers and discussions of this conference whereas others had to be omitted.

As I see it, our problem has undergone two significant changes during the last few decades. First of all, there was a widespread view, often called the Burckhardtian view, although it was not Burckhardt's view, that the Renaissance, at least in some of its strands, was basically pagan and anti-Christian. This notion which had many contrary facts to contend with, was opposed by Pastor with a kind of compromise, by stating that there are two contrary strands in the period, one Christian and one pagan. It was later opposed in a tour de force by another exaggerated view when Toffanin claimed that Renaissance humanism was a Catholic reaction against the heretical tendencies of the Middle Ages. Our present approach is I believe more objective and more tentative, and this is also the approach underlying the substantial recent volumes of our chairman : what did the Renaissance and especially Italian humanism contribute to religious thought, and vice-versa, what did the Church and the medieval tradition of religious thought contribute to Renaissance humanism ? We consider these questions as significant, and several of us have had occasion to address ourselves to them. but they cannot even be asked, let alone answered, if we start with the dogmatic assumption of a Renaissance all pagan or half pagan or all orthodox. The second change which I want to mention is related to the first one. The Renaissance, and especially the Quattrocento, has been traditionally considered as a foil to the Reformation, and as an interlude between the theology of the scholastics and the theology of the Reformers, both Protestant and Catholic. We continue to explore the links that connect Renaissance thought with the Protestant and Catholic Reformation, and on the other hand with medieval thought, but we are also trying to understand, in religious thought as in other areas, the peculiar physiognomy of the Renaissance, and to discover also in its religion and theology traits that are distinctive and significant and that are not merely remnants of the preceding or seeds of the following period.

Adding now a few words about Renaissance humanism and Platonism in their relation to Christianity and to the theology of their time, I cannot help restating my own views. I am afraid they are well known to you, but they have also been misunderstood, and I cannot resist the temptation to explain them to such a distinguished captive audience. I hope I shall hear now or in our other sessions some criticism, and I promise to mend my ways if some of this criticism strikes me as valid and as based on facts that I have not sufficiently considered.

Let me first talk about humanism. My refusal to define humanism in terms of any particular philosophical or theological doctrines, and my attempt to define it instead through a set of intellectual concerns or scholarly disciplines are due to some very simple factual observations. In trying to define humanism, we must not focus on a few interesting ideas expressed by one or a few humanists, but we must take into account the sum-total of intellectual interests that characterized the movement as a whole in the opinion of its representatives and their contemporaries. Their range of interest combines intellectual and professional concerns that at other times including ours are not combined but disparate. The humanists were not only moralists but also grammarians and rhetoricians, poets and writers, translators and copyists, historians and classical scholars, and many of them, perhaps the majority, were nothing but grammarians or rhetoricians; they were not concerned as a group with theology or metaphysics, natural philosophy or logic, medicine or law, mathematics or astronomy. I never meant to say that humanism made no contribution to philosophy or theology. I did not even say that the moralists among the humanists were not philosophers; I merely said that they were not professional or technical philosophers. The humanist profession as a whole was a scholarly and literary profession, and those members of the profession who were interested in philosophy combined philosophy with scholarship and literature, as at other times philosophy may have been combined with theology or with the sciences. Taken as a broad group, the humanists were neither Christian nor anti-Christian. As individuals, most of them were Christians, and some of them were sufficiently interested in religious and theological subjects to write about them. Vice-versa, the Church and the clergy of the fifteenth century were not identified with humanism, but some or rather many clerics were humanists, not only the members of religious orders whom I have treated in a recent paper but also the members of the secular clergy from the pope down to many parish priests. In the sixteenth century, humanism as such was neither Catholic nor Protestant. We find individual humanists who were Catholic believers or members of the clergy or religious orders, others who were Protestants and even Protestant theologians, and again others who were members of other religious groups or who were unbelievers. Our task is to define precisely what humanism is (I am not trying to do that now), and then to explore its contribution to the religion and theology of its time. I find much of this contribution in the style of writing, in the scholarly and critical treatment of religious texts such as the Bible and the Church Fathers, in the critical treatment of Church History, finally (and this is most difficult to prove) in the preference for certain problems.

I am now coming to my last point, Renaissance Platonism. In my view, the Renaissance Platonists, such as Ficino or Pico, were not merely a special group of humanists among others. They had a humanist training, to be sure, but they were professional philosophers, metaphysicians in a way none of the earlier humanists had been. I

happen to be a philosopher, and hence I cannot ignore these distinctions
(to offer a variation on a remark recently made by one of our friends
and colleagues, the history of philosophy is too important a subject to
be left entirely to the non-philosophers). I still believe that Renaissance
Platonism was a deep and important and even influential current of
thought. However, we have learned in recent years that its institutional
and professional basis was slender, as compared with humanism and
Aristotelianism, and that a large bulk of the technical literature produced by philosophers through the sixteenth century and beyond was
Aristotelian. Now the Renaissance Platonists, Ficino, Pico and others
intended to be Christians. Although imbued with ancient Neoplatonism
and its doctrines, they conceived of Platonist metaphysics as a rational
counterpart and support of Christian theology. Whether they succeeded
in this attempt is a question that has been much debated by scholars.
The fifteenth century Platonists were Catholics, and so were many of
their followers in the sixteenth century. But the Cambridge Platonists
of the seventeenth century who continued the tradition in a modified
way were Protestants and even theologians. And the relationship between Platonism and the Catholic Church in the sixteenth century
was not always peaceful, as the case of Francesco Patrizi shows
not to speak of Giordano Bruno. I should say about the Platonists
as well as about the humanists : individual scholars and thinkers
made their individual religious and theological choices that were
not predetermined by their general scholarly or philosophical concerns. I believe for the Renaissance, as I do for our own time, in
the freedom and autonomy of different cultural concerns and traditions.
Persons genuinely devoted to rational philosophy and to scholarship
usually are not and should not be willing to sacrifice their cultural do-
mains on the altar of religious or political orthodoxy or relevance. I
do not admire the sixteenth century for its intolerance and religious
wars. If there is anything I admire it is the way in which its philosophers, classical scholars, mathematicians carried on its work in
cooperation and mutual exchange of ideas, beyond the seemingly
insurmountable barriers of religious diversity and conflict. I think this
is a most important lesson that we should learn for our own time, to
continue our work with conviction against the increasing onslaughts
of Philistine indifference and barbarous hostility.

2. LAST SUPPERS AND THEIR REFECTORIES

CREIGHTON E. GILBERT

Queens College (C.U.N.Y.)

This paper proposes that a certain kind of interplay exists in the late Middle Ages and early Renaissance between a religious image and some contemporary religious texts. The art historian in an interdisciplinary context finds himself not quite part of the family. On the one hand, he is at an unfair advantage because twentieth century average man only knows Renaissance religion from its works of art, being far more likely to recognize the name of Leonardo and the *Last Supper* than Jan Hus or the *Imitation of Christ*, to cite the most famous tokens of other kinds of history. On the other hand, his materials have unusually little continuity with others. Histories of politics, law, society, religion, philosophy, literature, easily slip into each other, and all tend to be included under intellectual history, which tends merely to mean the history whose data are words (including, in the Renaissance, music). The odd non-verbal emphasis of the history of art is related, I think, to the foreignness seen in art historians' efforts to exploit religious and other texts. Without the natural continuum, the art historian must construct verbal associations with much random labor and without the expertise his colleagues can bring to neighboring subjects. He is also prone, in his eagerness, to lean repeatedly on a few texts he has found, to press their partial analogies into parallels, and to use antiquated research in other fields not merely as if it still were authoritative, but as if it were identifiable with the data it analyzes or edits; to be sure, art historians' naive use of Migne and Pastor has many analogies in other historians' regrettable citation of what Wölfflin and Berenson said in 1895. The art historian does well, by exception, when the text he uses has its own visual implication, as with an emblem book or perhaps a manual of mythology, and the fine results he then obtains have been all the more admired by others discouraged by their more awkward attempts. What follows assumes all these hesitations, and seeks to improve the technique.

It will also refer to a specific fallacy, as I consider it, related directly to the theme of this symposium. Today art historians rightly reject as anachronistic earlier interpretations of Renaissance images as being realistic dramas without symbolism; such readings are seen to have been the product of "modern" nineteenth century assumptions about progress and secularity. But by a too strong reaction it has now been inferred that the images must be symbolic with the systematic firmness of medieval works. The fallacy, I would say, is in the unstated assumption of only two possible alternatives, so that when one is disproved the other must be applicable. I will here suggest a third approach, which seems to me illustrative of early Renaissance culture, and in the process show explicitly what seems to me wrong with a particular "medieval" reading of Last Suppers.

About Leonardo's *Last Supper* it is well known, among many other things, that it is in a monk's dining room, a refectory. We are surely right to accept the "obvious" implication that a parallel is intended between the painted people and their observers performing the same actions. (This paper will, in a sense, in discussing the relation of the painting to the room, be a metaphor of the problem of the relation of the image to its age.) The claim that, in fifteenth century Italy, people consciously adopted this sort of thinking about parallels, can be supported not only by the frequency of *Last Suppers* in refectories and their infrequency everywhere else, but by other kinds of data, including writings giving directions about what art ought to do. Leonardo's single perspectival space, continuing steadily from our room far into the painted room, supports the demand of the period that painting at its best is at its most realistic, in the sense that reality in a painting is undifferentiated from reality outside it. For this attitude the best evidence is probably Alberti's statement that what the painter wishes to do is fill his surface with colors as if this surface were a glass, upon which we are seeing everything behind the glass.[1]) A painting is a window pane. There are a few literal illustrations of this formula; an elegant one is Pesellino's small Madonna in the Norton Simon collection, where a frame is painted around the figures.[2]

The identity of the painted world and the real world is posited more emphatically perhaps, in a way allowing for fewer instances, when the painting is called not a window but a mirror. In the case of the window, of course, the segments on the two sides of it need not look alike, but in a *Last Supper* they do have this further mirror—like relationship.

---

[1] L. B. Alberti, *Kleinere Kunsttheoretische Schriften*, ed. Janitschek (1887), 69.

[2] C. Gilbert, *Major Masters of the Renaissance* (Waltham, Mass., 1963).

Alberti again provides for this definition when [1] he attributes the invention of painting to Narcissus finding his own mirror image : "What else is painting, than to embrace with skilled technique *(artificioso)* the surface of the water ?" In a Last Supper the figures might mirror the eating monks (Vasari [2] in a typical anecdote has Leonardo threaten to use the annoying prior's face for Judas) or the artist (according to the same story teller,[3] in Castagno's *Death of the Virgin* Judas was a self portrait). The notion that artists constantly portray themselves became such a cliché that it got a variety of comments, including one by Savonarola, as Chastel[4] has shown. Conversely—as it were in a mirror-image of this idea—Ficino remarks that observers will start to reflect the emotions of painted figures.[5] Leonardo, in two texts that Chastel has put side by side, on the one hand complains that "the painter who works from habit, without reasoning, is like the mirror that reproduces in itself all that appears in front of it, without taking cognizance of it," and on the other hand approves that "the mind of the painter should liken itself to a mirror which always takes on the color of the thing it reflects, and is filled by as many images as there are objects before it."[6]

A different category of text documents a fifteenth century desire to think the Last Supper into one's own environment. Two historians have recently cited an example each. Brucker *(Renaissance Florence, 1969, 208)* cites the constitution of a confraternity in 1410 which calls on the governors each Holy Thursday to "wash the feet of the bretheren, and offer a simple meal, to commemorate this day on which Christ washed the feet of the disciples and then shared a meal with them." Baxandall *(Painting and Experience in Fifteenth Century Italy, 1972, 46)* cites a handbook for girls on how to pray, of 1454, telling them to fix in their minds places in Jerusalem, using a city they know, and including among the places the supper-room where Christ had the Last Supper, and then to form in their minds people they know to represent the people of the passion. Both would in different ways urge

---

[1] *Ed. cit.*, 93.

[2] G. Vasari, *Le vite* (Milan, 1963), III, 397.

[3] *Ed. cit.*, II, 508.

[4] A. Chastel, *L'art et l'humanisme à Florence au temps de Laurent le Magnifique* (Paris, 1959), 398.

[5] C. Gilbert, "On Subject and not-Subject in Italian Renaissance Pictures," *Art Bulletin*, XXXIV (1952), 205.

[6] A. Chastel, ed., *Léonard de Vinci par lui-même* (1952), 94-95.

us to recreate the supper kinaesthetically as a means to moral improvement, and they present this notion in a way that makes it seem to have been conventional rather than idiosyncratic. This link from the Supper to our environment does not mention painting, and the previously discussed texts linking painting to our environment do not mention the Supper. But we may tentatively blend the two sets with their common factor, so that when we do indeed read a text of 1405, telling us to associate children's gestures with the Christ child's gestures, as a means to moral improvement, and to do this with the aid of paintings, we may infer that it too is not idiosyncratic, and tells us much of the drives to represent certain themes in certain styles.

Cardinal Giovanni Dominici in his *Regola del governo di cura familiare*, about 1405, written for rich laymen, just the sort of people who ordered paintings, advises us how to bring up children to love God : in our houses we should have pictures of holy children, "which your son, still in swaddling clothes, may delight in as something like himself, and be swept up by the likeness," *si diletti come simile e dal simile rapito*.[1] He continues with many examples, including the Child held by the Virgin, with a pomegranate, nursing, sleeping, standing—it is significant these were indeed common images, and interesting that the pomegranate and so on are unhinged from the specific symbolisms they certainly had had earlier. Dominici then explains that, in the same way as paintings are useful in this way for the ignorant, living creatures are for the higher, and scripture for the highest. "In the first mirror let your children be mirrored when they open their eyes," in the second when they can speak, in the third when they can write. Thus the ethical value and the mirror image both appear here, if we are willing also to take on the stated suitability for the ignorant. (I think we should, making a presumption that once established the notion of this type of visual "Book of the Ignorant" received more extended acceptance.)

Thus our commonsensical belief that *Last Suppers* belong in rooms where people sup gains support when we explore ideas about the nature and function of painting in the period. And we shall observe that in Renaissance Florence they do not appear in other loci (with qualifications : they in are included in Passion cycles, they exist in small scale images, and a variant to be discussed that is a Last Supper in a broad but not a strict sense.) What this does not prepare us for is that this "natural" situation begins abruptly about 1450. Before then, Florentine refecto-

---

[1] C. Gilbert, art. cit., 206-07; G. Dominici. *Regola del governo di cura familiare*. ed. Bargellini (Florence, 1927).

ries were frescoed otherwise. It is interesting that good scholars have asserted the contrary, that the Last Supper was standard in earlier refectories, with what reason we shall see. To judge from the few examples we have, these earlier refectories seem to have had their own standard theme, the Crucifixion. This is not true in the late fourteenth century refectory of S. Maria Novella, frescoed with a Madonna and Saints in a pseudo-altarpiece. It is small relative to the room, which probably had other frescoes, but if it did not, the un-surprising inference is simply that at this earlier date there was indeed less uniformity. But the two more fully surviving fresco decorations of fourteenth century Florentine refectories both have as their central themes interesting and elaborate Crucifixions.

At the Franciscan convent of S. Croce, in the 1330's, Taddeo Gaddi painted it (fig. 1) in the version that may be called *albero della croce* (Va-sari's term) or *lignum vitae* (the name of the book once thought to be by St. Bonaventura which is its source). In it medallions hang from the cross and other branches of the tree, showing the whole narrative of Christ's life, in Taddeo's case reduced to tituli. Below the tree, the lower part of the wall shows a Last Supper, as a kind of predella. The same combination occurs in the second refectory, at the Augustinian convent of S. Spirito, about 1360, painted in my opinion by Nardo di Cione and an assistant. This is a narrative, not an exhortatory, Cruci-fixion, again with a Last Supper in the predella area. In her excellent *Mural Painters of Tuscany*, the best book on the relation of frescoes to their walls and rooms, Borsook speaks of S. Croce as if it showed a Last Supper in the same way as later refectories; for her the Supper "dominates the scheme" and is the "earliest surviving example of what became in Florence the favorite subject for refectory murals."[1] It is surely wrong to say that the Supper dominates an adjacent image several times its size, and I would hold that Borsook has been bemused by the "natural" but later pattern in refectories. What S. Croce does show is two odd tokens that the analogy between painted eaters and observing eaters is already being pursued at this date. The first is the very remarkable framing system of the scenes on the wall. Above the *Supper* the five scenes, the *albero della croce* and the four smaller ones at its sides, have frames in common that mark their front plane and equate it with the wall, in the ordinary way, but when these frames continue down, they are behind the figures of the *Supper*, which is

---

[1] E. Borsook, *Mural Painters of Tuscany* (1960), 131.

thus conceived of as in front of the wall and in the refectory with us. This produces alternatively, as has been said,[1] "a painting behind a reality" or a reality in front of the paintings, a supper continuous with our supper. The second piece of evidence for the concern with a continuity from our eating to the paintings with eating, is in the choice of the smaller scenes beside the *Crucifixion*. Each of the four tells a story about a saint, but they do not seem to make a neat set. Both Borsook and Vertova [2] have suggested analogies among them, in ways that to me seem less persuasive than that three of them are additional scenes of eating, I think a unique such case. The fourth is not; this *Francis Receiving the Stigmata* strikes me as meant to be seen as an extension from the central area in the *Crucifixion* where Francis kneels and embraces the foot of the cross : here he kneels and receives the five wounds from Christ crucified appearing as a seraph. The other three scenes would be seen as extensions from the Supper below. (Borsook calls the upper two scenes a pair of wilderness miracles and the lower two a pair of dining room scenes; the fact that one of the two wildernesses includes a dining room seems to me to disturb that reading. Vertova says all four scenes refer to aspects of the love of God or man, but in one of these cases, the Benedict story, the interpretation that it deals with "faith in God's love of man" seems too indirect to have been grasped in such a sense.)

In these three scenes each saint has a different relation to eating. Benedict above right (who, oddly and alone, is not one of the saints seen below the cross in the main scene) is seen in his cave where he usually gets food dropped by a priest with a rope, which the devil breaks, whereupon Christ in the form of an angel visits the priest, shown eating in a room, with the upbraiding words : *tu tibi delicias preparas, et servus meus malo loco fame cruciatur.* Magdalene, lower right, anoints Christ's feet as he is dining in the house of Simon and telling his host that he welcomes her because of her love. Louis of Toulouse, lower left, a Franciscan who had visited Florence, shows his *charitas* by serving a banquet to the poor. I can find no common

---

[1] U. Baldini, "Taddeo Gaddi, Bernardo Daddi," in : *Giotteschi a S. Croce (Citta di Vita,* IV)(1966), 403.

[2] Borsook, *op. cit.,* p. 131-132; L. Vertova, *I Cenacoli Fiorentini* (1965), 21-23, a fundamental collection of materials, execptionally thorough and with sound comments. Because of its value the disagreements I have with it are indicated in what follows with more detail than for other books.

doctrinal points among these three dinners, not to mention the Last Supper, and so propose that the obvious analogy is the intended one, the inducement to us dining in the refectory to imitate these saints in the other parts of our lives too, as Dominici's infants imitate the images in their rooms.

Two walls on which suppers are painted underneath Crucifixions do not add up to a norm, but there are others, surprisingly not considered in this relationship. When Castagno about 1450, at the convent of S. Apollonia, painted the first of our familiar Last Suppers for a refectory (fig. 2), he put it under a Crucifixion. Thus the formula is the same, the shift is in the emphasis. Earlier the Crucifixion had been bigger, now the Supper is. In this case the special importance of the Crucifixion is marked by its occupying the center of the wall, between two other scenes of the Entombment and the Resurrection, so that the set violates the usual desire at this date to arrange scenes in chronological sequences. (This center area is also the widest of the three, a fact controlled by the windows. The Crucifixion is not, however, given the center because it is the scene that needs the most room. It has fewer figures than the Entombment. It is an interesting corollary, I believe not explored in the Castagno literature, that the Entombment, which in the ordinary chronological scheme would have got the wide center space, here has a particularly crowded composition of figures, unlike any other by the artist, and also a forceful collision of these figures which finds thematic focus in the kiss on Christ's dead lips. It is an attractive speculation that Castagno first took it for granted that it would fill the roomier center space and so designed it to use that area, but was then told to put the Crucifixion there and so squeezed the Entombment composition tight, with brilliant results.)

The new observation that the whole Castagno wall has a precedent in the whole Gaddi wall (even the triptych system in the upper areas of both may be relevant) provides an explanation for a puzzling element in Castagno. That is the disjointed spatial relation between the upper scenes and the Supper, the Supper being further in front. (A typical hypothesis was Vertova's valiant but unconvincing idea that the three scenes were to be seen not so much above the supper as behind it, in a transition between the earlier willingness to paint tiers of frescoes on a chapel wall and the later demand for the "realism" of a single scene per wall.) The puzzle has been reinforced by our common habit of reading all frescoed scenes in isolation like so many easel paintings, not as a set on a wall, and here further by the much inferior state of preservation of the upper scenes. The many writers who have rightly called Gaddi's Supper a precursor of Castagno's in its internal composition have not mentioned this similarity, that both set the Supper in front of the wall plane, while the upper scenes are set at that plane and behind it. The only change from Gaddi in Castagno is the modern Brunelleschian perspective.

Castagno's perspective arrangements are worth further comment at the risk of digression. They are not as accurate as the traditional praise of them suggests, but not as inaccurate as suggested by Hartt.[1] Some of his criticisms disppear if we read this as a distant perspective; even the front of the room is far from our eyes, not at the "picture" plane as in the usual case and as one might quickly assume. This is proper because the refectory is a very long room, and the viewer is most logically to be imagined half way along it. Hence the whole painted room of the supper is background. Since perspective diminution is fastest at the beginning and narrows in the distance, these squares of floor and ceiling rightly do not grow measurably smaller from unit to unit as they are further away, but are virtually identical in the tiny depth that they all share. (In principle, so long as there is some type of reading that will yield a result including accuracy on the part of the painter, we must select this as having been the one employed, rather than one involving inaccuracy even if it is a more usual perspective scheme, because we know that the artist desired to be accurate and that he had been technically trained. Squares of unchanging depth are incompatible with perspective accuracy if their depth is large on the scale of their width, but if it is slight they can be an accurate rendering of a distant part of a floor or ceiling.)

The observation that Gaddi's formula is being repeated, presumably with the same purpose, of including the Last Supper space in our space, is pleasant for a broader reason, involving the status of Castagno's fresco in the history of quattrocento art. It is a work commonly cited for the quattrocento love of perspective. That has bothered me because it is not typical of the artist. He and his immediate contemporaries, Pollaiuolo and Verrocchio, tend to reject their predecessors' preference for figures in balance with their measured environment, in equipoise with cubic containers of air larger than themselves while of lesser density—Masaccio, Uccello, Lippi, Angelico, constantly show this kind of world—substituting for it a greater absolute and relative

---

[1] F. Hartt, *History of Italian Renaissance Art* (1970), 222.

stress on the figure, with the environment given less than equal weight, reduced sometimes to a shallow niche, or to an infinite open sky silhouetting the figure, a flat wall, or plain color. The Last Supper, an exceptional work where Castagno comes close to the older artists, tends when emphasized by historians to obscure this shift between generations, and make balanced perspective schemes the steady vehicle of a century. In an earlier study I proposed to decrease this effect by analyzing what Castagno does in this perspective, building a masonry structure just twice as wide as it is deep (as shown most clearly by the hooks of the drapery) but, very inconsistently, arranging the figures to occupy space at least five times as wide as it is deep. Since we react to the fresco invariably on the basis of the latter spatial character, it emerges that Castagno is indeed, as usual, emphasizing the figures to the detriment of the environmental structure, not keeping them in harmony like his predecessors. The extreme neat accuracy of perspective drawing in detail here is that of one who had learned it as a lesson while a student, not that of the older artists who had taken part in developing its laws and found it an exciting vehicle. Yet despite all that I had not been able to explain why in that case Castagno built this perspective room at all. Now, though, the reference to Gaddi explains this too; it was requred iconographically. And it is not only here (as Mr David Wilkins noted) that Gaddi's idea was alive in the early quattrocento, for it was followed in another fresco, Masaccio's Trinity, with the same purpose, to identify the lower part with the observer's experience. In fact that lower part with the skeleton, projecting in front of the wall plane, addresses the viewer with the well known words, hardly possible to better in their insistence on sharing a world with us, "as I am so you shall be," while above this, at and behind the plane of the frame, the higher world of the Trinity presides.

Castagno's refectory is not the last in which the Last Supper and Crucifixion are associated in some way. In Leonardo's case we easily forget that the one other image with which his Supper shares the room is a Crucifixion, on the opposite wall. This fresco, of equal size with his, by the unknown Donato da Montorfano, dated 1495, is inevitably far more old-fashioned in style, so it is natural that we do not take into account that the dates are the same. Clark, interestingly, nearly does, and then misses the occasion.[1] He rightly speaks of Leonardo as starting probably in 1495, and as nearly finished in 1497, and then in a

---

[1] K. Clark, *Leonardo da Vinci* (1952), 90.

note mentions Montorfano's work as of "only two years before" the latter date, instead of as of the same year as the former date. Leonardo having been slow, as is famous, we must thus think of the frescoes as started together, as part of the same scheme, a startling modulation in our view of Leonardo. The use of the two opposite walls, however, symptomizes the new realism of the single tier and confirms the improved status of the Supper.

There is an even later Florentine refectory wall with a small Crucifixion frescoed above a large Supper, which has been much neglected. At the Dominican convent of San Marco, in 1536, Giovanni Antonio Sogliani placed below the Crucifixion not a Last Supper but the scene of St Dominic and his Monks Fed by Angels (fig. 3).[1] From the point of view of our approach, holy eating painted in a dining room to edify the observing eaters, the shift from the Last Supper is not important, and Vertova has rightly included this with quite a few other variant meals painted in refectories in her book called *I Cenacoli Fiorentini*.[2] If anything, this holy meal is even more a mirror of the Dominican observers, and Vasari does not surprise us with his report that the painted monks were portraits of the San Marco monks. He also tells us that, on getting the commission, Sogliani hoped to show off his skill with an elaborate Christ feeding the Five Thousand (itself illustrating the interchangeability of holy eating scenes) but the monks insisted, in Vasari's marvelous phrase, on something with qualities more "positive, ordinarie e semplici." And he continues with one of most illuminating statements anywhere on the problem of the relative weight of patron and artist in iconographic decisions, never exploited so far as I know. Sogliani would have done better with his own theme, he says, "because painters express the concepts of their own minds better than

---

[1] L. Vertova, *op. cit.*, 75 ff.

[2] To art historians, especially native English speakers, the word "cenacolo" means "Last Supper". It is therefore worth recalling two other equally valid senses. The basic meaning is a dining room. Thus if Vasari says that someone painted the *cenacolo* in Milan, he need by no means refer only to the Last Supper; he also probably is not saying that he painted on a wall of the refectory, but that he produced a painted room, the illusionary space where Christ dines. From this also derives the use of the word to mean other kinds of supper paintings, which we are more likely not to realize. An early use is the document specifying that Pontormo will paint "lo cenaculo de la despensa," which is his *Supper at Emmaus*, J. Rearick, *The Drawings of Pontormo* (1964), 226-27. The reference to the cenacolo being *in* the *despensa*, a room where food is served, shows that cenacolo means not the room but the painting.

those of other people," yet, on the other hand, "it is only decent that he who spends his money should get satisfaction."[1]

This Supper is also congruent with a Last Supper compositionally, of course. In a scornful critique, a rare case of any attention being paid to the fresco, Adolfo Venturi finds strangely old fashioned and literal echoes of Castagno.[2] Besides, the presence of eleven figures, when any number could have been freely selected, seems to echo the Last Supper design as exemplified in Castagno, with twelve behind the table, changed to the nearest odd number to make the main figure perfectly central. (Indeed the non-centrality of Christ seems to have been an annoyance until Leonardo solved the problem by ending the isolation of Judas in front of the table.)

Venturi rightly spoke also of ritualistic qualities in the design, and Vertova of its archaism. They could have supported this suggestion concretely, with a citation from a chronicle of the convent, noted by Wackernagel,[3] reporting that this refectory contained a Crucifixion by Fra Angelico. This presumably no longer existed when Sogliani's was painted (two identical scenes in one room are nearly though not absolutely impossible) [4] so that Wackernagel is reasonable in his suggestion that Sogliani's is a replacement, painted over it, probably because it was in bad condition. There is a parallel in the unnoticed fact that the "archaic" design of Sogliani's Supper is copied from a known composition by Angelico, surviving today in two predella panels (fig. 4).[5] Indeed the monks would have had to show Sogliani a model, when they demanded that he paint that subject. Angelico, who painted this whole convent, almost certainly painted a supper of some kind on this very wall, since every other quattrocento refectory in Florence has one, yet there is no trace of it. There is now instead, on the wall Angelico would probably have used, Sogliani's Supper copying an Angelico design with exceptional, archaic, fidelity. We may thus entertain the attractive hypothesis that Sogliani's fresco replaces Angelico's original

---

[1] Vasari, *ed. cit*, IV, 399 ff.

[2] A Venturi, *Storia dell' arte italiana*, IX-1 (1925), 400-01.

[3] M. Wackernagel, *Der Lebensraum des Künstlers in der florentinischen Renaissance* (1938), 133.

[4] In the Sistine Chapel, the calling of Peter and Andrew is represented both in a fresco by Ghirlandaio and, in another Christ cycle below, on a tapestry by Raphael. This seems to be very exceptional, and one can think of several reasons why special allowance might have been made. The question deserves enquiry.

[5] Reproduced in J. Pope-Hennessy, *Fra Angelico* (1952), plate 37 and fig. 171.

in this location. Since both upper and lower halves of the wall, Crucifixion and Supper, lead by independent paths to a copy of Angelico,
we can further reconstruct hypothetically a major lost work by him.
Besides the recorded Crucifixion, the Supper must have existed unless
there were already a fourteenth century Supper on this wall when
Angelico began his frescoing campaign in the convent (this is the suggestion of Vertova, unaware of the record of Angelico's Crucifixion in
the room.) The reconstructed work neatly fits our newly recovered
tradition of Crucifixions on top of Suppers—indeed, before now the
reconstruction of that pair of scenes might have been rejected as a
bizarre or awkward compound, but it is now seen to fit the conventions
also. Since the chronicle reports "a Crucifixion" in the room, it is
likely that this was the major element in the fresco, with a smaller
supper below, following the fourteenth century scheme. It would have
been painted during Angelico's campaign in the convent, about 1436-
45. Thus Castagno's reversal of the sizes of the two parts about 1450
really is the innovating example, and we can date the change closely.[1]

Sogliani's work, before we explained it as a reworking, had also
seemed odd as the one isolated case long after Castagno where the
Crucifixion was still painted above the Supper; in all other refectories
after 1450 the Crucifixion is at most found elsewhere in the room, as
in Leonardo, and in the first example to reflect Castagno's innovation,
Stefano d'Antonio's very minor Last Supper of 1465 in the refectory
of the hospital of San Matteo,[2] with the Last Supper by itself on the
wall just as it generally is later. Thus the archaism of Sogliani appears
as extreme and sharp in this respect, as in the details of composition,

---

[1] Another indication that Fra Angelico's fresco existed is that it surely was the fundamental influence on Pontormo's *Supper at Emmaus*. Among suppers, the Emmaus theme
generally does not belong to this paper, since the small quantity of figures evidently
tended to exclude it from the large wall spaces at the end of refectories. But Pontormo's
was in a dining room, as noted above 356, n. 2. It seems to have been a particularly
illusionistic mirror of its observers, probably painted in a door frame, on floor level,
on the scale of life, with extremely vivid portraits of the monks of the convent, and
with other realistic details such as the still life. This is in contrast with the sense of
motionless ritual abstraction set up by the stance of the figures and the composition
they produce. In criticism, the naturalistic aspects have been thought to contradict
Pontormo's usual mannerism, or else their unresolved contrast with the rigid poses has
been considered particularly mannerist. We can now relate both qualities in different
ways to tradition, the first connected with the specially strong sense of realism of the
dinners in dining rooms, the portraits of the convent monks specifically reflecting Fra
Angelico, while Pontormo's rigidity relates, as Sogliani's does, to the sensed archaism of
the source.

[2] L. Vertova, *op. cit.*, 37-40.

both suggesting the same explanation, that he is going over an old fresco of Angelico's.

A special interest attaches to the Last Supper by Cosimo Rosselli, not in a refectory, but part of the Passion cycle of the Sistine Chapel in Rome, of 1481 (fig. 5). In general design it is wholly dependent on recent ones by Ghirlandaio, but it has several extraordinary features. We are asked to accept an octagonal room, five of its sides shown, the other three to be extrapolated in front of the picture plane. As this front plane are the painted figures, perhaps waiters, watching the event from outside it. Both these inventions are not Rosselli's, but are to be connected with new devices worked out during the painting of this cycle by others of its painters, Perugino and Ghirlandaio, as I have suggested elsewhere.[1] (Perugino seems to have taken the lead in spatial tricks, not octagons but equally striking ones, and Ghirlandaio in the tricks with outside viewers as well as with genre actors. Evidently the ambitiousness of the cycle and the collaborative work were exciting and stimulating to the crew of bright young artists, none of whom had ever worked on such a grand production before.) Part of Rosselli's relatively less resolved experiment is the inclusion of three small scenes above the Supper, which occupy the airy area above the benches that Ghirlandaio's Supper composition had first introduced. The three scenes reflect the three above Castagno's, one may point out, so it is a notable change that the Crucifixion is moved to the right, in its chronological place. Between 1450 and 1480 it would seem that devotional emphasis had lost ground. By a related spatial experiment, we see this Crucifixion asymmetrically, in its diagonal place on a minor side of the octagonal room, and so see Christ in the angle of casual perspective. This is a very early example of informality applied to the ritually important theme of the Crucifixion, contemporary with a different design bearing the same implication in a miniature by the Master of Mary of Burgundy. Later Cranach, Tintoretto and others develop it dramatically. It is possible here so early, and in such a timid painter, no doubt because it is small and in the background; the next case in central Italy, I believe, is the backgrounds of altarpieces by Signorelli, who was a member of the Sistine crew. It is likely that it was formulated in discussions among the artists, not by Roselli as an individual. We are likely to pass by his work since he is so dull,

---

[1] C. Gilbert, "The Renaissance Portrait", *Burlington Magazine*, CX, 1968, 284. Rosselli's fresco is reproduced by Vertova, fig. 23.

and the alert complexity of some of its inventions is indeed surely to be explained in this indirect way.

Thus Castagno's fresco makes the shift on the refectory wall from a Crucifixion (with a small Supper below it) to a Supper (with a small Crucifixion above it, at first). His great influence has been considered puzzling, since the convent was in such strict clausura that his work is not mentioned by Vasari or any other early source. Rather then supposing that it was visible for a brief early period, I would think it more plausible that the later Suppers found their model in Castagno's second Supper, now lost, in the refectory of S. Maria Nuova.

As texts were quoted at the beginning of this paper to show the aptness of a Supper to refectories in the quattrocento, it is also incumbent to show how Crucifixions would seem apt in the previous century. It is a help here that the earliest in our series of Crucifixions was of the *lignum vitae* type, which thus can be related with assurance to that Franciscan text. Its author had a well organized mind, and it is worth quoting the whole of this first page, in which he explains the purpose of his work :

> "The true worshipper of God, and disciple of Christ the Savior of all, who was crucified for him, desiring to come to resemble Him perfectly with all his might, must beyond all his other actions with his whole mind intend and seek to carry Jesus Christ's cross in his mind and in his flesh, so that he may truly say and feel within himself the word of Paul the Apostle written at the head of this book, *Christo confixus sum cruci*, that is, I am nailed to the cross with Christ. And truly he merits this feeling and sensation and is worthy to test within himself—whoever that is who is neither ignorant nor ungrateful for the passion of Jesus God and man and goes over in his mind the pain and suffering and love of Jesus crucified, with such a vivid memory and recollection and such sharp understanding and willingness for love and kindness, that he may truly say the word that the bride said of her beloved bridegroom in the Song of Songs : 'My beloved has become in my heart as a bundle of myrrh, which shall remain forever in my arms.' Therefore, so that love and feeling may be lit up in us, and our thought be formed in habituation and firmly planted in our memory without being forgotten, I have studied how to collect this bundle of myrrh, that is the pain and suffering and love of Jesus, from the holy grove of the Gospel, where Jesus Christ's life and passion and glorification is copiously treated, and this bundle is assembled and arranged in few words linked together."[1]

The assembling and arranging is on a tree, to assist our memory, "and this tree is the cross." (It is thus not proper to say of Gaddi's fresco that Christ is shown not on the cross but on the tree of life in Eden.) But what surely is striking, after the earlier part of this paper,

---

[1] *Mistici del Duecento e del Trecento*, ed. Levasti (1935), p. 163 ff.

Fig. 1. Taddeo Gaddi: Frescoes of Refectory Wall, S. Croce, Florence

Fig. 2. Andrea del Castagno: Frescoes of Refectory Wall, S. Apollonia, Florence

Fig. 3. Giovanni Antonio Sogliani: Frescoes of Refectory Wall, S. Marco, Florence

Fig. 4. Fra Angelico: St Dominic Served by the Angels, predella panel of Coronation altarpiece, Louvre, Paris

Fig. 6. Francesco Botticini: Last Supper, predella panel of altarpiece, Museo della Collegiata, Empoli

Fig. 5. Cosimo Rosselli: Last Supper, Sistine Chapel, Rome

Fig. 7. Fra Angelico: The Communion of the Apostles, fresco in a cell at S. Marco, Florence

Fig. 10. Paolo Veronese: The Feast in the House of Levi, Venice, Accademia, detail of central figures

Fig. 8. Ercole de' Roberti: The Institution of the Eucharist, predella panel of altarpiece. National Gallery, London

Fig. 9. Tintoretto: The Communion of the Apostles. S. Giorgio Maggiore, Venice.

is the emphasis on the *likeness* between Christ and the observer, who is stimulated to "resemble him perfectly," to carry his cross and feel his pain. Such resemblance and echoing of actions is just what we had found in the observer of the suppers. Yet it is decidedly different to identify yourself with Christ nailed to the cross and with Christ eating. To define this difference will be my essential way of suggesting a change in attitudes between late medieval and early Renaissance.

Before pursuing this, however, I must consider in detail an alternative explanation, which assigns the importance of both the refectory themes, Crucifixion and Supper, to the Eucharist, which, it holds, is being symbolized. This view gains obvious support from the fact that the two events are indeed the most important ones surrounding the institution of the Eucharist, as the most elementary theologian would have understood. Thus when the Roman Catholic and Anglican churches made a recent agreement on defining Communion, the *New York Times* (December 31, 1971) explained to its readers : "Communion is the rite in which Christians commemorate the actions of Jesus at the Last Supper, including the partaking of bread and wine," and, after a few more details, "Catholics have thought of Communion as a reenactment of the sacrifice of Christ on the cross for man's sins." Thus it is very true that when we look at any Crucifixion or Last Supper, the Eucharist will be part of the implied reference, and Bonaventura alludes to the Eucharist in speaking of both events. But he also alludes to various other events, and always to explain the meanings of these scenes by singling out such reference to the Eucharist would, I think, be an incorrect exclusion of other possible emphases. In quoting in full his introductory words on the purpose for which he constructs the *lignum vitae* as a whole, for example, we find strong un-Eucharistic associations.

And just as we may think of the Crucifixion in very many other connections than the Eucharistic, so, more surprisingly, we may think of the Last Supper. This can be seen in another popular fourteenth century Franciscan text, the *Meditations on the Life of Christ*.[1] The author tells us that we should consider four things "principally" with regard to the Supper. "The first is the literal dinner; the second the washing of the feet; the third is how he instituted the Sacrament; the fourth is the most beautiful sermon that he made to them." Of the four, the author gives less attention to the second and the third, and

---

[1] *Ibid.*, 447 ff.

more to the first and fourth, giving strong visual evocations for both. Thus in the first he is interested in telling us that the table was a square about seven feet on each side, that three disciples sat on each side, and other such details. In the fourth he insistently adopts the imperative "look"; "Look at the disciples, how they stay sad with their heads down ... see John among the others, how he comes close to him affectionately, and how attentively and lovingly he looks at his beloved Jesus ... Now see the disciples ..."

Among the many meanings, of which several at a time may be intended for any one painting,[1] is it not likely that the Eucharistic meaning will be important in the cases of scenes in refectories ? This is Vertova's view.[2] Rightly rejecting an older view that the Suppers of refectories should be seen as historical reconstructions of the original drama—a nineteenth century approach, as if Leonardo were Renan— she finds that, instead, we must pay heed to the "sacramental and eucharistic" meaning. She is right that there is not only more than an anecdotal purpose, but a profession of faith. But when she goes further and proposes that the image is meant to transform the dining room "into a sort of oratory or chapel" where the fresco could bring the Redeemer into the room "in the absence of an altar" I think she is the victim of the opposite anachronism. I doubt that the fifteenth century monk or nun would think of a "sort of" chapel; there were, surely, consecrated altars and unconsecrated places, not to be assimilated to each other. To eat a meal in a dining room cannot be turned into taking communion by the presence of a fresco producing a metaphorical altar, indeed, that would probably be shocking or heretical.

---

[1] Here and later we confront a problem in current research in art history. Most symbols have more than one meaning, the most obvious example being words, which have several definitions each in any dictionary. "The lion symbolizes Christ but also the devil." They may also be multivalent, symbolizing more than one of their meanings at a time. But it is not sufficiently kept in mind, in my opinion, that they are likely to exclude some of their meanings from any particular instance of their use; the lion referring to Christ does not refer also, probably, to the devil. (We are not speaking in a context where subconscious references are of concern.) It appears to me that much recent art historical work has been harmed by excessive openness in this regard.Given a symbol, the scholar who finds that it has various meanings will present them all, and of course a possible link can usually be found. But this procedure seems to me a backward step, and we need to do the quite difficult job of controlling which few of the many symbolisms of a symbol are relevant each time. An illustration of the problem is offered below in connection with Leonardo.

[2] *Op. cit.*, 14.

It is always good to pray and meditate on Christ, and an image can assist one; this can happen in a refectory as it can before an outdoor shrine or in a room in a house before a Madonna, but the first is no more a chapel than the others. Vertova has, I think, been the victim of the trap of considering only two alternatives, so that, rightly rejecting nineteenth century realism as an explanation of the Suppers, she must try to attach them to the well organized church symbolism known in medieval theology. To me it seems that the texts cited above provide us with a third sort of reading, in which the function of the paintings is to give us a tool to imitate and resemble Christ and thereby to become virtuous, and the empirical realism of the paintings helps in this aim. The works become more ethical than ritual, while they remain also more religious than secular—more Renaissance than medieval while they are also more Renaissance than modern. This finding relates to a previous study, the same in which I cited Dominici's reasons for having paintings, which also discussed Giorgione's *Tempest* and the problem of the kind of meaning or theme it may have. The large number of scholars who feel that it must illustrate a particular passage in a text have not lost this conviction during fifty years of study which have failed to find the right one, and indeed do not admit that view to be a matter of faith rather than evidence; they have been trapped, I feel, by their correct understanding that the picture is not an impressionist vista, and their incorrect assumption that these are the only two possibilities.

In the case of the Last Suppers, one might try out a milder reformulation of Vertova's idea that their inherent Eucharistic reference would turn the refectories into virtual chapels. Do these Last Suppers, at least, choose their Eucharistic overtones to bring before us, among the various possible significances of the Supper? This question can be checked, I believe, by seeking a control group of other Last Suppers that are actually in chapels. If, in Vertova's concept, the Last Supper tends to evoke the presence of a chapel, it certainly ought to do so when it is in a true chapel. There is no collective study of such images, but a survey for this period has an interesting result; they are rare, and they do emphasize and actualize their Eucharistic aspects, by introducing an iconography different from the ones in refectories. The inference is that those in refectories had, at least, a lesser tie to the Eucharistic allusion.

It may be worthwhile first to observe in general that at this period in Italy paintings in chapels, i.e. altarpieces, do not so much function to assert that they are on an altar, as to assert the dedication of their altar differentiated from other altars. They state more emphatically that this is the altar of Saint Lucy than that this is a consecrated table. This function is indeed understood in our studies with so little difficulty that it is never stated, but perhaps that silence is disadvantageous in the present connection. These altarpieces and the refectory frescoes, I suggest, are alike in both having a tight link to their local particular purposes (in the refectory, to exploit the presence of eating) rather than a broad allusion, which the subject would carry anywhere, e.g. to the sacrament.

On the other hand, altarpieces do allude importantly to the qualities constant for all altars, notably in the fact that the saint to whom the altar is dedicated regularly receives only the second most important position, the chief one going to the Virgin and Child, reminding us that the saint is not the object but only the intermediary of the worship. More directly interesting to us is what happens to the predella, normally in fifteenth century Florence devoted to scenes of saints' lives. It is rather common for the series of scenes to be interrupted at the center by one showing the dead Christ in the tomb, and this even appears when a predella is otherwise absent. This is certainly a Eucharistic image, alluding to St Gregory's vision at the mass, of the Christ in the tomb, and its position in the altarpiece is adjacent to the center of the altar table. This small, but strong, reference to the Eucharistic context of the altar is not, however, a Last Supper.

We seem to find Last Suppers on altars when the dedication of the particular altar is appropriate, rather than as an element of altars in general. In such cases there are interesting examples of the replacement of the Christ in the tomb in the central predella panel by a Last Supper, interrupting a diverse series of biographical panels again.

A survey of the Last Supper as itself a theme for altarpieces can be developed from the data offered by Vertova in 1965 and by M. A. Lavin in 1967.[1] Mrs. Lavin has usefully divided the examples into two types, which she calls the Communion of the Apostles and the Institution of the Eucharist, a formula which it will be convenient to retain (even though the two are so closely related that they might equally well have interchanged the names.)

The Communion of the Apostles is best known from Joos van Gent's

---

[1] M. A. Lavin, *Art Bulletin*, Vol. 49 (1967), 1, note 4. Since this material is very useful, it should by the same token be used with the caution appearing infra, 391, n. 2.

altarpiece in Urbino, for the Confraternity of Corpus Domini, and Fra Angelico's fresco in a cell in San Marco (fig. 7). Here Christ administers the wafer to the disciples, who have left seats at the table and kneel before him, while he himself stands up in front of the table (though he does not in all other examples). In the Institution of the Eucharist the figures sit as in the Last Supper, but on the table the food has been replaced by the chalice and wafer, as on an altar; the most famous image of this is Bouts' altarpiece in Louvain, painted in 1464-67 for the brotherhood of the Sacrament, the only example outside Italy that I shall use. It is noticeable that the patrons of both altarpieces had a special, not simply the standard, concern with worship of the Eucharist, just as others might venerate a particular saint, and their altarpieces reflect this position.

It is certainly helpful to refrain from calling these images Last Suppers, though this is done for instance by Vloberg in his book on the Eucharist in Art [1]—which by the way, rightly in my view, virtually passes by the Last Suppers in refectories—in the case of Fra Angelico, though not of Joos van Gent. So likewise Panofsky [2] calls the Bouts a "most unusual Last Supper, where Christ, blessing the Host and Chalice, addresses the entire community of the faithful instead of announcing the denial of St Peter and exposing the traitor (and where) the very absence of dramatic tension converts the historical event into a sacred ritual." It does so, of course, because it is not a Last Supper in the more restricted sense; Bouts is simply showing a perhaps only normal sensitivity to his specific theme, not giving an unusual flavor to the supposed theme. The same is the case with an Italian instance which we can understand better by noting its closeness to Bouts. This is the small panel by Ercole de' Roberti (fig. 8), made for the center of a predella which had on either side a Gathering of the Manna and an Abraham and Melchisedek, both themes which recur from Bouts' set and have Eucharistic meaning.[1] They are also associated with the Last Supper in the *Biblia Pauperum*. Longhi described Ercole's panel as being, before Leonardo's, "the most meditated of Last Suppers, with

---

[1] M. Vloberg, *L'eucharistie dans l'art* (1946), 105 gff.

[2] E. Panofsky, *Early Netherlandish Painting* (1953), I, 492. It is conventional to speak of Bouts' work as the earliest example of the theme, but Parshall, *Burlington Magazine*, CXIV (1972), 248, has pointed out that it occurs earlier in Flemish miniatures, citing an example from the workshop of the Bedford Master, before 1415, reproduced by M. Meiss, *French Painting in the Time of Jean de Berry : The Boucicaut Master* (1968), fig. 101.

a fearfulness of a Mithraic rite ... the objects on the table severe and discreet ... in a static composition."[2] The objects are the chalice and wafer, and we may thus change the label from Last Supper and again find the work less special. The representation of Judas at the side turning away satisfies the requirement that he must not be shown as taking Communion.

Two other cases of this subject were identified by Mrs Lavin's sharp eye, which could easily have been missed for the interesting reason that they have just the same composition as the refectory Last Suppers, with the minute modification of adding the wafer and chalice. The first is a predella panel by Francesco Botticini (fig. 6). Mrs. Lavin left it in the isolation in which she found it, reproduced by itself for comparative purposes in a book on Leonardo da Vinci. Its context is richly documented. It is the central predella panel of an altarpiece (now in the museum of Empoli) commissioned in 1484 by a confraternity in that town, for a high altar, whose central section is a rare instance of not being an image at all but a niche for a host. The documents of commission specify that it was "ad honorem et reverentiam Sanctissimi Corporis Domini nostri Jhesu Christi, in quo sacrario seu tabernaculo dictum Sanctissimum Corpus teneri debeat et honorari,"[3] that is, it is an actual tabernacle as well as an altarpiece. The side panels of the triptych show two saints; the five parts of the predella show scenes of the saints' lives in the two outermost panels, and the three middle ones include, besides our Institution scene, distinctly smaller scenes of the Arrest of Christ and the Prayer in the Garden at its left and right, thus following a doctrinal rather than a chronological interrelation.

The second example is Cosimo Rosselli's fresco in the Sistine Chapel, discussed above among the Last Suppers, and perhaps properly so since it is in a narrative sequence of Christ's life. Yet just as it was the only one of those discussed that belongs in a chapel, it is likewise the only one to introduce the wafer and chalice.

Although outside our scope, in the seventeenth century, another fresco mentioned by Vertova [4] has special interest because it is in a chapel in Florence, a city where Last Suppers even in a large sense

---

[1] M. Davies, *Earlier Italian Schools (National Gallery Catalogues)* (1961), 461. This material does not appear in the first edition, of 1951.

[2] R. Longhi, *Viatico per Cinque Secoli di Pittura Veneziana* (1946).

[3] Documents published by G. Milanesi, in his edition of Vasari, *Le Vite* (1879), IV, 243.

[4] *Op. cit.*, 87-88.

seem not to appear in relation to altars otherwise, perhaps because the theme had developed such a special association with refectories. It is an altarpiece fresco, with chalices included not in its main spatial area but in the frame, along with allegories of Faith and the Church. It is in the very convent, S. Apollonia, whose refectory contains Castagno's Supper, and though most planners of altars may have rejected the theme because of its connection with refectories, as suggested, one still may suppose that these nuns took the rare step of selecting it just because of their special link with it.

The earliest example cited by Vertova and the earliest known to me of the other theme, the Communion of the Apostles, is also the central panel of a predella, in an altarpiece now in the Vatican gallery. It is by Niccolò di Tommaso, a painter of the third quarter of the fourteenth century in Florence,[1] best known for his iconographic innovation of the Nativity in the form seen by St. Bridget in a vision. It is under a large Crucifixion, which will interest us, but perhaps this is not of special importance since the altarpiece contains eight further passion scenes. It is unfortunate that Mrs. Lavin did not know this work, since it invalidates some of her suggestions on the theme of the Institution of the Eucharist.[2]

From the instances collected of these two themes, not quite Last Suppers, found generally in relation to altars and chapels in the

---

[1] B. Berenson, *Italian Pictures of the Renaissance, Florentine School* (1963), 162. It is reproduced by Vertova, fig. 8, with a different attribution.

[2] Mrs. Lavin's useful discussion of the two themes lists only a few examples, which is appropriate since it is brief. It is unfortunate only that she draws conclusions from these few examples as to general trends, which are invalidated by the addition of even a few more examples, and it is especially unfortuante that she did not make use of the material collected by Vertova shortly before. The Niccolò di Tommaso panel cancels her view that this composition, as known later in Joos and Angelico, first appears in the quattrocento, along with the corollary that it was stimulated into being by the Ecumenical Council of that period, and helps to cancel her view that the theme is rare in Italian paintings of all periods. Examples only from among these related ot the present topic easily triple her list. They include the altarpiece of 1506 by Marco Palmezzano, somewhat reflecting Joos (Forlì Gallery, reproduced by C. Grigioni, *Marco Palmezzano* (1956), fig. 18), the important altarpiece by Signorelli of 1512 for a Fraternità del Gesù, which a recent writer typically calls "a fresh and original way of representing the Last Supper" (reproduced by L. Dussler, *Signorelli* (1927), fig. 139), the various versions by Tintoretto and the one by Veronese to be discussed below, and even a copy of Joos made as late as the eighteenth century for the altar of the sacrament in the Cathedral of Jesi.

quattrocento, we can infer a rule that when the image of the meal of Christ and the disciples is in a chapel or on an altar, the wafer and chalice are shown, and when it is in a refectory, they are not shown. The deduction, that in the refectories it was not intended to allude to the Eucharist, seems sharpened in particular by the predella of Botticini and the Sistine fresco of Rosselli, which both follow the composition invented by Ghirlandaio for refectories, quite closely so indeed, but add the chalice and wafer to it when they are planned for chapels. A similar comparison might be made between the two frescoes in S. Apollonia, Castagno's and the much later one in a chapel. The only exception I can find where a Last Supper for a chapel shows no chalice and wafer has to be sought at such a distance that the fact seems to make it the exception to prove the rule : this is a fresco over the altar of the church of S. Martino at Castel Sant'Angelo in the Marches, near the larger village of Visso, painted about 1475 by Paolo da Visso,[1] in a very old fashioned style suitable to its place in mountains near the Abruzzi. Its special interest is that it has a Crucifixion above, and what is more a small Crucifixion, allowing the attractive speculation that it is a reflection from Castagno's Florentine formula of 1450. Such a single spillover of two unusual characteristics from the—very influential—work for a refectory to an altar is the kind of thing that should be expected to happen in real life, however inconvenient to the establisment of categories; we shall see much more of this in the sixteenth century. In any case it does not seem to invalidate the distinction offered above.

The opposite exception, a refectory Last Supper *with* wafer and chalice, seems not to occur until the seventeenth century. Then a huge canvas by Matteo Rosselli, in a refectory for Florentine nuns,[2] adds not only a chalice but a vision above of Mary with a flaming heart. It clearly manifests a conscious infiltration of sacramental interests into the refectory suppers in the Counter-Reformation, and thereby only underlines further their distinct non-sacramental character up to that time. Perhaps the S. Apollonia altarpiece at the same date, if we

---

[1] Reproduced by Vertova, fig. 7, with inadequate caption. The central predella panel of Andrea Sansovino's Corbellini altar at S. Spirito, Florence, is a Last Supper, which may also lack eucharistic tokens; an examination was inconclusive. It is curious if this is so, since the altarpieces of that church of the same period consistently include a central predella panel (often alone) with Christ in the Tomb.

[2] Vertova, *op. cit.*, 89-90.

may look at it as a critique of the earlier S. Apollonia refectory fresco, does the same. This shift in the Counter-Reformation certainly fits one of the traditional views about that period, shown for instance by Mâle, though we are not therefore required to follow it further into calling the Renaissance a secular age. It was suggested above that the allowance of only two alternatives has caused the justified rejection of the formula "Renaissance-secular" to produce an idea of a Renaissance indistinguishable in its religious statements from the Middle Ages, as in giving eucharistic values to Suppers. Perhaps it would have been better to say indistinguishable from the Counter-Reformation.

Having concluded with a firm distinction between Renaissance refectories and chapels, we should test it again by considering a particular example of the opposite argument, in terms of a recent proposal that Leonardo's Supper is a eucharistic work.[1] Of course in a very broad sense it is. The raw term "Last Supper" with its many possible directions of emphasis, has the Eucharist as one of the major ones, and of course a major meaning is never entirely absent from any instance of the term, just as a word in the dictionary which has a constellation of meanings, however one uses it, retains some reference to its leading significations regardless of how one wants to use the word at the moment. To say this may seem to beg the question, by allowing Eucharistic meanings in a work like Leonardo's and then finding a way always to discount them at will. But this is not the case, on the contrary. The contrary proposal, that Leonardo's particular composition of the Supper has Eucharistic meanings, must be meant to say that it has the intention of bringing the Eucharistic qualities to the fore; if it only means that such qualities are inevitably embedded because of the theme, *that* is to beg the question. The analysis therefore has to proceed on the level, however difficult it is to get agreement, of whether such references in a work like Leonardo's are the inevitable minimal ones unremovable from all Last Suppers, or whether they are given a leading role. The recent analysis, whether or not with this requirement in mind, does set out to meet this degree of proof. It finds that Christ's two arms "point out" the bread and wine, with the implication that Christ at this moment is showing the disciples that this is his body and blood. But I would note that neither hand is in fact

---

[1] This proposal was made in a lecture, not heard by me but reported to me by a graduate student, It will therefore be cited here anonymously, only as the case that might be made for such a proposal.

performing a pointing gesture. In one case, at most, the direction of the arm, when we read it as a line, points to a piece of bread, and in the other the fingers come near to a glass of wine and are in circular position so that they might grasp it. This might be called "passive pointing". There is no wafer, as distinguished from ordinary bread, and no chalice, as distinguished from ordinary glasses. In each case the bread and glass indicated are among many others scattered over the table. If we compare this with other works, it shows less unquestionable allusion to the Eucharist than any of the contemporary Suppers in chapels, with chalice and wafer, and about the same amount as those in refectories. The relation of objects to hands, the nature of the objects, and their lack of uniqueness, all leads us to say that Leonardo is either diluting his Eucharistic references, or, to give it a more positive rhetoric, is alluding to it by subtle hints. He would, moreover, share this degree of passive, diluted or subtle effect with all the other refectory Suppers in non-consecrated places, a degree less than that present in the ones on altars. This seems to me to work out to a definition of a Supper in which the Eucharistic reference is the sort inherent in the theme, as suggested above. Nothing is being done to emphasize the reference to the body and blood, while everything is done to bring out the attractiveness of the figures to us who are to imitate them.

There are numerous Last Suppers which are neither altarpieces or in refectories. Some are or were in chapels, such as the set of panels for the Silver Cupboard of S. Annunziata by Fra Angelico, a cupboard which contained chalices. It is of interest for showing both the Last Supper and the Communion of the Apostles in two separate panels, the best evidence for the distinction of these events in the views of this period. It has a sacramental emphasis, as does Angelico's frescoed Communion in a monk's cell. When the scene is part of a narrative cycle of Christ's life the Supper is usually not sacramental, even when it is a predella panel of an altarpiece, such as those by Castagno[1] and Signorelli [2]—simply one predella panel in a chronological series, that is, not the separate central one.

Surprisingly little attention has been given to the particular actions represented in the non-sacramental Suppers of the refectories. The sacramental ones, in which Christ holds up the host, clearly illustrate

---

[1] Reproduced by M. Salmi, *Paolo Uccello, Andra del Castagno, Domenico Veneziano* (1936), fig. 155.

[2] Reproduced by Dussler, *Signorelli*, fig. 129.

the text, this is my body, this is my blood. Of the others it is often said that they illustrate the text : One of you shall betray me, but that seems to be extrapolated from Leonardo's version. It is very original, and the moment that is isolated, Christ's gesture of spreading arms, and John in the process of fainting as the others react, all are unique. What we should notice as common to many is Christ blessing. There seems to be no textual authority for this, and it is not always plain whether the blessing is directed to John swooning, [1] to the food on the table, or to us. The last is clear in some of the most routine instances, e.g. the one of 1470 at S. Andrea at Cercina.[2] Vertova notes the blessing in some cases, but oddly not in the earliest, the Gaddi fresco at S. Croce, which is the starting point in this as in other formulations that were to become common; she says Christ "lifts his hand o quiet the apostles"[3] but his fingers are in the proper blessing pattern.[4] tThis pattern seems to start with the start of suppers in refectories, and replaces the older pattern seen in Byzantine images and in Giotto's narrative scene in the Arena cycle, where the emphasis is on putting a hand in the dish. The blessing thus may relate to the special value that the Supper acquires when it comes into refectories, the continuum with us, since the blessing may be directed at us, and even the blessing of the food would be suitable to the continuity with our meal, quite outside a church.

The double tradition which we have observed, of eucharistic Suppers for altars and chapels, and non-sacramental ones for refectories, has

---

[1] V. Aurenhammer, in his excellent brief article, "Abendmahl", *Lexikon der christlichen Ikonographie* (1959), 11-15, notes that there is no textual or early basis for John swooning, and suggests that it develops about the tenth century in a gradual extension from the text about Christ's love for him.

[2] Vertova, *op. cit.*, fig. 39.

[3] *Op. cit.*, 24.

[4] V. Aurenhammer, *art. cit.*, provides a useful sketch of the history of Last Suppers before the period considered here, and curiously enough also for the period after it, with relatively little on the Renaissance. He lays stress on Gaddi's fresco as the innovative one for the type we know, showing the long table, with figures behind it, and Christ centered. He cites as exceptions two earlier cases, in Verona and Pistoia, but there are certainly more, e.g. S. Ambrogio, Milan, pulpit. It is almost always agreed that Gaddi's was the first Last Supper in a refectory, but L. H. Heydenreich has kindly drawn my attention to the one in the refectory at S. Paolo fuori le Mura, Rome, of about 1180. (Reproduced by J. Wilpert, *Die römischen Mosaiken und Malereien der kirchlichen Bauen vom IV-XIII Jahrhundert* (1917), II, Plate 232 f.) It is very fragmentary, and its relation to the later tradition would require a special investigation.

a strong continuation in sixteenth century Venice, and may help to explain some things that have been vague there. Vertova rightly drew attention to the sacramental character of Tintoretto's often repeated Last Suppers.[1] The complicating factor is the influential role in establishing their design played by Leonardo's non-sacramental composition, so that a refectory design is being utilized in an image with stronger ritual values. This had had the difficult result of obscuring the precise theme that Tintoretto is painting. In his first Supper, at San Marcuola.[2] he supplements a rather literal derivation from Leonardo with two figures of women entering the scene from left and right, holding bread and a chalice respectively, and identifiable as Charity and Faith. Thus these extra allegorical figures, rather like those in the framing areas of the S. Apollonia chapel fresco later, are needed to turn the composition into a eucharistic one, as it must be since it is in a church. This serves to underline the absence of eucharistic reference in the main Leonardo composition. The notable absence of integration of these two concerns happens to be helpful for our understanding of how the Leonardo composition was used, but unsurprisingly was dissatisfying to Tintoretto, In his three later and well known Suppers, at Santo Stefano, San Rocco, and San Giorgio Maggiore (fig. 9),[3] the theme is not a Last Supper at all, as it is generally labelled in the literature,[4] but a quite standard Communion of the Apostles in the tradition of Joos van Gent at Urbino. Christ is holding out the wafer, which Peter leans forward to take in his mouth. We must thus rename these paintings, and also alter our analysis of Tintoretto's art, taking a different view on such questions as how intently he was concerned to vivify the dramatic situation, and how much physical drama he added to the traditional base. What has obscured the true theme is that in the first two paintings Christ is still seated, no doubt again reflecting the great force of Leonardo's example still. Then at San Polo [5] he stands up, behind the center of the table, and his arms stretch out with wafers in them, to give to the communicants, a brilliant amendment to his source and a solution to the need to use Leonardo's classic design while representing the Eucharistic event. In the great San Giorgio picture

---

[1] *Op. cit.*, 16.

[2] Reproduced by H. Tietze, *Tintoretto* (1948), fig. 20.

[3] *Ibid.*, figs. 178, 208, 275.

[4] A valuable exception is Aurenhammer, *art. cit.*, who includes them in his list of representations of the Communion of the Apostles.

[5] Tietze, *op. cit.*, fig. 140.

Christ stands up behind the table and walks among the disciples just as in Joos van Gent; the comparison of the fifteenth and sixteenth century pictures is full of suggestion, and makes us feel astonished at the obvious error in the name regularly given to Tintoretto's work. In two other Suppers, the badly damaged one at San Simeone and the one at San Trovaso,[1] Leonardo is followed not only in composition but in theme; for the first time we see the non-sacramental composition on an altar. I attribute this to the effect of Leonardo's work, which had become "the" Last Supper already, and would speculate that once so established, this originally non-sacramental composition was able to appear on altars without disturbing anyone. Yet this break in the previous distinction only affects two of Tintoretto's seven versions.

It was right of Vertova to introduce Tintoretto into her Florentine study; her view that all Last Suppers are sacramental indeed gains support from them, all of them being related to altars, even the one for the Scuola di San Rocco,[2] and thus tending to show sacramental details. But another contemporary group of Venetian suppers was made for refectories, by Veronese, and they once again lack eucharistic tokens, like *their* predecessors in the fifteenth century refectories in Florence. Though the contrast in style between Tintoretto and Veronese is traditional, this factor of diverse placing and function of their works seems not to have been taken into account. It is common to say that Veronese's Suppers are secularizing, but perhaps we can modify that interpretation.

Like the Suppers for the earlier Florentine refectories, Veronese's represent many scenes of eating, not just the Last one. Indeed that is rarely their focus, so that Vertova is justified in omitting them. Yet this was, of course, the original theme of the most famous Veronese Supper of all, and the one whose subject has been the topic of investigation precisely because it did not seem serious enough. This is the one now in the Venice Academy, painted in 1573 (fig. 10), for which Veronese had to answer to the Inquisition. It is clear that it was originally a

---

[1] *Ibid.*, fig. 88.

[2] Since we naturally think of the Scuola di San Rocco as not a church, it is worth while to recall the presbytery area of its large hall, separated from the rest by steps and a railing. The altar is dedicated to St. Roche, and the eucharistic images are at the sides, in their normal secondary status on altars. As the so-called Last Supper is at the left, the Multiplication of the Loaves and Fishes is on the right, and the Old Testament themes traditionally considered prophecies of the Eucharist, scenes of miracles about food, appear on the ceiling.

Last Supper, as Fehl has pointed out in vain.[1] This is shown first by
the fact that it was commisioned to replace a Last Supper by Titian,[2]
which had been burnt, for the refectory of San Zanipolo, a Dominican
convent, second, by the fact that it does indeed present Christ seated
with the twelve disciples behind the table, who are the dramatis
personae of the Last and of no other Supper. Indeed one can with
some surprise see the three main persons, Christ, John and Peter,
shown so normally that in a detail reproduction one would never label
the painting in any other way. To be sure, some of the other disciples
are hard to track down. And third, Veronese said so in his testimony,
calling it "Last Supper" and mentioning the twelve disciples.[3] It is
there, though, that the trouble starts, which has led to the confusion,
since he calls it "Last Supper in the House of Simon," according to
the transcript. This makes no sense, and has been accepted by historians as showing that a lack of clarity about the theme was Veronese's
own, and permissible in our enquiries too. But a few lines later Veronese
mentions the theme of the "Feast in the House of Simon" separately,
in a way that shows he knew the exact difference, as indeed he would
since he had painted it not long before. The plausible explanation then
for the confused phrase is that it is the scribe's, affected precisely by
the rapid succession of reference to the two subjects, in a way note-
takers at art historical lectures should be able to appreciate. Testimony
indeed was given that before the trial, the Inquisition had proposed to
the Dominicans that they resolve the trouble by getting Veronese to
change the subject, by the expedient of removing a dog and painting
a Magdalene in its place, thus making the picture into a Feast in the
House of Simon. Not only was this not done, but we can still see the
dog, just at the point near Christ's feet where Magdalene would indeed
appear kneeling in a Feast in the House of Simon. Veronese, as we
know, promised to make changes but instead merely changed the title
inscribing it conspicuously as the Feast in the House of Levi. This was
a real acceptance of the spirit of the Inquisition's demands, which had
complained that buffoons were unsuitable to the Last Supper, since
in the house of Levi Christ ate with publicans and sinners. Hartt [1]

---

[1] P. Fehl, "Veronese and the Inquisition," *Gazette des Beaux-Arts*", VI-58 (1961),
325 ff.

[2] S. Marconi-Moschini, *Gallerie dell'Accademia di Venezia, Opera d'arte del secolo XVI*
(1962), 83-85.

[3] E. G. Holt, *A Documentary History of Art* (1958), II, 56 ff.

has rightly pointed this out, though he is not right in saying Christ is talking with such persons; he is still talking with Peter and John, intact from the Last Supper composition, and characters not properly included in the Levi story. Indeed confusion has reigned among the best writers, Blunt saying that the theme was the Levi story from the start and that Veronese did make changes,[2] Holt saying that at first the theme was the feast in the House of Simon, Hartt that the first theme cannot be ascertained.

When we see Veronese's painting as part of the tradition of Last Suppers for refectories, continuing at least since Castagno, we clarify its attitude and achievement, I believe. Like the earlier ones it is interested in everyday reality and remote from the eucharistic ritual. By the time of Andrea del Sarto and perhaps even Stefano d'Antonio this approach had already led to introducing the waiters at the meal, and Veronese extends that aspect greatly but does not shift direction. It was the inquisitors who wanted to change traditions of imagery, in what we might consider a "Counter-Reformation" sense, similar to the behavior of the Dominicans in Florence a generation earlier who made Sogliani do something more "ordinary and simple," and the nuns a generation later who got Matteo Rosselli to make the refectory supper wholly liturgical. Neither Sogliani's patrons nor Veronese's inquisitors yet went that far. It is worth underlining that the inquisitors, complaining of much that Veronese did and even of encouragement to heresy, never referred to the absence of any eucharistic reference in his work, though there is none. We may infer that none was expected; such confirmations ex silentio of our thesis that in refectories none ever was, seem legitimate to mention when the text that is silent is a list of indictments.

By the same token, Veronese made a proper defense, that he was doing what was normal, that painters are permitted to add "figures according to the stories," and was surprised at the excitement. Hence it seems better to follow not the interpretation of Blunt that Veronese ignored his theme in favor of his decorative interests, or that of Marconi that he was asserting the freedom of the artist, both, it seems to me, approaches of later times, but rather Fehl's argument that Veronese was indeed sensitive to his subjects.[3] An excellent confirmation for

---

[1] *Op. cit.*, 562.

[2] A. Blunt, *Artistic Theory in Italy* (1940), 116.

[3] Fehl goes beyond the evidence only, I think, where he suggests that the figures

this, indeed a sort of control object, is found when Veronese does paint a Supper of the Eucharistic kind, in fact a Communion of the Apostles (Brera), consistent with the several by Tintoretto, yet far more direct and simple in its exposition of the ritual action.

From this Venetian reaffirmation of the distinction of two kinds of Supper paintings, in refectories and chapels, we may return to our central interest in two kinds of refectories, with suppers and with crucifixions. I had suggested that they have in common the urging of resemblance and even identity between observers and observed, but that in the two cases this has very different implications for the observer's approach to God. While eating, to identify with a supper is effortless enough; to identify with Christ nailed to the cross calls for the strongest effort to imagine oneself other. In the later period, of the suppers, the priest as pedagogue comes to meet his pupils in their own context and creates a mirror of that environment; in the earlier period, the pupil is expected to do it all. In the later age we find Christ to be like us, as in the infantile images of Dominici, so that we can readily be like him; earlier, we must force ourselves to copy his incredible action. Both cases emphasize Christ's human aspect, living or dying, but in the later approach he is like all other men, earlier he had been the greatest man, feeling the greatest pain and greatest love, qualities that reinforced his human nature, with a body and with human feelings, and we had been forced to recognize and to repeat this.

This approach to the crucified Christ, taken from the introduction of the *Lignum Vitae* text, is emphasized here because of the striking and well-known fact that in the period and region of that book's composition the painted image of Christ crucified developed a comparable special quality. The painted crosses of thirteenth century Tuscany and nearby regions are the most remarkable and probably the most numerous paintings of their age there, and the most remarkable sculptures of the same locus are the wooden groups of Depositions from the Cross, identical in evoking the pain and mourning of Christ. For the purposes of the present essay I would like to contrast them with the most typical images of Christ seen in immediately preceding cultures. As is well known again, Byzantine mosaic apses and French church

---

suggest a eucharistic meaning. He does not give distinct evidence for this, and one may suppose that, not having had before him the factors of the previous tradition discussed here, he supposed that in an image attentive to the theme such a meaning must be contained.

porches as well as Italian echoes of both show him as the Lord, in the one case the *pantocrator*—as he is labelled at Monreale—in the other as the final appeals judge, in the Last Judgment. We are not to think of resembling him, but obeying him, and he is unlike us, not human but divine. I do not know what, if any, literary illustrations of that attitude exist. But I would now like to summarize three views by men about Christ, which can be associated with three successive epochs. He is (1) the divine ruler, (2) the greatest of men, (3) a man like ourselves. In the third case, where my illustrations are the refectory Last Suppers, they are not the most frequent Christ images of their age, but with Leonardo they produced perhaps its most classic image of him, and Dominici's text suggests that the most commonplace Christ icon of the quattrocento, the Madonna and Child panel, shares their approach in this respect.

To explore the first of the three epochs would be to go far afield; leaving it simply as a contrasting boundary, I would like to add a few details about the second, in terms of the painted crosses of the dugento, in the particular case of the painter who seems to have been the innovator of the suffering Christ, Giunta Pisano. It seems interesting that these works are the first to exemplify several apparently independent phenomena about painting and its social role, so basic that they usually are not even formulated explicitly. It is with them, and other contemporary dugento panels, that painting makes paintings its chief vehicle, as they have been since, not mosaics or stained glass or even fresco, all vehicles in which the surface of something else is partly covered with color. Here the paintings become autonomous. It is with Giunta again that the artist first emerges as part of the social phenomenon of art. Not all medieval art is anonymous by any means, but names belong to a single work and to nothing of any other sort; with Giunta and from then on we have a group of works, other biographical documents, an evolution of style, travels, influences, and thus a biography, the work appears the product of a personality. Both these new qualities of paintings and painters are related to the emergence, in the same Tuscan non-feudal towns, of capitalist society; the autonomous painting is among other things a commodity of trade and a manufactured good, the painter among other things an entrepreneurial venturer. He is also, outside feudalism, a free agent who will develop his individuality, as we traditionally say of the Renaissance— the new "humanity" appears both in the painting and its maker. In Giunta's painting, it appears in the abolition of the small scenes theretofore included on crosses, and the use of this freed area to let the body writhe. This is a triple dose of modern change, removing a medieval scheme in which a set of images appears in various classified sizes and importance in a feudal, contract-society manner, newly evoking instead the physical body of Christ, and doing these things as an artist's decision. All this might seem to be an assertion that the Renaissance begins with Giunta Pisano, and the temptation to keep pushing it back is of course always present. But his Byzantine stylized drawing is enough to remind us that he is as medieval as are the small commercial communes where he worked, however much they too contain nuclei of modern society shifted to the city from the manor, with social control by committees of merchants. Rather than forms of the Renaissance, all these may be considered that class of medieval forms that could most easily become fertile for the Renaissance, though in their own time atypical mutants.

Nevertheless, among the pattern of three epochs sketched here, we may be drawn to assert a great break between the first two, from divine to human God, rather than the second two, from superior human to similar human. The second pattern, the superior human God, would then for me mark the "late medieval," while the third would be of the "early Renaissance." Among the caveats to such formulas, existing in quantities, one might cite the persistence of older patterns—Bonaventura's view that we should respond to Christ's pain is still Ignatius Loyola's, or rather perhaps *again* Ignatius Loyola's. Conversely, new inventions are not invented, but are the coming to dominance of what had existed in a recessive corner—there are a few painted crosses in the twelfth century. In the context of such stipulations the reader may be willing to consider the preceding materials.[1]

---

[1] K. M. Swoboda, "Die Apostelkommunion in den Bildern Tintorettos," *Jahrbuch des Österreichischen Byzantinistik*, XXI (1972), 251-268, a Festschrift for Otto Demus, regrettably reached me only when this paper was in the press. It is agreeable that I reached the same conclusions on the earlier and later themes of Tintoretto, the main ubject of Swoboda's study. My paper is an implied critique of his view of the sources, a main topic here and a minor one in his case.

PHOTO PERMISSIONS AND CREDITS: Alinari (3,5,6), Anderson (10), Fondazione Cini (9), National Gallery, Londen (8), Service d'Etudes et de Documentation, Musée du Louvre, Paris (4), G. F. S. G., Florence (1,2,7).

QUERIES ON "LAST SUPPERS AND THEIR REFECTORIES"

CLIFTON C. OLDS

The University of Michigan

Professor Gilbert asked that his paper be considered a query. This critique of his very interesting study should be considered nothing more than that. As one more familiar with the art of northern Europe, I merely wish to raise a few questions which occurred to me as I read Professor Gilbert's paper and which he and/or others have probably also considered and perhaps disposed of.

I think I am correct in stating that Professor Gilbert has observed a number of phenomena hitherto ignored or at least misread by scholars dealing with this material. His analysis of the illusionistic aspects of the *Last Supper* of Taddeo Gaddi and the persistence of those aspects in the fifteenth and sixteenth centuries is extremely enlightening. His discussion of Tintoretto's and Veronese's *Suppers* adds important new dimensions to our knowledge of these often puzzling paintings. And tucked into the corners of his main thesis are some especially provocative suggestions concerning such problems as the subject of Fra Angelico's lost fresco in the *refettorio grande* at San Marco. There are much more important and central issues raised by his paper, however. To my mind, one of the most interesting of his observations is that the "meaning" of a given representation of the *Last Supper* is apparently conditioned by its site, not only in terms of the response of the viewer but more specifically and more importantly in terms of the intent of the artist and his patrons. That *Last Suppers* painted in or for chapels should include specifically eucharistic elements, whereas those painted on the walls of refectories should omit the chalice and the host, thus diminishing the sacramental aspect of the scene, should probably not surprise us. The art historian is constantly forced to admit that works of art which he once tended to consider under a single thematic heading are in reality very different indeed, so different in fact that the theological significance of variations on a theme often tends to overshadow the common thematic bond linking those variations. Professor Gilbert has effectively subdivided the subject commonly known as the *Last Supper* and has shown that this subdivision is historically valid, citing such texts as the *Meditation on the Life of Christ*, in which the literal, the symbolic, the sacramental, and the didactic aspects of the theme are all considered. In so doing he has demonstrated clearly the "interplay between religious ideas and certain novel images" which he establishes as the central focus of his paper.

I am not quite so convinced by Professor Gilbert's second principal thesis, i.e. that there is a significant shift of emphasis away from the *Crucifixion* as the principal theme of refectory decoration and toward the *Last Supper*—a shift he sees taking place in Andrea del Castagno's frescoes of the late 1440's and which he interprets as a reflection of a shift in man's attitude toward Christ (from "the greatest of men" to "a man like ourselves"). I would agree with him that the *Last Supper* painted on the wall of a refectory not only was intended as one unit in a *spatial* continuum involving the area of the dining hall itself, but also provided an *ethical* contunuum embracing those who observed it. I also agree that it is much easier to "join" Christ and the Apostles in the act of breaking bread then it is to join Him on the cross. What I question is whether the shift he observes actually takes place at the time and at the site he suggests. We know that the idea that an image, either physical or envisioned, could and indeed *should* elicit a strong sympathetic and even imitative response on the part of the viewer was current in western thought long before Giovanni Dominici's *Regola del Governo di Cura Familiare*, and the works of art inspired by the idea anticipate the third of Professor Gilbert's categories as often as they correspond to the second. Fourteenth-Century Germany produced a great many "compassion crosses", but the image of St. John resting his head on the bosom of Christ—an image related to if not extracted from the *Last Supper*—was just as popular. These are northern images, to be sure, but to my mind they complicate the neat chronological divisions established by Professor Gilbert. And to return to the frescoes of Florence, I am not certain that I can agree that the *Crucifixions* of the Fourteenth Century dominate their *Last Suppers*. In the frescoes of Sta. Croce and Sto. Spirito the *Crucifixion* takes up more space, it is true, but the *figures* of the *Last Supper* are in fact larger or as large as those of the *Crucifixion*, and the illusionistic "advance" of the *Last Supper* into the world of the viewer, so accurately analysed by Professor Gilbert, seems to me to *enhance* the significance of the latter scene. It is extremely difficult to compare the two scenes in terms of importance or impact since we deal with two very different compositions—one horizontal and the other essentially vertical—and this leads to another problem. The frescoes of the fourteenth-century refectories decorate high, timber-trussed halls whose end walls include an ample triangular "gable" ideal for the traditional composition of the *Crucifixion*. The groin-vaulted refectories of the fifteenth century are relatively low of ceiling, the more modern design transforming the wall area from a vertical or at least square profile to an essentially horizontal one. In a sense, there is no *room* for a *Crucifixion* in most fifteenth-century refectories, at least not above a *Last Supper* unless the former element is much reduced in size (as in Cosimo Roselli's fresco in the Sistine Chapel) or unless it is squeezed uncomfortably into place (as in Giovanni Antonio Sogliani's fresco in San Marco). This observation in no way invalidates Professor Gilbert's contention that the *Last Supper* supplants the *Crucifixion* in later fifteenth-century refectories, since the artist could have eliminated the *Last Supper* and retained the *Crucifixion*, merely adjusting the latter scene to a horizontal format. I would guess, however, that the monks of Florence, faced with a choice forced upon them by architectural realities, chose a subject which had *already* competed successfully with the *Crucifixion* on the walls of earlier refectories and which lent itself more harmoniously to the walls of the later ones. In short, the shift may owe as much to formal problems as it does to philosophical ones.

Finally, there is a peculiar fact concerning the patronage of the monuments which Professor Gilbert cites as illustrating the shift he describes. The three frescoes in which he sees the *Crucifixion* dominating the *Last Supper* are those in Sta. Croce, Sto. Spirito, and Fra Angelico's lost fresco recorded in the Chronicles of the Monastery of San Marco. The first of these institutions is Franciscan, the third Dominican, and the second Augustinian—the order with which the other two mendicant orders were most closely associated. The two frescoes in which he sees the shift beginning are Castagno's *Last Supper* in the convent of S. Apollonia and (perhaps) Castagno's lost fresco for the refectory of Sta. Maria Nuova. The first of these convents is Benedictine and the second is associated with that order (Sta. Maria Nuova was founded by the Camaldolesi). The Cross was of significance to every order, of course, but it had particular significance in the literature of the Franciscans and would have been of paramount importance in a monastery dedicated to the Holy Cross. One deals with so few monuments here that it would be foolish to draw any specific conclusions from these facts, and it is important to remember that by the end of the fifteenth century *Last Suppers* were as common in mendicant refectories as they were in those of the Benedictines. On the other hand, it would be interesting to explore further the possibility that at one moment in Florentine history the Benedictine Order found reason to alter a formula previously associated with the mendicants. It would not be the first time that iconographic alterations reflected differences in thought among the Orders.[1]

INTERVENTION ON CREIGHTON GILBERT'S "LAST SUPPERS AND THEIR REFECTORIES"

DAVID WILKINS
University of Pittsburgh

Professor Gilbert asserts that the central theme of the decoration of the fourteenth-century refectories is the Crucifixion, and that during this period the Last Supper is secondary in importance. This is true in terms of the amount of wall area given over to each representation and is especially obvious in photographs. When standing in the refectories at Santa Croce and Santo Spirito, however, I find that the Crucifixions are subsidiary to the Last Suppers. The latter are closest to us (I believe they are raised above a dado only so that all present may see them) and their figures are on our scale or are slightly larger. The Crucifixions are above our normal sight lines so they require a special upward glance. They are exalted and remote, while the impact of the Last Suppers is immediate.

One problem which should be investigated concerns the actual function of these refectories : did they serve as more than a dining room ? If so, did these additional uses change from the fourteenth to the fifteenth and sixteenth centuries and what effect might this have had on the iconography (and scale ?) of these rooms ? There is art historical evidence that the ecclesiastics ate while listening to readings (*The Illiterate St. Humility Miraculously Reads a Text in the Refectory of Santa Perpetua*, from the *St. Humility Altarpiece* in the Uffizi,

---

[1] See e.g. Erwin Panofsky, "A Letter to St. Jerome : A Note on the the Relationship between Petrus Christus and Jan van Eyck," in : *Studies for Belle da Costa Greene*, Princeton, 1954, 106.

Sienese, fourteenth century; Fra Angelico's *St. Dominic and the Dominicans Fed by Angels* from the *Louvre Coronation;* the pulpit in the refectory of the Badia Fiesolano). What texts were read and what relationship might they have had with the images represented in the hall?

Surely the meals of the ecclesiastics were accompanied by some sort of ritual which might also be of importance, such as prayers before and after the meal. The descriptions of the Last Supper in the Gospels actually include some suggestions of appropriate rituals which might have found their way into monastic life. In John the meal is followed by the lengthy and moving Sermon to the Apostles (13:31-17:26); following this example, might not the prior have chosen the hour after the meal to preach to his brothers? It is a temptation to connect this Sermon to those Last Suppers where the Apostles seem so clearly to be meditating (Castagno's is the best example), but the Sermon took place after the departure of Judas, who is always present in Last Suppers. Both Matthew (26:30) and Mark (14:26) mention that the group sang a hymn before proceeding to Gethsemane; this too would provide an appropriate precedent.

Professor Olds has pointed out that the limiting of refectory decoration to the single scene of the Last Supper in the later examples might be related to a more limited architectural format. Also relevant here, I believe, is the Renaissance aesthetic which preferred a single unified image to the multiplicity favored by the Gothic taste of the fourteenth century. The change can be documented in altarpiece format, for example, and these refectory frescoes might provide yet another example. In any case, it is significant for Professor Gilbert's arguments that the single image which survives is the Last Supper and not the Crucifixion.

The text by Cardinal Dominici he cites leads Professor Gilbert to suggest that the purpose of these Last Suppers in refectories is in part ethical: "Seeing Christ eat, we will be encouraged when we eat to be like Christ in other respects." I have often wondered to what extent the *Imitatio Christi* might be expanded to include the rest of the Christian pantheon and I would suggest that in this case, with monks gathered around tables in a refectory, the ethical inspiration might be enlarged to include the *imitatio apostolorum.*

3. PREACHING FOR THE POPES*

JOHN W. O'MALLEY

University of Detroit

In Erasmus' dialogue *Ciceronianus*, Bulephorus describes a sermon he supposedly heard preached before Pope Julius II on a Good Friday.[1] It is easy to infer, as Pastor does, that Erasmus is recounting for his readers the substance of a sermon at which he himself was present when he visited Rome in 1509.[2] If that is the case, the sermon as summarized by Bulephorus exemplifies a most inappropriate substitution of pseudo-Ciceronian rhetoric and pagan learning for a central Christian mystery. The exordium and peroration, together almost longer than the body of the sermon itself, were filled with elaborate praise of the Pope as *Jovis optimus maximus*, whose power was unlimited and whose omnipotent right hand brandished a thunderbolt. The preacher used the body of the sermon to parade before his listeners tedious and irrelevant stories from Greek and Roman history. Bulephorus finally betrays his disgust by saying, "In such fine Roman fashion did that Roman speak that I heard not a word about the death of Christ."[3] Our worst suspicions about the quality of religion

---

* For quotations from the sermons I have standardized the punctuation and the Latin orthography. I have employed the following procedures in listing folio numerations : (1) when two numerations are given in the text, I have used the one in the upper right-hand corner; (2) when no numeration is given, I have supplied my own, but indicated this fact by enclosing the numeration in parentheses. See the Appendix for full bibliographical information on the sermons. I would like to express my gratitude to the American Philosophical Society for a Grant-in-Aid which made possible the research on which this paper is based.

[1] Erasmus, *Opera omnia*, I (Leiden, 1703), 993-994.

[2] Ludwig Pastor, *Geschichte der Päpste*, 4th ed., III (Freiburg, 1899), 754. Since the English edition of Pastor (St. Louis, 1923) often omits material which the fourth German edition contains, references will be to the *Geschichte* or to the *History* as required or convenient.

[3] Erasmus, I, 994 : "Tam Romane dixit Romanus ille, ut nihil audirem de morte Christi." Erasmus makes a similar judgment about university sermons in his letter to Albert of Brandenburg, Oct. 19, 1519, *Opus epistolarum*, eds. P. S. and H. M. Allen, III (Oxford, 1922), 104.

and theology at the papal court have thus been confirmed, this time by the prince of the humanists himself.

Subsequent scholarship, when it deigned to take notice of the sermons at the papal court at all, accorded with Erasmus' negative assessment. Burckhardt does not specifically discuss the sermons at the papal court, but his general evaluation of Renaissance preaching is well known : the sermons were concerned with problems of conscience, were empty of doctrinal content, and had only a temporary effect upon their hearers.[1] Savonarola was his chief example. These sermons typified the difference between southern and northern piety : the former produced a "mighty but passing impression," whereas the latter "worked for the ages."[2]

Pastor, who was himself influenced by Burckhardt, saw in the mendicant "preachers of penance" one of the "most cheering signs, in an age clouded with many dark shadows."[3] He esteemed the moral earnestness of the preachers. Curiously enough, he comments on the sermons preached at the papal court only occasionally and in the most generic terms, but he does leave the reader with the impression that by and large in these sermons classical form disguised, deformed, and even displaced the Christian substance.[4] When Pastor calls attention to the *Ciceronianus*, it is obvious that he feels Erasmus was not describing an isolated case. His lamentation over the "extravagances" which some Renaissance preachers allowed themselves would seem, therefore, to have a certain application to the sermons preached before the popes :

> We hear of preachers whose sermons were overcharged with vain learning, or full of hair-splitting theological questions, and again, of others who condescended too much to the taste of the populace. The newly revived pagan philosophy was too often brought forward in the pulpit at the expense of Christianity. Passages from the works of heathen poets and teachers replaced the customary quotations from the Fathers. The glamour of the new learning obscured the old simple doctrines, and heathen Mythology was mixed up with Christian dogma. Equally objectionable was the conduct of those preachers who, instead of aiming at the conversion and edification of their hearers, thought only of making a name for themselves. Such men invented all sorts of miracles, sham prophecies and silly fables, ... dealing

---

[1] *The Civilization of the Renaissance in Italy*, II (New York, 1958), 450-463, as well as I, 243-244.

[2] Burckhardt, II, 450.

[3] Pastor, *History*, V, 33. See also *ibid.*, I, 97.

[4] Pastor, *Geschichte*, e.g., III, 250-251, 524-526, 754.

with politics and all sorts of worldly matters, and leaving out the one thing necessary.[1]

Since Pastor's day the sermons preached to the popes during the
Renaissance have received even less attention. The article on "Oratoria
sacra" in the *Enciclopedia cattolica* passes them over without mention,
as does the otherwise informative article on "Preaching" in the *New
Catholic Encyclopedia*. Even more significant is the fact that Johann
Baptist Schneyer's recent and impressive *Geschichte der katholischen
Predigt* does the same.[2] We might easily thereby conclude that no
comment on these sermons is offered because no comment is deserved.

While working on a somewhat different subject last summer, I began
to scan some of these sermons in various Roman libraries. Gradually
I became persuaded that they deserved more attention than they had
hitherto received and that they had significance for the interpretation
of the Roman religious scene in the late Quattrocento and early Cinquecento. At the very least, they provided some new data, for they do
not seem to have been seriously utilized by historians since the days
they were printed. It was at this juncture that I decided to change
slightly the focus previously announced for my presentation to this
Conference by limiting myself to a discussion of these sermons.

At some time in the near future I intend to do more extensive
research on this topic. Right now my work on it is in a very preliminary stage. I am still searching for sermons, and I cannot profess
to have read even all the ones I have already discovered. Nonetheless,
I feel that I can speak with some authority on those sermons I have
actually studied, although considerable research remains to be done
on them. I hope that my findings are of interest.

In the Appendix I list the fifty sermons which I am at present
prepared to discuss. Some of these sermons were chosen very deliberately because of specific themes developed in them, especially the
theme of the "dignity of man," while others of them were chosen
rather at random simply to give a coverage of various pontificates and
liturgical occasions. I suspect that these sermons are fairly representative, but I cannot be assured of that fact until I complete my research.

---

[1] Pastor, *History*, V, 180-181.

[2] (Freiburg, 1969). Anscar Zaw art does provide a few helpful bits of information in
his *The History of Franciscan Preaching and of Franciscan Preachers*, Franciscan Studies,
VII (New York, 1928). See also Thomas Käppeli, "Predigten am päpstlichen Hof von
Avignon," *Archivum fratrum praedicatorum*, XIX (1949), 388-393.

To these fifty printed sermons I join a "letter" of Giles of Viterbo which is found only in manuscript and which until now has been ignored by scholars.[1] I have prepared a critical edition of it, with introduction, which will appear in *Viator*, 3 (1972), 389f. This document, though buried in a collection of Gile's *epistolae familiares*, is in fact a sermon intended for the eyes of Julius II. As our discussion concludes, it will become obvious why I thought this document significant enough to be included with the other sermons.

THE SETTING AND THE SOURCES

The documents under discussion really range over five pontificates —from Sixtus IV to Leo X—and are fairly evenly distributed among them. There is one sermon from the pontificate of Clement VII, included simply because of its theme and occasion : an Ash Wednesday sermon on the dignity of men. These sermons were composed by twenty-seven different preachers, if we include in that number Giles of Viterbo. Better than half of the preachers were mendicant friars. The others were secular priests or laymen (and possibly clerics in minor orders), and one was a bishop, Stephanus Thegliatius (Stefano Tagliacci). Most of these men were Italians, but a few were Spaniards and one was a German. Figures like Mariano da Genazzano, Pietro Gravina, and Giles of Viterbo are relatively well known. Many of the others are extremely obscure. For some of them I have so far uncovered only the sketchiest biographical information. In the Appendix I try, whenever possible, to give some brief indication of their careers.

The heterogeneity of background, accomplishment, and ecclesiastical status of the preachers is best explained by the procedures regulating the assignment of the sermons. The regular and recurring occasions for sermons attended by the pope and the cardinals were the Sundays of advent and lent (with the exception of Palm Sunday), and the liturgical solemnities of St. Stephen (Dec. 26), St. John the Evangelist (Dec. 27), the Circumcision of Christ (Jan. 1), Epiphany (Jan. 6), Ash Wednesday, Good Friday, Ascension Thursday, Pentecost, Trinity Sunday, and All Saints (Nov. 1). The mendicant friars had a carefully

---

[1] Two copies of this document are extan t. The better version is found in the Biblioteca Nazionale, Naples, MS V. F. 20, fols. 256r-281r, henceforth cited simply as Naples MS. The second copy is in the Biblioteca Angelica, Rome, MS lat. 1001, fols. 11r-23v.

guarded monopoly on the Sundays of advent and lent, and these were
assigned to them in a definite and unvariable sequence : to the Dominicans, the first Sunday of advent and lent; to the Franciscans, the
second Sundays; to the Augustinians, the third Sundays; to the
Carmelites, the fourth Sundays; and to the Servites, the fifth Sunday
of lent and the feast of the Epiphany.[1] The so-called procurators
general of these orders, or their substitutes, had the duty of preaching
these sermons, under the general direction of the Master of the Sacred
Palace, the pope's official theologian. The position of Master of the
Sacred Palace was always filled by a Dominican. To him fell the duty
of selecting at his own discretion preachers for those occasions not
already pre-empted by the mendicants.[2] Sermons were to be submitted to him before they were delivered in public, but we know that
at least on occasion this provision was not honored.[3] The popes were
not altogether passive before the choices of the Master of the Sacred
Palace. Johann Burchard, the papal Master of Ceremonies, tells us,
for instance, of the reproof Alexander VI administered to one of them
for entrusting a sermon to a certain Battista Casale, whom Burchard
describes simply as "a student with long hair."[4]

The sermons were preached in the Vatican chapels, St. Peter's
basilica, the Lateran cathedral, the lenten stational churches, etc., as
occasion and custom required. All of the sermons we are discussing
were intended for the ears of the pope, but in a few instances, due to
some last-minute change of plans, the pope did not actually attend.
They were preached during Mass in a strictly liturgical context, and
they must be carefully distinguished from other orations at the papal
court which were more political or occasional in character, such as
the *pro obedientia* orations offered to new pontiffs on behalf of various
Christian monarchs or states. Of the many sermons which were preach-

---

[1] See Johann Burchard, *Diarium sive rerum urbanarum commentarii (1483-1506),*
ed. L. Thuasne, 3 vols. (Paris, 1883-85), *passim* and esp. I, 293. See also Florentinus,
Epiph. (6), fol. 13r.

[2] See Burchard, I, 283; III, 191. Zawarts asserts, p. 256, that Sixtus IV "introduced
the custom that a preacher with classical training hold office as preacher in the papal
chapel," but he gives no source for this information.

[3] See Burchard, I, 228-229.

[4] Burchard, III, 191, Ash Wednesday, Feb. 9, 1502 : "Sermonem fecit Baptista
Casalius, Romanus, scholaris laicus, cum capillis longis, de quo Papa fuit valde turbatus,
et dixit magistro palatii si deinceps aliquem talem admitteret ad orandum, quod vellet
eum privare officio."

ed for the popes, only a small proportion were printed and have thus come down to us.

The sermons are of reasonable length; most of them would probably have taken under a half-hour to deliver. Burchard, in fact, leaves us with the impression that brevity was highly appreciated, and Leo X supposedly insisted that the sermons not exceed fifteen minutes.[1] In general they are thematic. They set out to develop a specific idea or doctrine suggested by the liturgical occasion or the liturgical texts. Some of them, however, simply try to recount for their listeners the "sacred history" of the event which is being commemorated, as we see in the sermon by Ludovicus Ferrariensis on Christ's temptation in the desert for the first Sunday of lent. In a few instances we have nothing more than an extended moral exhortation, almost without intellectual content, as in the sermon of Nicolaus Schönbergt for the same liturgical occasion some years later.

Usually the sermons are divided into two or three distinct parts, announced for the hearers at the beginning, but in no instance do they labor the logic of the division or protract it into subdivisions. The sermon by Bernardinus Carvaial on Christ's circumcision is the unique example among these sermons of a professed attempt to proceed *scholastico more*, but even here we note that the use of definitions of terms, answers to objections, etc., which we associate with scholasticism, is moderate. Of all the sermons under discussion, those of Nicolaus Schönbergt are the most scholastic in their conception and in their Latinity. With few exceptions the other sermons move along in a classical, but reasonably simple, style, and they are filled with quotations and paraphrases, not from scholastic or pagan authors, but from Scripture and the Fathers of the Church. Thus we come to a consideration of the sources or the "authorities" upon which these sermons were based.

One of the few sermons Pastor specifically comments upon is the panegyric in honor of St. John delivered by the Roman humanist Pietro Marso during the pontificate of Innocent VIII in 1485.[2] Pastor

---

[1] Burchard, e.g., I, 235, 442; II, 281, 434, and esp. 365 : "... sermonem fecit [Ascension, 1497] quidam frater Thadeus, orator predicatorum, qui fuit brevissimus, propterea ab omnibus laudatus." On Leo X, see Zawart, p. 257.

[2] See Burchard, I, 173, for a description of the occasion. Burchard does not name the preacher but describes him as "quidam discipulus Pomponii." The sermon was received "absque omnium laude."

says : "The wealth of classical reminiscences which the reader en-
counters stands in singular contrast to the subject of the speech, praise
of John the Evangelist."[1] Pastor simply could not have read the sei-
mon and passed such a judgment! The sermon, a somewhat abstract
rehearsing of John's virtues, especially his virginity, is replete with
quotations or paraphrases from the Old and New Testaments, with a
special preference shown for St. Paul. Moreover, there are five or six
quotations each from St. Jerome and St. Augustine and one from
Gregory the Great. If a "singular contrast" occurs in this sermon, it
results from the juxtaposition of this "wealth" of *Christian* "reminiscences" alongside one brief quotation each from Plato and Seneca and
a very perfunctory mention of Aristotle. No matter what our final
judgment on the quality of this sermon might be, it certainly cannot
be criticized for substituting pagan sources for Christian ones.

Marso's panegyric is not an exception. Critical editions of the sermons would be required to determine with scientific accuracy the
precise incidence of reference to various sources. However, even without
such detailed studies, it is clear that Scripture was the source these
preachers quoted most liberally and that second to Scripture came the
Fathers of the Church, especially Augustine and Jerome. Occasionally
in sermons which deal with a more philosophical subject, such as
Marso's on human immortality, the references to classical authors are
more numerous. But these "authorities" are either rejected as ignorant
of Christian truth or are seen as confirmatory of it. Stephanus Gorgonius' sermon on immortality, by way of exception, is very philosophical
in its argumentation, but it can hardly be interpreted as trying to
replace Christian belief by philosophical reason. With Baptista Signorius' sermon on the unity and trinity of the Godhead, there is extensive
use of pagan sources, and Signorius comes precariously close to saying
that the mystery of the Trinity was available to man without revelation. I submit, nevertheless, that his views on this subject are best
interpreted along the orthodox lines of his fellow Augustinian, Giles of
Viterbo.[2] The sermon of Alexander Cortesius on Epiphany and particularly the long sermon of Andreas Brentius (Andrea Brenta) on
Pentecost make more ample use of classical sources than do the other

---

[1] Paster, *Geschichte*, III, 250 : "Der Reichtum an classischen Reminiscenzen, welcher
hier dem Leser entgegentritt, steht in seltsamem Gegensatze zum Gegenstand der Rede,
dem Lobe des Evangelisten Johannes."

[2] See my *Giles of Viterbo* (Leiden, 1968), pp. 24-28.

sermons we are discussing, and Brenta was not loath to display his familiarity with classical learning. There is no question, on the other hand, of this learning swamping the sermon's theme and submerging it.

More important than the simple quantity of references to various sources is, of course, the underlying attitude towards them. By and large the attitude of these preachers does not seem to differ from that of the scholastic tradition of the High Middle Ages, at least as that tradition is represented by St. Thomas. There is explicit rejection of pagan cults, even by Brenta.[1] The preachers say or assume that the philosophers, when they were not in actual error, were at best ignorant of the fulness of Christian truth. Marso, product of Leto's Roman Academy though he was, repeatedly asserts the proposition that that truth was unattainable *puris naturalibus*.[2] Nonetheless, two of our preachers take care to indicate to us that Christian truth, though above reason, does not contradict it, and this seems to be the assumption others are working with.[3] If syncretistic tendencies are operative in these preachers' approach to antiquity, they must be understood in the light of the above considerations[4].

Scholastic authors are referred to very sparingly by name, and only rarely do traditional scholastic terms such as *potentia absoluta* and *ordinata*,[5] *actus* and *potentia*,[6] *materia prima*,[7] and Marso's *puris naturalibus* [8] appear. This does not mean that the preachers were uninfluenced by scholastic doctrine. In some instances, indeed, direct dependence is certain.[9] But they eschewed scholastic arguments and

---

[1] Brentius, *Pent.*, fols. 68, 69ᵛ; Florentinus, *Ador.*, fols. 11ᵛ-12ʳ; *Pass.* fol. 18ʳ, "Graecia mendax."

[2] Marsus, *Immortal.*, fols. 94ʳ, 95ʳ. See also Ferrariensis, *Supr. die*, fol. 151ʳ; Totis, *Ult. fin.*, fol. 140ʳ.

[3] Ferrariensis, *Advent. Christi*, fol. 143ʳ; Totis, *Ult. fin.*, fol. 140ʳ.

[4] See the balanced presentation of this question in Charles Trinkaus. *In Our Image and Likeness*, II (Chicago and London, 1970), 502-504. See also my *Giles of Viterbo*, pp. 19-39, esp. 34-35.

[5] Maroldus, *Sent. verit.*, fol. 121ʳ; Marsus, *Immortal.*, fol. 95ʳ.

[6] Maroldus, *Sent. verit.*, fol. 122ʳ.

[7] Florentinus, *Epiph.* (1), fol. 2ᵛ.

[8] Marsus, *Immortal.*, fols. 94ʳ, 95ʳ.

[9] Note, for instance, the similarity of phraseology between Terasse and St. Thomas on the question of God's communication of secondary causality to His creatures : Terasse, *Div. prov.*, fol. 36ᵛ : "... nec propterea defectus virtutis arguendus in Deo, sed magis suae bonitatis abundantia laudibus extollenda est." Thomas, S.T., I. 22.3 : "... non propter defectum suae virtutis, sed propter abundantiam suae bonitatis, ut dignitatem

scholastic distinctions in their sermons. Marso explicitly rejects "inane disputations,"[1] and Augustinus Philippus Florentinus confesses to a Socratic ignorance concerning the nature of God.[2] Although the other preachers are not so explicit as are these two, they in general imply that for them living and loving were far more important than theological subtleties, which in any case were inadequate to the mysteries being discussed.[3]

If theological disputation was inadequate as well as irrelevant to Christian life, the Scriptures certainly were not. The very frequency with which they were quoted or paraphrased indicates the esteem in which they were held. Guilelmus Bodivit insists that pastors of souls who neglect the study of Scripture will find no excuse on the day of Judgment.[4] For Ludovicus Ferrariensis, Scripture is the principal weapon against the temptations of the Devil.[5] And for Florentinus the Scriptures have an inner force and vitality which cause them to penetrate to the soul and to transform it.[6] Of all the books of the Bible which are quoted by these preachers, the Pauline epistles probably are the most frequent. But among the popular verses from

---

causalitatis etiam creaturis communicet." See also Burchard, I, 228-229, for the concern of the Master of the Sacred Palace over an advent sermon by the procurator general of the Franciscans in which the Scotist, rather than the Thomist, opinion on the Immaculate Conception was preached, Dec. 10, 1486.

[1] Marsus, *Johan.*, fol. 52^r.

[2] Florentinus, *Trin.*, fol. 4.

[3] For example, Florentinus, *Verit.*, fol. 9^v, and *Trin.*, fol. 6^r : "Amare Deum dum sumus in corpore plus possumus quam vel eloqui vel cognoscere. Amando plus nobis perficimus, minus laboramus, illi magis obsequimur." See also Marsus, *Johan.*, fols. 51^v-52^r : "Minime laboremus, minime disputemus, sed sic vivamus ut a Christo diligi amarique mereamur ac demum bene mori contigat, et reditus illuc pateat ubi beati aevo sempiterno fruuntur. Hoc nos tangit. Hoc ad nos pertinet. Hoc agamus, patres. Inanes disputationes et de Lyra in campo scripturarum acumina penitus omittamus. Quod cito quem instituebat his verbis suasit Paulus, in cuius pectore Christus resonabat, ipso dicente, An experimentum quaeritis eius, qui in me loquitur Christus [2 Cor. 13.3]? Summas aut quaestiones et contentiones et pugnas legis devita. Sunt enim inutiles et vanae. Hoc quod Paulus cito scripsit, omnibus praeceptum esse putemus." See also Gravina, *Ascens.*, (fol. 4), and Signorius, *Sum. Deo*, fols. 204^v-205^r.

[4] Bodivit, *Trin.*, fol. 63^v.

[5] Ferrariensis, *Pugna*, fols. 148^v-149^r.

[6] Florentinus, *Verit.*, fol. 9^v : "Idipsum [amorem divinum] autem facillime consequimur si non cessabimus litteras sacras nocturna versare manu, versare diurna. Latet enim in illis caelestis vis quaedam viva et efficax, quae legentis animum, si modo illas pure humiliterque tractaverit, in amorem divinum mirabili quadam potestate transformat."

Scripture, the most significant for our purposes is taken from the Prologue of John's Gospel : *Et Verbum caro factum est, et habitavit in nobis* (1.14).

DOCTRINES AND THEMES

What is characteristic of these papal sermons is that their content is doctrinal. An operative distinction was made between academic theology and the central tenets of the Christian faith. The preachers had no intention of entering into the former, but they consistently addressed themselves to the latter. Among the various doctrines which the sermons discuss, three emerge as particularly prominent : the doctrine of the Incarnation and Hypostatic Union of the two natures in Christ, the unity and trinity of the Godhead, and a third which is somewhat vaguer and more diffuse but which can be gathered under the doctrine of divine providence. There were doubtless many reasons recommending these particular doctrines to the preachers, but for the first two, certainly, there was one reason which was obvious : these doctrines constitute the central Christian mysteries as these are found in the New Testament and as they were propounded by the Fathers and councils of the Early Church.[1] For centrality and antiquity, they had no rivals, and they could never be relegated to the limbo of mere theological subtleties. Moreover, they were the ones which the liturgical occasions and texts themselves tended to suggest, especially as regards the Incarnation and Hypostatic Union. However, we must recall that great latitude in selection and focus was possible in this regard. In any case, for all three of these doctrines we should hesitate to attribute their popularity simply to the preacher's arbitrary choice and to his seeing in them opportunity for intellectual or rhetorical display. The

---

[1] See, e.g., the oration of Giles of Viterbo opening the Fifth Lateran Council, 1512, Mansi, XXXII, 670 ,: 'Atqui sine synodis stare non potest fides; absque synodis igitur salvi esse non possumus. Verum quod ratione dicimus, ut etiam experimento probemus, cogitandum nobis est, tres esse credendarum rerum radices, e quibus universa ecclesiae fides manat. Prima, divinae naturae unitas est. Altera, eadem in natura parentis, sobolis, amoris felicissima Trinitas. Tertia, in virginis utero prolis divinae conceptio. In quibus veluti in altissimis apicibus ac sanctissimis montibus, et reliquae fidei partes novem et pietas universa fundata est." Trinkaus points out, I, 142, that Lorenzo Valla felt that "God's benefits in particular to man which are manifested through the Scriptures" were "Divine Providence, the Incarnation and Atonement, Salvation."

first and the third, particularly, were felt to be of the deepest practical import for the conduct of Christian life.

The prominence of the mystery of the Incarnation and Hypostatic Union certainly is due in part to the fact that whole sermons were specifically addressed to it, as were Ferrariensis' on Christ's advent and Vasques' *De unitate*. It is also due to the fact that long sections of sermons on other subjects discussed it, as did Maroldus' *Sententia veritatis*, Mariano da Genazzano's sermon on the Passion, and Marcus Antonius Ticinensis' for the second Sunday of advent. Most important of all, perhaps, this mystery was seen in other sermons as holding the underlying meaning for all the events of Christ's life. The significance of the feasts of the Circumcision,[1] Epiphany,[2] Ascension,[3] and All Saints[4] was made to relate to it. It was the foundation for the Church.[5] It initiated the Redemption.

What is noteworthy among a number of our preachers, in fact, is the tendency to see the Incarnation as in itself redemptive and not to reserve man's salvation exclusively to Christ's passion and death. As Thegliatius states in his sermon for All Saints : "... in the Virgin's womb and on the cross he [Christ] kissed us and renewed all reality."[6] Such a theological viewpoint was important in the thinking of some of the Fathers of the Church like Irenaeus, Athanasius, and Cyril of Alexandria.[7] According to this viewpoint, the foundations for man's divine sonship or even "deification" were established by the Incarnation, and thus man's redemption was inchoately effected. This critical question of filiation and deification we shall meet again when we come

---

[1] See, e.g., Lollius, *Circumcis.*, fol. 41.

[2] See, e.g., Maroldus, *Epiph.*, fols. 12ᵛ-13ʳ; Florentinus, *Sacram.*, fol. 8ᵛ; Cortesius, *Epiph.*, fol. 31ʳ.

[3] See, e.g., Totis, *Ult. fin.*, fol. 138ᵛ; Gravina, *Ascens.*, (fols. 1ᵛ-2ʳ).

[4] Thegliatius, *Omn. sanct.*, fol. 63.

[5] Marsus, *Johan.*, fol. 48ᵛ : "... Verbum caro factum est, et habitavit in nobis. Quae doctrina divinitus inspirata fidelium stabilivit ecclesiam."

[6] *Omn. sanct.*, fol. 63ᵛ : "Si quidem veniens, et nos non Moysi, non prophetarum, sed proprio ore in virginis utero ac in cruce deosculans omnia innovavit, iuxta illud, Ecce nova facio omnia [Apoc. 21.5], pro qua [sic], ut Apostolus ait, Debemus in novitate vitae ambulare [Rom. 6.4] et non veterem sed novum hominem imitari." See also Florentinus, *Epiph.* (8), fol. 17ᵛ. The attribution of a specific efficacy to the Incarnation is not unrelated to the scholastic dispute about whether the Incarnation would have taken place if Adam had not sinned. Giannozzo Manetti, the Florentine humanist, takes up that question and answers it affirmatively, as quoted in Trinkaus, I, 426-427 (n. 56).

[7] See the article "Grace," *Dictionnaire de spiritualité*, VI (1965), esp. 715-721.

to the question of the "dignity of man." For the moment it is enough simply to point out that from such a starting point each event of the life of Christ can be seen as an extension or reflection of the Incarnation and as having redemptive value. Mariano da Genazzano puts it simply, while still proposing a special efficacy for Christ's suffering and death : "There is nothing in the whole life of Christ, as he is born and as he dies, which is not part of our redemption."[1]

Any very protracted consideration of the mystery of the God-made-man naturally leads to questions concerning the unity and trinity of the Godhead.[2] Our preachers' reflections on this subject, therefore, were not confined exclusively to Trinity Sunday, although the two sermons by Bodivit and Florentinus given on that occasion are completely devoted to it. Signorius' sermon for the third Sunday of advent, *De summo Deo*, is on this same subject, as is a large portion of Brenta's Pentecost sermon. Reflections on the divine unity and trinity, however, are not nearly so pervasive as are those on the Incarnation, in part probably because resort to the technical language of the councils and the Fathers was almost inevitable. In any case, the Trinity was a mystery to be believed, a mystery far beyond the human mind's capacity to understand.[3] For Brenta, furthermore, this mystery of the three Persons in the one God was the source and archetypal pattern for the harmony, unity, and concord which should reign in the universe.[4]

Schönbergt's *Quarta oratio* and Terrasse's *Oratio de divina providentia* deal exclusively with the question of providence and God's orderly governance of the world. The harmonious constitution of the universe, however, was an important conviction for many of the preachers we are dealing with. Sometimes this conviction was expressed through the idea of providence. At other times the key ideas were those of *pax* and *concordia*,[5] whereas Maroldus and Lollius insist upon God's constant abiding presence in the world.[6] The divine Spirit inspired even the philosophers, says Signorius,[7] and Martinus

---

[1] Genazano, *Pass. Christi*, fol. 237ʳ : "Nihil est enim in omni vita nascentis Christi vel morientis quod non pars redemptionis nostrae sit."

[2] See, e.g., Cortesius, *Epiph.* ,fol. 31ʳ.

[3] See Signorius, *Sum. Deo*, fols. 203ᵛ, 204ᵛ-205ʳ; Florentinus, *Trin.*, *passim*.

[4] Brentius, *Pent.*, fol. 75.

[5] Marsus, *Steph.*, fol. 117ᵛ; Brentius, *Pent.*, fol. 75; Marcellus, *Omn. sanct.*, (fols. 2ᵛ, 6ᵛ).

[6] Maroldus, *Epiph.*, fol. 6ʳ; Lollius, *Circumcis.*, fol. 40ᵛ.

[7] Signorius, *Sum. Deo*, fol. 200.

Azpetia reminds us at some length that Christ promised that on the
cross he would draw all things to himself (John 12.32).[1] In terms
reminiscent of Cusa and Ficino, Florentinus tells us that under a
diversity of cult and ceremonies the same God is being worshipped
throughout the world.[2] Among Christians the deepest possible unity
prevails because of their incorporation into the Mystical Body of
Christ and the union of each member of that Body with Christ, its
head.[3] In short, one of the fundamental themes of the sermons, no
matter in what formal category expressed, was that the universe as
God's creation was or ought to be a universe of unity, concord, and
harmony.

In such a context we should not be surprised that considerable
emphasis is given to the virtue of charity, which besides had much
to recommend it to the preachers. Marso, once again using a scholastic
expression, extols it as "the form of all the virtues."[4] One of the most
telling commendations of charity comes from Ferrariensis. He puts
into the mouth of Christ the reproach that what he found most reprehensible about men was not their delivering him up to death, but
their exercising no mercy or piety towards one another.[5] Although man
was to be restored to the tranquility and concord of Original Justice,[6]
he had not been created that "he might pass his days with hands tied,
but that he might be active."[7] The activity thus commended often
relates directly to the question of trying to establish peace among the
Christian princes and, paradoxically, to taking military measures to

---

[1] Azpetia, *Pass. Dmni.*, fol. 128ᵛ-129ʳ. For Erasmus on this verse from John's Gospel,
see Ernst-Wilhelm Kohls, *Die Theologie des Erasmus*, I (Basel, 1966), 55, as well as II,
72-73 (nos. 136 and 137).

[2] Florentinus, *Trin.*, fol. 4ᵛ : "Aliquod esse numen in universo, quem Deum nostri
dixerunt, non modo sacrorum canonum auctoritas praedicat, ... non solum insuper
omnes quae sub caelo sunt nationes caerimoniarum et cultus diversitate illi sacra canentes
confitentur, verum et universa quoque rerum natura proclamat." See Ficino, "De
christiana religione," *Opera omnia*, I (Basel, 1576), 4, and Cusa, *De pace fidei*, eds.
Raymond Klibansky and Hildebrand Bascour, *Opera omnia*, VII [Heidelberg] (Ham-
burg, 1959), 15.

[3] See, e.g., Ticinensis, *Advent.*, (fol. 4ᵛ); Genazano, *Advent.*, fol. 56ᵛ; Florentinus,
Pecc., fol. 15ᵛ.

[4] Marsus, *Johan.*, fol. 51ʳ. See also Marcellus, *Omn. sanct.*, (fol. 4ʳ).

[5] Ferrariensis, *Supr. die*, fol. 152ᵛ.

[6] Florentinus, *Sacram.*, fol. 7ʳ; *Pecc.*, fol. 15ʳ.

[7] Florentinus, *Sacram.*, fol. 7ʳ : "... in paradiso voluptatis collocasse, non ut revinctis
manibus feriaret [sic], sed ut operaretur, ..."

contain or defeat the Turks. But it is generally viewed in a more specifically religious context of prayer, acts of virtue, and diligent praise of God. There is very little, if any, consciousness of man as the builder of the earthly city, and Marso, indeed, comes close to an explicit rejection of this idea.[1] What was important, as Florentinus never tired of reminding his hearers, was transformation of life.[2]

The doctrines of the Incarnation, Trinity, and divine providence certainly do not exhaust the themes which these preachers treated. There were sermons on sin, on grace, and on immortality, among other topics. There were also significantly extensive passages dealing with the problem of the Jews' persistence in their unbelief.[3] But these doctrinal or moral issues are either considerably less prominent than the other three, or else they can reasonably be subsumed under them.

If it is enlightening to consider which doctrines and theological questions received extensive treatment, it is also enlightening to consider which ones did not. There is, for instance, no formal theological treatment of the role of the papacy in the Church. It is true that in exordiums and perorations, which *pace* Erasmus were of appropriate length, the pope was at times addressed in the most flattering and extreme terms. Signorius, in fact, proposed him as "our God," as "the image of the Trinity."[4] But in those several sermons where we have discussion of the nature of the Church, what is emphasized is its sanctity and its condition as a reflection of the heavenly Jerusalem.[5] Christ is its head.[6] Curiously enough, the only time the famous Petrine text from the sixteenth chapter of St. Matthew is discussed, the preacher interprets the "rock" upon which the Church is founded to be Christ.[7] In other words, in these sermons there is very little preoccupation with questions of jurisdiction, primacy, apostolic succession

---

[1] Marsus, *Johan.*, fol. 48. See Trinkaus, I, 228-231, 245-250, 282-285, 292-293, for a significantly different emphasis in certain figures.

[2] Florentinus, *Epiph.* (1), fol. 4ʳ; *Verit.*, fol. 9ᵛ; *Epiph. MDXX*, fols. 2ʳ, 3ʳ, 5ʳ. See also Arzius, *Natura*, fol. 4ʳ, as well as William J. Bouwsma, *Venice and the Defense of Republican Liberty* (Berkeley and Los Angeles, 1968), 29-30, and Donald Weinstein, *Savonarola and Florence* (Princeton, 1970), 190-191.

[3] Cortesius, *Epiph.*, fol. 30ᵛ; Ferrariensis, *Advent. Christi*, fol. 145ʳ; Maroldus, *Epiph.*, fol. 7; Marsus, *Immortal.*, fol. 97; Vasques, *Unit. et simpl.*, fols. iiiᵛ-vʳ.

[4] Signorius, *Sum. Deo*, fol. 197ʳ.

[5] Thegliatius, *Omn. sanct.*, *passim;* Ferrariensis, *Conform. eccles.*, fols. 157ʳ-158ʳ.

[6] Ferrariensis, *Conform. eccles.*, fol. 157ᵛ; Marsus. *Johan,*, fol. 48ᵛ.

[7] Thegliatius, *Omn. sanct.*, fols. 62ᵛ-63ʳ. Marso tells us the Church is founded on Peter, *Johan.*, fol. 50ʳ, but see *ibid.*, fol. 48ᵛ.

and the like even on those relatively few occasions when the Church
was formally discussed.[1]

Outside a somewhat lengthy and not particularly enlightening discussion of Mary's sanctity in Maroldus' *Sententia veritatis* and a recounting by Canalis of her sorrows at Christ's death, no serious attention is given to Mariological issues.[2] The sacraments, also, play a
remarkably small role in these sermons. Florentinus deals with baptism
relatively at length in his sermon on the sacraments. Baptism, as well
as the Eucharist, is mentioned by Azpetia.[3] The others are scarcely
touched upon. Indulgences and pilgrimages are never once discussed,
and except for a paragraph on the question of the authenticity of
Christ's foreskin in the Lateran's collection of relics, the bodily remains
of the saints are not discussed either.[4] There are no miracle stories.
The preachers are silent about Purgatory. Brenta well summarizes the
religious spirit operative in these sermons : "Our cult of God is a
spiritual one, and it consists in thinking honest thoughts, speaking
helpful words, doing good deeds, and storing up in heaven a wealth
of piety which no accident or evil fortune can snatch away."[5]

Brenta's statement leads us to the important question of Pelagianism and Semi-Pelagianism. Did the religion espoused in these sermons
basically subscribe to the save-yourself tenets of Augustine's adversa-
ries in the fifth century, and was there operative in them a Renaissance
view of the "autonomy of man" which would contradict the canons of
the Councils of Carthage (418) and Orange II (529) ? No matter what
answer is eventually forthcoming, we must recall, first of all, that the
preachers give no evidence of being preoccupied with the theological
relationship of grace and free will, and, as we know, the decrees of the
Council of Orange II against those who would later be known as Semi-
Pelagians were not available to them.[6] Secondly, we must recall what

---

[1] There is one explicit anti-conciliarist st atement, Vazques, *Unit. et simpl.*, fol. vii[v],
and a implicit rejection of conciliarism, Ferr ariensis, *Conform. eccles.*, fol. 159[v].

[2] We know, however, that they were at least on occasion the subject of sermons,
e.g., a sermon of Ambrosius Coriolanus (Cora, Coranus) on the Virgin's conception in
1472, Hain # *5685. See also Burchard, I, 228-229.

[3] *Pass. Dmni.*, fol. 129[v].

[4] Carvaial, *Circumcis.*, fol. 9[v].

[5] *Pent.*, fol. 68[v] : "Spiritu namque Deum co limus honesta cogitando, bene dicendo,
recte agendo, et in caelo pietatis thesauros qui nullo fortunae aut casus impetu eripi
possint reponendo." See also *ibid.*, fol. 76[r].

[6] See Harry J. McSorley, "Was Gabriel Biel a Se mipelagian ?" in *Wahrheit und*

has already been said about the explicit refusal of many of them to admit that man was capable of attaining the truths of Christian revelation without the grace of revelation. Moreover, they are insistent upon the insufficiency of "the Law," and of nature for man's salvation,[1] they invoke the absolute necessity of grace,[2] and in explicitly Pauline terms confess that that grace would not be grace unless freely given.[3]

Nevertheless, there is an area of unclarity. Schönbergt's *Tertia oratio*, for instance, is a very naturalistic and moralistic exhortation to resist temptation, without any effective role attributed to grace, and he does not seem to have seen any very radical deficiency in man even after the Fall.[4] Perhaps more telling is the fact that the very authors who insist so vigorously upon the necessity and gratuity of grace occasionally slip into expressions which are capable of a Semi-Pelagian interpretation. But the casual and untechnical nature of the preachers' treatment of the relationship between grace and free will makes it difficult to resolve ambiguities with any satisfaction.[5]

What is certain is that these preachers hoped by their sermons to move their listeners to a better way of life, to encourage them to practice the art of "good and holy living." This phrase, so often on their lips, was of course Cicero's.[6] Its meaning, however, was translated in terms of Christ's example and message.[7]

Verkündigung, Festschrift Michael Schmaus, eds. L. Scheffczyk et al., II (Munich, Paderborn, Vienna, 1967), 1109-20.

[1] Ferrariensis, *Advent. Christi*, fols. 143ᵛ, 145ʳ; *Gratia*, fol. 154; Totis, *Induere*, fol. 144ʳ.

[2] Azpetia, *Pass. Dmni.*, *passim;* Ferrariensis, *Advent. Christi*, fol. 144ᵛ; Lollius, *Circumcis.*, fol. 42ᵛ.

[3] Florentinus, *Pass.*, fol. 19ʳ. Cf. also Totis, *Induere*, fol. 142ᵛ; Vasques, *Unit. et simpl.*, fol. xvʳ.

[4] *Tertia*, fol. 119ᵛ : "... [after the Fall] difficilius operetur bonum, ac saltem mediocriter non peccare non possit."

[5] Probably the most extended statement is by Ferrariensis, *Gratia*, fol. 156ᵛ : "Verum tametsi gratiam istam quibuslibet virtutis actibus nemo posset promereri, aggredi tamen arduum virtutis iter quisque tentet. Studiosis namque operibus Deus optimus maximusque tantum tribuit ut qui per eiusmodi actus, Deo optimo monente, quoad possunt recti iustique evadere nituntur, his gratiam conferre certa atque immutabili sententia decreverit."

[6] Cic. *Off.* I.6.19. See, e.g., Brentius, *Pent.*, fol. 75ʳ; Ferrariensis, *Advent. Christi*, fol. 141ᵛ, 143ᵛ; Marcellus, *Omn. sanct.*, (fol. 2ᵛ); Thegliatius, *Pent.*, (fol. 2ᵛ); Vasques, *Ciner.*, fols. 4ᵛ-5ʳ. On this phrase and especially its relationship to *doctrina* and *bene dicere*, see Gioacchino Paparelli, *Feritas, Humanitas, Divinitas : Le componenti dell' Umanesimo* (Messina and Florence, 1960), p. 43.

[7] See the helpful observations by Trinkaus on the relationship between the activism

For the rest, the preachers expected their listeners to react to the great truths they were propounding for them with the appropriate emotions, emotions which of course varied with the subject matter. However, if one emotion predominates more than others, it is that of joy—joy at the Incarnation,[1] joy over Christ's abiding presence,[2] joy even over the final outcome of Adam's fall and Christ's death, as interpreted with the liturgical formula of Holy Saturday's *felix culpa*.[3] Finally, there was joy over the recognition of the marvellous dignity of man, a dignity which derived from man's relationship to Christian mystery.

THE DIGNITY OF MAN

The theme of the dignity of man recurs with amazing frequency in these sermons preached to the pope and his court. It predominates, for instance, in the Ash Wednesday sermon by Hieronymus Arzius for Clement VII in 1531 and in the Ash Wednesday sermon by Dionysius Vasques for Julius II, preached just a few weeks before the pope died in 1513. Coincidentally, the Epiphany sermon for that same year of 1513 by Florentinus also stressed man's dignity. The first part of Ticinensis' advent sermon deals explicitly with this theme, and Totis' sermon on man's final end also treats of it *passim*. It appears, furthermore, at critical points in a number of other sermons, so that we can safely assert that in some form or other the question of man's dignity is a major theme in these sermons, taken as a whole.

We perhaps should not be surprised that this is the case. Most of these preachers seem, at the very least, to have been exposed to the humanist tradition and, therefore, exposed to the dignity-of-man theme in its humanist form. Moreover, Renaissance theory that panegyric was more effective than scolding in producing moral change might well have had special attraction for preachers.[4] The theme of man's dignity would thus seem to fit these sermons into the tradition

---

inherent in Renaissance rhetoric and the emphasis on God's grace, I, 32, 46-47; II, 633, 649.

[1] Ferrariensis, *Advent. Christi*, fol. 145ᵛ; Maroldus, *Epiph.*, fol. 12ᵛ.

[2] Florentinus, *Trin.*, fol. 6ʳ; *Sacram.*, fol. 8ᵛ.

[3] Azpetia, *Pass. Dmni.*, fol. 131ᵛ; Marsus, *Immortal.*, fol. 97ʳ.

[4] See Erasmus' letter to John Desmarais, 1504, *Opus. epist.*, I (1906), 398-403.

of what Harry Levin calls the Renaissance "rhetoric of congratula-
tion."[1] But it is probably premature to speculate at length as to why
there should be this emphasis on man's dignity. What is important for
the moment is that it was present and that it was present to a pervasive
degree.

The range of arguments favoring man's dignity is broad and subtle,
but it can be reduced to two very general headings : 1) arguments
deriving in some way from man's nature or his creation by God,
2) and arguments deriving from grace or from man's redemption by
Christ. Charles Trinkaus has convincingly shown the pivotal role
the image-and-likeness verse from Genesis played in the general humanist tradition on the dignity of man. The preachers at the papal court
also latched onto that verse, and it is quoted or paraphrased frequently.[2] Simply by reason of his creation man already has a sublime dignity, which indeed prompted Marso to refer to him in seemingly Hermetic terms as the *divinum animal*.[3]

Important in the story of creation is the fact that all things were
made for man, and that man himself has the power to command the
birds of the air, the fishes of the sea, etc. The preachers utilized this
fact to impress upon their hearers man's great worth. As Ticinensis
says : "And everything was made for man, as for a single end, and
indeed we read that some have even gone so far as to adore him,
because of his immense dignity."[4] "Ours is a singular dignity," observes
Arzius. In terms clearly inspired by Pico's *Heptaplus*, he continues :
"The earth and the sea serve man, heaven does battle for him, and the
spirits of heaven care for his salvation and well-being."[5] Through the

---

[1] *The Myth of the Golden Age in the Renaissance* (Bloomington, Ind., and London,
1969), p. 145.

[2] For example : Arzius, *Natura*, (fols. 3^r, 5^r); Florentinus, *Epiph.* (1), fol. 2; *Epiph.
MDXX*, fol. 3^v; Gorgonius, *Immortal.*, (fol. 3^v); Marsus, *Immortal.*, fol. 96^r; Ticinensis,
Advent., (fol. 2^r); Vasques, *Ciner.*, (fols. 1^v, 3^r, 3^v), etc.

[3] Marsus, *Steph.*, fol. 113^v. Cf. Hermes Trismegistus, *Pimander*, in Ficino, *Opera*,
II, 1849 : "Homo siquidem animal est divinum, nec est cum terrenis brutis, sed cum
diis caelestibus comparandus."

[4] Ticinensis, *Advent.*, (fol. 2^r) : "Et propter hominem omnia facta sunt, tamquam
propter unum finem, hominem ipsum ob immensam eius nobilitatem aliquos ut deum
iam adorasse legimus." This is possibly an allusion to the famous line from the *Asclepius*,
in Ficino, *Opera*, II, 1859 : "Propter hoc, o Asclepi, magnum miraculum est homo,
animal adorandum et honorandum."

[5] Arzius, *Natura*, (fol. 5^r) : "Singularis nostra est dignitas, cui terra, maria, elementa,
animantia cuncta deserviant, cui militet caelum, cui superni spiritus salutem bonumque

nobility and beauty of the union of body and soul, man was for Ticinensis a "microcosm."[1] For Arzius and Vasques he was, as citizen
of the heavens and as lord of the earth, the true binding force of the
universe. Both preachers borrow without acknowledgment Pico's
phrase, *mundi copula et hymenaeus*, and Vasques quotes several lines
from the exordium of Pico's famous "Oration."[2] According to Marso,
man's excellence consists in his being created in the image and likeness of God, which means that he is immortal, for all things divine
are immortal.[3]

---

procurent, quem denique mirifico amore omnia prosequantur, qui omnium est pulcherrimum vinculum et dulce pignus amoris." Cf. G. Pico della Mirandola, *De hominis dignitate,
Heptaplus, De ente et uno*, ed. Eugenio Garin (Florence, 1942), p. 304 : " 'Magnum, o
Asclepi, miraculum est homo.' Hoc praecipue nomine gloriari humana conditio potest,
quo etiam factum ut servire illi nulla creata substantia dedignetur. Huic terra et elementa, huic bruta sunt praesto et famulantur, huic militat caelum, huic salutem bonumque
procurant angelicae mentes, siquidem verum est quod scribit Paulus, esse omnes admi-
nistratorios spiritus in ministerium missos propter eos qui hereditati salutis sunt desti-
nati. Nec mirum alicui videri debet amari illum ab omnibus in quo omnia suum aliquid,
immo se tota et sua omnia agnoscunt." See also, e.g., Florentinus, *Epiph.* (1), fol. 2ʳ;
Epiph. (8), fol. 17ʳ; Ferrariensis, *Supr. die*, fol. 150ᵛ; Vasques, *Ciner.*, (fol. 4ʳ). According
to Gregory of Nyssa, the image of God is present wherever there is power to command;
see E. Garin, "La 'dignitas hominis' e la letteratura patristica," *La Rinascita*, #4, I
(1938), 128.

¹ Ticinensis, *Advent.*, (fol. 2ᵛ) : "Sic homo cuius animi et corporis tanta est pulchritudo
et nobilitas ut microcosmos, quasi parvus mundus, ab antiquis dictus est, cuius arbitrii
liberum imperium liberaeque potestates in manu sua sunt." On man as microcosm in
the Renaissance, see Garin, pp. 103, 114, 125; Trinkaus, II, 974 (index). See also Rudolf
Allers, "Microcosmus from Anaximandros to Paracelsus." *Traditio*, II (1944), 318-407,
and M.-D. Chenu, *La Théologie au douzième siècle* (Paris, 1957), pp. 34-44.

² Arzius, *Natura*, (fol. 3ʳ) : "... mundi copulam et hymenaeum, caelorum civem,
terrenorum dominum ad Dei factum denique imaginem, ..." Vasques, *Ciner.*, (fol. 4ʳ) :
"O magna opera Domini! O vas admirabile formatum ex limo! Et quis figulum non
amet, non admiretur, non adoret? Homo, inquit, pulvis. Homo ex pulvere. Et quid
homo? Homo creaturarum internuntius, homo superorum concivis, inferorum dominus,
homo sensuum acumine, rationis indagine, intelligentiae lumine interpres naturae, homo
stabilis aevi fluxique temporis interstitium, homo mundi copula et hymenaeus!" Cf.
Pico, *De hominis dignitate*, p. 102 : "Horum dictorum rationem cogitanti mihi non satis
illa faciebant, quae multa de humanae naturae praestantia afferuntur a multis : esse
hominem creaturarum internuntium, superis familiarem, regem inferiorum; sensuum
perspicacia, rationis indagine, intelligentiae lumine, naturae interpretem; stabilis aevi
et fluxi temporis interstitium, et (quod Persae dicunt) mundi copulam, immo hymenaeum,
ab angelis, teste Davide, paulo deminutum [Ps. 8.6]."

³ Marsus, *Immortal.*, fols. 95ᵛ-96ʳ. See also Gorgonius, *Immortal.*, (fol. 4ᵛ). On the
relationship between immortality, divinity, dignity, divinization, see the article "Divini-

One of the most marvellous qualities of human nature is its thirst for the divine. God is not so cruel as to deny us the quenching of this thirst, maintains Totis, and He calls us to His friendship.[1] But part of man's dignity consists in the fact that he was endowed with free will, that the Creator deigned to share His causality with him, that he in some mysterious way can choose to fulfill or to frustrate his desire for God.[2]

Even more significant is Vasques' long apology before Julius II in 1513 for man's basic indeterminancy and his potential "to be whatever he desires."[3] For Vasques, man's dignity is superior to the angels' not because of some static excellence, but because of his unlimited capacity to merit grace and to ascend to an ever closer union with God. Although arguments from indeterminancy reach back to the patristic tradition, Vasques is certainly dependent upon Pico's famous

---

sation" in the *Dictionnaire de spiritualité*, III (1957), esp. 1376-78, and Trinkaus, I, 213, 217-219, etc.

[1] Totis, *Ult. fin.*, fols. 139v-140r, and esp. 140r : "O mira conditoris nostri benignitas, caritas ! O excellentissimam hominis dignitatem ! Non dicam, inquit, vos servos sed amicos, quia quaecumque audivi a patre meo nota feci vobis [Jo. 15.15]. Hoc divinus Plato nescivit, hoc Aristoteles ignoravit." See also Ferrariensis, *Gratia*, fol. 154; Signorius, *Sum. Deo*, fol. 198r; Vasques, *Ciner.*, fol. 4v.

[2] See, e.g., Terasse, *Prov.*, fols. 34v, 36v, 38v; Maroldus, *Epiph.*, fol. 14r; Ticinensis, *Advent.*, (fol. 2v).

[3] Vasques, *Ciner.*, (fol. 6) : "Memento, homo, quia pulvis es. Minoratus quippe ab angelis homo est non solum quia non spiritus, sed ex spiritu constitutus et corpore, verum etiam quia eo spiritu constans qui propterea quod in sui primordio, ut Aristotelico utar eloquio, est velut rasa tabula, cum inter essentias intellectuales locum obtineat quem inter physicas nuda materia, ob idque fit omnium spirituum aptissimus, qui possit vacuo inanique subiecto maritales exhibere complexus, ut sint duo in carne una, homo unus, qui unde paulominus ab angelis minoratus is inde in orbe fit qui possit eousque gloria et honore coronari ut universis opibus quae patravit omnipotens manibus opificis antecellat, tanto excellentior angelis effectus quanto differentius prae illis liberum voluntatis arbitrium, adeptus non unico, ut angeli, merito, qui gratiam quidem primam accipientes non quantam elegissent, negato eis augmenti curriculo, in gratiam consumatam pervenerunt, sed multis meritorum accessionibus et, ut ita dicam, in dies inundantis gratiae diluvio altissimum felicitatis culmen pro votis accipiat .... ipsi certe angeli, quamvis non ab initio, paulo mox tamen ut conditi sunt id habuere totum quod sibi fuit in perpetuas aeternitates conferendum. O summam erga hominem benignitatem opificis ! O felicem, si ea non abutatur, hominis dignitatem, cui universa (ut ita loquar) semina inseruit conditor Deus, cui datum est id esse quod velit. Potest si velit in bruta descendere et obrutescere, ... Potest, si voluntas ferat, excellenti quadam unione caritatis unus cum Deo, mirabili dictu, spiritus factus in divinam prae caeteris sortem ascendere."

"Oration" for his formulation of it. Significantly, he places a stress on grace which is missing from the "Oration."[1] Within a year or so of Vasques' sermon, Florentinus took up Pico's thesis in the presence of Leo X. He basically agrees with Pico's view of man as self-determining and multipotential. But this view does not preclude, in his eyes, man's having a proper end prescribed for him by God.[2] Arzius, preaching before Clement VII in 1531, sees in man's spiritual nature a multipotentiality which implies him capable of becoming whatever he wishes, "heaven or earth," and capable of effecting in himself a "stupendous and radical metamorphosis." In this sense, again in Pico's terms, man is truly a Proteus, a chameleon.[3]

---

[1] Cf. Pico, *De hominis dignitate*, p. 106 : "'Poteris in inferiora quae sunt bruta degenerare; poteris in superiora quae sunt divina ex tui animi sententia regenerari.' O summam Dei patris liberalitatem, summam et admirandam hominis felicitatem! cui datum id habere quod optat, id esse quod velit. ... Nascenti homini omnifaria semina et omnigenae vitae germina indidit Pater; ..." See also 426, n. 2 above. On the patristic tradition, see Trinkaus, II, 506-507. For Pico's position on grace, see Giovanni di Napoli, *Giovanni Pico della Mirandola e la problematica dottrinale del suo tempo* (Rome, 1965), pp. 453-458.

[2] Florentinus, *Verit.*, fols. 8v-9r : "Sapientissimum rerum omnium architectum Deum, beatissime pater, ferunt nonnulli, hoc quem videmus mira arte mundo fabricato, super-caelesti regione mentibus decorata, universo animantium generi propria ut cuiusque tam exigebat natura et forma et sede concessa, homini tandem, post cuius utpote creaturarum omnium praestantissime genituram et fetus natura receptui cecinit, in mundi meditullio constituto nec certam sedem, nec propriam faciem, nec munus ullum peculiare dedisse, ut quam cuperet sedem, quam expeteret faciem, quae munera vellet, ea ipsa pro voto proque sua sententia et eligeret et possideret. Eundem hominem praedicant neque caelestem, neque terrenum, neque mortalem, neque immortalem factum. ... Haec diligenter perspecta etsi longe minora veris non arbitramur, quia tamen Dei perfecta sunt opera, ad praescriptum aliquem et certum finem hominis vitam a Deo optimo maximo institutam constanter asseveramus." Cf. Pico, *De hominis dignitate*, pp. 104-106 : "Iam summus Pater architectus Deus hanc quam videmus mundanam domum, divinitatis templum augustissimum, archanae legibus sapientiae fabrefecerat. Super-caelestem regionem mentibus decorarat. ... Statuit tandem optimus opifex, ut cui dare nihil proprium poterat commune esset quicquid privatum singulis fuerat. Igitur hominem accepit indiscretae opus imaginis atque in mundi positum meditullio sic est alloquutus : 'Nec certam sedem, nec propriam faciem, nec munus ullum peculiare tibi dedimus, o Adam, ... Nec te caelestem neque terrenum, neque mortalem neque immortalem fecimus, ut tui ipsius quasi arbitrarius honorariusque plastes et fictor, in quam malueris tute formam effingas.' "

[3] Arzius. *Natura*, fols. 3v-4r : "... ille, quod dictu est mirabile, si caelum esse vult, caelum est. Si terram fieri placet, terra est. ... Stupenda sed verissima metamorphosis ilico evadit, et ita quod vult evadit, ut cum eo sit magis unum, quam quod ex materia et forma coalescit, ut Proteus, chamaeleon, versipellis naturae non ab re dicatur."

The argument thus gradually moves from man's excellence as created in the image and likeness of God to his transformation or even "deification" as redeemed by Christ and subject to the workings of grace. The image and likeness, deformed by sin, is restored and even perfected by the grace of the Redeemer, so that man becomes more truly a son of God than ever before. He is, in fact, divinized.[1]

Grace is the "new Law," not written on tablets of stone but infused into our souls, whereby we "put on Christ" (Rom. 13.14; Galat. 3.27).[2] It is the inner light and warmth by which we are "transformed into Christ," says Florentinus.[3] For Maroldus, this internal "erudition" is superior to all external examples.[4] Cortesius asks his hearers to consider how much they owe to Him who snatched them from the power of darkness and translated them into the kingdom of the son of His love (Colos. 1.13).[5] For Ferrariensis nothing is more conducive to man's dignity than to be able to do those good and just things which others are incapable of doing. This capacity derives from grace and constitutes man's dignity.[6] Through the sacraments, according to Florentinus, the charity of God has been poured into our hearts by the Holy Spirit, who now dwells within us.[7] In another sermon he reminds his listeners that God created their souls in love, and that through love they will transform themselves into gods.[8]

Cf. Pico, De hominis dignitate, p. 106 : "Quis hunc nostrum chamaeleonta non admiretur ? aut omnino quis aliud quicquam admiretur magis ? Quem non immerito Asclepius Atheniensis versipellis huius et se ipsam transformantis naturae argumento per Proteum in mysteriis significari dixit."

[1] See "Divinisation," Dictionnaire, III, 1370-1459.

[2] Totis, Induere, fol. 142v : "Sed quaenam est lex ista non scriptis tradita, mentibus autem indita atque impressa ? Lex ista nova, patres optimi, non aliud divi Thomae ac aliorum theologorum sententia quam gratia Spiritus sancti nostro animo infusa, gratia fidei quae per dilectionem operatur, qua ad credendum sperandumque summeque diligendum aeternum et incommutabile bonum agendumque omnia illius amore ita dirigimur atque inclinamur ut nihil certius putemus, nihil facilius promptiusque et maiori cum voluptate agamus. Hac eminentissima gratia Christum consequimur atque induimus, per quem gratia hominibus teste Iohanne facta est [Jo. 1.14]. Haec est splendidissima et nuptialis illa vestis qua exuti homines ab aeterno convivio turpiter eiiciuntur, quae sine argento emitur, sine periculo exquiritur, sine labore obtinetur, sine consensu nostro non amittitur."

[3] Florentinus, Epiph. (1), fol. 4r.

[4] Maroldus, Epiph., fols. 13v-14r.

[5] Cortesius, Epiph., fol. 31v.

[6] Ferrariensis, Gratia, fol. 155v.

[7] Florentinus, Sacram., fol. 8r. See also Totis, Induere, fol. 144r.

[8] Florentinus, Trin., fol. 6v.

The Incarnation was the event which made possible this transformation. The Word's becoming flesh dignified human nature with
an excellence which far surpassed the excellence of man's creation
in God's image and likeness. "God became man, that man might become god."[1] This concise formula, wittingly or unwittingly borrowed
from a sermon of Pseudo-Augustine, was paraphrased by Florentinus
to describe what had taken place.[2] Vasques repeats the same idea in
slightly different words.[3] For Thegliatius the Incarnation sealed the
nuptials between the son of God and "our humanity."[4] Carvaial states :
"In the fact that he is called Emmanuel, which means with-us, is
designated the cause of our salvation, which is the union of divine
and human natures in the person of the son of God."[5] By emptying
himself, taking the form of a servant, and being born for us, he restored
to us our dignity, says Ferrariensis.[6] Ticinensis exclaims at the Incarnation : "O, how immense is the kindness of the eternal Father!
How great is the dignity of man! How incomprehensible the sublimity
of Jesus Christ, of whom it is truly said and proclaimed that he is
perfect God and perfect man!"[7] At the Incarnation, according to Ti-

---

[1] Ps. Aug., Sermo spurius 128, PL, XXXIX, 1997 : "Factus est Deus homo, ut homo
fieret Deus." This is a simplified version of a formulation which is genuinely Augustinian,
e.g., PL, XXXIX, 1504, and XXXVIII, 909 and esp. 1012 : "Deos facturus qui homines
erant, homo factus est qui Deus erat." The Pseudo-Augustinian formula was popular
and was quoted, e.g., by St. Thomas, S.T., III.1.2 : "Quinto, quantum ad plenam parti-
cipationem divinitatis, quae vera est hominis beatitudo et finis humanae vitae; et hoc
collatum est nobis per Christi humanitatem. Dicit enim Augustinus ..., Factus est Deus
homo, ut homo fieret Deus." Petrarch paraphrases the formula, De remediis utriusque
fortunae, II, 93, in Opera omnia, I (Basel, 1554), 211. It also occurs, slightly amplified,
in Thegliatius' sermon to the Fifth Lateran Council, Mansi, XXXII, 920. The idea
antedates Augustine, of course, and can be traced back as far as Irenaeus, e.g., Contra
haereses, V. praef., PG, VII, 1120 : "... Verbum Dei, Iesum Christum Dominum nostrum,
qui propter immensam suam dilectionem factus est quod sumus nos, uti nos perficeret
esse quod est ipse."

[2] Florentinus, Sacram., fol. 8ᵛ.

[3] Vasques, Ciner., (fol. 7ᵛ).

[4] Thegliatius, Omn. sanct., fol. 63ᵛ.

[5] Carvaial, Circumcis., fol. 15ᵛ : "In eo enim quod dicitur Emmanuel, quod inter-
pretatur nobiscum, designatur causa nostrae salutis, quae est unio divinae et humanae
naturae in persona Filii Dei, per quam actum est ut Deus esset nobiscum particeps."

[6] Ferrariensis, Advent. Christi, fol. 143ʳ.

[7] Ticinensis, Advent., (fol. 3ʳ) : "O ingens igitur aeterni patris benignitas! O quam
magna hominis dignitas! O incomprehensibilis Iesu Christi sublimitas! De quo vere
dicitur et praedicatur quod est perfectus Deus et perfectus homo."

cinensis, the Lord conferred greater dignity upon human nature than he did even to the angels—to the man Christ He conceded the supreme grace, and of Christ's plenitude we have all received (Jo. 1.16).[1]

Despite their extolling the redemptive efficacy of the Incarnation, the preachers did not mean to deny the traditional focus upon Christ's death as a saving event. Azpetia and Florentinus view it in their Good Friday sermons as an expression of God's love for men.[2] The emphasis is not on the depths of man's depravity which would require such a salvation, but upon the immense quantities of God's love which inspired it. Azpetia goes on to quote the verse from Holy Saturday's "Exultet," the liturgical hymn whose author was probably St. Ambrose : "To redeem a slave, You handed over Your son !" Marso quotes the same line in his sermon for Ascension Thursday. Both preachers continue to quote from this same hymn with its assessment of Adam's sin as the *felix culpa*, a truly "happy sin" because it merited so great a Redeemer. Azpetia then cites Augustine as his authority to maintain that as a result of the benefits conferred upon man by Christ's redemption, man was in a better condition than he would have been if Adam had not sinned.[3]

These benefits of the Redemption were finally and fully achieved when Christ ascended to the right hand of the Father. It was at that moment, says Marso, that our humanity was exalted above the choirs of angels.[4] It was at that moment, says Gravina, that human nature took its place above the very stars.[5] Our mortality was thus transferred into the very heart and home of immortality : "O, dignity of the human race, dignity never before heard of in all the ages of the world."[6]

The "sermon" of Giles of Viterbo is perhaps a suitable way to conclude our discussion of the dignity of man. Although Giles addressed this document to his good friend in Rome, Antonio Zoccoli, he at least hoped Zoccoli would bring it to the attention of Julius II, as the peroration makes clear. The document probably dates from sometime

---

[1] Ticinensis, *Advent.*, (fol. 2ʳ().

[2] Azpetia, *Pass. Dmni.*, fol. 127ʳ; Florentinus, *Pass.*, fol. 19ᵛ.

[3] Azpetia, *Pass. Dmni.*, fol. 131 ; Marsus. *Immortal.*, fol. 97ʳ. This same text is utilized by Benedetto Morandi, as quoted by Trinkaius, I, 441 (n. 48).

[4] Marsus, *Immortal.*, fol. 98ᵛ. The idea occurs, e.g., in Leo the Great, Sermo 78, PL, LIV, 396.

[5] Gravina, *Ascens.*, (fol. 4ʳ).

[6] Gravina, *Ascens.*, (fol. 2ʳ) : "O nullis antea saeculis auditam humani generis dignitatem !" See also Totis, *Ascens.*, fols. 138ᵛ, 141ʳ.

between 1503 and 1506, with the outside limits in both directions
reaching from 1503 to 1513. In my edition for *Viator*, I have entitled
it "Man's Dignity, God's Love, and the Destiny of Rome." The text,
which runs twenty-six pages in typescript, echoes and develops many
of the above arguments for man's dignity resulting from the Incarnation. Specifically, Giles insists upon man's transformation, even divinization, through the power of the Incarnation, and he alludes to the
formula from Pseudo-Augustine.[1] Through God's transforming love in
our hearts, man becomes "God" or a "son of God" and is rendered
immortal.[2] In this text Giles does not emphasize the excellence of
man's creation in God's image and likeness, nor the deprivation or
even depravity coming from Original Sin, but the surpassing sublimation effected by the Word's becoming flesh. In that event divinity and
humanity were joined in holy nuptials.[3] The resulting dignity did not
assign man to a static place of honor in the universe but imposed upon
him a mission to respond in love. Man must respond by doing "the
one thing necessary" (Luc. 10.42), by fulfilling Christ's command "to
love one another as I have loved you" (Jo. 15.12).[4]

Giles's sermon would be important merely as a representative compendium of arguments and texts we have seen. However, it has one
characteristic which makes it distinctive. It relates the theme of man's
dignity to the dignity and destiny of the city of Rome. This relation-

---

[1] Naples MS, fol. 257r : "Qui fit ut homo, sanguis et caro (ut nostri dicunt), in Deum
transeat, hoc est, evadat Deus Deusque efficiatur ? Sed quid id mireris quod homo fiat
Deus ? Nam Deus effectus est homo, et Verbum caro factum est." *Viator, loc. cit.*, ll. 18-21.

[2] Naples MS, fols. 257v-258r : "Qui igitur Spiritu Dei aguntur, quod ait Apostolus,
filii Dei sunt [Rom. 8.14], hoc est, qui divino amore flagrant ex Deo nati sunt [Jo. 1.13].
Sed qua id ratione ? Quia Verbum caro factum [Jo. 1.14]. Vides ideo factum ut habitans
in nobis ignem amoremque in nobis excitaret, quo absumpta mortali natura immortales
ex Deo nasceremur. Horum vero omnium ratio amor est, cuius gratia Deum hominem
effectum praedicabam." *Viat.*, 33-38.

[3] Naples MS, fols. 258r-259r. *Viat.*, 33-62.

[3] Naples MS, fols. 258r-259r.

[4] Naples MS, fols. 259v-260r : "Amore ille ad nos descendit, amore ad illum ascenden-
dum est nobis. Amore ille a viventibus seiunctus moritur, ut ipsi amore iuncti viveremus.
Sed tanta Deus pertulit nostra causa, quid mercedis exegit ? Num fortassis ut sua nos
causa moreremur invicem ? Non plane. Sed facili mercede contentus praecepit dumtaxat unum, ut ipsi inter nos invicem amaremus. Non multa iussit, non multa in evan-
gelio sunt, non multa facienda sunt homini. Porro unum est necessarium, verbum
Domini est. Non igitur multa, si unum. Sed quod tandem id unum ? Non intelligo quod
praecipias unum. Nolo mortalem interpretem. ... Audite vocem Domini, si oves (id
quod putemus) estis Domini. Vox eius est, mediusfidius ! Audite obiter ! Hoc est praeceptum meum ut diligatis invicem sicut dilexi vos." *Viat.*, 75-90.

ship is completely missing from Giles's text on man's dignity published
some years ago by Eugenio Massa,[1] and I am not aware of any other
instance in Renaissance writing where such a relationship is found.
Thus the theme of man's dignity is invested with a new meaning as
it contributes to the sacral mystique of the city of Rome.

Jerusalem rejected Peter and the other apostles, so they sought a
new city that might be worthy of the new religion. That city, really
chosen by God himself, was Rome. As the city of the new religion,
Rome must be inspired by love. It must be worthy of its destiny.
Under the leadership of the successor of Peter, it must be defended
from its internal and external enemies.[2] At this juncture Giles seems
to be calling for a reform of the Church and for the actual taking up
of arms against the Turks.[3]

In any case, Rome must be faithful, simple, without guile. It must
be without ambition and without greed.[4] Like the other preachers,
Giles has nothing to say about jurisdictions, primacies, and canon law,
but he has much to say about "the one thing necessary," if we may
borrow that phrase from him as well as from Pastor. Rome was chosen
by God in love, and Rome must respond with love. A bold rhetoric
animates the last part of the sermon as the nuptials between divinity
and humanity are specified in the form of the nuptials between Christ
and Rome.[5]

---

[1] Eugenio Massa, *I fondamenti metafisici della 'dignitas hominis' e testi inediti di
Egidio da Viterbo* (Turin, 1954). Trinkaus discusses this text, II, 526-529.

[2] Naples MS, fols. 280ʳ-281ʳ. *Viat.*, 588-613.

[3] On Giles's attitude towards war against the Turks, See my *Giles of Viterbo*,
127-130. This question plays a small but significant role in his address honoring Manuel I
of Portugal before Julius II, Dec. 21, 1507, which I published in *Traditio*, XXV (1969),
265-338, "Fulfillment of the Christian Golden Age under Pope Julius II." See esp.
274-275, 324-327, and the peroration, 338.

[4] Naples MS, fol. 278ᵛ : "Ipsa utpote princeps superstes omnium eris—modo fida
sis, bona fide sis, innocens, iusta, casta, pia sis, modo non aliena sed mea sis, sis integra,
sis simplex, sis sine dolo malo, sine luxu, sine ambitu, sine auri cupiditate, sponsi sis
amans tui sponsique amicorum amicarumque omnium." *Viat.*, 545-549.

[5] Naples MS, fol. 277ʳ : "Ecce Spiritus loquitur : caput caeli Christus, caput terrarum
Roma. Roma princeps, Christus princeps. Si is sponsus calestis sponsam in terris quaerit,
principem princeps ducat, rex reginam, terrarum imperatricem caeli atque terrarum
imperator. Mea es, mea, o septimontia Roma ! Salve, o felix sponsa ! Salve, Tarpeia
rupes ! Salvete, colles sacri ! Salve, Aventine ! Novus ad te Romulus, tanto Romulo
potior quanto homine Deus !" *Ibid.*, fol. 278ʳ : "Amore Deus ductus est ut homo fieret,
amore ut sese traderet, amore ut moriens sanguinem atque aquam funderet, ut te
[Tibrim] dextrumque latus tuum consecrarem. Sacro igitur ego te, ac ter appello, voco'

Conclusion

In a very brief space we have considered fifty-one distinct documents, authored by twenty-seven different men. Chronologically we have spanned half a century. Such a procedure suppresses individual differences and perforce gives a false impression of homogeneity. Perhaps the healthiest thing to do at this point, therefore, is to insist that no two sermons and no two preachers are identical in style, viewpoint, and theological treatment of subject. Moreover, what we have presented here has been in the form of a first exploratory essay into a *terra incognita*. Nonetheless, if we keep these important qualifications in mind, we can still reflect fruitfully upon our efforts.

First of all, we must reject the impressions about the content and quality of the sermons at the papal court which we inherited from Erasmus, Burckhardt, and Pastor. No matter what new data further research discovers, we now know that at least a significant body of that literature does not correspond to what those authors led us to believe. This preaching prided itself on its command of scriptural and patristic sources; whenever the classics played a role, they were subordinated to these other sources. Although there was often a vigorous element of moral exhortation in these sermons, not even the mendicants (with the possible exception of Schönbergt) could be described as "preachers of penance." These preachers were preachers of doctrine. We must assume many of them had a scholastic training, but they avoided scholastic arguments in their preaching and showed a decided preference for those Christian doctrines which preoccupied thinkers during the patristic era. They tried to relate these doctrines, abstract and abstruse though they sometimes were, to the lives of their hearers. If the papal court during the Renaissance was in many respects "pagan" or "exceedingly worldly," it certainly was not so in the quality of the sermons it heard.

What was the nature of the religion or piety proposed in these sermons? It was doctrinal and attitudinal. It did not rest on the performance of innumerable and specified external practices of devotion, such as pilgrimages and the veneration of relics, nor was a great deal of emphasis placed on the sacraments themselves. Given the setting in which these sermons were preached, there is amazingly

---

nuncupo amoris fluentum, iubeoque salvum sospitem sospitatoremque esse mortalium et sanctorum beatorumve amorum praeceptorem. " *Viat.* 507-513, 530-535.

little in them that is supportative of ecclesial institutions. This fact
by no means implies that the preachers questioned or denied these
institutions, but it simply shows that these were not invariably in the
forefront of their consciousness when they were called upon to speak.

Despite the important ethical concerns expressed in the sermons,
the religion they propound cannot be described principally as ethical,
if by that term we mean simply the performance of morally correct
acts. The preachers invited their hearers to contemplate with them
some of the central Christian mysteries, and they hoped to evoke from
the same hearers the proper attitudinal and affective response—belief, wonder, joy, gratitude, love. Thence would follow a life appropriate
to these attitudes and affections. They realized full well, however, that
the love or charity with which the Christian life should be inspired
was not theirs to give. It was poured into the hearts of their listeners
by the Holy Spirit.

The preachers wanted to impress upon their hearers the fact that
they were Christians, that is, that their lives were of a special quality
because they believed Christ's message and because they were the
recipients of Christ's salvation. What comes through in these sermons
is their strongly Christological patterns of thought and expression. If
Erasmus did not hear about Christ in the Good Friday sermon in 1509,
he listened to a sermon very different from the ones we have been
investigating.

The theme of man's dignity, as it emerges in these sermons, is
explicitly anchored to belief in Christ's Incarnation and Redemption.
Indeed, the ramifications of these two mysteries blur into one another
and stretch from the moment of Christ's conception in the Virgin's
womb until his ascension to the Father's right hand. In some contrast
with the texts discussed by Charles Trinkaus in his recent book, the
emphasis in these preachers is on the Christological mysteries rather
than on the fact of man's creation in God's image and likeness. We
are dealing here precisely with a difference of emphasis, for Trinkaus
also calls attention to the importance of the themes of Incarnation,
deification, etc. We are dealing, furthermore, with a difference which
is in part explainable by the different literary forms involved. I feel,
therefore, that my researches confirm Trinkaus' thesis about the
basically religious, and even theological, inspiration of the theme of
man's dignity in the Italian Renaissance for the period under discussion. In this theme as propounded by our preachers, we find data to
support Trinkaus' assertion that the Renaissance vision of man was

based on "possibly the most affirmative view of human nature in the history of thought and expression." It was a vision projected "within the inherited framework of the Christian faith."[1]

There is certainly more to be said on this question. The Christian mysteries are adduced as the foundation for man's dignity. But what were the sources inspiring such an interpretation of the mysteries? The Fathers clearly were important. At times certain scholastic principles, divested of scholastic dress, seem to have been operative. I have been able to establish specific dependences of Vasques, Florentinus, and Arzius on Pico della Mirandola. Occasionally the preachers speak in terms suggestive of Ficino's Platonism. But the degree of importance and the impact of all these relationships is not very clear. Even less clear is the relationship of the dignity-theme to the doctrine of deification in the Hermetic literature.[2] We need a closer analysis of the texts in question, and we need a comparison of them with other texts which deal with similar themes.

Studies are also needed to clarify for us with further detail the more general problem of the religion preached in these sermons. However, even now we can at least venture the opinion that there are no remarkable discordances between it and what I have elsewhere described as operative in the writings of Giles of Viterbo. Indeed, I do not find in it any remarkable discordances with what I would understand as basic to Erasmus' religion, which in many respects it seems to anticipate. What I am trying to say, at a minimum, is that this style of religion and religious discourse can be clearly distinguished from scholasticism and from the crude devotional and juridical piety which

---

[1] Trinkaus, I, xiv.

[2] See Trinkaus, II, 498-504; *Dictionnaire*, III, 1375; and Weinstein, pp. 198-199, with bibliographical references. Hermes is mentioned by name by six of our preachers. In Ferrariensis, *Advent. Christi*, fol. 143ᵛ, and Maroldus. *Epiph.*, fol. 13ʳ, the mention is casual. The mentions by Arzius, *Natura*, fols. 4ᵛ-5ʳ, and by Capitaneis, *Omn. sanct.*, fol. 3ᵛ, are brief, but suggest some familiarity with the Hermetic writings. Gorgonius actually quotes him twice, approvingly, on the nature of the soul, *Immortal.*, (fols. 2ʳ, 4ᵛ). Signorius, characteristically, refers to him most frequently, *Sum. Deo*, fols. 196ᵛ, 200ᵛ, 202ʳ, 202ᵛ, 203ʳ, in his attempt to authenticate the fact of the divine unity and trinity outside the canonical Scriptures. Even in Signorius' case, Hermes is placed rather indiscriminately in the company of other "philosophers" like Aristotle, Plato, and Cicero—with the exception of the significant line, fol. 202ʳ : "... ut si eam [disputationem] legas, Salomonem Ioannemque legisse te reputes, nec ultra Christianam desideres pietatem." For a discussion of similar statements by Giles of Viterbo about Plato, see my *Giles of Viterbo*, p. 24.

Erasmus so often decries for us in scathing terms. The emphasis on inner attitudes and especially the emphasis on God's gift of charity, which is the basis for the continuation or restoration of *pax* and *concordia* in the universe, are specific characteristics which are common. Also common is the strong Christocentrism, which qualifies and specifies the description "anthropocentric" sometimes applied to humanist religion. Most important of all, perhaps, is the viewing of the process of the individual's response to the great mysteries of his religion "as the transformation of a total personality through love."[1] Bouwsma sees such an emphasis on transformation as characteristic of the spirituality of the Italian Renaissance. Our sermons certainly confirm that judgment.

We might submit, finally, that Trinkaus' term, "rhetorical theology," is an accurate and suggestive one for describing this spirituality.[2] The term serves to distinguish this style of religion and religious discourse from "monastic theology" and "scholastic theology." More important, it suggests that it is a body of literature held together by certain common presuppositions about the nature of truth and religion, and that its ultimate objective was "practical" or "active," i.e., persuasional. Not abstract speculation, but transformation of life was its goal.

Appendix

In this Appendix I have tried to supply the essential bibliographical information for the sermons, including the shelf-number of the copy I actually used, incunabular number, and the name of the pope before whom the sermon was delivered. Then follows brief biographical data. In square brackets I give the abbreviation for the sermon as it appears in the notes. Libraries are abbreviated as follows :

Ang. Biblioteca Angelica, Rome
Vall. Biblioteca Vallicelliana, Rome
Vat. Biblioteca Apostolica Vaticana, Vatican City

1. Arzius, Hieronymus. *Oratio de natura, bello, et pace utriusque hominis* (Rome, 1531). Vall. Inc. Q. V. 175 (29). (Clement VII). Doctor of Sacred Theology. Professor of Metaphysics, University of Rome. [Arzius, *Natura*].

2. Azpetia, Martinus de. *De passione Domini in pontificia capella oratio* (n.p., n.d.)

---

[1] Bouwsma, p. 30.

[2] Trinkaus, I, 126-128, 141-142, 305-307, etc.

[Rome : G. Lauer or Euch. Silber, ?]. Ang. Inc. 457 (20). Hain #2238. (Alexander VI). Apostolic Protonotary. Master of Arts and Theology. [Azpetia, *Pass. Dmni.*].

3. Bodivit, Guilelmus (O.F.M.). *Sermo habitus in missa papali, Romae, MCCCCLXXXV, in die Trinitatis* (n.p., n.d.) [Rome : Steph. Plannck, 1485]. Ang. Inc. 457 (9). Hain # *3349 (or 3350). (Innocent VIII). Doctor of Sacred Theology. [Bodivit, *Trin.*].

4. Brentius, Andreas. *In pentecosten oratio* (n.p., n.d.) [Rome, 1483]. Vat. Inc. Ross. 1882, fols. 67ʳ-76ᵛ. Hain #3778. (Sixtus IV). "Roman philologist" (Hain). [Brentius, *Pent.*].

5. Canalis, Mathias. *Oratio de passione Domini* (n.p., n.d.) [Rome : Steph. Plannck, ?]. Ang. Inc. 457 (15). Hain # *4303. (Innocent VIII). "Servitor et praeceptor" (Burchard, I, 350) of Matteo Cibo, nephew of Pope Innocent VIII. [Canalis, *Pass. Dmni.*].

6. Capitaneis, Thomas de Celleonibus ex (O.P.). *Oratio in festo omnium sanctorum* (n.p., n.d.) [Rome : Steph. Plannck, 1483]. Ang. Inc. 476 (1). Hain # *4377. (Sixtus IV). Professor of Sacred Theology. Orator for the Most Christian King of France. [Capitaneis, *Omn. sanct.*].

7. Carvaial, Bernardinus. *Oratio in die circumcisionis Domini* (n.p., n.d.) [Rome : Steph. Plannck, 1484]. Ang. Inc. 476 (2). Hain # *4546. (Sixtus IV). Master of Arts and Theology. Created cardinal by Alexander VI, 1493, at request of Ferdinand of Aragon. Spaniard. [Carvaial, *Circumcis*]..

8. Cortesius, Alexander. *Oratio habita in aede d. Petri in Epiphania* (n.p., n.d.) [Rome, 1483]. Ang. Inc. 476 (5). Hain # *5773. (Sixtus IV). A "magister registri supplicationum" (Buchard, I, 402). [Cortesius, *Epiph.*].

9-13. Ferrariensis, Ludovicus (O.P.). *Orationes quinque* (n.p., n.d.) [Rome, ?]. Ang. Inc. 457 (23). Hain #6983. (Innocent VIII and Alexander VI). Procurator General of Dominicans. Taught philosophy at Ferrara and theology at the University of Padua.

    9. *De adventu Christi* (1) [Ferrariensis, *Advent. Christi*].

    10. *De pugna Christi cum daemone* (2) [Ferrariensis, *Pugna*].

    11. *De suprema mortalium rerum die* (3) [Ferrariensis, *Supr. die*].

    12. *De divina gratia* (4) [Ferrariensis, *Gratia]*.

    13. *De conformitate ecclesiae militantis ad ecclesiam triumphantem* (5) [Ferrariensis, *Conform. eccles.*].

14-22. Florentinus, Augustus Philippus (O.S.M.). *Orationes novem coram Iulio II et Leone X* (Rome : Jacobus Mazochius, 1518). Vall. Inc. Q. V. 175 (1). (Julius II and Leo X). Procurator General of the Servites. Professor of Theology.

    14. *In Epiphania Domini* (1) [Florentinus, *Epiph.* (1)].

    15. *Dominica de trinitate* (2) [Florentinus, *Trin.*].

    16. *De sacramentis* (3) [Florentinus, *Sacram.*].

    17. *De veritate* (4) [Florentinus, *Verit.*].

    18. *De multiplici adoratione* (5) [Florentinus, *Ador.*].

    19. *In die Epiphaniae* (6) [Florentinus, *Epiph.* (6)].

    20. *De peccato* (7) [Florentinus, *Pecc.*].

    21. *In Epiphania* (8) [Florentinus, *Epiph.* (8)].

    22. *In dominica de passione* (9) [Florentinus, *Pass.*].

23. Florentinus, Augustus Philippus (O.S.M.). *Oratio die Epiphaniae, MDXX* (n.p., n.d.). Ang. Inc. 550 (7). (Leo X). [Florentinus, *Epiph. MDXX*].

24. Genazano, Marianus de (O.E.S.A.). *Oratio coram Innocentio VIII dominica tertia adventus habita* (n.p., n.d.) [Rome : Steph. Plannck, 1487]. Ang. Inc. 476 (10). Hain #*7553. (Innocent VIII). Professor of Sacred Theology. Preacher. Prior General of Augustinians. [Genazano, *Advent.*].

25. Genazano, Marianus de (O.E.S.A.). *Oratio de passione Iesu Christi* (n.o., n.d.) [Rome : Euch. Silber, 1498]. Ang. Inc. 7 (17). Hain #7555. (Alexander VI). [Genazano, *Pass. Christi*].

26. Gorgonius, Stephanus Basignanas (O.Carm.). *Oratio de animae immortalitate* (n.p., n.d.) [Rome, 1518]. Vall. Inc. Q. V. 182 (24). (Leo X). Theologian. [Gorgonius, *Immortal.*].

27. Gravina, Petrus. *Oratio de Christi ad coelos ascensu* (n.p., n.d.) [Rome : Steph. Plannck, 1493]. Vall. Inc. Q. V. 175 (5). Hain #7925. (Alexander VI). Humanist. Poet at Naples with Pontano and Sannazaro. [Gravina, *Ascens.*].

28. Imolensis, Ludovicus (O.F.M.). *Oratio in die S. Stephani* (n.p., n.d.) [Rome : Steph. Plannck, ?]. Ang. Inc. 457 (17). Hain #*9162. (Sixtus IV). Professor of Sacred Theology. "Minister provincialis" of Franciscans in Bologna. [Imolensis, *Steph.*].

29. Lollius, Antonius Geminianensis. *Oratio in die circumcisionis Domini* (n.p., n.d.) [Rome : Steph. Plannck, 1485]. Ang. Inc. 476 (7). Hain #*10180. (Innocent VIII). Chaplain of the cardinal of Siena (Piccolomini). [Lollius, *Circumcis.*].

30. Marcellus, Christophorus. *Oratio ad Iulium II pont. max. in die omnium sanctorum in capella habita* (n.p., n.d.) [Rome, ?]. Vat. Barb. G. VIII. 125 (3). (Julius II). Apostolic Protonotary. Designated by Julius II Archbishop of Corcyra. [Marcellus, *Omn. sanct.*].

31. Maroldus, Marcus (O.P.). *Sententia veritatis humanae redemptionis* (n.p., n.d.) [Rome : Steph. Plannck, 1481]. Ang. Inc. 476 (23). Hain #*10778. (Sixtus IV). "Haereticae pravitatis inquisitor." Master of Arts and Theology. [Maroldus, *Sent. verit.*].

32. Maroldus, Marcus (O.P.). *Oratio in Epiphania* (n.p., n.d.) [Rome : Joh. Gensberg, 1475 (cf. fol. 9^r)]. Ang. Inc. 24 (2). Hain #*10779. (Sixtus IV). [Maroldus, *Epiph.*].

33. Marsus, Petrus. *Oratio in die S. Stephani* (n.p., n.d.) [Rome : Steph. Plannck, ?]. Ang. Inc. 457 (18). Hain #*10785. (Innocent VIII ?). Disciple of Leto, associa- with Roman Academy. Canon of S. Lorenzo in Damaso. [Marsus, *Steph.*].

34. Marsus, Petrus. *Panegyricus S. Iohannis evangelistae* (n.p., n.d.) [Rome : Steph. Plannck, ca. 1485]. Ang. Inc. 476 (9). Hain #*10789. (Innocent VIII). [Marsus, *Johan.*].

35. Marsus, Petrus. *Oratio in die ascensionis de immortalitate animae* (n.p., n.d.) [Rome : Steph. Plannck, ?]. Vat. Inc. Ross. 1882, fols. 93^r-98^v. Hain #*10791. (Innocent VIII). [Marsus, *Immortal.*].

36. Rodericus de S. Ella. *Oratio in die parasceve* (n.p., n.d.) [Rome : Steph. Plannck, 1477]. Ang. Inc. 476 (4). Hain #*13933 [sic : *13931]. (Sixtus IV). Master of Arts and Theology. [Rodericus, *Parasc.*].

37-41. Schönbergt, Nicolaus (O.P.). *Orationes vel potius divinorum eloquiorum enodationes facundissimae* (Leipzig : Wolfgangus Stoeckel de Monaco, 1512). Ang. Inc. 7 (8). (Julius II). Procurator General of the Dominicans. After 1510, Professor at the University of Rome. German.

    37. *De admiranda Christi pugna et eius imprimis necessitate* (1) [Schönbergt, *Prima*].

    38. *Secunda oratio. Nox praecessit, dies autem appropinquavit* (2) [Schönbergt, *Secunda*].

39. *Tertia oratio. Ductus est Iesus ab desertum a Spiritu ut tenteretur a diabolo* (3) [Schönbergt, *Tertia*].
40. *Quarta oratio. Nox praecessit, etc.* (4) [Schönbergt, *Quarta*].
41. *Quinta oratio. Ductus est Iesus in desertum* (5) [Schönbergt, *Quinta*].
42. Signorius, Baptista Genuens. (O.E.S.A.). *Oratio de summo Deo* (n.p., n.d.) [Rome, 1485]. Ang. Inc. 7 (14). Hain #14732. (Innocent VIII). Procurator General of the Augustinians. Professor of Theology. [Signorius, *Sum. Deo*].
43. Terasse, Petrus (O.Carm.). *Oratio de divina providentia* (n.p., n.d.) [Rome : Steph. Plannck, 1483]. Ang. Inc. 476 (6). Hain #*15369. (Sixtus IV). Bachelor of of Sacred Theology. [Terasse, *Div. prov.*].
.44. Thegliatius, Stephanus. *Oratio habita in die omnium sanctorum* (n.p., n.d.) [Rome: Euch. Silber, 1492]. Ang. Inc. 476 (12). Hain #15459. (Alexander VI). Archbishop of Patras and Antivari from 1475. [Thegliatius, *Omn. sanct.*].45.
45. Thegliatius, Stephanus. *Sermo habitus in materia fidei contra Turcorum persecutionem* (n.p., n.d.) [Rome, ca. 1481]. Ang. Inc. 33 (4). Hain #*15461. (Sixtus IV). [Thegliatius, *Mat. fid.*].
'46. Ticinensis, Marcus Antonius (O.F.M. ?). *In adventu dom. II MD oratio* (n.p., n.d.) [Rome : Steph. Plannck, 1500]. Ang. Inc. 1 (6). Reichling #345. (Alexander VI): Doctor of Arts and Theology. [Ticinensis, *Advent.*].
47-48. Totis, Timotheus de, de Mutina (O.P.). *Sermo quod omnino datur ultimus finis creaturae rationalis et quid illud sit et quod Christus ut ad illum invitaret nos hodie ascendit; Sermo eiusdem qualiter possimus Iesum Christum induere, coram Alexandro sexto* (n.p., n.d.) [Rome : Euch. Silber, ca. 1496]. Ang. Inc. 7 (9) Hain-Cop. #5843. (Alexander VI). Professor of Theology. [Totis, *Ult. fin.*] [Totis, *Induere*].
49. Vasques, Dionysius (O.E.S.A.). *Oratio habita Romae in apostolica sacri palatii capella in die cinerum* (Rome : Jacobus Mazochius, 1513). Vall. Inc. Q. V. 175 (3). (Julius II). Professor of Sacred Theology. "Capellanus apostolicae sedis." Spaniard. [Vasques, *Ciner.*].
50. Vasques, Dionysius (O.E.S.A.). *De unitate et simplicitate personae Christi in duabus naturis oratio praeclarissima* (Rome : Jacobus Mazochius, 1518). Vall. Inc. Q. V. 175 (2). (Leo X). [Vasques, *Unit. et simpl.*].

ADDITIONAL ON "PREACHING FOR THE POPES"

PAUL OSKAR KRISTELLER
Columbia University

I have been very much interested in Professor O'Malley's paper which presents extensive and solid documentation on an important subject that has so far received almost no scholarly attention. Since I have been aware of the problem for some time and have touched on it repeatedly, I venture to suggest a few addenda to Professor O'Malley's study, hoping that he may decide to enlarge it and to treat the subject in a longer monograph.

First of all, I have come across a few additional sermons of the type he discusses, and should like him to add them to his list and to include them in his study. There are several such orations by Aurelius Lippus Brandolinus and by his brother Raphael Brandolinus. The Biblioteca Publica in Evora, Portugal, from one of whose mss. Father O'Malley published an important text of Giles of Viterbo,[1] also contains a miscellaneous volume that has the shelf mark Incunabulos 27-94. It is partly manuscript and partly printed. Among its printed sections, it includes many sermons discussed by Father O'Malley, and several additional pieces of the same type.

Furthermore, there is another group of sermons that might be included, namely the sermons in praise of Thomas Aquinas delivered on his day at S. Maria sopra Minerva to which the members of the papal court were regularly invited. Several of these sermons are by famous humanists such as Lorenzo Valla and Johannes Antonius Campanus. The sermon by Valla is much earlier than the specimens discussed by Professor O'Malley. I briefly deal with this material in my booklet, *Le Thomisme et la pensée italienne de la Renaissance* (Montreal and Paris, 1967, p. 72-79). Several more sermons of the type under investigation appear in mss..

I published a sermon on St. Stephen delivered by the French humanist and theologian, Guillaume Fichet [2] where I also discuss the genre. More texts may be found in the Fondo Vaticano Latino and the Fondo Chigi of the Vatican, and in scattered papal mss. that might be located through the works of Eugene Muntz on the history of the Vatican Library. Also Burchard's Diary may serve as a starting point for the names of additional authors, and with his help further sermons might either be identified in catalogues of early printed books and of mss., or be recorded as lost.

Some additional types of sermons might be included if Prof. O'Malley is willing to enlarge the scope of his study outside of Rome. There are sermons or orations delivered at chapter meetings of religious orders, at the beginning of theological disputations, in honor of individual saints or on certain holidays, not to speak of funeral orations, or of

---

[1] *Traditio* 25 (1969), 265-338.
[2] *Mélanges Eugène Tisserant* 6, *Studi e Testi* 236 (1964), 459-97.

the lay sermons delivered in confraternities such as the ones mentioned by Professor Trexler.

In addition to the doctrinal content of the sermons and to the patristic and classical quotations discussed by Professor O'Malley, some attention may be given to the rhetorical form and style of the sermons, the use of Ciceronian periods and clausulae, the choice of classical words and the avoidance of technical scholastic terms. Of special interest is the pattern followed by the sermons. I suspect that most of them follow the disposition into five parts prescribed by classical rhetorical texts, and use many of the rhetorical figures discussed in the same treatises. In the case of Fichet, I found and published a set of glosses accompanying his sermon that turned out to be a rhetorical analysis of the sermon, using a number of terms and concepts taken from Fichet's own *Rhetorica*. It indicates a rhetorical awareness of the writers of these sermons that we can explicitly document in this instance and that may be assumed to underlie also some of the other sermons.

In comparing the humanist sermons not only with medieval sermons but also with the medieval *artes praedicandi* listed by H. Caplan and summarized by Th. Charland, it might be seen that many of the humanist sermons omit the *divisio* prescribed by the medieval textbooks, tend to add prologues of the classical kind, and even have these prologues precede the *thema*, the scriptural verse on which the sermon is based.

In other words, the influence of humanist secular oratory on sacred eloquence may be identified not only in the classical quotations and in the themes (dignity of man, immortality of the soul) but also in the form and style of the sermons that are being considered.

Moreover, it might be useful to pay attention to the status and personality of the authors of these speeches. It is important to know in each case whether the speaker is a member of a religious order or of the secular clergy or a layman. In each case attention should be given to his life and other written works, and we also may try to find out which of the speakers, including clergymen and members of religious orders, may be classified, on account of their training and other writings, as humanists.

The result of this would seem to be that there was in the Italian Renaissance a large body of sacred eloquence that was influenced in its form and content by the secular oratory, thought and scholarship of the period, without giving up the basic religious and theological content demanded by the occasion. In the case of lay speakers, it might be asked how this genre is related to the traditions of lay preaching that in Italy go back at least to Albertano da Brescia. In the case of clerics, the literature considered would provide additional proof of the fact that in fifteenth century Italy the more educated part of the clergy was deeply permeated by the secular education and learning of the time and made its own contribution to this learning.[1]

I should like to conclude with a general remark that I believe I have made at least once before. The prejudice that has prevented an adequate study of the sermons discussed by Professor O'Malley has been well described in his paper. I should suggest that we reverse the judgment along the following lines : Art historians have for a long time admired the way in which Renaissance painters and other artists applied classical and modern forms of expression to the religious subject-matter treated in their work. It would be quite consistent and appropriate for literary and cultural historians to recognize the same fusion of religious content and classical or modern form in the humanist sermons that Professor O'Malley has been discussing. It reflects the taste and style of the period in another medium but in the same way as does the religious art of the time, and we should learn to appreciate it rather than to reject it, if we want to understand the literature and civilization of Renaissance Italy of which it is a significant part and expression.

---

[1] See my article, "The Contribution of Religious Orders to Renaissance Thought and Learning," *American Benedictine Review* 21 (1970), 1-55.

4. ERASMUS AND THE "JULIUS" :
A HUMANIST REFLECTS ON THE CHURCH

JAMES K. McCONICA

Pontifical Institute of Mediaeval Studies, Toronto

The problem of defining the doctrine of Erasmus is familiar to all students of northern humanism. It is part of the larger question of the tenets of Christian humanists in general, and of the characteristics of style and moral concern that distinguish them from their contemporaries in 14th and 15th century Europe. If it is true that important contributions of recent years have done a great deal to clarify this question, especially by drawing attention to the influence of pre-scholastic ideals of rhetoric and persuasion,[1] we still need much careful study of individual thinkers, especially in the north of Europe, to make clear both their affinities with and departures from the teachings of scholastic theologians, and from the common doctrine of late medieval preaching and devotional writing.

The need for such clarification is apparent from studies about Erasmus, which still show the legacy of the time when the chief objective of scholarship was to claim him (or disown him) for some confessional purpose. Although most writers will acknowledge that Erasmus is peculiarly difficult to pin down, that his thought is 'protean', that he eludes our confessional categories, such attempts end all too commonly with one more essay on a particular phase of his thought, comparing his doctrine to that of Luther, or the late scholastics, or the teachers of the *Devotio moderna*. They await the deserved and inevitable criticism that points to texts that were overlooked, or nuances that should have been considered. Although studies of this type must certainly be done, they do not promise of themselves to reproduce the characteristic voice of Erasmus, or give an account of his appeal and important originality among his contemporaries.

---

[1] For example, E. F. Rice Jr., *The Renaissance Idea of Wisdom*, Cambridge, Mass., 1958; Hannah H. Gray, 'Renaissance Humanism : the Pursuit of Eloquence," *Journal of the History of Ideas*, 1963 (XXIV), p. 497-514; Charles Trinkaus, *In Our Image and Likeness : Humanity and Divinity in Italian Humanist Thought*, 2 volumes (London, 1970).

Although Erasmus manifestly proclaimed doctrine all of his life, by his own most explicit confession he was not a doctrinal thinker. This suggests that it should be rewarding to deal with his method, as a number of recent studies have done in investigation of his hermeneutics, exegetical principles and educational method. There is another possibility, and that is to try to cope with the rhetorical character of his thought by studying it, so to speak, in motion. It is an important truth about Erasmus, as it is about a few other highly influential thinkers (and perhaps preeminently about the man to whom he is so often compared, Voltaire) that it is not so much the content of his ideas as the way in which they take flight, their intonation, the circles in which they are discussed, above all the engaging and dominant personality behind them, that gives them their importance. We are dealing with a writer of great magnetism, of complex and sophisticated culture, and it is a danger that our study will fasten on aspects of this culture to seek conceptual explanations, while we forget to listen to the voice of the spirit. If we do this we are bound to give a misleading impression of conceptual clarity, or completeness, or of the want of these qualities, and in the process to misrepresent even his doctrinal significance. The thought of Erasmus is like a brilliant, strong and elusive moth that struggled forth from the apparently unpromising chrysalis of Netherlandish pietism. We learn something when we see it pinned for scrutiny, but we must also see it fly. If we do not do this, we are in danger of mistaking the sum of his thought for his achievement, and of diminishing a commanding figure by consideration of influences on his development and a confused search for originality.

The disputed dialogue, the *Julius exclusus*, offers the opportunity to consider a controversial document not simply as ideology, but also as event. Under the aspect of doctrine, the essay that follows may be considered a study of Erasmus' ecclesiology. From the historical point of view, the subject also involves an important problem of authorship, and an evangelical method that Erasmus made peculiarly his own, that of the satirical *pièce d'occasion*. It is also, as Robert Adams has shown us,[1] an event in the life of the English humanist community of the day. As such, our subject characterizes the voice of evangelical humanism [2] as the by-product of common endeavour and shared con-

---

[1] *The Better Part of Valor : More, Erasmus, Colet and Vives on Humanism, War and Peace 1496-1535* (Seattle, 1962).

[2] I use the term 'evangelical' throughout this essay to describe those who pursue the

viction, a confessional statement by one on behalf of many bound together by the invisible ties of reforming purpose and spiritual aspiration, stated appropriately in the form of a dialogue. Finally, the satire arises from important events in the forum of public policy, and has therefore a character that perhaps is only properly described as prophetic, in the sense that it attempts to locate a great event of the life of the Church in the providential purpose of God for his covenanted people. If we can to some degree recreate this moment in the life of Erasmus, we might hope to say something about the mutation of received doctrines of the Church in the quicksilver of rhetorical fervour. At best, we would hope to capture a glimpse of his convictions taking flight.

The *Julius exclusus* deals with the events surrounding the schismatic Council of Pisa-Milan and Julius II's Fifth Lateran Council, and in its present form at least, it was composed after the death of the Pope in February 1513—probably shortly after.[1] If it was written by Erasmus the period with which we are chiefly concerned is therefore the time of his third and most extended visit to England, beginning in 1509 and lasting, with breaks for business visits to the continent, until July 1514 when he left England for Basle. It is fair to say that in the span of his entire life, no years were of more fundamental importance for his final achievement. It was a climax to the earlier years of study, a period of withdrawal, in fact, in which the vast editorial foundations of his evangelical and scholarly achievement were cemented into place.[2]

---

ideal Christian life as one based upon or imitating that of the early Christians in the Gospels, Acts and Epistles. An 'evangelical humanist' is one who wishes to bring to bear upon those Scriptural sources the critical textual disciplines of humanism in order to recapture the Gospel message in its early purity with a view, not to advancing theological speculation, but to a fresh proclamation aimed at the conversion of life and manners.

[1] W. K. Ferguson, editor, *Erasmi opuscula* (The Hague, 1933), 41. The last events of the Lateran Council referred to in the dialogue are those of the Third Session which ended 3 December 1912. Julius' illness returned in January, and he died on the night of February 20-21, 1513. The likely time of composition thus falls during one of the periodic gaps in Erasmus' correspondence. After a letter of 11 November 1512 (Ep. 267 in the edition of P. S. Allen, *Opus Epistolarum Des. Erasmi Roterodami* (Oxford, 11 vols., 1906-47), hereafter cited as *EE*) two prefaces only survive from January 1513 (Epp. 268. 269) and the next letter is that of 11 July 1513 from Cambridge, addressed to Colet, This reveals that Erasmus has finished the collation of the New Testament and is starting on his edition of Jerome, and is delighted by the daily company of his assistant Thomas Lupset : see Appendix, and Ep. 270, *l.*58 f.

[2] On Erasmus' business at this time see the convenient account by H. C. Porter in

When we come to reflect on the unexplained gap in his correspondence in these years from 1509 to 1511, we should not entirely discount the possibility that, among other things, he wrote far fewer letters than he did when he was less totally preoccupied.[1]

The Erasmus who stayed in 1509 and 1510 in the household of Thomas More was in full possession of new energy, a man who had in a sense digested the Italian world he had heretofore regarded with awe. If, as seems likely, there is serious personal meaning in the Terminus emblem he gathered for himself during his visit to Italy,[2] we may also think that he had succeeded in coming to terms with the first part of his life and in accepting certain limitations, so that he now felt fresh resolution toward the enterprise of what would prove to be the greatest years of achievement. With the *Adagia* in the press in their new, full-dress version, with confidence born of the warm reception accorded to him by the mandarins of humanistic Italy, and with fresh energy drawn from the hard-won mastery of Greek, the first expression of his new spirit emerged in the *Moriae encomium*.[3]

He was also filled with the Italian politics of his day. On his way to Italy, in June 1506, and again in 1511, Erasmus had enjoyed the company of several Parisian humanists who were thoroughly immersed in advocacy of the royal cause against the Pope, notably Pierre Gringoire and Fausto Andrelini. In the months just prior to the second of these visits, when he stayed briefly in Paris to see the *Moria* through the press, Gringoire had published satirical pieces that bore directly on the theme of the later *Julius exclusus*.[4] On his return from Italy,

---

Erasmus and Cambridge : the Cambridge Letters of Erasmus (Toronto, 1963), 38-61; also James D. Tracy, *Erasmus the Growth of a Mind* (Travaux d'humanisme et renaissance CXXVI) (Geneva, 1972), 127.

[1] Léon.-E. Halkin, 'Érasme, de Turin à Rome,' in *Mélanges d'histoire du XVIe Siècle offerts à Henri Meylan* (Travaux d'humanisme et renaissance CX) (Geneva, 1970), 5, points out that the survival of correspondence is very thin for the whole period starting with his departure for Italy in 1506. See also, J. K. Sowards, 'The two lost years of Erasmus,' *Studies in the Renaissance* IX, 1962, 161-86, where he follows Renaudet in suggesting that the disappearance of letters from this period may be related directly to Erasmus' fear of being compromised over the reputation of Julius II. See the same author's 'Erasmus in England 1509-1514,' *Wichita State University Bulletin) University Studies* No. 51) (1962), 3-20; P. S. Allen, *The Age of Erasmus* (Oxford, 1914), 143, and the account by H. C. Porter, *op. cit.*, 100-103.

[2] See J. K. McConica, 'The Riddle of "Terminus",' in *Erasmis in English*, A Newsletter Published by University of Toronto Press, 2 (1971), 2-7.

[3] See Margaret Mann Phillips, *The 'Adages' of Erasmus* (Cambridge, 1964) 100.

[4] Charles Oulmont, *Pierre Gringoire* (Paris, 1911), 245 f. On Erasmus' early friendship

Erasmus found his English friends in an excited state over national policy since the accession of the young King Henry VIII. Their disappointment at the drift of England toward a *rapprochement* with the Roman court and against the common enemy, France, is the essential background to the humanist campaign for peace in the early years of the reign of Henry VIII, so well described by Robert Adams.[1] Adams' work makes it unnecessary here to be concerned with the story of that policy and of the energetic opposition to it of Colet, More, Warham and Erasmus. He has fitted the composition of the *Julius exclusus* convincingly into this campaign, along with Erasmus' adage on war for the 1515 *Adagia* and the long epistle to Anthony of Bergen, the abbot of St. Bertin, on 14 March 1514. To this should be added the devastating portrait of Pope Julius in chapter 59 of the *Moriae encomium*, which was ready for the printer early in June 1511, and must have been completed during the preceding winter.[2] It is noticeable that nothing like this criticism had yet occurred in England. We can agree that the important thing is the close association of a small group of highly talented and zealous men, reacting together to a succession of events that triggered their deepest emotions. It is impossible to overlook the fact that present in the group just at that time, like a potent catalyst, was a man whose intellectual range, foreign origins and literary genius allowed him to spreak with more fluency, point and daring than any of the others. Those who object that the *Julius exclusus* is too scathing and vehement for Erasmus should consider this background.

Apart from these and other works that show Erasmus' continuing preoccupation with the policies of Pope Julius,[3] it was in these same years, but before the death of Julius, that Erasmus wrote the stinging satirical poem that was first brought to light by J.-B. Pineau and

---

with Andrelini in Paris see *EE* I, Ep. 84 (Dec. 1498) and Ep. 127 (Andrelini's commendatory letter prefaced to the first edition of the *Adagia*, 1500). Renaudet commented, *Érasme et l'Italie* (Travaux d'humanisme et renaissance XV, Geneva, 1954), 122, n. 6, 'Il reste difficile d'imaginer Andrelini capable d'une œuvre aussi vigoureuse.' For More's report that Etienne Poncher was said to have ascribed it to Andrelini see E. F. Rogers, editor, *The Correspondance of Sir Thomas More* (Princeton, 1947), letter 83, *ll.* 880-4.

[1] *Op. cit.*; cf. J. D. Tracy, *op. cit.*, 135 f., and J. J. Scarisbrick, *Henry VIII* (Berkeley and Los Angeles, 1968), 25-6.

[2] Mrs. Phillips has pointed out the connection with the new version of the *Adagia; op. cit.*, 102-3.

[3] See Appendix to this article.

Wallace Ferguson. Their conclusion that it was an authentic piece by Erasmus which in sentiment and phrasing makes a remarkable parallel to the later dialogue has been strikingly confirmed by the recent discovery of another manuscript copy in Erasmus' hand, also addressed on the reverse side to Thomas More. Mysterious abbreviations provide further evidence to suggest that when he wrote the satirical poem, Erasmus was already thinking of a contrast between Pope Julius and St. Peter.[1] Whether it was sent to More from Cambridge or from Paris, this epigrammatic poem was certainly an intimate by-product of that collaboration in the house of Bucklersbury that produced the *Moriae encomium*, the 1515 *Adagia*, the *De copia*, the *Utopia* and a body of further work whose precise genesis remains in the realm of conjecture.

On 14 March 1514, three months before leaving England altogether, Erasmus wrote to Anthony of Bergen with a tone of personal involvement that makes the letter, despite some personal pleading, a convincing source for his inner state at this time.[2] It marks the end of the English experiment, of a time begun with optimism borne of promises not only of personal support for the rest of his life, but of continued royal favour and a realm at peace. He has been disappointed in all three expectations, and although he is not really bitter, he is more than ready to return to the continent. He speaks of the imminent war, and the sudden change the prospect of war has wrought in the character of England. "Besides, while it is a kind of exile to live anywhere in this island, our confinement is closer still at present by reason of the wars, so that one cannot even get a letter out. I can see vast disturbances in the making and what their outcome will be is not clear; may God in His mercy vouchsafe to quiet the storm that now afflicts Christendom." At this point he moves into an eloquent and moving consideration of the inexplicable and tragic human instinct that drives "the whole human race, not merely Christians, to war." He then proceeds :

> There are popes and bishops, and men of discretion and honour, through whom petty issues of this kind can be resolved without conducting incessant wars and

---

1 For text see, Ferguson, *op. cit.*, 36-7; on the recent MS, C. Reedijk, 'Een Schimpdicht van Erasmus op Julius II,' *Opstellen door Vrienden en Collegas aangeboden aan Dr. F. K. H. Kossmann* (The Hague, 1958), 186-207; and J. K. Sowards' introduction to *The Julius Exclusus of Erasmus* (tr. Paul Pascal) (Bloomington, 1968), 19-20.

2 *EE* I, Ep. 288, *ll.* 74-86, 105-7, 131-2.

throwing Heaven and earth to confusion. It is the proper function of the Roman Pontiff, of the cardinals, bishops and abbots, to settle disputes between Christian princes; this is where they should wield their authority and reveal the power they possess by virtue of men's regard for their holy rank. If Julius—a pope who was by no means universally approved of—succeeded in rousing such a hurricane of wars, surely Leo, who is scholarly, honourable and devout, will succeed in quieting it ? Julius' pretext for going to war was a threat to his own safety; but even though its cause has been removed, the war still goes on ... If there are any rights that offer occasion for war, they are crude rights, which smack of an already decadent Christianity, overburdened with worldly possessions. ... I shall rush to embrace you, as soon as I can escape from England.

As a concluding reflection on this momentous time in England, and as a statement of his attitude to the Papacy, this letter leads appropriately to our discussion of the *Julius exclusus* itself. Up to this point we have been trying to indicate the mental and emotional climate of the time when the *Julius exclusus* would have been written. If it was the work of Erasmus, it helps to explain why it took the form it did, and why the evidence about the authorship is as it is. More importantly, it illustrates the characteristic environment of this kind of humanist activity : familial, critical, operating in the full glare of public activity and world event, at once intimate and (through the printing press) public, although the public addressed is an assembly of individuals like the writers themselves, not (in any collective sense) an "audience". It illustrates also a time of great importance both in the life of Erasmus and in the development of English humanist writing, a time in which the personal relationships between Erasmus and his English friends were so perfectly resonant that they produced some of the major achievements of the European Renaissance. It could not go on forever in this way, and with this we reach perhaps the interior forum of Erasmus' own personality. We see in the letter to Anthony of Bergen a sense of closing boundaries both political and spiritual that appeared earlier in restrained allusions between Erasmus and Ammonio, once England went to war.[1]

Emile Telle has said that in these years, peace was Erasmus' "*souci primordial*,"[2] and it seems that for Erasmus, there was a particular

---

[1] *EE* I, Ep. 245, *ll.* 19-29; Ep. 247, *l.* 14 f.; Ep. 262. After England joined the Holy League, Greek was always used when need was felt to speak of Pope Julius and his policies.

[2] Emile V. Telle. 'Le *De Copia verborum* d'Érasme et le *Julius exclusus e coelis*,' *Revue de littérature comparée* XXII (1948), 441-7.

sorrow in the conversion of England to a policy of war. In an earlier
essay I have tried to explore something of the profound meaning of
pax and *unanimitas* in the mental and emotional makeup of this
Christian grammarian. It cannot be better expressed now than in a
letter of October 1499 to Colet, in which we can study a telling flow
of association. "I need hardly add that your style—calm, tranquil,
unaffected. flowing like a pellucid stream from the great riches of
your mind; even and consistent, clear and simple and full of modesty,
without a trace of anything tasteless, involved or confused—moved
me and delighted me enormously, so that it seemed to me that I could
clearly perceive a kind of image of your personality, reflected in your
letter. You say what you mean and mean what you say; your words
are engendered not in your vocal chords but in your heart, and they
choose to be the servants, not the masters, of your thought."[1] In this
passage, in an important sense, is all that England meant to Erasmus
up to his return in 1509; when he left in 1514, he felt that it was being
replaced by a world of very different values.

Almost all scholars today agree with the view of P. S. Allen and
Wallace Ferguson that the *Julius exclusus* was written by Erasmus in
England shortly after the death of the Pope in the late winter of
1512-13, and was circulated in manuscript copies of open anonymity
to his friends.[2] Quite recently J. K. Sowards has provided a general
account of the modern work on the *Julius* question where he himself
favours the authorship of Erasmus. The case against Erasmus is now
much weaker even than Sowards indicated. The only writer to be considered seriously as an alternative author of the dialogue is Fausto
Andrelini of Forli, whose initials it seems they were that appeared on
an early edition of the *Julius*. Wallace Ferguson pointed out forty
years ago that Fausto had never written anything at all like it,[3] and
recently a Belgian scholar has discovered two hitherto unknown letters
of Fausto that strongly reconfirm the judgement of Ferguson. The two
manuscripts found in the Condé museum at Chantilly were written in
the important years of 1509-10 and 1510-11 in the form of poetic
letters from the Queen, Anne of Brittany, to her royal husband.[4] Like

---

[1] *EE* I, Ep. 107, *ll.* 57-64.

[2] See Appendix.

[3] *Op. cit.*, 47.

[4] G. Tournoy-Thoen in *Humanistica Lovaniensia* XVIII, ed. I. Ijsewijn (Louvain,
1969), 43-55.

other works by Fausto, and in accord with the general tone of the
French satirical works emanating from the official campaign of Louis
against Julius, they reveal a strong if tacit desire to avoid the im-
putation of schism, and to assert not a religious, but a political motive
to Louis. In these two letters opposing Julius, the attitude to the
conflict, in the words of the editor, "is entirely different from that of
the author of the *Julius*. As an agent of French policy, Fausto does
not attack the pope except on the political plane, accusing him of
having injured a King who had always been his faithful servant. There
is no reforming enthusiasm, no genuine religious convictions in these
works, but at best a pompous rhetoric." He feels at the same time that
the rather stale and antiquarian style rules them out as works by a
man who could have written the Julius.[1]

In the same vein, another recent discovery, by Cornelius Reedijk,[2]
has proved that one of Erasmus' approved printers, Thierry Martens
of Louvain, printed an edition of the *Julius* in 1518, and that Erasmus,
for all his public protestations against publication of the dialogue, was
present in Martens' offices in Louvain in the very weeks when the
Julius must have been set in type and printed. As many have observed,
Erasmus never directly denied writing the *Julius;* his great claim was
to have had nothing to do with its publication. On at least one important occasion, this claim was false. At the same time, there are
considerations that point to a real filiation with the French satirical
campaign, perhaps dating to that visit to Paris in April 1511 to oversee
the printing of the *Moriae encomium,* and perhaps relating precisely
to work by his friend Andrelini.[3] Since the epigrammatic poem on
Julius was almost certainly written at that time, it becomes conceivable
that the *Julius exclusus* was developed by Erasmus from some suggestions in a political piece written by Fausto. The further suggestion
has been made that it was Andrelini himself who proposed that the
publisher in 1518 fix his initials to what was probably a Paris edition
to draw the fire from his old friend, whose hand was recognized in the
work from the very first.[4]

---

[1] *Ibid.,* 48-9.

[2] 'Érasme, Thierry Martens et le *Iulius exclusus*,' *Scrinium erasmianum* II, ed. J.
Coppens (Leiden, 1969), esp. 368 f.

[3] Tournoy-Thoen, *op. cit.,* 49.

[4] *Ibid.,* 50; cf. J. van der Blom, ' "F.A.F." Poeta Regius, de auteur van de Julius
Exclusus,' *Hermeneus* 42, No. 4 (March-April 1971), 258-65, 256-7, for an overly-in-
genious explanation.

There is an important reason for insisting on the link with Andrelini apart from several minor indications of style and circumstance and this brings us to the main thematic interest of the *Julius* itself. Every objection to Erasmus' authorship of the *Julius* brought by a serious scholar from Augustin Renaudet to Stange and Gebhardt, and not excluding the late Pierre Mesnard, has been inspired, it seems, less by a conviction that the evidence of circumstance weighed against Erasmus, than that the contents of the *Julius* itself were inconsistent with Erasmus' views of European politics in general and of the Church in particular. In a word, they have found it too pro-French and conciliarist. Before we examine the text itself, a brief résumé of the story may be of some assistance.

At the outset of the *Julius*, the Pope appears at the gate of Heaven with his personal "genius," attempting entry with his single key, the key of power. He admits that he has never had the other, the key of knowledge. An aroused St. Peter, amazed at the appearance of the caller and the stench of the horde of ruffians with him, questions him about his identity and right to enter. Julius is thus driven to a recital of his deeds as Pope, a naive and belligerent list of tyrannous exploits.

Astonished at his boasting, St. Peter then questions Julius about his retinue, about the motive for his wars and conquests, and then about the reason a schismatic Council had been convened against him. When the Pope explains his objections to a General Council, Peter suggests that not the power of the papal monarchy, but the general interest of the Christian commonwealth should be the true concern of the Vicar of Christ.

Julius then explains how he disposed of the Council of Pisa, and willingly reveals his detestation of the "barbarians" or non-Italians in Europe. He adds an account of his manoeuvres in setting the kings of Europe at war with one another. Peter concludes that Julius has acted more like the Vicar of Satan than the Vicar of Christ, provoking Julius into a boastful and slightly wounded account of his success in enlarging the Kingdom of Christ, that is, the wealth and outward ornament of the Church. When St. Peter continues to object that nothing of all his vain account amounts to more than the most worldly kind of achievement, lacking any tincture of spiritual worth, the climax of the piece is reached when Julius in reply, mockingly derides the rustic simplicity of the early Church, subject to poverty, toil, danger and vexation of all kinds. When he compares this derisively to the splendour and worldly power of his own pontificate, the Apostle is provoked to an eloquent and brilliantly conceived rebuttal in the name of the evangelical virtues, drawn directly from his own Epistles and those of St. Paul. He refuses to open the gate of Heaven, and advises Julius to use his gang of cutthroats to build himself a new Paradise, defensible against the oncoming assault of evil demons. Julius instead looks forward to storming the walls of Heaven when his numbers are further increased by the scores of thousands of men soon to die in further battles on earth.

The first and dominant purpose of this work is evangelical. In the opening scene, with St. Peter and Pope Julius in confrontation, is the essential theme of the whole dialogue, not the assertion of a conciliarist or Gallican position as such, but the contrast between the contemporary Papacy at its most secular and the spirit of the apostolic Church. It is thoroughly in keeping with Erasmus' moralistic outlook and with his characteristic lack of interest in legal and constitutional problems. Julius himself—sanguinary, belligerent and bedizened with the trappings of imperial splendour—is larger than life, despite fidelity to detail. There are stains placed on his reputation, such as his alleged syphilis, his personal luxury, his illegitimacy and pederasty, which were the common coinage of contemporary pamphleteers. Although the central figure of the *Julius* is certainly the person of the Pope himself, he is enlarged to become a vehicle for the standard vices of the papal court of his day, a symbol of secular policy and worldly degradation contrasted to the simple strength of the fisherman, his predecessor. The author's target is not simply a single personality in a particular political situation but an institution corrupted, in his eyes, by over-blown pretensions that reveal their falsity in the periodic scandal of spectacularly corrupt popes. Among these, Julius II was not only the most recent example, but one who had failed in the responsibility most urgent to Erasmus and his English friends—the pastoral guidance of Europe towards peace. By failing in this, he had also lost the character most essential to promote the work of the Holy Spirit. This glaring failure to act as the shepherd of Christian unity and concord is the dominant note of Erasmus' reiterated critique of Julius II. It undoubtedly outweighed by far the scandals of private immorality that could with more justice have been invoked against the reputations of some of Julius' predecessors, but the author's purpose is to show that the papacy, having failed in its fundamental responsibility, is indeed totally corrupt, a point made with this embroidery of rumoured vices around the name of Julius. It might be added at this point that the author of the *Julius*, like Erasmus, is likewise uninterested in the considerations of high policy that could be adduced, and were adduced, to justify the disedifying political involvements of the Pope. He is interested, however, in the particularities of day to day affairs, as Erasmus was, and shows an intimate knowledge of this that Erasmus' own correspondence in the years from 1509 to 1515 could well explain.

The Pope's claims to recognition are a catalogue of incongruous achievements, their scandalous nature pointed up by the continuing exchange with St. Peter. High birth, wealth, ruthlessness, simony, military conquest, infidelity to his treaty commitments and aggrandizement of the revenues of the Church—these are his titles to respect. Among them is the first reference to the Lateran Council : Julius has easily defeated the schismatical conciliabulum with a sham counter-council, and driven out the nail with a nail.[1]

The Council of Pisa is here designated by the derisory term "conciliabulum" applied by the adherents of the papal party, and it is further described as schismatical, as indeed it always is in the dialogue. Although this expression is here in the mouth of Julius, there is nothing to suggest that it is not the opinion of the dialogue's author as well. As we will see, the quarrel over the respective legitimacy of rival councils is not the heart of the matter in the *Julius*, nor was it for Erasmus. In his dedication of the Jerome to Leo X, dated 21 May 1515, Erasmus referred to Pisa as *"illud schisma"*. Although any other designation would have been remarkable to the eyes of Leo X, it need not have been mentioned at all, and it is clear that Erasmus himself regarded the termination of the schism as a genuine and important achievement of the new Pope.[2] Like the author of the *Julius*, Erasmus placed a heavy share of the blame for the schism at the feet of Julius II, and the same dedication contains the essence of Erasmus' charge against Pope Julius in a restrained criticism : with the accession of Leo X the world has passed from an age of iron to an age of gold. Others may celebrate the wars of Julius, but they must confess that these glories were won through the suffering of multitudes.[3] Where Julius showed his greatness by stirring the whole world to war, Leo's higher greatness is testified to by the restoration of universal peace;

---

[1] Ferguson, *op. cit.*, *ll.* 199-201.

[2] *EE* II, Ep. 335, *l.* 82; cf. Tracy, *op. cit.*, 137, n. 78.

[3] *EE* II, Ep. 335, *ll.* 76-7, 93-7.

he understands the papal role correctly.[1] It is interesting to see how much influence Erasmus felt a Pope could wield, and this conviction was certainly allied to his pastoral ideal for papal policy.

In the central part of the dialogue, dealing with the rival councils, the summoning of Pisa by the Emperor and the King of France is represented as the work of those who held that the Roman court was a scandalous abomination. The more purely political motives of the rulers are passed over in silence. In the development of the discussion there are passing references to familiar points of the conciliar tradition. Subjects may take power from a sovereign who abuses it, an argument that recurs in Erasmus' writings on political matters.[2] To this Julius replies that a General Council cannot be held without the Pope's consent. There follows a remorseless pursuit of the question of deposition by the figure of St. Peter, with the clear implication that a pope can be deposed for notoriety. The real object of the debate, however, emerges in the contrast between the general good of Christendom and the worldly pretentions of papal supremacy, not in an assertion of a conciliarist solution of the Church's problems.[3]

Julius' manoeuvres to defeat the rival council are vividly sketched and the opposition cardinals are represented as inspired only by motives of reform. It is the extended development of this part of the dialogue that is most difficult to square with the known priorities of Erasmus, and although they do not contradict these, it is here we might allow for the influence of another author with interests more like those of Andrelini. The late Cardinal d'Amboise, sometime rival to Julius for the see of Peter, is cited as the chief agent behind the Pisan Council along with Carvajal, another disappointed candidate.[4] There is evident partiality here in the concealment of the personal

---

[1] *Ibid.*, *ll.* 109-10, 113 f., 122-3 f. On this comparison between Leo X and Julius II, compare the *Dulce bellum inexpertis*, ed. Y. Rémy and R. Dunil-Marquebreucq, *Erasme, Dulce bellum inexpertis*, Collection Latomus VIII (Berchem-Bruxelles, 1953), *ll.* 1219-26.

[2] Ferguson, *op. cit.*, *ll.* 460-2 and note. The claim of Julius' notoriety was used by the jurist Filippo Decio before the convocation of Pisa, but became useless after the Pope convened his own Council. Cf. H. Jedin, *A History of the Council of Trent*, tr. Dom E. Graf, I (Edinburgh and London, 1957), 108-10.

[3] Ferguson, *op. cit.*, *ll.* 537-9; when Peter asks Julius if he thinks the only thing to be heeded is the royal dignity of the supreme Pontiff and not the general interest of the Christian commonwealth, the reply of the Pope is a crude repudiation of the pastoral responsibilities of his office : 'Ad suum quique commodum spectat; nos nostrum agimus negotium.'

[4] *Ibid.*, *l.* 591 f. and notes.

ambitions of both the "council fathers" named, but since the object of the satire is to show the venality of a papacy given over to the achievement of its ends by purely worldly means, it does not of itself constitute evidence for purely French sponsorship of the dialogue. The conduct of the delegates to Pisa is also represented in the highest terms, and their programme given as one of purely reforming intent.[1] Again, the author seems not to have wished to represent the Council of Pisa with historical accuracy but with polemical purpose, in this instance through the advocacy of a reform programme that actually follows, not Pisa's, but evangelical sympathies. It should be noticed that the tenets of this programme—a return to simplicity of life at the Roman court, abolition of pluralism and commendation, the promotion of popes and bishops for merit only, the suspension of bishops given to drink or fornication—these tenets touch at no point on conciliar positions as such. They are never remotely close to the actual programme of Pisa. The author's aim is clear : the pope and cardinals are to be reduced to a condition of apostolic simplicity. This is the essential message.

It might be natural to see the *Julius exclusus* as a French propaganda piece if these passages were isolated. Even the most recent commentator seems to accept the view that the dialogue has a discernible pro-French bias,[2] as perhaps it has. No one has yet pointed out, however, that apart from the passage on Pisa itself, the French are placed in no very favourable light. The first reference to that country is to the part French money played in purchasing the papal tiara for Julius.[3] The next is to the part played by France in Julius' unjust overthrow of Giovanni Bentivoglio of Bologna, a siege at which we may recall

---

[1] *Ibid., ll.* 625-6 f., 99, n. 639; cf. L. Sandret, 'Le concile de Pise (1511),' *Revue des questions historiques* XXXIV (1883), 442 on the establishment of the commission on reformation of the Church, and 446 and 448 f. on the actual fate of these proposals for reform. Georg Gebhardt, *Die Stellung des Erasmus von Rotterdam zur Römischen Kirche* (Marburg, 1966), 394, observing that the author of the *Julius* clearly wished to make the moral superiority of the Pisan Council stand out clearly, does not seem to realize that the portrait of the Council in the *Julius* has little to do with the actual historical events at Pisa.

[2] J. K. Sowards in his introduction to the translation by Paul Pascal, 9.

[3] Ferguson, *op. cit., l.* 171; in connection with the views of some on the antithesis of France and the Papacy in the dialogue, it should be added that this allegation actually exaggerates the involvement of France in the election of Julius II. Cf. Carl Stange, *Erasmus und Julius II, eine Legende* (Berlin, 1937), and Karl Schätti, *Erasmus von Rotterdam und die Römische Kurie* (Basel, 1954), 44 f., where such views are put forward.

Erasmus was present, and which caused him to shift his travel plans until the papal party was safely installed for a winter in the city.[1] Later in the dialogue, when Julius' success against the schismatic Council has been related, St. Peter grimly concludes that the French were justly punished for their part in promoting his election.[2] Once again the point is utterly familiar in the writings of Erasmus : princes and popes alike are involved in betrayal of their trust and Christian responsibilities for the sake of selfish, secular ambition.

If the Pisan council is treated with an evangelical unction so lavish as to raise the suspicion that it is being tacitly satirized itself, the credentials of the Lateran Council in turn are represented at their very worst. It is a caricature of a Council of the Church, composed entirely of Julius' own creatures.[3] At the same time the account of the work of the first three sessions of the Lateran Council is by no means inaccurate : they were given over entirely, amidst a great deal of ceremony, to the attack on the rival council. Again the point of the contrast is the fatal dissipation of the Church's energy in political maneouvre when reform is so badly needed. The passage concludes with an observation that scarcely amounts to an endorsement of Pisa ; the council that "wins" the contest will be that backed by the most money and it is that council that will be held to be legitimate.[4] If councils are venal, so are princes. Their religious policies are governed by their political interests, a fact that Julius turns to advantage for his own ends.[5] It is the same view exactly that we find in Erasmus' letter to Anthony of Bergen and in the *Dulce bellum inexpertis*, where it is plain that for Erasmus, the most cogent objection to conciliar politics is precisely this conviction that owing to the ambitions of princes, the authority of councils is as much compromised by profane self-seeking as is that of the papacy symbolized by Julius II.[6]

---

[1] Ferguson, *op. cit.*, *l.* 351.

[2] *Ibid.*, *ll.* 959-61, where the Latin is susceptible of a more trenchant interpretation than is given in Pascal's rendering.

[3] *Ibid.*, *l.* 570 f. and Ferguson's note, 85, *l.* 574. It is implied that Julius moved about the date of the opening to discourage attendance ; Ferguson comments upon the possible connection with the disappointment Erasmus himself experienced. Compare this with Erasmus' highly critical view of the political and bellicose motives of the cardinals in the *Querela pacis*, ed. Mme. E. C. Bagdat (Paris, 1924), sections XLI, XLII and notes 187-9.

[4] Ferguson, *op. cit.*, *ll.* 660 f. and 706-13.

[5] *Ibid.*, *l.* 839 f.

[6] For extended comment upon, 'Summa jus summa iniuria' with respect to the dealings of princes, see *EE* I, Ep. 288, *l.* 68 f. ; cf. *Bellum, op. cit.*, *ll.* 1091-1140.

The judgement on the claims of Julius II for admission to the
Celestial City which is the conclusion of the dialogue, may lack artistic
resolution, as Sowards suggests,[1] but it brings the theme back to the
dominant note of the opening scene in the contrast between evangelical
counsel and worldly power. The Church of Christ is not to be equated
with its clerical hierarchy and its worldly endowments : it is the body
of the faithful united by the spirit of Christ. Its head is Christ; its
virtues are poverty, purity of doctrine and contempt of the world. Its
ministers must use their pastoral office to restore the dead to life, not
to trouble mankind. It glories in its sufferings, not in its worldly
triumphs. This passage, in the form of a speech (the first) by the figure
of Peter, suddenly alters the tone of the dialogue to that of serious
evangelical discourse; there is a movement here rather like that at
the close of the *Praise of Folly*.[2] For the first time, the bluster and
vanity of Julius is punctured, and this is achieved by the Word on the
lips of the Fisherman. Although the impudent and unabashed pope
continues his defiance to the end, his ultimate fate is clear. Yet in the
dialogue's final moment there is a tribute to the office he has so grossly
disfigured. St. Peter is not surprised that so few souls now come his
way, when the Church is ruled by such men as Julius, but he concludes
that there must be some health in the Christian body when such a
despicable person is honoured simply because of the title of Pope.[3]

The *Julius exclusus* is not then intended to be a conciliarist treatise
as such, despite the remarkably one-sided treatment of the opposition
between the Council of Pisa-Milan and the Fifth Lateran Council. The
spiritual authority of Peter is also clearly asserted; he is the holder
of the keys and the commission of Christ to pasture his sheep and
guard the faith.[4] It is precisely because of this that Julius' deliquency
is so bitterly condemned. But the dialogue is not concerned to debate
such claims. Its message can be expressed much more clearly if we
turn to that part of the New Testament to which Erasmus' manuscript
notes on the satirical poem about Julius point, to the first Epistle of
Peter. In that Epistle, addressed, like the poem's cryptic notes, to
the "exiles of the dispersion in Pontus, Galatia, Cappadocia, Asia and
Bithynia," the author seeks to recall these Christians to the new life

---

[1] Introduction cited, 29-30.

[2] Ferguson, *op. cit.*, *l.* 1060 f.

[3] *Ibid.*, *l.* 1222 f.

[4] *Ibid.*, *l.* 1070 f.

which must infuse those who are "born anew," as "aliens" and "exiles" in this world. The whole emphasis is on the virtues of Christ, on the imminent judgement of the last days, and on the virtue of suffering in Christ's name. The portrait of the ways of the Gentiles in chapter 4 : 3-6 is like a memorandum from which the author of the *Julius* might have developed his account of the achievements of the Pope, and in chapter 5 : 1-4 we have a climactic text that seems perfectly to sum up the message of the dialogue :

> So I exhort the elders among you, as a fellow elder and a witness of the sufferings of Christ as well as a partaker in the glory that is to be revealed. Tend the flock of God that is your charge, not by constraint but willingly, not for shameful gain but eagerly, not as domineering over those in your charge but being examples to the flock. And when the chief Shepherd is manifested you will obtain the unfading crown of glory. ... Humble yourselves therefore under the mighty hand of God, that in due time he may exalt you.

Even the eschatological warning note of final judgement is there to summon up the satire's vision of Pope Julius, the domineering pontiff, before the astonished gaze of St. Peter.[1]

The conciliar elements in the thought of the *Julius exclusus* are much too general to qualify its author as a party man. They are chiefly a recognition of the authority of the *congregatio fidelium* in matters of doctrine and observance, reference to the right of deposition and an evident disregard for the claims of papal monarchy, along with appeals to the general good of Christendom. On two occasions the author refers to the possibility of a true council in which, it is evident, the Pope would preside.[2] But there is too little evidence to draw conclusions about the respective weight of the papal and conciliar elements. We are dealing here with an attitude to church authority formed by a rhetorical, evangelical purpose, distinct from any of the traditional conciliarist positions, but sharing common features with the core of the conciliar tradition.

In fact, the author of the *Julius* was thoroughly at home in the ecclesiology of Erasmus, who saw the Church as the body of Christ,

---

[1] Compare Erasmus' annotation on this text; J. Leclercq, *Opera Omnia Des. Erasmi Roterodami*, 10 vols. (Lugduni Batavorum, 1703-6) (cited hereafter as LB), vol. VI, 1055 D. : the precepts of the Prince of the Apostles should be inscribed in golden letters in every bishop's palace; however, 'nunc episcoporum vulgus nihil audit ab assentatoribus doctis nisi dominia, ditiones, gladios, claves, potestates : atque hinc fastus quorumdam plusquam regius, saevitia plusquam tyrannica.'

[2] Ferguson, *op. cit.*, *ll.* 698-9 and 950-1.

the evangelical gathering of the Kingdom. In its contemporary institutional structure he found a profound distortion of its original nature. He recognized the papacy as a legitimate and potentially salutary office of headship, but for the developed claims of the medieval papacy, amplified now with Renaissance splendour, he had no regard. The Lateran Council itself was no true council in his eyes since it was not a consultation of the universal Church.[1] In the *De interdicto esu carnium*, published in August 1522, these misgivings about the true authority of the Council *vis-à-vis* the Christian people as a whole are linked to Erasmus' sense of the pastoral inertia of the Church. He points out that the Fifth Lateran Council had issued innumerable constitutions, but the silent apathy of the people is enough to abrogate them. When the opinion of the multitude is not contrary to the Gospel, it must not be overlooked, for then the voice of the people is the voice of God.[2] Here there is clear common ground with conciliarist views about authority residing in the Church as a whole, but there is no trace of any thought that this authority must find some particular constitutional expression. In the technicalities of debate about what constituted a true council Erasmus seemingly had as little interest as he had in any of the refinements of the medieval debate about ecclesiology. What mattered was that the participants in any Council—like the faithful as a whole—should be infused with the spirit of Christ. If the participants lacked this spirit the Council, whatever its legal form, was certain to be futile. If we accept the view that the *Julius exclusus* is essentially a vivid statement of an evangelical and humanist position on the question of Church authority with some roots in conciliarist thought, but that it is not, in any simple sense, a conciliarist or Gallican tract,[3] we should naturally expect Erasmus to be a prom-

---

[1] *EE* V, Ep. 1268 to Willibald Pirckheimer, 30 March 1522, *ll.* 35-6 : 'De conciliis non ausim aliquid dicere, nisi forte proximum Concilium Lateranense concilium non fuit.' This opinion was shared at Trent by several of the Spanish bishops and the Emperor's confessor; cf. Jedin, *op. cit.*, I, 132 and n. 2. It is a view thoroughly consistent with the apparent ecclesiology of the *Julius exclusus*.

[2] LB IX, 1290 D, specifically with reference to the Lateran Council.

[3] This in opposition to the view especially of Stange, *op. cit.*, 84. 'Es kann nämlich keinen Augenblick zweifelhaft sein, dass nur ein Franzose oder ein französisch gesinnter Italiener den Dialog geschrieben haben kann. Es war soeben schon davon die Rede, dass die Absicht des Dialogs darauf gerichtet ist, die öffentliche Meinung zugunsten Frankreichs und gegen den Papst zu beeinflussen.' The present writer has analysed Erasmus' ecclesiology in, 'Erasmus and the Grammar of Consent,' *Scrinium erasmianum* II, 82 f.; a recent essay by Harry J. McSorley, 'Erasmus and the Primacy of the Roman

inent spokesman of such a view. In my opinion, the ecclesiology of the *Julius* does not weaken but further strengthens the case for his authorship.

Beyond this, we have here the problem of "Erasmianism". There is doctrine in it to be sure, but like the apostolic preaching he so much admired, the doctrine is presented not as system but rhetorically to bring conversion of spirit. In analysis of his works we must therefore be conscious of the circumstances that inspire especially his more occasional pieces. Taken apart from the precise circumstances that seem to have produced it, the *Julius* might be adduced to support almost any anti-papal theory. In fact, the one it supports is unmistakably the view of a party, and at the same time, quite idiosyncratic in the general tradition.

If we can produce another piece very much like it, in theme and occasional character, by the same suppositious author, we may hope further to strengthen our case. Another interesting production well within the decade bears a curious resemblance to the *Julius exclusus*. It too, appeared without any open connection with the name of Erasmus, and it too may well have been a joint effort in which Erasmus had a major share. But unlike the *Julius*, the *Consilium cuiusdam* received his open and passionate endorsement. The title of the work gives its theme quite copiously, and it has been rendered, "Advice of one who desires with his whole heart that due consideration be paid both to the dignity of the Pope and to the peaceful development of the Christian religion."[1] It has been attributed to various reformers, including Zwingli, but it was published with the public support of the distinguished Dominican prior of Augsburg, Dr. Johann Faber, its part author, perhaps (as the editor suggests) to enhance the prospect of its receiving a favourable hearing in Rome.[2] For his part, Erasmus

---

Pontiff : between Conciliarism and Papalism,' should also be examined for discussion of the literature and some instructive texts. This paper was read in Los Angeles on 5 September 1972 to the International Congress of Learned Societies in the Field of Religion.

[1] Also edited by W. K. Ferguson in the *Erasmi opuscula*, 338-61. See also H. Jedin, *op. cit.*, I, 192 and n. 2; Renaudet, *Études Érasmiennes (1521-1529)* (Paris, 1939), 198, 208; and his *Érasme, sa pensée religieuse et son action (1518-1521)*, Paris, 1926, p. 90-3; Craig R. Thompson, *Inquisitio de Fide*, Yale Studies in Religion No. XV (New Haven, 1950), 20-21: Schätti, *op. cit.*, 83-4; Tracy, *op. cit.*, 184-6.;

[2] Ferguson, *op. cit.*, 338-9; *EE* IV, p. 357, introduction to Ep. 1149. The best account of the career of Faber is that of Nikolaus Paulus, *Die deutschen Dominikaner im kampfe*

used his personal influence throughout 1520 and perhaps as late as 1522 to promote the scheme for reconciliation that it contained.[1] Through the critical year 1520 he entertained the hope that he might act as mediator between Rome and the adherents of Luther. Luther's unrelenting aggressiveness, especially in the *Babylonian Captivity*, eventually drained his hope for compromise, and after the Edict of Worms the scheme was virtually abandoned.[2] It is instructive to compare it to the *Julius* as a statement on a slightly later and much more important crisis in the life of the Church, and particularly for the view of the Church that it reveals.

The *Consilium* advances the principle that doctrinal difficulties should be resolved not through an appeal to infallible institutional authority, papal or conciliar, but through the deliberation of a select committee of learned men. This notion is to be distinguished from that of referring disputed theological problems to learned authority, which was of course perfectly familiar. The immediate background to Erasmus' and Faber's suggestion is to be found in conciliar experience of the 15th century, and envisages the adjudication of a small committee of wise and learned theologians over rival claims to doctrinal truth behind which there is an underlying unity. An obvious precedent is Nicholas of Cusa's suggestion in the *De pace fidei*, written in 1453 just after the fall of Constantinople, that a few wise men and scholars selected from among the various leaders of the world's religions could easily come to full agreement and bring about true religious concord. While there are elements in Cusa's thought that are plainly missing in the *Consilium*, both treatises resort to a learned consensus to repair a confessional breach in the interests of *concordia*. Once more, the work that we follow Wallace Ferguson in attributing to Erasmus contains idiosyncratic elements directed at the current crisis.[3]

The *Consilium* hoped to avert both the schism and religious war.

---

gegen Luther (1518-1563) (Freiburg, 1903), 292-313; also P. Kalkoff, 'Die Vermittlungs-politik des Erasmus und sein Anteil an den Flugschriften der ersten Reformationzeit,' *Archiv für Reformationsgeschichte*, 1 Jahrgang (1903), 6-23.

[1] *EE* V, Ep. 1329, 1352, to Adrian VI, December 1522 and March 1523. On Erasmus' general propaganda in favour of the *Consilium* see G. G. Krodel, 'Luther, Erasmus and Henry VIII.' *Archiv für Reformationsgeschichte* 53, (1962) 60-78; 74, n. 80.

[2] Ferguson, *op. cit.*, 341-3; Craig R. Thompson, *op. cit.*, 21 f.

[3] A certain cousinage with contemporary neo-Platonic syncretism is also likely; cf. Trinkaus, *op. cit.*, II, c. 16, Part 3, 'Pico's Pursuit of Theological Concord', on Giovanni Pico della Mirandola.

A committee of arbitration should be established, composed of the Emperor and the Kings of England and Hungary, to whom the Pope would delegate full authority to designate arbiters from men both learned and of impartial reputation.[1] Although, as it stated, knowledge in matters of the faith is the peculiar office of the Roman Pontiff, not to be taken away from him, nevertheless for the common good it might be allowed that in this instance the business be committed to others, to men of distinguished learning and proven integrity, above suspicion of susceptibility to venal motives.[2] These men should examine the dispute, rescue what is true from Luther's writings and correct his errors; the standard used, of course, would be "evangelical truth." Luther should be persuaded by argument, but if he persisted obstinately in the face of findings by such arbitration, he should pay the extreme penalty.[3]

Here again is a proposal conspicuously outside the main stream of discussion on authority in the Church. Is it conciliarist ? It is utterly *ad hoc*, yet of the greatest interest for the presuppositions it reveals. In effect, it proposed to assemble a Christian synod of a new type, combining the traditional authority of the Pope, the Emperor and representative princes (nominated for their impartiality in this dispute and conceivably, for their good relations with Erasmus) to support the decisive judgement of a committee marked both by learning and by probity. The proposal's sponsors felt that such a body would have far more chance of eliciting consent to its decisions than would any of the usual agencies, and that it would, in fact, in some way speak finally for the whole of the Christian body. The emphasis upon the integrity and good character of the judges recalls Erasmus' contention that unless its members were wholly receptive to the spirit of Christ, no organ of the Church's authority, however constituted, could act with valid credentials.[4]

---

[1] Ferguson, *op. cit.*, 359, *ll.* 134-6; in July 1520 Erasmus attended the meeting of Henry VIII and Charles V near Calais and tried to influence Henry to act as a mediator between Rome and the Emperor on the one hand, and Luther on the other. *EE* IV, Ep. 1118, introduction; Kalkoff, *op. cit.*, 19 f.; Krodel, *op. cit.*, 73.

[2] Ferguson, *op. cit.*, 359, *ll.* 127-33.

[3] *Ibid.*, *l.* 97 f. and *ll.* 145-6 : "Quod si Lutherus tum quoque perstiterit in his quae damnata fuerint ab arbitris, erit ad extrema remedia veniendum." Compare Erasmus to Albert of Brandenburg in 1519, *EE* IV, Ep. 1033, 101, *l.* 64 f. : "Postremo Christianum est, opinor, sic favere Luthero ut, si innocens est, nolim eum improborum factionibus opprimi; sin errat, velim sanari, non perdi ..."

[4] Ferguson suggests that the alternative appeal to a general council *(ll.* 155-8) is

We need not prolong the discussion to show other parallels with the thought of Erasmus or to probe the deep theological issues that it raises. It does bear directly on our theme because it illustrates and amplifies those characteristics of humanistic and evangelical thinking that we are endeavouring to capture. Some would say that the *Consilium* is donnish, but some donnish communities have wielded almost as much power as that envisaged by the *Consilium*. Like the *Julius exclusus*, as a *pièce d'occasion* it shows its humanist origin, as it does in its disregard of medieval ecclesiology. Conceived and written under pressure, infused with a passionate sense of urgency, both works offer highly personal comments that reflect the intimacy, self-assurance, mutual confidence and notable intellectual freedom of the humanist coterie. Both works are constructed from the historical materials of the Scriptural and Patristic heritage, and the views of both are informed and shaped by practical, evangelical ends. In the *Consilium*, where the ecclesiological focus is most clear, the delegated authority of the traditional secular and spiritual leaders of Christendom is ratified by the Holy Spirit, and it is notable that this holy and learned tribunal is to be not a consultative, but final, authority to settle the great question of the day. It is also constituted, after the tenets of evangelical humanism, as a body likely to be more persuasive than conventional authorities. When you consider the breathtaking claim here proposed, and its audacity in the perspective of tradition, what is perhaps most remarkable is that the authors seem so untroubled by the implications of their own proposal.

We are also able to see something of the tensions in conciliar thinking on the eve of the Reformation. As various scholars have shown in recent years, the association of conciliar theory with the call for reform of the Church in head and members was the result of the Great Schism and the tradition of papal-imperial controversy. But there was nothing inevitable about this association of ideas,[1] and in the years after the Council of Basel it is by no means clear that many of those who called

---

not the work primarily of Erasmus, but a concession to the German conciliar position espoused by Faber, *op. cit.*, 346. Erasmus' insistence upon Luther's good character echoes his sentiments about the learned commission in the *Consilium* : for him it constituted evidence that there was much that was good in his doctrine. On this attitude see the writer's essay, 461, n. 3 above, and Roland Bainton, 'Erasmus and the *Wesen des Christentums*,' in *Glaube Geist Geschichte*, ed. G. Müller and W. Zeller (Leiden, 1967), 200-06.

[1] Jedin, *op. cit.*, I, 32 f.

for a General Council to reform the Church were in any strict sense
conciliarists in principle.[1] Indeed, it has been observed recently that
by the early years of the sixteenth century, "conciliar theory, despite
its previous history, was becoming increasingly irrelevant to the question of ecclesiastical reform, whether conceived in Protestant or
Catholic terms."[2] It would appear that the advent of Christian humanism, nourished from sources that predated medieval conceptions and
consciously indifferent to the legacy of scholastic thought, could complete the rupture between the call for reform and conciliar theory, at
least for some. Once the unity of Christendom was clearly broken the
idea of a resort to learned consensus had obvious practical value alike
to *politique* statesmen and to churchmen seeking an alternative doctrine of authority. The proposal embodied in the *Consilium* then, anticipates in part the many colloquies of the sixteenth century on matters
of doctrine, from the Colloquy of Poissy to the private debates in
Cecil's household on the nature of the eucharist.[3] Like the *Julius*, it
reveals a wholly new mentality facing the institutional problems and
politics of Europe. Alienated from an apparently incorrigible papacy,
disillusioned by the spectacle of rival councils whose most serious
purposes were purely and patently political, and disabused of the
expectation that Europe's princes would or could undertake the reformation for which they so fervently longed, the humanist intellectuals almost unconsciously developed a personal approach to the whole
question of doctrinal authority, one that set aside the legal and in-

---

[1] Francis Oakley, 'Almain and Major : Conciliar Theory on the Eve of the Reformation,' *American Historical Review* 70, No. 3, (1965) 689.

[2] *Ibid.*, 688-9.

[3] Jean Carbonnier in 'Le Colloque de Poissy,' *Foi et Vie*, 60, no's 5-6 (1961), 43-52,
notes (46, n. 3) the need for a study of the sixteenth century religious *disputatio*. Certainly
it is clear that while much attention has always been given to the contentions between
religious groups, even at the most difficult times there were those interested in conversations to reconcile differences. Of the three types of *disputatio* distinguished by
Carbonnier none would seem exactly to fit the conditions envisaged in the *Consilium*.
It had some of the character of the 'disputatio-arbitrage' where both contestants seek
to convince a superior authority recognized and thought to be impartial (as in the Swiss
debates) and some of the 'disputatio-conciliation' resulting in an accord through mutual
concessions (as at Marburg, Worms and Ratisbon). None of these envisaged final authority for the judges themselves. On the debates in Cecil's household see J. K. McConica,
English Humanists and Reformation Politics (Oxford, 1965), 238; a recent discussion
is Basil Hall's, 'The Colloquies between Catholics and Protestants 1539-1451,' in *Studies
in Church History* 7 (1971), 235-66.

stitutional conceptions of recent centuries to invoke the authority of
learned men of probity—tribunes very like themselves—who would
act as the spokesmen for the enlightened conscience of the Christian
people as a whole, while the visible Church lay in fragments about
them. It is an idea as remote from the passions of popular religion as
it is from the calculating strategies of secular policy that they commonly
deplored. As an intra-mural remedy to the crisis of authority in the
Church, it was fatally vulnerable in the heat of theological warfare
after Luther's revolt, since in place of systematic rigour it relied for
acceptance upon that very consensus of Catholic belief that was now
in question, just as Erasmus' notion of proceeding with doctrine would
in practice have suspended the functioning of the Church's magis-
terium. The limitations of this coterie mentality are almost too easy
to demonstrate, but such notions came naturally to men who knew
and trusted and respected one another as much as they did who laughed
and read and ate and prayed together around the Bucklersbury house
of Thomas More and the Church of St. Thomas Acon, in the years
when a terrible old Pope and disappointing young king were casting
a vexatious shadow over what had seemed at first the brilliant promise
of an age of peace.

APPENDIX

BIBLIOGRAPHICAL NOTE ON THE AUTHORSHIP OF THE JULIUS EXCLUSUS

There is a general review of the history of the question in Wallace
K. Ferguson's editorial preface to the *Julius exclusus* in his *Erasmi
opuscula* (The Hague, 1933), 41 f. It was also discussed by P. S. Allen
in the introduction to Ep. 502 of *Opus epistolarum Des. Erasmi Roterodami*, 11 volumes (Oxford, 1906-47) volume 2, 418-20 (hereafter cited
as *EE*), and in Allen's *The Age of Erasmus* (Oxford, 1914), 184-9.
From the same period there is the important study of J.-B. Pineau,
Érasme et la papauté (Paris, 1923) and his article, "Érasme, est-il
l'auteur du Julius?" which appeared in *Revue de littérature comparée*,
5 (1925), 385-415. For a listing of the editions of the dialogue see
Ferguson, *op. cit.*, 55 f. J. K. Sowards has reviewed scholarship on
this question in the introduction to *The Julius Exclusus of Erasmus*
(tr. Paul Pascal) (Bloomington, 1968) and in his, "Erasmus and the
Making of the *Julius Exclusus*," Wichita State University Bulletin,
vol. 40, no. 3 (August, 1964) (University Studies No. 60), especially 4,
n. 8 and 5, n. 13.

Contention over the authorship of the *Julius exclusus* began with its publication. It was hailed at once as the work of Erasmus by a wide section of the informed community of learning, men who included Willibald Pirckheimer, Conrad Grebel and Martin Luther. Erasmus as promptly issued denials, although of a markedly equivocal character, and the ground was prepared for prolonged debate. It may be noted that certain significant positions are held in common by interested scholars. The dialogue is highly Erasmian in style, as contemporaries themselves insisted, and in content it agrees closely with what we know from other evidence of Erasmus' views on Pope Julius II. Apart from the passage noted above in the *Moriae encomium*, there are evident parallels in other works from the same period that are cited by advocates of Erasmus' authorship : the *Sileni Alcibiadis, Dulce bellum inexpertis, Querela pacis*, and the preface to his edition of Suetonius. Emile Telle has pointed out significant parallels with another work in, "Le '*De copia verborum*' d'Érasme et le '*Julius exclusus e coelis*," in *Revue de littérature comparée*, 22 (1948), 441-7, and Roland Bainton's essay in the Lau *Festschrift*, cited below, notes the remarkable parallel between the description of the entry of Julius II into Bologna in the *Julius exclusus* and Erasmus' portrait of the "high priest" in his Paraphrase of Mark 11.

At an appropriate moment a manuscript of the dialogue in Erasmus' hand, apparently in incomplete form, was held by Thomas Lupset, whose retention of it provoked sharp and anxious inquiry by Erasmus. There was evidently another copy in Erasmus' hand known to his intimates in Basel as early as August 1516; see Allen's introduction to Ep. 502, above, 419. Moreover, Erasmus wrote an epigrammatic poem on Julius II for Thomas More which is a close parallel in thought and phrasing to the anonymous *Julius*. This was first published by Pineau in *Revue de littérature comparée*, 5 (1925), 385 f., and edited by Ferguson in *Erasmi opuscula*, 35-7. Its authorship was questioned by Cornelius Reedijk in *The Poems of Desiderius Erasmus* (Leiden, 1956), Appendix II, 2, 391-3, but Reedijk has since reported the discovery of a copy in Erasmus' autograph, identifiable through the watermark as having emanated from the Paris region between 1503 and 1513; see 449, n. 1 above. Erasmus' denials, although unvarying, hardly confronted the question of authorship but concentrated rather on the dialogue's publication, for which he consistently maintained he was not responsible.

The election on 11 March, 1513 of Giovanni di Medici to succeed

Julius II as Pope Leo X clearly altered the situation for Erasmus. This was the Pope from whom he would secure the protective and approving patronage of both the New Testament and the edition of Jerome, and from whom he would receive the desired dispensation to end forever the canonical perils of his illegitimacy. J. K. Sowards has recently advanced the view that Erasmus' indebtedness to Pope Julius for similar favours, including possibly the granting of his doctorate in theology, also contributed to his reasons for denying the authorship of the *Julius* : "Even Erasmus was unwilling to face the consequences of such blatant ingratitude." See, "Erasmus and the 'Other' Pope Julius," *Wichita State University Bulletin*, vol. 48, no. 1 (February, 1972) *(University Studies* No. 90).

On 28 June, 1516, Lupset wrote Erasmus a letter revealing that both Colet and Erasmus had written to him to ask about certain things he had taken, apparently without authorization *(EE* II, Ep. 431). Begging the pardon of Erasmus, he says that he would have given them to the scribe-messenger, Peter Meghen, if he had not thought it safer to retain them until Erasmus' return. He promises to restore them in their entirety, and untouched. Erasmus' indignation over the episode suggests that he did indeed trust the discretion of Meghen, and was above all concerned to have the manuscripts back in his own possession.

The next clue comes from More on 15 December 1516' reporting that Lupset has restored to him some sheets ("aliquot quaterniones") which he has had for some time, apparently because Erasmus has ordered him to do so *(EE* II, Ep. 502, *l.* 9). The evidence that Erasmus directed Lupset to leave them with More is *EE* III, Ep. 664, *ll.* 28-30. Among these papers is the "Julii Genius"; that the sheets in question are manuscripts is determined by the next phrase—all are in the hand of Erasmus, but only in first draft, and none are entirely complete : "Tua manu omnia, sed prima tantum scriptio, neque quicquam satis integrum." (*l.* 12).

The following March, Erasmus told More of the delighted reception accorded the *Julius* in Brussels, where the satire was found to be written "quam festive et ... quam Erasmice." *(EE* II, Ep. 532, *l.* 24; cf. III, Ep. 961, *11.* 44-8, where Erasmus admits the style is "nonnihil Erasmicum.") He tells More to send what Lupset has returned to him —but by a reliable man *(EE* II, Ep. 543, *ll.* 9-10, 33-4). The following autumn, in a further abject apology to repair their relationship, Lupset admitted to Erasmus that the fault was a betrayal of books, insisting

that he was not to blame for this or for the fact that many were
alienated from Erasmus *(EE* III, Ep. 664, *ll.* 6-10). The whole 'matter,
often discussed, was fully dealt with by J. A. Gee, *The Life and Works
of Thomas Lupset* (New Haven, 1928) chapter 5, 53 f. Gee also pointed
out that such impetuous indiscretion was by no means out of character
for Lupset, for he more than once acted on his own responsibility in
serious matters without warrant for doing so *(ibid.,* p. 179-80).

　　Modern hesitations to ascribe the work to Erasmus stem from Henri
Hauser's critique of Pineau in *Revue de littérature comparée,* 7 (1927),
605-18. Hauser rested his objections principally on the contemporary
attribution to Fausto Andrelini of Forli, arguing that Pineau had not
proved that Andrelini did not write it. The considerable authority of
Augustin Renaudet was also brought to bear on the side of those
reluctant to ascribe the *Julius* to Erasmus, although initially he accepted P. S. Allen's analysis of the problem : "Erasme, sa vie et son œuvre
jusqu'en 1517," *Revue historique* 112 (1913), 241-74, 250 n. 4. He later
acknowledged that Erasmus had excellent practical reason to deny the
authorship of the dialogue after the election of Leo X, citing England's
entry into the papal alliance and Erasmus' dependence in Rome on
the Cardinals Riario, nephew of Julius II, and Grimani, indebted to
Julius for his advancement. But Erasmus, according to Renaudet, was
too critical both of conciliarists and of princes to have penned the
Julius : *Érasme et l'Italie* (Geneva, 1954), 112 ; "Discuter sur les droits
comparés du synode universel et du pape, du pape et des rois, n'était
pas son fait." Renaudet later agreed that the *Julius* is markedly
Erasmian in spirit, and called for fresh investigation of alternative
authorship on the ground that Erasmus had no interest in Pisa or the
antipapal policies of Louis XII; see his review of K. Schätti's *Erasmus
von Rotterdam und die römische Kurie* (Basel, 1954) in *Bibliothèque
d'humanisme et renaissance,* 17 (1905), 448-51, and compare the recent
comment of James D. Tracy in *Erasmus the Growth of a Mind* (Geneva,
1972), 137, n. 78, where in revising his earlier attitude which was
favourable to Stange's thesis (see below), he observes that Stange's
"contention that Erasmus was not a supporter of the French-sponsored
Council of Pisa, as *Julius exclusus* clearly is, has not been answered."
The present essay is directed in part precisely to this contention.

　　The case for Erasmus' authorship was put most firmly by W. K.
Ferguson, developing the position enunciated by P.S. Allen. Since
Ferguson's edition the most extensive study is Carl Stange's *Erasmus
und Julius II, eine Legende* (Berlin, 1937), where he raised questions

about the date of the first printed edition and refurbished the case for Andrelini. Working from somewhat similar premises, Pio Paschini in "L'autore del dialogo satirico contro Giulio II," *Atti dell' Accademia degli Arcadi*, ns. 13-14 for 1934-5 (Rome, 1937), 85-98, identified the author as Girolamo Rorario. This depends upon a great deal of conjecture about a work of which we have only a title—not the title of the *Julius exclusus*. In a detailed criticism of Paschini's thesis in the *Zeitschrift für systematische Theologie*, 18 (1941), 535-88, Stange came to the position that his hypothetical first edition of 1513 was withdrawn in the general hope for peace aroused by Leo X's election. The famous edition of 1517 was one in fact extensively rewritten by Erasmus, and came to be published, as has long been thought, by the indiscretion of Thomas Lupset.

This was the conclusion also of Roland Bainton, "Erasmus and Luther and the Dialog Julius Exclusus," in the *Festschrift Lau, Vierhundertfünfzig Jahre lutherische Reformation* (Leipzig, 1967), 17-26, Bainton here repeats Stange's suggestion that the incriminating autograph might have been a copy made by Erasmus himself from the original to keep his secretary from learning of his interest in such an explosive satire; cf. Stange, *Erasmus und Julius II*, 205. However it might equally be argued that to have a manuscript in his own hand circulating among his friends was foreseeably far more dangerous, and would have exposed him to the very risk he was allegedly trying to avoid. Certainly his intimates, including his scribes, must have known of his interest, if only to judge from the surviving correspondence, Erasmus' trust for Peter Meghen has been remarked upon already.

The most recent restatement of Stange's case came from Georg Gebhardt, *Die Stellung des Erasmus von Rotterdam zur Römischen Kirche* (Marburg, 1966), 377-95. Gebhardt accepts the view that the dialogue is both pro-French and conciliarist in outlook, and he thus finds it inconsistent with Erasmus' ecclesiology as it is set forth in the text of his study. While I do not agree with Gebhardt's thesis about Erasmus' ecclesiology, neither do I believe the *Julius* to be in any simple sense pro-French or conciliarist. In the present essay I seek to show that those traits of the dialogue have been much exaggerated, and that its essentially evangelical purpose is quite in keeping with the known views of Erasmus on the Papacy and the Church in general. Other material not listed here is discussed above in this essay.

THE MEANINGS OF "EVANGELICAL"

EUGENE F. RICE, Jr

Columbia University

Father McConica has read us an instructive paper. At one level it is a contribution to the debate on the authorship of the *Julius exclusus*. I shall not dwell on this point except to say that he has convinced me. His arguments make the attribution of the work to Fausto Andrelini of Forlì less plausible than ever and cogently buttress the case for Erasmus' authorship. In the continued absence of firm external evidence, we can still not be certain; but I think everyone will henceforth agree that it is very probable indeed that Erasmus wrote the *Julius Exclusus* and that he wrote it in the late winter of 1512-1513.

At another level, Father McConica's paper is a study of early sixteenth-century conciliar thought and of the relation of conciliar theory to the problem of ecclesiastical reform. He concludes with the provocative suggestion that Erasmus believed that "doctrinal difficulties should be resolved not through an appeal to infallible institutional authority, papal or conciliar, but through the deliberation of a select committee of wise and learned men," a Christian synod, according to Father McConica, of "a new type," and one without "any precedent in doctrine or event." These are large claims to novelty. They deserve the close attention of students of late medieval church history and political theory.

At yet another level, Father McConica is moving toward a definition of what he calls "Erasmianism," on the analogy of "Lutheranism" or "Zwinglianism." I believe I read him correctly when I say that in constructing his definition he puts a special emphasis on the idea of the evangelical. He speaks of Erasmus's "evangelical personality," of his "evangelical method," his "evangelical humanism," his "evangelical and scholarly achievement," his "evangelical light," his "evangelical attitude to the Papacy." More specifically, he argues that the "first and dominant purpose" of the *Julius Exclusus* is "evangelical," that its "dominant note" is the "contrast between evangelical counsel and worldly power," and that his attitude to the Church and ecclesiastical authority is shaped by "rhetorical, evangelical aims."

It strikes me that the adjective "evangelical" is not without difficulty; and I should like to devote the remainder of my brief remarks to an attempt to distinguish some of the different contexts in which the word is commonly used and abused and to suggest that even Father McConica has mildly abused it.

I think we should rather strictly limit "evangelical" to mean a deliberate emphasis on the Word of God localized in Scripture. One properly calls Luther's doctrine evangelical because it asserts the single authority of scripture in determining religious truth. Such a case is simple enough. On the other hand, deliberate emphasis on the Word of God localized in scripture can take a wide variety of forms, and is often linked and sometimes confused with ideas which have no necessary connection with it.

An example of this sort of ambiguity is the uncritical linkage of the notion "evangelical" with the notion of the *restauratio* or *renovatio* of the primitive church. "In the time of the primitive church one lived only with complete faith and complete charity," said Savonarola. "But how many are there in the world today who live thus!" So he preached repentance and the renewal and reform of the church. It seems to me confusing to call this message evangelical; it is better called prophetic, and was, in Savonarola's view, directly inspired by God.

Contrast Savonarola's call with a not dissimilar appeal for reform through a restoration of the sixteenth-century church to the likeness of the primitive church. It is by Lefèvre d'Etaples. "May kings, princes, magistrates and the peoples of all nations reflect on nothing else, embrace nothing so much, manifest nothing to the same extent as Christ, the vivifying Word of God and his holy Gospel. And may this be the sole effort and desire of all : to know the Gospel, to follow the Gospel, and everywhere to advance the Gospel. And may all hold firmly to what our ancestors and the early church, red with the blood of martyrs, perceived : that to know nothing except the Gospel is to know all things : *extra evangelium nihil scire est omnia scire.*" This appeal for renewal and reform is strictly and precisely evangelical.

Another sort of ambiguity arises from the increasing tendency I notice among students of the popular preaching, the popular piety and religion of the fifteenth and sixteenth centuries to speak of the "evangelization" of the lower clergy and of the laity. Some reforming efforts of this sort were plainly evangelical; others, I think, were not. Two examples of attempted diocesan reform, both French, one led by Denis Briçonnet in the diocese of St. Malo, the other by his cousin Guillaume Briçonnet in the diocese of Meaux, will make the difference clear.

In the summer of 1517 Denis Briçonnet returned to St. Malo from

Rome. He noted the "simplesse, ignorance, et insouffisance" of the laity and parish priests, chaplains and schoolmasters of his diocese. In order to remedy the situation he published an abridged French translation of Gerson's *Opus Tripartitum*. His choice was not unusual. Already in Gerson's own lifetime twenty-two dioceses had used the *Opus Tripartitum* to instruct clergy and laity in the elements of the Christian faith. In 1507 Etienne Poncher recommended its use in the diocese of Paris, followed in the next few years by the bishops of Evreux, Bordeaux, Langres and Chartres. The work was in four parts : on the virtues and contrary vices, on God's commandments and those of his church, on the sacraments, and on the Mass and how properly to celebrate it. Priests and curates were instructed to read one chapter at the early morning Mass each Sunday (at St. Malo the early Mass was especially for the young and for domestic servants, *jeunes et serviteurs*), to explain it clearly and simply, and to promise a twenty-day indulgence to all who listened well. Such a program has evangelical elements : to memorize the Pater noster and the Ten Commandments are evangelical exercises. But in its larger outlines the pedagogical and reformist impulse at work here is not in any strict sense evangelical. Its primary emphasis lay on matters other than the Word of God localized in Scripture.

The better known experiment of Guillaume Briçonnet at Meaux, in contrast, was, strictly speaking, evangelical, for it rested on a deliberate and active effort to distribute and popularize French translations of the New Testament and Psalms and on an organized program of preaching in which special attention was given to reading and explaining the text of scripture.

I barely scratch the surface of this matter. Further distinctions will occur to each of you. The problematical role of the notion of "evangelical" and related ideas in our period is of great interest and importance. It merits further investigation and discussion.

Let me return briefly now to Father McConica's paper and suggest why some (though by no means all) of his uses of the word evangelical disturb me. "Evangelical personality," for example. I am not sure what this phrase means. Jesus, by definition, was an evangelical personality. By extension, I can imagine that a human being who tries with some relative success to imitate Christ *(imitatio* or *filiatio Christi)* is properly called an evangelical personality. But despite the *philosophia Christi* I would still hesitate to call Erasmus that. On the other hand, when Father McConica defines Erasmus's "evangelical achievement" as his edition and translation of the Greek text of the New Testament, I am in complete agreement with him. Again, I am uneasy with the phrase "evangelical method"; and when Father McConica seems to define it as the "satirical pièce d'occasion," giving the *Julius exclusus* as an example, I am more than uneasy. His general reading of this text impresses me as uncommonly sensitive and perceptive. What I cannot yet see is why he considers it an example of "evangelical method" or goes on to argue that its "first and dominant purpose is evangelical." Using "evangelical" in this way widens the meaning of the word unnecessarily and clouds rather than clarifies our understanding of the text, the man and the period. There is nothing inherently evangelical about "reforming purpose"; or about "spiritual aspiration"; or about a passion for peace, concord, and social justice; or about a hatred of tyranny; or even, as I have tried to indicate, about efforts to renovate the contemporary church in image of the church of the apostolic age or contrasting the worldly power and pretensions of a secularized papacy with the simplicity of the primitive church.

I would not quarrel with the description of Erasmus as an "evangelical humanist" (it is better at any rate than "Christian humanist"—can anyone name a humanist who was not a Christian?), although he was much else besides; nor would I be surprised to discover, when Father McConica, one day, feels free to say with conviction "this *is* Erasmianism," that an evangelical impulse lies near its core. But I think that day will arrive the sooner if we can agree austerely to mean by evangelical something rather strict and literal.

INTERVENTION RE FATHER McCONICA'S APPLICATION OF THE TERM "EVANGELICAL" TO ERASMUS

WILLIAM J. BOUWSMA

University of California (Berkeley)

Like Professor Rice, I found myself also questioning the description of Erasmus as *evangelical*, and I share his view that this term should be limited to religious personalities or programs that emphasize the Scriptures as the word of God. But I am inclined to be even more restrictive. It was characteristic of our period that, although almost all (indeed, perhaps all) religious thinkers gave substantial attention to

Scripture, they read it in very different ways. One might demonstrate this, for example, by comparing their various commentaries on Paul's epistle to the Romans, a particular favorite. But some men read this text through Platonic or Neoplatonic spectacles, while others tried to wrestle with Paul's meaning in a more direct fashion; and just as their motives differed, so also did their understanding of the text. I am thinking particularly of the enormous differences in the understanding of the familiar Pauline dualism of flesh and spirit. One might, to be more concrete, compare Erasmus's *Enchiridion* (much of it comment on Romans) or Colet's treatment of this epistle with Luther's early lectures on Romans. If both types of treatment are described as *evangelical*, then I think the word tends to lose its meaning.

As long as we are clear about our terms, it may not matter much what language we employ; but it seems to me more useful to reserve *evangelical* for those who struggled to get through the hellenistic interpretation of Scripture, at least obscurely recognized this as the essential problem, and —whatever this may have meant to them—saw in the *direct* encounter with Scripture the key to religious and moral renewal. I think that humanism contributed to this effort, but not in its esteem for the religious value of the classics, an evaluation that in practice tended to obstruct any direct encounter by determining in advance the way in which the Scriptures were understood. The real contribution of humanism to this encounter—and here there are parallels in the approach to secular texts—lay rather in the new historical perspective that accompanied it and that was always in some tension with the concern to find contemporary value and relevance in the classics. This perspective enabled some thinkers to see ancient culture as a product of its own time, place, and circumstances rather than as an embodiment of ultimate truth that would necessarily aid in the understanding of Scripture. I would thus prefer to limit the term *evangelical* to those who approached Scripture on the basis of an absolute distinction between the Gospel of salvation and all secular culture. By this standard, it seems to me that Erasmus was not, for all his reformist fervor and his devotion to the Bible, an *evangelical*.

INTERVENTION RE FATHER McCONICA'S DISCUSSION OF THE ERASMIAN IDEA OF THE RESOLUTION OF DOCTRINAL DIFFERENCES IN COUNCILS OF LEARNED AND GODLY MEN

WILLIAM J. BOUWSMA

It may be that this proposal was not, after all, novel or very surprising. As early as the thirteenth century university scholars, especially at Paris, had discerned in Christendom not two but three sources of authority : not only the *imperium* and the *sacerdotium*, but also the *studium*, with a special responsibility for settling doctrinal questions. This position had been one of the strands composing the conciliar movement of the fourteenth and fifteenth centuries. Thus it may be that Erasmus was not so much creating a new idea as adapting an old one to the new conditions of his own time, especially to a new conception of religious scholarship and a new group of Christian scholars not any longer closely connected with universities. He may have absorbed the idea from one of those medieval (or at least non-humanist) writers he had read but rarely cared to acknowledge. On the other hand, the idea seems hardly striking enough to need explanation in terms of a literary source. It might have come quite naturally out of his high esteem for the insights and promise of his own humanistic theological method. At any rate it closely parallels the thirteenth century conception of the *studium*. Both, I take it, expressed a sense of the discrepancy between the administrative and jurisdictional responsibilities of the official hierarchy and the spiritual quality of doctrinal questions. Both, therefore, have the same ecclesiological implications.

THE AMBIGUITIES OF POPE JULIUS AND HIS ROME

JOHN ARTHOS

The University of Michigan

I am not in a position to review the implications of Father O'Malley's study if only because it represents the beginning of an investigation whose import we only partly see, nor am I able to speak substantively upon Father McConica's, which looks towards a consideration of the character of the mind of Erasmus—to assess that would be quite beyond my capacity. I shall attempt instead to offer a few thoughts that both papers have occasioned as they bear upon each other.

The irony is as agreeable as it is instructive—a paper that points to a certain simplicity and decency in honor at the Papal Court, with something of the purity the reformers of the time were pressing for, followed by a paper treating the famous and ferocious attack upon the very Pope who was listening to some of these sermons, treating of the Incarnation, of the dignity of man and of many central concerns neither coldly nor unchristianly.

The first thought that occurs to one, I think, after attending to Father O'Malley's paper, is a question about the pervasiveness of piety of this character. He gives us only a few examples, of course, but such as they are they seem to bear out Garin's observation that humanism and the Neo-Platonists in particular had effected a renewal of the inner life of thoughtful men. For by Father O'Malley's account these preachers, largely free of the habits of categorization, and largely untouched by the fashion of overloading Christian matter with pagan illustration; free also of the extreme practice of subordinating Christian doctrine and sentiment to the authority of the ancients, were yet expressing something other than the simplicity and ardor of a reconstructed primitive faith. It would seem they were indeed continuing something of that simplicity, colored, or reinforced, or newly clothed in the language humanism had given something of its own life to. These preachers—in these decades—some of them not known to fame, give witness to the power of the movement that was in effect displacing the excesses of recent scholasticism and countering the new pedantry, the charms of affectation that perenially tempt those who have learned something of ancient life. It appears that something had caught on where we thought it had not.

A second thought that occurs to one instantly has to do with the nature of the attention such sermons received at the Papal Court, particularly since Erasmus directed some of his sharpest criticism at a sermon he spoke of as delivered before Julius II, which, by his account, was as deadly dull as it was pretentious. The question now becomes for us, what indeed was the character of the interest Julius would have been giving these sermons?

Shortly before his death Julius had called the Fifth Lateran Council where one of the opening addresses, by Giles of Viterbo, had strongly called for reform in the Church, in the sweetness as well as energy of his character. And indeed among the passages from the sermons Father O'Malley quotes one wonders if it is not his influence that is counting for much. At other times, Giles of Viterbo had gone out of his way to call the attention of this Pope to what he believed to be urgent needs. Evidently he did not despair of getting his ear. And whether or not he himself obtained any successes, the Council did indeed acknowledge some demands, and among other policies one was effected through which the bishops were hereafter to supervise the sermons presented in their dioceses. I judge this was meant to restrain certain excesses often attributed to mendicant friars when they were developing the scholastic manner to extremes. The policy may not have been addressed to the particular abuses that Erasmus attacked so ferociously in the *Ciceronianus*, but to the degree that it took any account at all of the spirit of some of the recommendations before the Council it would have been as corrective of the abuses Erasmus was attacking as the very antithesis not only of Christian preaching but of Christian life. What Erasmus was to present so splendidly in the *Ecclesiasticus* was coming into honor already, although the counsel of perfection is of course always that. The inference accordingly supports the drift of Father O'Malley's paper—even before the actions of the Lateran Council Julius would have been responding to the movement.

To turn to another matter the papers call to our minds, we are led to think about the manner Erasmus adopts in attacking Julius.

Browning of course brought up many of the ideas that occur to us when we reflect upon worldly clergymen, yet he did not deny a fixed religiousness in the Bishop who was dreaming so passionately over the tomb he wanted for himself in Saint Praxed's church, imagining himself as he rested there waiting for Judgment Day listening to the blessed mutter of the Mass. Erasmus appears to have felt a less than comparable respect for Julius. In the *Exclusus* Julius is not shown doubting the being or the authority of Peter, but in the fate Erasmus was proposing for him we do not see him in his coffin enjoying the solace of prayers and incense. Erasmus, like Browning, exulted in the art of caricature, and we share in the enjoyment he found in annhilating his enemy. The hits, the slashes, the brilliance of phrase are as high-spirited as they are merciless. But the object of Erasmus's attack excites in us nearly as much hilarity as repulsion. Julius is such a determined failure, he is determined to put his worst foot forward. He plays the fool.

I am not able to judge the effectiveness of the technique, whether the method of caricature is as politically effective for good ends as satire can be—whether such a sketch can be as telling in the end as, say, Swift's *Modest Proposal*, or the incident in *A Tale of a Tub*, where evangelical enthusiasm, we learn, is being kindled by the lack of fresh air in a smoke-filled room. The question arises because we are forced to ask if Julius was indeed a fool. One may doubt his fitness for the post, one may agree to the condemnation of the importance he placed upon temporal power, but Erasmus comes close to condemning his energy. No doubt a soul at peace lacks the vivacity and certainly the tendentiousness we ordinarily attribute to evil, but one nevertheless raises a serious question about the seriousness of Erasmus. The question may appear sardonic but one may not avoid asking it—must the Pope be merely holy?

I would not of course build up the *Julius Exclusus* into an image in small of the range of Erasmus's values in working for reform, but I do ask if he has not here overshot the mark. And while I think we must accord Father McConica much of our accord in doing what we can to call attention to a lack of system, a lack of philosophic as well as doctrinaire cast to Erasmus's mind, one must believe that an intellect of such a character—free, imaginative, darting, half-poetical—is better at some things than at others, and in the long run, on this particular matter, Erasmus makes a serious mistake—he underestimates the enemy.

The excesses and faults of the man Julius and of his polices are obviously the right game although, as I have indicated, it is the man that is attacked more than the policies, but the very energy and worldliness that were so harmful were the instruments of a good so great that the spiritual character of the city of the Rome we know is continually fed by it. When we read in Rodocanachi how Julius worked with Bramante day in day out, year in year out, over the new basilica, over the colonnade, over the rejuvenation of innumerable churches; when we reflect upon the fierce contests with Michael Angelo; and when we read of his passion for jewels, believing, apparently with John Milton, that the streets of heaven could be no better paved than with diamonds and emeralds and pearls and when we see that he gave as freely as he spent, we are of course squarely up against the dilemma of all those who appreciate the values of asceticism—what business has beauty got do to with Christ? Or, more particularly, what has Bramante got to do with Christ?

Julius, by all the testimony, and by the evidence of his bequests, counted more on the glory of the Papacy than of his family. The buildings, the paintings and sculpture, the tiara were for the future of the Church. It was not only power he wanted for the Papacy, it was glory. To critics the distinction was not worth making, yet one may not accept wholly sympathetically the perspectives of those who in all earnestness appealed to the models of primitive simplicity, of some spirit of charity wholly unfettered by the demands of property. One must be even more diffident in supporting those who in criticizing, whether willingly or not, were aligning themselves with partisan interests—of France, or Venice. Father McConica has done well to emphasize the Arielilike freedom of this mind that could throw so bright a light yet, as we can see too well, even Erasmus could not either in principle or in his private affairs keep wholly disentangled from the world's great snare, and there was no Prospero to set him free in this life.

And so I return to the character of some of those sermons Father O'Malley has spoken of, heard by men with much else on their minds— the maintenance of authority, ambition, avarice, the Raffael Stanze, the statue of Moses, the new street from the Quattro Fontane to the Trinità—and while no doubt they were also attending much too often to long-winded, decadent theologizing as well as mere empty words, they knew they were being buffeted by the winds of change, they were alert to the ambitions and arrogance of the humanists, to the indignation and hostility of the reformers, to the endless restiveness of clerical rivals and political aspirants, they were—the portraits attest to this— convinced of the evanescence of all power, as of their lives. But I can imagine few persons more receptive than Julius to the idea that the

Incarnation was itself redemptive, just as I can imagine no one—unless it be Erasmus—more sceptical of the claim of men to dignity. I am supposing that the *terribilità* of Julius had as much religion, and as little, as Michael Angelo's.

In one of the sermons Father O'Malley tells of, the idea is developed that the Incarnation was in itself redemptive. Even the most tentative effort to grasp the import of this idea all but shatters the understanding. The Incarnation in any aspect certainly challenges to the depths the affirmations Platonism in any form depends on, and Michael Angelo, I believe, exhibited almost the complete derangement, the dilemmas, the dogma forces upon Neo-Platonists. I am suggesting that Julius, hearing a sermon broaching such a theme, would have sensed the tension, would have indeed known well enough that it was at work in the conception of the tomb the sculptor was to make for him. He would have been, in short, more than a little prepared for the introduction of such matters into the preaching at the Papal Court.

These and other questions haunt us as we try to reconstruct the life of the times and most especially of the Papacy, but the one that underlies them all finally is, I think, this—how much of the spirit that transformed the ancient world and helped effect the civilizing of the barbarians survived in the midst of iniquity? Did anything survive? Was it in fact alive in the reformers? The questions pressed further— do we in this age know what we are talking about when we agree to oppose to the excess and the corruption and the splendor of these courts and cities the example of Saint Peter or Saint Francis or Christ? For my part, I think I understand Colet when he speaks of a holy life, but More and Erasmus are more complex, and their criticism often shines with that brilliance that would throw out the baby with the bath. If to these questions we propose this answer—that indeed there did survive within the Lateran in the tending of the ceremonies, here and there in the very manoeuvering, traces of the authentic power and glory—we would have little enough to go on, but no less than if we were to suppose that all had vanished. In this cult of glory that so many intemperate and unholy men favored, what was there that gave such sustaining life to the monuments they left behind that, at times at least, Erasmus would not have had had erected, and that in the present we generally judge not inimical to the very piety Erasmus would have us honor above all else?

5. THE IMPERIAL MOTET :
BAROMETER OF RELATIONS
BETWEEN CHURCH AND STATE

LOUISE E. CUYLER

The University of Michigan

When the Church fathers at the Council of Trent set down their precepts concerning music for the liturgy, their concerns were immediate and pertained specifically to the Church's Latin rite. But because Western art music had been the handmaiden of the Latin church from the very beginning and had matured under her patronage, the musical consequences of Trent were both comprehensive and enduring. Summarily, liturgical music became a unique category with specific rules and inhibitions; as an inadvertent consequence, secular (that is, non-liturgical) music acquired new freedom and was induced to develop its own distinctive styles and idioms. This was one of the most influential changes ever to overtake Western music because, during the century before the Protestant Reformation, liturgical and secular music had drawn ever closer together. With the Josquin generation of Franco-Flemish composers (*ca.* 1480-1520), the musical aspects of the two styles virtually coalesced. A chanson or Lied, originally with earthy or amorous text, could serve as the *cantus prius factus* in a sacred polyphonic composition, and many a "Christe eleison" was sung to music that had formerly carried some such exhortation as "baisez-moi." Under other circumstances, sacred and secular texts were intermingled in motet-like compositions with musical texture resembling that of contemporary liturgical pieces. This cross-fertilization had produced results that were musically sound, whatever the judgment about the effect on the sacred liturgy : secular compositions drew discipline and expertise in syntax and architecture from such models as motets and Mass movements, while liturgical music assimilated some of the freedom and color of the less circumscribed worldly pieces. By the first decade of the sixteenth century, the principal criterion in designating a certain composition as sacred or secular was its text.

After about 1530, but especially following the Counter-Reformation and the Council of Trent, all this changed, for most of the Council's musical decrees were concerned with identifying secular elements and prohibiting them from the Latin liturgy. Many interesting musical forms were lost in the subsequent purge, but we shall be concerned in this paper with only one : a hybrid musical type to be designated the "paraliturgical" motet, which had flourished in the gray area between the sacred and the profane. One such paraliturgical type was the Imperial motet written traditionally to mark the accession of a new King of the Romans (German emperor) or a Holy Roman Emperor. As long as the ideal of a universal Church remained plausible, the Empire, as its secular arm, reflected a similar comprehensiveness; and the coronation of a new Emperor was itself a paraliturgical occasion. Indeed the Emperor took the holy order of deacon with his coronation, and afterward was privileged to sing the Gospel at Mass and to assist the celebrant in other ways. Thus a composition written to mark the occasion of a coronation was probably, and quite suitably, paraliturgical in style. In the relaxed times before Trent, it was likely to be performed in a liturgical setting.

The period from 1440 until about 1550 encompassed the heyday of the great Franco-Flemish school of composers. The same period saw the accessions of only three Holy Roman Emperors, for the Habsburg line at that time was singularly long-lived and the reigns of the three Emperors embraced those of seventeen popes. Each of the three secular monarchs, Friedrich III (reigned 1440-93), Maximilian I (1493-1519), and Charles V (1519-56), had at least one major Franco-Flemish composer as *Hofkomponist;* and each was honored with at least one monumental motet composed in connection with his accession. In examining motets written for the three men, we shall have an opportunity to observe a century-long evolution of the Franco-Flemish motet style. As a corollary, we shall remark upon the eventual detachment of the Imperial motet from its liturgical roots. For such detachment did indeed take place, parallelling the gradual estrangement of the Church and the Empire after the Protestant Reformation.

In 1440, when he was only twenty-five, Friedrich, the Duke of Styria and a minor Habsburg scion, was crowned King of the Romans. This office was a pre-Imperial post, and the election, which took place at Frankfurt, was probably more important to the Germans than any future acquisition of the "world crown"—that of Holy Roman Emperor. When Friedrich assumed his German office, the Church and the Empire were still linked by ancient tradition and they were probably even more interdependent than commonly, since each had arrived at a nadir of prestige. Friedrich's election took place in great haste, when Albert II died suddenly after less than two years in office.

Little is known about musical arrangements at the Imperial court at that early date. Until three or four decades ago, it had been assumed that Germany was slow to accept the learned polyphonic style practiced by the French during the thirteenth and fourteenth centuries and carried on by their Low Country successors during the decades after the onset of the Hundred Years War. Today, however, fresh evidence contained in a large manuscript collection known now as the Aosta Codex [1] confirms that Albert II and his successor, Friedrich III, were served by several Franco-Flemish musicians from the Liège district. One of them, Jean (or Johannes) Brassart, was an important composer who had served at the Papal court in 1431.

Two motets in the last portion of the Aosta collection definitely allude to events of the years 1439-40. Number 188, *O rex Fridrice tu pulcre pacis amice*, is obviously a gesture of homage to the new King of the Romans, and it is ascribed in the manuscript to Jo. Brassart. The ascription of the next motet, Number 189, was cut off in the binding, but the stylistic resemblance to Number 188 suggests that it, too, was composed by Brassart. This second piece, *Romanorum rex inclite*, has three-voiced polyphony overlaid to a tenor line derived from the Introit of the Gregorian Mass for the Dead, *Requiem aeternam*. It is clearly a *Trauermotette* for the dead Albert II. The principal text, shown below, lists six (possibly seven) men, all with French or Low Country names, and persons who, to judge from the exhortation "celeriter psallentes Christo regi," were members of Albert's *Hofkapelle*. Brassart, probable composer of the motet, heads the list :

ROMANORUM REX

Romanorum rex inclite,
Alberte, vita glorie
tibi sit eternalis.

---

[1] See Guillaume de Van, "A Recently Discovered Source of Early Fifteenth Century Polyphonic Music," in *Musica Disciplina*, Vol. II (1948) for a complete description of this manuscript. How the seminary in the obscure Piedmont village of Aosta came into possession of this treasure is not known, but much of northern Italy had close relations with the Empire during the late Middle Ages.

Fuisti princeps nobilis,
parens prudens et humilis
ecclesie filius.

Te diligebat populus
almanicus, bohemicus
ac tota religio.

Ergo Brassart cum Erasmo
Adam serva, Io de Sarto
Johannisque pariter

Tirion, Martin et Galer,
cantores celeriter
psall(entes) Cristo regi,

nostro summo creatori,
supplicando sue matri
ut sua per merita

perducat ad celestia
animam cum gloria
regis eternaliter.
Amen.

This composition is of considerable importance, first because it aids in dating the manuscript. It also testifies that Franco-Flemish polyphony was indeed known and probably liked in the Empire at a date considerably earlier than was once supposed.

Number 188, *O rex Fridrice*, is our principal concern, however, because it is the earliest of the paraliturgical, Imperial motets written during the period under consideration. This motet is polytextual : it comprises a *cantus prius factus* (the tenor) which uses the opening words and music of an Advent antiphon "In tuo adventu erue nos Domine"[1]; and an overlaid texture of three polyphonically related parts carrying the secular text *O rex Fridrice*. The plainchant antiphon segment which is the liturgical source of the tenor is shown below. Its choice as the basis for Brassart's composition is of symbolic importance, as will be shown presently.

---

[1] See *Paléographie musicale XII, Antiphonaire Monastique XIII siècle, (Codex 160 de la Bibliothèque de la Cathédrale de Worcester)*, 8. This Codex contains the Office of the Benedictine use, and it will be recalled that several of Germany's greatest churches were priories of the Benedictine Order—for example Sts. Ulrich and Afra at Augsburg, an important free Imperial city.

Ex. 1 Antiphon "In tuo adventu," from Worcester
Antiphonaire (Paléographie musicale XII)

    .In   tu – o   ad – ven – tu   e – ru – e   nos   Do – mi – ne

This motet is constructed on isorhythmic principles, which marks it
as essentially conservative, even anachronistic, because motets so
structured are encountered less and less frequently after approximately
the third decade of the fifteenth century. The isorhythmic plan of the
tenor projects a four-fold repetition of the antiphon segment "In tuo
adventu," the note values in each successive *talea* being decreased
systematically through application of a progressively diminishing proportional formula. Within the omnipresent symbolism of late medieval
art, the implication of this is clear. The tenuous state of the Empire
in 1440 might well have caused its people to plead "In thy coming
Lord bring us to the light"; and "Domine" could, in dualistic inference,
include the new young King of the Romans, for whose reign hopes
must have been high. As for the isorhythmic plan of diminishing
proportions, this, needless to say, symbolizes, through its sense of
growing tension, the increasing fervor of the petitions. The proportional
scheme for the four successive stages of isorhythmic dispersion of the
antiphon are shown below, each *talea* in the tenor carrying a progressively shorter segment of the superimposed secular text.

	Mensural signs	Equivalent time signature, unreduced	Proportional Reduction	Total Yield in Notes
I	☉•	$\frac{9}{1}$	——	45 ▢• (perfect breves).
II	☾•	$\frac{6}{1}$	$\frac{2}{3}$	45 ▢ (imperfect breves) or 30 ▢• (perfect breves)
III	⌽	$\frac{3}{1}$	$\frac{1}{2}$	45 ○ or 30 ○•
IV	⌽	$\frac{3}{2}$	$\frac{1}{2}$	22 ½ ○ or 15 ○•

The initial note values assigned in the successive statements to the first word of the antiphon, "In," are :

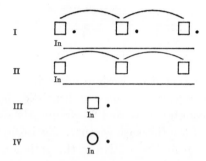

The first line of the secular text is detached and set in two voices to precede the beginning of the isorhythmic tenor. The remainder of the text is set to three-voiced polyphony, above the isorhythmic tenor. The concurrence of the reiterated antiphon (in tenor) with portions of the secular text, and the mensural signs for the successive sections are shown below :

Antiphon in four isorhythmic taleae	*Secular Text in three-voiced polyphony*
	[O rex Fridrice, tu pulcre pacis ami(ce),]
I ☉ In tuo adventu erue nos Domine	cleri protector ac utilis populi rector existis vere, qudo cuncti possunt videre. Austriam nunc regis post mortem incliti regis Alberti clari : te sibi nunc comparari cupio tam pie, tum nocte tum quoque die. O cristi genitrix, sis principis auxiliatrix, ut te iuvante, patriam regat velud ante
II ☾ In tuo adventu erue nos Domine	rex hanc regebat, et firma pace tenebat : hic te reliquit quem pacem ponere scivit. Clerus ac populus, tum proprius tum alienus, nunc vocibus oret, te cantu virgo decoret.
III ⊘ In tuo adventu erue nos Domine	Nos nympha pia, exaudi, virgo Maria, ut, extrema dies, sit nobis celica quies, cum sanctis omnibus hoc prestet trinus ac unus.
IV ⊘ In tuo adventu erue nos Domine	Amen.

Twelve years after his election as *Romanorum rex*, Friedrich journeyed to Rome for his coronation as Holy Roman Emperor and, concurrently, his marriage to Elnora of Portugal. This was to be the last Imperial coronation at Rome and many details of the occasion are set down in *Weisskunig*,[1] which Friedrich's son and heir, Maximilian, had prepared to preserve the glories of his own and his father's reigns. There is no information about the music used, however, and no Imperial motet written for this occasion is known.

In many respects, Friedrich's fifty-three year reign was a disastrous one, and the pious hopes expressed in his coronation motet were never fulfilled. In 1459, however, Elnora of Portugal bore him a son who survived : Maximilian, whose subsequent marriage to Mary of Burgundy (1477) brought the Netherlands within the Imperial domain. Maximilian's own coronation as King of the Romans took place in 1486, while he was yet a resident of the Low Countries as regent for his son, Philip, following Mary of Burgundy's death. Old Emperor Friedrich III was still living, but wisely arranged his son's election as a precautionary measure to assure Maximilian's accession upon Friedrich's death. An elaborate musical entourage accompanied Maximilian on the pilgrimage to Frankfurt for his election, then to Aachen for his coronation; but no known composers are named in Jean Molinet's elaborate account of the assembling of the personnel for Maximilian's *Chapelle*.[2] The Austrian archduke-regent was deeply resented by the people of his wife's domain and it is not surprising to find that no Low Country composer wrote a motet to mark Maximilian's election as *Romanorum rex*. Also, old Emperor Friedrich's living presence made the prestige of Maximilian's new post prospective rather than immediate.

Maximilian became Emperor-presumptive at his father's death in 1493, but during the next fifteen years, his desire to journey to Rome for his anointing as Holy Roman Emperor increased to an obsession. A variety of circumstances impeded the fulfillment of his wish, not the least of them the withholding of required funds, instigated by such North German princes as Friedrich the Wise of Saxony who feared that Maximilian's acquisition of the Imperial title might diminish his (Friedrich's) power and the growing autonomy of his Saxon domain. Friedrich's arrogance was closely linked, it goes without saying, to the increasing militance of reformers such as Luther. And the essential bond between the universal Church and the Empire constituted an

---

[1] See *Kaiser Maximilians Weisskunig*, new edition, Kolhammer Verlag (Stuttgart, 1956).

[2] See Molinet *Chroniques*, 3 vols. (Brussels, 1935-7), Vol. I, 470 ff. (Bibl. Royale de Belge, Ms. 15848).

early Renaissance example of what we now call the "domino theory." For the Empire needed the Church's claims of universality to bolster its own grandiose pretensions. Maximilan knew this full well, and the increase in his religious fervor during the last dozen years of his life probably stemmed as much from pragmatic as from spiritual considerations.

In 1506, Philip the Fair, Maximilian's only son and heir, died suddenly while he was visiting Spain. Thus the need for Maximilian to confirm his Imperial title with a Roman coronation became more urgent, for only in the role of Emperor did he have the prerogative of naming his successor. To expedite matters, Maximilian chose to convene the Reichstag at Constance, a free Imperial city which had been the scene of Emperor Sigismund's Ecumenical Council almost a century earlier; the express purpose of this Reichstag was to persuade the electors and princes of the Empire to provide funds for Maximilian's coronation journey.

The money was made available with surprising dispatch and the pilgrimage to Rome was undertaken during the fall and winter of 1507-08. However, Maximilian's retinue was blocked below the Brenner Pass by the Venetians; Pope Julius II probably had a hand in the move, for aspirant Emperors had been unwelcome visitors in Rome since at least two centuries. At Trent in the South Tyrol, on 4 February 1508, Maximilian took the title Emperor-elect with Pope Julius' permission and as much pomp as he could muster. His aborted Roman coronation was the major disappointment of Maximilian's life and may have been the cause of some of his capricious behavior during the next few years.

The great Flemish composer, Heinrich Isaac, who, after 1496, was a kind of roving *Hofkomponist* for Maximilian, was living at Constance at the time of the Reichstag, perhaps as a diplomatic emissary for the Emperor.[1] It was he who composed the splendid motet, *Virgo prudentissima* to mark Maximilian's prospective coronation at Rome. *Virgo prudentissima* is one of the noblest compositions of its type written during the early Renaissance and it is the epitome of the paraliturgical motet. Its permeation with liturgical material may be seen as symbol-

---

[1] Maximilian often employed non-professionals for diplomatic posts, for example Barbireau, another Flemish composer, at the court of Queen Beatrice of Hungary, around 1490.

izing the final drawing together, before the Reformation, of Church
and Empire.

The liturgical nucleus of this composition is the antiphon for the
Magnificat at First Vespers of the feast of the Assumption of the
Blessed Virgin Mary, shown below.

Ex. 2 Antiphon *Virgo Prudentissima* [1]

August 15

(Virgin most prudent, whither are you going, glowing brightly as the
dawn? Daughter of Sion, you are all beautiful and fair, serene as the
moon, bright as the sun.)[2]

Although the dogma of the Assumption did not become an article of
faith until fairly recent times (1950), the feast of the Assumption
(August 15) had been celebrated widely from ancient times and throughout the Catholic world. In medieval Germany, the feast took on certain
secular overtones, for it initiated a month-long celebration of the
harvest, known as the *Frauendreissiger*. The choice of an antiphon
from this Office of the B.V.M. could have stemmed from several considerations: mid-August must have been approximately the time when
Maximilian's trip to Rome became a firm prospect; and the *Frauendreissiger*, glorifying the harvest, could have suggested, symbolically,

---

[1] *Liber usualis* (Tournai and New York, 1956), 1600.

[2] Translation from *Lauds, Vespers, Compline in English*, The Liturgical Press (College-
ville, Minn., 1965).

the new harvest of prestige accruing to the Empire with the confirmation of Maximilian's Imperial title. We might recall, too, that the
German's designation for the Assumption is *Mariäs Himmelfahrt*,
which may have seemed to link it with Maximilian's own prospective
journey. In any case, Vadian,[1] one of a group of humanists who were
residents of St. Gall in the vicinity of Constance, prepared a lengthy
prose paraphrase of the liturgical antiphon. This paraphrase, in two
partes, is written in the manner of a massive trope; for it commences
with the salutation "Virgo prudentissima" and closes, many lines later,
with reference to the closing words of the antiphon. In his musical
setting, Isaac intertwines the model antiphon in still more intimate
fashion by recalling it, intact with its plainsong, at intervals during
the through-composed setting of Vadian's paraphrase. In the quotation
of Vadian's text shown below, the segments of the source antiphon
are placed in the left-hand column, as they occur in conjunction with
the paraphrased text in the musical setting.

VIRGO PRUDENTISSIMA

Source Antiphon as supplementary text	*Vadian's paraphrase*
	Virgo Prudentissima, quae pia gaudia mundo attulit ut sphaeras omnes transcendit et astra sub nitidis pedibus radiis et luce chorusca liquit. Et ordinibus iam circumspecta novenis ter tribus atque ierarchiis excepta supremi ante dei faciem steterat patrona reorum. Dicite qui colitis splendentia cul-
Virgo prudentissima	mina Olimpi, Spiritum proceres archangeli et angeli et alme virtutesque throni vos principum et
quo progrederis,	agmina sancta vosque potestates et tu dominatio
quasi aurora	coeli flammantes cherubim cerbo seraphinque creati,
valde	an vos letitie tantus perfuderit umquam sensus ut
rutilans	eterni matrem vidisse, tonantis consessum, coelo
filia	terraque marique potentem reginam, cuius numen
Syon	modo spiritus omnis et genus humanum merito veneratur,
	adorat, adorat.

---

[1] Vadianus = Joachim von Watt, 1481-1551. Vadian was educated at the University
of Vienna where he was a protégé of the great humanist, Konrad Celtes, whom the
Emperor Maximilian had called to the University's faculty when he sought to rehabilitate
it. Vadian received his laureate crown from Maximilian in 1514. After the Reformation,
Vadian was one of a large group of humanists from the Constance-St. Gall region who
adopted the new faith.

Secunda Pars

Vos Michael, Gabriel, Raphael testamur ad aures
illius ut castas fundetis vota precesque

Tota
formosa
et
suavis
es

pro sacro Imperio, pro Cesare Maximiliano.
Det, virgo omnipotens
hostes superare malignos;
restituat populis pacem
terrisque salutem

Hoc tibi devota carmen Georgius [1]
ante ordinat Augusti cantor,
rectorque capelle

pulchra
ut luna

Austriacae praesul regionis
sedulus omni,
se in tua commendat studio
pia gaudia mater.

electa
ut sol.

Praecipuum tamen est illi
quo assumpta fuisti,

quo tu pulchra ut luna
micas, electa es ut sol.

Isaac's polyphonic setting [2] is a splendid tour de force of early
sixteenth century motet style. Although six voice parts appear, the
counterpoint is essentially five-voiced, since the tenor moves in and
out independently to underlay the plainchant antiphon in longer note
values. Each *pars* commences with the two highest voices paired in
close imitation. The voice lines reflect contours of the source antiphon
and proceed in various voice pairings alternated with sections of fuller
texture. Each *pars* closes with a brilliant choral *tutti;* at the end of the
secunda pars, the text "ut sol" is inspiration for an extended Plagal

---

[1] The reference is to Georg Slatkonia, who was Imperial choirmaster, and later
(1513) Vienna's first bishop. He is shown seated at the rear of the car with the *Hofkapelle* in the *Triumphzug,* and his memorial plate is on the rear wall of St. Stephens
Cathedral, beneath the present choir balcony.

[2] The motet *Virgo prudentissima* is found in the 1520 publication of Grimm and
Wirsung of Augsburg, *Liber selectorum cantionum.* This anthology was prepared by
Ludwig Senfl, Isaac's pupil and successor as *Hofkomponist,* and was dedicated to the
Prince-Archbishop Matthäus Lang of Salzburg. The inferred dedicatee, however, is the
dead (1519) Emperor Maximilian, for all his favorite composers are included, and several
of the twenty-four motets allude to him. A modern edition of *Virgo prudentissima* may
be found in L. Cuyler, *The Emperor Maximilian I and Music* (Oxford University Press,
1973).

coda, with "ut" assigned generally to the note C, and "sol" to the modal *finalis*, G.

During the years immediately after 1508 and the collapse of his coronation plans, Maximilian gave repeated evidence of his conviction that the destiny of the Empire was linked inseparably with that of the Church. In 1510, following the death of Bianca Maria Sforza, his second wife, Maximilian commenced machinations which were designed to make him Pope as successor to Julius II, who was ailing. The plans came to nothing, partly because the Fugger bank at Augsburg was too canny to underwrite the scheme; but Maximilian continued to assert his belief that the posts of Pope and Emperor were essentially linked in a single but dualistic office; and he used the title *Pontifex Maximus*, after the fashion of the pagan emperors, on many of his documents.

Symbolic affirmation of this link can be seen in a happening of Holy Week 1512, which may be considered a miracle, or simple folklore, according to the point of view. At Trier, close to the border of the Netherlands, the Emperor found, under the high altar of the Cathedral, a garment deemed to be Christ's seamless cloak,[1] for the possession of which, after the Crucifixion, the soldiers had cast lots rather than divide it. The discovery of this seamless garment may have seemed a token of the inseparable Church and Empire to the aging Maximilian. Although no learned motet about the holy cloak of Trier is known, the event proved to be an inspiration for raconteurs and balladeers.[2]

Maximilian died just in time (1519) to avoid witnessing the catastrophe he had foreseen and feared. The Protestant Reformation, along with the exploration of the New World, made claims of universality for either Church or Empire more difficult to sustain, and the two drew apart. An interesting concomitant of this growing independence was that the Imperial motet lost its close liturgical ties.

Many events in the life of Emperor Charles V were marked by musical compositions, for Maximilian's grandson and successor had in his employ at one time or another several talented composers; Pierre de la Rue and Nicolas Gombert are perhaps the most distinguished. The third motet chosen for citation in this paper celebrates not only Charles but his two predecessors in the Imperial office, along with his dead father (Philip the Fair), and his brother Ferdinand who was to

---

[1] See John, 19, 23-24.

[2] See Liliencron, *Die historischen Volkslieder der Deutschen* (Leipzig, 1867), which includes a long narrative ballad entitled "Wie der heilige Rock funden ward." as No. 266.

succeed him as Emperor. The motet, *Felix Austriae domus*, may have been written when, in 1526, Ferdinand took the title King of Bohemia.[1] following the death at Mohács of young King Louis of Hungary, who was twice Ferdinand's brother-in-law.[2]

Felix Austriae domus [3] was composed by Gombert and it is truly an all-Habsburg motet; significantly, it has neither a *cantus prius factus* nor any liturgical connotation whatsoever. What does survive in it from the older motet tradition is the musical texture. Four-voiced imitative polyphony, carrying the principal text, is kept sprightly through the meter and use of active rhythms; just before the midpoint of the composition, a fifth voice (quinta pars) is added, carrying a supplementary text and moving much more slowly than the surrounding texture. This fifth voice has a certain resemblance to the traditional *cantus prius factus* of earlier compositions but its text is non-liturgical and the music is apparently not that of a pre-existent chant. The principal text, which is totally wanting in verbs, is a salutation to all the recent Habsburgs, whose power was summarized in Emperor Charles V. The text of the *quinta pars* is a pious prayer with possible humanistic overtones : *naturae genitor* seems to recall *beata Dei genitrix* and similar salutations that abound in Marian portions of the Latin liturgy. The "Habsburg" text and the supplemental text of the fifth voice are shown below.

Text of the Quinta Pars	*"Habsburg" Text*
	Felix Austriae domus
Naturae genitor	felicius Romanorum imperium
conserva morte redemptos	felicissima res christiana
fac nos tuo dignos	trium piorum Caesarum.
servitio famulos.	Friderici prudentia
	Maximiliani clementia [4]

---

[1] Schmidt-Görg, *Nicolas Gombert* (Bonn, 1938), 200, so states, but without documentation.

[2] Louis's wife was Marie, sister of Charles V and Ferdinand; and Ferdinand's wife was Anna of Hungary, Louis's sister. The two couples were the principals at the famous double marriage at the *Congress of Vienna*, in 1515, although the Emperor Maximilian stood proxy for his grandson, Ferdinand.

[3] The performance by the University of Michigan Collegium Musicum for this conference may be the first in modern times. The transcription was prepared by me from photostats of the voice parts as contained in Ott, *Novum et insigne Opus musicum*(1537), kindly provided by the British Museum.

[4] In his *Paul Hofhaimer* (18), H. J. Moser has misinterpreted this word as "dementia" and thus, by inference, defamed Maximilian !

Caroli potentia,
duorum regum Philippi et
Ferdinandi gloria.

Father of natural things	O happy house of Austria,
preserve from death the redeemed,	still happier empire of the Romans,
make us servants worthy of	happiest Christian state
your service.	of three upright emperors.
	O the prudence of Friedrich,
	the mercy of Maximilian,
	the power of Charles,
	the glory of the two
	kings Philip and Ferdinand.

The accession of Charles V was followed, within a very short time, by Luther's excommunication and also by the death of Josquin Després, the greatest of the Franco-Flemish composers. Thus while the Empire was acquiring a new, young monarch, it lost to the Reformation the allegiance of a large bloc of North German territory; and music lost its mentor, the man who was the acknowledged nucleus of two generations of Franco-Flemish composers. In a peripheral reflection of all these circumstqnces, ceremonial pieces such as the Imperial motet, as exemplified by *Felix Austriae*, ceased to borrow from liturgical compositions. Gradually over the next few decades the distinctions between sacred and secular music became much more precise, and such paraliturgical compositions as *Virgo Prudentissima* were rendered anachronistic. In the broadest sense, the musical recommendations of the Council of Trent were but affirmation of changes that humanism and a changing aesthetic had already made inevitable.

MUSIC AND RELIGION IN THE HIGH RENAISSANCE AND THE REFORMATION

LEWIS LOCKWOOD
Princeton University

Professor Cuyler's paper presents a valuable conspectus of one sector of the repertoire of the ceremonial motet, and her restriction of the primary material to motets for the Habsburg Emperors has the merit of showing continuity of function while recording decisive changes in style and technique. It goes without saying that these changes in style embrace musical literature beyond the motet and include both sacred and secular polyphony. The paper is particularly welcome because the entire field of the Latin motet is one of the most important yet least studied of the major musical genres of the late Middle Ages and the Renaissance.

While the paper is convincingly focussed on works by Brassart, Isaac, and Gombert, covering the span from about 1440 to about 1530, it suggests a number of problems for further research and thought, of which I shall briefly mention a few. 1) How far back beyond the mid-fifteenth century can the earlier history of this type of work be traced? Years ago Professor Leo Schrade called attention to commemorative polyphonic compositions in the repertoire of the Latin *conductus* of the 12th and 13th centuries, including not only the traditional genres of the *planctus* and the moralistic admonition to princes but also a series of works for the coronation of French kings.[1] Despite the vast differences in outlook and style that separate the 12th-century conductus from the 16th-century motet, some threads of continuity may perhaps be traced.

(2) It should be reemphasized that these Habsburg motets are samples of a genre that covers a wide range of ceremonial works of many kinds, written by composers of every artistic level and often for major events in which they took part. Close to the date of the Brassart composition, for example, is the famous motet by Guillaume Dufay on the text *Nuper rosarum flores*, written for the consecration of the Duomo of Florence in 1436.[2] And a long list of major works by first-rank composers could be compiled from the following century, when motets of this type were furnished for every sort of occasion. A recent first attempt to survey this field is Albert Dunning's book *Die Staatsmotette*,[3] which offers a useful beginning although it is inevitably far from fully comprehensive. There remains the major problem of establishing a truly adequate perspective on the history of the motet as a whole, within which this special branch can be seen to function. This is especially true with regard to the problem of the liturgical and non-liturgical status and usage of various motet-types.

---

[1] Leo Schrade, "Political Compositions in French Music of the 12th and 13th Centuries," *Annales Musicologiques*, I (1953), 9-63.

[2] Published in *Guglielmi Dufay, Opera Omnia*, Vol. 1/2 (ed. G. de Van), 70 ff.

[3] Utrecht, 1970.

(3) The broader implications of the performance of such works should be considered in the light of late medieval and Renaissance patronage. Such compositions were meant to enhance the artistic and political solemnity of a state occasion. They employ music as a means of symbolic expression of the stature of the ruler : the music is written for him, about him, is normally produced by a composer in his service, and is performed by his own musicians. This last point suggests that it is not only the musician who gains prominence by paying homage to his lord, but the lord whose importance is enhanced by his commemoration through a means of artistic expression of which he is the subject.

The naming of the musicians in Brassart's funeral motet seems to be linked to a later tradition; similar groups of musicians are expressly named in Compère's motet *Omnium bonorum plena* and in Josquin's *Déploration* on the death of Ockeghem. The maintenance of a skilled group of singers was not only an ideal necessity for a Christian prince, in order to ensure the proper observation of the daily Office and Mass, but it was also an obvious form of display. At the Field of the Cloth of Gold, in 1520, when Henry VIII met Francis I, their respective musical chapels met in rivalry parallel to that of their knights in chivalric combat; at a solemn Mass the two choirs sang the movements of the Mass in alternation, with some motets at the beginning and end.[1] Similarly, the meeting at Nice in 1538 of Pope Paul III, Francis I, and the Emperor Charles V included the presence of all three musical chapels, and the performance of works by their principal members; among those written for this occasion was the motet *Jubilate Deo*, by the Spanish composer Morales, then in Papal service.[2] In this connection I can also mention a hitherto unknown motet for Charles V by the famous Italian composer Costanzo Festa, written in 1536 while Festa was in the service of Pope Paul III. This work is lost but we know of its existence through a letter by another Papal singer, who sends it to the Duke of Ferrara with the remark that it had been written upon

---

[1] See Paul Kast, "Remarques sur la musique et les musiciens de la Chapelle de Francois 1er au Champ du Drap d'Or;" also Hugh Baillie, "Les Musiciens de la Chapelle Royale d'Henri VIII au Camp du Drap d'Or," and Sidney Anglo, "Le Camp du Drap d'Or et les Entrevues d'Henri VIII et de Charles Quint"; all three essays in J. Jacquot, ed., *Les Fêtes de la Renaissance*, II : *Fêtes et Cérémonies au Temps de Charles Quint* (Paris, 1960).

[2] See *Cristóbal de Morales, Opera Omnia*, ed. H. Angles, Vol. II (1953).

the Emperor's personal motto, "Plus ultra."[1] This motto was widely understood by contemporaries to symbolize the aspirations of Charles V to extend his empire; the motto, when conjoined in emblems with the Pillars of Hercules connoted especially the enlargement of the Imperial domain to include the New World beyond the Atlantic.[2] This illustrates a situation in which a dedicatory motet is written not by a member of the patron's establishment but by a singer in a rival chapel who deliberately chooses a text uniquely associated with an outside patron, presumably in hope of some form of benevolence. It also illustrates the wide range of personal and textual associations open to this branch of the contemporary Latin motet.

(4) A last element of the background to the ceremonial motet that I can mention here is the parallel literature of the ceremonial or commemorative Mass. This too is a very large repertoire, extending from the late 15th century to the end of the 16th century and in a sense far beyond. The tradition seems to have begun, or at least have become widespread, with Josquin's Mass *Hercules Dux Ferrarie*, written between 1471 and 1505 for Duke Ercole I d'Este of Ferrara.[3] In works of this type that followed Josquin's prototype, there is a clear tendency to employ a second text alongside the text of the Mass Ordinary, either in the final movement or throughout, or at least to imply a second text by deriving the subject of the Mass from a non-liturgical source. Works of this type corresponding to Gombert's motet for Charles V include Gombert's own Mass *Sur tous regretz*, subtitled *A la incoronation*, which was undoubtedly written for the

---

[1] The source is an unpublished letter from the singer Antonio Cappello to Duke Ercole II d'Este of Ferrara, dated from Rome on April 25, 1536 and preserved as part of a group of six letters by Cappello written between 1536 and 1540, all in the Archivio di Stato di Modena, Archivio per Materia, Musica e Musicisti, B. 2. The relevant portion of the text is : "Ill(ustrissi)mo et Ecc(ellentisi)mo S(ignore) et Patrone mio oss(ervandissi)-mo : ... M(esser) Costa(n)tio Festa, compositore et cantore qui della cappella, [della] S(anti)ta di N(ostro) S(ignore) à questi giorni passati compose à sua M(aesta) un mottetto sopra q(ue)l suo motto di plus ultra. Et havendogli io detto quanto V(ostra) Ex(cellen)tia se deletta di musica glie parso cosa, che a me parimente è stata gratissima farnela parte-cipe, acciò ch(e)lla intenda ch(e) l'è servidore et quando saprà di farle servigio, ogni volta ch(e) haurà cosa che gli pare degna di lei, se offre à farnela sempre partecipe. Et così V(ostr)a Ecc(ellen)za havrà qui alligata questa sua compositione ..."

[2] See M. Bataillon, "Plus Oultre : La Cour Decouvre le Nouveau Monde." in J. Jacquot, ed., *op. cit.*, 13-27; also in the same volume, Frances A. Yates, "Charles Quint et l'Idée d'Empire," 57-97.

[3] Published in *Josquin des Pres, Werken, Missen*, II (Amsterdam, 1937).

coronation of Charles at Bologna in 1530.[1] Even more explicit tributes
to political figures are the series of Masses written after that of Josquin
for later Dukes of Ferrara, and a work by the composer Lupus entitled
Missa Carolus Imperator Romanorum Quintus.[2] That works of this type
were regarded as important forms of glorification is evident from the
occasional transfer of a Mass from one patron to another, no doubt
by a copyist aiming to please the recipient of his work. Thus Josquin's
Mass *Hercules Dux Ferrarie*, based on a subject derived from the very
name of the patron, is recopied for Maximilian's son, the Archduke
Philip the Fair, as *Missa Philippus Rex Castilie*[3]; later it was copied
for Frederick of Saxony, the friend of Luther, as *Missa Fridericus Dux
Saxsonie*.[4] The association of the Mass with the glorification of a
secular prince is one more indication of the freely reciprocal relationship of the polyphonic Mass to secular music in the period before about
1560; a more familiar symptom of this is the widespread use of secular
polyphonic compositions themselves as antecedents for the composition
of many polyphonic Masses.

This raises for brief final consideration the broad but vital issue of
the interpenetration of secular elements into sacred music in the 16th
century, particularly in the periods of religious upheaval and transformation. The subject is so broad that once again I can only allude
to what seem to me a few unresolved problems. To begin with, the
broad distinction between "secular" and "sacred" seems to me far
too blunt to suggest the complexities inherent in the relationship
between musical and religious movements of the time. The terms
themselves are inadequate even for the broad level of categorization
at which they normally function, since at the very least we need to
reckon not with bifurcation but with a fourfold division that would
distinguish the musical domain of the "popular" from that of the
"secular," and the "liturgical" from the "sacred." Nothing in the
history of music in the age of the Reformation and Counter-Reformation is more striking than the co-existence of repertories representing

---

[1] Published in *Nicolai Gombert, Opera Omnia*, ed. J. Schmidt-Görg, Vol. II.

[2] Preserved in Munich, Bayerische Staatsbilbiothek MS 19, fols. 50v-79. A Mass
entitled *Plus oultre* has also been ascribed to one of the composers known as Lupus or
Lupi (see L. Finscher, article "Lupi, J." in *Die Musik in Geschichte und Gegenwart*,
VIII, 1317.

[3] In Brussels, Bibl. royale, MS 9126, fols. 72v-82r, doubtless copied for the Archduke
Philip the Fair between 1498 and 1506 (I am indebted for information about this MS
to Professor Herbert Kellman).

[4] Thus in Jena, Universitäts-Bibliothek, MS 3, fols. 15v-28r.

different levels of musical expression suitable to different modes of religious thought and action, whether Catholic or Protestant, whether formal or informal; a broad spectrum of approaches to the role of music is visible among the leaders of both camps. Among Protestant reformers as among Counter-Reformation prelates there were not only sharply divergent views on the suitability of music to worship but, more crucially, a variety of views on the degree of complexity of musical style that was to be considered compatible with the communication of sacred texts. On both sides there is a visible demand for a type of music that would give religious texts a suitably serious mode of expression and render the words intelligible enough to guarantee them their full ethical effect. It follows that since music that is too complicated divides a text among many voices it must be simplified to make the words intelligible : this argument, when advanced by churchmen, is actually identical with the opposition to counterpoint voiced by the proponents of expressive dramatic song in the late 16th century; in fact both views stem from the same humanistic doctrines.[1] From this point of view the prohibition of secular elements is actually less important in itself than the question of simplicity of style. Thus Luther, who was of course deeply musical, sought to formulate a means of musical expression suitable to the church, and incorporated as much as possible of the accumulated musical experience of German congregations into the chorale literature and its polyphonic outgrowths. As Konrad Ameln wrote with great acumen some years ago, "In the Protestant church the decisive point, which is also in keeping with Luther's theology, is that secular material is rendered holy through its absorption into church music. The incorporation of secular music into sacred functions is seen as a confirmation and continuation of older practices."[2]

A different emphasis is visible in Calvin's approach, which is profoundly imbued with a learned and humanistic view of the relation between music and spiritual observance through vernacular prayer .In his preface to the Geneva Psalter (1543) Calvin restates the view of

---

[1] See the remarks of Claude Palisca in *Report of the Eighth Congress of the International Musicological Society, New York*, 1961, Vol. II (Kassel, 1962), 121, as contribution to a panel discussion on "Relations between Religious and Secular Music in the 16th Century." See also my monograph, *The Counter-Reformation and the Masses of Vincenzo Ruffo* (Universal-Edition, for the Fondazione Giorgio Cini, 1970), 127-135.

[2] See *Report of the Eighth Congress of the International Musicological Society, New York, 1961*, 118.

Saint Augustine that music is a "gift of God" that must be properly
used because "there is hardly anything in the world with more power
to turn or bend ... the morals of men, as Plato has prudently considered; and ... it has a secret and almost incredible power to move our
hearts in one way or another."[1]

Similarly, among the leaders of the Counter-Reformation there were
widely diverse positions. In one sector were those whose major concern was with the purification of Catholic liturgical polyphony from
the alleged contamination of secular music; here the Mass is the main
focus of concern, as in Bishop Cirillo Franco's letter on sacred music
of 1549.[2] In this document we see an eloquent appeal for intelligibility
of text along with a rejection of secular subjects for the Mass; as
Cirillo writes : "What the devil has the Mass to do with the armed man,
or with Philomena, or with the Duke of Ferrara ?" The eventual result
of this view is the official decree produced at Trent in 1562, but the
long-range effect of the combined demand for intelligibility and exclusion of secular elements is not very widespread; in fact it is visible
only in the works of a few composers. Certain Masses by Palestrina
belong to this camp, with some others by his Roman contemporaries;
so do the later Masses of a few North Italian composers such as Costanzo Porta and Vincenzo Ruffo. A much more pliant attitude towards
secular and even popular music is visible in the *laudi spirituali* produced at Rome through the work of San Filippo Neri in the period
from 1550 onward; these works in the vernacular draw directly on
currents of popular music and thus on the wellsprings of traditional
Italian popular religious feeling. Even when partly transformed into
polyphonic forms by composers like Animuccia, they retain a link to
simple forms of Italian secular music.

To conclude, even these brief examples suggest an enormously
varied tapestry into which are woven many different combinations
of sacred and secular elements adapted to special purposes. From this
point of view the broad distinction between "sacred" and "secular"
is an abstraction that stands high above the specific musical realities
of the time and by itself provides no more than a simple conceptual
framework that will have to be more carefully refined.

---

[1] Translated in Oliver Strunk, *Source Readings in Music History* (New York, 1950),
347.

[2] Published from a 16th-century MS source in P. de Angelis, *Musica e Musicisti
nell' Arcispedale di Santo Spirito in Saxia* (Rome, 1950), 39-44; the letter was originally
published in Aldo Manuzio's *Lettere Volgari ... Libro Terzo* (Venice, 1565), 114-118.

EPILOGUE

ERASMUS' GODLY FEAST

MYRON P. GILMORE

Harvard University

Most of us when confronted with an abstract and comprehensive rubric such as "Late Medieval and Renaissance Religion" seek some particular referent or specific example which may help us to understand it better and discuss its meaning. In my case when I come to the second part of this title, "Renaissance Religion," the figure who comes first to my mind is that of Erasmus. I propose to recall briefly one of his most genial and charming professions of faith as presented in his colloquy, *The Godly Feast*.

The colloquy opens with the invitation of the host Eusebius to eight guests to come to dinner at his house in the country. After a tour of the pleasant garden and gallery, they go to table and during the course of dinner scriptural passages are read out, first from *Proverbs*, second from *Corinthians* and third from *St. Mathew*. The guests participate in explicating the true meaning of these passages. Here we have the Erasmian insistence on the direct acquaintance with scripture on the part of laymen and the exposition of the Bible unencumbered with scholastic commentary.

Interspersed with these exchanges are other characteristic elements of Erasmus' religious opinions. There is a long tirade on the familiar theme of the worthlessness of ceremonies and sacraments when observed only by custom rather than by inner conviction. The host Eusebius reflects on the waste of money in reliquaries and in certain monastic establishments. He has seen the tomb of Thomas à Becket in Canterbury laden with precious jewels which might have been better used to relieve the necessities of the poor. He has also seen the Certosa of Pavia, all built of white marble within and without, from top to bottom. What, he asks, is the good of pouring out so much money to enable a few lone monks to sing in a marble church which even to them is a burden because it is constantly overrun with tourists? Host and guest make it clear that they are devoted to practical works of charity, sending what remains of the roast to a poor woman who is a neighbor, going out to comfort a dying friend or to try to settle a quarrel between two stubborn men. At the end the departing guests are given presents, among which are four manuscripts, the Book of *Proverbs*, the *Gospel of Mathew*, the Pauline *Epistles* and Plutarch's *Moralia*.

Plutarch's appearance in this company recalls one of the most famous passages in the colloquy—the discussion of the relation of the Greek and Roman classics to Christian morality. Eusebius declares that whatever contributes to good morals should not be called profane and he confesses that he sometimes comes across pagan writings, even those of the poets, so purely and reverently expressed that he cannot but believe that their authors were moved by some divine power. He considers that the spirit of Christ must be more widespread than we understand and that the company of saints includes many who are not in our calendar. Cicero must have been divinely inspired. The other guests join in : Chrysoglottos maintains that no Christian could speak more reverently than Cato, and the theme reaches its climax of emotion in the exclamation of Nephalius on reading Plato, "Sancta Socrate, Ora pro nobis !"

On the walls of the dining room are six pictures. Three are from the *New Testament*. There is a last supper of Christ and His disciples, then the fateful birthday feast of Herod, and the rich man Dives robed in purple and dining sumptuously, while Lazarus lies dying at the gate, hoping for some crumbs from the table but about to be received into Abraham's bosom.

The other three pictures Timotheus says he doesn't recognize and the host explains that the first is the voluptuous banquet of Anthony and Cleopatra, in which Cleopatra has already swallowed one pearl in her wine and is reaching for another, the second shows the Lapiths fighting with the drunken Centaurs and the last portrays Alexander the Great intoxicated after a victory celebration, in the act of piercing with his spear his comrade in arms Kleitos, the brother of his old nurse. The host explains that all these examples, taken from classical history and mythology, are intended to reinforce Christian morality by warning us against the dangers of gluttony and intemperance.

The compatibility of classical literature and Christianity had of course been much discussed throughout the middle ages from the time of the Church Fathers and many were the explorations of the uses to which to put the gold and silver vessels brought by the Israelites out of Egypt. In the later middle ages we think perhaps particularly of the *Ovide moralisé* and the *De laboribus Herculis* of Salutati. It seems to me, however, that in the lifetime of Erasmus, in literature and in art, philosophy and theology, in the north as well as in Italy, this theme was more completely elaborated and more vividly expressed than it had hitherto been. Let me mention two examples where it is most concretely realized in art and architecture.

Two little chapels, jewel cases of carved marble, are buried almost secretly in the lower depths of that perfect Renaissance construction, the ducal palace at Urbino. These chapels are arranged side by side, one dedicated to the remission of sins and the other to the muses. The Pardon Chapel has on its lintel and within the following inscriptions :

HAEC QUICUMQUE PETIT MUNDO PIA LIMINA CORDE
HIC PETIT AETERNI FULGIDA REGNA POLI

ACCIPITE SPIRITUM SANCTUM ET QUORUM
REMISERITIS PECCATA REMITTUNTUR EIS

The corresponding inscriptions in the Chapel of the Muses are :

BINA VIDES PARVO DISCRIMINE IUNCTA SACELLA
ALTERA PARS MUSIS ALTERA SACRA DEO EST

QUISQUIS AD ES LAETUS MUSIS ET CANDIDUS ADSIS
FACUNDUS CITHARAE NIL NISI CANDOR INEST I[1]

The influence of the teaching of Vittorino da Feltre, of whom Federigo da Montefeltro had been a pupil, was thus commemorated.

A more humble example is furnished by a papal bureaucrat. Tommaso Inghirami, humanist secretary of Julius II and Leo X, had the nickname of Phaedrus because he had taken the female part in Seneca's play *Hippolytus*. Going one morning from the Vatican to the Lateran where he had a canonry, riding on his mule reading a manuscript, he passed under the arch of Constantine. A cart drawn by two bullocks and piled high with sacks of grain was coming through in the opposite direction. The sacks toppled and knocked Inghirami off in such a way that he fell under the wheels of the cart. He invoked Christ the Saviour with Saints Peter and Paul and was miraculously saved. He commemorated the incident in an ex voto which can still be seen in the Sacristy of San Giovanni Laterano. We see him setting out from the Vatican and then in the center prostrate with a piteous expression on

---

[1] On the Urbino chapels and their inscriptions see Pasquale Rotondi, *Il Palazzo Ducale di Urbino* (Urbino, 1950), pp. 357-82.

his corpulent face about to be run over by the cart. The colosseum
and the arch of Constantine are accurately reproduced and the miraculous saviours hover in the heavens at the upper right of these Roman
monuments.[1]

Erasmus records that he knew and loved Inghirami during his so-
journ in Rome in 1509.[2] The latter was then prefect of the Vatican
Library. His portrait was painted by Raphael and, although there is
no documentary evidence, he may well have been among those who
participated in the development of the iconographic program for the
Stanza della Segnatura where Raphael gave classic expression to the
belief in the compatibility of Greek philosophy with Christian theology.

In their enthusiasm for the idea of Sancte Socrate it may be admitted
that the men who shared this belief were unwilling to explore the
profound differences between the classical world and Christianity. The
existence of a beautiful harmony was above all asserted in the realms
of ethics and aesthetics and little attention was paid to the profound
incompatibilities that existed for example between the Greek view of
immanence and the Judeo-Christian tradition of transcendence or the
Greek conviction that knowledge is virtue and the Christian dogma
that the intellect is of no avail against a will profoundly corrupted by
original sin.

It is precisely because the belief in a harmonious relationship was
expressed by the pen of Erasmus and the brush of Raphael that we
are in danger of concluding that it is *the* religion of the Renaissance.
The great value of this conference is that it has given us an opportunity to consider what other forms of religious belief and observances
co-existed with the religion of Erasmus. We need to hear the voices
of Savonarola's *fanciulli* and of father confessors and mystics : we
need to follow the intricate arguments of scholastic theologians and
to explore as well the thought of those humble people—the ploughboy
and the housewife, even the prostitutes and the Turks—to whom
Erasmus hoped that his *Paraphrases* would bring the *Philosophia
Christi*.

Florence was undoubtedly one of the most literate communities in
Christendom. We may suppose that everyone understood in some
sense the nativities, crucifixions, and last suppers which the Flor-

---

[1] The ex voto is reproduced in Denys Hay, ed., *The Age of the Renaissance* (London,
1967), p. 125. Cf. J. Klaczko, *Julius II* (Paris, 1898), pp. 221 ff.

[2] Allen, ed., *Opus Epist. Erasmi Rot.*, vol. V (Oxford, 1914), p. 246.

entines saw painted on their walls. But how many would have been able to endow with any moral or religious significance the scene of Alexander throwing his spear at Kleitos or the battle between the Lapiths and the Centaurs even though sculptured by Michelangelo ? It is always useful to remind ourselves that the religion of Erasmus was and remained the religion of an intellectual élite.

In thanking again our hosts of The University of Michigan I may be permitted to quote one more line from *The Godly Feast*. Timotheus, taking leave of his host Eusebius, exclaims, "Who could be bored in this house ?"